Consumer Economic Problems

Fifth Edition

By

W. HARMON WILSON
Editor of THE BALANCE SHEET
Vice-President, South-Western Publishing Co.

AND

ELVIN S. EYSTER
Chairman, Department of Business Education, Indiana University

SOUTH-WESTERN PUBLISHING CO.
CINCINNATI 27 CHICAGO 5 SAN FRANCISCO 3 DALLAS 2
NEW ROCHELLE, N. Y.

G16

Copyright, © 1956

By South-Western Publishing Company

Cincinnati, Ohio

All Rights Reserved

The text of this publication, or any part thereof, may not be reproduced in any manner whatsoever without permission in writing from the publisher.

Library of Congress Catalog Card Number: 56–7416

H257

*Printed in the
United States of America*

PREFACE

The Fifth Edition of CONSUMER ECONOMIC PROBLEMS reflects twenty years of growth and development of a popular textbook in consumer-economic education. While many characteristics of the previous editions have been retained, the Fifth Edition differs in that new topics have been added, factual data have been brought up to date, and many changes in subject matter and methods of presentation growing out of the suggestions of teachers and students have been made.

In line with current and popular objectives of consumer-economic education, the following objectives and concepts are developed in CONSUMER ECONOMIC PROBLEMS:

(1) To understand the minimum economic principles and the common business practices that are essential for the wise management of one's personal business affairs and that are generally helpful in the pursuit of one's occupation or profession;
(2) To get the most value and the most satisfaction out of the time, effort, and money that are expended for food, clothing, shelter, personal services, and all other economic goods and services;
(3) To plan and operate a well-balanced financial program, considering needs and wants on the one hand and income and expenditures on the other;
(4) To work toward a higher level of living for all the people in a democratic society;
(5) To understand fully one's responsibility to be constantly alert to the economic problems confronting consumers, business firms, and government and to participate actively in their solution.

In this textbook the basic principles of economics and the practices of business considered to be of importance to everyone have been introduced in the discussions of specific problems encountered by consumers. The emphasis is placed upon the application of an economic principle to the solution of a consumer problem rather than upon the theory. Many economic principles and concepts thus are discussed more than once in their relationship to several different problems. To illustrate, the effect of the division of labor or occupational specialization is introduced in the treatment of marketing and is discussed in a later chapter in its relationship to sharing income and wealth. The legal aspects of consumer buying and credit, likewise, are discussed several times in their relationships to specific consumer problems.

Though it is not the primary purpose of this book to provide training in business practices and procedures, some of this type of information is presented because of its indispensability to the conduct of personal business affairs. Guides and principles for solving consumer problems are given in summary form for the convenience of the reader. The responsibility to study and understand the economic problems of consumers and to contribute to their solution is stressed.

It is hoped that through the use of this textbook those who study it may not only become more efficient in handling their personal business affairs but that they also may participate in solving the economic problems of business and government through intelligent voting on economic issues.

In this volume there is both an adequate range of subject matter and problem material to permit selections and omissions to accomplish any desired emphasis for a semester course. For a year course there is plenty of material if it is all covered.

The authors take this opportunity to thank the many teachers who have offered suggestions and criticisms. We particularly acknowledge the extensive suggestions offered for improvement by the following: Martha Byrne, Brother Leo V. Ryan, Ernest Walker, Jane M. Welch, John H. Linn, Horton Amidon, Gerald Cresci, Herbert Sunderman, Ruth B. Woolschlager, Arthur Broetje, John J. Gibba, Charles Fuhr, M. Randolph Grimmett, James A. Burt, Ernest A. Dauer, F. J. Schlink, Miriam Calmenson, Mary P. Brantley, John P. Weise, Richard Hanula, James M. Duff, and Arthur C. Daniels.

W. HARMON WILSON
ELVIN S. EYSTER

TABLE OF CONTENTS

PART I. YOUR ECONOMIC WANTS AND NEEDS

Chapter		Page
1.	How Can We Live Better?	1
2.	How Our Needs Are Met by Business	13

PART II. BUSINESS AND GOVERNMENT SERVE CONSUMERS

3.	How Business Is Organized and Operated to Serve You	28
4.	The Functions and Services of Marketing	48
5.	How Government Affects the Consumer	66

PART III. PROTECTIONS FOR CONSUMERS

6.	Private Agencies That Protect Us	85
7.	How Government Agencies Protect and Serve Us	101
8.	Legal Relations for Our Protection	125

PART IV. PRINCIPLES OF CONSUMER BUYING

9.	General Principles of Buying	149
10.	How to Interpret Advertising	169
11.	Standards, Grades, and Labels as Guides in Buying	187

PART V. SPECIFIC PROBLEMS IN BUYING

12.	Getting the Most for Your Food Dollar	206
13.	How to Buy Foods	217
14.	How to Buy Fabrics, Clothing, and Shoes	240
15.	How to Buy Home Appliances and Automobiles	259
16.	How to Buy Furniture and Floor Coverings	277
17.	How to Buy Drugs and Similar Articles	295

PART VI. HOW BANKS AND CREDIT SERVE YOU

18.	How Your Bank Operates	312
19.	How to Use Your Bank	328
20.	How to Obtain and Use Credit	350
21.	Important Principles of Installment Buying	366
22.	How to Obtain a Small Loan	389

PART VII. MANAGING YOUR PERSONAL FINANCES

Chapter | Page
23. How to Keep Personal and Family Budgets 407
24. How to Keep Personal and Family Records 420
25. Planning Your Savings Program 430
26. Principles of Investing Your Savings 451
27. Information You Need About Investments 467

PART VIII. BUYING INSURANCE PROTECTION

28. How Insurance Protects You 483
29. Social Security 506
30. Features of Life Insurance Contracts 521
31. How to Buy Life Insurance 539

PART IX. OBTAINING A HOME

32. Renting or Buying a Home 554
33. Financing the Purchase of a Home 572
34. Legal Problems of Obtaining a Home 586

PART X. ECONOMIC PROBLEMS OF THE CONSUMER

35. Wealth, Production, and Income 603
36. How We Share in the National Income 620
37. The Functions of Money and Credit 638
38. How Values and Prices Are Established 656
39. How Business Conditions and Prices Affect Us 673
40. How the Consumer Buys Services with Taxes 691

INDEX 715

Chapter 1

How Can We Live Better?

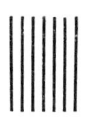

> **Purpose of the Chapter.** All people have wants and needs for goods and services. Most of us spend the major part of our time and effort in trying to satisfy those wants and needs. Problems arise in using one's earnings and savings in getting the things we need and want. This textbook is devoted to a study of those problems.
>
> You will find answers to these questions:
> 1. What is the nature of our wants?
> 2. How are our economic wants and needs satisfied?
> 3. Who is a consumer?
> 4. What factors affect our level of living?
> 5. What is economic voting?

What Are Our Wants? Our wants are of two kinds, intangible and tangible. The *intangible wants* include the desire for love and affection of our family, respect and admiration of our friends and acquaintances, recognition of our achievements, and freedom from worry and anxiety and other things that take away the joy of living. *Tangible wants* consist of our desire and need for the other necessities of life, such as clothes, food, and shelter. We also want such other tangible things as athletic and sporting goods, record players, television receivers, books, and magazines. We want money income regularly to provide the tangible things we want.

The intangible wants may be thought of as personal and in a sense the spiritual wants of man, whereas the tangible wants are for material things and for services such as dental care and laundry or dry cleaning. Both kinds of wants are important for our happiness and our contentment in life. The intangible wants cannot be bought with money, but our personality, character traits, habits, and attitudes affect them. The tangible wants have a money value. They are the economic wants and needs of man.

How We Satisfy Our Economic Wants. We get the economic goods and services, that is the tangible things, we need primarily by working. Almost everything we have and use is the result of work that either we or someone else has done. By working we earn, and with the money we earn we buy the things we want and need. Sometimes we do not spend the money we have earned but save it to buy things we will need at a later time. Thus, savings really represent accumulated purchasing power.

In a lifetime we use or consume many economic goods and services. Small children, retired people, and some others cannot work and earn to provide for their present economic wants. Thus, they must use and consume things either that have been saved or that are being earned by others. It is the responsibility of each of us during the working period of our lives to work and produce at least as much as we will use or consume during our whole lives. And if we are to contribute toward better living for the nation as a whole, we shall have to produce more in our lives than we use.

How well our economic wants are satisfied depends not only upon how much we earn but also upon how wisely we spend what we earn. *Economics* is the study of man's efforts to satisfy his wants and needs of material things and services. Economics includes one's productivity, earnings, and savings as well as the satisfying of his wants for economic goods and services. *Consumer economics* is a study of the use of one's earnings and savings in obtaining the economic things he wants and needs, such as food, clothing, recreation, education, and medical care.

Who Is a Consumer? Every person is a consumer because he uses or consumes economic goods and services.

Not only are you a consumer when you buy and use groceries and automobiles and clothes, but you are also a consumer when you make use of educational opportunities offered in a school, or obtain legal advice from a lawyer, medical service from your physician, or a haircut from your barber. The retail merchant himself is a consumer when he buys food, recreation, and other things for himself and his family. Therefore, a *consumer* is any person who engages in the process of spending money and using economic goods and services.

Level of Living. Most of us would like to buy more goods and use more services than we are buying now. We would like for our money to go farther. In other words, we would like to live on a higher economic level than we are at present. Your level of living is measured by the quality of the home you live in, by the kind and amount of food you are able to use, by your ability to travel and take vacations regularly, by the monthly accumulation of your insurance and investments, by the savings you are laying aside for a rainy day. The level of living is much higher in some countries than in others; it is higher in some parts of this country than in other parts, and it is higher for some people within a community than for others in the same community.

The *level of living* consists of the goods and services that an individual or family regularly obtains. A *standard of living* is similar to a goal or a guide. Many of us set standards that we should like to attain. There really is no standard in the true sense of the word; but when we use this term, we usually are thinking of a certain degree of success in satisfying our needs and wants.

Your level of living depends in large part upon how much income you receive and upon how wisely you spend it. Obviously, the greater your income is, the more goods and services you are able to buy to satisfy your wants. Likewise, the more wisely you spend your money, the better your wants are satisfied. But there are other factors that also affect our level of living. For example, if the supply of the goods you want is very limited, you may not be able to get what you want. Or, if prices in general are very high, your income may not be large enough to permit you to buy what you want. Our level of living is also influenced by inventions of such conveniences as automobiles, dishwashers, and power lawn mowers. Modern methods of manufacturing make many of these products available to us at a cost we can afford to pay. It is easily seen that how well our wants for goods and services are satisfied is dependent upon many factors.

We have some control over our income. In general, the harder one works or the better one serves in his job, the greater are his earnings. Of course, we have control of the spending of our income. We may spend wisely, or we may make unwise choices and thus spend foolishly. Aside from control over our earnings and expenditures, our level of living is dependent largely upon the general conditions that prevail in our occupation and in the country at large. Let us examine some of those factors.

How Can We Raise Our Level of Living? The reason we work is to produce economic goods and services that people want. We receive wages or income for the work we do. In general, the more we, as individuals, produce by our work, the greater will be our income.

If we want to raise our level of living, we must do it by increasing our individual production which in turn will increase the total production of all people. This means that we must strive for the greatest efficiency. To do that we must have educated and skilled workers. We must take advantage of modern machinery, modern power, and modern science. It also means that we must not artificially restrict production except to avoid overproduction to the extent that there is more than can be consumed. As a result of these factors, we will get more goods at lower prices.

As individuals, we often set our own standards and strive to accomplish them. The degree of success in obtaining our own standard of living is often dependent upon our personal abilities, the extent to which we use our abilities, the degree to which we follow a plan, and the breaks that we get in life. But, also as individuals, we are affected by the efficiency of other people.

Let us assume, for example, that each group of 100 people working at different tasks could supply the group with the goods and services needed. If they all work slowly and only a few hours a day, the total produced by the group will be very little. If they all work fast and efficiently, production will be high and they will all have more goods and services to enjoy. If they use no tools, production will be low. If they use modern tools and equipment with gasoline, electric, or steam power, their production will be higher; each person will turn out more goods or render more service.

Courtesy, The Advertising Council, Inc.
The Better We Produce, the Stronger We Grow

Let us assume that each one of these 100 people performs one job or service and has complete control over what he does. If one cuts down his production of a vital product or service, the supply will not meet the demands of the group. The other 99 will beg for it, plead for it, and bid for it. In terms of what they are willing to trade for it or pay for it in money, the price will be high. Thus one person who restricts his production may benefit himself by getting more total income by charging a higher price for less goods or services, but all the other persons in the group suffer. By restricting his production, he is not helping to raise the level of living for all people, but may help to lower it.

As the result of the scarcity or shortage of the product or service created by this one individual, the efficiency of the other 99 people will probably also be impaired. The curtailment of one such item as transportation would slow down all other production and would make it more difficult for the other 99 people to get along.

The restriction of production in this case enables the producer to get a higher price for each unit of what he does produce. He may not increase his total income however, because fewer people may be able to buy his product at the price that is asked.

On the other hand, restrictions, whether by people in the fields of marketing, farming, or labor, tend to lower the level of living for everyone although a restriction by a certain group may help that group. Of course, there are times in a modern free system when certain individuals or groups may overproduce. This is good for all others, but it is bad for the group that overproduces. Somebody gets hurt economically while others get the benefit.

Purchasing Power of Dollar Affects Level of Living. We are all very conscious of the money we have or the

Real Wages Have Gone Up; Hours of Work Have Gone Down

We have made progress in several ways. Our real wages are greater; our hours of work are shorter; in many cases our work is easier because of the use of machinery.

Courtesy, The Advertising Council, Inc.

SINCE 1850
REAL WAGES
UP 3½ TIMES

HOURS A WEEK
DOWN FROM 70 to 40

money we are earning. The amount of money that we have or earn, however, is not so important as what it will buy. That is an important fundamental of economics.

Let us assume that Jack Cook graduates from high school and starts earning $40 a week. He finds that he can buy his food, clothing, shelter, personal services, and amusement and still have $5 left that he can save.

Ten years later Jack Cook has advanced in his work. He is a more valuable man; and so far as money income is concerned, he is doing well because he is now earning $80 a week. He is still single, but something has happened that affects Jack. A law of economics has been at work.

Although he is earning $80 a week and has a more important job, Jack is not getting along as well. He is just as careful as ever in his spending. He eats as economically as possible and is not extravagant in the buying of clothing or anything else, but now Jack is still able to save only $5 a week because the prices of what he buys have increased. In other words, Jack is worse off than he was ten years ago because, even though he has had more experience, is a more valuable worker, and is getting more cash income, it requires $75 instead of $35 a week to live. His money will buy less. Even the $5 that he saves may buy less when he wants to spend it. The purchasing power of a dollar has decreased, thus affecting Jack's level of living.

How Prices Affect Our Real Income. Prices of goods and services wanted by consumers increased generally from 1939 to 1955. The graph on page 8 shows that if all goods and services wanted by consumers are considered together, a dollar would buy 51.9 per cent as much in 1955 as in 1939. This means that a person would have needed an income almost twice as large in 1955 as in 1939 in order to buy the same amount of goods and services.

Prices do not always go up, causing the purchasing power of the dollar to decrease. There are times when prices of goods and services go down. Under such conditions the purchasing power of the dollar increases, and as a result one can maintain his level of living on less money than when prices were higher.

Average Amount of Consumer Goods and Services That One Dollar Would Buy

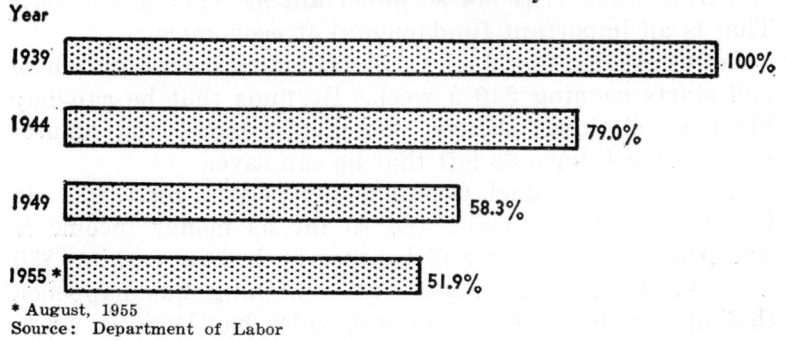

Year	
1939	100%
1944	79.0%
1949	58.3%
1955 *	51.9%

* August, 1955
Source: Department of Labor

Changes in Purchasing Power of Consumer's Dollar

The amount of money one earns is not so important as what that money will buy. A person's *real income* is measured by the amount of goods or services he can buy with his wages or salary. Let us assume that five years ago a carpenter received $2.50 an hour for his labor and that he could buy two and one-half pounds of beef steak with that amount of money. If five years later he still receives $2.50 an hour for his labor but the money received for it will buy only two pounds of beef steak, his wage per hour in terms of what he can purchase is less than it was five years ago. If he could buy three pounds of steak now for $2.50, the wages he receives for one hour of labor, his real wages have increased. Real wages rather than dollars received as wages affect our level of living.

Economic Voting. Every economic choice you make is really an economic vote. Your choices and those of all other people taken collectively affect the standard of living generally. Everything you buy or fail to buy is an economic choice. You are deciding first whether it is better to keep your money for some future use or to spend it immediately. You are making choices between two different brands or types of goods, or between one type of article and another.

In this choice of economic voting you are serving as one of the final judges as to whether some business firm will succeed or fail. The highly skilled businessman tries to determine what customers will buy, but he may guess wrong. Consumers have the power to determine the success of a business. Actually they decide what goods and services will be offered on the open market.

In government you also have economic choices. The government collects money from you and from everyone else to provide services for you and for others. Even though you may not pay taxes directly to Federal, state, or local governments, you are still being taxed through the goods and services you buy. Throughout your lifetime you must help to make decisions as to whether it is better to buy services through government taxes, to buy services from private business enterprise, or to perform these services yourself.

In labor unions and many other types of organizations, such as groups of manufacturers, groups of merchants, and farmers, the freedom to exercise a vote or a choice helps to determine how we all shall live. If all individuals and all groups act unwisely or too selfishly, we all suffer because of the bad choices and bad decisions that are made.

Economic Problems of the Consumer. Consumers are concerned primarily with establishing and maintaining a high standard of living. They want the money they have earned to buy for them as much economic goods and services as possible. Their problem is not one alone of wise spending, but it also involves making economic choices which in turn determine what goods and services shall be available, what business firms shall remain in business, what controls and regulations government will exercise over business, and what protections will be provided consumers.

We have gradually developed a system of government under which business is controlled and consumers are protected. We still operate under a relatively free enterprise system, but it is a system that is regulated and controlled. We try to prevent honest people from getting hurt in business dealings, and our aim is to prevent unethical or dishonest practices.

We need to know some of the rules of our economic life so that we will know how to play the game and deal with other people. We need to know a great deal about economics and business in order to earn a high level of living for ourselves. The important factors in planning your economic life will be developed as you complete this course.

> *Important Factors for Consumers in Understanding Their Problems*
>
> 1. How business and government affect consumers.
> 2. The protections consumers have.
> 3. General principles of buying consumer goods and services.
> 4. Specific problems encountered by consumers in buying.
> 5. The use of banks and credit by consumers.
> 6. Problems of managing one's personal finances.
> 7. Procuring protection and security through insurance.
> 8. Obtaining a home.
> 9. Basic economic principles.

TEXTBOOK QUESTIONS

1. Of what do our intangible wants consist?
2. What are tangible wants?
3. How do we get the goods and services we want and need?
4. With what does the study of economics deal? Consumer economics?
5. Is a businessman a consumer? Why or why not?
6. What is meant by "level of living"?
7. What determines your standard of living?
8. Do we all have the same standard of living?
9. What are some of the ways in which we can raise our level of living?
10. How do machines help us raise our level of living?
11. What would happen to our level of living if everybody slowed down production?
12. What is meant by the purchasing power of the dollar?
13. Why does the purchasing power of the dollar vary?
14. What is meant by real wages or real income?
15. Which is the more accurate measure of our standard of living, real wages or money wages?
16. What do we mean by "economic voting"?

Ch. 1] How Can We Live Better? 11

DISCUSSION QUESTIONS

1. Discuss the problems of the individual and the nation in raising the general level of living of everyone and point out some of the handicaps.
2. Discuss why one's level of living may not depend entirely upon his income.
3. Explain how savings represents accumulated purchasing power.
4. Name some ways in which your family can vote economically.
5. Explain why an increase in real prosperity cannot be measured in terms of wages.
6. Planning one's economic life, that is, to have adequate earnings and to use one's savings and earnings wisely involves many factors. What are these factors and what should one know about them?

PROBLEMS

1. In the table below are some imaginary examples to illustrate the relations between wages and the cost of living. The first year (No. 1) is the base year used for comparison and is therefore 100 per cent. The second year (No. 2) is worked out for you as an example.

    In this example the increase of $10 in the average wage, as shown by the figures for Years 1 and 2 in column (2), has been recorded in column (3). The per cent of increase (25%), as shown in column (4), was determined by dividing the increase in the average wage, $10, by the average wage in the first year, $40. The per cent of increase in the Cost of Living Index (8%), as shown in column (6), was determined by subtracting the Cost of Living Index for Year 1 in column (5) from that index for Year 2.

    (a) Complete the figures in the table.

(1) YEAR	(2) AVERAGE WAGE	(3) AMOUNT OF INCREASE OR DECREASE IN WAGES OVER FIRST YEAR	(4) PER CENT INCREASE OR DECREASE IN WAGES (COMPARED TO BASE YEAR)	(5) INDEX OF COST OF LIVING	(6) INCREASE OR DECREASE IN INDEX OF COST OF LIVING (COMPARED TO BASE YEAR)
1	$40 (Base)	0	0	100 (Base)	0
2	$50 (Example)	$10	25%	108	8 Inc.
3	$55			120	
4	$60			121	
5	$55			130	
6	$50			120	
7	$40			110	

(b) Explain what has happened to wages, what has happened to the cost of living, and how well off is the worker in the seventh year as compared with the first year.

2. Part of the story of wages and prices is illustrated in the previous problem, but there is another way to analyze wages and prices as shown in the table below. The first year is used as a base year with which other comparisons can be made. The purchasing power of the dollar in this particular year is considered to be 100 per cent. The second year is used as an example. In this case each dollar is worth 95 cents, which means that it is worth 95 per cent of what it was worth the previous year in terms of what it will buy. Therefore, how much will $42.00 in wages buy? Answer ($42 × .95 = $39.90).

(a) Complete the rest of the table.

YEAR	AVERAGE WAGES	DOLLAR PURCHASING POWER	BUYING POWER OF WAGES
1	$40.00 (Base)	100% (Base)	$40.00
2	$42.00 (Example)	95%	$39.90
3	$45.00	92%	
4	$48.00	90%	
5	$50.00	85%	
6	$58.00	80%	
7	$65.00	60%	
8	$70.00	50%	

(b) Explain what has happened in these eight years to wages and their purchasing power.

COMMUNITY PROBLEMS AND PROJECTS

1. From governmental sources, the library, banks, local newspapers, or any other reliable sources, collect information in regard to prices and wages and make analyses, if possible, similar to those in Problems 1 and 2 in this chapter. Study these figures and prepare your own interpretation.

2. In this chapter have a discussion of the level of living and the standard of living. Prepare a budget for a young married couple of what you consider to be the requirements they should save for rent, clothing, food, transportation, medical care, recreation, contributions, personal care, etc. Do not include any purchases of furniture or equipment but in transportation include the cost of operating an automobile if you assume that one is owned. This will be a minimum budget requirement. Compute the separate amounts and the total of wages made to provide your desired or expected level of living.

Chapter 2

How Our Needs Are Met by Business

> **Purpose of Chapter.** Our needs for goods and services are met through the processes known as business. This chapter will provide an understanding of the important role of business in the lives of people in general and of consumers in particular.
>
> You will find answers to these questions:
> 1. What is business?
> 2. How are consumers needs and wants met by business?
> 3. What factors in business especially affect the meeting of our needs?
> 4. How are business, labor, and consumers interdependent?
> 5. What is our stake in business?

What Is Business? *Business* is a general term that applies to several types of organizations that strive to make a profit by rendering various kinds of personal services or creating usefulness in goods.

How Business Helps Consumers. In earlier times pioneer families produced most of the goods they consumed. They made their own clothes, produced their own food, and provided their own personal services such as laundry, shoe repair, and recreational facilities. They were very nearly independent. The average family worked together both as a producing unit and as a consuming unit. Their economic life was very simple.

Times have changed. Today we know very little about most of the things we eat, wear, and use, for we do not make them but buy them. We work at an occupation or profession to earn money. Then we use the money to buy the goods and services we want. Our economic lives are dependent upon many factors. Therefore, we need to understand the business and economic factors that affect consumers.

How Business Developed to Meet Our Needs. Let us look back a moment and see the change in the relation between consumers and business a century or two ago and today. Again referring to the pioneer, he produced what his family used and practically no more. After a time, a few enterprising men produced a surplus of one commodity which they liked to make and felt they made well. The sought to exchange (*barter*) this surplus commodity for something else their family needed but what they did not want to make or could not make as economically or as well as someone else made it. Thus, barter and later organized trading and marketing became common aspects of business.

As barter became common, a man sometimes wanted to dispose of a surplus of some item but did not want to choose immediately another item in exchange for it. He wanted to wait until he needed the other item or perhaps wait until he found exactly the kind and quality of goods his family could use best. This led to the concept of money which enabled man to dispose of his surplus at the market place, accept money for it, and thus defer the selection of other things of value in its place until a time later. Thus, he "stored" his purchasing power for use later. Money also is a medium of exchange and a standard of value.

As business developed, some men had need to buy more economic goods than they had "accumulated earnings" or "purchasing power" to pay for, so they borrowed money. This led to the rather elaborate and complicated plan of finance and credit that is common in business today. Finance is a very important phase of business enterprise.

As man produced less and less of his families' needs at home and sought to buy goods with money he had earned, factories sprung up to produce a particular article or group of articles in large quantities. Usually, they produced the article more economically and also better than it could be made at home because they specialized in making a few commodities or maybe only one. The making of one article exclusively in large quantities is known as *mass production*.

In order to get the products produced on farms and made in factories to the people who need them and want to buy them, wholesalers, jobbers, and retailers came into the picture. The process of getting the finished product to the one who needs it and wants to buy it is known as *distribution*. The process by which distribution is carried out is known as the *marketing system*.

Much careful planning is required to produce goods in large quantity, finance a business enterprise, and distribute the finished product to consumers. Many decisions have to be made, and risk of losing one's investment is at stake. Assuming the risk, planning for the business, and making the decisions are the functions of owners and managers.

Our Economic System. Let us review a moment. Earlier the wants and needs for economic goods and services were satisfied directly by a man producing practically everything he and his family used. Now, the wage and salary earners in a family work to earn money which in turn they use either immediately or later to buy as many of the economic goods and services they can afford or want. Man's needs and wants are no longer satisfied directly as in early days. But they are satisfied indirectly. The process through which our economic wants and needs are satisfied is complex. It involves production, finance, distribution, and good management. The process by which your needs for economic goods and services are indirectly satisfied is known as the *American economic system*, sometimes referred to as the free enterprise or the private enterprise system or the profit and loss system. We shall learn more about our economic system in the next chapter. This system has been and is a powerful influence in making America great.

What Is the Function of Business? Consumers want various kinds of services and goods, and businessmen attempt to satisfy those wants of people. This is done by creating various kinds of usefulness, such as: (a) producing goods in a form that people will want (*form utility*), (b) making goods and services available at a time when people will want them (*time utility*), and (c) making goods and services available in the proper place (*place utility*). For example, wheat grain converted into flour and into a fresh loaf of bread is form utility; if it is available fresh in the morning, when needed, it has time utility; if it is available at a convenient location for the consumer to obtain it, it has place utility. Economists also recognize *elementary utility*, which means products provided by nature; and *possession utility*, which means that nothing is useful unless it is possessed by someone. However, from the point of view of our study of business and how it serves us, we are concerned with form, time, and place utility.

The teacher, the lawyer, the physician, the banker, and the musician perform economic services just as surely as any business firm that manufactures or sells a product. People who render services are satisfying a human want.

It can be easily seen therefore that business serves us by providing shelter, food, clothing, equipment, tools, transportation, communication, and numerous kinds of services.

The People Who Render Business Services

1. Basic production—approximately 8 million workers (farming, fishing, forestry, mining, etc.).
2. Processing or manufacturing—approximately 14 million workers (steel, automobiles, furniture, printing, etc.).
3. Distribution—approximately 15 million workers (wholesaling, retailing, transportation, communications, etc.).
4. Services—approximately 12 million workers (finance, law, amusement, medicine, beauty culture, etc.).

What Does Business Do? Remember that all businesses are formed and operated to render a service or supply goods to fill wants. Each operator of a business hopes that he will be able to make a profit by filling these wants successfully. The filling of these wants is a complicated process. Some products go through many hands. A few products are sold directly by the farmer to the consumer. Some businessmen serve consumers directly, but some businessmen serve other businessmen, who in turn serve addi-

---

MATERIALS, PRODUCTS, AND SERVICES USED BY THE AUTOMOBILE INDUSTRY

Minerals and Mine Products

Iron	Nickel	Sulphur	Silica
Copper	Zinc	Oil	Soda
Lead	Coal	Gas	Chromium
Tin	Lime	Aluminum	Asbestos

Agricultural and Forest Products

Cotton	Lumber	Padding	Insulation
Wool	Fibers	Carpets	Rubber
Leather	Oils	Fabrics	

Chemical and Other Manufactured Products

Tires	Solvents	Alloys	Machine Parts
Hose	Plastics	Steel	Wire
Paint	Acids	Cast Iron	
Lacquer	Glass	Malleable Iron	

Economic Services

Transportation	Finance	Grading	Storing
Communication	Insurance	Assembling	Personal Services

↓

The Automobile Manufacturer

↓

THE AUTOMOBILE CREATES THE NEED FOR, SUPPLIES GOODS TO, OR HELPS TO SUSTAIN THE FOLLOWING SERVICES AND RELATED BUSINESS:

Research	Public Sanitation	Recreation	Finance
Product Development	Education	Highway Restaurants	Insurance
Publications	Highway Construction	Tourists	Dealers
Engineering	Trucking	Roadside Markets	Parts Manufacturing
Advertising	Railroad Freight	New Construction	Refining
Police Protection	Public Transportation	Real Estate	Filling Stations
Fire Protection	Marine Freight	Farm Equipment	Service Garages
Public Health			

Here Is How One Industry Uses Goods and Services, Produces Goods, and Creates or Sustains Other Business

tional businessmen. The ultimate goal is a product or service that will serve a consumer. For example: (a) basic raw materials are produced on farms, in mines, and in forests, and are processed by manufacturers to furnish fertilizer, goods, and equipment to the farmer; (b) the farmer is financed by banks, (c) the farmer produces raw materials in the form of food and fiber; (d) foods and other products are processed by manufacturers and distributed to consumers. Throughout the entire endless process there are many people rendering services in a business way.

New products often create new businesses and new businesses create jobs. New products often create the need for additional materials, products, and services. For example, let us take a look at the automobile industry and see what happens. Let us see what kind of materials and services are needed and what kinds of business and activities the automobile industry creates and serves. These processes and functions are illustrated in the chart below.

Specialization Helps Us Get What We Want. Business provides many of the economic goods and services that consumers want through specialization. Under *specialization,* sometimes referred to as *division of labor,* a worker performs a particular task or job while other workers do something else. For example, a person may perform a certain task in making a shoe, such as attaching the eyelets for laces while, other workers may sew the upper to the sole or attach a heel. He performs a part of the total labor involved in making the shoe.

When every worker performed every task involved in making an article or commodity, production was slow and consequently cost of production was high. Specialization benefits both producer and consumer by lower costs. When cost is low, more people can buy; therefore, manufacturers can make more to sell.

It is not difficult to find an employee who can make castings for an automobile, another who can assemble parts, and still another who can paint and finish the car. But, to find one man who can do all of these tasks equally well would be almost impossible. Specialization makes possible more effective use of human abilities. It enables manufacturers to make more nearly complete use of their plants and equipment. Buildings and equipment can be used more advantageously.

We have many products and services that without specialization would be unavailable to use. The cost of many of the goods and services we use daily would be prohibitive if there was no division of labor; that is, if every person who works performed all of the labor that goes into the making of a product.

In 1920 an Hour's "Take Home" Pay Would Buy—

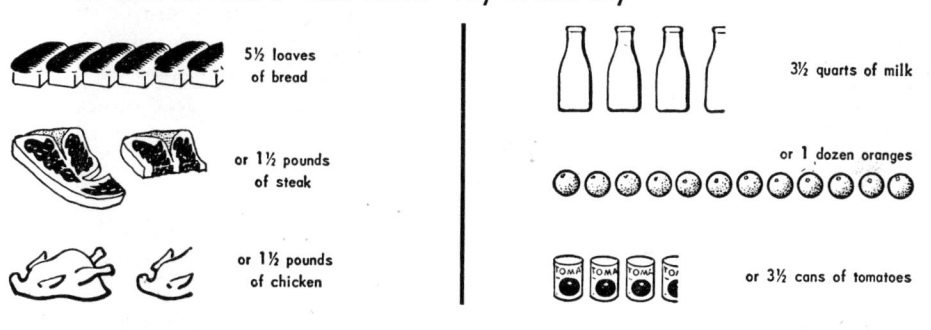

5½ loaves of bread

or 1½ pounds of steak

or 1½ pounds of chicken

3½ quarts of milk

or 1 dozen oranges

or 3½ cans of tomatoes

In 1954 an Hour's "Take Home" Pay Would Buy—

10 loaves of bread

or 2 pounds of steak

or 3 pounds of chicken

7 quarts of milk

or 3 dozen oranges

or 9½ cans of tomatoes

Source: U. S. Department of Agriculture

Efficient Methods of Production and Distribution Have Raised Our Standard of Living

Mass Production Lowers Costs. Abundance of power and the use of machines have made mass production possible. Mass production refers to the practice followed by many business firms of making one or at most only a limited number of different products and producing them in large quantities. Specialization is one of the factors that makes mass production possible. Through the use of power and machines a worker's production can be much greater than by doing the work by hand. Hence, because his output is greater his wages have steadily increased. Costs of the commodities he makes are lowered by use of power and machines; hence, more people are able to buy the commodity.

Harold M. Lambert

A Part of the Story of Men, Machines, Power, and Mass Production

This machine used in the Ford Motor Company for drilling crankshafts is typical of modern machinery created by man to make man's work easier and to make it possible to produce more goods for everyone at lower costs.

Science has helped business develop specialization and mass production. Manufacturing processes and products have been improved, and new machinery has been developed. New uses have been discovered for many raw materials that have been available in great quantities. Nature has been put to work for us in the modern laboratory and factory. When we made the clothing, food, and other commodities we wanted in our homes, our needs could not be supplied so well as they are today under modern division of labor and mass production.

There was a time, for instance, when an automobile was made in a small machine shop by only one or two men. Now under mass-production methods and straight-line assembly procedure, more than a hundred men may help in the final assembly of each automobile, each man performing only one or a few related tasks.

What Mass Production Means to You. What have been our benefits from specialization and mass production? Mass production has created greater human comfort, less fatigue, more leisure, and an average longer life. The farmer may work hard, but with his modern tractor and the electrification of his equipment, he can produce many times what the same man could have produced a hundred years ago. The same thing is true in factories where specialization has developed mass production.

Mass production has also brought many improvements in the materials that we use. Some items could not be made in small quantities at a price that you and I could afford to pay. It is only through mass production that we can get many things that we need. Take, for instance, aluminum ware. Do you think that you could develop a small plant in your home to make aluminum ware?

Mass production has lowered the price that consumers must pay for nearly everything that we use. This does not mean that you and I can pay for everything that we want, but on an average we all have more than our grandparents and our great-grandparents had. From an economic point of view, we have more goods and services to enjoy. Money

ITEMS	1914	1952
Dress (Cotton)	4.67 hours	2.5 hours
Suit (Men's Worsted)	75.1 hours	23.2 hours
Bread (1 pound)	17 minutes	6 minutes
Milk (1 quart)	24 minutes	8 minutes

National Industrial Conference Board

This chart shows the hours of labor the average factory worker had to give in 1914 to earn enough to pay for some typical products compared to hours required in 1952.

The Purchasing Power of Labor

prices have gone up, but a day's work will pay for more than ever before, and that is the real measure of prices.

It is evident that specialization and mass production have tremendously increased the total quantity of goods and services and have also improved the quality while cutting the cost.

Specialization and Mass Production May Create Conflicts. One hundred years ago most family units were producers and consumers. As we have become more highly specialized, we have developed group interests. Some of the major group interests are those of farmers, factory laborers, merchants, manufacturers, bankers, and professional men.

Usually labor unions want higher wages, shorter working hours, and better working conditions. They sometimes restrict labor and production. Merchants want to eliminate as much competition as possible. Generally speaking, they do not like sales taxes. Manufacturers want tariffs on competing foreign goods to protect themselves, but they do not want tariffs on things that they import. Some of them want to pay low wages and are often opposed to legislation favorable to labor. Likewise, bankers and professional groups have their special interests. These conflicts of group interests lead often to regulations, laws, and practices that are good for certain minority groups and that may not be good for the other groups and for consumers. Since everyone is a consumer, it is important that he know how to protect his special interests as a consumer.

Organized Marketing Helps Us. Imagine how difficult it would be for each of us to obtain the food, clothing, and other things we need directly from the producer of them. Our marketing system performs that service for us and also through advertising acquaints us with products and services for sale. Perhaps you may think the marketing system costs too much, and it is wasteful in some instances; but the functions performed are essential. Since the field of marketing is competitive, only the most efficient firms can survive in the long run.

Our marketing system makes it possible for you to buy almost anything you want if you have the money to pay for it. This magic has been brought about by a complicated system that will be discussed in detail in Chapter 4.

Of course we can all perform some of the functions of marketing if we have the time to do so. We can go directly to the farm and buy eggs if we have the time and the means of transportation. For the average family, however, it is more expensive to get the eggs in that way than it is to buy them at a store.

Sometimes the farmer and other producers give up some of the specialization in the hope of making more profit. For example, the farmer may decide to try to peddle vegetables, eggs, and poultry from door to door in the city. As a result, he will get a higher price than if he sold them to a wholesaler, but he might make less profit.

Problems of Choice. In the process of specialization each of us has learned to know his own task well. We have become efficient producers, but we have become poor consumers. We know less and less about what the other fellow produces. All along the lines of our activities we have lost touch with the direct sources of information that were common to our grandparents. Our lack of firsthand knowledge is not the only problem facing the consumer. Goods have changed also. In fact, they sometimes change so rapidly that experts and specialists have difficulty keeping themselves familiar with all new products and the changes in old products. Consequently, the process of determining quality has become a difficult one. While your grandmother could distinguish the grades of plain woolens, cotton goods, or silks, today you have to contend with numerous grades and weaves of woolens, new combination fabrics, entirely new cotton goods that grandmother never knew, and new synthetic yarns that are woven into many types of new fabrics.

In the food lines there have also been many changes. Your grandmother bought sugar and crackers out of a barrel, and beans out of a hundred-pound sack. She judged her coffee by its taste and aroma. Today goods are put up in attractive cans and beautiful packages of all sizes and shapes. There are many brands, many grades, and many advertising claims. We certainly have to develop a new means of judging the merchandise, since we have had no experience in producing all these items.

This matter of choice is a part of the whole problem of economic voting. You as an individual, along with millions of other people, have a tremendous power in your possession in controlling what you get and how you get it. In order to exercise your power of economic voting, you must have the knowledge that will enable you to make wise choices.

Interdependence Creates Problems. In this period of specialization a great chain of interdependence has developed—interdependence between individuals, between communities, between states, and between nations. The chain of interdependence is endless and hard to trace, for each person who receives money for his work or his goods uses this money to buy what is produced by many others.

We cannot have a prosperous society unless all of us who are dependent upon each other receive the goods and the services that we need. For instance, the farmer can be prosperous only if people in the city pay satisfactory prices in sufficient quantity for the goods produced on the farm.

Manufacturers can prosper only if the farmers and the city dwellers buy their machinery and other goods.

Consumers are dependent upon business for the goods and services they need; labor needs the jobs created by business in order to make a living; and owners and managers of business are dependent upon labor for production and upon consumers for a market for their product in order to operate their business at a profit. Thus, it is easily seen that each of the three groups is closely linked with the other two. The interdependence among the groups makes cooperation necessary.

INTERDEPENDENCE OF WORKERS

THE FARMER SELLS HIS PRODUCT TO THE GROCER

THE GROCER SELLS FOOD TO THE AUTOMOBILE WORKER

THE FARMER AND THE GROCER BUY THE CARS THE AUTOMOBILE WORKER MAKES

Graphics Institute for "Planning Your Future" by Myers-Little-Robinson; McGraw-Hill Book Co.

All People Benefit from Business. Our level of living in America is the highest ever known in any country of the world. The indications are good that it will go still higher. American business which may be compared to a three-horse team comprised of owners and managers, labor, and consumers makes this standard of living possible.

As consumers we are almost wholly dependent upon business for the economic goods and services we need. Business serves us; without business our present-day economic life would be impossible.

It is desirable that each of us understands what business is, how it operates, and how it affects us. We need to understand what the American Economic System is, how it operates, and its influence on our level of living.

Summary of How Business Meets Our Needs

1. Business meets our needs through production, distribution, finance, and management.
2. Machines, power, and mass production have lowered production costs making many goods available to consumers at lower prices.
3. Specialization has contributed to lower costs and has increased the productivity of many people.
4. Organized markets make available to you goods and services from all parts of the world.
5. Owners and managers, labor, and consumers are interdependent. What is good for one group must not be detrimental to another.
6. Our high level of living is the product of American business.

TEXTBOOK QUESTIONS

1. What essential changes that affect consumers have taken place in business from pioneer days to the present?
2. What is meant by the American Economic System?
3. What is meant by specialization or division of labor?
4. How does specialization affect the producer and the consumer?
5. How does mass production affect consumers?
6. How do specialized groups sometimes come into conflict in their economic interests and goals?
7. Why does the consumer have such a problem of making choices in buying goods and services?
8. Explain how interdependence among individuals, communities, and states creates problems.
9. How do people in general benefit from business?
10. In what way do consumers have a stake in the success and prosperity of business?

DISCUSSION QUESTIONS

1. Give examples illustrating how pioneer men supplied the wants and needs of their families directly and how our needs are supplied indirectly.
2. What are some of the primary factors comprising the American Economic System?

3. Explain some of the advantages of specialization.
4. It is still possible for an individual to make cloth and to prepare some of his food. For instance, one could buy a bushel of oats and make rolled oats for breakfast cereal. Rolled oats that you buy in a package in a store cost about ten times as much as the raw oats from which it is made. Would you recommend that every family prepare its own rolled oats? Why?
5. Three groups of people have special interests in American business. They are owners and managers, labor, and consumers. Why is it that what is good for one of the three groups must not be detrimental to the others?
6. In what way does marketing accept consumers?

PROBLEMS

1. This chapter includes a brief discussion of the conflicts that arise among certain groups of specialists, such as farmers, city workers, manufacturers. Write a theme according to the instructions of your teacher, developing further all the group conflicts that you can think about. Show how some of these conflicts can be detrimental to all of us but how compromises of their aims could help all of us.
2. In this chapter are mentioned the three basic economic utilities (form utility, place utility, and time utility) which are provided through business services and functions. In the case of breakfast cereal, point out as many as you can of the persons or businesses that have contributed each of the three basic utility values in cereal.
3. In this chapter there is a discussion of specialization, machines, power, and mass production as they contribute to the welfare of all of us. Assume that you had to make a shirt or dress for yourself. Estimate the amount of time that would be required for you to grow the cotton; harvest it; make the thread; make the cloth; and make the shirt or dress. From this analysis explain how you benefit by not having to make everything you need.

COMMUNITY PROBLEMS AND PROJECTS

1. For a period of the past week make a list of all the different kinds of specialists who have served you in some way.
2. Give several examples of mass production factories that require so great an investment that ordinarily no single individual could organize one.
3. Make a list of specific examples of modern machinery that have made it possible to increase production and lower costs.

Chapter 3

How Business Is Organized and Operated to Serve You

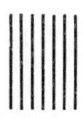

> **Purpose of the Chapter.** In the life of the consumer there are daily dealings with business. If you expect to be served to the best advantage by business, you need to know something about the purposes of business and how business is organized to serve you. A study of this chapter will help you to have a better understanding of business.
>
> You will find answers to these questions:
> 1. How big is business?
> 2. How does business operate?
> 3. How does business affect us?
> 4. How is business organized to serve us?

How Big Is Business? As our nation has grown from an agricultural nation to an industrial nation, fewer people are needed to raise our farm products because machinery has made farm production more efficient. More businesses are required to serve us because of our wants and needs of machinery and other types of goods and services.

How big are these individual businesses and how many of them are there? The following table includes figures from the United States Department of Commerce, Survey of Current Business, showing the sizes and types of industries and types of organizations. A more detailed description of the types of organizations will be given later in this chapter. Observe that most businesses are run by individuals and are small. Most large businesses are corporations.

Number of Firms in Operation by Type of Organization
(Thousands)

INDUSTRY DIVISION AND SIZE CLASS	ALL TYPES NUMBER	ALL TYPES PER CENT	INDIVIDUAL	PARTNERSHIP	CORPORATE	OTHER
All industries	3,839.7	100.0%	2,667.6	691.2	411.7	69.2
0– 3 employees	2,856.3	74.4	2,235.3	475.7	109.2	36.1
4– 7 employees	490.8	12.8	277.1	110.6	91.1	11.9
8–19 employees	301.1	7.8	119.9	66.4	103.2	11.6
20 or more employees	191.6	5.0	35.3	38.6	108.1	9.6

Businesses are also measured by the size of the investment or the size of sales. Later in this chapter will be found some information as to the amount of investment per employee in several kinds of industries.

What Are the Elements of Business? A large American business is so complicated that it is almost beyond the power of description. However, there are four fundamental factors or elements used by business in rendering services or supplying goods to customers. These four fundamental elements are (1) *natural resources*, such as land, oil, coal, mineral, forests, and water; (2) *labor*, such as railroad engineer, electrician, construction worker, miner, factory worker, or clerk; (3) *capital*, such as a factory, factory building, railroad, oil refinery, or machinery; and (4) *management*, such as designing, research, planning, directing, and supervising.

Natural resources are quite evident, but when we refer to labor we mean manpower in its broadest sense which includes physical labor, mental labor, and technical skills. These are all performed by individuals who are free men in the United States and may work where they wish, when they wish, as long as they wish, and for any wages they wish, provided no laws are broken.

In the economic sense capital refers to any buildings, equipment, or actual physical property used in business besides raw materials. Most important among these capital goods is machinery because machinery has had such a great

30

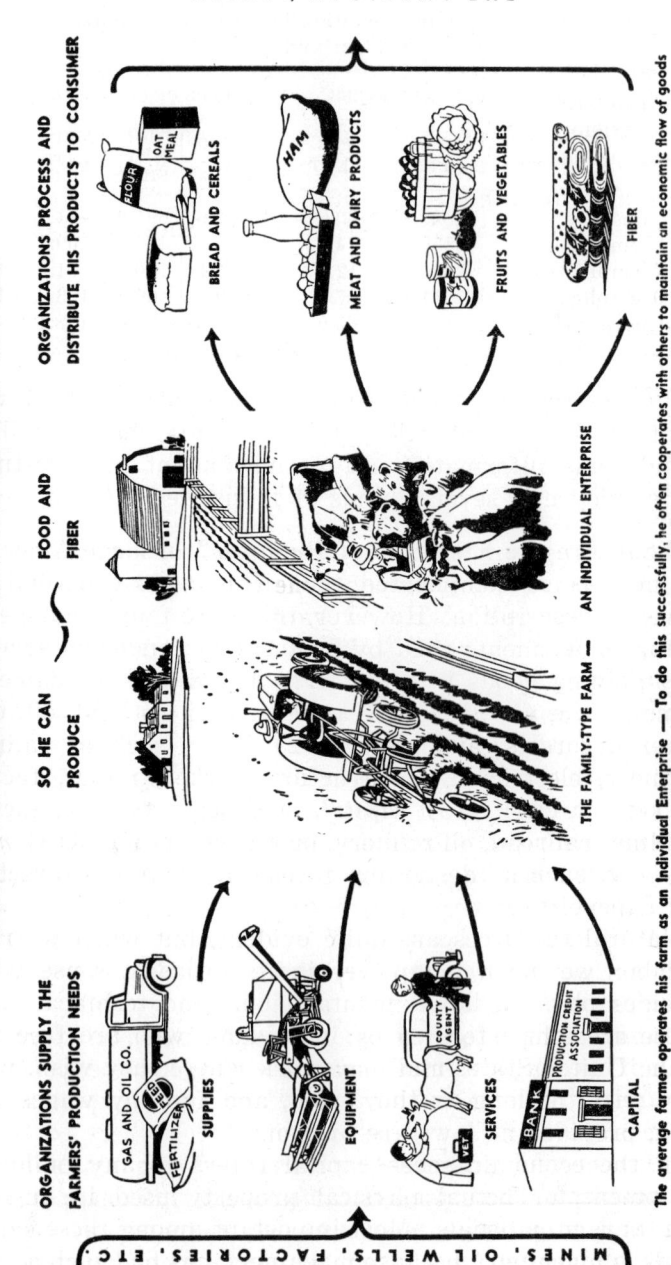

effect upon the happiness and prosperity of people in the United States. According to a study by the 20th Century Fund, man supplies less than 6 per cent of the energy used to produce all our goods and food. Man has learned through the use of better tools to multiply his productive capacity. Tools and machines make it possible to produce sixteen times as much food or goods as every man could produce with his own efforts.

There has always been a certain amount of fear that machines will replace men and will throw them out of work. Machines have made our country great, strong, and prosperous. Machines have given us many things we otherwise could not have. Machines have made it possible for most families to own an automobile. If an automobile were made by hand, it would be so expensive that few people could afford to buy one.

Before one jumps to the conclusion that machines are evil and create unemployment, one should ask himself some of these questions? Would I want to give up the use of a shovel and use my hands? Would I want to give up the use of a lawn mower? Would I want to give up the use of a vacuum sweeper? Would I want to give up the use of an automobile and walk instead of ride? Would the worker want to give up an electric drill or drilling machine and do it by hand? All of these are machines, and they are made by machines. Many products that we use today could not be produced at any price if it were not for modern machinery. Machines are definitely the muscles of business which lighten the burdens of workers and increase their efficiency so that we all have more and better things for lower prices.

Management is the key to a successful business operation. Even if we had the most valuable land, abundant natural resources, the most modern buildings and equipment, and the most intelligent and industrious labor, there could not be a successful business without good organization and management. The same principles apply in a one-man business and in a large business, but management becomes more complicated in a large business. Ideas must be created, designs made, plans drawn, workers hired, raw materials obtained, equipment purchased or built, and all of these factors put together efficiently. These are the functions of management.

What Is Free Enterprise? In our American economic system we say that we enjoy personal liberty, private property, and free enterprise. We may do pretty largely as we please if we respect the rights of other people and do not break any laws. We may own or use private property. We may sell it or give it away. From the point of view of business and the consumer a *free enterprise system* (also called *private enterprise*) means essentially that a businessman may produce anything he wishes and as much of it as he wishes. He may sell it to anyone who wishes to buy it at a price anyone is willing to pay. It means that the businessman operates in a free market without price fixing, without rationing, and without restrictions as to what he produces, how much he produces, where he will sell his products, or to whom he will sell it. There are certain exceptions, especially in time of war.

Freedom and Choices in Business

1. Buy
2. Sell
3. Select a location
4. Start a business
5. Advertise
6. Produce
7. Set prices
8. Compete
9. Invest money
10. Make a profit
11. Manage
12. Make decisions
13. Own property
14. Go out of business

Under a free enterprise system anyone may start a business by himself or with anyone else provided he does not break any laws. He has several choices of how he may organize his business. These will be discussed later. The businessman has an incentive to invest his money and to devote his time and effort to the business with the hope and expectation that he can earn his own wages and perhaps extra profit to compensate him for his risks and the money he has invested. He may keep his profits except the share that is collected by government for taxes.

Free enterprise, through its incentive profit system has caused the discovery and development of natural resources. Recent developments in uranium mining are good examples of this incentive. The personal freedom of the free enterprise system and the incentive rewards lead to new inventions and better ways of doing things. Many of the rewards of private enterprise are not great, but some of them are. The possibility of a reward of large profits causes thousands of individuals to start new businesses each year and encourages existing businessmen to strive to do better in providing goods and services for consumers.

How Does Competition Work? Competition is probably the most important aspect of a free enterprise system because it is part of the incentive profit motive. *Competition* means the privilege of one business to do the same thing as another business. It means the privilege of selling to the same customer and to sell as many goods or services as he can at whatever price he chooses provided he does not break any laws. Under a competitive system everyone is free to make a better product or to render a better service; he is not only free to do these, but competition is the driving force in business. He is free to compete with anyone else for his share of business. He may undersell his competitor and may make just as much profit as possible through his ability.

Competition is probably the greatest means of protection for the consumer because each businessman is forced to try to make the best product or render the best service if he wants to stay in business, and he tries to sell it to as many customers as possible and to make as much profit as possible. His profit is always limited by competition. The profit motive urges the businessman to try to produce efficiently and to try to give the customer what he wants. Therefore, the consumer really determines what the businessman does. He also determines the price that the businessman can charge because the consumer has the privilege of buying from anyone he chooses at whatever price he chooses. He may keep his money or spend it.

We sometimes speak of the free enterprise system or the *competitive system* as a *profit system.* It is also a *"voting" system* because every time a customer makes a purchase, he is voting in favor of one product or service instead of another. If there are two stores selling the same kinds of product side by side, the customer has the choice of voting or deciding in which store he will make his purchases. When he goes into a grocery store he probably has several choices of canned goods. He votes again as to how he will spend his money. If the price of one article is too high, he has the choice of taking another. If he does not like one kind of automobile, he may select another. If he does not like one color of automobile, he may select another.

When You Buy, You Are Voting

The great Dr. Charles F. Kettering, scientist and industrialist, has said, "I believe not only in the profit system, I believe in the double profit system. I will admit that I don't know a great deal about business because I've been a mechanic all of my life, but I do know this much about it: If I make an article and can sell it to you for more than it cost me, I have made a profit; but that profit doesn't do me very much good unless you are convinced that the article I sold you is worth more to you than the price you paid for it; and that is the second profit. If the customer does not make a profit which is even larger than you, the manufacturer, make, you cannot stay in business.

"We have the double profit system in every part of this country. That's what stores are; that's what advertisements are: Voting and electioneering places for their articles, whether it be a drill press, a neck-tie, or a hat. The man who can keep on making something and giving his customer a profit is the one who is getting the most votes, and that man is sure to succeed."

Of course, it is true that a consumer may sometimes think that a product is selling at too high a price. If he believes this, he does not have to vote for it (buy it). He can be sure however that in the long run competition will control prices unless there is a scarcity of goods and services which sometimes arises in war time.

Sole Proprietorship—A Type of Business Organization. A *sole proprietorship* is sometimes called an *individual proprietorship* or an *individual enterprise*. Such an enterprise is one that is owned and managed by one person. That person is the only one who receives the profits. He is a *capitalist* because he owns the business and receives the profits (anyone else who owns property from which he earns an income is a capitalist); he is a *laborer* because he performs some of the work and services. He may run the business in any way that he sees fit and make his own decisions provided he does not break any laws. The income that he receives from the business may be hardly enough to pay himself decent wages. On the other hand the income may be great enough to pay him decent wages and also an income on the investment that he has in the business.

The sole proprietorship is the simplest form of business and it is usually an example of the smallest type of business. Very few, if any, large businesses are operated as a sole proprietorship.

Characteristics of a Sole Proprietorship

1. Serves people by producing or distributing goods or by rendering a service.
2. Profit goes to the sole owner.
3. Owner makes decisions of policy.
4. Owner manages.
5. Owner provides the money for investment in the business except what he borrows.
6. Owner usually works in the business.
7. Owner is responsible for the acts and is liable for debts of business.

Partnership—A Form of Business Organization. A partnership is sometimes called a *copartnership*. A *partnership* is a type of business owned by two or more persons. Each may invest the same amount in the partnership or different amounts. If there are any profits above their wages, they generally share in the profits in proportion to the investment that each has in the business. In most states there are specific laws that regulate the formation, ownership, operation, and management of partnerships. These laws determine the rights and the responsibilities of partners. They also protect persons who loan money to the partnership or who do business with it. All partners are individually and jointly responsible for the operation of the business and for any debts of the business. There are special types of partnerships, referred to as *limited partnerships*, which permit a partner to participate without the usual liability for debts.

The purpose of a partnership usually is to combine the talents, labor, experience, and property of all partners in the hope that a profit can be earned for each partner. One of the advantages of a partnership is that two or more people share in the management. Each may have special

---

Characteristics of a Partnership

1. Serves people by producing or distributing goods or providing services.
2. Decisions are made by majority votes of partners.
3. All partners share in management.
4. By agreement, management responsibilities may be delegated to other persons.
5. Partners contribute the capital needed.
6. Partners are joint owners and share in the profits according to agreement.
7. Expenses of the business are borne by the partnership.
8. Generally partners are together liable and individually liable for debts to the extent of all the property they personally own. (There are exceptions in a limited partnership or when there is a silent partner who does not participate in the business, but merely invests in it.)

ability which will make the business a more successful business than one operated by one person with limited ability. Two or more partners usually can also provide more money to finance a business than can just one person.

Corporation—A Form of Business Organization. An important form of business organization is the *corporation* which is owned by *stockholders*. The ownership in a corporation is represented by *shares of stock*. Ownership of one or more shares of common stock in a corporation entitles the owner to help select members of the *board of directors* who manage the corporation. Members of the board of directors usually delegate much of the responsibility for the management of business to *officers* who are selected by the board of directors. The officers usually consist of at least the president, the treasurer, and the secretary. The chairman of the board of directors sometimes also serves as an active manager of the business.

A distinct advantage of a corporation over a partnership or a sole proprietorship is that the owners of a corporation are not responsible personally for the debts of a corporation; however, they may lose what they have invested in shares of stock if the corporation fails.

A corporation is in a sense an artificial being or person created or authorized by the state laws in which the corporation is organized. The purposes for which a corporation is organized are stated in its *charter*, which is the written legal evidence issued by the state showing the right of the corporation to exist and to do business.

In addition to the laws of the state which govern a corporation and the privileges and limitations stated in the charter, the stockholders vote on and approve a set of *bylaws* which become additional regulations under which the board of directors, the officers, and employees may operate the business.

For all practical purposes the officers of a corporation operate the business themselves or through hired employees, but are subject to the regulations of the board of directors, the stockholders, the provisions in the charter, the provisions in the bylaws, and the state laws under which the corporation is organized. Of course, any corporation must abide by the laws in other states in which it may operate and must abide by Federal laws if it operates in more than one state.

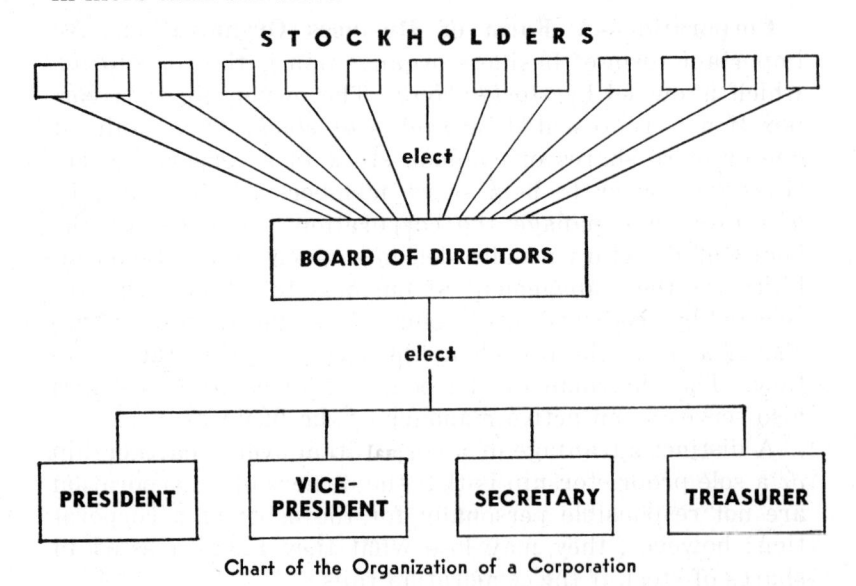

STOCKHOLDERS

elect

BOARD OF DIRECTORS

elect

PRESIDENT | **VICE-PRESIDENT** | **SECRETARY** | **TREASURER**

Chart of the Organization of a Corporation

Generally, there is a stockholders meeting once a year at which time the members of the board of directors are elected and major business of the corporation are voted upon (state laws provide that certain decisions must be decided by stockholders). The law usually requires a corporation to send each stockholder, at a specified time in advance, a notice of the time and the place of the meeting. If the stockholder cannot attend the meeting personally, he may be represented by someone else. The written authority to allow someone else to represent a stockholder is called a *proxy*.

A *close corporation* is one that does not offer its stock for public sale. It is frequently owned by just a few stockholders, some of whom may be actively engaged in operating the business in the same manner as partners operate a business. A close corporation, under the laws of most states, does not need to make its activities known to the general public since its securities are not offered for general sale. It must, however, submit reports to stockholders and to the state from which it obtained its charter.

An *open corporation* is one that offers its stock for general sale to anyone who wishes to buy it. Stocks of these corporations may be listed and quoted for sale on organized *stock exchanges* or may be sold privately as unlisted securities by brokers and dealers.

An open corporation must provide stockholders annually with a financial statement and must make certain financial figures available to the public. Under certain conditions the Federal Government regulates, through the Securities and Exchange Commission, the sale of corporation securities

---

Characteristics of a Corporation

1. Ownership is divided into equal parts called shares of capital stock.
2. Common stockholders own the business.
3. Common stockholders elect directors.
4. Directors formulate general plans and policies and elect the officers.
5. Officers in a small corporation usually consist of a president a secretary, and a treasurer.
6. Officers have charge of the active management of the business.
7. Officers have the privilege of employing additional persons if necessary to manage the business.
8. A corporation is authorized by a state through a charter.
9. Laws of the state, the charter, and the bylaws are the rules under which a corporation operates.
10. If a corporation operates in more than one state, it is subject to certain Federal laws.
11. A corporation may borrow money.
12. Common stockholders receive profits through dividends in proportion to the number of shares owned.
13. Preferred stockholders generally have no voice in the management or policies of the corporation but usually receive a fixed dividend before common stockholders.

and the publication of financial information of corporations. These regulations will be discussed in Chapter 7.

Large corporations require many millions of dollars, and they are owned by thousands of individual stockholders. It usually is impossible for a few individuals to provide personally the amount of money needed to start and to operate a large corporation. Therefore, banks and other dealers in securities often take over the function of selling securities for a corporation. These securities may be in the form of common stock, preferred stock, bonds, or notes which are discussed in detail in Chapter 27.

Although there are many more businesses operated as sole proprietorships and partnerships than there are corporations, the corporation is probably the most important type of business. Most of the very large businesses are corporations. Their stock is owned widely by individuals, banks, insurance companies, and others.

Cooperative—A Form of Business Organization. A *cooperative* is a special form of business corporation. It is a "legal person" created by the laws of the state and distinct from its members. It continues to exist regardless of the individual deaths or the withdrawals of members. In contrast with an ordinary business corporation the cooperative serves only as an agent for its members. In theory the members of a cooperative are the owners and users of a service, but in actual practice some cooperatives sell to and deal with the general public.

Under the principles of operating a cooperative, profit above the cost of operation is returned to the members in proportion to the amount of business that each member does with the cooperative. This is common practice although it is not followed by all cooperatives. However, one practice that is usually followed by all cooperatives is in allowing each member to have only one vote regardless of the number of shares owned.

Types of Cooperatives. There are many types of cooperatives including those engaged in agricultural marketing, farm purchasing, credit unions, cooperative housing, cooperative health, newspapers, insurance. Credit unions are a form of consumer cooperative. These are discussed in more detail in Chapter 22. There are several other types of consumer cooperatives. Some consumers believe that the amount of profit taken out during the process of distribution is unjustified and unnecessary. Consumers who are willing to perform some of the functions of distribution themselves may band themselves together in a cooperative association, commonly known as a *consumer cooperative* or a *retail cooperative*. The objective of this type of cooperative is to pass on to the members of this cooperative any savings that result from the enterprise.

Characteristics of a Cooperative

1. Cooperatives are organized to serve their members (although some sell to the general public).
2. Members elect the board of directors to manage the cooperatives.
3. Members decide questions of policy at meetings of members.
4. The board of directors is responsible for management of the cooperatives and may employ people to carry out the functions.
5. Each member has one vote, although there are some exceptions.
6. Member-patrons are the sole owners of the business unless nonvoting preferred stock is sold.
7. Member-patrons supply the needed money and capital by purchasing shares of stock or paying membership dues.
8. Money may be borrowed by a cooperative.
9. Cooperatives pay a fixed interest rate on stock.
10. Profit is returned to members in the form of patronage refunds.
11. If the cooperative fails, the liability of members is limited to investment in the cooperative.

Some consumer cooperatives are relatively small, the members being confined to a certain group of people, such as the postal employees in a city. They are frequently organized in a city and are frequently organized as retailing establishments or as credit unions. Some deal only with their own members; however, some also sell to anyone.

Businessmen Organize Cooperatives, Too. Many kinds of regular sole proprietorships, partnerships, and business corporations organize themselves in the form of cooperatives. The Associated Press is a world-wide news gathering cooperative for various newspapers. Thousands of individually owned grocery stores, jewelry stores, drugstores, and other types of businesses unite and jointly form cooperatives and own and operate their own wholesale houses.

Public Utilities—A Type of Busines. Such services as telephone, gas, water, electricity, and transportation are often provided by business firms that are known as *public utilities*. Some public utilities are owned by a government unit, such as a town, township, or city. These are said to be publicly owned. These companies usually are given the exclusive right to provide a service to the consumers of a certain geographical area. This right is granted to assure the utility company that no other company will be permitted to compete with it in providing the same kind of service to consumers in its territory. This protection is necessary because of the exceedingly high cost of building water and gas mains or electric and telephone lines by which such services are made available to the consumers. Pipe lines and telephone or electric lines are permanent, and the investment in them cannot be recovered by removing them if they are no longer used. Uncontrolled competition might force the abandonment of such equipment or make it unprofitable for the public utility to remain in operation.

The public utility company usually is given the privilege to operate and to provide a particular kind of service in a given territory by the state, the city, and sometimes by the Federal Government. This privilege or right to operate is known as a *franchise*. In accepting a franchise, the public utility company assumes certain responsibilities and agrees to abide by certain regulations relative to its management, operation, and rates.

Public utility companies provide many essential services for consumers at rates that consumers can afford to pay. Most services of public utilities would be impossible for the consumer to provide for himself. Thus public utilities are important factors in meeting the wants and needs of consumers in modern life.

Monopoly. When conditions are such that it is not advisable or economical for more than one public utility to provide a service for a given territory, the firm to which the right to provide the service is granted is said to have a *monopoly*.

A monopoly exists in business when there is no competition. There are no real monopolies in the United States today except in the field of public utilities. However, the world production of diamonds is pretty largely controlled by a monopoly, and we must pay the price asked by the monopoly.

Though many public utilities are virtually monopolies because they may be free from competition in a particular territory, the rates charged for their services are regulated and controlled by the city, the state, or the Federal government. The rates are regulated to insure consumers the services at a fair and reasonable cost. Rates also are established to produce sufficient income to pay all expenses, to provide for proper maintenance and repair, and to provide a reasonable profit for the owners of the company if it is one that is privately owned.

Legal Authority for a Business Organization. In the previous discussion it was pointed out that sole proprietorships, partnerships, and corporations are organized under state laws and are regulated by state laws. As will be seen in a later chapter, businesses that operate in more than one state are regulated by Federal laws.

Except in a few unusual cases, such as the Federal law authorizing charters for national banks, the Federal Government does not give a group the legal right to incorporate. The exceptions are the charters issued to the American Legion, the Boy Scouts of America, the American

Red Cross, and a few others, but these are not regular business corporations.

Business and Jobs. The previous discussion in this chapter has already pointed out how new products and new investments create jobs. Management plays a major role in organizing business activities so that jobs are available. Money is needed to create jobs because in business money is needed for capital goods, such as buildings and equipment, before there is a place for a worker and a job to perform. The creation of new jobs by business is therefore dependent upon the available capital which must be provided by investors who are willing to take a risk of investing their money in business. In modern manufacturing industry the average investment per worker is $13,281 as illustrated in the table below.

	Average Investment per Job in Manufacturing Plants	
NUMBER OF COMPANIES	INDUSTRY	TOTAL
83	All manufacturing (average)	$13,281
7	Food	16,996
9	Paper	16,142
5	Plastics	10,754
9	Chemicals	38,117
14	Other nondurable goods	10,955
13	Electrical machinery	10,305
9	Other machinery	13,248
8	Other fabricated metal products	10,460
9	Other durable goods	11,125

But, Business Is Not Free. In this chapter we have spoken of free enterprise, but actually, in the United States business operates under many governmental regulations. The purpose of governmental regulations is fundamentally to prevent honest people from getting hurt in business dealings and to prevent unethical or dishonest practices. These regulations tend to control business on the one hand and to protect consumers and businessmen on the other hand. Some of these regulations will be explained later.

Ch. 3]   How Business Is Organized and Operated   45

> ### Summary of How Business Is Organized and Operated to Serve Us
> 1. Business provides goods and services to fill our wants.
> 2. The elements involved in business are material, labor, capital, and management.
> 3. We operate under a free enterprise system, but with governmental controls.
> 4. Free competition helps us to get better products at a reasonable price.
> 5. The consumer is an important factor through his voting in the competitive system.
> 6. Businesses are organized in many ways.
> 7. Business creates business, goods, and services.
> 8. Business creates jobs.
> 9. Business is regulated by laws.

TEXTBOOK QUESTIONS

1. In terms of number of employees, are most businesses large or small?
2. When we speak of natural resources as an element or factor of business, what do we mean?
3. Besides natural resources, what are the other three factors or elements of business?
4. Of the energy or power used in business, approximately what per cent is supplied by human energy?
5. What is the estimate of how much men produce with tools or machines as compared with what he could produce with his own efforts without tools or machines?
6. Essentially what do we mean by a free enterprise system or private enterprise system?
7. What is meant by the competitive system and how does it work?
8. Why is the competitive system a voting system?
9. Why are most monopolies regulated by government?
10. Give at least two characteristics of a sole proprietorship.
11. How are the profits of a partnership generally distributed?
12. Generally, what is the responsibility of partners in regard to debts?
13. In what way is a corporation owned?

14. Who elects the board of directors and the officers of a corporation?
15. What is a close corporation?
16. What is an open corporation?
17. Through what legal authority is a corporation usually organized?
18. What is the difference between a preferred stockholder and a common stockholder?
19. In a cooperative, how many votes does a member generally have?
20. In a cooperative, who elects the board of directors to manage the enterprise?
21. Tell how a grocery store operator may be a member of a cooperative with other store owners.
22. What are some of the business services that are often organized as public utilities and frequently as monopolies?
23. What is a franchise in relation to a public utility?
24. In major industry, what is the average amount of money per worker invested by business in buildings and equipment?

DISCUSSION QUESTIONS

1. Some individual workers and unions are fearful of machines and the introduction of new machinery is often opposed by some people. Mention an example and discuss the good and bad effects of the use of machinery instead of hand work.
2. Management is sometimes looked upon as an unnecessary cost by uninformed people. Explain the functions of management as an essential element in business.
3. Why do we say that many commodities or services should be profitable to both the buyer and the seller?
4. What freedoms would be lost if all businesses were owned and operated by a government?
5. It has often been said that consumers are voting their economics processes every day and are deciding the fate of businesses. Explain what is meant by this.
6. From the point of view of an investor in a sole proprietorship, partnership, or corporation which type of organization has the least risk in regard to acts or debts of the business?
7. Explain why you feel a franchise for a public utility is necessary or desirable.
8. It is often stated that anything that retards or prevents the assemblying of capital for a business restricts general economic progress. If this is true, explain why it is true.

PROBLEMS

1. In your school library, locate books on business law, business organization, or bookkeeping in which are given the characteristics of single proprietorships, partnerships, and corporations. Prepare a report on the advantages and disadvantages of each of these three forms of business organization.
2. From your own knowledge and opinions and from information that you can gain from businessmen or from library reading make a list of the ways in which business enterprise has freedom to do as it wishes. Make another list of the ways in which business is regulated and does not have complete freedom.

COMMUNITY PROBLEMS AND PROJECTS

1. Make a list of business firms in your community or city that specialize in (a) making a product that is used by individuals or families as consumers, (b) making a product that is used by other business firms in the making of their products, and (c) rendering a service to individuals and to families.
2. Interview one of the officers, preferably the president, of a consumer cooperative enterprise in your community. Prepare a report giving the nature of the cooperative enterprise, number of members, requirements for membership, how the cooperative is managed, the volume of business and the savings for consumers during the past year and the basis for distributing the savings to the members.
3. From your proper state official, a local bank, a lawyer friend, or some other source, obtain information as to the requirements in your state for organizing a corporation and making a list of the requirements and procedures.
4. Make a list of the special utilities in your community, such as those providing water, gas, electricity, transportation, and telephone. Find out and report whether they are owned by individuals, partnerships, corporations, or the community, such as the city or any other public authority. If possible, find out how rates are established and regulated and report these facts.

Chapter 4

The Functions and Services of Marketing

> **Purpose of the Chapter.** Most of the relationships that a consumer has with business pertain to buying goods and services. If you are going to be an effective buyer, you need to understand the marketing system, its functions, and its services so that you may use the marketing system to the best advantage. A study of this chapter will help you to understand something about the marketing system with which you must deal daily.
>
> You will find answers to these questions:
>
> 1. What are the economic functions of marketing?
> 2. What are some of the services performed in distribution?
> 3. How do goods and services reach us?
> 4. Can any of the marketing functions and services be eliminated or combined?
> 5. What are some of the costs of distribution?

Functions of Marketing. The marketing process is sometimes called *distribution* or *the distributive system*. This system includes all of the functions that have to do directly with satisfying the wants and needs of individuals; but it does not include the productive or manufacturing process. Marketing makes goods available at a time (time utility) and at places (place utility) needed by consumers. Some of the functions of the system involve the actual physical handling of goods and others involve services. These functions are as follows:

48

Ch. 4] FUNCTIONS AND SERVICES OF MARKETING   49

> *Economic Functions of Marketing*
> 1. Assembling
> 2. Storing
> 3. Grading and standardizing
> 4. Stimulating demand (advertising and selling)
> 5. Merchandising
> 6. Transporting and communicating
> 7. Financing
> 8. Risk bearing

The exact channels of distribution for various products are not the same, but the functions are always the same. Certain middlemen may be eliminated by combining some functions, but it is not possible to eliminate any of these basic functions.

(1) Assembling—A Function of Marketing. The assembling of goods is one of the first steps in marketing. *Assembling* means accumulating or gathering goods from various sources. Many individuals and businesses are engaged in assembling goods. For example, raw materials are

Courtesy General Motors

Materials Are Assembled in Many Places to Make Automobiles

assembled for manufacture. Wholesalers assemble many types of manufactured goods from many different manufacturers located in many different places and make these available for the retailer. The retailer assembles a considerable variety of goods from different wholesalers. Creamery stations, grain elevators, and stockyards are also important agencies in the assembling of products for consumers.

(2) Storing—A Function of Marketing. Storing is a function that is performed during many stages of the process of delivering goods from producers to consumers. The businesses that assemble goods in large quantities hold them for the demand of those to whom they sell. We ordinarily think of cold-storage plants, commercial warehouses, and grain elevators as places of storage.

In all stages in the distribution process, goods must be stored, either temporarily or for a long period of time. The manufacturer, the wholesaler, and the retailer, however, must have on hand a supply of goods to serve those to whom they sell.

Quick Freezing Brings Fresh Foods to the Consumer

Materials and foods are stored in many ways. Freezing is used both in transporting and storing foods.

Birds Eye Frosted Foods

Many people fail to realize the extremely important function of storage. Without storage many products could not be enjoyed. They would not be available at the proper time and at the proper place. This fact is especially true of such products as meat, eggs, and fresh veegtables. Fresh meat is available in practically every community at all times of the year. Eggs are stored during seasons of high production for use in seasons of low production. Fresh vegetables are available during the twelve months of the year in most cities and towns. These foods are available as the result of cold storage. The introduction of quick-freezing methods of storage brings to our tables fresh fruits and vegetables in all seasons, preserved with their original flavors.

(3) Grading and Standardizing—A Function of Marketing. Grading has rapidly become an important function of distribution. Tobacco, wheat, corn, and other agricultural products are carefully graded as they are assembled and marketed. They are sold in large lots on the basis of grade. Meat especially is marketed on the basis of inspection and grading. Grading determines the differences in value.

The Federal Government and many associations organized to promote standards are performing an important function for the consumer. Many products can now be bought to meet standard specifications and are marked as to grade. Canned food products—as will be discussed in more detail later—are now being graded for the protection of the buyer. Grading and standardizing save time and money in buying.

(4) Stimulating Demand—A Function of Marketing. The preceding functions deal with the accumulation and the preparation of goods for distribution through the various channels on their way to the consumer. Those who have collected goods, stored them, and graded them cannot assume that people who want these goods will seek them. It is an entirely false assumption that if you have a good product, "customers will beat a path to your door." Personal selling and advertising are therefore used to stimulate demand for goods.

Elias Howe was the inventor of the sewing machine. He died a poor man because he could not sell his sewing machine. A whole generation of women lived after its invention without the help of the sewing machine. This happened because selling and advertising were not used to tell women about it and to educate them to its use. There was no merchandising organization to distribute the machine. Selling and advertising finally did the job and look what the sewing machine means to us today. Similar stories have repeated many times in our history. Do you suppose for instance that women would be wearing nylon hose today if it had not been for the force of selling and advertising which taught women to use a better product and made that product available?

PERSONAL SELLING. The most common type of personal selling is practiced by the retail clerk who both serves the customer by providing information and demonstrating the product and also by attempting to convince the customer that the product or service should be bought. Personal selling is being practiced every day by thousands of people: Technical engineers sell when they try to show manufacturers how expensive new equipment will enable them to reduce manufacturing costs and produce better products. The manufacturer has salesmen to sell his product. Clerks sell goods to consumers over the counter.

There are two general methods of stimulating demand. The first method is to pass on to each member in the distributive system the responsibility of selling the product at a particular stage in distribution. Under this method the manufacturer may sell to the wholesaler, the wholesaler sells to the retailer, and the retailer sells to the consumer.

Without Demand There Would Be Low Production and High Cost

The retailer has the final responsibility of selling the product to the consumer.

ADVERTISING. The second method is to create consumer demand. Under this plan the manufacturer buys advertising space in newspapers and magazines, uses time on radio and television, and uses various other means of mass advertising to tell consumers about his goods, thus causing them to want his goods in preference to others. Under this method the function of selling is partially reversed. The consumer demands the product from the retailer; the retailer buys it from the wholesaler; and the wholesaler buys it from the manufacturer.

In actual practice the two methods are almost always intermingled; the manufacturer advertises to the public, but he also has salesmen to call on wholesale dealers. The wholesaler or manufacturer, in turn, may advertise to the public; but he will also send salesmen to call on retailers. In recent years, however, manufacturers have tended to go directly to the consumer with a mass advertising message to create direct consumer demand. Creating consumer demand gives the manufacturer better control over his distributive system, provided he is successful in his advertising efforts. Great sums of money are expended annually for advertising.

Advertising performs certain useful business and economic functions. However, there have been some criticisms of the wastefulness of advertising in some particular cases. From an economic point of view, the following are the purposes and the functions of advertising:

(a) *To provide a necessary means of widespread communication from the producer to the consumer in a democratic and capitalistic type of society.* Unless there were some means of advertising, a producer would never be able to communicate with customers on a wide scale. Without advertising, consumers in San Francisco might never learn of a product manufactured in New York.

(b) *To create a demand for a particular product or type of products.* This function might be considered as a part of the first function. Advertising has educated us to accept and to use new products or improved products. It has educated us to demand certain types of foods, and in many ways it has changed our eating habits. In this respect it has performed a useful social function.

(c) *To get a premium price on brands over and above the average price of unbranded goods or of competing brands.* By establishing in the minds of buyers a preference for a particular brand, it has been possible in many cases to get a higher price for that brand of merchandise. In some cases this function works to the disadvantage of the consumer when the price is higher than that of other goods of equal quality. Some consumers, however, are willing to pay a premium price to be able to identify a brand of established quality.

(d) *To get wide distribution, mass production, reduced costs of distribution, reduced costs of manufacture, and therefore reduced prices to the consumer.* This process of obtaining mass distribution and lower prices is often used to compete with other companies. At the same time, it tends to push prices down for the consumer and to force other competitors to operate equally efficiently or to go out of business.

(e) *To speed the process of distribution.* It is a well-known fact in business that advertising helps to move goods off the shelves of individual merchants. It therefore reduces the time that the goods are held on the shelves, it reduces the amount of money that the merchant has tied up in merchandise, and it reduces the time that he has his money tied up. In business terminology, advertising increases the turnover of merchandise. By increasing the turnover, there is lower cost for the merchant, and the consumer gets fresher goods. The merchant will either make a greater profit, or the consumer will enjoy lower prices. It is a well-established fact in business that a merchant must charge a higher margin of profit on goods with a low turnover than he charges on goods with a high turnover.

(5) Merchandising—A Function of Marketing. After demand has been created, it must be satisfied. Merchandising is the actual process of filling demands for products. It is particularly important in retail stores, and in such cases includes the following:

1. Arrangement of counters and other store facilities.
2. Display of goods.
3. Window displays.
4. Procedure and personnel for showing and demonstrating goods to prospective customers.
5. Delivery service.
6. Systematic credit policy.
7. Installation and repair service.

Not every retailer performs all these functions, but he must perform some of them. For instance, a retailer may have no delivery service, and he may not need to perform installation and repair service; but he probably does have to perform the other functions.

A very important function in the merchandising of household equipment is installation and repair service. For instance, if a person buys an electric refrigerator, he wants to be assured that it will be installed properly, will operate properly, and can be repaired if the need presents itself.

(6) Transporting and Communicating—A Function of Marketing. Transporting and communicating represent indispensable services in the distributive system. Such means of transportation and communication as railroads, boats, airplanes, trucks, telephones, and telegraph and postal service help each person obtain the goods that he needs.

The wonders of transportation and communication enable a person to telephone or telegraph to Hawaii and have fresh flowers delivered in Chicago in twenty-four hours, or a buyer in New York City to transmit orders to Florida and have fresh fruits or vegetables sent by fast railway express, motor carrier, or airline in an amazingly short time. Modern refrigeration makes it possible to transport almost any kind of food to any place in the United States so that everybody may enjoy fresh foods twelve months out of the year.

(7) Financing—A Function of Marketing. Whenever goods are assembled, stored, or graded, or any of the other functions of distribution is performed, money or credit is needed. Suppose, for example, that a farmer stores his wheat in a grain elevator until he can sell it. He will have to pay for the storage and will probably need to borrow some money until he can sell his wheat. On the other hand, if the operator of the grain elevator buys the wheat to hold for future sale, he must have the cash with which to pay the farmer, or he must borrow the money.

When a product such as wheat is stored, a receipt is given to the person who has stored the product. This receipt can be left with a banker or an individual as security for a loan. If the loan is not paid, the product that is stored becomes the property of the person who has lent the money.

(8) Risk Bearing—A Function of Marketing. Taking a risk means bearing the chance of a loss. Constant risks occur all along the line of distribution. These risks include theft, fire, breakage, spoilage, shrinkage, and a drop or a rise in prices. Insurance can be obtained to provide protection against most risks. Limiting or eliminating other types of risks must be obtained through good management.

If a person in the distributing system takes a risk, he is entitled to a profit for his risk. The cost of risk bearing is therefore included in the price that the consumer pays.

Speculation on our organized markets is another form of risk bearing that is important in our distribution system. Speculators are willing to offer a purchase price on a commodity months in advance, even before it is produced. Other speculators are willing to sell for future delivery goods that they do not have.

What Is a Market? The word *market* is used in a variety of ways. When a businessman says that he has a good market for his goods, he means that there is a good demand for them. If he says that he has a large market for his goods, he means that these goods are distributed over a wide geographical area or that there are many people who are his customers.

The word market is also used to refer to a place used for buying and selling. In many cities there are public market squares where produce merchants and farmers gather to sell to people who are seeking their products. Exchanges are markets. The New York Stock Exchange, for instance, is a security market. The Chicago Board of Trade is a grain market. The word market is used in still another way. For instance, if a person says, "How is the stock market today?" he has reference to the trend of prices and conditions in the entire United States, although most transactions are centralized in New York City.

Wholesale Markets. A *wholesale market* is distinguished by its practice of trading only in large lots. A large lot may be one hundred cases, a carload, or an entire shipload of goods. Wholesale markets are classified as (a) general wholesale markets, (b) commission markets, and (c) auction markets. Dealers and brokers operate in all types of markets. A *dealer* buys with the hope of selling goods at a profit. The *broker* acts as an agent in buying for someone else. He does not take the title to the goods, but assists in the transaction between the buyer, whom he represents, and a seller.

Dealers are ordinarily the principal operators in general wholesale markets. A dealer takes the title to goods and sells the goods in smaller lots to other wholesalers, to retailers, or directly to consumers. For example, dealers may buy hogs and cattle that have been brought to a central marketing place and sell them to packing houses, who are the wholesalers. These wholesalers sell the meat to retail stores and the retail stores sell the meat to consumers.

Commission Markets. *Commission markets* are ordinarily operated by commission merchants. A *commission merchant* takes possession of the goods and acts as an agent in handling them. He usually does not actually own the goods, but in some markets he may actually buy the goods instead of acting just as an agent for the seller. He attempts to sell the product entrusted to him at the highest price he can obtain, although he sometimes follows special instructions from the seller as to the price he should obtain. For his services he obtains a fee known as a *commission*. There are commission markets in all large cities. Products that are commonly sold on these markets are fruits, vegetables, and poultry.

Suppose, for example, a farmer brings fifty sacks of potatoes to a commission merchant in Cincinnati. In the absence of specific instructions with regard to the price at which the potatoes must be sold, the commission merchant will sell them at the highest price that he can obtain on the basis of bids offered by buyers. For his services he will charge either a percentage of the sale or a fixed amount.

An *auction market* is one in which buyers congregate and bid for products that are offered for sale. Fruits, tobacco, and furs are frequently sold in this manner. Important tobacco auction markets are located in Lexington and Louisville, Kentucky. Important fur markets are located in St. Louis and New York.

The wholesale markets of the United States are concentrated in sections where they can serve most effectively the concentrated areas of population.

Retail Markets. A *retail market* is the final outlet in the distributing system—the final link in the chain between the producer and the consumer. There are more retailers than there are business proprietors of any other type. Grocery stores, department stores, filling stations, meat markets, shoe stores, and clothing stores are representative types of retail markets. These are places to which consumers may go in order to obtain the goods they want.

Organized Markets. An *organized market* is a place where buyers and sellers can congregate for the purpose of trading in securities or products. Such a market is commonly referred to as an *exchange*.

Organized commodity markets are located in many parts of the country. Some of the smaller exchanges maintain close contact with the larger exchanges. Canned food, cottonseed, grains, feed, eggs, hides, lard, lead, potatoes, rubber, silk, minerals, sugar, tobacco, wool, and many other products are sold on organized exchanges in various parts of the country. Products are sold on the basis of grades and frequently by samples.

Organized markets or exchanges provide a nationwide means of buying and selling. They benefit the seller by providing an assured market of a wide scope so that he does not have to depend upon selling his products locally. They benefit the buyer by providing a relatively sure and constant supply of goods. They also tend to establish and to stabilize prices. For instance, one can determine very quickly the price of a commodity by looking at the latest market quotations. These quotations are published in the newspapers and are often broadcast over the radio.

Organized markets also provide a means of speculation that is used by businessmen to hedge their operations. *Hedging* is a system whereby businessmen can buy raw materials sold on an organized market and yet avoid the usual risks of fluctuating prices. Hedging is too technical to discuss at this point.

Scope of Markets. In general, markets are considered to be (a) *local,* (b) *regional,* (c) *national,* or (d) *international.* International markets are frequently referred to as *world markets.*

The large geographical area of the United States has enabled many businesses to develop large national markets. There is an interesting contrast between a manufacturer's potential market in the United States and a manufacturer's potential market in one of the small European countries. The manufacturer in a small European country not only has a small market but also has a barrier of tariff between his country and other countries. A large national market encourages production in large quantities. As this type of production is usually economical, the consumer benefits. For instance, if an automobile manufacturer were limited to a market the size of Michigan, the company could not produce automobiles in large numbers. Both the cost of production and the price to the consumer would therefore be high. Automobile manufacturers have a national market, and some have international markets.

Not all products or services can reach out into the national market. The nature of the product or the service and various other influences tend to restrict the market. Laundries, for instance, are usually confined to local communities. Without establishing branches, a laundry seldom finds it profitable to solicit business at greater distances than twenty or thirty miles. A single retail meat market is necessarily confined to its own neighborhood. It sometimes enlarges its territory by delivery service.

The marketing of vegetables at one time was confined to areas close to the points of production. The marketing areas for these products have, however, been extended to almost every point of the United States through the use of transportation and storage facilities. Nevertheless, the market for seasonal fresh vegetables is usually confined to relatively small areas around producing regions. For instance, during the producing season, it would be foolish for a person who raises beans in Missouri to attempt to sell fresh beans in New York City if beans are produced economically within a few miles of New York City. Certain regions, such as the South and the West Coast, have national markets for fresh fruits and vegetables during the seasons when other regions cannot produce these foods.

Place of the Middleman. A *middleman* is one who performs a marketing service between the producer and the consumer. Some of the most common types of middlemen are wholesalers, jobbers, commission merchants, and retailers. The term *jobber* arose out of the custom of certain dealers to buy from producers in quantities called "job lots." Jobbers and wholesalers are now almost indistinguishable because they serve essentially the same purpose. If middlemen perform useful services at reasonable cost, their existence is justified.

Criticism of the middleman may be attributed largely to a lack of understanding of the functions he performs. Many buyers fail to realize that after goods are produced many additional services are required before consumers can enjoy these goods. These services are performed by the middlemen.

Ch. 4]   FUNCTIONS AND SERVICES OF MARKETING   61

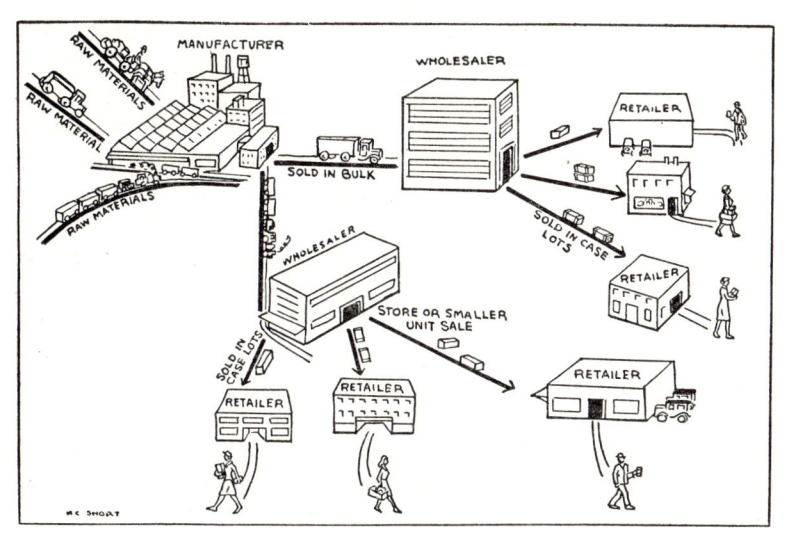

The Distribution System Involves Sales in Progressively Smaller Lots

A wholesale grocery company, for example, collects a wide variety of food products and other grocery items from all parts of the United States and even from various foreign countries. These goods may be obtained in large lots from canneries, jobbers, commission merchants, manufacturers, and importers. Buying in these large quantities is economical. The goods are transported to the warehouses of the wholesaler, are stored, and are then sold in smaller lots to retailers. During all this time the wholesaler has his money invested in the goods going in and out of his warehouses. Without the assistance of a middleman, such as this wholesaler, the small retailer would not have access to this wide variety of products, or he would have to assume the function of collecting a large variety of goods.

Direct and Indirect Marketing. Distribution through the wholesaler and the retailer is frequently referred to as *indirect marketing*. Indirect marketing has acquired its title because products pass through several hands in going from the producer to the consumer.

Direct marketing or *direct selling* is the process by which the producer sells to the consumer directly or through his own representatives. Well-known manufacturers sell directly to the consumer.

There are various attempts at times to make the distributive system more economical or at least more advantageous to some persons who are interested in the marketing system. For instance, farmers have organized numerous cooperative marketing associations, which perform some of the functions of buying, assembling, storing, transporting, financing, risk bearing, and selling. None of the processes is eliminated, but some of the benefits go to the farmers. A specialist takes over the functions of operating the cooperative on behalf of the farmer. He then spends more of his time in producing his crops and therefore gains a personal advantage. If by his action the whole process becomes more efficient, the consumer also sometimes receives a benefit.

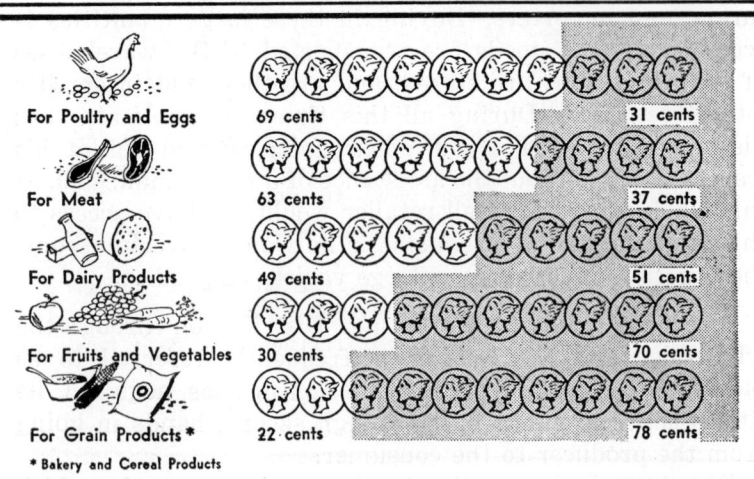

THE FARMER'S SHARE OF YOUR FOOD DOLLAR

The Farmer Gets: 45¢   The Marketing System Gets: 55¢

For Poultry and Eggs	69 cents	31 cents
For Meat	63 cents	37 cents
For Dairy Products	49 cents	51 cents
For Fruits and Vegetables	30 cents	70 cents
For Grain Products*	22 cents	78 cents

* Bakery and Cereal Products

The price spread between the actual production cost and the final retail price is not the same for every product. This price spread is not all profit. Out of each share, each middleman must pay his own costs. Actual net profit in many cases is small.

If you will examine the essential functions performed in the marketing or distribution processes, you will easily see that they can be combined, but they cannot be eliminated. Therefore, any improvement in our marketing system must come from increased efficiency, not from eliminating functions. The same functions have to be performed regardless of who does them or how they are done. For example, the chain store or the supermarket eliminates the wholesaler, but it performs the wholesale function itself.

How Much Does Distribution Cost? Studies made by the Twentieth Century Fund, an unbiased organization for the study of economic problems, report that, out of every dollar which the consumer spends for goods and services, an average of about 41 cents goes for production and 59 cents goes for the services of distribution. The difference between the 41 cents, which is the cost of production, and the final selling price is referred to as the *spread*. In this case it is 59 cents, which represents the cost of distribution. Not all of this is profit. In fact, net profit is usually only a small part of this amount.

Summary of Effects on the Consumer

1. There are certain fundamental economic functions performed in marketing or distribution.
2. There are several different kinds of markets and of channels of distribution, and not all products and services follow the same pattern of distribution.
3. Economic functions of marketing may be combined, but they cannot be eliminated.
4. Any particular middlemen may be eliminated, but his functions and services cannot be eliminated.
5. Any savings in the cost of distribution must come from increased efficiency.
6. The spread between the original cost of the product and the final retail price is not all profit; most of it represents payment of wages and other expenses of providing the services.

TEXTBOOK QUESTIONS

1. What are the eight economic functions of marketing?
2. What is meant by (a) assembling goods? (b) storing goods?
3. Why is advertising considered an essential economic function of marketing?
4. How does the function of grading and standardizing goods aid in the distributive system?
5. What activities are included in the merchandising function of retail stores?
6. Why are banks necessary in the distributive system?
7. If a person says, "There is a good market for this product," what does he mean?
8. What distinguishes a wholesale market from a retail market?
9. Name some products that can be bought in organized markets.
10. What functions of distribution enable people in most parts of the United States to enjoy fresh foods of practically all kinds during the twelve months of the year?
11. What is meant by direct marketing or direct selling? Does it eliminate any fundamental function of distribution?

DISCUSSION QUESTIONS

1. (a) Are there any advantages to the consumer in allowing farmers to peddle products without restriction in cities? (b) Are there any disadvantages?
2. Do you think we could get along without the services of the wholesaler? Explain your answer.
3. "The commission market helps the farmer to make more money." Is this statement true? Explain your answer.
4. Explain in what way storage may have aided in distributing the food that you consumed in your morning meal.
5. What happens to the distributive system if farmers become bankrupt in great numbers?
6. If manufacturers could no longer make profits, what would happen to the distributive system?
7. How do the transportation and storage functions reduce the profits of producers in some regions?
8. A manufacturer of fountain pens sends an agent to your door to attempt to sell a pen to you. Does the manufacturer perform distributive functions in addition to the functions of manufacturing and selling?

9. Name some mail order houses that sell in large areas directly to the consumer and explain in what way you feel they eliminate certain functions of distribution.

PROBLEMS

1. What has refrigeration done for distribution, particularly as it affects the consumer?
2. State the advantages of the storage of wheat in large elevators from the point of view of (a) the grower and (b) the consumer.
3. List as many as possible ways in which risk is involved in distribution.
4. To discover the interdependence of people, make a study of the products which you have at home in your medicine cabinet and in your kitchen pantry. Make a list of these products and indicate where each is manufactured. Can you draw any conclusions as to certain places where many products are manufactured and other locations where there is not much manufacturing?

COMMUNITY PROBLEMS AND PROJECTS

1. List various local businesses within a radius of your school that is designated by your teacher and consider four types of businesses that you select, such as bread manufacturers, drug stores, automobile dealers, and manufacturers of shoes. Classify them according to the markets that are available to them, such as local, national, or international; and in the case of local markets, try to define how far you feel their local markets extend.
2. Select some product with the approval of your teacher and make a study of it with the aid of any library material or information that you can obtain from that business. Write a report as to how it is produced or distributed and where it goes.

Chapter 5

How Government Affects the Consumer

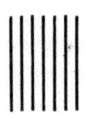

> **Purpose of the Chapter.** In a democratic form of society, such as ours, government is fundamentally a service organization created by the people and responsible to the people. Through our elected representatives and through our votes on taxation we determine what services will be provided by government and the amount and the kinds of taxes that are collected. We should therefore "buy" government services at least as carefully and thoughtfully as we buy any other kind of goods or services. The purpose of this chapter is to point out the general ways in which government is organized to serve consumers and how much these services cost.
>
> You will find answers to these questions:
> 1. Are any governmental services free?
> 2. What are some of the types of services performed by government?
> 3. What businesses are operated by government?
> 4. How does government serve and regulate business?
> 5. What governmental regulations serve and protect the consumer?
> 6. How much do governmental services cost?

Free Governmental Services. Some people assume that services provided by government are free because they do not specifically pay a certain amount of cash when they use a governmental service. But, are they free? The cost of governmental services must be paid from public funds, which come either directly or indirectly from consumers. The cost of government must be taken out of the total production of all people and if the taxes collected by government did not go for these purposes, the money would be available for other uses.

Taxes are included in the cost of every article or service that we buy; taxes are included in the cost of rent and in the cost of owning a home. For example, when we buy a dozen oranges for 60 cents, that price includes not only the amount that goes to the grower and to the various distributors, but some of it is also to pay for taxes, which are a part of the cost of doing business. These taxes have been paid all along the line by the grower, the trucker, the wholesaler, and the retailer.

The more service we obtain at public expense, the higher the cost of government; and the higher the cost of government, the more taxes we pay. When we consider buying an article for personal use, we ask ourselves whether we need it and whether our budget can stand it. However, when we request our legislators to vote for another service or for a new building or bridge, do we consider the question of whether we and other consumers are willing and able to pay for it by paying higher taxes? Some elected legislators promote certain ideas, not because they have been requested to do so, but because of an attempt to get votes. This decision of buying government services faces the consumer directly when he votes on local tax decisions.

As citizens, we participate in making the regulations and rules by which we are governed. We do this by voting for legislators whose points of view about government we approve. We also pay for the costs of government; and, as consumers, we use the services provided by government. Our interests as citizens and our interests as consumers in government are almost identical.

Once a governmental service is provided at public expense, all consumers help pay for it through taxes and often through higher prices even though many of them may not need or want the service. Our interest, therefore, is to see not only that our government provides services for the general good of people but also that the government does not provide services and special benefits that are nonessential.

The majority of people believe that government should produce only those services that are not and cannot be provided by individuals and private enterprise. Illustrative of the services that cannot be provided by private enterprises are national defense, police and fire protection, conservation of natural resources, general hospitals, public health, education except college, and institutions for unfortunate people. Those persons who lean strongly toward socialism, however, believe government should assume the responsibility for providing as many services and for producing as many commodities as possible.

Government Performs Many Services. If you were the only person who lived in the United States, you would be entirely independent; your work, your actions, and even your thoughts would not affect anyone else. At the same time you would be wholly dependent upon yourself. You would have to protect yourself. You could turn to no one for help, nor could you exchange commodities with others. No need would exist for laws or regulations.

By Exercising Their Right to Vote, Citizens Help to Make Decisions of Government in Economic Matters

To fulfill our responsibility as voting citizens we must understand the economic problems and issues affecting consumers by expressing our opinions and points of view. By voting, we can determine the kinds and extent of the services and benefits that our government will provide.

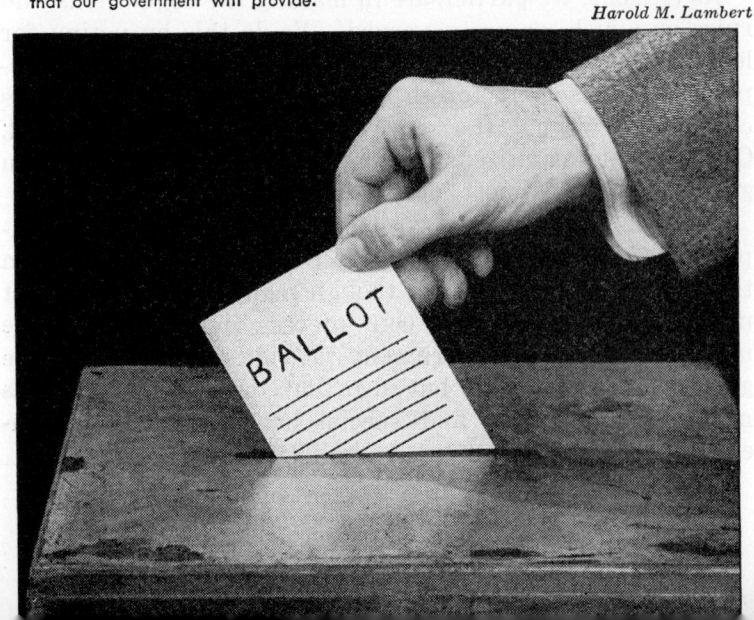

Harold M. Lambert

In a society people help each other. They cooperate in making and doing things that would be difficult or impossible alone. Under a system of specialization or division of labor people become dependent upon one another and upon government to supply the services and the goods they want. The more complex the problems of working and living together, the greater is the need for government.

Government serves citizens in many ways. In addition to giving protection to citizens, government also gives other services needed by its citizens, such as are shown in the table below.

Services Provided Through Taxes

1. Police, fire, military, and coast-guard service.
2. Legal title records.
3. Health and sanitation.
4. Garbage collection and sewage disposal.
5. Inspection: weights, standards, quality.
6. Schools, universities, and research laboratories.
7. Legislative and executive services.
8. Postal service.
9. Transportation service.
10. Courts, prisons, and jails.
11. Welfare and relief agencies.
12. Water, electric, and gas systems.
13. Street lighting and cleaning.
14. Maintenance of streets, sidewalks, highways, bridges and waterways.
15. Parks and recreational activities.
16. Civic museums, auditoriums, and libraries.
17. Harbor and terminal facilities.
18. Unemployment insurance and old-age pensions.
19. Inspection of building construction.
20. Regulation of admission requirements for professions.
21. Forestry and reclamation service.
22. Employment service.
23. Price supports and subsidies.
24. Bank deposit insurance.
25. Information and consultation services.

While all governmental services are intended to serve society in general, some groups of citizens benefit directly from certain services and others only indirectly. Old-age assistance, unemployment insurance, and price supports for eggs and cotton are examples of services or benefits to special groups of citizens.

There is a tendency for state governments to take over services previously given by local governments and for the Federal Government to take over or contribute substantially in providing services formerly rendered by state governments. For example, road building and maintenance were at one time almost wholly functions of local government. In recent years, they have been practically absorbed by the state governments with the financial assistance of the Federal Government.

Some of the services provided by government are not used by individuals but are provided for all of the people collectively. Inspection of food processing plants to insure clean and wholesome food is an example of services for the good of all people. The use of many governmental services by consumers is voluntary; however, a few, such as provisions for social security, are compulsory for those persons to whom the laws are applicable.

In Chapter 7 you will find discussed in more detail some of the governmental services that are of more specific and direct interest to the consumer in his activities of buying and investing. In later chapters you will find more detailed discussions of governmental services pertaining to old-age insurance, unemployment insurance, wages, interest rates, advertising, bank deposits, and other problems of consumers.

Government Operates Businesses. Ordinarily we think of commodities and services as being produced under competitive conditions by individuals and by private enterprises for profit. Upon examination, however, we find that many services and some commodities are produced by government without profit and under noncompetitive conditions. Whether consumers actually pay less through taxes for a service provided by government without profit than they would pay for the same service provided by a private enterprise that makes a profit is an unsettled question.

Many of the services provided by government are financed wholly through public taxation. No direct charge is made to the persons using them; however, in some cases the person using a service pays a portion of the cost. Electricity generated by the Tennessee Valley Authority is paid for in part by the user. Of course, in cases in which the user pays only a portion of the cost of the service, the remainder is paid from public funds raised through taxation.

In some cases the government has become a producer in order that, through research and experimentation, a new product may be developed and made available to consumers. Aluminum, synthetic rubber, and synthetic gasoline are examples of products that have been developed experimentally and produced at least in the initial stages by the government. In some cases private business has bought these businesses from the government.

Ewing Galloway
Our Federal Government Develops and Operates Electric Power Resources

The Post Office Department and other governmental activities are really businesses that are operated by governmental agencies. Some of these will be discussed in more detail in later chapters.

Government Aid to Business and Agriculture. The Federal Government has aided business in many ways. One type of service to business is the gathering, compiling, and distributing of statistics and information relative to payrolls, wages, prices, volume of production, finance, costs, and many similar aspects of business. These data are collected by such agencies as the Department of Commerce, the Bureau of Labor Statistics, and the Federal Reserve Board.

The Bureau of Standards has given an invaluable service to business by testing materials and establishing standards. Many divisions of the Department of Interior and the Department of Agriculture primarily serve producers. Following World War II the Reconstruction Finance Corporation loaned millions of dollars to railroads, banks, insurance companies, and manufacturing companies when loans from other sources would have been almost impossible. During the Second World War many industries engaged in war production were subsidized (financially helped) by the Federal Government. In some cases our Federal Government has built steamships and has leased them to private owners at a price the owner could afford to operate them. This is a form of subsidy. The first synthetic rubber plants were financed by the government and operated by private industry. The rubber was urgently needed and since private industry could not produce it at a profit, the Federal Government assisted. Airlines and steamship companies have in some cases really been subsidized in the form of very liberal compensation for carrying mail. The aids to business paid by the Federal Government are often overlooked or taken for granted. The foregoing examples are only a few.

Government aids to business are almost too numerous to mention. Many of these aids to business are indirectly aids to the consumer because they help business to operate more effectively for the benefit of the consumer. Some of these additional aids to business are navigation services on rivers or lakes, weather reports, financial services through the Federal Reserve Bank, protection of honest businessmen from dishonest competitors, development of standards, and many others.

The aid of government to some phases of business is more direct and more concrete than that of providing statistical information and determining standards. For example, in an effort to guarantee a substantial income to the producer of such commodities as potatoes, eggs, butter, and cotton, the government may regulate the prices of these commodities by buying and storing or otherwise disposing of sufficiently large quantities of the products to keep prices at a level satisfactory to the producer. Without governmental control, if potatoes or eggs are plentiful, the market price drops; consequently the consumer is able to buy at a relatively low price; however, the return to the producer is also low. Under governmental control of prices, the market price is maintained at a relatively high level, from which the producers of the commodity benefit by realizing a better income.

But, the Consumer Pays Twice. The theory of subsidizing business and agriculture is that this aid is needed for the general welfare of the nation. The theory of this kind of aid is that the safety and welfare of the whole country is benefited by protecting the farmer. However, when someone such as a farmer is subsidized, the consumer really pays twice. He not only pays a higher price for the commodity he wants, even though it is plentiful, but through taxes he also pays the cost of the product bought by the Federal Government in order to keep the price up for the producer.

In other instances, the Federal Government regulates the amount of a product produced or grown, as the case may be. Regulation of the number of acres of wheat planted is a typical example. By reducing the amount of wheat grown, the market price of that product is forced up by the demand for it. Consequently, the wheat farmer may have a return as great by planting 85 per cent of his land in wheat as he would have had without governmental regulation if he planted 100 per cent of his land in wheat. In order to induce the wheat farmer not to plant too much wheat, the Federal Government may make a direct payment to him for reducing the amount of wheat he grows. These payments are based upon the estimated net income that might have been earned if the unused acres had been planted and the crop had grown.

Price supports and subsidies for special groups of producers, whether farmers or manufacturers or distributors, are of vital interest to consumers. They are beneficial to consumers in that some of the products and services would not be available to them if the producers were not protected by price supports or did not benefit from subsidies. They are not beneficial if some groups of producers through political pressure are successful in obtaining the benefits of price supports or subsidies even though their products could be produced and distributed satisfactorily without

---

Why Government Regulations of Business Activities and Practices Are Imposed

1. To curb monopolistic trends; to regulate and control prices, rates, and services of enterprises that can operate effectively only as monopolies; and to prevent practices in restraint of trade.
2. To control quality of products and services, primarily in protection of consumers.
3. To regulate prices on products and services as protection for consumers and to prevent unfair trade practices among businesses.
4. To protect business owners and managers from unfair methods of competition and unfair trade practices.
5. To protect investors by controlling the practices of financial institutions in issuing stocks, bonds, and other securities.
6. To control public utilities, which usually are monopolistic in nature, especially as to rates, services, and managerial policies.
7. To promote some aspects of business by curbing others.
8. To promote safety, health, and good working conditions.

governmental aid. A situation of this kind results in unfairness to the producers of other products for whom governmental aid is equally justifiable but who do not seek governmental aid. These producers help pay for the subsidies and other aids given to the business firms that receive them.

The issue of vital importance to consumers is: What kinds of products and services should be subsidized or protected by price supports, and to what extent?

Government Regulation of Business. In theory our laws that regulate business are designed to protect honest businessmen from unscrupulous competitors, to protect the consumer from bad business practices among competitors, and to protect the consumer directly from dishonest businessmen. Some of these laws are designed to prevent the

---

Methods Used by Government to Regulate Business

1. Control of entry into business by requiring licenses, permits, and certificates.
2. Government ownership and operation of businesses that are difficult to control when privately owned and operated.
3. Conducting periodic and special investigations of business practices by the officials of governmental agencies that are authorized by law to make such investigations.
4. Requiring businesses to file detailed and summary reports of business transactions revealing business practices.
5. Regulation of prices and rates.
6. Regulation of advertising selling practices.
7. Control of business and professional activity by requiring licenses and permits to be renewed periodically.
8. Stimulating or curbing business activity through taxation.
9. Regulation of interest rates and credit.
10. Labor legislation regulating employee-employer relations, hours, wages, safety, and health.
11. Regulation of the amount of production of industries dealing with natural resources, such as oil, coal, metals, and wood.

following: monopolies that will control prices and supply, fraud through the mail, adulterated and misbranded food, false advertising, deceptive practices, unsatisfactory working conditions, fraud in selling securities, and many others which will be discussed in more detail in later chapters.

While businessmen generally regard government regulation of business as interference, they recognize that certain regulations are necessary and desirable. The primary concern of the businessman is that only the regulations that are absolutely necessary shall be authorized, that these regulations shall be reasonable, and that they shall be administered in a fair manner.

Protection of Citizens by Government. No governmental service or activity is more important to its citizens than protection. We must feel secure not only from physical harm and discomfort but also from injustices involving our personal rights and freedoms.

National defense and internal police protection are among the most important protective services provided by government. The army, navy, and air corps provide protection from invading foreign powers and protect our possessions located in other parts of the world. This protection we take for granted in times of peace, but it is of vital importance to us in times of world unrest and war. In times of war the amounts spent on national defense are very large. In 1953, approximately 50 of the 75 billion dollars spent by the Federal Government were spent for national defense. This was 67 per cent of the total amount spent. The 50 billion dollars did not include approximately 6.5 billion dollars expended for interest on the public debt much of which was incurred during war or 4 billion paid for services and benefits for veterans. The annual expenditures for national defense comprise the largest item in the Federal budget. The money spent for defense comes from taxation.

The Federal Bureau of Investigation, state police departments, and local police protect us from physical harm and injustices from people within the country. Protection from fire, flood, storms, and other disasters is provided by the Coast Guard and local agencies. The total amount spent for national defense and internal security is reflected not only in direct taxes but in higher prices of commodities wanted by consumers.

Most of the protective services furnished by government cannot be provided economically or cannot be provided at all by consumers themselves. Therefore, as consumers we have an interest in the kinds and extent of the protective services provided by government. We want those services provided efficiently and economically.

Governmental Operations Are Extensive. To provide services and benefits for citizens, our governmental units operate the world's most extensive business. The combined operation of local, state, and Federal governmental units in the United States requires millions of public employees and billions of dollars annually to pay the total costs. Every person working for the government is one less to help pay the costs of government.

Of approximately 60 million people who were gainfully employed in 1950, 6 million were employed by the Federal, state, and local governments. This means that of every ten persons gainfully employed one was working for the government. In 1900, one of every 23 gainfully employed persons was employed by the government. From 1900 to 1950, the total number of persons employed increased from 27 to 60 million, an increase of 122 per cent; governmental employment increased during the same period from 1.2 to 5.9 million, an increase of 392 per cent.

The combined expenditures of Federal, state, and local governments in the United States in 1953 were a little less than 100 billion dollars or approximately $623 for every adult and child. Approximately $466 a person was spent by the Federal Government, and $157 by state and local governments combined. Since the average consumer had an income of approximately $1,700 in that year, governmental services cost an average of 35 to 40 per cent of an average consumer's annual income. Consumers, therefore, have a deep interest in the business affairs of government.

78   BUSINESS AND GOVERNMENT   [Part 2

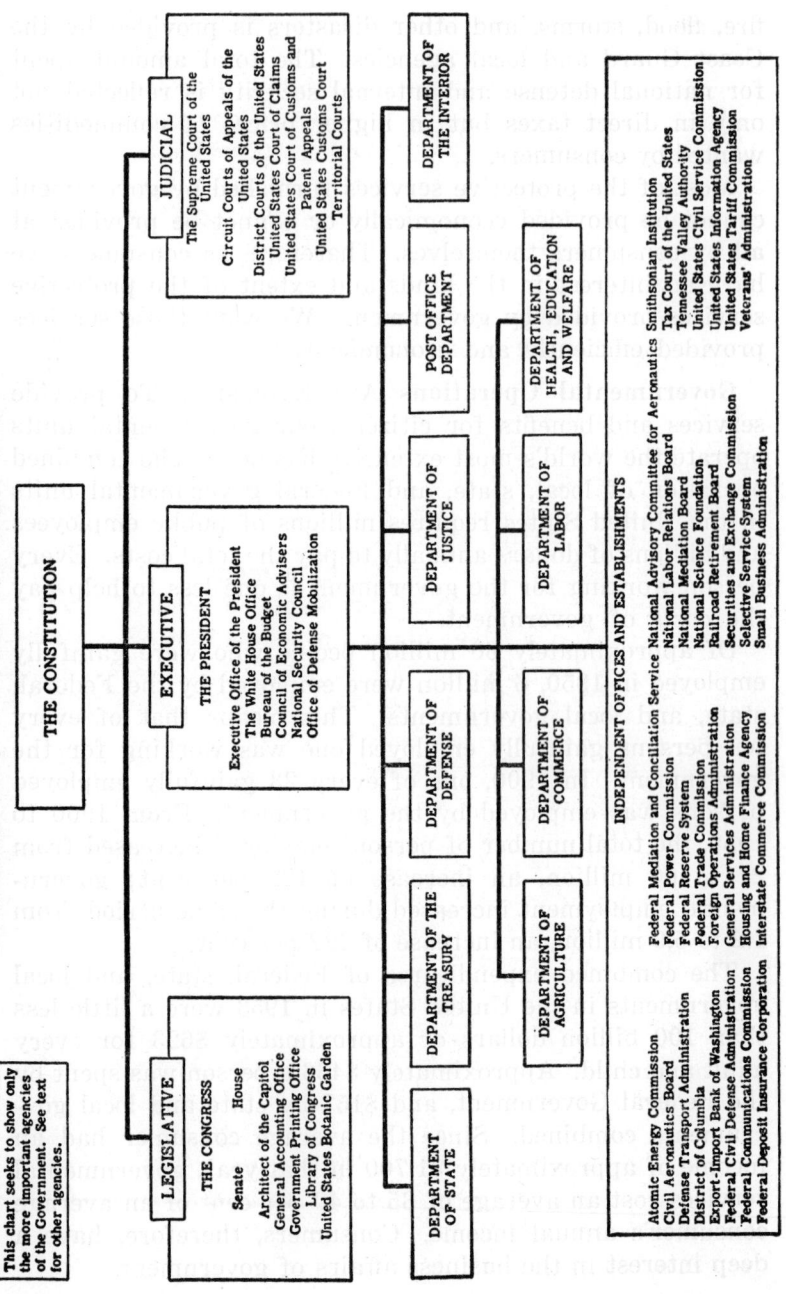

GOVERNMENT OF THE UNITED STATES

THE CONSTITUTION

This chart seeks to show only the more important agencies of the Government. See text for other agencies.

LEGISLATIVE

THE CONGRESS

Senate House

Architect of the Capitol
General Accounting Office
Government Printing Office
Library of Congress
United States Botanic Garden

EXECUTIVE

THE PRESIDENT

Executive Office of the President
The White House Office
Bureau of the Budget
Council of Economic Advisers
National Security Council
Office of Defense Mobilization

JUDICIAL

The Supreme Court of the United States
Circuit Courts of Appeals of the United States
District Courts of the United States
United States Court of Claims
United States Court of Customs and Patent Appeals
United States Customs Court
Territorial Courts

Departments

- DEPARTMENT OF STATE
- DEPARTMENT OF THE TREASURY
- DEPARTMENT OF DEFENSE
- DEPARTMENT OF JUSTICE
- POST OFFICE DEPARTMENT
- DEPARTMENT OF THE INTERIOR
- DEPARTMENT OF AGRICULTURE
- DEPARTMENT OF COMMERCE
- DEPARTMENT OF LABOR
- DEPARTMENT OF HEALTH, EDUCATION AND WELFARE

INDEPENDENT OFFICES AND ESTABLISHMENTS

Atomic Energy Commission
Civil Aeronautics Board
Defense Transport Administration
District of Columbia
Export-Import Bank of Washington
Federal Civil Defense Administration
Federal Communications Commission
Federal Deposit Insurance Corporation
Federal Mediation and Conciliation Service
Federal Power Commission
Federal Reserve System
Federal Trade Commission
Foreign Operations Administration
General Services Administration
Housing and Home Finance Agency
Interstate Commerce Commission
National Advisory Committee for Aeronautics
National Labor Relations Board
National Mediation Board
National Science Foundation
Railroad Retirement Board
Securities and Exchange Commission
Selective Service System
Small Business Administration
Smithsonian Institution
Tax Court of the United States
Tennessee Valley Authority
United States Civil Service Commission
United States Information Agency
United States Tariff Commission
Veterans' Administration

How Foreign Policy May Affect Consumers. Foreign policy is a dominant factor in determining the political and economic relations between the United States and other nations. Our political and economic relations with the other nations of the world may have either favorable or unfavorable effects on our economic conditions. The economic welfare of individual consumers is directly dependent upon economic conditions within the United States.

Foreign policy is a significant factor in establishing and maintaining completely friendly relations with other nations. When friendly, cordial relations exist between nations, we have not only a two-way flow of economic goods but also an exchange of cultural, scientific, and technical information between the nations from which both benefit. If there is mistrust, jealousy, or a feeling of ill will between nations, commerce and the exchange of information are reduced, if not eliminated.

Foreign trade enables us to obtain many raw materials and products that we need and want. It also provides a market for the raw materials and products that we produce. Generally speaking, good foreign trade relationships with other nations has a favorable effect on economic conditions in the United States. Foreign policy thus has an indirect but significant effect on business and hence on consumers.

The foreign policy of the United States in protecting our economic and political interests influences the attitudes of other nations toward the United States. Whether these attitudes are cordial and friendly or hostile determines the extent to which preparation for national defense is necessary. Many times hostile relations and war between nations have resulted from economic and political misunderstanding and conflict.

Consumers' Interest in Public Finance. The management and control of the financial aspects of government are referred to as public finance. In other words, *public finance* deals with the revenues, expenditures, and debts of government. It is clearly a phase of economics that is of significance to consumers because the consumer is the one who pays the bill.

The sources of government income are taxes, fees and fines, special assessments, and revenue from government-owned industries. One of the major problems of legislators is to keep costs of government as low as possible and at the same time provide the services needed. Another problem is to devise ways by which the revenue may equal or exceed the expenditures of government. The burden of most taxes, fees and fines, and special assessments ultimately is on consumers.

From 1929 to 1953 Federal expenditures increased approximately 2,717 per cent and state and local expenditures, 226 per cent. Consumers, businessmen, and legislators have expressed great concern over the increase in expenditures of the local, state, and Federal governments.

Expenditures of Federal, State, and Local Governments for Selected Years

YEAR	FEDERAL EXPENDITURES (MILLIONS)	STATE AND LOCAL EXPENDITURES (MILLIONS)
1929	2,648	7,689
1934	6,393	8,055
1939	8,966	9,303
1940	9,183	9,095
1941	13,387	8,974
1942	34,187	9,175
1943	79,622	8,496
1944	95,315	8,773
1945	98,703	9,130
1946	60,703	11,115
1947	39,289	14,669
1948	33,791	16,700
1949	40,057	20,565
1950	40,167	21,825
1951	44,633	22,134
1952	66,145	23,584
1953	74,607	25,135

Sources: Survey of Current Business, Table 9, Office of Business Economics, U. S. Department of Commerce, and Statistical Abstract of the United States, U. S. Bureau of Census.

How far can the trend of increasing cost of government go without making us an insolvent nation? What percentage of national income may be paid to the government in taxes without seriously impairing our standard of living? What will be the effect on business and economic conditions if the cost of government and the amount of public debt continue to increase? What can be done to curb the trend of higher costs of government? Every consumer and taxpayer, and that includes all of us, has much at stake in the answers to these questions. Our standard of living, the possibility of accumulating personal savings, and the opportunities for employment all are dependent upon the issues raised by these questions.

Public debt results from governmental expenditures exceeding revenue. In only three of the years from 1930 to 1953 did the Federal revenue exceed expenditures. Those years were 1947, 1948, and 1951. During this same period from 1930 to 1953 the public debt increased from approximately 16 billion dollars to more than 266 billion dollars or more than 1563 per cent. This debt increased from $131.51 to $1,666.11 per person. The interest on the public debt in 1953 was more than 6 billion dollars. This amount for interest alone is greater than the total annual cost of the Federal Government for any year prior to 1934 except the years during and immediately following World War I. The increase in the cost of government and in public debt since 1930 is almost too great for one to comprehend.

Every citizen has an obligation to learn all he can about the financial affairs of government. An understanding of the problems of public finance is essential for every consumer if he is to vote intelligently on economic issues.

Summary of How Government Affects Us

1. Governmental services are not free; we all pay for them.
2. Governmental services are extensive and are continuing to grow.
3. Government performs many services for us that we could not provide satisfactorily as individuals or smaller groups.
4. Government aids and subsidizes agriculture and business with some direct benefits to consumers.
5. Government regulates business for the protection of business and the consumer.
6. The cost of government is high and is continuing to grow.
7. We should ''buy'' governmental services carefully through our votes.

TEXTBOOK QUESTIONS

1. Many people speak of free government services. In what way are they free or not free?
2. In what way is electing a public official or a legislator an act of buying public service?
3. Name some governmental services from which certain groups of people receive the primary benefits.
4. Name some services provided through taxes?
5. Name some businesses that are owned and operated by government.
6. In what ways does government aid business?
7. Explain how consumers pay for price support programs in two ways.
8. Name some ways in which business is regulated for the protection of consumers.
9. In 1950, about how many people were gainfully employed? How many were employed by Federal, state, and local governments?
10. In 1953, about how much was spent for all types of government expenditures for every adult and child in the United States?
11. What per cent of the average yearly income of $1,700 per person in the United States in 1953 is the cost of government?
12. How may foreign policy affect the economic welfare of consumers?
13. What is meant by public finance?
14. Explain why the costs of government are increasing.
15. From 1930 to 1953 how much has the public debt increased?
16. How much greater was the public debt per person in 1953 than 1930?

DISCUSSION QUESTIONS

1. Explain why laws and regulations are necessary when people live together in a community or state.
2. Explain why the more services a government provides for its people the more complex and costly government becomes.
3. In what way do consumers have a financial interest in the business affairs of government?
4. Why do not consumers protect themselves individually from injury or physical loss instead of depending upon government?

5. Discuss the various ways that the people of your community are protected by the local, state, and Federal governments.
6. What would be the arguments against a plan for education in which public funds would not be used for education and parents would use the taxes thus saved to provide education for their children?
7. If the Federal Government should increase materially the kinds and extent of the services it now offers to consumers, what would be the effect upon business firms that produce services and commodities for profit?
8. The postal rates for letters and other classes of mail do not provide sufficient income to pay the costs of the Postal Department, and the Federal Government bears the remainder of the cost. What are the arguments against eliminating postal charges entirely and permitting all mail to be carried free of charge?
9. Give some examples of government regulation of business activities from which consumers benefit.
10. Discuss how business firms are affected by foreign policy.

PROBLEMS

1. In your school or public library obtain the file of the local and state newspapers for the past month. Make a list of the items of economic importance of interest to consumers in your community that are featured in editorials and news stories.
2. Using a reference, such as the *World Almanac and Book of Facts* or the *Information Please Almanac,* which probably will be found in your school library, determine: (a) What was the per capita income for the average person in your state for the latest year for which such data are available? For the average person in the United States? For the average person in the region in which you live? (b) What has been the trend in income per capita in your state for the past five years? For the United States? (c) Compare the receipts and expenditures of the United States Government for each of the last 20 years showing the deficit or surplus.

COMMUNITY PROBLEMS AND PROJECTS

1. Make a study locally to determine the services for consumers that are given by local and Federal Governmental agencies and paid for from public funds.

2. From local government officials and from any other sources available to you, prepare a list of the buildings, bridges, roads, and other public works in your community that were paid for, at least in part, from Federal funds. Also give on the list the names of the local, state, and Federal agencies that co-operated in the construction of the project and the amounts each contributed.
3. The Federal Government of the United States spent more than 68 billion dollars in 1954. The main items for which this amount was spent are as follows:

	EXPENDITURES (MILLIONS)
National defense	$46,522
Veterans' services and benefits	4,256
International affairs	1,720
Social welfare, health, and security	1,990
Agriculture and agricultural resources	2,557
Natural resources	1,213
Transportation and communication	1,611
General government	1,209
Interest on the national debt	6,382
Other (including education and research)	957
	$68,417

a. Compute the percentage that each class of expenditure is of the total federal expenditures for 1954. Construct a bar chart showing the percentage spent for each main item of the total expenditure.

b. Payments to veterans and payments for interest on the public debt are primarily costs of past wars. Assuming this statement to be true, what per cent of the total federal expenditures for 1954 resulted from past wars and from outlays for national defense?

c. Which of the classes of items of expenditures are for services or benefits to the citizens and business firms of the country?

d. What per cent of Federal expenditures for 1954 was spent for items of special or direct benefit to the citizens and business firms of the country?

Chapter 6

Private Agencies that Protect Us

Purpose of the Chapter. In some of the previous chapters you have learned in a general way how business is organized to serve consumers. There are other types of business organizations and private agencies that are organized more specifically to aid and protect consumers. Some of these specific ways of aiding and protecting consumers are discussed in this chapter.

You will find answers to these questions:

1. What are the purposes and functions of Better Business Bureaus?
2. How are consumers aided and protected by organizations such as the American Medical Association and American Dental Association?
3. How do standards established by business aid the consumer?
4. How do laboratory tests and labels aid in protecting the consumer?
5. What are the services available through consumer organizations?

Better Business Bureau. The better business bureaus of the United States were originally organized to improve the quality of advertising by fighting unethical advertising. Today they are concerned with all unfair trade practices, but still concentrate their main efforts on advertising and promotional schemes. At one time they were more concerned with unfair competition, but now they fight against the unfair treatment of consumers.

One function of a local better business bureau is to check carefully the practices of local businesses in order to prevent any unfair trade practices. Standards are usually specified for truthful advertising and fair public relations. The local bureau also investigates the various promotional schemes of new businesses that enter the community. Some local better business bureaus conduct newspaper campaigns to warn people against fraud and deception.

Functions of Better Business Bureaus

1. Elimination of the causes of customer complaints against business by—
    A. Preventing unfair treatment.
    B. Promoting fair advertising and selling practices.
    C. Promoting informative advertising.
    D. Fraud prosecution.
2. Cooperation with educators and business to provide students with sound knowledge of the functions of our economic system.
3. Adult education to teach employees, their families and other customers about money management, better buymanship, and a better understanding of sound business-consumer relations.

Many of these bureaus investigate soliciting schemes and promotional schemes. Anyone has the privilege of calling the local better business bureau for information and advice. In many communities the members of the bureau will not contribute to any soliciting scheme until it has been approved by the bureau. Consumers can protect themselves if they will get in touch with the bureau immediately whenever there is any question of an unfair trade practice. Even after a person has been injured or swindled by an unfair trade practice, he should get in touch with the better business bureau. This serves two purposes: first, to acquaint the better business bureau with what is going on in the community; and second, to get a possible adjustment through the assistance of the bureau.

Detection and prosecution of fraud is an important function of better business bureaus. When complaints are received, they are investigated. If fraud is evident, the person responsible is warned and the fraud is publicly exposed. If these methods do not stop the practice of fraud, the better business bureau often prosecutes the offender through the courts.

The National Better Business Bureau (operating on a national scale in a similar manner to local bureaus) publishes various pamphlets specifically for the benefit of the consumer. These pamphlets provide warnings and information with regard to specific types of commodities and lending institutions. These pamphlets were developed by the Boston Better Business Bureau. They are distributed through the National Better Business Bureau and can be obtained at a small cost through any local bureau. Examples of some of the many "Facts" are shown in the illustration on page 88.

People Without Money Can Get Legal Aid

Legal Aid Societies. Under the belief that getting justice should not depend upon one's ability to pay fees and hire a lawyer, organizations that are generally called *legal aid societies* or *legal aid organizations* have been formed throughout the various states. These organizations are found principally in the larger cities. They are often sponsored by lawyers in order to provide an organized method of handling cases for persons who cannot afford to obtain legal assistance. Therefore, if a consumer does not have the money to fight his own legal battles to protect himself, legal assistance is often available to him if a real need for it exists.

American Medical Association. The American Medical Association is probably one of the most respected non-

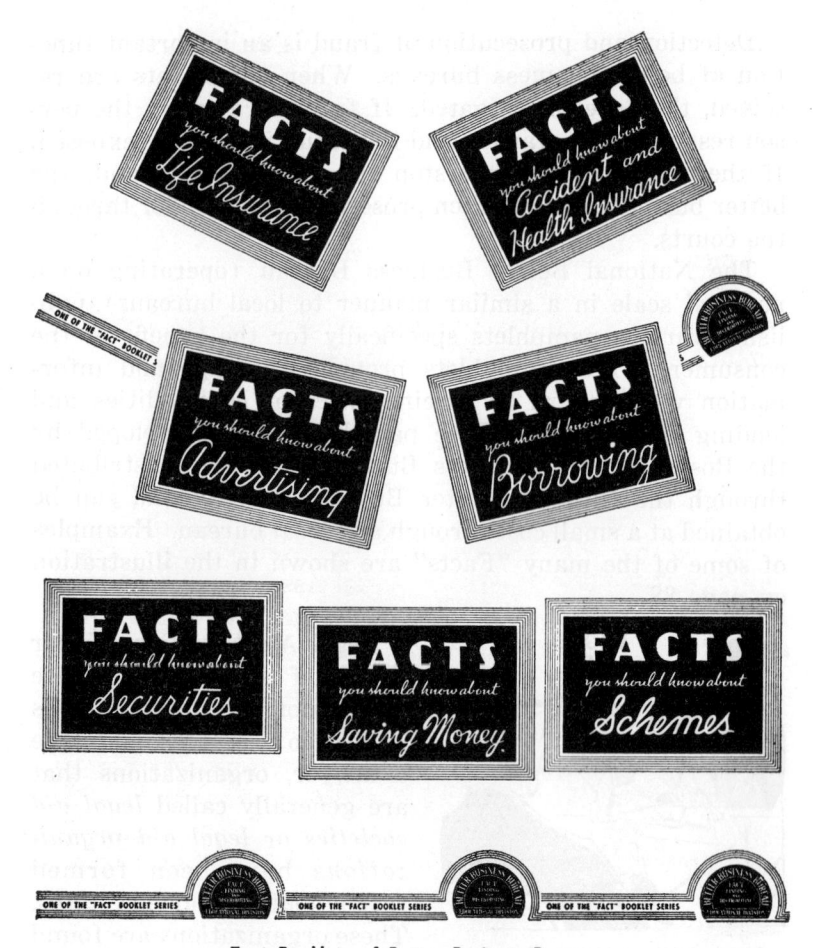

Fact Booklets of Better Business Bureau

public agencies for the aid and the protection of the consumer. This association maintains a Council on Pharmacy and Chemistry, a Council on Physical Medicine and Rehabilitation, a Council on Foods and Nutrition, a Committee on Cosmetics, and a Committee on Pesticides; it also has a staff of laboratory investigators. Useful information is made available to medical societies and the general public. Substances offered to the medical profession are evaluated. The association issues annually a book, *New and Nonofficial Remedies,* containing descriptions of proprietary articles that conform to the rules of the association.

Another service of the American Medical Association that is of interest to consumers is the publication of a magazine entitled *Today's Health.* Advertising in this and other publications of the Association must be approved.

American Dental Association. The American Dental Association maintains the Council on Dental Therapeutics which gathers and disseminates information to assist the dental profession in the selection and use of therapeutic agents (agents that have value in treatment of mouth and teeth with antiseptic or healing values). The Council studies products that are also offered for sale to the public which are reputed to have therapeutic or cosmetic value. At the present time the council examines only dentifrices and mouth washes that are designed to prevent dental decay or gum diseases. The American Dental Association has not yet approved any of these to use the seal of acceptance. However, the study of these products is being continued.

National Board of Fire Underwriters. The National Board of Fire Underwriters maintains laboratories that are operated on a nonprofit basis for the purpose of giving information on the merits of materials and appliances that may involve hazards of life, fire, theft, or accident. The laboratories are known as the Underwriters' Laboratories, Inc. They operate somewhat independently on a self-supporting fee basis serving anyone who wants a product inspected.

Tests are conducted in the laboratories on the basis of predetermined standards. Information on these standards may be obtained by writing to a testing laboratory of the National Board of Fire Underwriters. The major work of the laboratories consists in inspecting various materials and appliances to ascertain whether they meet the minimum standards of safety. The board publishes annually a list of important appliances and materials, such as electrical appliances, fire-protection appliances, oil and gas appliances, and automotive appliances, that have been approved by it.

The consumer can profit from the services of the underwriters' laboratories by purchasing only equipment or material that has been approved. Approved equipment and material can be determined from the published lists and also from the labels on the products. A product that bears the label of the Underwriters' Laboratories has been inspected and approved in the factory in which it was produced. The seal appears in various forms, sometimes merely with "U. L." stamped into or impressed on the article.

A Sample Label of the Underwriters' Association

American Gas Association. Manufacturers of gas-operated equipment and appliances have the privilege of sending their products to the American Gas Association laboratories, which are located in New York City and in Cleveland. These products are tested for safety, durability, and efficiency. If they meet the standards set up for each type of equipment, the manufacturer is permitted to use a seal of approval. This distinguishing mark of approval has become so important in marketing gas appliances that over 95 per cent of the gas-operated appliances that are manufactured bear this seal of approval. It must be borne in mind that this seal of approval indicates only that the product meets a certain minimum standard of quality. There will naturally be a difference in quality among the products that bear this seal of approval.

Seal of the American Gas Association

American Standards Association. The American Standards Association is a group that represents business, government, and the public. It does not directly formulate standards, but it serves to coordinate the efforts to develop standards. The standardization program that most directly affects consumers is carried on through a committee known as Consumer Goods Standards Board on which are represented the American Home Economics Association, the National Retail Trade Goods Association, the American Association of University Women, and other groups. Many standards developed in this way are directly helpful to the consumer. For example, when one buys a standard household electric light bulb from any manufacturer, it will fit a socket made by any manufacturer. Similar standards apply to hundreds of other items and standards of quality have also been set up.

ASTM Standards. The American Society for Testing Materials (ASTM) is a nonprofit, technical society organized in 1902. Its membership, comprised of corporations and individuals drawn from industry, government, and the sciences may be classified into three groups: consumers of raw materials and semi-finished and finished products; producers of materials; and a general-interest group of leading engineers, scientists, educators, test experts, research workers, and others interested in materials and testing. It works through technical committees which are responsible for the development of standards and methods of testing materials.

Although not developed or intended generally for use by the ultimate consumer in making purchases, ASTM Standards are important helps in maintaining standards of quality and uniformity for materials which eventually reach the ultimate consumer or serve him in the form of manufactured goods, buildings, or public works. The standards are used widely for making quantity purchases by manufacturers, distributors, large stores, cooperatives, and institutions.

A Special Seal for Garments

National Association of Dyers and Cleaners. The National Association of Dyers and Cleaners maintains a research and testing laboratory. In order to bear the seal of approval of this association, fabrics and garments must meet certain standards as to shrinkage and color fastness.

Private Laboratories. In a discussion of private agencies for consumer protection, it is desirable to include various types of laboratories that test foods and other merchandise. Such laboratories may be classified as follows:

(a) Laboratories maintained by private companies for testing their own products and purchases.
(b) Laboratories of some schools and universities that will conduct a test for anyone who is willing to pay a fee for the service.
(c) Private laboratories that will do testing on a fee basis for anyone who submits a product.
(d) Laboratories retained by or owned and operated by associations.

A company laboratory is organized primarily for the benefit of a particular company and its customers. For instance, one large chain-store grocery company has a completely equipped laboratory that is used to test all merchandise before it is bought. Upon the basis of its test the laboratory authorizes or rejects any proposed purchase. Some of the great corporations operate scientific laboratories for testing their own products. This in itself is a service to consumers. However, some stores and mail-order houses go further; through detailed information on labels, they pass on to consumers facts discovered by their laboratories.

The proving grounds and the testing laboratories of our large corporations indirectly affect the consumer, for they tend to raise standards of quality. For example, the automobile manufacturers have large proving grounds used to test new devices and new models of automobiles before they are offered for sale. If this testing were not conducted, the consumer in many cases would not get his money's worth. He would do the experimenting rather than the producer. Producers usually feature in their advertising certain tests that have been made on the proving grounds or in the laboratories. The wise buyer will weigh the results of such tests.

Quality Seals

The laboratories of some schools and universities are operated only for the benefit of the institutions, but occasionally the facilities of such a laboratory are available to any client who is willing to pay an established fee.

Numerous laboratories are open to individuals or organizations for the purpose of testing various types of products, ranging from foods to chemicals, clothing, and heavy machinery. The National Bureau of Standards of the United States Department of Commerce publishes a directory of commercial testing laboratories and college research laboratories. This directory indicates the types of commodities that can be tested by each laboratory. Some of these laboratories will test items such as clothing, shoes, or food for a fee ranging from one dollar to ten dollars.

The United States Testing Company is an agency that serves many manufacturers, department stores, and individuals. The label issued by this organization is illustrated on this page. Standards of quality and descriptive terms are established by the United States Testing Company and when a product is tested and found to meet these standards, the manufacturers may use the label of the United States Testing Company on its product. The product must not only meet proper standards of performance tests, but the advertising and promotional claims for the product must also be found to be valid and truthful.

FLUORESCENT LAMP BALLASTS

The Manufacturer guarantees by affixing this Label that these **FLUORESCENT LAMP BALLASTS** duplicate samples found by periodic examination to comply with
"SPECIFICATIONS FOR FLUORESCENT LAMP AUXILIARIES"
which are sponsored by the Certified Ballast Manufacturers.
ELECTRICAL TESTING LABORATORIES, INC.
NEW YORK, N. Y.   11-45

CERTIFIED
E.T.L.
SPEC.NO.6

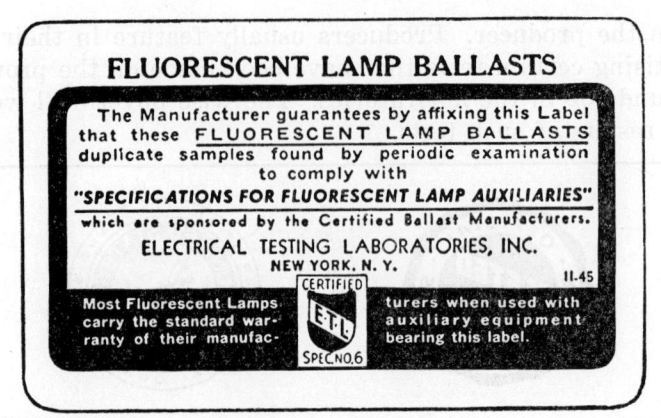

Most Fluorescent Lamps carry the standard warranty of their manufacturers when used with auxiliary equipment bearing this label.

Certification Label of ETL

Any manufacturer or distributor that receives the Certified Merchandise Seal of Quality enters into an agreement requiring quality control and check tests. If at any time in the future it is found that the product does not measure up to the proper standards, the privilege of using the seal of quality is withdrawn.

The Electrical Testing Laboratories, Inc. is a privately operated laboratory that tests and awards seals of approval on electrical apparatus. One of the most common products that a consumer will find carrying this label (ETL) is the portable electric lamp, including the lamp shade. Certificates are awarded on the basis of safety, durability, effectiveness, convenience, and absence of objective features. Some lamps may bear both the ETL and IES labels.

Consumers' Research Organizations. There are two organizations that solicit membership on a fee basis and furnish members with bulletins and guides: Consumers' Research, Inc., Washington, New Jersey; Consumers Union of U. S., Inc., Mt. Vernon, New York.

Such organizations are operated on a nonprofit basis for the benefit of their members.

The direct benefit of these organizations is limited largely to the subscribers. As these organizations are operated largely for members, however, they have greater freedom in making tests and in reporting the information.

Testing Mattresses

Consumers' Research, Inc.

Consumers' Research, Inc. Consumers's Research is the outgrowth of what was originally a small club for the study of consumers' goods. Consumers' Research is now a national organization with laboratory facilities at the headquarters in Washington, New Jersey, and elsewhere.

Consumers' Research tests products that are most widely distributed and most inquired about by those who use its services. *Consumers' Research Bulletin,* issued monthly, presents in nontechnical language reports on products that have been tested or studied in the laboratory or by other means by experts and consultants. These bulletins are not confidential and anyone or any organization may subscribe. The *Annual Cumulative Bulletin,* which furnishes a convenient summary of a wide range of findings in one volume, is issued in September and is available to individual subscribers at an additional charge. Those who wish to obtain this book alone for personal individual use without the other part of the service may do so.

Products that have been examined and reported on are classified on the basis of quality as (a) recommended, (b) intermediate, or (c) not recommended. The fact that a particular product is not listed in a bulletin usually means that the product has not yet been examined.

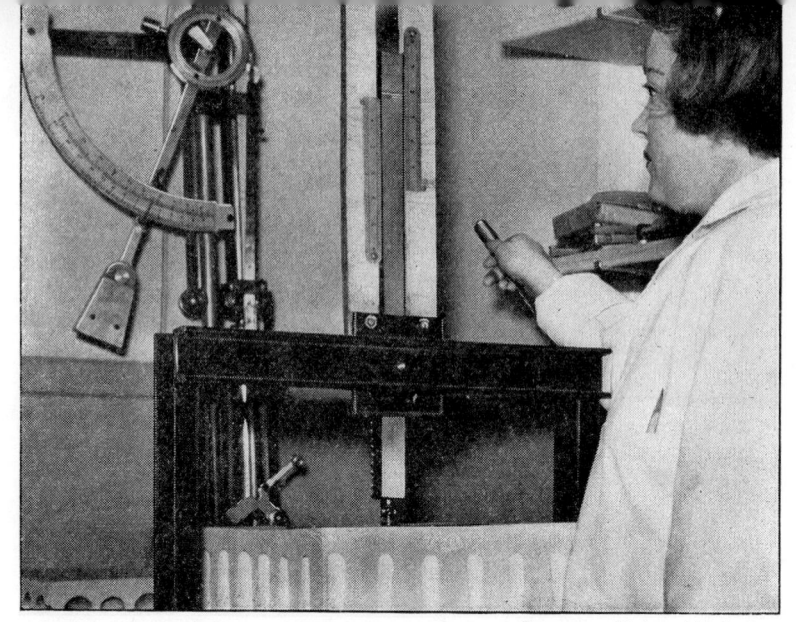

Consumers Union of U. S., Inc.

Testing Foam Rubber

Consumers Union of U. S., Inc. This nonprofit testing organization, with offices and laboratories in Mt. Vernon, New York, reports on consumer goods and services. The annual subscription includes eleven issues of the *Consumer Reports* and the annual Buying Guide.

Most of the product ratings are based on tests made in Consumers Union's laboratories, but tests are also made by a large number of technical specialists in university, government, and private laboratories, acting as consultants on special projects.

In addition to ratings by the brand name of many products, Consumer Reports also contains general buying advice and special features, including departments on Health and Medicine, Consumer Economics, Gardening, and a Movie Poll. Samples of products tests by Consumers Union are purchased by the organization's shoppers in the open market. No products are ever accepted as gifts or loans from manufacturers or distributors. Products are rated as "Best Buys," "Acceptable," or "Not Acceptable," with the "Acceptable" products generally listed in order of estimated over-all quality. A "Best Buy" is not always the highest quality product; it is a product found to offer outstanding value for its price.

Consumers Union is governed by a board of directors consisting of scientists, engineers, economists, educators, social workers, and other persons having no connection with commercial interests. Each subscriber has the privilege of becoming a member of Consumers Union by voting in the annual election of directors. Subscribers also assist in the formation of Consumers Union's policies by their answers to a detailed questionnaire.

American Home Economics Association. The American Home Economics Association has devoted some of its main efforts to the education and the protection of the consumer by furnishing buying information and by encouraigng suitable legislation and the use of proper standards. The association publishes a monthly magazine and bulletins on buying and the protection of the consumer.

Magazines and Newspapers. Magazines and newspapers have been performing a great amount of service for the average consumer. Some of the publishers maintain testing laboratories, and others have an advisory or consultation service for the benefit of consumers. Much advertising is rejected because the goods fail to meet the claims. In some cases products are tested and are given seals of approval that may be carried on the labels and in the advertising. Some of the testing is conducted with a view to aiding the advertisers and developing editorial material for the articles that are published.

Good Housekeeping magazine and *Parents' Magazine* maintain testing services, as a result of which any product that is accepted for advertising is guaranteed or approved by the magazine. The seal indicating approval may be carried on the label and in the advertising.

In the case of *Parents' Magazine*, there is a Commendation Seal that may be used under stipulated conditions. The seal of *Good Housekeeping* is used with the legend "Replacement or refund of money guaranteed by *Good Housekeeping* if not as advertised therein."

In some cases, such as *Parents' Magazine* Consumer Service Bureau, products are sent out to technical testing laboratories, such as the United States Testing Company, for neutral, unbiased tests, and the products are then assigned to consumer advisors who use the products in order to give them a practical test. *Parents' Magazine* claims to publish advertisements only of products and of services which it believes to be suitable for families with children.

National Canners Association. The National Canners Association has been responsible for setting up certain minimum standards for sizes of cans, quality, fill, and description of the product. Members are encouraged to pack their products in accordance with these standards.

Summary of Private Protection

1. Better Business Bureaus are organized to prevent unfair treatment, unfair advertising and selling, and fraud; and to promote informative advertising.
2. In many cities there is a Legal Aid Society that will furnish legal help if you cannot afford it.
3. American Medical Association and American Dental Association make regular studies of medical and dental preparations and devices.
4. Standardizing and testing agencies often provide labels signifying quality.
5. There are two organizations, Consumers' Research and Consumers Union, that are primarily organized to provide information to members in regard to the quality of products and services.
6. Some magazines test products and issue seals of approval or commendation.
7. The National Canners Association is responsible for setting up certain standards and means of identification of canned foods.

TEXTBOOK QUESTIONS

1. What are some of the functions performed by the better business bureaus in promoting fair trade practices?
2. Who may utilize the services of a better business bureau?
3. In most large cities how can a person without money obtain legal advice or assistance?
4. In what ways does the American Medical Association provide protection to the consumer?
5. In what way does the American Dental Association help protect the consumer?
6. What two main functions are performed through the tests conducted in the laboratories of the National Board of Fire Underwriters?
7. What does the seal of the American Gas Association mean?
8. How does the American Standards Association influence the development of standards?
9. What are some of the factors that determine whether the National Association of Dyers and Cleaners will approve a garment or fabric?
10. Name three of the types of private laboratories that test foods and other merchandise.
11. What kinds or classes of products are tested by Consumers' Research, Inc.?
12. Under what classifications are products rated by Consumers Union, Inc.?
13. How does the American Home Economics Association benefit the consumer?
14. What statement appears on the seal of *Good Housekeeping*?
15. In what way does the seal of approval of *Parents' Magazine* guarantee or approve a product?
16. To what extent has the National Canners Association contributed to the protection of the consumer?

DISCUSSION QUESTIONS

1. Suppose a door-to-door salesman calls on you and you would like to obtain information as to the reliability of him or his company in case you place an order with him and make a down payment. From what source might you be able to obtain help or advice?
2. At one time the American Medical Association approved products and allowed manufacturers to carry seals of approval. How do you feel that the present practices of the association help protect the consumer?

3. How do the laboratories of the National Board of Fire Underwriters save money for all of us?
4. "The activities of the American Standards Association save many thousands of dollars each year." Do you think this statement is true? Why?
5. Why do you think some manufacturers organize an association and use a seal indicating that products of the members of that association meet certain requirements?
6. Some manufacturers oppose such organizations as Consumers' Research, Inc., and Consumers Union, Inc., whereas others approve them. How do you account for the difference in attitude?
7. Some of the reports issued by consumer research organization are often a year old and sometimes older. Are these reports valuable? Discuss.
8. Some people assert that the scientific laboratories maintained by periodical publishers are operated for the benefit of manufacturers and therefore render little service to buyers. Do you think this assertion is true? Why?

PROBLEMS

1. Prepare a complete list of the products that are advertised in a current issue of some popular magazine. Opposite the name of each product indicate whether there is any seal, label, certified test, or testimonial used to indicate the standard of quality of the product. Indicate the specific proof that is given.
2. Make a list of food products and drugs that you find bearing seals or labels of approval. Indicate the particular seal or label for each product. If you find any seal or labels with which you are not acquainted, inquire about the conditions under which these are awarded.

COMMUNITY PROBLEMS AND PROJECTS

1. If you are in a community where there is a better business bureau, contact the bureau and find out some of the activities in which it has engaged recently, and obtain a description of some of the latest examples of frauds about which consumers in your community should be warned.
2. Investigate the services that are performed by some periodical publisher in testing and approving products and in issuing information for the benefit of consumers. Write a report on your findings, and evaluate the services performed.

Chapter 7

How Government Agencies Protect and Serve Us

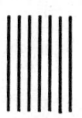

> **Purpose of the Chapter.** The primary purpose of government is to protect the rights of individual citizens. Many agencies or divisions of government have been created to carry out this objective. Although consumers benefit indirectly from the services of all government agencies, the functions of some of the agencies are very closely related to the interest of consumers. In this chapter we shall learn how government agencies help and protect consumers.
>
> You will find answers to these questions:
> 1. What government agencies offer services for the information and protection of consumers?
> 2. What is the nature of the information and protection provided for consumers by government?
> 3. What are the services offered by the various government agencies?
> 4. How may one obtain and use effectively government services?

United States Department of Commerce

Benefits to the Consumer. The primary purpose of the United States Department of Commerce is to serve business; however, in serving business, consumer interests are also served. Setting of standards for business is an indirect aid to consumers. Testing of products indirectly aids consumers. Encouraging the use of self-certifying labels makes useful information available to the consumer. These services to business and others that also help consumers are presented here.

National Bureau of Standards

Air View of National Bureau of Standards

The Bureau of Standards In Washington affects all of us in our daily lives. It is an institution that has helped us to live better by aiding government and business and indirectly aiding the consumer.

National Bureau of Standards. Although the National Bureau of Standards issues no regulations or orders, it probably exercises more influence on our daily lives than any other government agency. It has in its custody the standards of length, weight, and volume by which instruments for measurement of the inch, ounce, and pint may be calibrated. Radio wave lengths, the length of a second of time, and a degree of temperature are all measured by standards maintained by the Bureau.

The Bureau makes tests of products for quality and performance mainly for Federal agencies, but it will occasionally do testing for others if facilities are not available elsewhere. The testing, calibration, and certification of standards and standard measuring apparatus are services the Bureau renders not only for the Federal Government and state and city governments, but also for scientific societies, educational institutions, and business firms.

Among other services of the Bureau from which consumers benefit is the development of codes pertaining to safety, building design and construction, and plumbing. Federal specifications are prepared to serve as guides to departments of government in purchasing many kinds of materials and products. These *Federal specifications,* which really are standards of acceptable quality or performance as a basis for government bids, are available to business firms and the public. One of the most valuable services of the Bureau is the development of methods of testing such commodities as cement, paint, rubber, and textiles.

Information pertaining to a wide range of subjects in science, mathematics, and technology is available free upon request. Most of the other services are free to governments, but a nominal fee is charged the public and business firms.

Simplified Practices and Commercial Standards Recommendations. The Commodity Standards Division of the Office of Technical Services in the Business and Defense

Radio Station, WWV, Bellville, Maryland, Broadcasts Official Time Signals by a Musical Note

Measurement of time is critically important to industry, science, aviation, rail transportation, and in almost everything else we do. Time signals enable all of us to check our watches and clocks regularly to be sure that they are accurate.

National Bureau of Standards

Services Administration of the Department of Commerce issues bulletins on current simplified practices pertaining to commodities ranging all the way from flashlight batteries to shoe laces. *Simplified practice* means reduction of excessive variety of manufactured products or of methods. One of the primary advantages in the establishment of standards has been the elimination of unnecessary variations in size, grade, color, shape, and nomenclature of products. The standardization of the sizes of bricks and bolts is a good example. The recommendations for simplified practices are developed by voluntary cooperation among manufacturers, distributors, consumers, and other interests. This activity has an important value to consumers because, for example, manufacturers make about two standard sizes of garden hose instead of many.

The Bureau of Standards Tests Hosiery

Hosiery is only one of the thousands of products tested by the National Bureau of Standards. These tests are going on daily in an attempt to find ways of developing better quality through better processes and by setting standards of quality.

National Bureau of Standards

Another function of the Commodity Standards Division is the establishment of standard quality requirements, methods of testing, rating, certification, and labeling of commodities which are known as Commercial Standards Recommendations. Manufacturers are encouraged to use self-certifying labels on their products. On these *self-certifying labels* the manufacturer states that his goods conform to commercial standards. Many pamphlets are available from the Division at a nominal cost pertaining to standards for wearing apparel, appliances, electrical equipment, hardware and tools, household supplies and furnishings, and many other commodities for consumer use.

Copies of the lists of effective Simplified Practice Recommendations and Commercial Standards, respectively, may be obtained from the Commodity Standards Division, Office of Technical Services, Department of Commerce.

Other Services of the Department of Commerce. Although consumers benefit indirectly from practically every activity of the Department of Commerce, some services are more closely related to consumers than are others. Mention of a few will be sufficient to indicate their value to consumers.

The Patent Office encourages invention of new commodities and processes by issuing patents to protect the rights of inventors. This benefits consumers by making new things available to them. The Bureau of the Census issues statistics on population, occupations, and many other aspects pertaining to the lives of all people. The Office of Business Economics, although created primarily to serve business enterprise, publishes statistics useful to people on wages, costs, income, and debts. The Weather Bureau's forecasts and warnings are protections to consumers against loss due to extreme variations in temperature and rainfall.

United States Department of Agriculture

The United States Department of Agriculture is one of the executive departments of the Federal Government that offers important services for the information and protection of consumers. In addition to the many services provided for the benefit of farmers, it provdes commodity standards and grades for many foods and farm products, meat inspection service, and other marketing services that are helpful to consumers. Several of the regulatory laws designed for consumer protection are administered by this Department.

The Human Nutrition and Home Economics Research Branch is an agency of the Department of Agriculture that seeks to develop new knowledge about nutrition; better consumer use of food, fiber, and other products; and efficient household management. One of the significant contributions of this agency to consumers is the preparation and distribution of bulletins pertaining to such topics as composition and nutritive values of foods, diets, home preservation of foods, new and improved cooking methods, food plans for families and recipes.

The Home Economics Research Branch helps consumers by publishing information pertaining to the simplification of household procedures, time-saving devices and practices, money management, and guides for buying clothing, textiles, and household equipment.

The Agricultural Marketing Service, an agency of the Department of Agriculture, provides marketing services of tremendous value not only to consumers but also to distributors such as food wholesalers and retailers.

The function of the Federal Food and Drug Administration is to develop and enforce standards for foods; whereas the Agricultural Marketing Service has the responsibility for grading of the various common kinds or types of food. *Grading* is the process of determining the quality of foods. In addition to grading foods at the meat packing plant or at the cannery, the Agricultural Marketing Service has the responsibility for inspecting meats and passing on their wholesomeness and fitness for human food.

Federal grades have been established for meats, poultry, eggs, butter, cheese, processed fruits and vegetables, and fresh fruits and vegetables. The method of designating grades varies from one food commodity to another. For example, the grade of canned fruits and vegetables ordinarily is designated as A, B, and C, fresh fruits and vegetables by U. S. No. 1, U. S. No. 2, etc. The grades of foods and their meaning will be explained further in Chapter 11.

Grades of foods and food products indicate to the consumer the quality of food he is buying. Through inspection and analysis the fitness for human use is determined.

Department of Health, Education, and Welfare

Consumers may look to the Department of Health, Education, and Welfare for information and protection pertaining to health. The activities of the Department concerning health are centered primarily in the divisions of Public Health Service and the Food and Drug Administration.

Public Health Service. The principal activity of the Public Health Service is the prevention of disease and the protection of health. Close cooperation is provided with medical, dental, nursing, and other social service groups, and with schools and governmental bodies of states, counties, and cities. For instance, one of the activities of the Public Health Service has been to set up standards for milk and to promote the adoption of a standard milk ordinance in cities. This Service deals largely with groups rather than with individuals.

The Federal Food and Drug Administration. The Food and Drug Administration, which is one of the divisions of the Department of Health, Education, and Welfare enforces the following laws: Federal Food, Drug, and Cosmetic Act; Tea Importation Act; Import Milk Act; Caustic Poison Act; and Filled Milk Act. The primary function of the Administration is the development and enforcement of food and drug standards. The activities of the Administration are directed mainly toward promoting purity, standard strength, and truthful and informative labeling of the essential commodities covered by the provisions of these five acts. These laws are among the most important of all Federal laws for the protection of consumers.

Enforcement is carried out by inspection of factories for sanitary conditions, raw materials used, and controls in processing, packaging, and labeling products for shipment. Imported foods and drugs are analyzed and examined after arrival in this country. Although inspection is carried on continuously, when violations are suspected, specimen products are picked up at their destinations for examination and analysis. Retail drugstores are kept under observation to prevent the selling of dangerous drugs without a doctor's prescription. Violations of the pure food and drug laws are reported to the Department of Justice for seizure of the commodities in question or criminal prosecution.

Laboratories are maintained in Washington to test samples of commodities covered by the pure food and drug laws and to develop methods for the detection and proof of adulteration of food and drug commodities for human consumption.

Federal Food, Drug, and Cosmetic Act. Consumers are protected by prohibiting the sale and transportation across state lines of foods, drugs, and other devices that are adulterated, misbranded, or that fail to meet other standards. If the quality of a commodity is not acceptable for interstate commerce, its sale and use will be very small within the state where it is manufactured. The Federal Food, Drug, and Cosmetic Act protects consumers by making it illegal to move or sell such goods in interstate commerce. Foods, drugs, and cosmetics are considered illegal in interstate commerce if they are adulterated, misbranded, label defaced, or if a false guarantee is given.

Food Standards. Any food that is injurious to health is barred from interstate commerce. Unsafe amounts of harmful ingredients may not be added to any food product. The Law makes it mandatory that harmful sprays on fruits and vegetables be thoroughly washed off before shipments of the products may cross state lines. Any type of food that may be contaminated during the process of manufacture or packing may be subjected to the regulations of the Food, Drug, and Cosmetics Act.

Ch. 7] GOVERNMENT AGENCIES THAT PROTECT US 109

The Law permits the Food and Drug Administration to set minimum "standards of identity" for foods after conducting public hearings. That is, for each commonly named food, it can write a definition with minimum standards. Only foods meeting these standards can be marketed under that name. Foods that do not meet the standards, but that are clean and wholesome, may be marketed but must be labeled "substandard." Even these must meet all standards of sanitation and nutrition. It will be observed that the purpose of the law is to protect the consumer by setting some standards. However it is also recognized that some foods are still safe and wholesome but may not be up to standard.

Drug Standards. Proper use of drugs may be of great value to individuals; improper use may be highly dangerous. Many individuals attempt to diagnose their own physical ailments and then treat their illness by the use of drugs. Except for standard home remedies as recommended for the home medicine cabinet by the Food and Drug Administration, the individual who is not medically trained should

Dough for Bread That Will Be Sold in Another State Is Subject to Inspection by the Food and Drug Administration

The Federal Food and Drug Administration sets standards for and inspects only foods that are sold from one state to another, but many products manufactured and sold locally are influenced by these standards in order to meet competition.

Food and Drug Administration

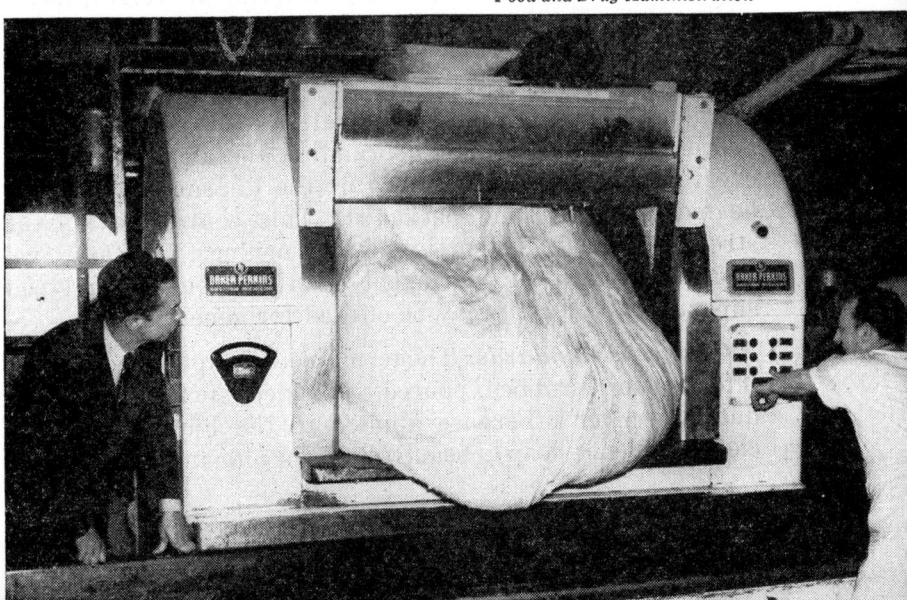

not be permitted to obtain drugs for such promiscuous use. Thus, the Federal Food and Drug Administration has set up certain controls over drugs in regard to their sale. Under the provisions of the Federal Food, Drug, and Cosmetic Act the term *drug* applies to articles recognized by the official United States Pharmacopoeia, the official Homeopathic Pharmacopoeia of the United States, the official National Formulary, or any supplement to any of them.

The so-called health devices governed by the Act are instruments, apparatus, and contrivances for use in the diagnosis, cure, mitigation, treatment, or prevention of disease in man or other animals. The term also applies to devices that affect the structure or any function of the body.

For the protection of the consumers the sale of adulterated drugs is prohibited in interstate commerce when they are found to be contaminated, impure, or unsanitary, making them injurious to health. Further, drugs are considered to be adulterated if the strength or quality differs from established standards or if coloring has been added that has not been certified.

One of the purposes of the Federal Food, Drug, and Cosmetic Act is to protect consumers from misbranding of drugs. Drugs must carry labels giving in terms ordinarily understood such information as the name of the manufacturer or distributor; quantity in terms of weight, measure, or count; adequate directions for use and warnings against misuse; and complete description and amounts of ingredients.

The Food and Drug Administration not only attempts to prevent adulteration and misbranding, but also dictates how every remedy that is approved by the Pharmacopoeia shall be manufactured and packaged. This control covers the strength, dosage, instructions, and warnings. The approval of a new remedy is contingent upon a tryout under strict supervision before it may be offered for general sale.

Cosmetic Standards. The term *cosmetic* applies to articles intended to be rubbed, poured, sprinkled, sprayed on, introduced into, or otherwise applied to the human body for cleansing (not soap), beautifying, or altering appearance.

Consumers are protected from adulterated cosmetics by their sale being considered illegal in interstate commerce when they are contaminated, impure, or unsanitary, thus making them injurious to health. Cosmetics are also considered to be adulterated if they or the containers in which they are packed contain a substance that is poisonous or injurious to users under ordinary conditions of use of the cosmetic or if they contain coloring that has not been certified. Hair dye containing coal tar ingredients must have a label cautioning users that it may irritate the skin or may cause blindness if gotten in the eyes.

The label on cosmetics must not be false or misleading. It must identify the manufacturer and distributor; contain an accurate statement of the quantity in terms of weight, measure, or count; statements pertaining to directions for its use or cautions against possible injury from misuse as prescribed by the law must be easily understood. Cosmetics not meeting the qualifications for labeling are considered misbranded.

Other Food and Drug Acts. The Tea Importation, Import Milk, and Filled Milk Acts are concerned with the fitness of imported foods for human use. The Caustic Poison Act is to prevent the sale of vegetables, fruits, and other foods that may be contaminated or unfit for human use due to the use of insecticides and preservatives.

Federal Trade Commission

The basic objective of the Federal Trade Commission, which was established in 1915, is the maintenance of free competitive business as the keystone of the American economic system. The principal functions of the Commission benefit consumers in some way.

Several laws have been enacted to enable the Commission to carry out its functions. Amendments to the laws have been made from time to time. We shall not attempt to study the provisions of the laws separately.

Promote Free and Fair Competition. One of the principles upon which the idea of free enterprise is based is that

> *Principal Functions of Federal Trade Commission*
>
> 1. Promote free and fair competition through prevention of price-fixing agreements, unfair methods of competition, and unfair or deceptive practices. (Sherman Antitrust Act, 1890; Clayton Act, 1914; and Federal Trade Commission Act, 1914.)
> 2. Prevent price discrimination among buyers and arrangements among business firms that result in lessening competition. (Robinson-Patman Act, 1936; Miller-Tydings Act, 1937; McQuire Act, 1952.)
> 3. Safeguard consuming public by preventing use of false and deceptive advertisements. (Federal Trade Commission Act, 1914; Wheeler-Lea Act, 1938.)
> 4. Enforce truthful labeling of wool and fur products. (Wool Products Labeling Act, 1939; Fur Products Labeling Act, 1951.)
> 5. Protect consumers from dangerously inflammable wearing apparel or fabrics by preventing its sale. (Flammable Fabrics Act, 1953.)

there shall be unrestricted but fair competition among farmers who produce agricultural products, manufacturers who make commodities, wholesalers and retailers whose function is to get commodities to the people who want and need them, and individuals in their occupational and professional pursuits. Unrestricted but fair competition forces us to strive continuously to improve our product or service, to develop better and more effective methods and procedures of doing our work, and to expect only a reasonable financial return for our efforts. Consumers benefit from competition by way of better products and services and lower prices.

These benefits to consumers are threatened whenever price fixing agreements, boycotts, or other methods of unfair competition are entered into by any economic group whether the group is comprised of farmers, laborers, manufacturers, businessmen, or professional people. Any business practices that curtail competition are adverse to free enterprise.

Three basic acts have been passed by Congress to foster free private enterprise. The first one passed in 1890 which essentially was to prevent monopoly (i.e., control of an industry or a service by one business firm) was The Sherman Antitrust Act. Many years later in 1914, the Clayton Act which really supplemented the Sherman Act was passed to control arrangements among business firms, such as discrimination in price, interlocking directorates, and other practices that would have an adverse effect on competition. The Federal Trade Commission Act of 1914 created the Federal Trade Commission as an agency to enforce laws designed to prohibit unfair methods of competition.

Prevention of Exclusive Deals and Price Discrimination. Another principle upon which the concept of free enterprise is based is that goods or services should be offered to all purchasers at the same price, allowances being made for differences in costs due to quantity, method and place of delivery, and specifications. Selling goods on the condition that the buyer promises not to make purchases from the seller's competitors or that he will purchase all of his requirements of similar commodities from the seller, substantially lessens competition and in the long run is detrimental to the consumer. Such agreements are considered to be in restraint of trade.

The Robinson-Patman Anti-Discrimination Act passed in 1936 makes it unlawful for a manufacturer, wholesaler, or any other type of distributor to discriminate among his customers as regards price, discount, or services. For instance, it is not lawful for a manufacturer to sell to one distributor at a lower price than he does to another, provided the conditions of the sale are the same. One of the purposes of this law was to prevent unusual discounts from being given to one customer when another might be required to pay the standard price.

Fair Trade Laws. Under the provisions of the anti-trust laws and the Federal Trade Commission Act, agreements between a manufacturer and a wholesaler or a retailer to fix retail prices were held to be in restraint of trade and considered to be unfair competition. In 1937, the Miller-Tydings Act was passed which amended the anti-trust laws so that state legislatures could legalize price fixing contracts between a manufacturer and a wholesaler or retailer. By 1941, all except three states had passed "fair trade laws."

In general, these state laws permit a manufacturer or distributor of a trade-marked or otherwise identifiable commodity to enter into contract with a wholesaler or retailer not to sell the goods at less than the price stipulated in the contract, which usually is the manufacturer's nationally advertised price. Such agreements are not permissible, however, between two groups of manufacturers or between groups of wholesalers, or between groups of retailers.

In most states a commodity becomes subject to the state's fair trade law when one wholesaler or retailer agrees not to resell it at less than the manufacturer's stipulated price. Any other wholesaler or retailer, even though he has not signed such an agreement, is considered to have engaged in unfair competitive practices if he "willfully or knowingly" advertises or sells the commodity at less than the stipulated price. The United States Supreme Court ruled in 1951 that price fixing agreements were not binding on wholesalers and retailers who had not signed such contracts. However in 1952, the McGuire Act specifically made nonsigners subject to minimum price agreements.

Controversy on Fair Trade Laws. Many arguments in favor and against price fixing agreements and the provisions of the state fair trade laws are advanced. Those in favor maintain that fair trade protects consumers from questionable merchandising practices of merchants who resort to "bait advertising" and unethical price cutting to force competition out of business. It is claimed by some that fair trade laws protect consumers from monopoly practices in distribution by giving small businessmen a chance to compete on equal terms with large distributors, who normally buy in large quantity and can sell for less. Others claim that the retail prices of some articles are actually lower on the whole in states in which they are under fair trade laws than in states in which they are not. It is contended that cut prices offered by discount houses are actually misleading because they often do not include delivery, installation, or service. In some instances where a commodity is not under fair trade laws, small retailers have discontinued handling the commodity because they could not compete with prices offered by discount houses at 30 to 50 per cent less than the nationally advertised price of the manufacturer.

Manufacturers insist that price fixing results in better quality merchandise and in lower costs to the consumer because "cut throat" competition is eliminated. Many manufacturers of nationally known durable goods such as refrigerators, ranges, and air conditioners favor fair trade laws. Likewise, the manufacturers of patented drugs and cosmetics generally advocate the legal enforcement of stipulated retail prices.

Probably the strongest argument against fair trade is that it keeps prices up by protecting the inefficient merchant. Many people who oppose the fair trade laws believe them to be wholly contrary to the principles of free competition because retailers who have neither agreed to nor signed price fixing contracts are bound by the agreements others have made.

Consumers often argue that they are entitled to the benefits of lower prices that result from competitive price cutting. The argument of manufacturers that selling at a stipulated price thus reducing competition will improve quality is refuted by many consumers and retailers. Retail chain stores selling goods such as groceries and drugs insist that they should be permitted to pass on to the customers the benefit in prices resulting from their large volume of sales. It is held that the fair trade laws reduce competition.

A study of the effects of fair trade laws indicates that although there are certain disadvantages to consumers, there are also advantages in retail price fixing. Some retailers who are able to buy in large quantities at lower costs sell merchandise at lower prices than competing small merchants, thus driving the latter out of business. After the competition is removed, the large merchant may then raise his prices to any level he chooses.

Some stores advertise well-known brands of commodities at very low prices in order to bring people into their stores.

As a result of the bait advertising, customers may believe prices of all commodities in that store are lower than in competing stores. Repeat bait advertising has been carried so far in some instances that customers will buy only when a well-known brand is on sale. This injures the manufacturer and other dealers who are trying to sell at a reasonable price.

Some merchants attempt to ride on the reputation which has been built up for merchandise through regular channels. They offer no services, but sell on a "take it or leave it basis." Although it may be argued that this is a legitimate practice, the whole distributive process would break down if all merchandise were sold in this manner.

Strong arguments are advanced on both sides of the fair trade issue. A solution satisfactory to all interested parties has not been reached.

Federal Control of Advertising. The Federal Government's power over advertising rests in a number of agencies. The Federal Trade Commission is concerned especially with deceptive advertising. The first regulations pertaining to deceptive advertising were concerned with "unfair methods of competition" that would be damaging to an advertiser's competitors. In response to a feeling that the interests of consumers should also be protected in advertising, the Wheeler-Lea Act, as an amendment to the Federal Trade Commission Act, was passed in 1938. The following provisions of the amendment are significant to the consumer:

(a) In general, all unfair methods of competition in commerce, as well as unfair or deceptive acts or practices, are declared unlawful.

(b) It is unlawful to publish or distribute false advertising in order to induce purchases of foods, drugs, devices, or cosmetics.

(c) Publishers, radio broadcasters, advertising agencies, and other advertising mediums are relieved from liability under the Federal Trade Commission Act unless they refuse to furnish the Commission with the name and the address of the manufacturer, packer, distributor, seller, or advertising agency that has caused the distribution of such advertisements.

(d) False advertising is defined as being "misleading in a material respect," including the failure to reveal facts as to consequences that may result from the use of the advertised commodities.

An illustration of deceptive or false advertising would be to state or imply that a pain killing drug such as aspirin will cure a decayed tooth when it really does nothing more than relieve the pain which is a symptom. Another case of deception in advertising is to state or imply that a fabric, such as cotton, will not shrink. Statements that cotton will not shrink more than a certain percentage are permissible. In examining thousands of advertisements annually the Federal Trade Commission finds relatively few that are actually deceptive or false.

The Federal Alcoholic and Tobacco Tax Division of the Treasury has the responsibility for policing advertising pertaining to alcohol. The Alcohol Division objects to statements such as "no hangover," "it's good for you," and "our brand will help you to success."

The Food and Drug Administration is concerned with advertising and labeling of products in its area; the Department of Agriculture, with misleading labeling and advertising of seeds; the Federal Communications Commission with radio and televison broadcast commercials; and the Securities Exchange Commission with advertising of security issues.

State Control of Advertising. There are numerous state laws supplementing the Federal laws that represent barriers against deceptive and fraudulent advertising. Probably the most famous law is the *Printers' Ink* Model Statute. The 1945 revision of the Model Statute is shown at the top of the next page. This statute, substantially, is in use in 26 states and the District of Columbia. Seventeen other states have adopted variations of it. Thus, 43 of the 48 states have adopted the principle of the *Printers' Ink* Model Statute. The states that do not have such laws are: Arkansas, Delaware, Georgia, Mississippi, and New Mexico.

The Model Statute provides the basis for the operations of the Better Business Bureaus.

Printers' Ink Model Statute

Any person, firm, corporation or association or agent or employee thereof, who, with intent to sell, purchase or in any wise dispose of, or to contract with reference to merchandise, real estate, service, employment, or anything offered by such person, firm, corporation or association, or agent or employee thereof, directly or indirectly, to the public for sale, purchase, distribution, or the hire of personal services, or with intent to increase the consumption of or to contract with reference to any merchandise, real estate, securities, service, or employment, or to induce the public in any manner to enter into any obligation relating thereto, or to acquire title thereto, or an interest therein, or to make any loan, makes, publishes, disseminates, circulates, or places before the public, or causes, directly or indirectly, to be made, published, disseminated, circulated, or placed before the public, in this state, in a newspaper, magazine or other publication, or in the form of a book, notice, circular, pamphlet, letter, handbill, poster, bill, sign, placard, card, label, or over any radio or television station or other medium of wireless communication, or in any other way similar or dissimilar to the foregoing, an advertisement, announcement, or statement of any sort regarding merchandise, securities, service, employment, or anything so offered for use, purchase or sale, or the interest, terms or conditions upon which such loan will be made to the public, which advertisement contains any assertion, representation or statement of fact which is untrue, deceptive, or misleading, shall be guilty of a misdemeanor.

Wool and Fur Products Labeling. Proper, informative labeling of wool and fur products has been made compulsory for the protection of consumers. The Federal Trade Commission was given jurisdiction over the Wool Products Labeling Act of 1939 and the Fur Products Labeling Act passed in 1951. Under these laws products made of wool or of fur each must be identified with a stamp, tag, or label giving specific information as to the kind, name, and grade of the wool or fur used in the product.

A *wool product* is any product made wholly or in part of new, unused wool, reprocessed wool, or re-used wool. The label for such a product must indicate the class of wool used, the percentage of the fibers that are actual wool, and whether it is loaded or weighted in any way. The name of the manufacturer, distributor, or retailer must also be on the label.

A fur product means any article made in whole or in part of fur or used fur. *Used fur* is a term applied to fur in any form which has been worn or used by an ultimate consumer. *Waste fur* refers to mats or plates made from ears, throats, or scrap pieces which have been severed from the animal pelt.

The Fur Products Labeling Act makes it illegal to misbrand furs, advertise falsely, or invoice fur products improperly. A *Fur Products Name Guide,* prepared by the Federal Trade Commission and the U. S. Department of Agriculture, gives the true names of hair, fleece, and fur-bearing animal from which fur products are made. The names given in the Guide must be used to designate on the label the kind of fur used in an article.

Protection from Flammable Fabrics. Some synthetic fabrics are highly flammable and burn with an intense heat making them highly dangerous when used in wearing apparel. The Flammable Fabrics Act, passed in 1953, prohibits the manufacture for sale and sale of any article in commerce of wearing apparel made of fabric that does not meet the Commercial Standard for Flammability of Clothing Textiles prepared by the Commercial Standards Division of the Department of Commerce. The enforcement of the Flammable Fabrics Act is under the Federal Trade Commission.

Administration of Trade-mark Regulations. Trade-marks are of great value to consumers in identifying the products of specific manufacturers. They also have promotional value to the manufacturers. The Trade-mark Act of 1946 conferred upon the Federal Trade Commission the authority to administer and enforce the Act. The law specifies how trade-marks may be used.

Other Public Agencies

United States Department of Labor. The Department of Labor among other responsibilities is concerned with promotion of the welfare of wage earners, improvement of their working conditions, and advancement of their opportunities for profitable employment, all of which are of interest to consumers. The Bureau of Labor Statistics collects and publishes regularly data in regard to retail prices, wholesale prices, employment, wages, hours of work, and cost of living.

The Consumer Price Index calculated monthly by the Bureau of Labor Statistics is of great value to consumers who use it. The index is a measure of the average change in prices of goods and services customarily purchased by families of wage earners and clerical workers.

Consumer Price Index—United States Average, by Groups of Commodities, August, 1955 (1947-49—100)

All items	114.5
Food	111.2
Housing	120.0
Apparel	103.4
Transportation	125.4
Medical care	128.0
Personal care	115.8
Reading and recreation	106.3
Other goods and services	120.4

United States Post Office Department. For the protection of individuals and business firms postal laws declare it illegal to use the mails for the promotion of lotteries and for sending materials pertaining to schemes to defraud. Explosives, poisons, firearms, intoxicants, and certain narcotics are not mailable. Placing in the mails letters of extortion containing threats to injure the reputation of any person or to accuse him of a crime is considered a criminal offense. It is illegal to send through the mails indecent, obscene, defamatory, or subversive matter. Violations of postal laws carry very heavy penalties.

Federal and State Regulation of Securities. Federal legislation administered by the Securities and Exchange Commission protects the interests of the public and investors against malpractice in the issuance and sale of stocks and bonds in interstate commerce. These securities laws require public disclosure of information that will enable prospective investors to make a realistic appraisal of the securities and the possible risks in their purchase. Registration of issues of stocks and bonds is required before sales may be made.

Many states have securities laws commonly known as *blue-sky laws* that apply to the issuance and sale of securities.

State and City Protection. In some states laws have been set up for grading the quality of such items as fruits and vegetables. Many states and cities have set up regulations for controlling the quality of milk and other foods sold in local markets. The health departments of those states and cities require products to measure up to specified standards. Most cities require the regular inspection of scales and measures. Many other local regulations tend to protect the consumer.

CITY OF CINCINNATI
DEPARTMENT OF SAFETY
PUMP
EXAMINED AND SEALED
I. VAN CLEEFF,
Supt. Markets, Weights, Measures
Office, Sixth and Plum Sts.   Market House
Phone CHerry 5300, Line 303   Cincinnati, O.

A City Inspector's Seal

Summary of Government Services to Consumers

1. The Federal Government provides much valuable information which otherwise would not be available to consumers.
2. Standards and regulations to insure purity, potency and truthful and informative labeling of drugs and cosmetics protects consumers.
3. The Federal Government promotes free and fair competition among business firms and among individuals, thus assuring better products and reasonable prices.
4. The consuming public is safeguarded by preventing use of false and deceptive advertising.
5. Truthful labeling and description of wool and fur products is enforced by the government.
6. State and city governments give many services that are protections to consumers.

TEXTBOOK QUESTIONS

1. What is the primary purpose of the United States Department of Commerce?
2. What is the primary purpose of the National Bureau of Standards?
3. (a) What standards are maintained by the National Bureau of Standards? (b) What testing service is performed by the National Bureau of Standards? (c) What codes and specifications are prepared by the National Bureau of Standards?
4. What is meant by "simplified practice"?
5. What are the advantages of having standards?
6. Give a summary of the services provided by the United States Department of Agriculture.
7. (a) What is grading? (b) For what items have Federal grades been set?
8. How does food grading benefit the consumer?
9. What is the principal activity of the Public Health Service?
10. (a) What laws are enforced by the Federal Food and Drug Administration? (b) How does the Federal Food and Drug Administration enforce these laws? (c) What are the benefits to the consumer of the activities of the Federal Food and Drug Administration?
11. (a) How does the Federal Food, Drug, and Cosmetic Act protect consumers? (b) What food standards, drug standards, and cosmetic standards are enforced by this act?
12. What is meant by the setting up of "standards of identity" by the Food and Drug Administration?
13. What information must the label on cosmetic products contain?
14. How does the Federal Food, Drug, and Cosmetic Act affect the labeling of drugs?
15. What is the basic objective of the Federal Trade Commission?
16. What are the principal functions of the Federal Trade Commission?
17. What acts have been passed by Congress to foster free private enterprise?
18. What is the Robinson-Patman Act?
19. What are the Fair Trade Laws?
20. (a) What are the arguments in favor of fair trade laws? (b) What are the arguments against fair trade laws?
21. In what way does the Federal Trade Commission have control over advertising?
22. What is the *Printers' Ink* Model Statute?
23. Under the Wool Products Labeling Act and the Fur Products Labeling Act, what do the following terms mean: wool product, used fur, waste fur?

Ch. 7]   GOVERNMENT AGENCIES THAT PROTECT US   123

24. What is the *Fur Products Name Guide*?
25. How are consumers protected from flammable fabrics?
26. (a) What are trade-marks? (b) How are they regulated?
27. In what ways is the United States Department of Labor of interest to the consumer?
28. What is the Consumer Price Index?
29. What protections are afforded consumers by the United States Post Office Department?
30. What does the Securities and Exchange Commission regulate?

DISCUSSION QUESTIONS

1. (a) What services are provided to consumers by the United States Department of Commerce? (b) Of what value are each of these services to the consumer?
2. Imagine that the United States Department of Commerce, including the National Bureau of Standards, should suddenly disappear. Describe some of the problems which might face the consumer.
3. How do the tests that are made by the National Bureau of Standards for individual manufacturers help all consumers?
4. In what way does the standardization program of the National Bureau of Standards help you as a buyer?
5. (a) How do the grading and inspection services of the Department of Agriculture aid the consumer? (b) How can you as an individual benefit from these services?
6. Do you think the standards set up by the Department of Agriculture for grading milk will help a local consumer of milk? How?
7. (a) Why were the recent polio vaccinations given to school children free? (b) What agency of the Federal Government provided this service?
8. On which would you place more reliance: an advertisement of a particular product, or the label on the product?
9. Assuming that you buy a product sold in interstate commerce on the basis of an advertisement in a magazine and find that the article does not conform to the quality or the description in the advertisement, what means of protection have you?
10. If a manufacturer of an article tells completely truthful facts in radio advertising of an article offered for sale but the article proves injurious to the consumer, is there any action that the consumer may take for his protection?
11. (a) Is a garment labeled properly if the label on it states "100% wool" and it is made partly from reclaimed wool?
(b) Is a garment labeled properly if the label states truthfully that it is made from 50 per cent reprocessed wool and 50 per cent re-used wool, but the lining is of rayon?

12. If you were a manufacturer, could you sell the same item to one customer for $1.50 and to another for $1.00 under the same conditions of sale?
13. In order to eliminate competition and cut down costs, two large wholesale hardware companies agree between themselves to divide the territory into two parts, one company covering one part and the other covering the second part. Is this permissible?
14. Are you in favor of or against fair trade laws? Give all the reasons you can for your opinion.

PROBLEMS

1. Examine the products in your medicine cabinet at home. Study the labels and find out whether the products comply with the regulations of the Federal Food, Drug, and Cosmetic Act. List under the name of each product the contents and the quality; whether or not artificial coloring or adulteration is present; and other similar facts.
2. From a magazine or a newspaper obtain an advertisement giving a rather complete description of a food, drug, cosmetic, or device. Analyze the advertisement to see whether it, in your opinion, violates the Federal law.
3. (a) Make a list of all the services you have observed that were provided for you today by a government agency. (b) Which of these services were probably not provided for your grandfather when he was your age? (c) Explain why these services might not have been provided for your grandfather.

COMMUNITY PROBLEMS AND PROJECTS

1. Find out what the Better Business Bureau of your community does. Then prepare a talk on how the *Printers' Ink* Model Statute provides the basis for the operation of the Better Business Bureau.
2. Visit with a farmer in your community and find out what services he uses that are provided by the United States Department of Agriculture. While talking with him, try to learn how he thinks these services could be improved; then decide whether or not you agree with him.
3. (a) Go to a hardware or drugstore and make a list of ten items for sale that are sold under the fair trade laws, and ten items that are not sold under the fair trade laws; be sure to list the price for which they are for sale. (b) Go to another similar store and check the prices for which the same items are for sale. (c) Compare the lists and explain why some prices are the same and some are different.

Chapter 8

Legal Relations for Our Protection

> **Purpose of the Chapter.** Every day you do certain things that involve legal relations with someone else. For this reason you need to know your legal rights and responsibilities and when you need legal advice. There are many other important kinds of legal relations, but in this chapter you will learn about the most common legal problems of the consumer and particularly those involved in the buying activities.
>
> You will find the answers to these questions:
> 1. Under what circumstances do you need expert legal advice?
> 2. What are the common types of contracts that you are likely to enter into daily?
> 3. What contracts may be oral or written?
> 4. What kinds of contracts are binding on a child?
> 5. What kinds of agreements may be broken?
> 6. What can you do if a party to a contract fails to perform his obligations?

When to Use Legal Advice. In this world of specialization it is sound practice for one to go to a doctor when he is ill. Likewise, it is sound business procedure to obtain competent legal advice on important problems. Some of the problems on which an individual should consult a lawyer are the writing of an important contract, the writing of a will, and protection against law suits. In selecting a lawyer, one should be careful to avoid the so-called shyster who is often too eager to take a case or who solicits a case. It is a practice among reputable lawyers to wait for the client to request legal counsel. Only lawyers who are members of the local or state bar association should be considered. When in doubt, ask the advice of some reputable businessman or consult a member of the local legal aid society.

If you ask a lawyer a question, his answer will be given to you in what he calls an *opinion*. Most lawyers will never state definitely what the answer is because it depends upon many circumstances. What appears to be true may not be true when all of the facts are known. For example, two judges in different courts, giving decisions on what may appear to be identical sets of circumstances, may give completely opposite decisions. Sometimes these decisions are reversed by higher courts.

Some "Yes" and "No" Answers

Here are some questions that bring up common problems and show you how easy it is to get into a legal situation.

THE ANSWER TO EACH OF THESE QUESTIONS IS "NO":

1. Is a contract binding if it is entered into under pressure or a threat?
2. Is a contract binding if it involves breaking the law?
3. Is an agreement of a boy fourteen years of age to buy a bicycle binding?
4. Is it necessary to sign a written order for the purchase of a suit of clothes in order for the contract to be binding?
5. Are you obligated to return or pay for merchandise sent to you that has not been ordered?

THE ANSWER TO EACH OF THESE QUESTIONS IS "YES":

1. Is a contract binding if it is signed without being read?
2. Is a contract binding if you sign it just to get rid of a persistent salesman?
3. Is a contract binding if you misunderstand part of it?
4. Is an installment sale agreement a contract?
5. Must a contract to purchase real estate be in writing?

Although many things in law appear to be definite, it must be borne in mind that any statement in the field of law cannot be completely definite without knowing all the circumstances. Therefore, any of the statements in this chapter are general statements of law and represent additional reasons why in many cases you should consult a lawyer.

What Is a Contract? A *contract* is an agreement between two or more competent parties that creates an obligation enforceable by law. If one of the parties does not carry out his part of the agreement, the other party may resort to a court action.

When you buy goods in a store on account, you make a contract with the store to pay the cost of the merchandise. If you leave shoes in a repair shop to be fixed, a contract is made on the part of the repairman to fix the shoes and on your part to pay the prescribed charges. When you rent a house, you enter into a contract to pay the rent; and the owner obligates himself to let you have possession of the property. Many other situations exist in everyday life that involve contracts. Buying life insurance, buying fire insurance, shipping merchandise, or accepting a position, all involve contracts.

The basis of a contract is an agreement between the parties. But not all agreements are contracts because some agreements do not have all the essentials of contracts. Ashworth agrees to go hunting with Stillwell; but if Stillwell changes his mind and decides not to go, he is not breaking a contract. On the other hand, if Ashworth and Stillwell make

---

Elements of a Contract

1. There must be offer and acceptance.
2. The parties must be competent.
3. The purpose must be legal.
4. There must be a consideration.
5. It must be in required form.

arrangements to go on a hunting trip together and arrange for a professional guide to provide them with hunting equipment, food, and lodging, they have entered into a contract with the guide. They are both responsible to the guide for carrying out the contract or for settling it in some satisfactory manner if they change their minds. It is also quite possible that a court would decide that there was a contract if both or either had made certain preparations and spent any money for mutual benefit.

Offer and Acceptance (Mutual Assent). Mrs. Burton bought a stove and had it sent out to her home. She used it for two weeks; and when the store asks for payment, she insisted on returning it although she has no complaint as to its performance. She insisted that she had never accepted it because she had not paid for it. Courts would undoubtedly hold that there was an offer and an acceptance. On the other hand, if she had ordered it sent out on approval, an

A Cash Purchase at the Grocery Store Is an Example of a Simple Contract

Almost everyday we enter into contracts which may be oral or written. They may be expressed or implied. You should learn to know your rights and responsibilities in regard to these contracts.

Ewing Galloway

acceptance would not have been indicated until she had signified her approval or had kept the stove an unreasonable length of time without expressing dissatisfaction or a willingness to return it. *Mutual assent* in simple terms means the making of an *offer* on the part of one person and the *acceptance* of the offer on the part of another.

The essential characteristics of an offer are: (a) the proposal must be definite; (b) the proposal must be made with the intention that the *offeror* (person making the offer) be bound by it; (c) the proposal must be communicated by words or actions. For instance, if you were to offer to work for an employer for "all that you are worth," the offer would be too indefinite to be the basis of an enforceable agreement. If an offer is made in obvious or apparent jest, it is not a real offer. Most advertisements are not offers. They are usually merely invitations to buy or invitations to make an offer to buy. For instance, if you see something advertised and you send your money but the order cannot be filled because the merchant is sold out, you have not entered into a contract. Likewise, if one walks into a store and finds goods on display with a price marked on them and the goods are obviously offered for sale at that price, the proposal has been communicated and he has made a contract when the money is accepted by the clerk for the purchase of those goods.

Acceptance Is Indicated by:

1. Specific indication that the buyer accepts the goods.
2. Use of the goods.
3. Detention of the goods for an unreasonable length of time.

Under the principles of law, it is not considered that there is mutual assent unless both parties have freely, intentionally, and apparently assented to the same thing. Acceptance has much to do with the way that the offer is made and terminated. If acceptance is required to be made in a special manner, it must be made in that way. For instance, acceptance may be requested by mail or by a certain deadline. If it does not conform to these requirements, it is not a legal acceptance. However, if the acceptance is later approved by the offeror, the agreement becomes binding.

As in the case of an offer, the acceptance must be indicated by some word or act. For instance, one cannot be bound against his will by an offeror who states in his offer, "If I do not hear from you by ten o'clock, October 10, I shall consider that you have accepted this offer." The acceptance must also be made by the party to whom the offer was made. If someone has made an offer to you and you tell a friend about it, the person who made the offer does not have to recognize an acceptance by your friend. The acceptance may be in the form of a definite promise that completes the mutual agreement, or it may be made in the form of some act. For instance, if a boy is offered $1 for cutting a lawn, the act of cutting the lawn is evidence of accepting the offer.

As a general rule, when offers are made by letter with the acceptance to be made by mail, the offer is considered to be accepted when the acceptance is deposited in the mail. Likewise, if the acceptance is to be made by telegram, the agreement is considered to be completed when the message is given to the telegraph company.

When an Offer Is Made by Mail, the Contract Is Formed When the Acceptance Is Mailed

How Is an Offer Terminated? An offer can be terminated in many ways. It may be terminated at a definite time stated in the offer. If no definite time is stated, it will be terminated in a reasonable amount of time, which often has to be determined by the court if a dispute arises. Definite refusal of the offer or a *counteroffer* (a new offer by the person to whom the original offer was made) will terminate the original offer. The withdrawal or revocation of the offer before it is accepted is a clear termination. Other unusual circumstances that terminate offers are death or insanity of the offeror.

Ordinarily, if an offer is made for a specified length of time, it may still be revoked before the expiration of that time if proper notice is given of the withdrawal. However, if a general offer is made to the public, such as a reward published in a newspaper, it is still in effect unless it is withdrawn in the same way that it is offered.

Keeping an Offer Open. Offers are sometimes kept open for specified periods of time by a special contract that is known as an *option*. If the offeror receives cash or something of value as an inducement to keep an offer open for a certain specified time, the offer cannot be withdrawn for the period of time covered by the option. This is an important type of offer that is used in large transactions. For example, a person considering buying a home or a company considering buying a new factory would want time to consider the matter with the assurance that if a decision is made to buy the property, the original quotation of the price would be accepted.

Options are very useful in many types of negotiation leading up to a sale. It is important, however, that an option be in writing and signed by the person granting it.

Who Is Competent to Make a Binding Contract? The Ridge Hardware Store accepted a properly signed order for a bicycle for $40 from Bob Hansen, age 12. When the bicycle arrived from the factory, the price had risen and the dealer insisted on getting $50 for the bicycle or canceling the contract. He argued that the original agreement was not binding because Bob Hansen was a minor and was, therefore, incompetent to contract. This agreement is binding, however, on the dealer. Bob could cancel the contract if he wished. A situation such as this and many others are involved in contracts with minors and certain other types of people.

The question of competence of parties determines who is legally qualified to make contracts. Anyone who is not other-

Ewing Galloway

Neither the child nor the parents of the child are responsible for some of the contracts made by a child who is not of legal age, but they are responsible for some contracts. The legal age is not the same in all states.

A Minor's Contract to Buy a Bicycle May Be Voidable

wise prevented by law from making enforceable agreements may make a contract. In many cases children (*minors*, or those who are not of legal age) are not competent to contract and may not be required by law to carry out agreements. There are, however, some exceptions to this rule, such as contracting for necessaries. When a minor makes an agreement with an adult, the adult is required to fulfill the contract if it is legal; but if the minor chooses to *rescind* (cancel) the contract, he can, in most cases, escape his responsibility.

Usually contracts made by a minor are *voidable* (that is, they may be broken) by the minor. He may break them while he is still a minor or within a reasonable time after he becomes of age. If he reaffirms the agreement after he becomes of age, it becomes a binding contract. The voidability of a contract applies generally whether it has been fully performed or only partially performed.

Contracts made by minors to acquire reasonable necessaries are binding upon the minor. A contract by a merchant to furnish jewelry, tobacco, or sporting equipment to an ordinary minor is voidable, but a contract to furnish necessary clothes or food is not voidable if the amounts charged are reasonable and the goods are needed and are actually delivered. On the other hand, if all these necessaries of life are provided by the parents, any contract made by the child to obtain them is voidable. A contract by a poor child to buy expensive clothing beyond his means would be voidable also.

Howard Martin, age 20, signed a contract for the purchase of an automobile. The dealer questioned him as to his age, and he assured the dealer that he was 21 years old on his last birthday. When the dealer notified him that he was ready to deliver the car, Howard refused to accept it, asserting that he misrepresented his age at the time of making the contract and, therefore, he could not be held responsible. In some states a minor is held responsible if he deliberately misrepresents his age; but if a child, age 12, were to misrepresent his age, the dealer might find it difficult to hold the child responsible because of his obvious young age. The reason for this principle of law is that a minor who misrepresents his age places the other party in an unfair position, particularly if the minor is close to twenty-one years of age. However, it is assumed that if a much younger child misrepresents his age, the other party would enter into the agreement knowing that the person is a minor.

Other persons who are not competent to contract under certain conditions are intoxicated persons and insane persons. The reason for making voidable all contracts made by these persons, except those for the reasonable value of necessaries actually furnished, is obvious: it is considered that they are not capable of exercising their own judgment. In certain states there are special laws applying to contracts that may not be made by convicts, foreigners, or married women, but there is a wide variation in these laws in various states.

> ### Some Other Examples in Regard to Competent Persons
>
> 1. A person who cannot read is bound by a contract if it has been read to him and is understood by him before signing.
> 2. A person who cannot read or write, but who signs a contract with an "X" or other symbol is bound by the contract if it has been read to him and if he understands it.
> 3. Generally, a person who has made a contract while a minor may repudiate or affirm the contract when he becomes of age, but failure to repudiate it generally makes the contract binding.

The Purpose of the Contract Must Be Legal. A contract is not legal unless the subject or the purpose of the agreement is legal. This is referred to as *legal bargain*. In fact, in most cases, when the subject of the purpose of the contract is not legal, there is not even a contract. Neither party can be held under the agreement.

Some examples of illegal bargains are those involving agreements to steal, to accept stolen goods, or to commit any other crime. All agreements to wager or gamble are illegal except in the cases of certain states in which betting on horse racing has been legalized. For instance, if you make a bet with somebody, you have not made a legal

An Agreement to Commit a Crime Is Not Enforceable

contract; but in a state where betting on horse races is legal, your placing of a bet is a legal contract.

In all states there are so-called *usury laws* that establish the highest contract rate of interest that may be charged. If a contract is made and interest is charged at a higher rate, the contract is an illegal contract. Exceptions to these laws are the small loan regulations that permit licensed small loan organizations to charge higher rates.

It is always illegal to enter into any contract to obstruct justice, such as an agreement to give false testimony or an agreement to avoid giving testimony.

Generally speaking, when a certain type of business or professional man is subject to licensing, any contract made with one who is unlicensed is void. For instance, in most cities electricians and plumbers are licensed. If you make an agreement with an unlicensed electrician or plumber, the agreement is not a legal contract.

In almost all cases, agreements that restrain trade unreasonably are void. Examples of such agreements that are void are those involving control of prices, limiting production, creating a monopoly, creating an artificial scarcity, or causing unreasonable injury to competitors or to consumers.

Anyone buying stolen goods does not get a valid title to the goods. They must be returned to the rightful owner if the ownership can be proved.

Consideration in Contracts. J. R. Jackson, a wealthy member of Summit Hills Country Club, offered to give his old set of golf clubs to a caddy at the end of the golf season. He changed his mind and did not give them to the caddy. The caddy insisted that a contract had been made. Mr. Jackson insisted that there was no *consideration* on the part of the caddy in the nature of goods, money, services, or promises. If the caddy can prove that the clubs were promised him as a reward for caddy service or any other favor to Mr. Jackson, he probably can consider that there is a contract; but in the absence of such proof, there is no contract. It is simply in the nature of a promise to make a gift. A gift without a consideration is not considered a contract.

Ordinarily the promise made in an agreement is not enforceable unless something of value is received for the promise. The value may consist of goods, money, services, refraining from doing something that one has a right to do, or giving up a privilege. A common example of a consideration is the down payment made to a merchant when an agreement has been reached for the delivery of a piece of furniture. When one takes a job, the employer promises to pay for the services and the employee promises to perform the duties required in the job. A landlord may pay a tenant a certain sum of money to give up his lease and vacate the property. The amount paid is the consideration for the giving up of a legal right on the part of the tenant if the lease has not expired.

Proper Form of Contracts. Mr. and Mrs. Waltham bought a house from the Oval Realty Company for $10,000 on an oral agreement. This is not a regular contract because the law requires that agreements of this type must be in writing. However, they can make other purchases orally that are legal contracts.

Generally speaking, there are two main types of contracts, (a) *oral* and (b) *written*. Most contracts may be made informally merely by the exchange of a few words or the performance of certain acts. Certain contracts must be made in special form specified by law.

These Contracts Must Be in Writing

1. An agreement to answer for the debt, default, or obligation of another person.
2. An agreement that is not to be executed or performed within a period of one year after it is made.
3. An agreement to buy or sell real estate, including land, buildings, minerals, or trees.
4. An agreement to sell goods in excess of the amount specified by state law for which contracts must be in writing. (Exceptions are when there has been a part payment or part of the goods have been delivered.)
5. An installment contract.

Ordinarily, oral evidence of a sale is sufficient when the price does not exceed the amount set by law in a particular state. If it exceeds this amount, it must be in writing. The table on page 138 shows the maximum for oral evidence in each state. Note that in two states written evidence is required in all sales. In six states no written evidence is required. If the requirements are not met, the oral agreement to sell goods is legal, but is voidable by either party. It may be carried out by mutual agreement.

Agreement May Be Indicated by Shaking Hands

Contracts for work and labor, including materials, generally need not be in writing. Contracts for medical or dental services need not be in writing regardless of the amount involved. A contract for the painting of a house need not be in writing, although it should be to avoid any misunderstanding.

Express or Implied Contracts. Contracts may be classified in another way. They are said to be either express or implied. An *express contract* is one that arises out of an agreement expressed by oral or written words. If you orally agree to buy a refrigerator at a specified price and the dealer agrees to sell it to you at that price, you have made an express contract that is legally binding. An *implied contract* is one that is made through an agreement implied by the acts or the conduct of the parties involved. If you pick up an article in the store and hand the required amount of money to the clerk, who wraps up the article and hands it to you, you have made an implied contract. If you board a streetcar or a train, you imply by your act your willingness to pay the proper fare, and the carrier implies that he will transport you as a passenger.

A great many contracts do not have to be in writing because the offer, acceptance, payment, and delivery of goods

Maximum Amounts for Which Sales May Be Proved in the Various States, Alaska, the District of Columbia, and Hawaii without Written Evidence

State	Amount	State	Amount
Alabama	$500	Montana	$ 200
Alaska	50	Nebraska	500
Arizona	500	Nevada	50
Arkansas	30	New Hampshire	500
California	500	New Jersey	500
Colorado	50	New Mexico	50
Connecticut	100	New York	50
Delaware	500	North Carolina	none required
District of Columbia	50	North Dakota	500
Florida	all sales	Ohio	2,500
Georgia	50	Oklahoma	50
Hawaii	100	Oregon	50
Idaho	500	Pennsylvania	500
Illinois	500	Rhode Island	500
Indiana	500	South Carolina	50
Iowa	all sales	South Dakota	500
Kansas	none required	Tennessee	500
Kentucky	500	Texas	none required
Louisiana [1]	none required	Utah	500
Maine	500	Vermont	50
Maryland	50	Virginia [2]	none required
Massachusetts	500	Washington	50
Michigan	100	West Virginia	none required
Minnesota	50	Wisconsin	50
Mississippi	50	Wyoming	50
Missouri	30		

[1] Sales of $500 or more must be proved by two witnesses or by one witness and other acceptable evidence.
[2] Contracts of sale or contracts to sell for future delivery must be in writing.

often occur within a short space of a few seconds or a few minutes. In general, a contract should be written instead of oral when there is any chance for misunderstanding or disagreement between the parties and when a written contract is required by law.

When a written contract is required by law, both parties are not bound until the contract is signed properly by both parties. Evidence of an agreement signed by one party binds that party to the agreement, but not the other until he signs. Exceptions are certain kinds of agreements such as an order signed by the buyer. It may not need to be signed by the seller to be a valid contract.

The Primary Essentials of a Written Contract Are:

1. The date and place of the agreement.
2. The names and the identifications of the parties entering into the agreement.
3. A statement of the purposes of the contract.
4. A statement of the money, the services, or the goods given in consideration of the agreement (an act to be performed, refraining from any act, or the relinquishing of a privilege by a party, also consideration).
5. The signatures of both parties or the signature of legal agents.
6. In the case of some contracts witnesses are required, and in such cases the witnesses must sign in accordance with the provisions of the law.

A *bill of sale* is a written contract with which many consumers are acquainted. It is required in most states for the transfer of ownership of such items as automobiles or refrigerators. Even in states where a bill of sale is not required for these items, it is often desirable to obtain one because it provides evidence of ownership after the transaction has been completed.

In states where the bill of sale is used, it is usually necessary to register the bill of sale with the proper county authority so that the ownership of the property can be established.

Defective Agreements. From the foregoing discussion you have learned what constitutes a valid or enforceable contract. When an agreement fails to include all the essentials, it is not a contract. If James Hirsh orally agrees to buy a car for $2,600 from the City Motor Company, the contract is not enforceable because it is not in writing.

Agreements that are not enforceable may be classified as void or voidable. When an agreement is *void*, it has no legal force or effect. In other words neither party can enforce the agreement. A *voidable contract* is one that may be broken (rescinded or voided) by one or both of the par-

> **Examples of Voidable Agreements**
>
> 1. If there is fraud in the form of misrepresentation.
> 2. If a person makes an agreement as a result of threat or the use of violence.
> 3. If there has been undue and unfair influence and pressure to the extent that one person has not reached the agreement through the free exercise of his own judgment.
> 4. If one party fails or refuses to fulfill his part of the contract, the second party may rescind or void the contract.

ties. Such an agreement is enforceable if the party or parties having the option to reject it choose not to do so.

Ordinarily a mistake made by one party, such as the quoting of the wrong price, does not make the contract void or voidable. Mistakes that make a contract void include mutual mistakes as to the existence of the subject matter or a mistake as to the indentity of the parties. For instance, a man agreed to sell a certain dog at a definite price, but later it was found that the dog had died before the agreement was made. The agreement was void because of mistake as to the existence of the subject matter.

Preventing Fraud and Misunderstanding. Never sign a contract in blank or with part of the figures or conditions left to be filled in. If someone hurries you or suggests that you sign the contract with the rest of the information to be filled in later, your suspicion should be aroused.

Do not sign a contract with the understanding that supplementary agreements will be made later. Be sure that all agreements are in the contract. In the absence of substantial proof with regard to oral agreements or supplementary written agreements, only the agreements stipulated in the contract are enforceable.

Warranties. Under an old principle of law of "Let the buyer beware," it is assumed that the buyer must be pretty largely responsible for knowing what he gets. However, when a seller, in making a sale, makes promises that an article will operate in a specific way or that it has a certain specific quality, he makes statements on which the buyer has a legal right to rely in regard to the quality of the goods. These promises or representations are called *warranties*.

There are two types of warranties: (a) *express* and (b) *implied*. For example, if a merchant states definitely that cloth is pure virgin wool, that is an express warranty. A written guarantee is also an express warranty. An example of an implied warranty is one in which the buyer has a right to expect that the article purchased will serve the purpose for which it is sold, although there is no definite statement in regard to it. For instance, if one buys a stove, he has a right to expect that the stove will operate; if it does not operate, the buyer has a legal recourse. If one goes into a restaurant and orders food, there is an implied warranty that the food is fit to eat. If you become poisoned, the restaurant owner is liable. If it can be proved that the manufacturer or processor of the food was responsible because of improper processing or handling of the food, that person may also be liable for any damages resulting from the sickness.

Generally speaking, when a buyer has an opportunity to inspect the goods, there is no implied warranty that the goods are of a particular quality; but there is an implied warranty that they will serve the purpose for which they are intended. If the buyer does not inspect the goods but relies largely on the judgment and honesty of the seller, there is an implied warranty that the goods will be satisfactory. When a sample is used to indicate the kind and quality of the goods, the seller impliedly warrants the goods to correspond with the sample shown in kind and in quality. When merchandise is purchased by description, such as by specifications, the seller impliedly warrants the goods to correspond to the description.

"Trade puffs" or "trade talk" are not warranties and should not be relied upon by the buyer. A *trade puff* is a general claim, such as "This is the best merchandise you can buy," "This is the most popular item on the market," or "This suit is very becoming to you."

Remedies for Breach of Warranty. In the case of misrepresentation or if goods do not fulfill the reasonable expectations of a warranty, there has been a *breach of warranty*. Several different remedies are available in case of a breach of warranty. The following general recourses are open to the buyer: (1) to keep the goods and to deduct from the price the amount of the damages; (2) to keep the goods and to bring an action against the seller for damages; (3) to refuse to accept the goods and to bring an action against the seller to recover damages; (4) to rescind the contract (break, void, or refuse) and to refuse to receive the goods or, if the goods have been accepted, to return them to the vendor and to recover the price that has been paid.

Passing of the Title. When a cash sale is made, the title passes immediately. This means that the seller ceases to own the goods and the buyer becomes the owner. When a sale on credit is made, the title passes immediately; the buyer merely has an agreement as to the time when he will pay for the goods. Ordinarily C.O.D. sales result in a transfer of the title at the time the goods are shipped; the seller merely does not give possession of the goods until the charge has been paid.

The Buyer Need Not Accept Delivery If the Seller Violates His Contract

When one buys something on approval, the title does not pass to him until the article has been approved and an acknowledgment of its acceptance has either been given or implied.

In the case of installment sales in which the conditional contract is used, there is really not a sale until all provisions of the contract have been fulfilled. The seller has a right to reclaim the goods. If payments are not kept up, the buyer may in that case lose what he has paid and may even have to pay something extra if he does not fulfill the provisions of the contract. When the provisions of the contract are fulfilled, the title then passes to the buyer.

In a sale subject to return, the title passes at the time of the sale; but if the goods are returned, the title reverts to the seller.

Remedies of the Seller When Buyer Fails to Perform. If the buyer of merchandise fails to perform his part of the contract, the seller may select any of these remedies:

(a) The seller may sue for payment (if the title has passed). When the buyer refuses or neglects to pay, the seller may sue for the price of the goods.

(b) The seller may sue for damages (if the title has not passed). When the buyer wrongfully refuses or neglects to accept and pay for the goods, the seller may sue for damages. The amount of damages will usually be the difference between the contract price and the market price.

(c) The seller may rescind the contract. When the buyer repudiates the contract, or when he cannot perform the contract or fails to perform it, the seller is allowed, under most laws, to rescind (cancel) the contract.

Remedies of the Buyer When Seller Fails to Perform. If the seller fails to perform his obligations, the buyer has the choice of one of the following remedies:

(a) The buyer may obtain possession of the goods or the value of the goods (if the title has passed and payment has been made). When the seller wrongfully refuses or neglects to deliver the goods, the buyer may sue for the possession of the goods, for the recovery of the value that has been paid, or for damages.

(b) The buyer may sue for damages (if the title has not passed). If the seller wrongfully refuses or neglects to deliver the goods, the buyer is entitled to damages for nondelivery. The amount of the damages is ordinarily the difference between the contract price and the market price at the time and the place of delivery. The amount may also include any other damages for loss resulting from the failure to fulfill the contract.

(c) The buyer may insist upon the fulfillment of the contract. The buyer has the right to sue for specific performance if damages will not be adequate compensation or if they cannot be computed. When the buyer sues for specific performance and wins the case, the seller is ordered by the court to carry out the original contract.

(d) The buyer may refuse to accept goods. If the seller has broken his part of the contract or in any way has failed to carry out his part of the contract, the buyer may refuse to accept delivery of the goods or may return them if delivered. If damages have resulted, he may also sue for damages.

Goods Not Ordered. You do not have to accept goods that you have not ordered. Some firms and other organizations follow a practice of sending unsolicited merchandise in the hope that persons receiving them will send a remittance. If you receive such a package, you may refuse to accept it, you may return it, or you may hold it subject to whatever the sender wishes to do with it. However, you must not use the merchandise or in any way indicate an acceptance of it unless you intend to pay for it. On the other hand, if you are in the habit of receiving and accepting such merchandise, you may be responsible unless you return it or notify the sender that you do not accept it.

Goods Entrusted to Other Persons. If you leave an automobile with the City Garage for repairs, the City Garage may hold the automobile if it wishes until you have paid the bill. This claim against the car is referred to as a *mechanic's lien*. If you send clothing to a laundry and it is damaged, you have a claim against the laundry for the damage. If an automobile is entrusted to a garage or a parking lot for safekeeping, the garage or parking lot is responsible for its safekeeping. This is especially true if you are given a parking ticket that is a receipt for your car and if you are required to leave the keys in the car so that it can be moved. However, if you regularly place your own car in a lot and take the keys with you, the operator of the parking lot is generally not liable.

Ewing Galloway

The Operator of a Parking Lot Is Responsible for the Safekeeping of Your Automobile

If you rent or borrow an article, such as a lawn mower, you are responsible for taking reasonable care of it to prevent damage or theft. Likewise, if you take a lawn mower to a repairman and he damages it in the process of repairing it, he is liable because he is expected to exercise reasonable care and skill. He is assumed to have the skill to do the job for which he is paid.

Generally speaking, people who accept the property of others are responsible for it. On the other hand, if a neighbor brings you some jewelry and asks you to keep it while he is gone on a vacation, you are not responsible for its loss or theft if you exercise reasonable care over it.

> **Summary of Important Legal Principles**
>
> 1. When in doubt consult a lawyer.
> 2. Nearly everyone enters into several legal contracts daily.
> 3. A contract involves the elements of offer and acceptance, the competency of the parties, a legal purpose, consideration, and required form.
> 4. Some contracts must be in writing.
> 5. Some contracts are voidable.
> 6. There are specific remedies if a warranty is broken.
> 7. Some contracts are expressed or implied.
> 8. The seller has certain choices of remedies if the buyer fails to perform.
> 9. The buyer has choices of certain remedies if the seller fails to perform.
> 10. Generally when property is entrusted to another party that party is responsible for reasonable care in safe keeping.

TEXTBOOK QUESTIONS

1. Why is there not always a definite answer that a lawyer can give a client?
2. What is a contract?
3. Give the essential elements of a contract.
4. What are the three essential characteristics of an offer?
5. What evidence may there be that the buyer has accepted the goods?
6. How may offers be terminated?
7. What is an option?
8. Name some types of persons who are generally not competent to make a contract.
9. Give an example of a bargain that is not legal because of the subject of the contract.
10. Explain the difference between a promise and a consideration in relation to a contract.
11. What types of contracts usually must be written to be enforceable?
12. What is meant by an implied contract?
13. Give at least three good reasons for putting important contracts in writing.

14. Give an example of a voidable contract.
15. What is a warranty?
16. If there is a breach of warranty, what recourses are open to the buyer?
17. If a buyer of merchandise fails to perform his part of the contract, what possible remedies does the seller have?
18. If a seller fails to perform his obligations, what may the buyer do to protect himself?
19. If you are sent merchandise on approval which you have not ordered and which you do not want, what may you do with the merchandise?
20. What is your responsibility if you borrow something from a friend?
21. If a repairman loses or damages an article left with him for repair, what is his responsibility?

DISCUSSION QUESTIONS

1. Can you explain why there are quite different decisions given by courts in apparently similar or identical cases?
2. Mr. Martin insists that he will not fulfill a contract because he did not know all the terms of the contract when he signed it. His reason for not having read the contract carefully is that he finds it difficult to read fine print. He admits, however, that the signature on the contract is genuine. Is there anything he can do to avoid fulfilling the contract?
3. You are given a sales demonstration in a store. During the demonstration the salesman tells you many ways in which his product is better than some other product. Later you find that what he has told you is not true. (a) Do his statements constitute fraud? (b) Have you any legal basis for returning the merchandise and demanding your money?
4. You received through the mail some literature with samples of cloth from which shirts are made. You test the cloth in various ways, including washing it and counting the threads in each square inch. You keep these samples and order five of the shirts for $15. When the shirts are delivered, you find that they are poorly tailored and that the cloth does not seem to be like that in the samples. One of the shirts is worn and then washed. It fades badly. Then you count the threads in each square inch and find that the cloth is actually inferior to that in the samples. What recourses have you?
5. Besides the examples given in your textbook, can you describe an agreement that is void?
6. From the study of this chapter why is it apparent that one should consult a lawyer to handle important legal problems?

PROBLEMS

1. A general contractor, The Home Building Company, contracted to build a home for Harry Nelson with the written understanding that the furnace would heat each room in the house to 72° temperature when the temperature outside was 10° below zero. For two years after the house was completed, the weather was rather mild in winter and the temperature did not go below zero until the third winter. Then Mr. Nelson had difficulty heating the house and could not get the temperature above 70° in two of the bedrooms when the temperature went to 10° below zero. The contractor contended that Mr. Nelson did not know how to operate the furnace and refused to do anything for him. Was this a warranty? What do you think Mr. Nelson can do?

2. Arthur Knight arranged with Ace Building Company to build a home for him. He did some of the work himself and went to a furnace company and selected a furnace from the Hamilton Heating Company, which the heating company said would heat satisfactorily. After the house was completed, Mr. Knight could not get his furnace to heat the house to a warm enough temperature to suit him in cold weather. Was there any warranty, and does Mr. Knight have any claim against the contractor or the heating company?

COMMUNITY PROBLEMS AND PROJECTS

1. From your local newspaper watch for court cases that are reported and try to find at least one that involves a contract. What are the claims and what was the decision of the court? From facts available, what is your own opinion as to the fairness of the decision?

2. Write a simple contract between you and someone else, in which you agree to perform some task.

3. On April 3, Mr. Ladley made a legal offer by mail to sell Mr. Moore a house and lot for $7,000, $4,000 to be paid in cash upon the acceptance of the offer. On April 6 Mr. Moore mailed a letter to Mr. Ladley and enclosed a certified check for $4,000. The letter was delivered on April 10. On April 7 Mr. Ladley decided to withdraw the offer because he thought that the value of the property had increased. He wrote Mr. Moore withdrawing the offer. When Mr. Ladley received the check, he refused to accept it and returned it, claiming that the offer had been withdrawn. Mr. Moore brought a suit for breach of contract. Do you think Mr. Ladley had broken a contract?

Chapter 9

General Principles of Buying

> **Purpose of the Chapter.** There are certain general or fundamental principles of buying which apply in almost all kinds of buying. Before taking up the buying of specific products and services, the general principles are presented in this chapter. They will serve as general guides in the study of all specific buying problems.
>
> You will find answers to these questions:
>
> 1. In what way is buying a matter of making choices?
> 2. What are some specific shopping procedures and suggestions?
> 3. What are some legitimate bargain sales?
> 4. What is the best time of the year to buy certain products?
> 5. Should you buy in small quantities or large quantities?
> 6. Can you depend upon brand names, trade-marks, trade terms, labels, salesmen, and advertising?
> 7. What testing services are available?
> 8. What are some common mistakes in buying?

Buying Is Choice Making. Buying is always a matter of making choices. Choices must be made (a) between wants and needs, (b) between luxuries and necessities, (c) between one product and another of the same kind, (d) between two entirely different kinds of products, or (e) between spending your money now or saving it for another purpose.

In an earlier chapter the great Charles F. Kettering was quoted as saying that no product is worth buying unless it is worth more to the buyer than the money he spends for it. If you will think carefully about every purchase that you make, there is less chance that unneeded and unwanted luxuries will be purchased under high pressure advertising and selling in preference to the filling of real needs of the family.

The real needs of the average family are relatively limited but wants can be increased almost without limit. As a result of high pressure advertising and selling and our rising standards of living, there is a tendency on the part of every person to want to "keep up with the Joneses" and to justify in his own mind that what really is a luxury is actually an urgent need.

The vast majority of families do not earn enough money to enjoy unlimited purchase of luxuries. In fact, many families cannot purchase all their real needs without very strict self-restraint in making their purchases. In the average family the tendency is to follow individual selfish urges in filling emotional wants rather than practicing individual self-restraint for the benefit of the whole family: if mother wants something, she may buy it on an emotional urge; if father wants something, he buys it without consulting the family; if children want something, they spend their own money without much thought or they put pressure on mother and father to obtain the things they want. If family purchasing is considered from the point of view of unselfish group needs, most families can get the most out of their income.

Even in the case of small purchases, a great amount of money can slip through the fingers of every member of the family in buying little things that merchants call *impulse items*. They are the little things in the nature of luxuries that sit by the cash register and are easy to pick up for 5 to 25 cents or even more, just on an impulse because the buyer has a little money in his pocket.

A Plan for Spending. Very few people earn so much money that they can buy all they want without considering whether or not they have enough money to pay for their purchases. Therefore a plan of buying is necessary. Although budgeting is presented in detail in Chapter 23, it is desirable to emphasize it at this point because of its relationship to buying. A budget is a plan of spending and saving. The plan will help you to determine how much to spend and how much to save. When the spending program is broken down into months and weeks, it should be checked periodically with the original plan to be sure that overspending is not taking place. It often must be revised and adjusted to take care of unforeseen problems as they arise.

Advantages of a Budget Spending Plan
1. It will help you to live within your income.
2. It will help you to save.
3. It will help you to determine what you can and must have so that you will not recklessly spend your money for foolish things and deprive yourself of things you really need.

Methods of Buying. Most people have a choice of several methods of buying. They may buy by telephone, from house-to-house salesmen, by mail from a catalog, or by shopping in stores.

Buying by telephone is convenient, but it deprives you of the privilege of careful shopping and comparing the merchandise. Usually buying by telephone is more expensive because it involves delivery service.

Buying from house-to-house salesmen is an easy way to obtain what you need, but it is not always a satisfactory way. Unless you take the trouble to make comparisons with other products, you may not be getting the best merchandise in this manner; and you may be paying more than is necessary. However, the convenience of buying in this manner is often an important advantage to some buyers.

Buying by mail is convenient because it can be done in the home; but it is also inconvenient because of the necessity of sending a remittance or paying for the package when it comes C.O.D. Waiting for the package to be delivered is another inconvenience. Selecting suitable merchandise is difficult by this method because you have to depend upon pictures and descriptions.

Harold M. Lambert

Intelligent Shopping Is One of the Best Means of Buying

Buying in stores, although it may be inconvenient, is generally the most satisfactory method of buying. Buying in stores permits you to see what is available and permits you to make comparisons within a particular store and among several stores. You have an opportunity to choose as to quality and price. Often you may either pay cash or charge it, and in many cases you have a choice of taking the merchandise with you or having it delivered.

Shopping Procedures. At the time of purchase the buyer often does not have an opportunity to make careful comparisons. When there is opportunity for it, comparison may be made casually and hastily, or it may be well thought out and reasonably scientific. The more scientific the procedure, the more chance the buyer has of getting value for his money. Before going shopping it is wise to determine needs rather than impulse wants and then to determine values as a result of shopping experience. If a mistake is made once, it should not be repeated. Learn from mistakes and remember correct decisions as guides in future buying.

Hints for Shopping

What to Do
1. Take a shopping list with you.
2. Do your shopping before you buy; avoid having merchandise sent on approval.
3. Make use of all buying information available, such as advertising, the salesclerk, labels, tests, and specifications.
4. In making comparisons, check not only the price but also the quality.
5. Watch scales and measuring devices.
6. Avoid rush periods in stores so you can shop with greater ease.

Where to Buy
1. Select a store with a reasonable range of varieties, sizes, and qualities.
2. Select a store that has labels and standards that aid in making intelligent selections.
3. Select a store with shopping conveniences that save time and energy.
4. Select a store with fair prices based on the quality and the service.
5. Select a store with services, such as credit and delivery, if you need them.
6. Select a store that is reliable.
7. Select a store that gives courteous service.

Intelligent buying demands the development of a consciousness of differences between products. One of many products may be good. Two products may be very similar. It is frequently difficult to determine the better of two products even under the most careful scrutiny. When such is the case, there is little danger of making an unwise selection.

Legitimate Bargains. The following paragraphs explain types of bargain sales that are conducted by reputable stores. The buyer must learn from experience what stores really offer bargains when such sales are conducted. Merchandise bought on sale is not a bargain at any price unless it is needed or will be needed in the future.

Examples of Bargain Sales

1. Remnant sales of merchandise which are odd lengths, sizes, and assortments.
2. Sales of soiled goods which may be returned goods, shopworn goods, or sample merchandise.
3. Preseason sales in advance of the regular season.
4. Preinventory sales to reduce stock of merchandise on hand.
5. Out-of-season sales of merchandise left over at the close of a season.
6. Odd-lot sales of merchandise such as irregulars or seconds.
7. Surplus stock sales resulting from overbuying of a merchant or overproduction of a mill.
8. Anniversary sales as a special event to stimulate business.
9. Special seasonal sales that offer bargains in season.

When to Buy. The preceding discussion of various types of sales gives some ideas as to when to buy. For instance, it is easy to observe that seasonal goods usually run through a definite cycle in price level. When offered in advance sales, they are usually sold at reduced prices. The buyer who is especially interested in the style of his clothing can frequently take advantage of such sales. At the beginning of a season style goods sell at the highest prices. As the season progresses, the prices are gradually lowered, for merchants hope to dispose of their goods before the end of the season.

There are important price cycles for many other products. For instance, in cities in which coal is used for heating purposes, it is usually sold at its lowest price in April and May and at its maximum price during the winter months.

Fresh fruits and vegetables usually sell at the cheapest prices during the summer. The prices of canned goods are lowest soon after the canning season. The illustration on page 155 shows the seasonal trends in the prices of some common foods. As one might suspect, products that are most difficult to store have wide fluctuations in price.

During periods of generally high prices the wise consumer will avoid buying everything that he does not really need. He will save his money and wait until prices are lower. Of course, certain things must be purchased regularly, such as food. Because the prices of different kinds of food fluctuate during the year, the wise consumer will avoid foods when they are at their highest prices and will substitute other foods that are available at lower prices.

Seasonal Price Trends of Common Foods

Consumers' Guide

Consumers can influence the prices of commodities by the way they buy them. If consumers refuse to buy a particular product, it is sure to come down in price.

Some Policies in Buying. In determining how to buy, let us think in terms of shopping procedure. The saving of time, energy, and money are the points to be considered in shopping procedure. The saving of money may be the primary consideration of one buyer, whereas the saving of time may be an important consideration of another. For instance, the buyer may save time and energy by ordering by telephone, but he may pay extra for delivery service and may not get the benefit of personal selection.

Buying in large quantities rather than in small quantities usually is desirable, provided the large quantities are needed. People who buy small lots of groceries from day to day, or even several times a day, are causing an economic waste of time and are paying more per unit than persons who buy in larger quantities. A housewife will, however, find it desirable to buy food in small quantities if larger quantities would spoil before they could be used.

Seasonal buying and quantity buying go hand in hand. In other words, if a person decides to enjoy the advantage of buying canned goods when prices are low, he must buy a relatively large quantity in order to profit by the reduced prices. Many families buy whole cases of canned foods at the end of the canning season and store these for use during the winter.

Guides in Buying Foods and Household Supplies

1. Buy in as large quantities as can be stored conveniently and used without waste from spoilage.
2. Keep informed of the regular prices of staple foods and household supplies in order to gauge the savings that will be possible through taking advantage of special sales.
3. Watch market conditions and know whether the general price trend is upward or downward. Take advantage of seasonal low points and of rising markets for quantity buying.
4. Consider the value of time and effort, as well as money,
   a. When deciding between charge-and-delivery and cash-and-carry stores.
   b. When deciding whether to buy in large or small quantities.
   c. When deciding whether to buy in bulk or in packages.
5. Keep on hand an emergency supply of foods that will provide at least one meal on short notice. A larger supply, however, is usually advisable.

The size of the package is an important element in the cost. Obviously, it costs more to put a certain food product into ten small cans than it does in one large can. In some instances, therefore, the cost of the package is an extremely important factor. Some foods that are ordinarily offered for sale in packages can be bought more economically in bulk. The wise buyer will learn to shop as infrequently as possible to save time and energy. He will also learn to buy in packages of a size that will be economical for his family.

Ch. 9] GENERAL PRINCIPLES OF BUYING 157

No definite rules can be laid down for buying, because there are many variables. Different quantities must be bought for families of varying sizes. The quantity to be bought will depend upon the amount of money available and upon the peculiar needs of the family.

Trade Names and Terms. There are many trade names and terms used in connection with various products. Most of these are not intended to be deceptive or misleading, but they are confusing unless a person knows what they mean and knows something about the differences in quality. For instance, stainless steel is a general term used to identify a steel alloy that will not tarnish so easily as ordinary steel, but there are many qualities of stainless steel.

Let us consider a few other common examples. Wool cloth may be made from all virgin wool, reprocessed wool, re-used wool, or a mixture of these with some other fibers. The dictionary defines parchment as the skin of a sheep. Parchment paper and parchment lamp shades, however, are very seldom made of skin; they are usually made of paper. Chinaware usually does not come from China; the word designates a type of clay from which the pottery is made. The product may or may not be better than a similar product made in China. Silverware is not sterling silver, but usually plated ware. Sterling silver is solid silver. For examples of trade names of furs and fabrics, refer to Chapter 14.

When Buying Woolen Products, Read the Labels

How to Read the Label. The buyer should read labels carefully to obtain information with regard to (a) the weight or the volume, (b) the grade or the quality, and (c) an analysis or a description of the contents. The labels of some private agencies have been discussed previously.

Until uniform grade standards have been established and are used for a particular product, it is impossible to rely upon the existing grade designations without knowing what those grades mean. Much of the terminology in use means one thing to the seller, but a different thing to the buyer. If the buyer takes the words at their face value, he is sometimes misled into believing the goods to be of a grade higher than they actually are. Furthermore, the terminology is made confusing by the wide variation in its use. In other words, buyers and sellers do not speak the same language. When this situation exists, grade designations are of very little value.

For instance, one would suppose that the "first" grade of butter is the best grade, but as a matter of fact it is the third grade when compared with government standards. To get the best grade of butter, one has to buy the "AA" grade. Similar confusing grades are used for other products.

As was explained in a preceding chapter, the Federal Food and Drug Administration protects the consumer from obtaining adulterated and misbranded products. Under the Federal law the labels on foods and drugs must not mislead consumers. For instance, if an article is artificially colored, this fact must be indicated on the label. All imitations must be definitely indicated. Ingredients in imitations must be declared. Although an imitation product may be wholesome, it may be inferior to the genuine product. If the consumer is to realize the full benefit of such protection, however, he must learn to read labels accurately.

Read the Label on a Package or a Can Before Buying

Suppose, for example, that you ask for a bottle of vanilla and are handed a bottle marked "Vanillin Extract." What does this name mean? It really means that the bottle contains a flavoring material that is a synthetic coal-tar product, whereas the genuine product is made from the vanilla bean. If the extract is colored to imitate genuine vanilla extract, this fact should be indicated on the bottle.

If you ask for egg noodles and are given a package merely labeled "Noodles," you are not getting what you requested. Egg noodles must contain egg solids to the extent of 5½ per cent by weight. Plain noodles contain no egg products.

When you buy jams, jellies, and preserves, do the labels on the containers mean anything to you? Do you expect to get pure fruits and sugar? If you wish to be sure to obtain a product containing nothing but pure fruit and sugar, you should buy one that has a label indicating what you desire.

The partial label below on this page illustrates the type of information that a consumer may find on a good label. If one learns to use such labels in buying, he will find that they not only serve as helpful guides, but also encourage other producers and distributors to use equally informative labels.

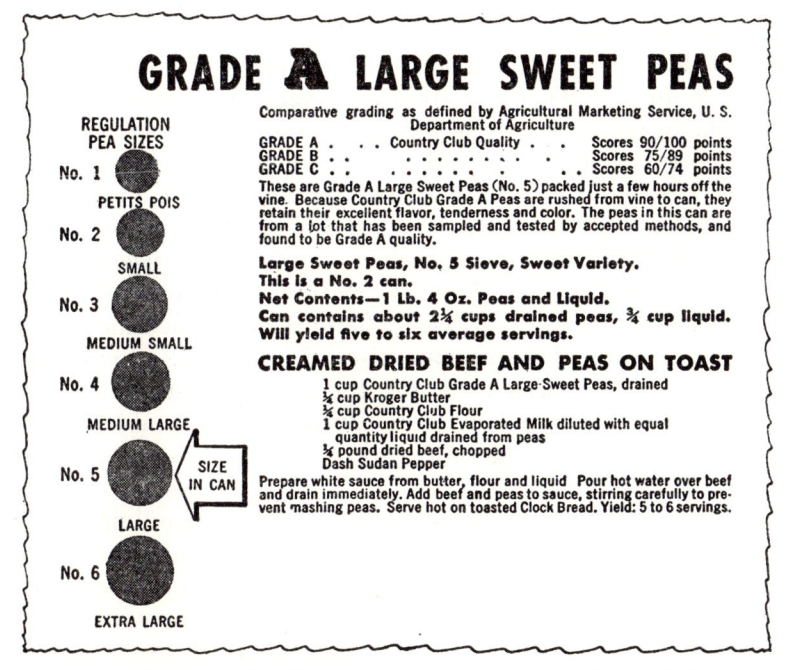

GRADE A LARGE SWEET PEAS

REGULATION PEA SIZES

No. 1 — PETITS POIS
No. 2 — SMALL
No. 3 — MEDIUM SMALL
No. 4 — MEDIUM LARGE
No. 5 — LARGE (SIZE IN CAN)
No. 6 — EXTRA LARGE

Comparative grading as defined by Agricultural Marketing Service, U. S. Department of Agriculture

GRADE A . . . Country Club Quality . . . Scores 90/100 points
GRADE B . . . . Scores 75/89 points
GRADE C . . . . Scores 60/74 points

These are Grade A Large Sweet Peas (No. 5) packed just a few hours off the vine. Because Country Club Grade A Peas are rushed from vine to can, they retain their excellent flavor, tenderness and color. The peas in this can are from a lot that has been sampled and tested by accepted methods, and found to be Grade A quality.

Large Sweet Peas, No. 5 Sieve, Sweet Variety.
This is a No. 2 can.
Net Contents—1 Lb. 4 Oz. Peas and Liquid.
Can contains about 2¼ cups drained peas, ¾ cup liquid.
Will yield five to six average servings.

CREAMED DRIED BEEF AND PEAS ON TOAST
1 cup Country Club Grade A Large Sweet Peas, drained
¼ cup Kroger Butter
¼ cup Country Club Flour
1 cup Country Club Evaporated Milk diluted with equal quantity liquid drained from peas
¼ pound dried beef, chopped
Dash Sudan Pepper

Prepare white sauce from butter, flour and liquid. Pour hot water over beef and drain immediately. Add beef and peas to sauce, stirring carefully to prevent mashing peas. Serve hot on toasted Clock Bread. Yield: 5 to 6 servings.

An Example of Specifications and Information on a Food Label

Many of the products, including food products, sold in stores today do not carry information in regard to standards or grades; but many labels, particularly on foods, do contain certain helpful information. This information can be relied upon to be generally truthful and accurate.

The contents indicated on labels are also important, for the size of the container is frequently misleading. Deceptive containers are now illegal if the products are sold in interstate commerce. In examining a label, one should look for the following information:

(a) Specific descriptive statements.
(b) Facts regarding quality.
(c) Facts regarding quantity.
(d) Grades or other similar designations.
(e) Certificate or other mark of approval.

Brand Names and Trial Use. A brand name or trademark is used for one purpose only: to encourage people to ask for the product again after using it the first time. The manufacturer of an established brand therefore usually strives to fulfill certain standards that the consumer will expect to obtain when he buys the product. In the absence of information that would permit comparison, the recognized brands of reputable producers are usually more reliable than other brands. If other information is available, however, the brand on a product should not be used as the only means of comparison. Certainly some branded merchandise sells at higher prices than other branded merchandise or unbranded merchandise. There will always be differences in prices even for the same quality of goods. However, a branded product produced by a reputable manufacturer is your guide for future buying after you have determined values.

Brand names or trade-marks, however, are important guides for a consumer, because after a person has tried a certain product, he can ask for the same brand again with reasonable assurance that he will get the same quality that he has used before. Reputable manufacturers attempt to maintain standards of products carrying their brand names.

Nearly all products carry a brand name now, but some branded products are not reliable; the manufacturers make no attempt to maintain standards. Quality may vary considerably from time to time, but the manufacturer that advertises his product intensively with the idea of building a reputation for the brand usually attempts to maintain a satisfactory standard.

Study the Labels and Identify Brand Names

Trial use is an important means of buying any product, whether it is trial use from a sample, trial of merchandise bought by a friend, or trial use from a small purchase before making a large purchase.

Testing. A previous chapter has disclosed that the United States Bureau of Standards makes tests of products, but does not make any tests for individuals. You can profit by these tests and standards only through the fact that manufacturers voluntarily label their products if they measure up to these standards.

Food products packed under the supervision of Federal agencies have been properly inspected and tested so that you have the assurance of protection. If the products have been inspected or tested, this information is indicated on the label.

There is constant scrutiny on the part of the Federal Government of the food, drugs, and cosmetics that are sold in interstate commerce, so in a general way you have protection from dangerous or harmful products; but unless there are state laws to protect you adequately, you have no assurance that products made and sold within a particular state are of satisfactory quality.

As has been pointed out, one may send a product for testing to the Agricultural Marketing Service of the United States Department of Agriculture. This kind of testing service is useful only in buying in relatively large quantities or in attempting to establish a conclusion as to the quality of a certain brand.

There are many private testing agencies that will test any kind of product for a stipulated fee. Anyone may use these agencies, but their principal advantage to the consumer is through the fact that individual manufacturers and retailers use these testing agencies in determining the quality of their merchandise and indicate this quality on informative labels. The table on page 163 provides an analysis of the various types of testing agencies.

There are certain simple tests that any individual may use when he is buying merchandise, and other slightly more complicated tests that may be performed in the home. Some of these means of identifying quality will be discussed in succeeding chapters pertaining to various types of goods.

Using Salespeople and Advertising. Demonstrations were formerly considered to be applicable only to mechanical products; but they are now applied to food products, pharmaceutical products, and cosmetics. In watching the demonstration of a cosmetic, one should ask oneself, "What will be the effect?" rather than merely, "How is it done?" In watching a demonstration of a food product, such as baking powder, the buyer should ask himself, "In what way does this product differ from other products?"

In observing demonstrations of mechanical appliances, it is usually possible to make comparisons. No wise purchaser will select the first make that he has examined. He should watch the demonstration of more than one make. The more demonstrations he observes, the greater chances there are that he will get his money's worth. Through a demonstration of a mechanical appliance, for instance, he gets specific information with regard to original cost, performance, cost of operation, length of life, amount of service, guarantee, workmanship, finish, and chance of obsolescence. If possible, the information obtained from a demonstration should be supplemented by that obtained from unbiased users of the product being considered.

A person may not be sufficiently familiar with workmanship and finish to be able to judge a single product,

Ch. 9]   GENERAL PRINCIPLES OF BUYING   163

ORGANIZATION	TYPE OF ORGANIZATION	IS ORGANIZATION CONCERNED WITH SALE OF THE PRODUCT?	PRODUCTS USUALLY TESTED	USE AND LIMITATIONS
U. S. Dept. of Agri. Marketing Service	Federal	No	Foods	For packers and processors, but available on a fee basis to consumers.
U. S. Dept. of Agri. Meat Inspection Service	Federal	No	Meat	On meat sold in interstate commerce.
U. S. Bureau of Standards	Federal	No	All types	Testing and standards for government purchase; manufacturers may have products tested.
Federal Food and Drug Administration	Federal	No	Foods, drugs, cosmetics	Testing done to enforce standards. Service not directly available to consumers.
American Medical Association	Professional members	No	Foods, drugs, medical appliances	Some products carry seal of approval but reports not easily available.
American Dental Association	Professional members	No	Dentifrices, mouthwashes	Some products carry seal of approval but reports not easily available.
Consumers' Research, Inc.	General members	No	Many types	Service available to members, limited facilities.
Consumers Union, Inc.	General members	No	Many types	Service available to members, limited facilities.
American Gas Association	Trade association	No	Gas appliances	Products tested and approved carry informative labels for consumer.
Underwriters' Laboratories, Inc.	Trade association	No	Electrical and safety devices	Products tested and approved carry informative labels for consumer.
Better Fabrics Testing Bureau	Trade association	Yes	Fabrics	Products tested and approved carry labels certifying specifications.
American Institute of Laundering	Trade association	No	Fabrics	Labels certify color fastness, shrinkage, and laundering qualities.
National Association of Dry Cleaners	Trade association	No	Fabrics	Labels certify color fastness, shrinkage, and cleaning qualities.
Manufacturers	Manufacturing	Yes	Many types	Test control aids consumers, but detailed information not always available.
Retail Stores	Sales	Yes	Mainly textiles, clothes, foods	Tests used in purchasing; information and standards made available to consumers on labels.
Independent Laboratories (Such as U. S. Testing Co.)	Independent	No	All types	Service available to anyone willing to pay fee, but cost is high.
Public Laboratories	Cities, states, etc.	No	Food, water, measures, weights	Used largely to enforce health and other local laws; tests available to consumers.
Magazine Publishers	Publishers	May be	Mainly foods, cosmetics, textiles, and household equipment	Testing for approval and standards for production guarantees; tests not directly available to consumers.

Testing Services

but a comparison with other similar products will give some basis for judgment. The free service furnished with an appliance can be evaluated definitely. The cost of extra service is very important.

Obsolescence is one of the important elements to be considered. In many cases obsolescence occurs when the manufacturer of the product has gone out of business. Under such circumstances it usually becomes difficult or impossible to obtain replacements or proper service for the product. Such a product is referred to as an "orphan."

Intelligent salespeople can and will give information if it is demanded. Sales propaganda should, however, not be

---

Some Typical Mistakes in Buying

1. Habitual bargain hunters often buy goods they do not need just in anticipation that they may need them.
2. Goods bought at auctions or other types of sales are not necessarily bargains.
3. Claims by agents that house-to-house selling eliminates the middleman's profit and therefore offers the greatest bargain are not necessarily true.
4. Consumers who buy at "wholesale" often pay just as high prices as at retail and may not get the choice merchandise they need.
5. "Bait" advertising that draws people into stores may lead them to purchase other merchandise that is not a good bargain.
6. People who buy in small quantities on a day-to-day basis are not getting the best bargains.
7. The person who insists on being the first to get seasonal fruits and vegetables or the first to get new styles will usually pay the highest prices.
8. Following a blind rule that all advertised merchandise is the best will cause a buyer to overlook good bargains in nonadvertised merchandise.
9. The cheapest is often not the best bargain.
10. People who buy household equipment from unknown manufacturers and retailers may have difficulty getting repair parts and service.
11. Buying all that merchants will sell the consumer on the installment plan often leads to financial disaster.
12. Habitual returning of merchandise bought on approval increases costs for everyone.

confused with real sales information. One should distinguish between glowing terms and facts that show what it has done for others.

The prospective buyer should ask questions and see that his questions are not avoided. If, in examining a product, a person does not readily observe what he wants to know, he should ask the salesperson. The failure of the latter to give a satisfactory answer will be based on lack of knowledge or unwillingness to tell the truth.

An Item Bought at an Auction May Not Be "Cheap" Unless It is Actually Needed

In Chapter 10 you will learn something about advertising. If you learn to read advertising properly, you can use the knowledge gained from advertising in the actual buying of merchandise.

Summary of Buying Principles

1. Buying is a matter of making many kinds of choices.
2. Buying should be based on budgeting.
3. The best way to buy is to examine and compare merchandise in terms of quality and price.
4. Determine your needs and go shopping to fill those needs rather than to do impulse buying if wants are developed on the spur of the moment.
5. There are recognized, legitimate types of special sales put on by reputable stores.
6. There are certain times of the year when certain types of merchandise can be purchased at lower prices than the regular.
7. Goods should be purchased sometimes in large quantities and sometimes in small quantities.
8. Brand names, advertising, salespeople, and labels are helpful guides if used properly.
9. Certain kinds of testing information are helpful.
10. Do not make the same mistake twice.

TEXTBOOK QUESTIONS

1. Give some examples of why buying is a matter of making choices.
2. Explain how a considerable amount of money can be spent and possibly wasted by a family on impulse items.
3. What should be the relationship between budgeting and buying?
4. Why is personal shopping in a store ordinarily a better way to buy than by telephone, from a catalog, or from a house-to-house salesman?
5. What types of hints can you offer in regard to good shopping procedures?
6. (a) What kind of special sale is advantageous to the person who is interested in style? (b) What kind of sale is advantageous to the person who is not interested in style?
7. As a season progresses, why do merchants gradually reduce the price of their seasonal merchandise?
8. Are the price cycles for various products the same?
9. What is the result of buying frequently and in small quantities?
10. Under what circumstances is it desirable to buy food in small quantities?
11. How can the person who has surplus funds take advantage of the price cycle in buying foods?
12. Give some examples of trade names or terms that are confusing.
13. What information besides grades on a label is helpful in buying?
14. Why are brand names or trade-marks used? Are these of any help to you?
15. Give some examples of testing services that are most directly available to consumers.
16. What might be some of the difficulties and risks of buying an item from a legitimate wholesale source?
17. Are advertisers and salespeople helpful in buying? If so, how?

DISCUSSION QUESTIONS

1. Explain how you can help yourself to stay within your budget and become a more careful buyer if you make a careful decision as to whether the item you are buying is worth more to you than the money you are spending for it.

2. To what extent does experience in buying and using commodities serve as an adequate guide in making the following purchases: (a) Suppose an article is expensive and will normally last many years. Will the consumer's experience in buying that article be of any value to him? (b) Suppose an article of a relatively low price is used frequently and bought rather often. Will the consumer's experience in buying that article be adequate as a guide? (c) Suppose an article such as tooth paste is bought frequently. Will the consumer's experience in buying that article be a suitable guide in making purchases?
3. What are some of the limitations to the benefits derived from buying in order to take advantage of low prices during price cycles?
4. Mrs. Hart prides herself on buying only nationally advertised goods. (a) What do you think of her practice? (b) Is she following good judgment? Why?
5. If you went into a strange grocery store for the purpose of buying peas, and found on the shelf two brands of peas, one of which was well known to you and the other was not known, what procedure would you follow in buying? Why?
6. (a) Name some products that do not lend themselves to trial use before the purchase is made. (b) Why do they not?
7. (a) In what ways do you think you could rely on the opinions of your friends and neighbors in buying? (b) In what ways do you think it would be unwise to rely on their opinions?
8. What guides can you suggest as to policies in buying in small or large quantities?
9. There is considerable controversy over the whole question of fixing prices on nationally advertised goods. Some stores sell goods at cut rates and some stores actually sell goods below the cost price as "bait" to draw customers into the stores. How do these practices affect the consumer?
10. For a family of six, what would you think of the policy of buying in quantities of (a) a bushel of fresh sweet corn, (b) a year's supply of potatoes, (c) two small cans or one large can of peaches?
11. (a) What articles do you think are most likely to be safe to buy by mail? (b) Which are least likely to be safe to buy by mail?

PROBLEMS

1. Make a list of the trade names or brand names of products that you have learned to be reliable. Give the name of the product with each trade or brand name. Indicate why these have proved to be reliable guides to you in buying.

2. From your local newspaper, over a period of a week, make a list of different kinds of special sales that, in your opinion, come under the classification of legitimate bargain sales as described in this chapter.
3. Make a list of at least six items (not more than four foods) and state the time for each when you think it is at its lowest seasonal price.
4. Analyze the reasons why you and your family buy from the places where you are accustomed to buy (a) groceries, (b) drugs, (c) clothing. Give a list of reasons for each classification. If you buy in more than one place, give the reasons.

COMMUNITY PROBLEMS AND PROJECTS

1. Make a study of the whole problem of "discount houses" that sell branded merchandise below regular prices, stores that offer merchandise at "wholesale prices," and the whole problem of fair trade laws and price cutting. Present all the facts that you can after talking to Better Business Bureau, regular retailers, and doing all the reading that you can.
2. Compare prices of foods in different sizes of cans in the same store, and figure the percentage of saving if a family can justify buying the larger size.
3. Compare prices on one-half peck, one peck, and one bushel of potatoes, and indicate for what size of family you think the different sizes of purchases would be most appropriate without running the risk of spoilage.
4. Compare prices on one-half peck, one peck, and one bushel of oranges (or in terms of pounds or dozens, depending upon the way they are sold), and determine which is the most economical quantity for your own family to purchase without running the risk of spoilage.
5. Make a study of some of the special sales of clothing or dry goods and report whether the store is selling at reduced prices its regular merchandise, or whether special merchandise is brought in for the sale.
6. Attend an auction with one of your friends and see if you can detect whether there is someone in the audience representing the auction who is serving as a "booster" or "house bidder" in order to keep the bidding going and provide some competition.

Chapter 10

How to Interpret Advertising

Purpose of the Chapter. Advertising is both criticized and praised. In a democratic free enterprise system it is an important factor in distribution because it is a means of mass communicating, educating, and stimulating demand for products and services. Advertising provides useful information to consumers, but consumers also need knowledge that will protect them from being influenced by the wrong kind of advertising. This chapter will help you to understand and interpret advertising as a guide in buying.

You will find answers to these questions:

1. What can be learned from advertising?
2. What are some arguments for and against advertising?
3. Who pays the cost of advertising?
4. What advertising appeals cause people to buy?
5. What are some of the characteristics of misleading advertising?
6. What questions should you ask yourself as you read an advertisement?

Then and Now in Advertising. When our country was young, production and distribution were very simple. Before production in factories, most consumers produced the goods they consumed, or they traded with nearby acquaintances. Stores often traded goods across the counter, and very little money changed hands. The first common form of advertising was the sign of the doctor, the merchant, the blacksmith, and other business establishments. In those days no means of mass production was known; therefore, there was no need for mass distribution.

Now we have mass production with producers and consumers widely separated. A complicated system of transportation and communication is needed to help producers reach the consumer. Advertising has become the means of telling the consumer in distant places what the producer has to sell. Under our present system of economics advertising is essential. Advertising helps both agriculture and business and it creates jobs.

Of course in a completely controlled society, advertising would not be so useful because producers would be told what to produce, and consumers would be able to buy only the goods placed at their disposal. We would have very few kinds of goods from which to make a selection.

Advertising Educates Buyers. We often overlook the fact that advertising has been a tremendous influence in the United States in the development of our standard of living by improving our diet, our health, our living conditions, our comforts, and our conveniences. This has been brought about through constructive education and by increasing our wants for things that now seem necessary although at one time they may have seemed unnecessary. It may be true that advertising has caused us to want things that we really do not need, but after all, we have a free choice in deciding what we need. It is therefore necessary for the consumer to be well enough informed so that he may intelligently decide what he needs.

If we study the history of food items, we get a good example of the influence of the educational value of advertising on our diets and our general health. Authorities dealing with the problem of diets long have advocated the use of orange juice, tomato juice, lettuce, fresh vegetables,

You Can Learn from Good Advertising

and many other forms of food that at one time were not common parts of the everyday diet. Very little progress was made in establishing these foods as a part of our basic diet until they were publicized by producers who promoted the sale of these food items through advertising by educating people as to the desirability of their use.

The story of popularizing desirable foods is somewhat parallel to the story of popularizing the acceptance of electricity, electric appliances, the telephone, sanitary plumbing, ventilation, lighting, refrigeration, radio, television, and many types of labor-saving devices that are now considered essential in the home. We can live without them, but who would want to live without them?

Could You Buy as Confidently if no Goods Were Branded and Advertised?

Does Advertising Really Help You? Have you ever stopped to study advertising long enough to discover whether you really get any helpful information from it? If it is of no value to you, then it is wasteful. If it is of some value, you should learn how to get the greatest value from it. Answering some of these questions will help to determine whether advertising is of any value to you.

Does Advertising Assure Quality? Not all advertised products are of a high grade, and not all unadvertised products are of a low grade. A businessman may sell a bad product once through advertising, but he cannot sell it twice to an intelligent buyer. That is the secret of why most advertisers and certainly all honest advertisers must produce and sell a good product. If they expect to stay in business, they must depend upon repeat sales to customers who have bought their product as a result of advertising. One advertisement which attempts to popularize the particular product will usually not sell enough goods to pay for its cost. It is the cumulative effect of advertising, getting consumers to buy, satisfying consumers, and causing repeat sales that gradually builds enough sales volume to pay for the advertising. It is therefore the desire of most advertisers to obtain and hold repeat business that causes them to strive constantly to develop and sell a better product.

What Are Your Answers to These Questions?

1. If you were a farmer, could you get all the information you want about the latest farm equipment without referring to advertisements?
2. Does advertising give you any information about the latest developments in household equipment?
3. Has advertising educated you in regard to television?
4. If all refrigerators were sold without trade-marks and trade names, would you feel safe in picking a good refrigerator?
5. If all canned foods were prohibited from carrying labels and trade-marks, do you think you could select foods wisely?
6. Do you ever read the newspaper to see what is offered for sale in your local stores?
7. Did you ever buy from a mail-order catalog?
8. Do you use advertising (posters, leaflets, or announcements) in your school to promote attendance at a school play or athletic event?

Some Arguments Against Advertising. Many critics, and particularly those who believe in a socialistic economic system operated by government, contend that advertising is a waste. They contend that the buyer has to pay for the advertising. They also contend that advertising is bad because it encourages people to buy things they really do not need. They say that there is too much emphasis on style and emotional appeals rather than on specific physical values. These critics object to the fact that advertising causes us to have new wants.

It is probably true that many of our purchases are unnecessary or at least they are unnecessary if we compare our present method of living with primitive living conditions of two hundred years ago. We could exist without tooth paste, hand lotion, vacuum cleaners, radios, automobiles, cosmetics, and many other things.

We could make our own tooth paste; we could make our own cereals out of raw grain; we could weave the cloth and make our own clothes; we could use a broom instead of a vacuum cleaner; we could live in thatched huts instead of a comfortable home; we could do without modern plumbing and many other things. The question is whether we want to go back to those conditions.

Just what is a necessity? When does a luxury become a necessity? Soap at one time was considered a luxury, but is it a luxury or a necessity now? Modern plumbing was considered at one time a luxury, but is it a luxury or a necessity now?

Because of our level of living people want many things that are not practical. They want more than warmth in clothing. They want style. Women want their hair to look attractive and their skin to be smooth. These are some of things that provide certain satisfactions; and in many of our purchases we are buying human satisfactions rather than practical things. We must be intelligent enough to determine for ourselves where the dividing line is between a luxury or a necessity.

How You Are Influenced. The professional seller is a trained specialist. He understands human behavior and the workings of the human mind. He presents his product so that it will attract attention, create desire, convince the consumer of its worth, and cause him to purchase it.

A businessman is essentially free to advertise and sell in a manner that will cause you to buy. It is to your advantage as a consumer to understand enough about advertising and selling techniques to enable you to evaluate advertising and selling so that you get the things you want at a fair price.

Appeals That Open Your Purse. There are two general types of sales appeal. The first is known as the *emotional*, or *human-interest, appeal*; the second, as the *rational*, or *reason-why, appeal*.

Experience has proved that, in the selling of many commodities, the emotional appeal is more effective than the reason-why appeal. The emotional appeal influences the buyer through suggestion. He is not invited to deliberate or compare; he is made to feel that the article that is advertised will please his senses or satisfy his desires.

The reason-why appeal requires a careful presentation of facts that appeal to conscious deliberation. This type of appeal must present logical reasons why the product or services should be purchased.

Within these two general classes of sales appeal, there are numerous appeals used by advertisers to stimulate sales. The following is a list of fourteen that are commonly used in advertising all general types of products:

(a) Health.
(b) Maternal affection.
(c) Appetite and taste.
(d) Attraction of the sexes.
(e) Economy.
(f) Comfort, pleasure, and luxury.
(g) Ambition.
(h) Beauty and appearance.
(i) Efficiency.
(j) Vanity, pride, and fashion.
(k) Safety.
(l) Sympathy.
(m) Envy.
(n) Fear.

The way in which the advertiser utilizes an appeal depends upon whether the appeal is emotional or rational. For instance, if clothing is sold purely for the sake of beauty or appearance or with the purpose of enabling the buyer to imitate someone else, the appeal is highly emotional. On the other hand, if the advertiser of men's clothing points out how attractive clothing and a good appearance will help a man in business, the appeal is somewhat rational.

The illustration on page 175 shows an advertisement with an emotional appeal and one with a reason-why appeal. Compare the two. Determine which one actually tells enough to enable the reader to determine the merits of the product.

Experts in selling and advertising study very carefully the appeals that are most effective in selling products. They find that some appeals are satisfactory for men, whereas they cannot be used satisfactorily with women; and vice versa. Style, for example, is an important consideration in selling shoes to women, whereas it is not quite so important

Ch. 10] HOW TO INTERPRET ADVERTISING 175

A Maiden's Dream

NEW SPRING SUIT
$49.50

Definitely new, sensational, and exciting. A designer's dream! For a thousand and one hours of blissful spring wear. Tailored for a slenderizing effect. In green and blue pastels. You will get a real thrill from one of these suits.

THE BATES STORE

An Emotional Appeal

New Tweeds

SELECTIONS FOR SPRING
$49.50

We have just received a new shipment of tailored tweed suits made of virgin wool fabrics in a wide range of colors and patterns. The lining is guaranteed for two years. Excellent for street or office wear. Alteration charges on any suit will not exceed $2.00.

THE BATES STORE

A Reason-Why Appeal

in selling them to men. Many tests will show that men consider the quality of shoes along with style, whereas women make style the paramount consideration. In choosing an appeal to be used, the seller or the advertiser must therefore consider the prospective buyer.

Who Pays the Cost of Advertising? Some critics contend that all advertising is wasteful because it influences people to buy when they should be allowed to make their own choices without such an influence. It is true that some advertising is wasteful; but, on the other hand, if one makes an honest analysis of the situation, he will see that without advertising it would be impossible to have mass distribution. Without mass distribution it would be impossible to have mass production. Without mass production it would be impossible to have manufacturing processes improved to the high degree to which we now are accustomed. Without improved manufacturing processes it would be impossible to have many of our commonly accepted necessities produced at a low cost. For instance, in 1922 a few thousand people with radio sets costing from $100 to $500 could make their friends envious by receiving radio programs. There are now more than 46,000,000 homes equipped with radio sets, which have cost in some cases as low as $20 a set. Advertising and mass production have brought about this change.

Sometimes critics cite examples of manufacturers who are able to produce and sell an item, such as a razor, for $5, $10, or $15. These critics attribute the high cost to advertising. One of the reasons for the high cost is patent protection, which enables the producer to get the price he wants. Lack of competition is another factor. Furthermore, during the early stages in the introduction of a product, it is necessary to charge a higher price to carry the burden of advertising until mass production results in lower production costs. Without advertising, a large market would not be created; low production resulting in high production costs would therefore tend to keep the price at a high level. In normal, unrestricted advertising and trade, however, when new competing products come onto the market, additional advertising causes wider use; and, through competition and mass production together, a lower price is made available to the consumer.

It is true that, in the case of luxuries such as exclusive clothes and cosmetics, advertising costs may run unusually high; but when one buys a luxury, he is not necessarily looking for economy. When one analyzes commonly advertised commodities, he finds the advertising cost rather low. For instance, in the case of a well-known shirt, only 64/100 of a cent goes into public information about it. In the case of a well-known brand of soup, only 36/1000 of a cent on each can is spent for advertising.

It may seem a waste to some people for an advertiser to pay $20,000 for a full-page advertisement in a national magazine, but you can estimate the cost of this advertisement per reader when you know that it goes into more than eight million homes. A television program may cost $40,000, but it often reaches as many as thirty million people.

Advertised products sometimes sell at higher prices than unadvertised products, but in the final analysis, it is not a question of who pays for advertising, but rather it is a question of the total cost of merchandising and whether this total cost is too high. It is frequently a choice between using more advertising or more direct selling. One of the best defenses of advertising is that, when it is well done, it is the cheapest way of selling. When this is true, it is to the advantage of the consumer. In the case of some products, it has been shown that the advertising costs are high because of pressure that is needed in selling those products. In the case of many other products, it has been proved conclusively that advertising has served an important economic function by gaining widespread distribution, low costs of production, and therefore the lowest possible price to the consumer. If it were not for this function of advertising in our distributive system, it can easily be seen that we would not enjoy some of the benefits that we enjoy today. It cannot be said that advertising is entirely good or entirely bad.

Other Benefits from Advertising. In England radio and television most stations and programs are operated by the government and are supported by taxes and licenses. The government decides what programs will be broadcast and there is a fee charged for possessing a radio or television set and for the privilege of listening to the programs broadcast by the government. In the United States radio and television stations pay taxes to the government instead of being supported by the government. They derive their income from the entertainment and advertising programs paid for by advertisers. These programs are available free to anyone who owns a receiving set. In the case of the United States consumers pay for radio and advertising programs by paying for the cost of advertising.

Have you ever estimated how much you would have to pay for some of our beautiful magazines if it were not for advertising? The subscription price of most magazines is only a small fraction of the cost of this magazine; the advertisers pay most of the cost.

Honest and Dishonest Advertising. Every buyer must recognize the fact that, although the majority of advertisers are honest, some are unscrupulous. Substantial and well-established business concerns recognize the fact that honesty, in advertising as well as in other relationships with consumers, must be the basis of permanent success. The publishers of magazines and newspapers recognize the fact that dishonest advertising reacts unfavorably against their publications as well as against the products advertised. Because of the importance of advertising, the Federal Government and also state governments have passed laws on this subject. The most important government agency in the supervision of advertising is the Federal Trade Commission. In a recent year the Federal Trade Commission examined more than a half million advertisements and

Sales Are Sometimes Not What They Appear to Be

made complaints to the advertisers in only seventy-two cases. One of the most effective promoters of honesty in advertising is the National Better Business Bureau and its affiliated organizations.

Misleading Advertising

The National Better Business Bureau publicizes various advertising schemes that are considered misleading and unethical. A few of the schemes are as follows:

1. Fire sales that are really not fire sales.
2. Puzzle contests that are so difficult and long that most contestants drop out after paying a fee and never have a chance of winning.
3. Work-at-home schemes that require applicants to pay for a course of instructions which they seldom complete.
4. Help-wanted advertisements that are really advertisements for the enrollment in a training program.
5. Bait advertising that attracts people to stores because of a bargain when only a few of the bargain items are available.
6. Advertisements of pure gold jewelry that has a very low gold content or which is gold-plated.
7. Wholesalers that advertise for retail trade.
8. Advertising at a false high price to give the impression of a reduction at the sale price.
9. Periodic practice of a business that advertises "selling out," "going out of business," or "fire sale" when actually the statement is not true.

Some Absurdities of Advertising. Let us consider some of the tactics of those who write advertisements that are supposed to educate consumers and to induce them to buy. Demands are placed upon the writers of advertising copy to use devices that will build up the maximum amount of emotion. Note just a few of the irrational appeals that are used: Turn to a page of a popular magazine and you will find the picture of a beautiful young woman with a statement that Miss So-and-So uses Such-and-Such face powder; turn to another page and you will see pictured an attractive young woman who is supposed to convey the idea that, if a particular product is good enough for her, it is good enough for you; turn to another page and you will find a grotesque picture warning you against dire results if you do not use a certain disinfectant or mouthwash. In advertisements you should search for statements relating to performance, quality, ingredients, and actual results.

Testimonials. It is common knowledge that debutantes, society leaders, political figures, film stars, and many other prominent people sell their names and photographs for use in the testimonial advertising of various products. They have been paid in money, publicity, or other forms. In fact, there are agencies that make a business of arranging contracts with clients who are willing to sell their names and photographs for such purposes. Obviously, testimonials that are obtained and used promiscuously cannot be sincere. In evaluating testimonials, one must therefore take this common practice into consideration. If a consumer is going to judge a testimonial upon its merits, the testimonial should come from a qualified person.

Testimonials Influence Many Buyers

Meaningless Statements. Pictures are not the only devices used to convey certain emotional impressions. Headings, slogans, verse, and humorous quotations also serve that purpose. Here are some examples of slogans:

"It's the Best"   "The Best Shoe Available"
"It Can't Be Beat"   "The Unusual Watch"
"The Perfect Dentifrice" "Better Than Any Others"

Do any of these statements convey definite assurance of quality, performance, or value?

Headings are interesting. Slogans sometimes catch the eye. Verse and humorous statements are frequently amusing. But these should not be allowed to influence buying. One should read the advertisement carefully, and then learn something about the quality of the product, the contents, the cost, and the performance.

It has been said that the public likes to be fooled. Most buyers are influenced by tradition, and many lack the incentive to investigate for themselves. Instead of taking the initiative, they wait until the seller does so. Flattery and the appeal to envy often induce a prospective purchaser to buy without consideration of quality, cost, or utility.

Informative Advertising. For many years advertisements of goods purchased by manufacturers have been phrased in terms giving exact descriptions of those goods. At present some advertisers of consumers' goods are featuring in their advertisements pertinent statements on standards, specifications, and performance.

It is now common practice of certain stores to give exact descriptions or sizes of dresses available, the name of the cloth, and the quality of the cloth. In advertising furniture, some stores give an exact description of the type of frame that is used, the type of springs, the kind of padding in the cushions, the kind of covers, the finish, and sometimes additional information. Others sometimes go a step farther and provide additional information in regard to the materials that are used. Some of the advertisements of merchants are backed up by helpful tags and labels.

From a consumer's point of view, an advertisement may be considered primarily good if it provides facts in regard to quality, standards, specifications, and performance. It can be generally considered not good if it fails to provide this information but instead appeals only to the emotions.

How to Read Advertisements. Advertisements should be read from two points of view: (a) to learn everything possible from the advertisements, and (b) to try to detect if there is any deception or misleading information. Some advertisements are neither informative nor deceptive. They are simply evasive or general, or they merely appeal to the emotions. The intelligent consumer will look for helpful information. Learn to distinguish between emotional appeals and rational appeals. Learn to evaluate testimonials and to discern the facts that are included.

Follow These Guides in Analyzing Advertisements

1. Do I need it?
2. What does the product contain and how is it made?
3. Is it beneficial?
4. How economical is it?
5. How long will it last?
6. How does its price compare with the prices of similar products?
7. Does it carry any seals identifying quality or any evidence of authoritative scientific tests?
8. What proof is used to back up the statements?
9. Is it harmless?
10. Are any of the advertising statements evasive or misleading?
11. Does the advertisement appeal to your intelligence?
12. Does the advertisement make you feel confident that, if you buy, you will be a satisfied customer.

Every large business has at least one buyer who is a specialist. Some concerns, such as wholesale grocers, have several buyers. Professional buyers devote all their time to buying. They sometimes have difficulty in distinguishing a good product through its advertising, and in the final analysis they must examine the product. The average consumer is an amateur when it comes to buying. His emotions are easily influenced in buying. Often he buys emotionally rather than rationally because the professional advertiser knows how to appeal to the emotions of the individual. One can become more than an amateur buyer if he learns to interpret advertising and to look beyond advertising.

If you believe that advertising can be improved and ought to be improved, you should cooperate with the advertisers that give you the information that you want and need. Have you ever analyzed your own buying habits to see how you are influenced? Check yourself on some of these points to see how wisely you are using advertising. From what you have learned in this chapter you should be able to evaluate your own answers.

Check Yourself

1. Do you buy on a basis of emotional or a reason-why appeal?
2. Are you influenced by facts and information or by high-sounding generalities?
3. Do you ever compare one advertisement with another and one product with another?
4. Do you buy the most advertised brand without further thought of quality or economy?

Some Legal Protections. In Chapter 7 you studied governmental protection, which includes the regulation of advertising. Chapter 6 introduced you to some private agencies that are interested in helping the consumer to get honest advertising. A knowledge of the information in these chapters will help you to evaluate advertising and to guard against unethical and dishonest advertising.

Some Legal Implications of Advertising. An advertisement of goods is not necessarily a legal binding offer in terms of a contract. It may be withdrawn at any time and becomes a contract only when it has been accepted according to the legal requirements of a contract. For that reason prices that are quoted in advertisements are not necessarily binding upon the seller; therefore, an advertiser has the right to change his prices without notice. For example, a store advertised a washing machine for $90. When Mrs. Jones went to the store to buy one, the store refused to sell it, contending that the price had risen and the new price was $100. There was no contract because an advertisement is considered merely an invitation to trade.

> *Summary of Principles of Interpreting Advertising*
> 1. Advertising helps agriculture and business and creates jobs.
> 2. Advertising is a means of communication and a means of educating which creates wants.
> 3. Advertising tends to raise our level of living by turning wants into needs and luxuries into necessities.
> 4. Some people contend that advertising is an economic waste.
> 5. From the point of view of business, advertising is an economical and often the cheapest way to sell a product.
> 6. Advertisers use emotional appeals as well as reason-why appeals.
> 7. An advertised product may sell at a higher price than an unadvertised product, but often it can be sold for less.
> 8. Advertising helps pay the cost of radio, television, magazines, and newspapers.
> 9. Some advertising is misleading, some is helpful and informative, and some is meaningless.
> 10. Advertising should be studied carefully as a guide in buying.

TEXTBOOK QUESTIONS

1. Explain why advertising is more essential now to manufacturers, merchants, and consumers than it was when our country was very young.
2. Give some examples of the educational value of advertising.
3. Why must advertising be honest and the product good if a manufacturer or merchant expects to continue in business and sell this product?
4. What are some of the objections to or complaints against advertising?
5. How has advertising helped you reach our level of living?
6. (a) What are the two general types of appeal that advertisers and sellers use in encouraging people to buy? (b) What are the differences between them?
7. Name at least five specific advertising appeals.
8. Who pays the cost of advertising?
9. Explain how advertising helps us to get good magazines and radio or television programs.

10. (a) What jurisdiction does the Federal Government have over advertising? (b) By what agency is control over advertising administered?
11. Give at least two examples of advertising that the National Better Business Bureau considers misleading.
12. Why is testimonial advertising often frowned upon?
13. Give some examples of shallow, meaningless statements used in advertising.
14. What suggestions do you offer as a guide in helping you to read advertisements?
15. Name some ways that you can check yourself to see how you are influenced in reading advertising.
16. If a price of an article is advertised, is this a legal binding contract?

DISCUSSION QUESTIONS

1. If advertising is used by producers or distributors to get a premium price on branded merchandise, is this purpose of advertising ever advantageous to you?
2. Give two examples of how advertising may force prices down.
3. Give your opinion of the arguments for and against advertising.
4. Discuss some of the advantages and the disadvantages of brands or trade names from the point of view of the buyer.
5. "Advertising has converted many luxuries into necessities." Explain this statement.
6. "An uneducated person is a toy in the hands of an advertising expert." Explain this statement.
7. When you buy clothes, what appeals influence you most?
8. Select some article, such as women's shoes, and think of some statements that might be made in advertising them that might be (a) emotional and (b) rational.
9. More than a billion dollars is spent each year for advertising. If advertising were discontinued, could we expect to buy the same goods in the same quantities for one billion dollars less?
10. Why is the question of who pays for advertising not important?
11. How may testimonial advertising of athletes sometimes serve a useful purpose?
12. What do you think of a statement such as this in an advertisement: "Used by the best families"?
13. Try to recall and describe a recent advertisement that you feel was informative. Give your reasons.

PROBLEMS

1. In magazines or newspapers in your home find advertisements that contain appeals to (a) health, (b) beauty, (c) economy. Paste these on a sheet of paper, and write opposite each a brief notation indicating how the appeal is emphasized.
2. Bring to class two advertisements of similar products, one giving few or no specific facts and the other containing several facts. List for each advertisement the specific facts that are given with regard to the product. If none are given, indicate accordingly. If it is impossible to find two advertisements of similar products, select advertisements of different products and then complete the same work.
3. Bring to class an advertisement containing a testimonial that, in your opinion, is not sincere and that probably has been purchased. Give your reasons for your opinion.
4. Pick out the best advertisement that you can find in some recent popular magazine. Submit it with a written statement as to why you think it is the best advertisement.
5. From five magazines or newspapers make a list of all the high-sounding titles and terms used in advertising products. This list should include meaningless, but attractive, slogans and descriptive terms. (b) After listing these terms, analyze their truthfulness, their intent, and their usefulness from the point of view of the buyer.

COMMUNITY PROBLEMS AND PROJECTS

1. If your community has a better business bureau, find out exactly what functions it performs in regard to maintaining the ethics of advertising locally. If possible, obtain some examples to report to the class.
2. Learn from a magazine or a newspaper publisher what regulations are placed upon the acceptance of advertisements. Ask specific questions with regard to how the truthfulness of advertising is judged and investigated. Write a report of your findings.
3. Make a list of items that you generally use or would like to use. Classify these in two groups: Necessities and luxuries. Try to name and explain some of these items that you have listed as luxuries for yourself which might be necessities for someone else. Explain why.
4. Watch your local newspapers for what you will consider false advertising and state why you feel it is false. Watch for court cases pertaining to false advertising or check with the local Better Business Bureau as to false advertising practices. Write a report of your findings.

Chapter II

Standards, Grades, and Labels as Guides in Buying

> **Purpose of the Chapter.** We want to make sure that the goods we buy are worth the money we give for them and that they have the characteristics and quality that meet our needs. The content, quality, and characteristics of many goods are not readily observable before we purchase them. Standards and grades on printed labels attached to the goods helps us know what the goods are before we buy.
>
> You will find answers to these questions:
> 1. What is the importance of standards?
> 2. What are standards, grades, and labels?
> 3. What government and private agencies formulate and enforce standards?
> 4. How can informative labeling help us?

What Is a Standard? Imagine trying to get along without standards. A *standard* is a unit of measure. A pound is a measure of weight; a foot, a measure of distance or length; and a gallon, a measure of liquids. How would we buy coffee, or fabric, or milk without these standards of quantity? How could prices be set? How could you indicate how much of a commodity you want?

There are other standards too. We designate the size of a shirt by neckband size; shoes, by length and width; and some articles, such as hats and sometimes dresses, by arbitrary numbers. Another kind of standard pertains to performance, such as the octane rating of gasoline or the heat units, known as British Thermal Units, in coal.

A standard ordinarily is thought of as a measure of quantity, weight, or extent, and sometimes of quality. A standard for consumer goods is usually a definition which states fully what the measuring stick is.

What Is a Grade? With the exception of foods, standards usually define a single level of quality of a commodity that is considered satisfactory. A drug, for example, either complies with the formulae of the official United States Pharmacopeia, which is known as the U.S.P. standard, or it does not. There are no degrees of conformance to the drug standard. But when applied to foods, standards often are established to define several levels of quality, each of which is known as a grade. For example, there are four grades of butter, each of which is defined by a standard. A *grade*, then, is really a term applied to standards of quality when more than one quality of a particular food is defined. The Federal Government agencies sometimes refer to the definitions as standards of identity, because the definition describes or identifies the standard or grade so it is recognizable.

What Is a Label? Back in the days when practically all food, clothing, and other necessities were prepared and made in the home, there was little need for standards and grades. Consumers purchased raw materials from which to make the things they needed. Processed foods and ready-made clothes were practically unknown. Purchasers could see what they were buying and in some instances they even tasted the food before they bought it. There were few choices to make, for usually the merchant had only one kind of coffee, shoes, or furniture to sell.

Now that most of the foods, drugs, clothing, and other things we buy are finished products and ready to be used, merchants keep in stock a variety of each kind of commodity from which we choose the one that appeals to us. Many commodities, such as foods and drugs, are in cans or otherwise packaged so that we do not actually see them until we use them. Standards and grades thus are very important to modern consumers. Standards indicate to us what the

Ch. 11] STANDARDS, GRADES, AND LABELS 189

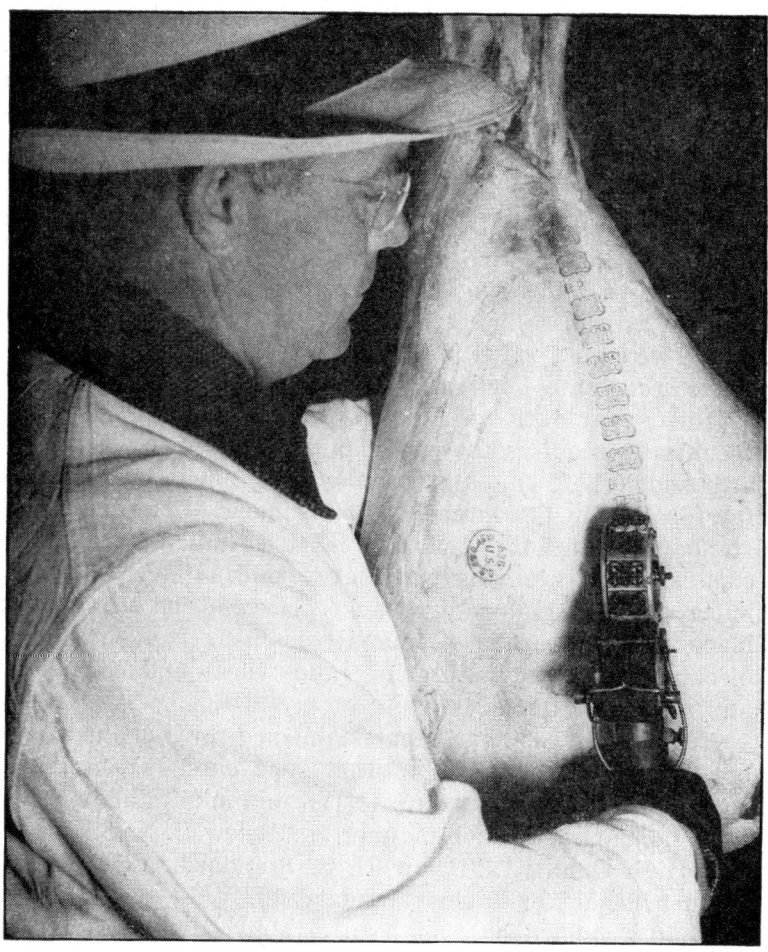

U. S. Department of Agriculture

Meat grades are examples of the many types of grades. Meat grades are based on standards of quality. Federal grades are prime, choice, good, commercial, and utility. There are grades for many other food products.

Grading of Meat

commodity really is, what it is made of, and what its characteristics are. If there are several qualities of a commodity, such as there are in foods, grade indicates the level of the quality.

A *label* is a written statement attached to an article or a commodity describing its essential characteristics. Standards and grades may be indicated on the label as well as other information of importance to consumers. A consumer should familiarize himself with standards and grades; he should read the labels on merchandise to learn the characteristics of the goods that he is contemplating buying.

Standards of the United States Department of Health, Education, and Welfare. Many Federal laws have been enacted to insure purity, quality, and truthful labeling of foods, drugs, and cosmetics. These laws provide control of imports as well as interstate shipments.

The Federal Food, Drug, and Cosmetic Act, which is administered by the Food and Drug Administration, an agency of the Department of Health, Education, and Welfare, specifically requires that reasonable definitions and standards should be formulated for food to promote honesty and fair dealing in the interest of consumers. Definitions and standards under the Act have been formulated for many classes of foods, among which are: milk and cream; fruit butters, jellies, and preserves; chocolate and cocoa products; macaroni and noodle products; shellfish; canned fruits; oleomargarine and margarine; and wheat and corn flour and related products.

After standards have been established for a canned fruit or vegetable, every food of that type entering interstate commerce must measure up to the minimum standards or must be marked in such manner as "Below U. S. Standard, Not High Quality," "Below U. S. Standard. Low quality but not illegal," or "Below standard fill."

If no standard has yet been established for a fruit or vegetable entering into interstate commerce, the common name of the food and the ingredients, if there are two or more, must be indicated. The ingredients must be named in the order of their predominance by weight.

Special dietary foods, such as those advertising vitamin concentrations, must indicate on the label the amount of the vitamin content. Foods fortified with vitamins by adding vitamin content must indicate this content.

When artificial coloring, artificial flavoring, or preservatives are used, the label must state this fact. Butter, cheese, and ice cream are exempt from this provision. However, in some states the coloring of margarine is prohibited entirely by state law.

If any food is an imitation, the label must be marked "Imitation."

Standards of the Federal Trade Commission. The Federal Trade Commission has the authority to enforce the standards and the labeling specifications of the Federal laws pertaining to the manufacture and sale of fur, wool, and synthetic fabric products.

Probably the greatest contribution of the Federal Trade Commission in serving the consumer is through the trade practice rules that are the outgrowth of conferences in all the major industries, including the hosiery industry, the silk industry, the fur industry, and approximately one hundred fifty others. When various standards of identification and standards of quality are established for an industry, the Federal Trade Commission recognizes these as standards for the determining of unfair trade practices. If any producer or distributor in interstate commerce violates one of these standards, the Federal Trade Commission can take action to prevent the practice. For instance, let us assume that a manufacturer of silk hosiery sells a product that is inferior in quality as based upon the standards that have been established. When this fact is discovered by the Federal Trade Commission, it will, through so-called stipulation, request the offender to sign an agreement to stop the practice. If he stops the practice, the case is not prosecuted; if he does not sign the agreement and stop the practice, hearings are held; and if he is judged guilty, the Federal Trade Commission issues a cease and desist order. This order has the effect of becoming law. If the order is ignored, the Commission may bring a court action to force the manufacturer to stop the unfair trade practice and the violation of the order.

Standards of the United States Department of Commerce. Many Federal agencies assist in the preparation and writing of Federal specifications. These specifications are used by government agencies as the basis for requesting bids on materials to be purchased. The specifications are listed in a publication known as *Index of Federal Specifications and Standards,* which is available from the Superintendent of Documents. Federal specifications are valuable to business firms that may be interested in selling their products to the government. The public also is interested in Federal specifications as standards of quality.

The National Bureau of Standards tests many products and materials for government agencies to determine whether or not they meet Federal specifications.

The Commodity Standards Division of the Office of Technical Services cooperates with a trade or industry in developing "commercial standards." Requests for the development of commercial standards originate with an interested industry group. A statement of a commercial standard includes: (1) its purpose and scope; (2) physical, chemical, or performance requirements; (3) methods of testing. An industry may, if it chooses, state in its advertising, on the labels of products, or on invoices that the specific product meets the requirements of a certain commercial standard. However, if such reference is made by the business firm to a commercial standard in contracts, labels, invoices, or advertising, the provisions are enforceable through usual legal channels.

The value of commercial standards to the consumer is that they indicate quality as approved by the industry making the product.

Standards of Trade and Technical Organizations. Many standards have been formulated and established by trade and technical associations for their respective commodities. These standards are very beneficial to consumers.

Standards of Underwriters' Laboratory. The National Board of Fire Underwriters sets up certain minimum standards of safety for materials and appliances that might involve hazards of life, fire, theft, or accident. The Underwriters' Laboratory maintained by this organization passes judgment on a product before it is permitted to carry the U. L. label.

Standards of U. S. Pharmacopoeia. Every ten years various medical authorities representing the U. S. Public Health Service, the Department of Agriculture, the U. S. Army, the U. S. Navy, and various medical societies and colleges meet to draw up standards of quality and purity for all known types of drugs and medicines. These are then published in a book called *U. S. Pharmacopoeia*, which is referred to as "U. S. P." No new remedy can be added to the official list until it has been properly tested and tried out under special supervision. When a consumer buys any drug or medicine with its contents described on the label on the basis of U. S. P. standards, he can therefore have reasonable assurance as to the quality and purity.

Standards of American Pharmaceutical Association. Another agency that establishes standards for drug products is the American Pharmaceutical Association. These standards are published in the *National Formulary*. When the letters "N. F." appear on a drug product, the consumer may have reasonable assurance of quality and purity.

Standards of American Institute of Homeopathy. This institute publishes annually a *Homeopathic Pharmacopoeia* of the United States, which set standards of identification for certain drug products. When the letters "H. P." appear on a drug product, they carry an assurance of standards similar to those previously mentioned.

Other Standards. There are other specialized agencies that set standards. The American Institute of Laundering sets standards in regard to the washability of fabrics. The Better Fabrics Testing Bureau issues a "color tested" seal for fabrics that meet its standards of color fastness.

Some states have established their own particular standards. For instance, there are several states that have grading and labeling laws applying to fruits and vegetables. Several have laws pertaining to bedding, including blankets, mattresses, and springs. These laws particularly apply to new and secondhand materials used in padding mattresses and upholstery. In some states labels used to identify the quality must not be removed from the product when sold.

Enforcement of Voluntary and Mandatory Standards. When voluntary standards have been established by private agencies and are so marked on the label, the consumer may be reasonably certain that the commodity at least meets those minimum standards. When minimum standards for such commodities and goods have been established under the agencies of the U. S. Department of Health Education, and Welfare and the Federal Trade Commission, they become mandatory for those products covered by the standards that are sold in interstate commerce. If these products do not measure up to the minimum standards and are sold in interstate commerce, they must be labeled in some manner as "Below U. S. standards, a good food, not high grade," or "Below U. S. standards, low quality but not illegal."

Government Grades of Foods and Food Products. In an earlier section of this chapter it was stated that the Food and Drug Administration of the United States Department of Health, Education, and Welfare is responsible for the formulation of definitions and standards for foods.

The Agricultural Marketing Service, a division of the United States Department of Agriculture, has two major responsibilities in regard to food. The one pertains to inspection of foods and food processing to insure wholesomeness, cleanliness, and fitness for human use. The second function is the administration for the grading of foods and food products for human use. Both are highly important services to consumers.

In order to arrive at a grade classification, certain standards must be established for every item. A scoring table is therefore arranged that is used as a guide in determining grades. For instance, in the case of canned tomatoes the following are the points that are considered:

Drained weight (solids without juice)	20 points
Wholeness (percentage of whole tomatoes)	20 points
Color	30 points
Absence of defects	30 points
Total	100 points

These standards for tomatoes are converted into grade designations as follows:

A total score of 90 to 100 is Grade A
A total score of 75 to 89 is Grade B
A total score of 60 to 74 is Grade C

Failure of a product to rate a specified number of points for any one factor may determine its grade regardless of the total score. For example, if a can of tomatoes contains some that are undercolored, they cannot be given a Grade A rating regardless of the total score. It must be borne in mind, however, that all three grades of tomatoes are thoroughly wholesome or else they would not be permitted to be sold in interstate commerce.

Products marketed under these standards may or may not be inspected by Federal agents, but if they purport to measure up to the standards, they must adhere to the standards.

It should be understood that grades describe the minimum quality that is acceptable; therefore, there is a possibility of a difference in quality between lots of the same grade designation.

United States grades of foods do not refer to quality alone, but also grades may indicate weight or size as in the case of eggs which may be graded as "Large," "Medium," and "Small" according to weight. Apples are usually graded not only for quality, but also for size, such as 2 to 2½ inches.

Grades for Fresh Fruits and Vegetables. Although the use of grades for fresh fruits and vegetables is optional, there are now Federal grades in use for 62 different fruits and vegetables, with 102 different standards. In the case of some fresh fruits and vegetables, such as tomatoes, both *shipping grades* and *consumer grades* have been established. United States shipping grades are usually designated as U. S. No. 1, U. S. No. 2, and so forth; whereas consumer grades are designated by letters such as U. S. Grade A and U. S. Grade B.

The official grades for fresh fruits and vegetables have not been commonly used in retail markets; however, with the current practice of packaging in small retail cartons grades are becoming more common. The official government grades vary for some products, but those for potatoes will serve as an example.

  U. S. Fancy   U. S. Commercial
  U. S. Extra No. 1   U. S. No. 2
  U. S. No. 1

Grades for Canned Fruits and Vegetables. In the case of every product there is a definite scale by which the grades are determined. The grade markings do not appear on the labels of all canned fruits, but they do appear on the labels of many. The purchaser has a right to demand canned fruits that have such markings.

The table on this page provides an explanation of the grades for canned fruits. This method of indicating grades is commonly known as the ABC method of grading. Other methods have been established by various associations, canners, and distributors; but there is no particular uniformity among the standards set up under these methods.

GRADE	QUALITY	COLOR	FORM	SIZE	SIRUP WHEN PACKED
A (fancy)	Very best	Very high	Free from blemishes; mature but not overripe	Very uniform and symmetrical	From 40 to 70 per cent sugar, depending on acidity of fruit
B (choice)	Fine	High	Free from blemishes; mature but not overripe	Uniform, symmetrical, usually smaller than A	From 30 to 55 per cent sugar
C (standard)	Good	Reasonably good	Reasonably free from blemishes; reasonably uniform in ripeness	Reasonably uniform and symmetrical	From 14 to 30 per cent sugar, or water pack
Substandard	Second	Below standard	Below standard; not uniform	Below standard; not uniform	Below standard for sirup or water pack

Quality Grades for Canned Fruits

Grades have been established for many canned vegetables such as corn, peas, beans, and tomatoes. The grade designations for canned vegetables are similar to those for canned fruits shown in the foregoing table except that the term "extra standard" is used to explain grade B in the place of the term "choice." Many canners are voluntarily labeling their products according to these designations.

The ABC grading may be used on canned fruits and vegetables in the following manner:

(a) The canner or distributor may do his own grading; but if he does, the grades must meet government standards.
(b) On the payment of a fee, a government grader will check sample lots and award grades for the entire lots, which permits the label to carry the statement "This grade officially certified by the U. S. Department of Agriculture."
(c) On the payment of a fee, an inspector will be stationed in the cannery for continuous inspection of every lot, in which case the label may bear the statement "Packed under continuous inspection of the U. S. Department of Agriculture."

Grades for Poultry, Eggs, and Dairy Products. Poultry being sold in interstate commerce must be graded and also must be processed in plants that are Federally inspected. The inspection mark may be used only on a ready-to-cook bird that has been examined by a Government inspector and passed as wholesome food. This mark denotes wholesomeness only—not grade (quality). It may be used without a grade mark.

The grade mark tells the quality (U. S. Grade A, B, or C), the style of processing (ready to cook), and the kind and class of poultry (for example, stewing chicken, young turkey). It also states that the product has been Government graded or Federal-State graded, and usually gives the number of the processing plant in which the grading was done. A ready-to-cook bird may carry the grade mark only if it also carries the inspection mark denoting wholesomeness.

The inspection mark is always a circle and the grade mark always a shield. The combined grade and inspection mark (a shield within a circle) may be used only on a ready-to-cook bird that has been both graded for quality and in-

Inspection and Grade Marks for Poultry

spected and passed as wholesome food. Processing plants that use the Government poultry grading and inspection services are permitted to use the grade and inspection marks designed by the Department of Agriculture. These official marks are used, under the immediate supervision of official graders or inspectors, on commercial labels. The label may be a metal clip placed on the wing, or a paper tag or sticker, or the label information may be printed on the consumer package.

There are four United States consumer grades for eggs—U. S. Grade AA, U. S. Grade A, U. S. Grade B, and U. S. Grade C. Each grade refers to a specific interior quality, defined by Government standards. Grade AA and Grade A

QUALITY FACTORS	SPECIFICATIONS OF EACH QUALITY FACTOR			
	AA GRADE OR U. S. SPECIAL	A GRADE OR U. S. EXTRA	B GRADE OR U. S. STANDARD	C GRADE OR U. S. TRADE
Shell	Clean; sound; normal.	Clean; sound; normal.	Clean; sound; may be slightly abnormal.	Clean; sound; may be abnormal.
Air cell ...	One-eighth inch or less in depth; regular.	Two-eighths inch or less in depth; regular.	Three-eighths inch or less in depth; may show movement not in excess of one-half inch.	May be over three-eighths inch in depth; may show movement in excess of one-half inch; may be bubbly or free.
Yolk	Well centered; outline indistinct; motion sluggish; free from visible germ development and other defects or blemishes.	Fairly well centered; outline moderately defined; may be slightly mobile; free from visible germ development and practically free from other defects or blemishes.	Outline well defined; may be mobile; may show slightly visible germ development and other definite but not serious defects.	May be plainly visible; may be freely mobile and cast dark shadow; and show clearly visible germ development but no blood; may show other serious defects.
White	Firm; clear.	Firm; clear.	Reasonably firm; clear.	May be weak and watery.

Summary of United States Standards for Eggs

eggs are of top quality. They have a large proportion of thick white which stands up well around a firm high yolk, and are delicate in flavor. Grade B and Grade C eggs are good eggs, though they differ from higher quality eggs in several ways.

Grade standards for milk and cream are based on the bacterial count; the highest grade has the lowest bacterial count. The United States Public Health Service has recommended grade standards for fluid milk. Many of the grade standards enforced by states and cities are similar to the standards established by the Federal Government. The United States Department of Public Health has established grades or tentative grades for several daily products, such as cheese, evaporated milk, dry milk, and ice cream. The highest quality of milk is Grade A.

A Grade Emblem for Butter

Every carton of graded butter is stamped with the shield-shaped emblem of the Federal Butter Grading Service. The grade names "U. S. Grade AA" and "U. S. Grade A" are the quality ratings most often seen on butter cartons in the retail store. For those who prefer a mild, fresh, sweet flavor, Grade AA is tops; Grade A is a very close second.

Grades for Meat. The grade and brand stamps which are affixed to meat and meat products are of two types: (1) the grade or brand names of the individual packers, and (2) the grade names of the United States Department of Agriculture. The official grading and stamping of beef was started in 1927. Later this service was extended to include lamb, mutton and veal.

The United States official grades of meat are described in Chapter 13.

Grade and brand names are applied to meat with a roller stamp which leaves its mark the full length of the carcass, or if cuts are being graded, the full length of the cuts. The marking fluid is similar to that used for the inspection stamp and is harmless.

Government Inspection. Well-trained Federal agents inspect food manufacturing and processing plants to insure wholesomeness of food prepared for human use. Establishments processing meats, poultry, and dairy products must be federally inspected if their products are to enter interstate commerce. Foods that have been federally inspected are stamped or marked in abbreviated form, "U. S. Inspected and Passed." A round stamp is always used on products that have passed federal inspection. The purple stamp is used directly on meats to show that they have passed federal inspection. The number appearing on the stamp indicates the establishment. On processed foods the stamp is printed on the label.

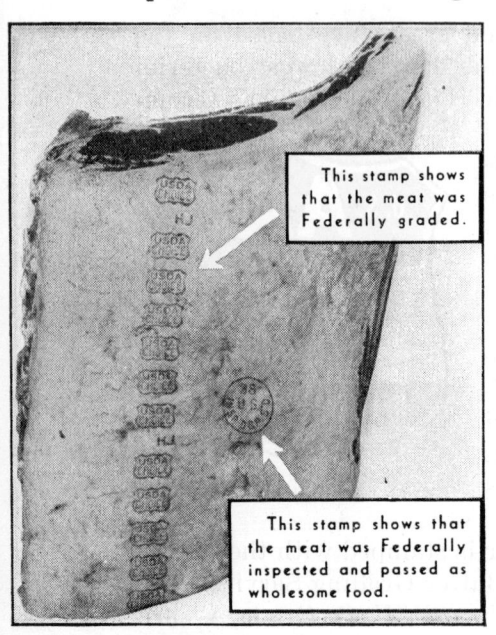

This stamp shows that the meat was Federally graded.

This stamp shows that the meat was Federally inspected and passed as wholesome food.

Graded and Inspected Beef

Informative Labeling. Good informative labels can provide the kind of information one wants and needs for good selection of the commodities we wish to buy. Good labeling should give not only quality standards and grades but also all of of the important facts you, as a consumer, want.

Informative labeling applies to many products, including appliances, clothing, and fabrics. In the case of fabrics, there are various terms used to indicate shrinkage, such as "preshrunk." If this term is used, the fabric should not shrink more than 2 per cent. Other information on fabrics and clothing may indicate the type of fiber used, the weave, the water repellency, the finish, the crease resistance, and other special features. You should learn the descriptive terms that you can depend upon.

U.S. GRADE B — EXTRA STANDARD

Packed under continuous inspection of the U. S. Department of Agriculture.

GRADE B (EXTRA STANDARD) EARLY VARIETY PEAS
This means that they meet the following standards:
1. Reasonably tender.
2. Reasonably uniform in color and size.
3. Surrounded by liquor which may be somewhat cloudy.
4. Reasonably free from skins, broken peas and other defects.
5. Must possess a good pea flavor.

GENERAL DESCRIPTION
Type . . . . Early Variety
Size . . . . No. 4 Sieve
Size of Can . . . . No. 2
Contents . . . . 1 lb. 4 oz.
Servings . . . . 4 to 5
Cups . . . . Approx. 2¼

U.S. GRADE C — STANDARD

Packed under continuous inspection of the U. S. Department of Agriculture.

GRADE C (STANDARD) TOMATOES
This means that they meet the following standards:
1. Small or large pieces.
2. Fairly red in color.
3. Fairly free from defects.
4. Possess a normal tomato flavor.

GENERAL DESCRIPTION
Type . . . . Slightly Salted
Size of Can . . . . No. 2
Contents . . . . 1 lb. 3 oz.
Servings . . . . 4 to 5
Cups . . . . Approx. 2¼

Portions of Labels Showing Both Grade and Description

Industry Standards for Informative Labeling. Some canners and distributors have developed types of labeling that they believe is better for the consumer than the A, B, C, or other grade labeling because it is more descriptive. It is often referred to as descriptive labeling. Descriptive labels for foods, for instance, would contain such information as: (a) style of the pack; (b) degree of maturity of the food; (c) number of units in the can, such as the number of slices of peaches; (d) the quantity in terms of cups if the units are small, such as cherries; (e) the quantity in terms of servings; (f) the size of the can; (g) the description of the raw product and the method of processing; (h) the suggested methods or ways of serving. It will be seen that this type of label has many advantages over the kind used with strictly grade labeling.

Progress in Informative Labeling. It is obvious that the use of fixed grades or general descriptive labels all provide a certain amount of helpful information to the consumer. Various groups of retailers have been active in the development of the so-called informative labeling practice. In developing informative labels, this organization—composed of consumers, producers, and distributors—attempts to find out the kind of information that will be most useful to the consumer in determining quality. The following illustration is the master outline for all such labels. Such labels have now become quite generally used, particularly in the textile field. Many chain stores, large department stores, and mail-order houses are using informative labels.

The National Consumer-Retailer Council suggests several ways by which the consumer can encourage and promote the informative labeling practice as follows:

OUTLINE FOR INFORMATIVE LABELS

It is understood, of course, that labels should conform to local, State or Federal regulations where such exist.

WHAT IT WILL DO (Performance)
Degree of color permanence; shrinkage or stretchage; breaking strength; seam slippage; resistance to water, perspiration, wind, wear; light, heat and power tests; power consumption; cost of upkeep; etc.

WHAT IT IS MADE OF (Composition)
Kind and quality of fiber, metal, wood, leather, ceramics, cement, rock, fur, plastics, petroleum products, rubber, paper, bone, chemicals, drugs; ingredients of food products; etc.

HOW IT IS MADE (Construction)
Size, weight, number of yarns per inch, weave, number of stitches per inch, finish, ply, cut, hand or machine made, pressed, molded, stamped, inlaid; etc.

HOW TO CARE FOR IT
Detailed instructions for washing and/or cleaning; precautions to be observed in cleaning or in storage; refrigeration; oiling and greasing; polishing; etc.

RECOMMENDED USES
Purposes for which it is most suitable; recipes; etc.

NAME OF MANUFACTURER OR DISTRIBUTOR
Name and address of the manufacturer or distributor.

1. Let the label be your guide in buying.

2. Patronize stores that label merchandise well.

3. When you find a label that is helpful, "think out loud" about it:
   (a) Comment on it to the salesperson.
   (b) Write a note to the store president, thus assuring that your recommendation reaches top executives.
   (c) If the label is a manufacturer's label, write him about it.
   (d) If the label is not a good one, comment on it to the manufacturer.

4. File the labels you find helpful. Instructions as to care may be needed throughout the life of the article. When it is necessary to replace the article from which you took the label, you can refer to your label file as a buying guide.

Pepperell Peeress Sheet

An exquisitely smooth percale, made of combed yarns. One of the finest, most luxurious cotton sheets you can buy.

This Pepperell product has been tested and approved by the Better Fabrics Testing Bureau.
PEPPERELL MANUFACTURING COMPANY
Boston, Massachusetts

WHAT IT IS MADE OF
Fibre Content: 100% American Mississippi Delta cotton.

HOW IT IS MADE
Thread count (after bleaching) averages: 202 threads to the square inch—103 lengthwise, 99 crosswise.
Weight averages 3.92 ounces to the square yard.
Finishing materials: less than 1%.

This luxurious sheet is made of the finest cotton yarns, combed to remove short fibres. Only the silkiest, longest fibres are used.
3/8-inch Tape selvage is tightly woven to offer extra protection against cracking and tearing.
4-inch hem at top, 1-inch at bottom. Stitched with small stitches, and the ends firmly caught.
Tellmark tab, in corner of sheet, makes it easy to tell the size without removing sheet from shelf.
Inspected 28 times during manufacture. Samples tested weekly to check quality maintenance.

WHAT SERVICE IT WILL GIVE
Breaking strength: Sheet fabric will withstand a pull of 79 pounds lengthwise, 87 crosswise. (Average figures.)
Shrinkage tests made on the rotary ironer basis show approximately 6% lengthwise and 1.75% crosswise.

This exquisite sheet provides the utmost in sleeping comfort. But the fine yarns and tight weave, which make it so smooth and even-textured, also give it extreme strength and durability.
Its lightness makes it easy to handle, and cheaper to launder at pound rates.

An Informative Label

> ### Summary of Use of Standards, Grades, and Labels
>
> 1. Some standards are measures of size, weight, and distance; others are used to measure quality.
> 2. Most standards of quality define the minimum quality that is satisfactory.
> 3. Many standards for consumers' goods are formulated, adopted, and enforced by the Federal Government.
> 4. States, cities, and trade and technical associations formulate standards that are valuable to consumers.
> 5. Federal standards for foods and drugs apply only to goods sold across state lines.
> 6. Most food grades refer to quality; however, some designate size or weight.
> 7. Foods that grade relatively low may be as sanitary and wholesome as foods that grade high.
> 8. Informative labels give information about standards, grade, content, and other characteristics of goods.
> 9. Consumers should learn what standards and grades mean.

TEXTBOOK QUESTIONS

1. Give at least one good example of why standards are important to you in buying some of the things that you need.
2. What is a grade as applied to a product?
3. What is a label and what information may be found on it?
4. Name some items for which the Federal Food and Drug Administration has established standards?
5. In what way does the Federal Trade Commission enter into the establishing of standards?
6. What is a commercial standard developed through the United States Department of Commerce?
7. What is the significance of the "U. L." label, and on what kinds of products are you most lkely to find it?
8. What is the significance of the "U. S. P." found on some drug products?
9. On what products are you likely to see the letters "N. F." and what do they mean?
10. What do the letters "H. P." mean on a product?
11. Give an example of how standards are converted into grades. Use tomatoes as an example.
12. What is the highest grade of eggs?
13. What are some of the helpful items that might be found on a good descriptive label on a food product?

DISCUSSION QUESTIONS

1. Distinguish between a standard and a grade.
2. Name some grades and descriptions of products that you have seen which have meant nothing to you.
3. Let us suppose that a standard is set by an industry and one member of that industry does not choose to meet this standard. Is there anything that can be done about it?
4. Explain how standards developed by industry through the United States Department of Commerce may be of some help to consumers.
5. Name some articles on which you have found the "U. S. P." standard on the label.
6. Can a canner or a distributor sell any food product that is below standard?
7. How would you attempt to take advantage of Federal grades in buying potatoes?
8. Discuss some of the advantages and disadvantages of the ABC labeling advocated by the Federal Government.
9. Give some of the arguments for and against informative or descriptive labeling without fixed standards for grades.
10. State your final opinion and summary of the question of the use of fixed grades as compared with descriptive labels without grades. What would be your choice?

PROBLEMS

1. Make a list of the food, medical, and clothing products in your home on which you find indicated any of the standards or grades described in this chapter. If you find any other grades that are not mentioned in this chapter, list these.
2. Give your own description of an ideal food label, either by a list of information it should contain or draw a model.
3. Present your idea of an ideal clothing label either by making a list of information it should contain or draw a model.

COMMUNITY PROBLEMS AND PROJECTS

1. From any product purchased recently in your home obtain a label that you think is helpful or not helpful as a guide to you in buying. Describe the information on the label that you think is helpful to you and the information that is either not helpful or the lack of information that you feel is needed.
2. File for future reference all labels that you find helpful. Paste these up in the form of a scrapbook with divisions for different classes of products, such as foods, clothing, drugs, furniture, and other items. At a time fixed by your teacher, submit this scrapbook for grading.

Chapter 12

Getting the Most for Your Food Dollar

> **Purpose of the Chapter.** The average family spends a greater percentage of its income for food than for any other commodity or service. No other factor has greater influence on our health, energy, and achievement than the food we consume. Therefore, the wise buying of food to provide for good nutrition within the limits of one's budget is one of the consumer's most important problems. The purpose of this chapter is to help you get the most for the money you spend for food.
>
> You will find answers to these questions:
> 1. What is involved in food management?
> 2. What functions do the various types of food have?
> 3. In what items of food are the principal food nutrients found?
> 4. What constitutes an adequate diet in content? in amount?
> 5. What practices help you get the most for your food dollar?

Food Management. Although the standard of living in America is high and the average American consumes more food than the average person in any other country, it is estimated that approximately one half of the families in the United States do not have good diets and satisfactory nutrition. This condition is not due to lack of available food, for our warehouses and storage bins contain enough food to feed many of the people of the world. Further, it is not due to insufficient family income, for families not having income for adequate food requirements comprise only a small percentage of the total; and most of these families can obtain financial assistance for food by applying to appropriate welfare and government agencies.

Poor diets and inadequate nutrition in most instances are due to a lack of knowledge about foods and their functions and about nutritional needs. This knowledge is essential for good food management which involves careful and deliberate planning, buying, preparing, and serving of foods. Wise *food management* means that the homemaker will plan the buying, preparing, and serving of food to: (1) provide ample amounts of the basic food nutrients the individual members of the family need—proteins, vitamins, and minerals; (2) supply the calories to meet individual requirements for growth and energy; (3) look good and stimulate appetite; and (4) fit the family budget.

Thus wise food management requires that one should know many things about nutrition requirements, foods and their functions, and preparation and serving foods. One also should know how to judge quality and price of food materials; about markets, grades, labels and protective regulations that insure uncontaminated and wholesome food. In this chapter and the one following we are studying primarily how to control the food dollar; that is, the economic aspect of food management. Courses in nutrition, food selection and preparation, and other aspects of food management are available in many high schools and colleges. Many helpful books and pamphlets on all aspects of food management are available for people who wish to study at home.

Spending the Food Dollar. The problem of acquiring sufficient quantities of the proper types of food is not difficult for families with adequate incomes. The only problem for such families is buying the proper food. A family with a moderate, a minimum, or a restricted income, however, must attempt to get the greatest maximum food values out of every food dollar that is spent. In getting the maximum value out of every food dollar, two cautions should be observed. First, the foods provided daily for the family must include the principal food nutrients needed by the human

> **Guides to Getting the Most for Your Food Dollar**
>
> 1. Plan the family food ahead—a week if possible, thus avoiding haphazard day-to-day buying.
> 2. Shop for the best buys in several stores, prices vary.
> 3. Find the best hour of the day and best days of the week to shop for fresh fruits and vegetables in your locality.
> 4. Buy staple foods in as large quantity as your storage space permits—prices often are less by the dozen or the case.
> 5. Select the most economical food items that will provide the principal food nutrients needed by the body.
> 6. Read weights on labels of cans and packages to compare costs.
> 7. Analyze critically "premiums" and so-called "food purchase plans" before buying.
> 8. Select the grade of food that is suitable for the method of preparation and serving you intend using.
> 9. Buy fruits and vegetables in season.
> 10. Watch for sales and week-end specials.
> 11. Remember that home prepared and home cooked foods cost less than those that are preprocessed and prepared.
> 12. Avoid waste by proper storage to prevent spoilage.
> 13. Learn to prepare food in a way to preserve maximum food values.
> 14. Learn to serve leftovers in a variety of attractive ways.

body. Second, the total food provided must be adequate in amount for all members of the family.

Families having restricted food budgets can reduce food costs by observing the practices listed under guides to getting the most for the food dollar.

Types of Foods. From the point of view of nutrition, there are three types of foods, as follows: (a) foods that provide fuels or energy for the body, which include *carbohydrates* and *fats*; (b) body-building foods, which are *proteins*; and (c) the regulatory foods, which include those that furnish *minerals, vitamins,* and the proper amount of bulk and water in the daily diet. Most of the things we eat contain a combination of these three types of foods.

Ch. 12]   GETTING THE MOST FOR YOUR FOOD DOLLAR   209

Since the human body needs some of each of the three types of foods daily for good nutrition, it is essential that the particular items of food we eat during a day should be selected to contain carbohydrates and fats, proteins, and minerals and vitamins. After careful study the United States Department of Agriculture and the National Research Council classified common items of food into seven groups known as the *Basic Seven Food Groups.* Some items of food should be selected daily from each of these seven groups. This will assure one of getting the basic nutrients his body needs in ample amounts for good health. The chart below lists the food items in each group and gives suggestions as to the amount of each that may be needed for an adequate diet.

GROUP ONE
GREEN AND YELLOW VEGETABLES...
some raw —
some cooked,
frozen or canned

GROUP TWO
ORANGES, TOMATOES, GRAPEFRUIT...
or raw cabbage or salad greens

GROUP THREE
POTATOES AND OTHER VEGETABLES AND FRUITS
raw, dried, cooked, frozen or canned

GROUP FOUR
MILK AND MILK PRODUCTS...
fluid, evaporated, dried milk, or cheese

GROUP FIVE
MEAT, POULTRY, FISH, OR EGGS...
or dried beans, peas, nuts, or peanut butter

GROUP SIX
BREAD, FLOUR, AND CEREALS...
Natural whole-grain
or enriched
or restored

GROUP SEVEN
BUTTER AND FORTIFIED MARGARINE
(with added Vitamin A)

★ U.S. NEEDS US STRONG ★
EAT THE BASIC 7 EVERY DAY

"United States Government Chart based on recommended dietary allowances established by the Food and Nutrition Board of the National Research Council."

7 Basic Food Groups Needed Every Day

What Functions Do Foods Perform? Each type of food has a definite function to perform in the human body. Since the body is a human machine, it must have fuel to provide energy just as any other machine has to have fuel. The carbohydrates and fats provide fuel for heat and energy. A *calorie* is a unit by which fuel energy is measured.

Since proteins are the body builders, we need them to build muscles and tissues and to take care of the necessary repairs of the body. Our blood, our hair, our nails, and all parts of our body require proteins for building and maintenance. Without sufficient proteins, children would stop growing normally. Their muscles would become soft and many of their organs would fail to function normally.

The most important regulatory foods may be roughly classified as (a) minerals and (b) vitamins. Of course, the body must take in a certain amount of bulk foods and water, but the bulk may be provided by any one of the types of food. There is usually no problem in taking water into the body because, besides the liquids that one drinks, water is taken into the body through many foods. For instance, a high percentage of fresh fruits and vegetables is water. Likewise, a high percentage of meat is water.

The most important minerals from a body-building and maintenance point of view are calcium and iron. *Calcium* builds bone and teeth and helps to keep one in good physical condition. *Iron* is an important part of our blood and must be constantly provided through food. Iron serves to build and maintain vigor. Lack of iron causes people to tire easily.

Probably the third most important mineral is *phosphorus*, although *copper* is also considered essential in small amounts. *Iodine* and other less important minerals are considered essential in small amounts. They all have a general regulatory effect on the body.

There are many types of known vitamins, and new ones are being identified by science. The principal vitamins, however, are: Vitamin A; Vitamin B_1 (thiamine); Vitamin B_2 (riboflavin or Vitamin G); Vitamin C (ascorbic acid); Vitamin D; and niacin.

Vitamin A is especially important for normal growth of children, and it is needed by adults to keep their eyes, skin, and body linings in a healthy condition. Some of the indications of the lack of Vitamin A are night blindness and lack of resistance to colds, sore throat, and pneumonia.

Vitamin B_1 is also important to help in the normal growth of children. It contributes to a good appetite and calm nerves. It assists the body in digesting sugars and starches. A lack of the proper quantity of Vitamin B_1 sometimes causes a poor appetite and nervous ailments.

Vitamin B_2 assists the body in using the fats and carbohydrates and helps the body to use the oxygen carried through the blood. A lack of Vitamin B_2 sometimes causes skin disorders and other discomforts and low vitality.

Vitamin C strengthens the muscles and teeth and is a safeguard against infections. Sometimes a lack of Vitamin C in the body is made evident by bleeding gums, aching joints, and a general feeling of discomfort. The absence of the proper supply of Vitamin C in one's system will eventually cause scurvy, which is a dread disease of people who have inadequate diets of fresh fruits and vegetables.

Vitamin D is the sunshine vitamin. It is absorbed through the skin from the sun's rays and may be taken internally through certain foods. It helps our bodies to assimilate calcium and phosphorus, which are so necessary to the well-being of our bones and teeth. It is therefore especially important to children, but adults also need it. One of the most common results of Vitamin D deficiency on the part of children is the serious disease of rickets.

Niacin is similar to Vitamin B_1 in that it helps to keep our nerves, skin, and digestion in a healthy condition. A prolonged absence of niacin in the diet will eventually cause the serious disease of pellagra.

Other less common vitamins have been identified or partially identified by scientists. Vitamins, other than those obtained in food, should be used only on the advice of physicians.

A study of the chart on page 212 will give you the functions and sources of the major nutrients needed daily.

PRINCIPAL FOOD NUTRIENTS, THEIR FUNCTIONS AND MAJOR SOURCES

NUTRIENT	FUNCTION	SOME IMPORTANT SOURCES
Carbohydrates	Chief source of energy. Aids in metabolism of other foods.	Sugars, cereals, starchy vegetables, fibrous vegetables.
Fats	Source of energy. Aids in use of some other foods. Insulative material for muscles and other body tissues.	Butter, margarine, vegetable oils, lard, and other animal fats.
Protein	Yields energy. Builds and repairs body tissues.	Meat, cheese, milk, eggs, poultry, enriched, restored and whole grain bread, flour and cereals, dried peas and beans, fish, lima beans, and nuts.
Vitamin A	Needed for growth, normal vision and to protect the body from infection.	Liver, sweet potatoes, citrus fruits, leafy, green and yellow vegetables, butter or margarine, egg yolk, whole milk, red salmon, yellow and red fruits, nuts, and cheese.
Thiamine (Vitamin B_1)	Essential to growth, good appetite and healthy nerves. Helps make energy value of foods available.	Lean pork, liver, dried peas and beans, enriched restored and whole grain bread, flour and cereals, other meats, eggs, green peas, potatoes, poultry, and fish.
Riboflavin (Vitamin B_2)	Essential to growth. Helps body use protein in building new cells.	Milk, liver and other variety meats, lean meats, eggs, enriched, restored and whole grain bread, flour and cereals, leafy, green vegetables, dried fruits, nuts, green peas, and beans.
Niacin	Essential to utilization of protein and to healthy skin. Helps prevent and cure pellegra.	Liver, fish, lean meats, poultry, enriched, restored and whole grain bread, flour and cereals, eggs, green vegetables, nuts, and potatoes.
Vitamin C (Ascorbic Acid)	Assists in the development of bones and teeth, body tissues and blood. Prevents and cures scurvy.	Citrus fruits, tomatoes, cabbage, green, leafy vegetables, cantaloupe, potatoes, berries, green pepper, cauliflower, pineapple, and turnips.
Vitamin D	Helps body use calcium and phosphorus in building strong bones and teeth. Helps prevent and cure rickets.	Vitamin D irradiated milk, red salmon, eggs, oily fish, liver, butter or fortified margarine.
Iron	Helps form hemoglobin necessary for red blood cells. Helps prevent nutritional anemia.	Liver, lean meats, shell fish, dried beans and peas, green, leafy vegetables, enriched, restored and whole grain bread, flour and cereals, eggs, and dried fruits.
Calcium	Helps build strong bones and teeth. Aids in clotting of blood. Necessary to the proper functioning of nerves and muscles.	Milk, leafy, green vegetables, shell fish, cheese, molasses, dried fruits, dried peas and beans, eggs, enriched, and whole grain bread, flour and cereals.

Ch. 12]

How Much of Each Food Do We Need? An adequate daily diet is comprised of a selection of foods including one or more from each of the Basic Seven Food Groups to supply enough of the food nutrients necessary for growth and vigorous health. One's diet should be checked frequently in order to see if it is adequate in respect to all of the essential food nutrients.

Assuming that the items of food we select include some from each of the Basic Seven Food Groups, the next question is what quantity of food should we eat. The energy produced by foods is measured

A NUTRIENT YARDSTICK

	MAN MODERATELY ACTIVE	WOMAN ACTIVE	BOY 13-17 YEARS	CHILD 4-6 YEARS
CALORIES	3,000	2,500	3,200	1,600
PROTEIN IN GRAMS	70	60	85	50
CALCIUM IN GRAMS	0.8	0.8	1.4	1.0
IRON IN MILLIGRAMS	12	12	15	8
VITAMIN A IN INTERNAT. UNITS	5,000	5,000	5,000	2,500
VITAMIN B$_1$ (THIAMINE) IN MILLIGRAMS	1.8	1.5	1.6	8
VITAMIN B$_2$ (RIBOFLAVIN) IN MILLIGRAMS	2.7	2.2	2.4	1.2
NIACIN IN MILLIGRAMS	18	15	16	8
VITAMIN C (ASCORBIC ACID) IN MILLIGRAMS	75	70	90	50

GRAPHIC ASSOCIATES FOR PUBLIC AFFAIRS COMMITTEE, INC.

Food Requirements of Adults and Children

by calories. The calories are consumed in keeping the body warm and in furnishing energy for muscular activity and body processes such as circulation, digestion, and respiration. If we eat more calories than are needed for body repair and physical activity, the surplus will be stored and we probably will increase in weight. A person becomes overweight because the total of the calories in his diet is greater than the calories he needed to furnish heat, body repair, and energy for physical activity.

The number of calories needed daily varies with age, sex, and amount of activity. The chart above will give you the approximate amounts of food needed by people of different ages. A child one year old needs approximately 1,200 calories to provide for growth and energy for activity. The number of calories required increases both for boys and girls while growing, then drops back unless they do heavy labor or engage in a great amount of other physical activity. A man doing heavy work and a football player during heavy practice or playing season may use as many as 4,500 to 5,000 calories a day.

	Breakfast	Lunch	Dinner
LIGHT	FRUIT — orange, grapefruit, or tomato juice BREADS—enriched or whole grain, with butter or Vitamin A margarine OR CEREAL—whole grain or restored—with whole milk BEVERAGE—coffee for adults —milk for children	NUTRITIOUS SOUP—cream soup or vegetable soup, for instance SALAD—fruit or vegetable OR DESSERT—fruit BREADS—enriched or whole grain, with butter or Vitamin A margarine BEVERAGE—milk, in greater quantities for children	PROTEIN FOOD, such as meat, fish, fowl, eggs, cheese, dried beans, soybeans, etc. VEGETABLES—yellow or green, at least one of each every day. Use raw frequently SALAD—fruit or vegetable OR DESSERT—fruit BREADS—enriched or whole grain, with butter or Vitamin A margarine BEVERAGE—milk and coffee or tea
MEDIUM	FRUIT — orange, grapefruit, or tomato juice BREADS—enriched or whole grain, with butter or Vitamin A margarine OR CEREAL—whole grain or restored—with whole milk EGGS—or some other protein food BEVERAGE—coffee for adults —milk for children	VEGETABLE PLATE, with yellow or green vegetables OR SALAD—fruit or vegetable BREADS—enriched or whole grain, with butter or Vitamin A margarine DESSERT—fruit, pudding, or some other simple dessert BEVERAGE—milk	PROTEIN FOOD, such as meat, fish, fowl, eggs, cheese, dried beans, soybeans, etc. VEGETABLES — one cooked, one or more raw, perhaps as a salad BREADS—enriched or whole grain, with butter or Vitamin A margarine DESSERT—fruit, custard or pudding, or some other simple dessert BEVERAGE—milk and coffee or tea
HEAVY	FRUIT—orange, grapefruit or tomato juice BREADS — enriched or whole grain, with butter or Vitamin A margarine CEREAL—whole grain or restored—with whole milk EGGS—or some other protein food BEVERAGE—coffee or milk	PROTEIN FOOD, such as fish, eggs, cheese, dried peas or beans, soybeans, peanut butter VEGETABLE—yellow or green OR SALAD — fruit or vegetable BREADS — enriched or whole grain, with butter or Vitamin A margarine DESSERT — fruit, or some simple dessert BEVERAGE—milk	PROTEIN FOOD, such as meat, fish, fowl, eggs, cheese, dried beans, soybeans, etc. VEGETABLES—at least two cooked vegetables, one yellow or green SALAD—fruit or vegetable BREADS — enriched or whole grain, with butter or Vitamin A margarine DESSERT — fruit, custard, pudding, or other simple dessert BEVERAGE—milk and coffee or tea

Home Economics Institute
Westinghouse Electric and Manufacturing Co.

Menus for Different Types of People

Examples of a Balanced Diet. The final goal of this chapter is to present for study some satisfactory meals that are appetizing and adequate. The table on the previous page shows how three meals a day can be planned from these various food sources to provide for light, medium, and heavy diets. A person working at a desk or doing other light work should use a light diet. A person on his feet and reasonably active daily should use a medium diet. A person who follows an active life, such as a factory worker or a farmer, will require a heavy diet.

Summary of Principles and Practices Underlying the Economical Use of the Food Dollar

1. Food management requires knowledge of foods and their functions and ability to plan, buy, prepare and serve food.
2. Good practices as to planning, buying, preparing, and serving of foods will aid in getting the most value from the food dollar.
3. Carbohydrates and fats, proteins, and minerals and vitamins must be supplied by food to keep the body going.
4. Everyone needs one or more items of food daily selected from each of seven basic groups of foods to insure proper nutrition.
5. The principal food nutrients required daily by the body should not be sacrificed in economizing on the food budget.
6. The amount of food needed varies with sex, age, and physical activity.

TEXTBOOK QUESTIONS

1. What are the objects of wise food management?
2. Name at least two ways to get the most for your food dollar.
3. Name the three different types or classes of foods as to functions.
4. What are the functions of the three main types or classes of foods?
5. (a) What is the function of Vitamin A? (b) What are some of the indications of a deficiency?
6. (a) What is the function of Vitamin B_1? (b) What are some of the indications of a deficiency?
7. (a) What is the function of Vitamin C? (b) What are some of the indications of a deficiency?

8. What are some of the important sources of carbohydrates?
9. What are some of the important sources of proteins?
10. Name the basic seven food groups.
11. About how many calories does a child one year old need; how many does an active working man or a football player need?
12. Give an example of a recommended light breakfast.

DISCUSSION QUESTIONS

1. If you are seeking an energy food, what kind of food will you need and from what source can it best be obtained?
2. If you are susceptible to colds and sore throat, what kind of vitamin may help you and from what natural food sources can it best be obtained?
3. If one has a poor appetite and is nervous, giving an indication of a deficiency of a certain vitamin, what vitamin is it and from what source can it best be obtained?
4. On the basis of food and vitamin requirements, what particular foods would you strongly recommend for children?
5. Many primitive people have strong bones and teeth. Can you give any possible reason for this fact?
6. Why does a factory worker need more calories than an office worker?
7. Can you give any reasons why manual workers usually require considerable meat?
8. Why do women usually avoid diets high in calories?

PROBLEMS

1. Suggest a diet for a child of a certain specified age.
2. On the basis of the general suggestions for a lunch for a heavy diet of an active worker, plan a specific lunch menu.
3. Plan a dinner menu that you think is appropriate for a woman office worker who sits at a desk each day. Give reasons for your selections.

COMMUNITY PROBLEMS AND PROJECTS

1. Keep a record of what you eat for an entire week without discussing the matter with your parents. Estimate the quantities that you eat. Then, on the basis of the facts you have studied in this chapter, determine whether you have been following a balanced diet.
2. On the basis of the menu given for a dinner for a medium diet in this chapter, prepare a menu indicating the quantities of each food needed and the cost for a family of two adults and one child of high school age.

Chapter 13

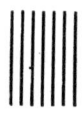

How to Buy Foods

> **Purpose of the Chapter.** In the preceding chapter you learned about food management, the kinds and functions of foods in nourishing the human body, and general guides to observe in getting the most out of your food dollar. The next step is to learn some of the more specific guides that may be helpful in buying the foods we need. In the space of a single chapter it is not possible to make a detailed study of the principles to be observed in buying all kinds of foods; therefore, our discussion will be confined to some of the more important items, which will be used as examples.
>
> You will find answers to these questions:
>
> 1. What is the importance to the consumer of labels and of United States food grades?
> 2. By what general characteristics may the quality of canned fruits and vegetables be judged?
> 3. What guides should be observed in buying canned goods?
> 4. How may the quality of meats, poultry, dairy products, and eggs be judged?
> 5. What are the essential points to look for and avoid in buying fresh fruits and vegetables?

United States Grades Indicate Quality of Food. Three important factors for consideration in buying foods for personal and family use are: (1) the wholesomeness or fitness of the food for human use; (2) assuming the food is wholesome, its quality or suitableness for different uses sometimes indicated by United States grade; and (3) cost of each grade in relation to the food budget.

Federal regulations assure us that foods sold and delivered across state lines are wholesome and suitable for human use. It would be also to the interest of consumers if each state had similar regulations for all food produced and sold within it.

Wholesome food may have several qualities. For example, there may be three or four qualities or grades of meat such as beef, each of which is entirely suitable for human use, but one of which is intended for stewing, another for roasting, and some suitable for other methods of preparation. There may be a wide range in the cost of the different qualities or grades. Qualities of some foods are indicated by grades, which are developed by the Federal Government. Grading is voluntary on the part of the producer or packer. Therefore, the problem of the consumer in buying is finding foods that are graded. Consumers should urge stores to carry both fresh and packaged foods that are Federally graded or graded on a similar standard by the state. Encouragement should be given to all food producers and processors to have their products graded. There is no better assurance of quality than a Federal grade stamp on food.

Consumers should not be misled by such designations as Extra Special, Exquisite, Superb, Supreme, Superior, Our Best, or any other designation that has no recognized meaning. These terms are used presumably to indicate quality by some producers and processors of foods who do not have their products graded according to United States Government standards.

In order to have the ability to buy foods wisely, whether fresh or packaged, one must have a good knowledge of food standards and must understand United States grades for the various types of fresh and packaged foods. One also should have the ability to judge the freshness and quality.

The Label Is Your Guide. The law requires that on the labels of all canned foods sold in interstate commerce the following information shall be given:

1. The legal name of the product.
2. The net contents in weight or fluid measure, depending upon the nature of the product.
3. The name and address of the manufacturer, packer, or distributor.

Although the Federal ABC grading is not mandatory on foods going into interstate commerce, there is certain information designated for various types of foods that is mandatory for descriptive purposes on the label of canned goods that are sold and delivered across state lines. For example, the style of pack of asparagus must be indicated as follows:

"Spears" or "Stalks"—3¾ inches or more of the upper end of the sprout.

"Peeled Spears" or "Peeled Stalks"—3¾ inches or more of the upper end of the sprout, peeled before canning.

"Tips"—Not less than 2¾ inches but less than 3¾ inches of the upper end.

"Points"—Less than 2¾ inches of the upper end.

In the case of green and wax beans, it is mandatory to indicate the style of pack as to whether it is whole, cut, or sliced lengthwise (shoestring, French style, or julienne). The style of pack must be indicated for nearly every fruit or vegetable. In addition, it is mandatory to indicate the variety of such foods as peas, peaches, and cherries, and to indicate the type of syrup for fruits. In order to buy intelligently, therefore, one must know something about the style of pack, the varieties of fruits and vegetables, and the standards for syrup.

Voluntary Labeling Information. It has been contended by the Labeling Committee of the National Canners Association that Federal grades are not sufficient in themselves because they are not completely informative. This committee has therefore set up for the industry a voluntary labeling practice that every member of the industry is requested to follow. The following are the five requirements of this labeling practice:

1. The terms must be simple and understandable by ordinary people, for when so, the label is self-explanatory.
2. The terms must be specific. Generalizations permit too much latitude in use and allow too much variation in consumer interpretation.
3. The terms must be standardized and used alike by all canners and distributors.

4. The terms must be readily enforceable under the misbranding section of the Food, Drug, and Cosmetic Act.
5. In order to achieve the third and fourth points, the terms must be based upon objective definitions and standards.

As a result of these recommendations, many canners now use modern descriptive labels giving such helpful information as variety, style of pack (whole, sliced, etc.), the amount of food in the container in cupfuls or number of pieces, consistency, tenderness, and recipes and suggestions for serving.

Form of Label Recommended by Home Economics Division, National Canners Association

An example of a label form recommended by the Home Economics Division of the National Canners Association illustrating mandatory and voluntary information for descriptive labeling is shown above.

Determining the Quality of Canned Foods. The average buyer of canned foods finds it difficult to rely upon his own judgment in determining quality. Some large buyers of canned foods employ experts to perform this function for them. Nevertheless, a person has an opportunity to determine quality largely by comparison.

There are positive characteristics that distinguish quality, and there are negative characteristics that distinguish lack of quality. These simple observations can be made at home. In trying to identify brands that are of a good quality, it is desirable to try different brands until adequate comparisons can be made. Some of the characteristics to observe when evaluating the quality of canned fruits and vegetables are listed below.

Quality Characteristics of Canned Fruits and Vegetables

Positive Characteristics

1. Fullness of can
2. Gross weight of contents
3. Volume of juice
4. Weight of juice
5. Net weight of food
6. Absence of defects
7. Clearness of liquor or juice
8. Character of liquor or juice
9. Color of food
10. Consistency
11. Crispness
12. Flavor
13. Aroma or odor
14. Maturity
15. Percentage of whole food
16. Tenderness
17. Uniformity of size
18. Uniformity of color
19. Nature of blemishes
20. Units per can

Negative Characteristics

1. Lack of uniformity in size
2. Lack of uniformity in texture
3. Overmaturity
4. Undermaturity
5. Discolored liquor
6. Too much liquid
7. Poor color
8. Broken pieces
9. Poor flavor
10. Foreign particles

The price of canned foods does not always indicate quality. When the contents of cans of foods are evaluated, it is sometimes found that those costing the most are average or below in quality, and conversely that those having an average or below cost sometimes are found to be of very good quality. Often, price and quality go together, but one should observe the quality of canned goods he has purchased to serve as a guide for future purchases.

Sizes of Cans. When canned goods are bought, the size of the can and the quality of the contents must be considered. There is so much variation in the sizes of cans that the buyer should familiarize himself with them. Over 80 per cent of the fruits, vegetables, and juices that are packed is in the nine sizes of cans listed below.

NUMBER OR NAME OF CAN	AVERAGE NET WEIGHT	APPROXIMATE CUPFULS
Buffet or Picnic	8 oz. or 7¾ fl. oz.	1
No. 1	10½ oz.	1⅓
No. 300	16 oz.	1¾
No. 1 tall	16 oz. or 15 fl. oz.	2
No. 303	16 oz.	2
No. 2	20 oz. or 1 pt. 2 fl. oz.	2½
No. 2½	29 oz.	3½
No. 3 cylinder	46 oz. or 1 qt. 14 fl. oz.	5¾
No. 10	6 lb., 9 oz. or 3 qt.	12

Contents of Cans of Various Sizes

The average weight of content and the number of cupfuls are based upon the average standard fill. There is always a certain amount of open space in a can. The exact weight will vary according to different kinds of fruits and vegetables because they do not have the same density.

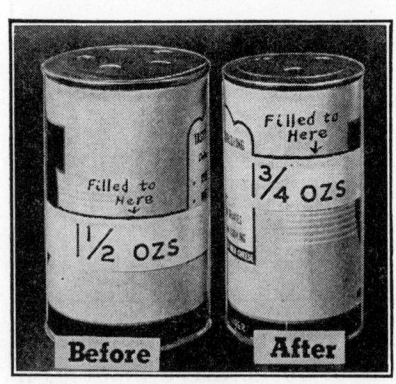

Some foods may be advertised at "three cans for 35 cents." This statement does not mean anything unless one knows the exact size of the can. If a can appears not to be of standard size, compare it with a standard can.

Food and Drug Administration

Consider the Contents, Not the Size of the Can—an Example of How the Food and Drug Administration Required a Producer to Avoid Deception in the Size of the Container

A Careful Buyer Reads All Labels

Ewing Galloway

Usually the larger the can, the less one pays proportionately for the quantity of goods bought. For instance, if a person buys a vegetable in No. 2 cans, he probably pays from two to four cents a pound less than if he bought the same food in No. 1 cans. If he buys fruit in No. 2½ cans, he probably pays three or four cents a pound less than if he bought the same fruit in No. 1 cans.

Guides in Buying Canned Goods. Depend to some extent upon a brand that you have learned gives you the quality and value that you expect for a particular purpose. If you buy a new brand, make some evaluation to determine its quality and value.

Note whether the label bears any indication of government standards or failure to meet government standards.

Read the labels carefully. Note the designation of size, weight, and grade, and any descriptive or informative terms used. Compare the product with other similar products to determine value.

Evaluate the cost by comparing the product with two or more similar ones after the specifications of each product have been determined.

Shop in more than one place, and compare products at home. Learn where the best values can be obtained.

Determine how much canned food should be bought at a time. If your requirements at any one time can be filled by one large can, do not buy two small ones, for the cost in the latter case will be greater. The size of package for greatest economy should be considered. In a comparison of purchases made in the same stores on the same days over a period of two years, the saving that resulted from buying in large packages ranged from 8 to 38 per cent, depending upon the quantity purchased and the difference in size of the packages.

If your budget will permit the purchase of a number of cans at one time, buy at special sales in dozen lots or in case lots.

Watch the appearance of the can. If the can is dirty, discolored, or rusty, examine it carefully. If the can has a small hole in it, do not accept it. If the ends are flat or

---

Summary of Guides for Buying Canned Foods

For Quality:
1. Learn brands of high quality by comparison.
2. Check the labels for standards.
3. Check labels for seals of approval.
4. Check the labels for informative descriptions.
5. Compare the costs.
6. Shop in more than one place.
7. Buy in economical amounts.
8. Select the quality and grade to fit your particular needs.
9. Watch for damaged containers.
10. Return food in original container if it is unsatisfactory.

For Personal Preference:
1. Look for the variety.
2. Look for the style.
3. Look for the sizes.
4. Look for the seasoning.
5. Look for the kind of syrup in the case of fruits.

slightly drawn in, but there is no noticeable flaw, the can is probably all right. If the ends are bulged, however, or if one end bulges out when the other is pressed, the food has probably spoiled.

When the can is opened, note the condition of the food and observe whether the quality is what you expected. If there is any doubt as to whether the food is good, return it to the merchant as soon as possible.

Decide what use you wish to make of the food. Lower grades of canned foods are often suitable for combination dishes, whereas the better grades may be more desirable for other purposes.

Methods of Packing and Packaging. All canned foods that are cooked have a partial vacuum in the open space in the can. This is accomplished by heating the food to expand it and drive out the air. The full can is then sealed and sterilized. When it cools, the can then has an empty space.

The so-called *vacuum packing* now used in the food industry indicates that the can is filled and sealed with a special sealing machine with a vacuum attachment that withdraws the air without heating. The can is then sterilized as in the regular process. Since air in contact with the food causes it to deteriorate or will eventually change its flavor, vacuum packing for such items as coffee, peanuts, and other similar items will preserve these for a much longer time than if they were in packages that admit air.

Another vacuum method in which transparent plastic bags or envelopes instead of cans are used is now utilized for packing commodities, such as luncheon meats, in which loss of moisture impairs both appearance and quality. Although the package is sealed, perishable goods packed by this method must be refrigerated.

Most foods except fresh fruits and vegetables are packaged before displaying them for sale. Some are packaged by the manufacturer or producer and others by the retailer. Some vegetables and fruits also are prepackaged. Likewise, meats, fish, and poultry are prepackaged in many of the modern food stores. Packaged goods have the advantage of greater sanitation, convenience, and identification.

Buying Frozen Foods. Many fruits, vegetables, and meats are available in frozen, packaged form. They are easy to use and can be economical too. Goods must be frozen quickly and stored at zero degrees Fahrenheit for best results. Some families have home freezers; others rent locker space in a frozen food storage plant. The ordinary home refrigerator is unsatisfactory for keeping frozen foods except for short periods of time in the ice-making section of the refrigerator. Meats ordinarily should not be stored in the home refrigerator for more than a week and other foods no longer than two weeks.

Most frozen fruits and vegetables that are available in stores were of good quality when frozen. However, fruits and vegetables lose flavor, color, and nutritional value when frozen, especially if kept too long. It is a good practice to plan so that frozen foods will be used within a few months. Ordinarily no frozen food should be stored in your freezer for more than a year.

For greatest economy foods should be purchased for freezing when they are in season and the price the lowest. Meats may be bought in large pieces as they come from the packing house at a saving over buying in small quantities; however, the large pieces will include all cuts of meat, some of which your family may not like as well as other cuts.

Packaged frozen foods may at times be available in quantities at a discount or on special sale. Such purchases are economical only if the food will be used before it deteriorates in flavor and food value.

How to Judge the Quality of Meat. Packers are not required to have their meat graded by the United States Department of Agriculture. The grading of meat is therefore entirely voluntary on their part. If consumers are not obtaining graded meat, however, they have the privilege of indicating a preference for it from local dealers. If graded meat is demanded, packers will be more likely to furnish this service.

The United States official grades, in their respective order for the different kinds of meat, are:

BEEF	VEAL	LAMB	MUTTON
Prime	Prime	Prime	
Choice	Choice	Choice	Choice
Good	Good	Good	Good
Commercial	Commercial		
Utility	Utility	Utility	Utility
Cutter	Cull	Cull	Cull
Canner			

Government graded meat from a locally inspected establishment is marked "Prime," "Choice," etc., while government graded meat from a federally inspected plant is marked "U. S. Prime," "U. S. Choice," etc.

Many packers have their own grade names, usually referred to as *brand names*, to designate the different grades of meat they are selling. Some of these brands closely parallel the government grades.

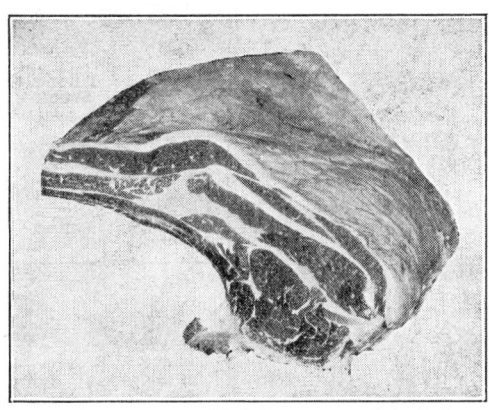

Good Beef Has a Marbled Appearance

U. S. Department of Agriculture

The consumer should remember that government inspection of meat is not grading of meat. While inspection is mandatory for all meat coming from plants that sell in interstate commerce, the grading is voluntary. Meat inspection was discussed in Chapter 11.

The food value of meat is not measured by its price. Many lower priced cuts are highly nutritious. The real cost of meat is measured by the cost per pound of an edible portion. You should know the various cuts and kinds of

Meat Cuts and How to Cook Them
BEEF CHART

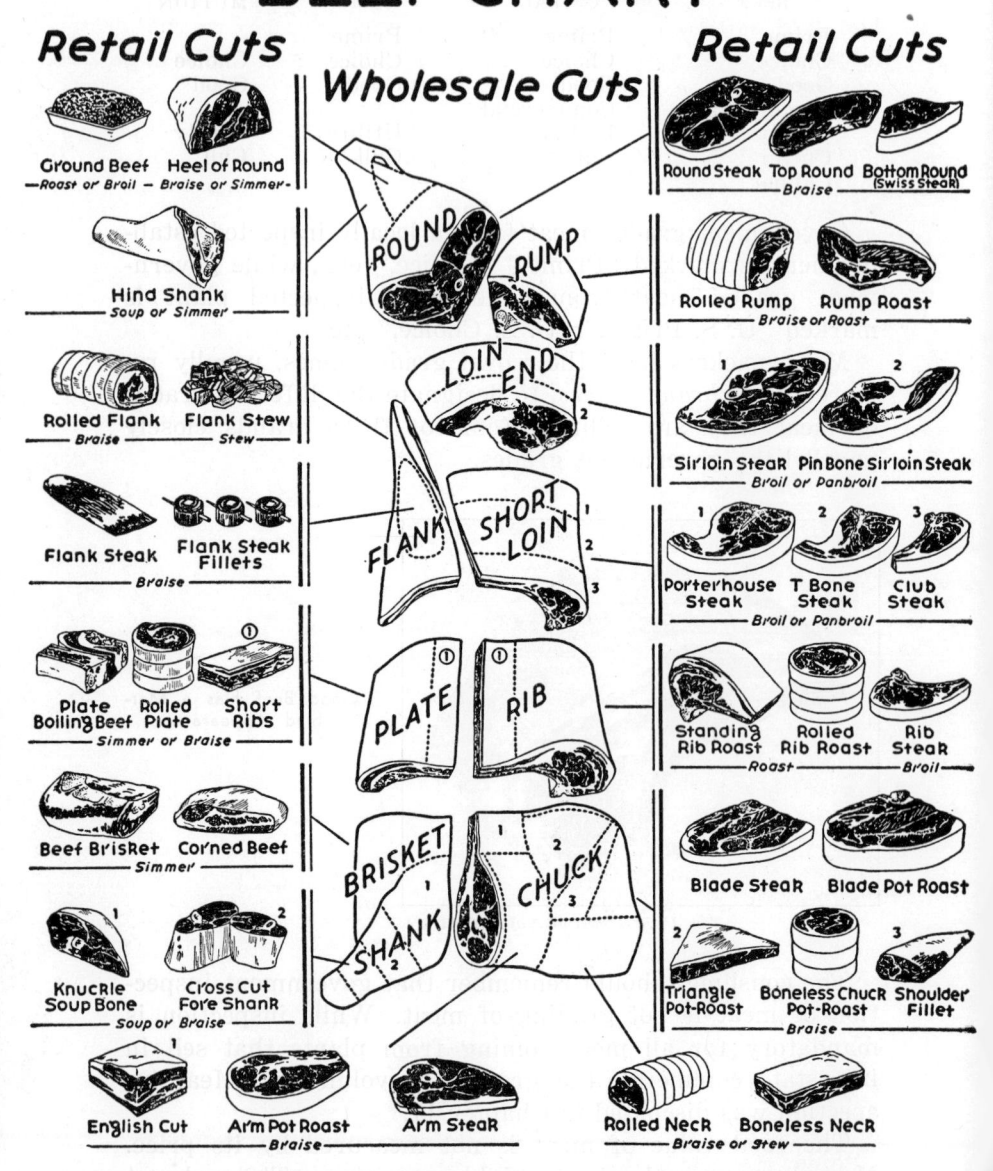

Retail Cuts

- Ground Beef — Roast or Broil
- Heel of Round — Braise or Simmer
- Hind Shank — Soup or Simmer
- Rolled Flank — Braise
- Flank Stew — Stew
- Flank Steak — Braise
- Flank Steak Fillets
- Plate Boiling Beef
- Rolled Plate
- Short Ribs — Simmer or Braise
- Beef Brisket
- Corned Beef — Simmer
- Knuckle Soup Bone
- Cross Cut Fore Shank — Soup or Braise
- English Cut
- Arm Pot Roast
- Arm Steak — Braise

Wholesale Cuts

- Round
- Rump
- Loin End
- Flank
- Short Loin
- Plate
- Rib
- Brisket
- Shank
- Chuck

Retail Cuts

- Round Steak
- Top Round
- Bottom Round (Swiss Steak) — Braise
- Rolled Rump
- Rump Roast — Braise or Roast
- Sirloin Steak
- Pin Bone Sirloin Steak — Broil or Panbroil
- Porterhouse Steak
- T Bone Steak
- Club Steak — Broil or Panbroil
- Standing Rib Roast
- Rolled Rib Roast — Roast
- Rib Steak — Broil
- Blade Steak
- Blade Pot Roast
- Triangle Pot-Roast
- Boneless Chuck Pot-Roast
- Shoulder Fillet — Braise
- Rolled Neck
- Boneless Neck — Braise or Stew

Ten Lessons on Meat, National Live Stock and Meat Board

A Good Buyer Should Know the Cuts of Meat and How to Cook Them

228

meats in order to select in accordance with your budget. The cuts of beef are illustrated in the chart on page 228. Similar charts may be obtained for pork, lamb, mutton, and veal.

The quality of meats may be judged by observing certain characteristics. The following chart illustrates some of the characteristics that should be observed in buying meats.

KIND OF MEAT	CHARACTERISTICS OF EDIBLE PORTION	
	LEAN	FAT
Beef	Well-marbled with fat, firm, smooth, in texture; light to dark red in color.	Fairly thick layer of white to yellowish white fat covering outside.
Veal	Firm, fine textured; grayish-pink in color.	Outside covered with thin layer; pinkish-white in color.
Lamb	Fine-grained in texture, firm; dull pink in color.	Firm, creamy-white to slightly pink in color.
Mutton	Firm; medium texture; dull red in color.	Very white; brittle.
Pork	Relatively fine-textured, firm, well-marbled with fat; light grayish-pink in color.	Firm, outside covered with medium thick layer; white in color.

How to Judge the Quality of Poultry. Ready-to-cook poultry that has been federally inspected and passed for wholesomeness may also be federally graded. The poultry grades are:

GRADE	CHARACTERISTICS
U. S. Grade A	Well-fleshed, full breast, "meaty" legs, no defects such as crooked breastbone or broken bones, good layer of fat well distributed, well bled, free of pinfeathers, skin not torn or bruised.
U. S. Grade B	Fairly well-fleshed and fattened and may show slight defects such as skin tears or discoloration. Not more than three such defects may appear on the breast of birds of this grade.
U. S. Grade C	Poorly fleshed and poorly covered with fat, could have been poorly bled and poorly picked, could have minor skin tears or bruises, may have some deformities or a broken bone.

Grades for Dressed Poultry

Some poultry processors use brand names to indicate differences in quality. Poultry carrying brand names may also carry U. S. grade and inspection labels.

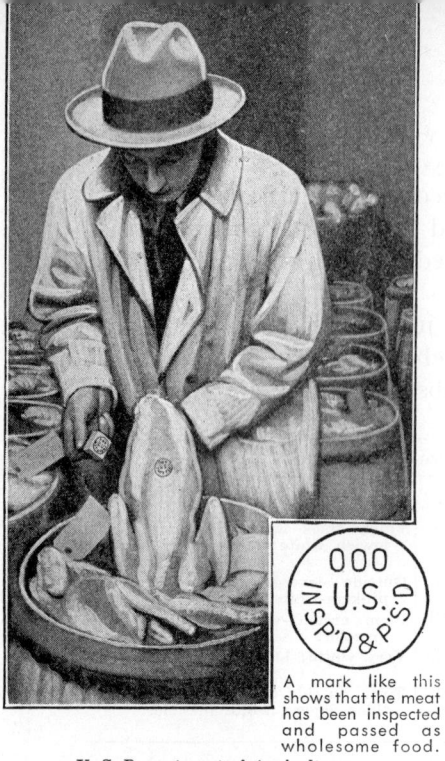

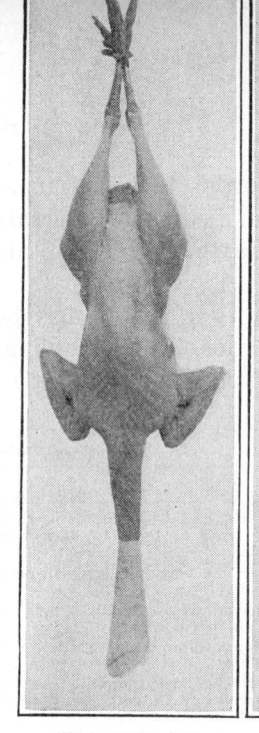

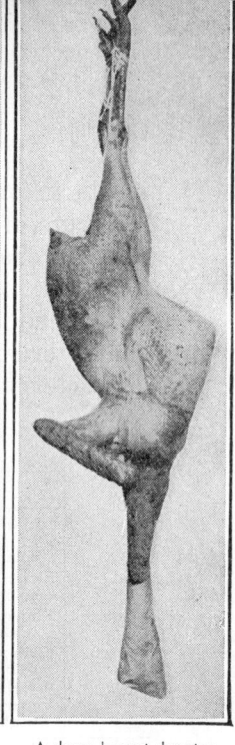

U. S. Department of Agriculture

Inspecting and Stamping Poultry

A mark like this shows that the meat has been inspected and passed as wholesome food.

Choice or Grade A turkey.

A sharp breast denotes low quality.

High and Low Grades of Poultry

Milk. Dairy products include milk, cream, butter, and cheese. The consumer may choose from among several grades of raw or pasteurized milk. The price of milk varies according to the grade, the grades usually being designated as A, B, and C. However, certified milk is of a higher grade. These grades are approved by the United States Public Health Service. Milk sold in cities is usually pasteurized. Grade A pasteurized milk is produced under more sanitary conditions and has a lower bacterial count than Grade B. Grade C milk must be labeled "cooking milk."

Departments of health in most cities have established rigid systems for controlling the inspection and the grading of milk similar to those of the Federal Government.

Cream. There are four classes of cream: heavy cream, whipping cream, medium cream, and light cream. They rank according to their content of butter fat, which may test from 36 per cent to 18 per cent.

Butter. Grades for butter have been established by the United States Department of Agriculture on the basis of flavor, body, color, and salt content. Although grading is voluntary, many manufacturers have their butter graded by Federal graders. The Federal grades are:

SCORE	GRADE
93 or above	U. S. Grade AA
92	U. S. Grade A
90	U. S. Grade B
89	U. S. Grade C

Grades of Butter

Grades AA and A are most commonly found in the retail market, although B and C are also marketed as table butter. In the scoring of the first three classes, maximum ratings are given to various factors in the following manner: flavor, 45 points; body, 25 points; color, 15 points; salt, 10 points; package, 5 points; total, 100 points. Butter that scores about 93 or 94 points is fine, sweet, fresh, mild, and clean. Butter scoring 75 to 88 inclusive is classified as cooking grade.

Cheese. American cheese is classified on several bases. On the basis of flavor it may be classified as fresh, mild, or aged; on the basis of texture, as close, medium close, or open; on the basis of color, as uncolored, medium-colored, or highly colored. Cheeses can be divided into four other general classifications: very hard, such as Parmesan; hard, as Cheddar and Swiss; semisoft, as brick and Roquefort; and soft as Camembert, cream, and cottage.

United States grades for Cheddar cheese, which is one of the most commonly used cheeses, are used in the wholesale trade but seldom in the retail market. The U. S. grades AA, A, B, and C are based on flavor, body and texture, color, finish and appearance, and additional factors according to the age of the cheese. For grading, Cheddar cheese is classed as fresh (current make), medium cured, and cured or aged. Cheddar cheese and other closely related types are sometimes called American cheese.

A great variety of cheeses are sold in American markets. Many of them are so-called processed cheeses. These are made from natural cheese after the natural cheese has matured. Natural cheese is mixed and blended to obtain a uniform fat content, flavor, moisture, and acidity. It is then pasteurized, molded into the proper form, and packaged. The pasteurization of cheese is essentially the same as that for milk.

Margarine. Margarine, which is technically referred to as oleomargarine, is a spread that is similar in characteristics to butter. When it is properly fortified with vitamins according to regulations, it contains essentially the same nutritional value as butter. All margarine, regardless of whether it is sold locally or in interstate commerce, is under government supervision in its manufacture. It is not sold by grade, but it must measure up to minimum standards. Most margarine is made from vegetable oils such as soybean oil, cottonseed oil, peanut oil, or cocoanut oil. Skimmed milk, whole milk, or powdered milk is usually added along with the required vitamins and salt. Anyone buying margarine has assurance that it is wholesome.

Eggs. In Chapter 11 there is a table illustrating the standards and grades of eggs set up by the United States Department of Agriculture. In many markets eggs are sold in cartons bearing the grade markings and the Federal seal of inspection. Even though a consumer may not buy eggs in cartons, it is sometimes possible to determine the quality by examining the wholesale carton from which they are taken.

Official U. S. Grade Label for Eggs in Carton

Eggs may vary in weight from about 30 ounces to 15 ounces a dozen. There are six different classes of eggs by weight: the jumbo or largest size has a minimum net weight of 30 ounces a dozen; the extra large, 27 ounces; the large, 24 ounces; the medium, 21 ounces; the small, 18 ounces; and the peewee, 15 ounces. It is to the customer's advantage to buy eggs by weight or by size. The following table, based on minimum weight of four sizes of eggs, shows how prices of grade A eggs of these sizes may be compared. The same figures may be used to compare the prices of eggs of any other grade.

WHEN EXTRA LARGE GRADE A EGGS (MINIMUM WEIGHT 27 OUNCES PER DOZEN) COST—	LARGE GRADE A EGGS (MINIMUM WEIGHT 24 OUNCES PER DOZEN) ARE AS GOOD A VALUE AT—	AND MEDIUM GRADE A EGGS (MINIMUM WEIGHT 21 OUNCES PER DOZEN) ARE AS GOOD A VALUE AT—	AND SMALL GRADE A EGGS (MINIMUM WEIGHT 18 OUNCES PER DOZEN) ARE AS GOOD A VALUE AT—
Cents per dozen	Cents per dozen	Cents per dozen	Cents per dozen
49	44	38	33
54	48	42	36
59	52	46	39
64	57	50	43
69	61	54	46
74	66	58	49
79	70	61	53
84	75	65	56
89	79	69	59
94	84	73	63

Comparing Values in Grade A Eggs, Based on Minimum Weight of 4 Sizes

The grade mark on a carton of federally graded eggs always carries the letters "U. S.," always tells the grade (quality) of the eggs and the size, and always states the date of grading which is an indication of freshness. A label as used on a federally graded egg carton is illustrated on page 232.

Judging the Quality of Fresh Fruits and Vegetables. A great amount of printed material is available to help you learn how to judge the quality of fresh fruits and vegetables. In addition to pamphlets and books published by the Department of Agriculture and home economics departments of colleges and universities, some packers' associations make available excellent helps to the consumer for the wise selection and proper use of their commodity.

Practices That Will Save Money in Buying Fresh Fruits and Vegetables

1. Make your own selection; do not order by telephone. Buy in small quantities unless you have a cool, dark place for storage.
2. Fruits and vegetables that are in season in the nearest marketing area are cheapest in price and often best in quality.
3. Do not handle fruits and vegetables unnecessarily. Handling increases spoilage and the retailer's overhead, both of which represent costs that must be passed on to consumers.
4. Avoid the purchase of foods that show decay. Distinguish between blemishes that affect only appearance and those that affect eating quality.
5. Whenever possible, buy by weight instead of by measure.
6. Do not always buy the best; but buy the grade that is wholesome, economical, and suitable for the purpose for which the food is intended.
7. Buy from more than one merchant. Compare prices and quality.
8. Determine the relative values obtained from a particular merchant, or from various merchants, by testing the foods at home.

The Consumer Education Department of the Household Finance Corporation has summarized in the following tables many of the points that the consumer should consider in buying fresh fruits and vegetables. You will be especially interested in the varieties of fruits and vegetables and in the points to look for and to avoid in buying.

BUY-POINTS FOR FRESH FRUITS

KINDS AND VARIETIES	BUY-POINTS
APPLES—*Cooking:* Baldwin, Ben Davis, Gravenstein, Rome Beauty, Northern Spy, Grimes Golden, Rhode Island Greening, Newton, York Imperial *All-Purpose:* Jonathan, Wealthy, McIntosh, Winesap *Baking:* Rome Beauty, Rhode Island Greening *Eating-Salad:* Delicious, Baldwin, Stayman, Gravenstein, Grimes Golden, Newtown, York Imperial, Northern Spy, Cortland	*Look for:* good characteristic color, firm fruit. *But avoid:* immature, unripened fruit; shriveled peel; soft or bruised fruit.

APRICOTS, PEACHES, PLUMS, NECTARINES
PEACHES—*All-Purpose:* Belle, Carman, Elberta, Elberta Cling, Hale. *Eating:* Elberta, Golden Jubilee, Hale, Hiley. *Canning, Pickling:* Early Rose, Hobson Cling, Elberta Cling
PLUMS—*Eating:* Burbank
Cooking: Damson, Green Gage, Italian

Look for: plump, fresh, firm fruit. Skin: smooth, unblemished, with characteristic color.

But avoid: overripe, noticeably soft, bruised or cracked fruit; shriveled or green fruit; brown, sunburned plums.

BANANAS—Yellow
Red (Claret)

Look for: yellow-flecked with brown for ready-to-eat; all yellow to eat or cook; yellow, tipped with green to hold for later use.
But avoid: overripe fruit or broken skins.

AVOCADO

Look for: fruit which yields to slight pressure in your hand.
But avoid: overripe or soft fruit, breaks in skin.

BERRIES—Blackberries, Boysenberries, Dewberries, Loganberries, Mulberries, Raspberries, Strawberries, Blueberries, Elderberries, Huckleberries, Currants, Cranberries, Gooseberries

Look for: plump, clean, bright, fragrant, full-colored fruit. Currants and gooseberries with stems. Cranberries firm, lustrous. Strawberries with hulls.
But avoids: crushed, overripe or moldy berries. Tough, soft or sticky cranberries.

CHERRIES—*Salads, Eating, Canning:* Bing, Black Tartarian, Napoleon, Royal Anne, Windsor
Pies: Montmorency, Richmond, May Duke, Late Duke

Look for: tender, firm, plump fruit. Bright characteristic red to black color. Stems on.
But avoid: damaged or spoiled fruit, poor color, overripe.

GRAPES—*Eating:* Thompson Seedless, Malaga, Muscat, Flame Tokay
Juice, Jelly: Concord, Catawba

Look for: plump and well-colored with stem firmly attached. Soft to touch when ripe. Well-filled clusters.
But avoid: moldy or wet grapes. Brittle stems. Straggly clusters.

GRAPEFRUIT, ORANGES, LEMONS, TANGERINES
GRAPEFRUIT: Duncan (many seeds), Marsh Seedless, Pinks (seedless)
ORANGES—*Slicing, Sectioning:* Naval, Pineapple, Temple
Juice: Parson Brown, Valencia

Look for: bright characteristic color. Well-shaped and firm. Heavy for size.

But avoid: fruit with soft spots, light in weight.

MELONS—Cantaloupe, Casaba, Honeydew, Watermelon

Look for: fragrant, well-shaped fruit. Hold ends between palms. Melon is ripe if it feels springy.
But avoid: soft, watery, overripe, bruised or flabby melons.

PEARS—*Eating:* D'Anjou, Bosc, Bartlett, Comice, Seckel, Winter Nelis
Canning: Bartlett, Bosc, Seckel, Kieffer
Pickling: Kieffer

Look for: fairly firm fruit. Large, smooth and fragrant. Yellow, russet or brown in color.
But avoid: soft or bruised fruit; brown spot, especially at stem or blossom end.

PINEAPPLE—Cuban
Mexican

Look for: compact fruit, heavy for size, fragrant, golden color. When ripe, spine pulls away from top easily.
But avoid: soft spots, dark color, decay at base.

RHUBARB

Look for: thick red or pink stalks. Tender, crisp, dark green leaves.
But avoid: wilted, flabby or stringy stalks. Wilted or too large leaves.

Money Management—Your Food Dollar, copyright by Household Finance Corporation

BUY-POINTS FOR FRESH VEGETABLES

YOU'LL WANT TO BUY	BUT AVOID	½ CUP SERVINGS PER LB.
Asparagus—Brittle, tender, straight, thick stalks; mostly green; smooth, compact, pointed tips.	Wilted, thin stalks; dried-out ends or loose tips.	About 2 (4-5 stalks each)
Beans, green and wax—Fresh looking; bright yellow or green; long, straight, smooth pods that break with a crisp snap; beans underdeveloped.	Wilted pods, enlarged beans, stringiness.	6
Lima beans, Peas—Plump, greenish-white beans with tender skins. Firm, tender, green, young peas. Fresh, well-filled pods.	Pods that are wilted, yellowish, flat, highly speckled or mildewed.	2
Beets, Carrots—Bright color; smooth, well-shaped roots. Carrots: crisp, tops off. Beet greens: fresh, deep color.	Beets with ridged skin; rough, scarred flesh; wilted leaves. Roots: blemished, shriveled, flabby or cracked.	Beets: 4 Carrots: Shredded 8 Cooked 5
Broccoli—Buds: unopened, tender, small, green or purplish-green. Fairly compact head, green leaves, tender stalks.	Open buds showing color of blossoms; tough, woody stalks.	3-4 (2 stalks per serving)
Brussels sprouts, Cabbage—Sprouts: firm, compact. Cabbage: solid, heavy head. Fresh, good green color.	Puffy look, wilted or yellowed leaves, discolored or decayed spots. Split cabbages.	Sprouts: 5-6 Cabbage: Raw 7-8 Cooked 4-5
Cauliflower—White or creamy white color. Compact, heavy for size. Fresh outer leaves.	Yellow or green tint, dark spots on surface, loose and spreading head.	3
Celery—Stalks: fairly thick, crisp. Fresh green or white. Good heart formation. Green or yellow leaves.	Stalks: limp, flabby, with growth cracks or damage. Wilted leaves.	Cooked 3-4
Corn, sweet—Husks: fresh, green. Crisp, brown silk. Ears: filled to tip; plump, soft, milky kernels. Refrigerated.	Yellow husks, shriveled or missing kernels. Worm-eaten ears. Unrefrigerated corn soon becomes starchy.	Cut off 2
Eggplant—Dark purple color. Uniform shape, solid, smooth-skinned, heavy for size.	Light-colored, wilted or flabby eggplant, brown spots.	4
Lettuce—Firm head; fresh, crisp, green leaves.	Wilted, bruised head. Slimy or discolored areas.	4
Potatoes—Clean, firm; shallow eyes. Medium size. Choose varieties to suit cooking method: baking, frying, French-frying, salads.	Surface defects, cuts, growth cracks. Withered, leathery, discolored or sunburned (green-colored) skin. Sprouted.	3-5
Spinach—Leaves: crisp, green, clean.	Coarse stems. Yellow, wilted or slimy leaves.	3-4
Sweet Potatoes—Plump, smooth, bright.	Growth cracks. Irregular shapes. Wrinkled, soft ends.	3-4

Money Management—Your Food Dollar, copyright by Household Finance Corporation

Grades of Fresh Fruits and Vegetables. Although the number and the names of grades established for the different varieties of fresh fruits and vegetables differ somewhat, the classification is, in general, as follows: best grade, U. S. Fancy; next grade, U. S. No. 1; third grade, U. S. No. 2. Many states have adopted their own grades, but most of these conform to the standards established by the United States Department of Agriculture. It would be to the consumer's interest to have grades developed that are especially adapted to consumer needs.

Summary of How to Buy Foods

1. Buy United States graded foods when possible; encourage stores to handle graded and well-labeled products.
2. Price and quality especially of canned foods are not always closely related.
3. Can and package sizes may affect cost per pound or cupful.
4. Methods of processing and packaging may affect cost of food.
5. A Federal food inspection stamp indicates wholesomeness of food; a grade, a specific quality of that food.
6. United States grades (that is different qualities) of meats, poultry, dairy products, and eggs are usually closely related to price.
7. The wise consumer will learn how to judge the quality of fresh fruits and vegetables.

TEXTBOOK QUESTIONS

1. In what way may Federal grades help you in buying foods?
2. Give some examples of kinds of information that are mandatory under the Federal labeling system for canned foods.
3. Give some examples of voluntary labeling information that the National Canners Association requests its members to place on canned foods.
4. Name some meaningless grade designations.
5. Even though a food sold in interstate commerce, from one state to another, may not bear Federal grades, what information is required on labels of canned foods?
6. Name at least five positive characteristics that determine the quality of canned fruits and vegetables.

7. Name at least three negative characteristics that determine the quality of canned fruits and vegetables.
8. What is the approximate average weight of canned fruits or vegetables that one should expect to find in a (a) No. 1 can, (b) No. 2 can, (c) No. 3 can, (d) No. 3 cylinder can?
9. What are the advantages of buying packaged goods?
10. What is vacuum packing?
11. To get the best results, at what temperature should foods be frozen originally? At what temperature should they be stored?
12. What means are used to protect the buyer of meat that is sold in interstate commerce?
13. What are the official grades of beef?
14. Name the characteristics of a good piece of beef.
15. What grading service is provided for dressed poultry?
16. Explain the grades of milk.
17. What are the factors by which butter is judged?
18. From what is margarine made?
19. (a) What is the range of weight of eggs? (b) What is the largest size called?
20. What grades of fresh fruits and vegetables are recognized by the United States Department of Agriculture?
21. Name at least two practices that will save money in buying fresh fruits and vegetables?
22. What are good points to consider in buying citrus fruits?
23. What are good characteristics to observe when buying green beans?

DISCUSSION QUESTIONS

1. Do you think a store has any advantage in selling merchandise that is marked according to standard grades?
2. What do you think is meant by Grade AA, which appears on the label of a canned food?
3. Explain a procedure that you would suggest for comparing canned foods on the basis of quality and value.
4. Why should a person beware of cans that have unusual sizes or shapes?
5. Some maple syrups that do not contain pure maple syrup are sold on the market. Is it legal to make such sales?
6. Which would you rather have on canned fruits and vegetables: (a) A regular ABC grading system, or (b) all of the voluntary information recommended by the National Canners Association?
7. Explain some of the dangers of relying on grade marks on packages of eggs.
8. Should one always attempt to buy Grade A jumbo eggs because they are the largest and best? Explain.

Ch. 13] HOW TO BUY FOODS 239

9. Why do you think it is difficult to enforce the use of quality standards for fresh fruits and vegetables?
10. On what basis should one buy citrus fruits: weight, juice, size, price?
11. If you were given an opportunity to handle green snap beans, what would be one of your first tests of freshness and quality?
12. Why do some people contend that the top grade of beef is not always the best for every purpose?
13. In the general rules for buying it is suggested that whenever possible one should buy by weight. Why is this important?

PROBLEMS

1. If a No. 1 can of food sells for 20 cents and a No. 2 can sells for 30 cents, what is the price of a pound in each case?
2. Canned tomatoes were advertised by one store as selling at 20 cents a "large can." Another merchant advertised a "large can" for 25 cents. The tomatoes were of approximately the same quality. Investigation disclosed, however, that those advertised in the first case were packed in No. 1 tall cans, whereas those advertised in the second case were packed in No. 2 cans. Was there any difference in the price of a pound? If there was, which can was the cheaper?
3. Assume that Grade A eggs weighing 24 ounces a dozen cost 48 cents. (a) What is the price per ounce? (b) In order to pay the same price, what should one pay for a dozen eggs weighing 20 ounces?

COMMUNITY PROBLEMS AND PROJECTS

1. Compare the contents of two or more cans of beans or of some other product. Note the price, volume, weight, taste, and other factors that can be used in determining the quality and the value. Make a comparative report on the quality and the price. Use the brand names to distinguish the products that you compare.
2. Collect a variety of labels from cans of similar products. Make a list of the information shown on the labels, and report your conclusions as to what criteria can be followed in evaluating these foods on the basis of the information given on the labels.
3. In your local stores see what information you can find in regard to grades of fresh fruits and vegetables. Write a report of the information you obtain and indicate how you obtained it.
4. Investigate to see whether your state has any state laws pertaining to the grading and marketing of fruits and vegetables and give a report to the class.

Chapter 14

How to Buy Fabrics, Clothing, and Shoes

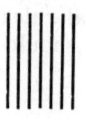

Purpose of the Chapter. Fabrics for use in the home and clothing for personal use require a substantial portion of the income of the average family. Among the things we buy as consumers, clothing ranks along with food and housing as a factor that contributes to our health, comfort, and satisfaction. What you get for your clothing dollar depends largely upon how well you plan your wardrobe and the skill you have in buying and caring for your clothing. The purpose of this chapter is to present the basic principles for buying fabrics and clothing, leaving to you the application of them in the buying of specific items of clothing.

You will find answers to these questions:

1. What does a consumer need to know about fabrics made from natural and man-made fibers?
2. What are the principles that may serve as guides in the selection of fabrics?
3. What are the basic principles for planning a wardrobe?
4. How should one select clothing?
5. What are the general principles by which the quality of clothing may be determined?
6. What are some guides for the wise buying of furs and shoes?

Kinds of Cloth. A *fabric* is cloth woven or knit from yarns. *Yarns* are made of threads and threads of *fibers*, which are natural such as wool and cotton, and some are man made such as nylon and rayon. Fibers that are relatively short in length, such as cotton and wool, are known as *staple fibers*. *Filament fibers* are very long. *Reeled silk* is a filament fiber; man-made fibers may be either staple or filament.

The *weave* of a cloth refers to the manner in which the yarns are interlaced or woven. The weave may be plain or patterned, tight or loose. The strength and durability of the cloth is affected by the kind of yarn used in it and also by the weave.

Fibers are often mixed or blended in order to give the cloth the characteristics desired. For example, wool and dacron are blended to obtain the warmth and resiliency of the wool and the strength and wrinkle resistant qualities of the dacron.

The attractiveness and serviceability of clothing, draperies, and other household commodities made of cloth depends upon the fabric from which they are made. The various fabrics or cloths have advantages and disadvantages which one should know when selecting clothing and fabrics for household purposes.

Natural Fibers. The four natural fibers commonly used in making cloth are cotton, linen, silk, and wool. The first two are primarily of cellulose, and the last two protein. Yarn or thread from which woolen fabrics are woven is made from the soft, curled fibers of the coat of sheep and some other animals. A characteristic of cloth made from wool fiber is that it holds its shape well and has a tendency to resist wrinkling much more than cotton and better than some but not all of the fibers made by chemical processes.

Fabrics are sometimes referred to as all wool, pure wool, and part wool. All wool or pure wool fabrics may be made either of wool that has not been used before, which is known as *virgin wool*, of wool that has been spun or woven before (but not used), but which has been *reprocessed*, or of wool that has been reclaimed from previously used cloth, *re-used wool*. Virgin wool cloth is usually considered more desirable because it is more durable.

Wool fibers are made into two types of yarn, one of which is known as woolen yarn and the other as worsted yarn. Ordinary *woolen yarn* is usually spun from a mixture of short and long fibers; *worsted yarn,* from fibers two or more inches in length that are combed so they will lie parallel when spun. Fabrics made from worsted yarns are hard surfaced and long wearing, while fabrics made from ordinary woolen yarns are fuzzy and somewhat uneven in appearance. Though they may be as warm, they do not wear as long as fabrics made from worsted yarn.

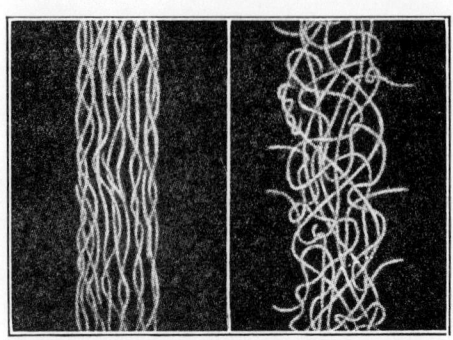

Forstmann Woolen Company

WORSTED YARN (Enlarged)
A single worested yarn spun from long fibers combed into a parallel position.

WOOLEN YARN (Enlarged)
A single woolen yarn made of short and long fibers mixed together and then spun.

Examples of Worsted and Woolen Yarns

Cloth made from the fibers that grow on the cotton plant is known as cotton. It is the most commonly used fabric in making clothing. Cotton in its natural state is nonabsorbent, but it may be treated chemically to make it absorb moisture readily. It is more inflammable than wool, and it does not have the luster or the body of wool and linen.

Cloth made from the fibers in the stems of the flax plant, which is a kind of tall grass, is called linen. It is a very durable cloth and is characterized by its smoothness, crispness, and luster. Though cotton is sometimes substituted for it, women especially like linen for summer dresses.

Silk worms make a very fine fiber that they wrap tightly around the cocoons in which they spend part of their lives. The silk fiber is very strong and has a high luster. When made into cloth, it wears very well unless it is damaged by chemicals in the dying process. If a piece of "silk" cloth splits or breaks after brief wear, this fact is a definite indication that the cloth is not pure silk.

Man-made Fibers. Several man-made fibers are used extensively in making fabrics for clothing. Some are used alone and some are blended with natural fibers.

Fibers made from cellulose or from corn protein are known as semi-synthetic; those produced from the combination of chemical elements are known as synthetic.

The characteristics and uses of the common man-made fibers are given in the chart on page 244. In addition to the man-made fibers listed in the chart, there are a few others that are being tested for use in making fabrics. Prices of man-made fabrics vary, rayon and acetate being the lowest in price and orlon and dacron among the highest in price.

Materials often called plastics are being used increasingly to make raincoats, slip covers for furniture, purses, luggage, and in some cases shoes and other articles. These materials vary widely in their usefulness and durability. Probably the best guide to buying articles made of these materials is the recommendation of a reliable store and product rating services such as those in Consumers' Research and Consumers Union.

Selecting Fabrics for Clothing and Home Use. When choosing fabrics, the general appearance may be observed and one may feel the softness and texture. It is impossible, however, to determine by observation the kinds and proportions of fibers of various kinds of which the cloth is woven. Other characteristics, such as color fastness, shrinkage, sensitiveness to heat in ironing, and reaction to cleaning fluids cannot be determined by observation. Most tests for kinds of fiber, color fastness, and other characteristics are too complicated to be performed by the consumer either in the store or at home. Consequently, he must turn to two sources for information about the fabrics in which he is interested. The label on yard goods and on clothes should give the buyer some information he needs to decide the suitableness of the fabric for his purposes. A reliable store in many instances can provide the information you need. In any event, it is desirable to buy fabrics at a store known for its reputation for fair dealing and standing back of its merchandise.

The closeness of the weave; that is, the number of threads lengthwise and crosswise through the cloth, is an important factor in the durability of different grades of cloth. In

CHARACTERISTICS OF MAN-MADE FIBERS

FIBER	MADE FROM	QUALITIES AND LIMITATIONS	COMMON USES
Acetate	(Cellulose) cotton linters, wood pulp	Soft texture and appearance, drapes well, lustrous, resistant to wrinkles; low strength, sensitive to heat	Curtains, draperies, upholstery, carpets, dresses, blouses, hosiery, underwear, linings, blankets
Acrilan	Chiefly from Acrylonitrile	Launders and dries easily, light weight; does not dye easily, static (clings); heat sensitive	Suits, dresses, blankets, pile fabrics
Dacron	Terephthalic acid Ethylene glycol	Resistant to wrinkle and abrasion, resilient, soft and lustrous feel, tough; low moisture absorbency, somewhat difficult to dye	Suits, shirts, blouses, sweaters, socks, thread, industrial uses
Dynel	Acrylonitrile and Vinyl chloride	Resistant to burning, does not shrink, resists chemicals, launders and dries easily; can be ironed only at low heat	Blankets, draperies, pile fabrics, work clothes, socks
Glass Fiber	Silica, sand, and Limestone	Very strong, resistant to sun, nonflammable, resistant to chemicals; low resistance to abrasion	Draperies, curtains; reinforcement for plastics, papers, and rubber; several industrial uses
Nylon	Hexamethylene-diamine and Adipic Acid	Strong, elastic, resists abrasion, light weight, launders well and dries quickly, deteriorates when exposed to sun; nonabsorbent, static (clings)	Dresses, hosiery, underwear, bathing suits, sweaters, blankets, upholstery, many industrial uses
Orlon	Chiefly from Acrylonitrile	Resists sun and rain, resilient, launders easily and dries quickly, light weight; dyes only to pastel shades, static (clings), low moisture absorbency, heat sensitive	Suits, coats, blouses, shirts, dresses, work clothes, many industrial uses
Rayon	(Cellulose) cotton linters, wood pulp	Soft, smooth, strong, absorbent, takes dye well and drapes well; wrinkles easily, weak when wet	Gloves, curtains, dresses, blouses, hosiery, underwear, suiting, carpets, ties
Saran	Vinyl chloride and Cinylidene chloride	Fire resistant, tough and durable; sensitive to heat	Upholstery, seat covers, luggage, carpet, outdoor furniture
Vicara	(Zein) corn protein	Soft texture, luxurious feel, dyes well, weak especially when wet	Chiefly as a blending fiber in suits, sports clothes, dress goods, linings

A filled cloth before washing.   A filled cloth after washing.

Consumers' Guide

Many weighted fabrics lose their luster and body after the first washing because the filler washes out.

Weighted Fabric Before and After Washing

cotton cloths percale, chambray, and gingham have approximately the same number of threads woven in each direction. Cotton broadcloth has more threads one way than the other, usually at least 136 threads vertically to the inch and 60 horizontally. A fabric with a high thread count is usually smoother, firmer, more even, and has more luster than one with a low thread count; although many fabrics, such as those used for sheets, are loaded or weighted with starch or some other compound that is washed out in the first laundering. In buying fabrics such as sheets the weight of the yarn is important in addition to the thread count.

The American Standards Association has classified sheets by types, such as Type 200, Type 180, Type 140, and Type 128, in which the numbers represent the number of threads in the *warp* per inch vertically plus the number of *filling* or crosswise (horizontally) threads per inch.

The *ply* of the yarn also may affect durability. A two-ply yarn is two threads twisted together. It is stronger than one-ply yarn. In a 2 x 1 broadcloth, two ply yarns are used vertically and single-ply yarns horizontally.

A consumer should familiarize himself with the various terms that he needs to know when selecting fabrics for either clothing or home furnishings. He needs to know the characteristics of various fibers, their properties when blended, trade names of man-made fibers, and meaning of such terms as thread count, ply of yarn, staple and filament fiber, and weave. Much of this information the consumer will have to learn for himself for it changes from time to time. Government pamphlets, leaflets issued by the American Home Economics Association, and booklets and brochures distributed by manufacturers of man-made fibers and of all kinds of fabrics will be very helpful in obtaining the information you need to buy fabrics wisely. A good practice is to compile your own buyer's guide which may be primarily a pamphlet and clipping file containing information you may need when buying.

Guides for the Selection of Fabrics When Shopping

1. Read the labels on garments and on bolts of fabrics to determine the kinds of fibers in the cloth.
2. Determine the amount of shrinkage to be expected.
3. Inquire if the fabrics are resistant to the soaps and detergents used in laundering and dry cleaning processes.
4. Consult the standards division or customer's information service in stores having such services relative to the suitability of the fabric for your purpose.

Look for Tags and Labels. Some manufacturers of clothing and fabrics use labels indicating the standards set up by the United States Bureau of Standards. Some of the trade associations require their members to use tags and labels indicating the quality of the clothing and the working conditions under which the clothing was manufactured. A truly informative label will provide information on such points as fibers used in the fabric, yarns per square inch, weight per square yard, sizing, finish, size of the garment, seams, how seams are made, strength of fabric, resistance to slippage, shrinkage, washability, resistance to sunlight and perspiration, and suggestions for laundering and dry cleaning.

The label can tell you whether or not the fabric meets the standards for the specific use you want it to serve. If the product is not labeled, see or write the store management insisting on goods with informative labels on them.

The types of information one should look for on tags and labels on fabrics are as follows:

(a) Under the rules of fair trade practices of the Federal Trade Commission terms, such as "preshrunk," "will not shrink," "completely shrunk," or "fully shrunk," may not be used unless no further shrinkage will occur. If such a statement is used, it must be qualified as in the following example: "Preshrunk; will not shrink more than 2 per cent under Commercial Standard CS 59-41." Such a statement on a garment gives assurance of adequate protection. The so-called Texturized process for woolen fabrics and the Sanforized process for cotton and linen fabrics have proved reliable.

(b) The seals or tags of approval of the American Institute of Laundering and the Better Fabrics Bureau are important guides in determining color fastness, shrinkage, and construction.

(c) Every garment made in whole or in part from wool and sold in interstate commerce must be labeled to indicate the percentage of wool and the type of wool.

(d) The Federal Trade Commission has ruled that all rayon fabric must be labeled *rayon*, and all acetate fabric labeled *acetate*.

(e) Brand names may be helpful to a buyer in identifying merchandise after experience using it.

(f) Special labels with regard to workmanship may disclose the types of seams, the method of sewing, the inner construction, the type of hem, or other features.

(g) Many buyers consider it important to look for union labels or other labels indicating the working conditions under which the clothing was manufactured.

(h) Besides the information mentioned above, look for information pertaining to tensile strength, tearing strength, and instructions in regard to cleaning.

(i) Any other kind of so-called protective label is meaningless unless the label indicates definitely what protection is provided.

Planning and Selecting Clothing. Some people always appear to be well dressed and yet many of them spend only a moderate amount of money for their clothing. They are able to do this through careful planning of their wardrobe, wise selection of their clothing, and observing the basic rules for buying clothing. Planning and selecting clothing are rather complicated, for not only does custom require us to have different kinds of clothing for sports, work, and social activities, but also there are many different kinds of fabrics and materials from which clothing are made. A comprehensive study of textiles and other materials used in making wearing apparel would require a great amount of time. Students not having an opportunity to take a course in textiles in high school or college should acquire all the knowledge they can through self study.

The following rules for planning your wardrobe and selecting your clothes suggests the topics about clothes that all people need to study continuously in order to make their clothing dollar go the farthest.

(a) Plan your wardrobe; buy each article to fit the plan.
(b) In developing your clothing plan, consider the things you do regularly—the places you go, therefore, the kinds of clothes you need.
(c) Examine present articles of clothing to determine their serviceability if repaired and renovated.
(d) Control the amount of each kind of clothing you buy so your needs are adequately met, but also so you benefit fully from each article before it is out of style.
(e) Select each article on the basis of its intended use. For example, do not buy high heels for sports activities or a sport jacket to wear to church.
(f) Compare values on the basis of quality, style, and purpose; ordinarily, middle price lines are more economical in the long run than extremely low priced or high priced lines. Shop at more than one store.
(g) Take advantage of sales.
(h) Select clothing having simple style and good design; they have longer usefulness and usually greater durability than those highly decorated and with extreme style.

Ch. 14] HOW TO BUY FABRICS, CLOTHING, AND SHOES 249

(i) Do not spend more for clothes than your budget allows.
(j) Learn all you can about fabrics commonly used in clothing, their characteristics, and how to care for them.
(k) Become acquainted with the different finishes of textiles such as moth proofing, water repellant, and wrinkle resistant treatments.
(l) Learn how to judge good workmanship and the quality of clothing.
(m) Launder, clean, press, pack, and store your clothing properly.
(n) Be sure to consider comfort and health as well as appearance and serviceability in selecting your clothing.

Some Guides in Determining Workmanship and Construction

1. The pattern in cloth should be matched at the seams so far as possible.
2. Cloth should be cut with the "grain" that is straight with the lengthwise or crosswise threads.
3. Buttonholes should be neatly and firmly made by using close, even stitches.
4. Seams should be deep enough to resist pulling out and allow for adjustment in size.
5. Raw edges of cloth at seams should be pinked or overcast to prevent fraying.
6. Stitches should be close together and even in length.
7. The handwork should be neatly and carefully done.
8. Collar and lapels should fit smoothly, sleeves hang straight from shoulder, and armholes should be smooth and free from wrinkles.

How to Judge the Quality of Clothing. The guides for checking quality of clothing are basically the same for women and for men. They apply generally to the various items of wearing apparel such as dresses, suits, coats, hats and millinery, gloves, underwear, hose, and shirts and blouses. Our purpose here is to learn the basic principles for judging the quality of clothing; you, then, may apply

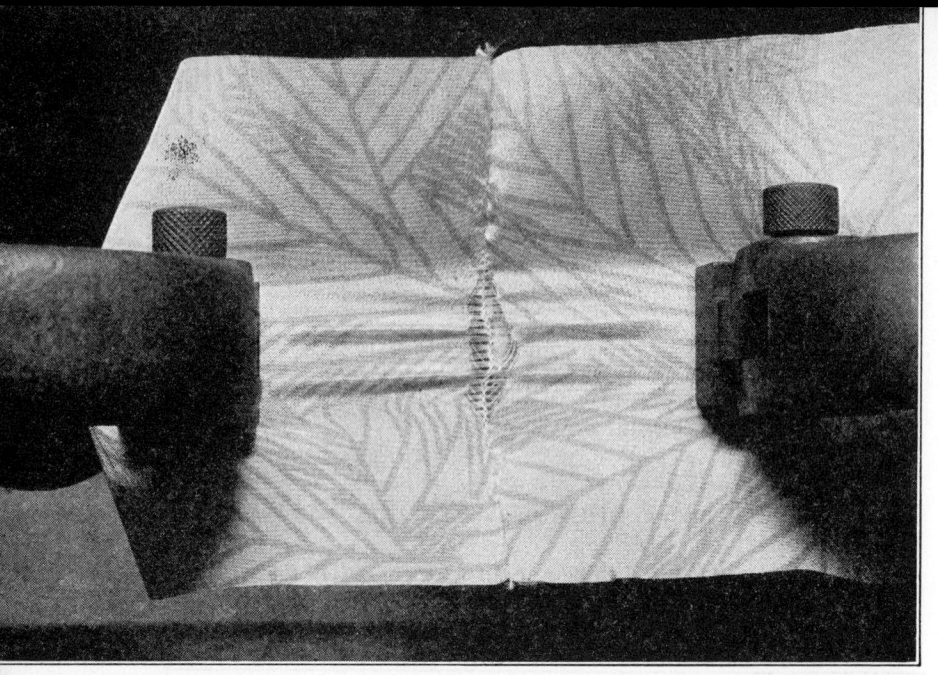

Bureau of Standards

One test of the fabric in clothing is to stretch it at a seam to find out if there is a slippage of the threads. This is also a good test to determine how well the garment is sewed together. In the test above the seam is rapidly pulling apart although the tension is not great.

Check the Seams Carefully
Some Clothing Pulls Apart Easily at the Seams Because It Is Not Woven Tightly

those principles in the selection of the specific articles of clothing you need.

Three important factors in the quality of clothing are good design, the material or materials of which a garment is made, and the workmanship and methods used in making it. We discussed earlier the general principles that may be used as guides in selecting fabrics for our clothing. Design is controlled by fashion; a consumer should always select items of clothing that are appropriate in design for the person wearing them. For example, a very heavy person should look for a suit in which the lines tend to run vertically rather than horizontally. Materials and their selection was discussed earlier. Now what about workmanship and methods of making the garment?

Looking for good workmanship and good methods of construction are equally as important as looking for suitable fabrics and good design. Workmanship can be judged by examining especially the manner in which the cloth has been cut and the care used in sewing and finishing a garment.

Ch. 14] HOW TO BUY FABRICS, CLOTHING, AND SHOES

The right size is important for comfort, appearance, and good wear. Clothing of good quality is cut generously in size and is clearly marked as to size.

You can develop a list of guides for determining the quality of each item of wearing apparel, such as underwear and lingerie, shirts and blouses, coats and suits, work clothes, hose, dresses, and casual or sportswear. Knowledge and experience are required to be a good judge of the quality of clothing.

How to Buy Furs. A lady buys a fur coat for its beauty, serviceability, and warmth. Furs vary widely in these qualities—some that are luxurious in appearance are not rugged and do not wear well. Others are highly durable but do not appear luxurious. The relationship between cost of furs and their serviceability is not close. Some that cost the most are the least durable. The amount of money you wish to spend and whether you want serviceability or beauty will be the deciding factors in the selection of a fur coat, stole, or jacket.

Buy furs only from stores or furriers who are reputable and who are known for fair dealing. Avoid sensational offers of bargains in furs. Buy only furs that are labeled in accordance with the Fur Products Act, which was passed in 1952. The law requires that all furs be correctly labeled with the true English name of the animal and the country of origin if imported. The names of furs used on labels must comply with the fur names established by the Federal Trade Commission, which is published under the title of *Fur Products Name Guide*. Abbreviations and ditto marks are not permitted on fur labels.

The names of many furs are given in the table on page 252 with an indication as to their durability and cost. Any fur or fur garment must be labeled to indicate whether it is composed of used fur; has been bleached or dyed; or is composed of paws, tails, or other undesirable parts.

How to Buy Shoes. Shoes are one of the most important items of wearing apparel from the standpoint of comfort and health and also from the standpoint of expenditure.

Name of Fur	Durability Low	Durability Medium	Durability High	Cost Low	Cost Medium	Cost High
Beaver			x			x
Ermine		x				x
Fox		x			x	
Hare (rabbit)	x			x		
Kid	x			x		
Lamb		x		x		
Lamb, Broadtail			x	x		
Lamb, Mouton			x	x		
Lamb, Persian			x	x		
Leopard						x
Marmot	x			x		
Marten			x			x
Mink			x			x
Muskrat			x		x	
Opossum		x			x	
Opossum, Australian		x			x	
Otter			x			x
Rabbit	x			x		
Raccoon			x			
Seal			x			x
Sheep		x			x	
Skunk			x		x	
Squirrel		x			x	
Weasel		x			x	

Durability and Cost of Furs

Important factors to consider in buying shoes are: (1) fit, (2) construction (how they are made), and (3) materials of which they are made.

Proper fit is essential for health and comfort. Fit is determined by length, width, and shape. Shoe length ranges from 1 to 13 in adult sizes and from 0 to $13\frac{1}{2}$ in children's sizes. The difference in length between whole sizes, that is between size 7 and size 8, is about one third of an inch. Width is designated by letters ranging from AAAAA, very narrow, to EEEEE, which is very wide. The difference in width is about one twelfth of an inch between sizes. A shoe is made over a form or mold which is known as a *last*. Thus, the shape of the shoe is determined by the last on which it was made. The shape of feet vary widely among people. Every person should look for a shoe that fits the shape of his foot.

Wise buyers realize that shoes cannot be bought like other clothing, but must be bought with the advice of a capable shoe-fitter.

Several different types of construction are used in making shoes. The main difference is in the way the sole is

---

Some Pointers on Getting a Good Fit of Shoes

1. Shoes should extend from one half to three fourths inches beyond the end of the longest toe.
2. The shape of the toe of the shoe should conform to the shape of the toes permitting them to lie flat and in natural position.
3. The ball joint at the great toe should be at the widest part of the shoe.
4. Shoe soles should bend easily and naturally at the base of the toes.
5. The shape of the entire shoe should conform to the general shape of the foot.
6. The shoe upper should fit the ankle snugly without pressure and should not gap when walking.
7. Some leathers and fabrics used in shoes favorably affect fit because of softness or flexibility.

attached to the upper. One type of construction is probably as satisfactory as another for the average person. Good workmanship is essential for comfort and durability.

The average person is not in a position to judge the specific quality of leather. Furthermore, there is no mark on shoes to indicate the grade of leather. It is advisable, therefore, to deal only with reputable shoe merchants.

The general quality of leather can, however, be detected by examination. Good leather is closely fibered, flexible, and firm. Poor leather is loosely fibered, stretches much, and is inclined to break when bent. The finish on poor leather sometimes cracks when the shoe is bent. Rough edges on soles and a rough finish on uppers are also indications of poor leather.

The uppers of shoes are made from many qualities and kinds of leather. Calfskin is probably the best kind for the uppers of dress shoes. Various other heavy skins are used as substitutes. Many varieties of special leathers are coming into use. These include the skins of reptiles, deer, ostrich, and kangaroo, and many substitutes for them. Many shoes are now made of combinations of leather and fabrics or leather and solid plastics. Soles and heels are frequently composition or rubber. Some of the fabrics, plastics, and composition materials are as serviceable as leather; however, some are not too long wearing. Shoes made of novelty leathers and special materials for styling effects present special problems that only the buyer can solve.

Comfort, Style, and Cost of Shoes. Rapid changes of style in women's shoes often have an important influence on price. Style also influences the price of men's shoes. Comfort should never, however, be sacrificed for cost or style, even though comfortable shoes may cost more.

The price of a shoe is governed largely by the process of manufacture, the quality of the leather, and the style. If a manufacturer has given special attention to style, it is possible that the buyer may be attracted by a shoe that has been made by a cheap process and of low-grade material. In general the higher-priced shoes are constructed better and are made of better leather than lower-priced shoes.

However, it is not always possible to determine quality or to predict comfort from the price paid for shoes. Probably it is more difficult to select shoes from the middle-price range with confidence as to their construction and quality than from the high- and low-priced ranges.

When you buy shoes, look first for as perfect fit as possible, and buy from reputable stores.

Summary of General Rules for Buying Fabrics and Clothing

1. Natural and man-made fibers have both advantages and limitations which need to be known by the consumer.
2. Wise selection of fabrics for clothing and for use in the home requires a general (not technical) knowledge of fabrics and of the terms used in describing them.
3. One should plan his wardrobe carefully and select clothing according to that plan.
4. Three important factors affecting the quality of clothing are good design, materials used in making, and workmanship and method of construction.
5. The principles applicable to the selection and buying of clothing in general may be applied specifically to any one type of wearing apparel such as furs and shoes.

TEXTBOOK QUESTIONS

1. Why is the weave of a cloth important to a buyer?
2. What is the reason for blending of fibers? Can you give a good example of fiber blending?
3. What are the natural fibers commonly used in making cloth?
4. What are the different types or grades of wool that may be used in a garment?
5. Explain the difference between worsted and woolen yarns.
6. Explain briefly the general characteristics of (a) cotton, (b) linen, (c) silk.
7. What is the major difference between semisynthetic fibers and synthetic fibers?
8. From the chart on page 244 list the qualities, limitations, and common uses of the following fibers: (a) acetate, (b) dacron, (c) nylon, and (d) saran.

9. Where can a customer selecting fabrics for home use obtain reliable information about those fabrics while he is in the store?
10. Explain the characteristics of a fabric with a low thread count as compared with one with a high thread count.
11. What is a "two-ply" yarn?
12. What kind of information should one expect to find on tags or labels of fabrics and garments?
13. What does "preshrunk" or "will not shrink" mean as applied to labels according to the rules of the Federal Trade Commission?
14. Why are planning and selecting a wardrobe difficult tasks?
15. What are three important factors in the quality of clothing?
16. How can a buyer of clothes judge the workmanship of the garment?
17. How does the Fur Products Act (1952) protect the customer buying furs?
18. Which is likely to be the higher in cost, Squirrel or Seal?
19. Which fur is likely to be the higher in durability, Muskrat or Ermine?
20. What are the three important factors to consider in buying shoes?
21. What are the most important factors as to the fit of shoes?
22. By examining shoes, how can the average person determine the quality of the leather?
23. What is the relation between price and quality of shoes?

DISCUSSION QUESTIONS

1. Why is it important for a consumer to know the characteristics of the various kinds of fibers of which fabrics are made?
2. (a) Should you always buy clothing of the best grade? (b) How can you determine which is the best grade? Discuss your answers to these questions.
3. What attitude may salespersons in stores take about your making tests of fabrics before buying?
4. Why are some fabrics weighted? How is this done? How may it be detected? What effect does it have on the fabric?
5. On the basis of the discussion in this chapter, explain the steps that are practicable in buying your own clothing.
6. A list of five guides for the selection of fabrics when shopping is given in the chapter. Discuss the meaning of each of these principles and how they may be applied when purchasing articles such as a skirt for girls or trousers for boys.
7. Even though some of the tests explained in this chapter cannot be conducted in a store at the time a purchase is to be made, how are they helpful to the buyer?

Ch. 14] How to Buy Fabrics, Clothing, and Shoes   257

8. What do the heat-conducting qualities of a fabric have to do with its seasonable use? Explain your answer.
9. From your study of this chapter, explain the importance of knowing something about fabrics and clothing before you buy.
10. What, in your opinion, provides you the safest guides in regard to shrinkage?
11. What are the factors of primary importance to consider before going to a store to select clothing of any kind?
12. Discuss the seven guides for determining the quality of clothing that are given in this chapter.
13. Name at least one fur you would buy if you wanted one among the lowest in cost but highest in durability.
14. Women are generally considered to have more trouble with their feet than men. Why do you think this condition exists?
15. From your observations, what is your opinion of the effect of style on the price and the wearing quality of shoes?
16. State some advantages of buying all your shoes at the same place.

PROBLEMS

1. Secure pieces of thread or yarn that are known to be wool, cotton, linen, silk, rayon, and nylon. Untwist each piece and examine the fibers of which it is made especially to determine resiliency, tensile strength, luster, and body. Prepare a report giving the characteristics of each type of fiber.
2. A person buys two summer suits. One suit can be laundered, but the other must be dry cleaned. The suit that can be laundered costs $20 and is expected to last two years. It will have to be laundered eight times during each summer at a cost of $1 each time. The other suit costs $30 and is expected to last three years. It will have to be dry cleaned four times during each summer at a cost of $1.50 each time. Figure the yearly cost of each suit, considering that the original cost in each case is divided equally over the number of years during which the suit will be worn.
3. If a broadcloth shirt sells at $3 and may be laundered 24 times before wearing out and another broadcloth shirt with fewer threads to the inch in the fabric sells for $2 and may be laundered 20 times, which is the more economical to buy? What other factors than the number of times a shirt may be laundered may influence your selection?
4. You should be certain that when you buy clothing your best buy is quality clothing. Remember that excellent quality is available in moderate and even low-priced garments if you know how to recognize it. Survey recently purchased garments by your family. Check each garment for quality asking the following questions:

(a) Are the seams stitched evenly?
(b) Are the seams generous?
(c) Are buttons securely fastened?
(d) Do the zippers work easily and have dependable locking mechanisms?
(e) Are the linings and pockets tightly woven of firm material?
(f) Do the fabric patterns match where the seams come together?
(g) Is the hem substantial?
(h) Is there any skimping around the shoulders, waist or hips?
(i) Is the garment guaranteed against shrinking?
(j) Is the garment fade-proof?
(k) Is the finish of the garment permanent?
(l) Is the garment wrinkle-resistant?
(m) Is the lining made of substantial material? Is it securely sewed into the garment?
(n) Does the lining lie flat and smooth?
(o) Were there any manufacturer's instructions with the garment on the proper care of it?

All these points are factors to consider in buying quality clothing. After analyzing several garments with these questions in mind, bring one of the garments to class and give a report as to why you believe it to be a quality garment or why you believe quality is lacking in the garment.

COMMUNITY PROBLEMS AND PROJECTS

1. Obtain samples of three distinctly different types of fabrics. Paste them on a sheet of paper, and opposite each classify the fabric and write an explanation of why you have classified the fabric as you have.
2. Obtain two different pieces of cotton fabric. Cut them into pieces approximately two inches square. Paste them on a sheet of paper, and opposite each give your opinion of the strength and the general quality of the fabric. Give an analysis of the thread count by marking off a one-inch square on each piece and counting the number of threads running lengthwise and crosswise.
3. Invite a representative of a women's apparel store, the store being selected by the members of the class, to come to the class to explain and demonstrate how to select and buy a fur stole. Be prepared to ask questions. Also invite a representative of a man's apparel store to explain and demonstrate how to select and buy a man's suit.

Chapter 15

How to Buy Home Appliances and Automobiles

Purpose of the Chapter. The purchase of home appliances, mechanical equipment for home and personal use, and automobiles is an important problem in the average home. Not only does the purchase of one of these items involve a major expenditure but also in many instances operating and service costs are dependent upon the wisdom of the choices made. The purpose of this chapter is to develop general principles that may serve as guides in the wise selection and buying of home appliances and automobiles.

You will find answers to these questions:

1. What are the general principles for the selection of home appliances?
2. How may specific guides in the selection of a particular type of appliance be developed?
3. What procedure should be followed in selecting a new automobile?
4. What factors should be considered in comparing new automobiles?
5. What principles should be observed in selecting a used automobile?

General Guides in Buying Home Appliances and Equipment. Many appliances are used to make the work of the home easier and more pleasant and to contribute to comfort and enjoyment. Some homes are equipped with practically all appliances that are available, but the budgets of most families make it necessary to buy only the specific appliances that will bring the greatest satisfaction.

Harold M. Lambert

The buying of a television set, a lawn mower, a garden tractor, power tools, and any other items in a home represent a major expenditure and should last a long time. Since they are not made frequently but involve considerable money, they should be bought carefully.

Buying a Television Set Involves a Major Expenditure

Among the many major appliances that are frequently purchased for the home are ranges, refrigerators, freezers, water heaters, dishwashers, food waste disposals, incinerators, furnaces, manual or automatic clothes washers, clothes dryers and ironers, vacuum cleaners, television receivers, radios, record players, sewing machines, and room or central air conditioners.

Very few houses have all of the appliances and mechanical devices that are available, but even if only a few are used, the money invested in them warrants very careful selection and buying. They represent a substantial portion of the total investment in a home. Most of the appliances have a life of many years. We do not repeat buying them as we do food and clothing. Therefore, the home owner does not obtain much practice in their selection and purchase. Consequently, it is important to know in advance how to select and how to buy wisely. Basic principles have been set up to serve as guides in this important phase of consumer activities.

The basic principles of selection and buying apply equally well to all types of both the major and small home appliances and mechanical equipment. In addition to these general guides for the selection and purchase of home appliances and laborsaving equipment, some specific guides may be considered in the selection of each type of appliance, such as ranges, refrigerators and home freezers, and vacuum cleaners.

Our study will be confined primarily to the basic principles of selection and buying applicable to all kinds of home appliances. In addition our study will include two or three illustrations of the application of specific principles to the selection and buying of each type of appliance, such as ranges and refrigerators.

Fourteen questions that may serve as general guides in selecting and buying major and small home appliances are given below:

Guides in Purchasing Home Appliances

1. Is the appliance actually needed?
2. What size or capacity is necessary to meet your needs?
3. What are the general specifications of the appliances made by various manufacturers?
4. What do you know about the dealer? Can you depend upon him?
5. What do you know about the manufacturer's reputation?
6. What operating cost may be expected?
7. What maintenance and service costs may be expected?
8. How readily available is service?
9. What is the guarantee?
10. What is the expected life and the probable trade-in value of the appliance?
11. What special care does the appliance require?
12. What has been the experience of other users?
13. Does the appliance meet the tests for safety?
14. What seals of approval does it carry?

Specific Guides in Buying Household Ranges. There are two major types of ranges for cooking purposes, electric and gas. The type of household range you buy depends not only upon the availability of gas or electricity but also upon the relative cost per heating unit, which varies from one community to another. After you decide upon the type of range that you should buy, several other factors should be considered in making the selection.

A person buying a gas or an electric range cannot be expected to have the technical knowledge to base his decision upon his own observations of the quality of the product. He can apply the fourteen general principles of buying home appliances, and he may consider the special guides for the selection of a range given below.

Specific Guides in Selecting a Range

1. Is the arrangement of surface burners satisfactory?
2. Are the oven and broiler adequate in size and located conveniently?
3. Can the heat be controlled for different speeds of cooking?
4. Are the oven, broiler, and surface burners easily cleaned?
5. Is the finish durable?
6. Is the oven insulation adequate?

Buying Refrigerators and Home Freezers. The rapid change from preserved and canned to fresh and frozen fruits, vegetables, and meats has made a food refrigerator a necessity in the home. Mechanical refrigerators use electricity or gas. Mechanical refrigerators are of three types: (1) the conventional type for short-term storage of foods with a small freezing unit for ice cubes, desserts, and small quantities of frozen foods; (2) the home freezer for the freezing and storage of foods for several weeks or months; (3) the refrigerator-freezer, which combines the two. The home freezer, either as a separate unit or in combination with the conventional refrigerator, is especially applicable to the needs of people with gardens and is useful for people in cities who like to buy food in large quantities.

As stated earlier, the selection and purchase of any home appliance should be based upon a very careful and detailed study of its general characteristics and intended uses. As an illustration of the kind of study that may be made for a specific type of appliance, six basic points for consideration in buying refrigerators and freezers are given. Similar studies could be made for each type of home appliance.

(a) Tests disclose that the following temperatures are necessary to preserve particular types of food under average conditions for short-term storage:

```
Milk, milk dishes, butter, broth,
    desserts ....................Not over 45° F.
Uncooked meats, poultry, covered
    jars of salad material .........Not over 47° F.
Berries, cooked meats ...........Not over 48° F.
Cooked vegetables, eggs, fats,
    left-overs ...................Not over 50° F.
Uncooked fruits and vegetables ..Not over 52° F.
```

The average temperature of a modern type of refrigerator should not exceed 45 degrees in the milk compartment and 50 degrees in the food compartment, when the outside temperatures average 80 degrees with occasional periods of 90 degrees or higher. The proper humidity is required to maintain the proper freshness of foods. The amount of humidity varies according to the type of cooling system, construction of the cabinet, and method of circulating air.

(b) Factors to be considered in determining the cost of operation are: relative cost of gas and electricity, rate of depreciation (normal is from five to ten per cent a year), and cost of maintenance service and repair.

(c) The storage space and freezing capacity must be adequate to meet the family needs. The rate and the capacity of freezing should be measured at a definite room temperature. In some mechanical refrigerators, fast freezing will cause the freezing of certain foods in other parts of the refrigerator and therefore will damage them.

A family of two will require approximately six cubic feet of refrigerator space. The minimum for a family of four is seven or eight cubic feet, and one additional cubic foot of space for each additional member of a family.

The cubic foot of space is not the only problem. The square feet of shelf space is important, because shelf space determines the practical, usable capacity. A refrigerator containing six cubic feet should contain from twelve to fourteen square feet of shelf space in order to make maximum use of the refrigerator.

(d) Construction affects the durability and serviceability of refrigerators. Cabinets of mechanical refrigerators and home freezers should be made of steel that will resist rust. The frames should be rigid and strong, and the exterior finish either lacquer or baked enamel. In the refrigerators of good quality the lining usually is seamless and is coated with enamel. The bottom of the compartment is sometimes made of porcelain to resist acids from foods that may be spilled. The racks should be of a good quality metal that will resist rust. Home freezers should be constructed of the same type of materials as conventional refrigerators; however, the bottom of the food compartment need not be porcelain because frozen foods seldom are spilled.

Specific Guides in Selecting a Refrigerator or Freezer

1. Does the cabinet meet your requirements for easy cleaning; durability of finish; resistance to scratching, staining, and chipping; and insulation?
2. Is the ice cube capacity adequate?
3. Are temperature controls clearly marked and easy to set?
4. Will the shelves accommodate containers of different sizes, bottles, and bulky foods?
5. Are the special compartments for meat, fresh vegetables and fruits adequate in size, conveniently located, and constructed to serve the purpose intended?
6. Is the size of the compartment for frozen foods satisfactory for the needs of the family? Can the temperature of the frozen food compartment be maintained low enough for satisfactory storage of food?
7. How much extra are you willing to pay for the convenience of such features as automatic door closer, foot or pedal door opener, sliding and adjustable shelves, special color, self-defrosting, and butter compartment?

(e) The insulation used in the walls, door, top, and bottom of the refrigerator or freezer is an important factor in operating cost. Several kinds of insulation are used in the construction of refrigerators and freezers. Testing agencies may be consulted for the relative efficiency of the different kinds of insulation materials. Insulation in home freezers is especially important because of the low temperature that must be maintained.

Insulation should be of a type that will not settle and that will resist moisture. Usually the insulation of good refrigerators is at least three inches thick and of good home freezers, four inches thick.

(f) Mechanical efficiency is measured by the amount of power or fuel consumed to operate the refrigerator or freezer. Dealers and manufacturers usually have information based upon tests that will enable you to compare the efficiency of different models and different brands.

Although a well-designed and well-constructed refrigerator or freezer should operate quietly, the possible noise and vibration nuisance should be considered.

Buying Other Labor Saving Equipment. The fourteen general guides in the selection and purchase of home appliances should be applied to all kinds of mechanical equipment for home and personal use. Specific guides similar to those mentioned for the buying of ranges, refrigerators, and freezers may be developed by the consumer and applied in the selection and purchase of other equipment, such as food mixers, water heaters, waste food disposers, automatic dishwashers, power lawn mowers, bicycles, and cameras.

A Warranty May Justify a Higher Price

Price should be considered as a relative matter. A machine that sells for $125.00 may be a bargain as compared with one that sells for $80.00.

All the factors of quality, length of life, and cost of operation must be taken into consideration with price. Whenever possible, the choice should be based on comparison of all the factors.

When you are considering purchasing a particular appliance, such as a room air conditioner, you will be interested in two aspects of the tests of that appliance made by agencies, such as private testing laboratories, Consumers' Research, Inc., and Consumers Union. Your first interest will be in the points tested. In other words, what did they test? Second, you will be interested in the results of their tests which are sometimes given as ratings.

Buying Automobiles. When one considers buying an automobile, he should first decide how much he can afford to spend. Then, he should examine and study the automobiles that fall in his price range. Very good and serviceable automobiles are found in each of the four or five price groups.

You will find from eight to ten different makes and models of automobiles priced within one or two hundred dollars of your price range. Ordinarily, the actual differences in quality and serviceability of the basic automobiles in such a price group are relatively slight. Therefore, the decision as to which one to buy frequently is based first on the buyer's personal preference and, second, on the extras and the special features that appeal to him. Having decided which two or three automobiles in a price group one likes best, consideration should then be given to special features available such as types of transmission, radio, heat and fresh air devices, and power steering and brakes. Again, the buyer will need to decide how much extra he can afford to spend for these features.

Though practically all of the automobiles manufactured today will give satisfactory performance, a buyer should not pay more than necessary to get what he wants. Some analysis should, therefore, be made so that values can be compared. A buyer should select the automobile that not only has the largest number of points that appeal to him but also that will serve his needs the best.

A sample check sheet designed to help you rate new automobiles in the same price group is given on page 268. This check sheet is to serve as an illustration of how you may make one of your own. You may, for example, believe other factors should be added to or substituted for those on the check sheet. You may also believe some factors merit a greater number or fewer points than are assigned on the check sheet.

Analyzing Delivery Prices of Automobiles. Some manufacturers of automobiles make a low-priced series and a high-priced series. Basically they are the same, but the higher-priced series may have stepped up horsepower through better carburation or a better quality of upholstery or a larger size of tires. In the low price field, the difference in price of an automobile in the low-priced series and one in the high-priced series is from $200 to $300.

An analysis of the cost of an automobile, similar to the one given below may be made by any prospective buyer.

Description of Low-priced Series Automobile

Two-door sedan, solid color, black tires, electric wipers, gasoline and oil filter, heater, six cylinder motor

Approximate factory-delivered price and dealer's profit		$1,700
Add: Federal tax	$165	
Freight	55	
Service (dealer)	25	245
Consumer's drive-away price		$1,945

A high-priced series automobile bearing the same description as the basic automobile may be priced to a consumer at $2,200.

The costs of selected accessories for either of the foregoing two automobiles are:

8-cylinder motor	$ 99
4-door body	44
White sidewall tires	27
Two-tone paint	15
Radio	75
Automatic transmission	180
Power brakes	33
Power steering	92
Tinted glass	33
Air conditioner	565
Electric seat and window controls	92

SAMPLE CHECK SHEET FOR COMPARING NEW AUTOMOBILES IN THE SAME PRICE GROUP

FACTOR FOR EVALUATION	POINT VALUE ASSIGNED TO FACTOR	AUTOMOBILE A	AUTOMOBILE B	AUTOMOBILE C
1. Delivered price, not including extras	40	40		
2. Additional cost of the extras and special features you want	30	30		
3. Fuel economy	30	30		
4. Economy in oil consumption	20	20		
5. Type of transmission	20		20	20
6. Cost of standard maintenance and repair	20	20	20	20
7. Riding qualities	20		20	
8. Roadability and ease of steering	20	20		
9. Body construction and workmanship	20			
10. Brake factor	15	15		
11. Horsepower, maximum	15		15	15
12. Engine revolutions per mile	15	15		
13. Acceleration	15		15	15
14. Compression ratio	15	15		
15. Gear ratio	10			
16. Tire size; battery capacity	10	10	10	10
17. Head, shoulder, and leg room	10			
18. Legibility of indicators and arrangement of controls on dash	10	10	10	
19. Quality of upholstery, trim, and finish	10			
20. Protection against door and body injury by other car doors	10			
21. Arm rests, sun visors, locks, lighter, horn button, and window controls	10			
22. Safety of driver and passengers	10	10	10	10
23. Owner's experience and satisfaction	10	10	10	10
Total	385	170	95	120

Instructions: Give the total points for a given factor to the automobile that you rate the highest.

Ch. 15]   HOW TO BUY APPLIANCES AND AUTOMOBILES   269

A prospective buyer should always analyze the drive-away price to see what he pays for.

An owner who wishes to trade his automobile for a new one should always analyze the price of the new automobile. He should make certain that the new automobile with its accessories is not overpriced to offset a larger trade-in allowance for the old automobile.

Automobile Depreciation. For practical consideration, depreciation of an automobile and decrease in value from obsolescence are the same. When a person drives a new automobile out of an agency and takes the title to it, he suffers a loss due to obsolescence, although the automobile has not depreciated because of wear or deterioration. If the automobile were to be resold immediately, the owner would have to accept a price lower than that he paid. Depreciation, on the other hand, results from wear.

Obsolescence Is an Important Factor in the Value of an Automobile

The depreciation to be expected on a low-priced automobile is approximately as follows:

YEAR	DEPRECIATION RATE
1st	25 to 30 per cent of drive-away cost
2nd	20 per cent of value at end of first year
3rd	25 to 30 per cent of value at end of second year
4th	20 per cent of value at end of third year
5th	20 per cent of value at end of fourth year

By the end of the fifth year most automobiles will have depreciated approximately 70 to 75 per cent of their original drive-away prices. In general, the higher the purchase price of the car, the greater the percentage of depreciation and the greater the total amount of depreciation.

Most people find that it is most economical to trade in a car at least every three or four years. Although an automobile may have been driven less in three years than another was driven in two, it is a common practice in the automobile industry to allow less for the automobile that has been driven three years than for the one that has been driven two. This practice is based on the fact that the older model has become more obsolete than the one that has been used only two years.

Gasoline and Oil Consumption. The consumer should know that every automobile burns more gasoline at a high rate of speed than it does at a reasonable rate of speed. Furthermore, there is a difference among automobiles. Some will burn more gasoline than others at certain rates of speed. The chart below shows the increase in quantity of gasoline used as miles per hour increase. For each of the five cars tested, the most economical rate of speed was from 25 to 35 miles per hour.

Every automobile must consume a certain quantity of oil because oil lubricates the mechanism. Nevertheless, some automobiles consume excessive quantities of oil. For instance, the following table shows the quantity of oil consumed by each of five automobiles in the same price class:

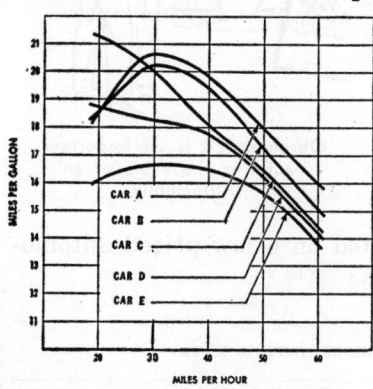

Source: *Consumers' Research Bulletin*, Washington, New Jersey, February 1955. Used by permission.

Gasoline Consumption

Automobile A	1,670 miles on a quart of oil
Automobile B	1,180 miles on a quart of oil
Automobile C	990 miles on a quart of oil
Automobile D	880 miles on a quart of oil
Automobile E	830 miles on a quart of oil

Oil Consumption of Five Automobiles

Buying Used Automobiles. Almost twice as many used automobiles as new automobiles are sold annually. From

75 to 90 per cent of new automobile buyers trade in their old automobiles. Usually, plenty of used automobiles are available. The prices vary according to the demand for them.

Most people are not able to judge the condition of a used automobile. Consequently, they must depend upon a reliable dealer. Well-established new car dealers feel a sense of responsibility to the purchasers of both new and used cars. Among the independent used car dealers are many

---

Points to Consider in Buying a Used Automobile

1. Decide how much you can spend for a used automobile.
2. Buy only from dealers who are known to be reputable.
3. Beware of exaggerated advertisements.
4. Do not be misled by "bait" advertising or "bargains."
5. Compare prices of comparable models by shopping among reputable dealers.
6. Keep in mind the total price to be paid for the automobile you are purchasing.
7. Do not be misled by high trade-in allowances.
8. Automobiles from two to three years old usually are the best buy.
9. Do not rely upon speedometer readings for actual mileage. The miles driven per year by the average owner is 10,000.
10. Do not pay extra for radio or heater; a maximum of 50 per cent of original cost should be paid for such items as automatic transmission, power brakes, and power steering.
11. External and internal appearances are indications of the care the previous owner has given.
12. An automobile that has a neglected interior probably also has been neglected mechanically.
13. Always test drive before buying.
14. If necessary, have a mechanic examine the car for you.
15. Check steering, wheel alignment, and brakes.
16. Observe how well the engine runs under various conditions.
17. Avoid automobiles that have been badly wrecked.
18. Examine your purchase contract in detail.
19. Is the used automobile guaranteed?

reliable ones, and also some whose practices may be questionable. In any event, make certain the dealer from whom you buy a used automobile is reliable.

Beware of exaggerations in advertising used automobiles. "Bait" advertising also is used by some dealers. Often, however, the advertised car is said to have been sold just before you as a prospective buyer arrived.

Inasmuch as depreciation rates are the highest on automobiles during their first two years, a model from two to three years old is probably the most economical to buy. Some kinds of automobiles are much more popular, both new and used, than others. The price of popular automobiles on the used car lot is usually considerably higher than the cost of used cars of a make that has not been so popular. Based upon the amount of potential mileage still in a used car, frequently those that are less popular are the best bargains. However, one should be aware when buying either a new or used car that the popularity of that particular kind of car affects its trade-in value when you want to dispose of it.

Automobile Supplies and Accessories. Tires, oil, and gasoline represent the major operating costs of an automobile. The problem of buying automobile supplies, of which these are the chief items, is so important that technical information should be obtained from some authoritative source. Consumers' Research, Consumers Union, and other testing agencies are in a position to furnish such information.

The most expensive product is not necessarily the best; but cheap tires, oils, or gasolines are frequently not economical. Some cheap oils may damage the engine, and some cheap gasolines may cause the formation of carbon and a loss of power.

Every manufacturer wants his automobile to stand up well. It is therefore advisable to study carefully the recommendations of the manufacturer in regard to the type of gasoline and type or grade of oil to use. So-called high compression engines require a high grade of gasoline with a high octane rating.

Probably no item of maintenance and care is more important than the proper oil in an automobile engine. Motor oils are classified as follows:

Regular or Service ML (light service). This oil is for engines having no special lubricating requirements and operating at moderate speeds.

Premium or Service MM (moderate service). This oil is for engines that do not have special lubrication requirements but that operate at high speeds.

Heavy-duty or Service MS (severe service). These oils contain bearing corrosion inhibiters and a detergent additive. They are especially for engines operating under severe conditions and for engines having special lubricating requirements, such as hydraulic valve lifters. This oil may be used in any car for any type of driving.

A good filter will help to keep the oil in good condition; however, all heavy duty oils look dark after use because the detergent holds carbon and other elements in suspension.

Summary of Guides in Selecting Home Appliances and Automobiles

1. The principles of the selection and purchase of home appliances in general are applicable also to each specific type of appliance.
2. Specific guides to supplement the general principles for the selection of home appliances may be developed separately by the consumer for each type of appliance.
3. Automobiles in all price groups will give satisfactory performance.
4. Comparison of automobiles in a given price group provides a reliable basis for selection.
5. An excessively large cost of special features and extras is often hidden in the consumers' drive-away price of an automobile.
6. On a quality basis used automobiles are more difficult to select than new ones.
7. An automobile buyer should use a check sheet or a similar device to evaluate the automobiles from which he will select one.

TEXTBOOK QUESTIONS

1. Why don't consumers know as much about the purchase of appliances as they do food and clothing?
2. What general guides may be followed in the selection and purchase of home appliances?
3. What are some of the general guides that may be used in selecting a range?
4. What is the maximum temperature that should be permitted in a refrigerator to preserve (a) milk, (b) uncooked meats, (c) uncooked fruits and vegetables?
5. What factors should be considered in determining the cost of operation of a refrigerator or home freezer?
6. What is the minimum size of a refrigerator for (a) a family of two, (b) a family of four?
7. Why is it not necessary that the bottom of the food compartment of a home freezer be porcelain?
8. What are some of the important construction features of a refrigerator or home freezer?
9. Make a list of as many guides for the buying of home refrigerators and home freezers as you can.
10. Name two organizations in the United States which have as part of their functions the testing and rating of home appliances.
11. When one considers buying an automobile, what should be one's first decision?
12. Name at least five factors to be followed in evaluating an automobile.
13. Describe what is usually the best bargain in a used car.
14. List the points that you consider most pertinent in buying a used automobile.

DISCUSSION QUESTIONS

1. Discuss how each of the guides listed on page 261 for the selection and purchase of home appliances may be applied when purchasing an ironer.
2. How would you determine if the manufacturer of a home appliance is reliable?
3. Discuss the importance of selecting an appliance made by a reliable manufacturer through a reliable dealer.
4. How much dependence should be placed on the statements of friends and acquaintances about their experiences in using a particular appliance?
5. Discuss the type of guarantee that you think would be acceptable if you were buying an electric refrigerator.
6. (a) If a gas-burning appliance bears the seal of the American Gas Association, what can you assume with regard to

Ch. 15] HOW TO BUY APPLIANCES AND AUTOMOBILES

the quality of the appliance? (b) If the appliance does not bear such a seal, is that fact an indication that the appliance is of a poor construction?
7. When you try to investigate the performance of an electric refrigerator, you find that styles in refrigerators change so frequently that it is impossible to form any conclusions unless a comparison is made with older models of the same refrigerator. What are some of the factors that could be investigated in order that you might base some of your conclusions on the experience of those who are using older models?
8. What factors should be considered in the purchase of a home freezer?
9. A dealer advertises the sale of the electric refrigerator of a bankrupt manufacturer at 75 per cent of the cost. (a) Would you consider such an electric refrigerator to be a bargain? (b) Would you buy one? Give your reasons.
10. From your knowledge of copper, enamel, and aluminum, what do you think would be the advantages and the disadvantages of washing machines made from each of these three kinds of materials?
11. What major classes of factors should be considered in selecting an automobile to meet your needs?
12. Discuss repair service as a factor in buying an automobile.
13. Can you see any reasons why one dealer might offer as much as $100 more for a secondhand car on a trade-in than was offered by another dealer?
14. In proportion to the original cost of the automobile, a large secondhand automobile can be purchased for less than a small used automobile of the same age. Why is this true?

PROBLEMS

1. A family that has a savings budget of $15 a month wishes to buy an electric refrigerator. The payments will amount to $15 a month for twelve months. The increase in the electric bill will average 85 cents a month. Past experience discloses that the average amount spent for ice during the warm weather is $18 a year. The family does not want to withdraw anything from its savings fund to use in paying the monthly installments. (a) Can a plan be worked out satisfactorily? (b) If the refrigerator will cost $180 and can be used no more than twenty years, do you think it will be a wise investment? Under what circumstances?
2. Prepare a list of factors that may be considered in evaluating a room air conditioning unit for home use.

3. A company that uses a large number of automobiles finds that the average costs per mile for the operation of each automobile are:

   Gasoline and oil $0.021
   Garage rent .... .003
   Repairs .... .01
   Insurance .... .003
   Depreciation .... .023

   (a) What should be the annual cost of operating an automobile that is driven 30,000 miles during the year? (b) On the basis of the costs listed above, what should be the monthly cost of operating an automobile if the owner drives the car about 10,000 miles a year and trades it in on a new automobile at the end of three years?
4. How much would it cost for three years, for one year, and for each mile to own and operate an automobile, assuming the following conditions: A used automobile cost $1,300; it may be traded in on another automobile at the end of three years at an allowance of $450; the average cost of gasoline and oil is 2¼ cents a mile; repairs and maintenance service cost $72 a year; insurance including bodily injury and property damage costs $80 a year; license and property taxes cost $18 a year; the average mileage is 10,000 a year. What would be the effect on the cost a year and the cost a mile if the automobile were driven 20,000 miles a year?
5. Develop as complete a list as you can of buying guides for a food mixer or for a power lawn mower.

COMMUNITY PROBLEMS AND PROJECTS

1. Assume that a young man who has a moderate income and who rides five miles to work every day is considering the purchase of an automobile. The automobile is also used for short shopping trips, pleasure, and some vacation travel. There are two adults and a four-year-old child in the family. Using the check sheet on page 268, investigate through literature available at automobile dealers and newspaper and magazine advertisements three automobiles that may meet this young man's needs. You may need some information about the automobiles that is not listed on the check sheet. Write a report on your findings. In the report, reproduce the check sheet. Explain your procedures and justify your conclusions as to which is the better for the young man to buy.
2. Besides the points given in this chapter, add all additional points that you can think of and prepare a rating chart for electric refrigerators and home freezers. With this chart proceed to make a comparison of two refrigerators or two freezers to try to determine the best buy.

Chapter 16

How to Buy Furniture and Floor Coverings

Purpose of the Chapter. The purchase of furniture and floor coverings is an important problem. These items are not purchased often; but when they are purchased, they deserve careful consideration, for they will be used a long time. The primary purpose of this chapter is to establish a few fundamental standards by which furniture and floor coverings can be judged without the necessity of a technical analysis.

You will find answers to these questions:

1. How can one's furniture problem be solved?
2. What guides should be followed in selecting wood and upholstered furniture?
3. What determines the quality of carpet?
4. What factors should govern one's selection of carpets?
5. What does a buyer need to know about linoleums and floor tiles in order to select wisely?

Selecting the Right Furniture. The householder should buy furniture and not allow himself to be sold furniture. In furnishing a home, it is desirable to know in advance the space to be filled and the amount of money that may be used. Of course, the ideal situation is one in which the funds available will permit the furnishing of all the rooms adequately. In many cases, however, the budget must be stretched considerably to buy the bare necessities.

Deliberation will help to eliminate unwise buying. There are two extremes to be avoided. One is a disproportionate expenditure for a few pieces of furniture at the sacrifice of

Carpet Institute, Inc.

Since furniture is often purchased to last a lifetime, there should be great care in selecting it. It should be both practical and attractive. Even inexpensive furniture can be attractive and practical. Shop carefully until you find what you want at the price you can pay.

Attractive and Practical Furnishings for a Teen-Ager's Room

other necessary pieces. The other extreme is the buying of unsatisfactory furniture at a low price in order to obtain a full suite.

In Chapter 23 there is a study of budgeting. When young married couples equip a home, the first step is to determine how much money can be spent; then make a list of requirements. The most urgent items should be purchased as the budget will permit; others will have to wait until there is a place in the budget for them.

The suitability of furniture depends largely on personal taste. Good judgment can, however, be formed by studying color combinations, by considering the space that is available, by observing the furnishings in other homes, and by examining the furniture in several stores. Many stores have good salesmen or consultants who will give free advice, but you can also hire a professional decorator.

Ch. 16]				Furniture and Floor Coverings				279

Except for the modern styles of furniture, most furniture of good quality and of good style is based on well-established patterns that, in most cases, were created centuries ago. The functional qualities of modern sectional furniture merit consideration. Tables, cases, chests, and other pieces are designed in related heights and proportions to be used singly, stacked, or grouped in many ways. Sectional furniture may be particularly advantageous where space is limited.

Furniture that is not comfortable is a poor investment. Therefore, the height and size of the persons who will use it should be considered in selection.

What Is a Good Furniture Wood? The type of wood has an important relation to the price of furniture. It also has an important relation to the quality and the wearing features. Some woods crack easily and show scratches readily. Those that are soft show marks easily. Others are subject to warping when exposed to moisture.

The ideal wood for furniture possesses enough hardness to resist normal wear, yet it is sufficiently soft to be worked with ordinary tools without splitting. It should also be subject to minimum swelling and shrinkage. The natural grains are attractive. No wood is perfect in all respects. Some woods have one desirable feature, but lack some other. The problem resolves itself into getting the best wood one can afford at a reasonable price.

Walnut is almost an ideal wood for furniture because it combines beauty, strength, and durability. There are various grades of walnut, most of which are good. Oak is a good wood for furniture because it is solid and substantial. It is so hard that it is not subject to scratching, as are many of the other woods.

Gum is one of the most widely used of the American hardwoods. It is used frequently by itself and in many cases in combination with other wood. It is not so desirable as the two previously mentioned woods because it is softer and is subject to scratching and warping.

Birch, maple, beech, chestnut, and cherry are also good woods for furniture. Mahogany is excellent, but most of it is imported and is therefore costly, although it is often not so costly as walnut.

The softer woods, such as poplar, spruce, and pine, are not so desirable for furniture because of their relative lack of durability. However, pine is preferred for some Early American furniture.

The average person who is not familiar with woods cannot rely upon his own judgment in distinguishing them. In selecting a piece of furniture, he should therefore be sure to observe whether it is made of more than one piece of wood, how much of it is solid, and what parts are made of veneer. Ask what kind or combinations of wood are used in its construction. Some of this information is given on labels.

WOODS USED IN FURNITURE

DESIRABLE AMERICAN WOODS	DESIRABLE IMPORTED WOODS	UNDESIRABLE AMERICAN WOODS
Walnut	Mahogany	Ash
Oak	Ebony	Cypress
Cherry	Primavera	Elm
Birch	Teak	Pine*
Maple	Rosewood	Redwood
Chestnut		Cedar
Gum		Fir
Beech		Hemlock
Basswood		Poplar
Hickory		Spruce
Sycamore		

* Soft, but preferred for some types of furniture such as Early American.

Types of Furniture Woods

The table above shows a list of the most common woods that are used in furniture. Those that are most desirable are indicated. Some of those listed as undesirable are used for cheaper grades of furniture. Some of them may make furniture just as sturdy as the better grades, but the furniture will be lacking in beauty. Some of the desirable woods for indoor furniture are not satisfactory for outdoor furniture. Cypress, redwood, and cedar are recommended for outdoor furniture because they will withstand weather conditions.

Veneer. As a general rule, but not always, furniture made of a solid wood is more expensive than a comparable piece made wholly or partially of veneer. Solid wood can be carved. If it is scratched or chipped, there is no danger, as in the case of veneer, that a thin surface layer of wood will be penetrated. The use of veneer, however, is not necessarily an indication of low quality. In fact, some of the best furniture today is constructed with veneer for the tops and panels.

Veneer consists of two or more thin layers of wood from 1/28th inch to 1/35th inch in thickness glued together. Veneer makes it possible to use a good piece of wood for the surface of furniture and a cheaper piece for those parts underneath the surface. Large panels and the tops of large tables are less liable to warp if they are made of veneer than if they are of a solid wood. Cheap veneer may blister, however, because moisture loosens the glue. It also may develop checks and cracks.

The mechanical construction of a piece of furniture may be perfect, but the beauty of the piece may have been lessened by carelessness in matching the grain of the veneer in a panel.

The beauty of the grain in the wood is one indication of quality, whereas the careful matching of the grain tends to indicate good workmanship. The illustration below shows how veneer is matched in creating attractive designs. Unusual designs may be created in this way. Drawer fronts, doors, and table tops made of veneer often have beautiful patterns.

When examining a piece of furniture, the purchaser should look underneath and inside it if possible. He should notice ends that can be examined. A place that is not covered with varnish and stain is preferable for examination. It is easy to distinguish ve-

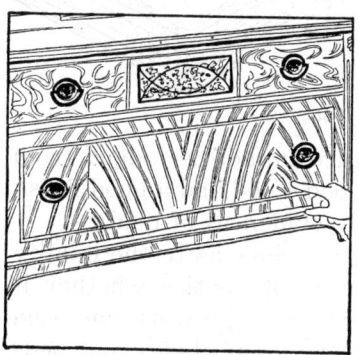

Well-Matched Veneer

neer from solid wood because veneer is composed of two or more thin layers of wood with the grains crossing. The purchaser should find out whether the furniture is made of just one kind of wood or of more than one kind.

The quality of veneer depends largely on (a) the care used in gluing, (b) the number of layers, and (c) the kind and the thickness of the veneer. The only way in which a casual observer can judge the quality of the gluing is to observe whether the veneer is coming loose in any place. This test is not absolute, however. It is often easy to determine the number of layers. When other factors are not considered, the veneer with the greater number of layers is the better piece of veneer. The illustration below shows five-ply and three-ply veneer. Although it is too much to expect the average person to be able to judge the quality of the wood used in a veneer, he can usually detect the thickness of the surface veneer. If this veneer is too thin, it will scratch easily or absorb moisture.

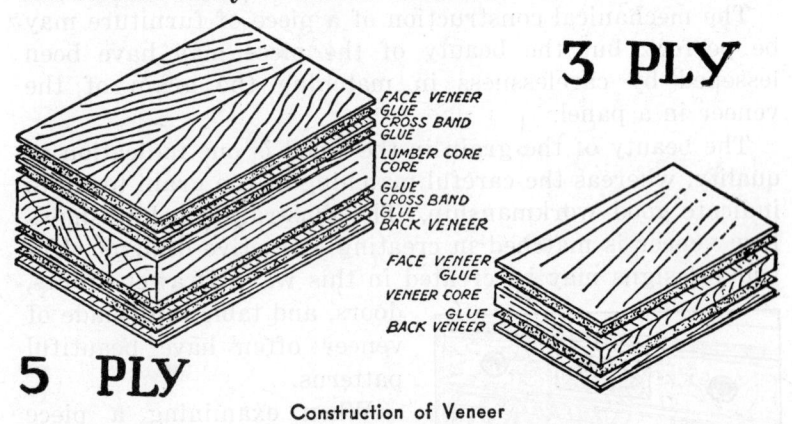

Construction of Veneer

Joints. A good piece of furniture cannot be judged from only the surface. Furthermore, good wood and a good finish should not be accepted as the only evidences of quality.

The back of any cabinet will give clues as to the quality of workmanship. The purchaser should notice whether it has been nailed or screwed and whether the work has been done poorly or neatly. The back posts of chairs and beds should be scrutinized carefully to determine how they have

Ch. 16] FURNITURE AND FLOOR COVERINGS 283

A

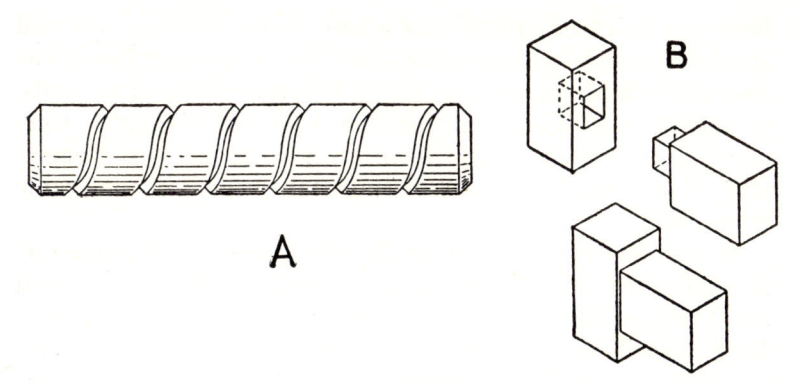

Dowel, and Mortise and Tenon Construction

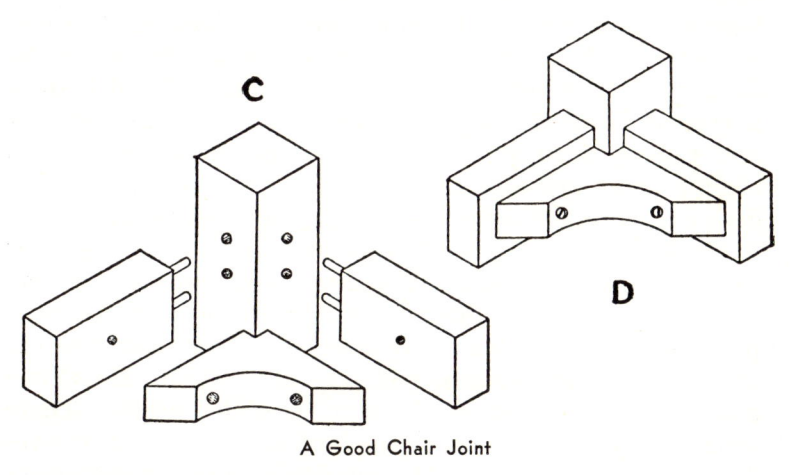

C **D**

A Good Chair Joint

E **F**

Good Construction for Drawers

been put together. All points where there will be stress and strain should have been reinforced when the furniture was manufactured. Fastening joints together with glue, nails, or screws usually does not provide adequate strength. Corner blocks, which should have been fastened with screws and glue, are important because they add considerable strength.

In the illustration on page 283, the example designated as A shows the dowel type of construction; that designated as B shows the mortise and tenon type of construction. Both types are desirable, for they help to strengthen furniture. Sometimes a combination of the two is used. Example C below shows how a chair joint is frequently put together, and example D shows the assembled joint. Combinations of A and B are sometimes used by employing the dowel with the mortise and tenon. Examples E and F show a typical dovetail joint and dado joint used in the construction of drawers. These joints prevent drawers from coming apart provided they have been well glued. The best drawers will have dovetails at the front and the back.

The drawer is one of the best indications of care in the construction of a piece of furniture, for many things can be observed from the drawer but not elsewhere in the same piece of furniture. The purchaser should observe whether the bottom is strong and will stay in position. He should also determine whether the drawer slides easily. There should be a center slide for the bottom and special grooves for guiding the drawer. The relative ease in the movement of the drawer will give some indication of whether the wood is well seasoned. If it sticks or jams when new, it probably will be worse later.

Finish. The finish of a piece of furniture can be judged largely by its smoothness and its durability. The finish can be tested by scratching the varnish on an obscure part of the furniture with the fingernail to see whether it comes loose easily, becomes chalky, or rubs off. The varnish should also be pressed with the finger to see whether it is sticky. The finish is probably satisfactory if it reacts favorably to these tests and if it is smooth and unmarked.

Furniture is frequently advertised as having "walnut finish" or "maple finish." These terms do not indicate the kind of wood or veneer. They merely indicate the kind of stain that has been used. The wood may be, and probably is, entirely different. A walnut stain, for instance, may be given to furniture made of pine; but this treatment does not improve the quality of the wood.

Frames of Upholstered Furniture. The frames of upholstered furniture are usually made of wood. Although most wood that is used in these frames is of an inexpensive variety, it must be strong and free of knots and cracks to avoid breaking. Ash, birch, and hard maple are good woods for this purpose.

The joints of upholstered furniture must be as carefully made as the joints of any other furniture, even though they may be covered. If possible, the purchaser should have the salesman display a cross section of the construction or have him turn the piece of furniture over so that the bottom construction can be seen and some of the joints can be felt.

In Buying Furniture, Look for Sturdy Construction

Stuffing in Upholstered Furniture. The stuffing or padding that is used in cushions and over springs may consist of sterilized hair, foam rubber, moss, down, kapok, palm fiber, cotton, or excelsior. The terms will be explained by a good dealer in furniture, and definitions are also given in leaflets distributed by the manufacturer of furniture. The first three are the most expensive. New cotton is also used in the upholstery of some of the better grades of furniture. Excelsior is the least desirable as well as the least expensive stuffing. Occasionally, in exceptionally low-grade furniture, shredded paper has been used. Before

Carpet Institute, Inc.

Check your budget when you buy furniture. Be especially careful in selecting upholstered furniture because there are many things that cannot be seen that determine quality. Check the covering and find out how it is made.

Home Furnishings Should Be Durable, Pleasing to the Eye, and Fit One's Budget

buying, therefore, it is wise to examine carefully any mattress or upholstered piece of furniture and to obtain some definite assurance of what has been used for stuffing.

Many states have laws pertaining to mattresses and other household furnishings containing padding or stuffing. On furniture that is upholstered, look for labels indicating whether the stuffing in the upholstery meets certain state requirements. This label will indicate the kind of material used for the stuffing or padding.

Coverings of Upholstered Furniture. The coverings of upholstered furniture are made of animal fibers, vegetable fibers, synthetic fibers, or leather. Woven fabrics may be a combination of animal, vegetable, or synthetic fibers. The animal fibers used for furniture covers include silk, wool, mohair, and horsehair. The vegetable fibers include cotton, flax, hemp, and jute. The principal man-made fibers used

OFFICIAL STATEMENT	Space to Attach
Manufactured of All New Material MATERIALS USED IN FILLING: **COTTON LINTERS** MADE BY **GOLD MEDAL FOLDING FURNITURE CO.** RACINE, WIS., U. S. A. VENDOR ADDRESS This article is made in compliance with the laws of the State of California, approved June 7, 1915; of Missouri, approved May 26, 1919; of New Jersey, approved March 4, 1913; of Pennsylvania, approved May 1, 1913; as amended; and of all other states of the Union which have enacted sanitary bedding laws.	**DO NOT REMOVE THIS TAG** under penalty of law This article contains SECOND-HAND MATERIAL consisting of KAPOK . . . . 50% COTTON LINTERS . . 50% Registry No___Permit No___ Space for New York State Inspection Stamp — This tag is attached as required by law as a certification that this article is as represented CONTENTS STERILIZED Sold by **JOHN DOE and SONS CO., INC.** No. 567 Greene St. New York City

Upholstered, Overstuffed Furniture and Bedding Are Required to Carry Informative Labels in Many States

in upholstering fabrics are rayon, nylon, acetate, and saran. The durability of natural and man-made fibers was explained in Chapter 14.

The table below provides a list of fabrics rated according to their durability for coverings on upholstered furniture.

FABRIC	CHARACTERISTICS
Brocade Bracotel Tapestry Satin	Attractive, but long threads on the surface are subject to tear and abrasion. Not good for hard use.
Frieze Plush Velvet	Attractive; will give good wear if firmly woven. Uncut pile is subject to catching and pulling.
Chintz Cretonne Denim Taffeta Homespun	Cheaper grades; of this group denim will give longest wear. Others are not suitable for rough use.

Fabrics Used for Furniture Coverings

Leather is used to a limited extent for upholstering. Good leather is relatively expensive. Some of the modern artificial leathers and plastics are very durable.

Generally speaking, fabrics that are firmly and closely woven from tightly twisted yarns are most likely to withstand heavy wear and the pulling that may result from catching the fibers on the surface. Loosely woven and soft fabrics are attractive, but they are subject to faster wear.

Guides in the Selection of Upholstered Furniture

1. The frame should be of hardwood, sturdily constructed.
2. Tempered steel springs should be firmly anchored to a steel base or to webbing.
3. Springs should be covered to keep dust out and filling in.
4. Springs should be tied or clipped together and fastened securely to the frame.
5. The padding should be generous and of good quality.
6. Padding should be covered to keep it in place and to provide a base for the top fabric.
7. Upholstering fabric should be durable, color fast, and easily cleaned.

Types of Carpets and Rugs. The thickness of the pile, the closeness of the weave, the height of the pile, and the quality of the fiber are more important than the type of weave. The types of weaves are as follows:

(a) *Cut-pile* carpets and rugs, including Oriental, Chenille, Wilton, Axminster, and Velvet.
(b) *Loop-pile* carpets and rugs, including Brussels and Tapestry weaves.
(c) *Flat-weave* rugs, such as those made of linen, cotton, wool, pulp fiber, and grass, which may be used either side up because both sides are alike.

In recent years a new type of construction known as tufted carpet or rug has been used extensively. Tufted carpets are really not woven. Loops or tufts of fiber are punched by a machine through a backing material which is then coated with a rubber-like compound to hold the tufts

Carpet Institute, Inc.

Carpets of Many Types of Weaves and Patterns, of Various Qualities, and at Widely Varying Prices Are Available for Home Use

in place. Many different fibers are now being used in making tufted carpets—cotton, wool, rayon, nylon, and other man-made fibers.

The fiber used has much to do with both wearing qualities and appearance. Over a long period of time wool has been recognized as one of the most satisfactory fibers for floor coverings. Cotton is durable and easily cleaned, but soils more readily than wool or rayon. When considering a carpet made of man-made fibers, inquire about the satisfaction it has given under actual wearing conditions.

Buy carpets and rugs from reputable dealers in whom you have confidence and who have had experience in dealing in floor coverings. The advice of a reliable dealer is the best assurance you can have of quality and serviceability.

Distinguishing Features of Rugs. The table on page 291 gives the features and quality of the basic types of rugs.

Rug Cushions. The length of life of any rug or carpet can be prolonged through the use of what is called a *rug cushion*. Such a cushion, which is placed under the rug or the carpet, prolongs the life of the rug.

Grass and Composition Rugs. Rugs are sometimes made of grass fibers and sometimes of a composition of wood pulp and other materials. The pulp is given special treatment so that the rugs will be hard and durable. Sometimes the pulp is combined with wool and other materials. The wearing qualities of a rug of this type depend largely upon the toughness of the fiber. In purchasing such a rug, one should therefore examine the fiber carefully with the fingernail to judge its toughness.

Another important consideration is whether the rug will hold its color under wear. Unless the color design has been woven into the rug, it will probably wear off in a short time.

Guides in Buying Rugs
1. Read the label.
2. Know the fibers and the amount of each used.
3. Examine the type of construction and kind of weave.
4. Know the ply of the yarn used and the number of tufts per square inch.
5. Observe the length of the pile.
6. Consider both serviceability and appearance.
7. Depend upon a reputable dealer for information.
8. Buy only from reliable dealers and stores experienced in floor coverings.

Smooth-surfaced Floor Coverings. Smooth-surfaced floor coverings are of several different types—enameled-surface felt base, asphalt tile, cork tile, linoleum, vinyl plastic, rubber, and vinyl asbestos. Each type has special characteristics.

FEATURES AND QUALITY OF THE BASIC TYPES OF RUGS

TYPE	DISTINGUISHING FEATURES	QUALITY	PATTERN
Oriental	Tufts tied separately; hand woven; unlimited colors	Long wearing; quality varies with the wool, length of fiber, fineness, and number of tufts per inch; luxurious in appearance	Unlimited; mostly individual expression of weaver
Wilton	Made from dyed yarn; cut-pile and loop-pile; may have several colors in combination; tightly woven; medium height pile	Wide range of quality depending upon fibers used and tufts per inch; from 95 to 128 tufts per square inch in highest quality; good quality wears exceptionally well; appearance, luxurious; easily cared for	Many patterns; tone-on-tone; sculptured; delicate and intricate designs
Axminster	Made of dyed yarns; colors do not show through back; can be rolled lengthwise only; heavy crosswise fiber in back to which pile is fastened	From four to eight rows of tufts per inch depending upon quality; 28 to 77 tufts per square inch; pile varies from ⅞ to ⅜ inches in depth	Unlimited patterns and colors
Velvet	High quality yarn; often in solid colors with design printed on after weaving; soft and pliable; smooth surfaced, occasionally hard-twist	Good quality is very durable; from 50 to 80 tufts per square inch depending on quality; pile from 3/16th to 5/16th inches in depth	Wide range of printed designs; many colors
Chenille	Woven from heavy cords rather than ordinary yarn; soft, luxurious pile; may be woven in widths to 30 feet; may be woven in irregular shapes	Good grades are luxurious in appearance and wear very well due to density of packed pile; some are difficult to keep clean	Usually tone-on-tone; may be textured or sculptured
Brussels	Similar to Wilton except pile is not cut; constructed of tightly looped wool	Durable; appearance very good	Patterns available; many color combinations
Tufted	Latex or rubber-like covering on back; many different fibers and combinations of fibers used; feels heavy	Quality varies widely; good grades have high count of tufts to inch; appearance good; durability and serviceability varies	Usually plain; may be tone-on-tone

Prices per square yard vary widely. Some are limited in their use. For example, linoleum and rubber should not be laid on a cement floor.

In most instances the wearing qualities and other service characteristics cannot be determined by examining a sample. Depend upon well-known manufacturers and reliable, well-established dealers for the information you need in selecting smooth-surface floor coverings.

Summary of Guides in Selection of Furniture and Floor Coverings

1. Furniture should be selected in accordance with an overall plan for the home.
2. Select furniture deliberately.
3. Learn to recognize good construction in wood furniture.
4. The quality of upholstered furniture may be determined by examining the frames, stuffing, and cover.
5. Quality of carpet is determined by thickness of pile, number of tufts per square inch, height of pile, and ply of the yarn.
6. Read the label in selecting furniture and floor coverings.
7. Buy furniture and floor coverings from reliable dealers.

TEXTBOOK QUESTIONS

1. What two extremes are to be avoided in buying furniture if it is necessary to budget the expenditures carefully?
2. What are the characteristics of a good wood for furniture?
3. (a) What is considered to be almost an ideal wood for furniture? (b) What is one of the most common American hardwoods? (c) What are some additional desirable woods for furniture?
4. Name some types of wood that are recommended for outdoor furniture.
5. Which is better for panels: solid wood or veneer?
6. What decorative advantage has veneer?
7. (a) Upon what does the quality of veneer depend? (b) In what way can one judge the quality of veneer?
8. What type of construction should be used to strengthen the posts of chairs and beds?
9. What type of construction should be used to fasten the corners of drawers in furniture?

10. What qualities should the wood in the frames of upholstered furniture possess?
11. (a) What are the most common types of stuffing used for upholstered furniture? (b) Which are the best? (c) Which is the least desirable?
12. What qualities should one consider in selecting upholstered furniture?
13. Give some examples of cloth used in upholstering furniture that are (a) not good for hard wear, (b) good for hard wear.
14. Over a long period of time, what fiber has proven to be most satisfactory for floor covering.
15. Of what value is a rug cushion?
16. Give the characteristics of the highest grades of Wilton rugs.
17. What types of smooth surfaced floor coverings should not be laid on cement floors?
18. Whom should the average purchaser of floor covering consult when he is planning to purchase a smooth surfaced floor covering?

DISCUSSION QUESTIONS

1. What do you think would be a good policy to follow in buying furniture for a home in which there are children?
2. How would you judge the value of a piece of furniture if it contained (a) oak and poplar? (b) walnut and gum? (c) gum and pine?
3. "If a piece of furniture contains veneer, it is not of high quality." Discuss this statement.
4. As the first step in judging the quality of a piece of furniture, one expert on the selection of furniture advocates removing and examining the drawer. What information is disclosed in this way?
5. If you were asked to examine a piece of furniture and to pass judgment on the merits of the finish, on what would you base your judgment?
6. (a) What means may be used for determining the kind of stuffing used in furniture? (b) What are the best types?
7. Even if you are not able to identify types of fabrics, how would you judge a good fabric for covering furniture?
8. How would you distinguish an Axminster rug from another type of rug?
9. (a) Explain some of the characteristics by which you could judge any rug. (b) How would you detect these?
10. What kinds of floor coverings are most satisfactory for cementing to a concrete floor? Why?
11. Give some reasons why ceramic tile is not used to any extent in northern states for floor coverings in bedrooms, dining rooms, and kitchens.

PROBLEMS

1. If a living room is twenty feet long by thirteen feet nine inches wide and has no obstructions protruding into it, how much will be the cost of having a rug made from strips of carpeting that are twenty-seven inches wide and cost $8.90 a yard? A floor border of fifteen inches will be around the rug, and five strips of carpeting are to run lengthwise with the room. If a fraction of a yard is needed, the charge for a full yard must be used.
2. A kitchen is eight feet wide by eleven feet long and has no obstructions protruding into it. Linoleum is available in strips three feet wide. Compute the cost of linoleum for the kitchen if the price is $3.00 a yard and the strips are to run lengthwise with the room.
3. In order to judge furniture on the basis of modern style and harmony in the home, it is desirable to know something about furniture styles. Obtain a book or magazine on furniture styles from the library, home economics department, or other source. Study the various styles and select one you believe to be suitable for your home. Give reasons for your choice. Include pictures of the furniture selected in your paper if possible.

COMMUNITY PROBLEMS AND PROJECTS

1. As a committee project, gather samples of cuts of rugs. Identify these rugs and prepare a display giving the identification and, if possible, some indication of quality. Before you begin this project decide where each committee member will secure samples of rugs. Plan your report and display of samples.
2. Make an analysis of the furniture in your home on the basis of (a) the kind of wood in the furniture, (b) the kind of construction used in the drawers and in strengthening the legs of chairs and tables, and (c) the use of veneer or solid wood. On the basis of the illustrations in the textbook, determine what kinds of joints have been used.
3. With the aid of the industrial arts department of your school or of a local furniture manufacturer, obtain samples of wood used in the making of furniture. Prepare each specimen by cutting them to uniform size, sanding, sealing, finishing, and waxing. Mount the specimens for display purposes describing under each the characteristics of the wood and its common use in making furniture.
4. Investigate to see what laws and regulations there are that apply to upholstering and bedding. Give a report to the class of your findings.

Chapter 17

How to Buy Drugs and Similar Articles

Purpose of the Chapter. There are many things that involve the health and welfare of individuals. There are too many of them to cover in detail, but in this chapter medical care, drugs, cosmetics, dentifrices, soaps, and related articles will be studied to acquaint you with some of the effective uses, dangers, and proper buying practices.

You will find answers to these questions:

1. To what extent may you safely give yourself medical treatment?
2. What are the recommendations and warnings in regard to eye care?
3. How may one go about selecting a hearing aid?
4. What are some guides in buying drugs?
5. What will cosmetics do?
6. Are cosmetics safe?
7. What are the advantages of different types of soaps and synthetic detergents?

Dangers of Treating Yourself. Every year there are thousands of individuals who fail to obtain proper treatment because they attempt to treat themselves. Thousands of individuals make mistakes in using otherwise helpful drugs. One of the greatest dangers is the promiscuous use of prepared cures that are bought over a drugstore counter as casually as chewing gum. Any sensible person can keep on hand and can use a certain number of standard home remedies, such as those recommended for the home medicine cabinet by the Food and Drug Administration. In all serious ailments, however, and in the cases of diagnosis of the ailments, a doctor should be consulted. Since many drug and curative devices are bought by people who are not experts, the government seeks to protect them from exploitation. As explained in a previous chapter, the Federal Government has set up certain controls over drugs in regard to their advertising and labeling.

One of the great dangers of treating yourself is that you guess at what is wrong with you and guess at the remedy. In neither case are you competent to judge. A doctor may guess, but it is a competent guess based upon evidence

---

Some Warnings on Medical Cures and Drugs

1. If you think you have anemia, consult a doctor because there is more than one type of anemia and the more serious type requires careful treatment.
2. Arthritis appears in the human body in so many forms that only an expert doctor can determine the proper and safe relief without injury.
3. Beware of advertised cancer cures; consult a doctor. With the early detection and proper treatment or surgery, there is a good chance of a cure.
4. If you have diabetes or suspect having this ailment, see a doctor promptly and follow his directions regularly.
5. Electro-magnetic devices are considered worthless.
6. Heat treatment for some ailments may give relief, but heat may be the wrong treatment for some ailments.
7. Many "magic" cures have been offered for high blood pressure, but if you have high blood pressure or suspect it, see a doctor and follow his advice.
8. The value of hormones is limited, but the possible danger from their use is great and should be administered only by a physician.
9. Many mineral waters are advertised to cure almost any kind of ailment, but in some cases, they will do more harm than good.
10. Beware of drugs advertised to reduce weight.
11. There are no known drugs that can cure tuberculosis except those that may be administered by a competent doctor. The principal cure is through rest, diet, and special treatments.

of your ailment. He is a specialist in identifying your ailment and prescribing a remedy.

Some Warnings on Cures and Drug Products. The American Medical Association, individual doctors, the Federal Food and Drug Administration, and the Better Business Bureaus have issued many warnings in regard to worthless, objectionable, and dangerous drugs and cures of various kinds. If one will learn to depend upon the advice of a competent doctor, he need not be concerned with some of these questionable cures. However, because of the temptation of many people to provide their own treatment, the following are issued as warnings.

Harold M. Lambert
Protect Your Eyes: They Are Precious Assets

Be Careful with Your Eyes. Eyes are such a precious asset and are so delicate that you should not gamble with treating them or fitting your own glasses without the aid of a competent oculist. An *oculist* is a physician who has specialized in the study of the eyes. He is competent to determine if there is anything wrong with the eyes and prescribe proper treatment or lenses. The oculist is sometimes an eye surgeon who is competent to perform delicate operations on the eye.

An *optometrist* is one who is trained to examine the eyes and prescribe lenses or exercises for correction of difficulties, but is not qualified to administer drugs for medical treatment.

Sometimes an optometrist also serves as an optician. An *optician* is the one who grinds the lenses. If a person is only an optician, he does not examine or treat the eyes, but simply manufactures the lenses to fill the prescriptions of the oculist or optometrist.

Oculists urge regular examinations of eyes and the correction of defects when they are evident. They call attention to many abuses of the eyes which come principally from concentrated reading under improper lighting conditions and improper posture that cause an eye strain. Under artificial lighting the following are recommended as conditions that will avoid eye strain: (1) proper quantity or amount of light, and, (2) the quality and distribution of the light. Sufficient light is important, but the quality of the light is also important because contrast between light

---

Guides in Buying Drugs

1. Rely upon a dependable doctor for prescribing drugs.
2. Learn from your doctor the names of manufacturers of dependable drugs and buy under brand names the drugs manufactured by those companies.
3. Be skeptical of new drug products until your doctor has assured you of their accepted use.
4. A drug clerk may be able to suggest some simple remedies, but a drug clerk or even a pharmacist is not a physician and is therefore not capable of making the same authoritative diagnosis and recommendation that a doctor would make.
5. Read the label for information in regard to dosage and warnings. If a drug is not sold in interstate commerce and is not covered by state regulations, sufficient information may not be given on the label. Buy only drugs for which the proper information is given on the label.
6. In determining the standard quality and reliability of a drug, check to see if it conforms to the standards of the United States Pharmacopoeia (USP), the official Homeopathic Pharmacopoeia (HP), or the National Formulary (NF).
7. Even though some drug preparations are more or less harmless for the purposes for which they are recommended, such drugs may be harmful if taken without the advice of a physician.
8. Some drugs may be harmless to certain individuals but harmful to others. Follow the advice of a physician in taking prepared medicines.
9. Beware of drugs with all-inclusive claims as to their uses.
10. Beware of any drugs that are to be taken internally to reduce weight. Most of these are injurious.

and dark causes eye strain and the location of the source of light may cause eye strain. An even distribution of light without striking the eyes directly and in adequate quantity is the ideal artificial lighting situation.

Experts have a scale by which the proper amount of light can be determined in terms of foot-candles. It is measured by a meter and roughly is as follows:

- 25 watt bulb— 5 foot-candles of light at a distance of 2 feet.
- 50 watt bulb—13 foot-candles of light at a distance of 2 feet.
- 60 watt bulb—17 foot-candles of light at a distance of 2 feet.
- 100 watt bulb—32 foot-candles of light at a distance of 2 feet.

For modern office and factory work 10 to 25 foot-candles is satisfactory. For ordinary reading or clerical work 20 to 50 foot-candles is satisfactory. For concentrated reading and fine close work 50 to 100 foot-candles is recommended.

A Good Personal Health Program

1. Periodic general examinations by physicians.
2. Regular examinations of eyes, teeth, ears.
3. Do not postpone treatments.
4. Scrub your teeth twice daily.
5. Study and read with proper lighting.
6. See a physician promptly in case of illness.
7. Obtain vaccinations and repeat necessary vaccinations when needed (especially for children).
8. Keep your weight normal.
9. Eat a properly balanced diet.
10. Fit shoes properly (especially for children).
11. Take preventative measures against diseases.
12. Get proper rest and recreation.
13. Practice good sanitation and cleanliness.
14. Avoid self-prescribed drugs.
15. Practice safety.
16. Buy hospital and surgical insurance if possible.

There are many warnings issued by competent authorities, but probably the most important warning is against ordering glasses by mail or without an examination. Great permanent damage can be done to the eyes by wearing improper glasses. Sun glasses are no exception to the rule. Most sun glasses are safe, but some are injurious if they are poorly made and cause distortion of images. They will not correct eye defects unless they are made to the specifications of an oculist or optometrist.

Hearing Aids. Doctors say that there are many cases of defective hearing that could have been cured if the defect had been discovered early enough. Examinations of children are therefore important. When in doubt consult a competent doctor.

When hearing defects become permanent, there are many aids that are now available. They are designed to aid persons with various different types of hearing defects. A list of accepted hearing aids may be obtained from the Council on Physical Medicine and Rehabilitation of the American Medical Association, or through the American Hearing Society.

What Is an Allergy? The use of the term *allergy* has become frequent. It simply means that a person is especially sensitive, or, in terms of the doctor, hypersensitive to certain substances. These may be foods or drugs that are taken internally or as injections; they may be cosmetics or any other substances applied to the surface of the body. Hay fever is caused from an allergy to certain pollen dust in the air at certain times of the year. Ragweed pollen is particularly offensive to persons who tend to have this allergy.

Some people are allergic to some of the new types of medicines and some of the old types of medicines. They cannot use these without becoming nauseated or ill. Their use may cause inflammation of the skin or certain parts of the body.

Allergies of the skin are especially noticeable because they can be seen and because there are so many substances that come in contact with the skin. Some people are said to be poisoned by certain types of weeds, grass, and other plant growth, whereas most people are not bothered by them. On the other hand, some people are allergic to certain kinds of cosmetics, lotions, soaps, and synthetic detergents. For instance, some people are allergic to substances that contain sulphur or tar. Doctors have developed tests that will determine whether one has a specific allergy.

Are Cosmetics Safe and Useful? On the whole, the cosmetic industry is legitimate and honorable, but it may get a bad reputation because of some unscrupulous manufacturers. Most of the products are of high quality and are safe to use.

The cosmetic industry also suffers disrepute because some people are allergic to various ingredients. In other words, some individuals are hypersensitive to substances that are not harmful in the least to the majority of persons. Such an ingredient may cause a skin irritation to a few persons, but may be used daily by others without injury. When one considers the great number of ingredients included in cosmetics, it can easily be seen how some of these ingredients may cause irritation to at least a few users.

Advertisements of Cosmetics Usually Have a Strong Emotional or Glamor Appeal

The preparations that are most liable to contain dangerous ingredients are hair dye, hair tonics, dandruff removers, hair beautifiers, freckle removers, skin peelers, skin bleaches, depilatories, and personal deodorants. Many of these will cause the hair to fall out or irritate the skin.

To go into an elaborate discussion of the advertising and the labeling of cosmetics would be futile because most people buy these products regardless of the irrational claims in advertisements and on labels. Most people buy beauty preparations in the hope that they will become or will remain beautiful. Advertisements that contain testimonials of attractive women or photographs of glamorous persons merely add to the self-satisfaction of the individuals who buy those products. Such advertising has principally one purpose: to satisfy certain human emotions. As a result most cosmetic advertising appeals to the emotions rather than to the common sense of the buyer.

Function of Creams and Lotions. Price alone is not an adequate guide to quality or effectiveness in the purchase of cosmetics. Many preparations available at reasonable prices contain pure ingredients that are helpful. Unless a cream or a lotion serves a definite purpose as a drug, its real purpose is to keep the skin moistened. Any other purposes claimed for it are questionable.

A study of cosmetics involves many points of view. In this study there is no attempt to decide whether cosmetics should or should not be used. The lists on page 303 point out what creams and lotions will do and what they will not do.

Food and Drug Administration
The Main Value of Facial Cream Is to Moisten and Soften the Skin

What Creams and Lotions Will Do

1. A cosmetic preparation is primarily a protection for the skin from the ravages of weather and time. It may help to prevent defects and deficiencies, but it will not cure them.
2. The massage that accompanies the application of cosmetics is helpful in delaying the formation of wrinkles.
3. The application of a cosmetic has a temporary effect on the outer skin but has no permanent effect.
4. The skins of most people have excretions of fat that tend to lubricate the skin. These excretions are washed away by soap and water. A cosmetic will help to replace them.
5. Some lotions for the hands and the face will form a protective coating and help to retain natural oil and moisture, thereby encouraging the healing of chapped hands and face.
6. If astringent lotions are strong enough, they will temporarily keep pores from functioning.
7. Any make-up preparation that temporarily coats the skin will serve as a slight protection in addition to enhancing the appearance, provided it is applied properly.

What Creams and Lotions Will Not Do

1. No cosmetic will bring about a permanent change in the nature of the skin. The general nature of one's skin depends largely upon the health and the cleanliness of the individual and upon inherited characteristics.
2. Wrinkles in the skin are caused by the effect of emotions and expressions on the face. The folding of tissues gradually causes wrinkles that cannot be erased by the application of oils or creams. Wrinkles can be avoided or partially removed by prolonged rest and relaxation and by a conscious attempt to avoid frowning and other unusual facial expressions. Such treatment is effective only in the case of young persons, however.
3. No cosmetic can nourish or feed the skin.
4. An astringent lotion, although producing a slight contraction of cells, will not shrink the pores. Sometimes these lotions cause annoying irritation.

Cautions About Cosmetics. When one studies the things that cosmetics will and will not do, he does not get the complete picture. The following is a summary of cautions on the use of cosmetics:

(a) Beware of preparations that contain a lead compound because such a compound may cause serious poisoning. Fortunately some preparations advertised as being radio-active do not have any radio-active substances in them. If they did, the preparations would be injurious.

(b) There are no creams or tonics that are known to grow hair.

(c) Nearly everyone is allergic to some kinds of preparations, usually resulting in skin irritation. To find out whether one is allergic to a certain cosmetic, apply it to a small area as an experiment.

(d) Only those skin-bleaching compounds that bleach the surface are safe. Their effectiveness is slight and slow. Bleaches that loosen the outer skin cause irritation and possible poisoning. Many of them contain mercury, which is dangerous to the human body.

(e) Skin peelers or freckle removers that require the removing of layers of skin are considered very dangerous, especially when used by the average individual.

(f) There are several types of hair dyes that will cause irritation and possible poisoning to some individuals. The safest procedure is to consult a dermatologist or some other expert on the use of such dyes.

(g) Some so-called deodorants act as antiperspirant agents. Most deodorants are harmless, but some will cause an irritation to certain people. While most of them are harmless to the skin, they will injure many types of fabrics.

(h) Many of the so-called skin lotions or astringents have no particularly useful purpose except to provide temporarily an invigorating feeling and a pleasant odor. The danger of such lotions lies in the fact that many of them contain alcohol or mild acids or other astringent agents that may tend to dry the skin.

(i) Many eye make-up preparations have potential dangers for individuals who use them. Those containing colors made from metallic salts or aniline dyes may cause permanent injury to the eyesight. Some dyes that may be used safely on the hair cannot be used safely on eyelashes.

(j) The lathering quality of shampoo is not necessarily an indication of the effectiveness of the shampoo. A shampoo should be judged on the basis of its effectiveness and its failure to dry the scalp.

(k) Electrolysis is the only known, safe method of removing surplus hair, but it must be used only by an expert. X-ray treatment is considered dangerous.

(l) Moles should be removed only by an expert.

Soaps and Detergents. A *soap* is defined as a fat with an alkali. Early soaps were made from animal fat and wood ashes. The ashes provided the potash, or alkali. Soaps today are made from many kinds of fats and many kinds of highly refined alkali agents. Other ingredients are often added.

A soap is a detergent, but not all detergents are soap. A *detergent* is defined as a cleansing agent and as we think of detergents today, they are synthetic solids or liquids that are combined with water for cleansing purposes. There are many hundreds of detergents that have been developed with various qualities for various purposes. Some of them are used on the body, some are used for washing clothes, and some are used for industrial purposes.

Uses of Soap. While soaps have many specialized uses in the various industrial applications, their use in the home is primarily for cleaning—for washing the face, hands, dishes, floors, walls, and other articles. Some products are formulated to be all-purpose cleaners. This means that they can be used for all kinds of cleaning jobs, such as washing clothes and scrubbing floors. However, these types of all-purpose cleaners would usually not be satisfactory for washing the hands and face. Toilet soaps, fine fabric soaps, and shampoos are designed for more specific tasks.

Soaps used on the skin or the hair should be mild or neutral. Such soaps will prevent irritation of the skin and excessive drying of the skin. The most that a toilet soap can do is to cleanse efficiently. An inexpensive mild or neutral soap will serve the purpose; but if the family budget will permit, one may indulge in soaps that are perfumed and colored, and can be obtained in small bars or in unusual shapes. These soaps, however, do not have any additional advantage for the consumer.

There are numerous soaps, such as floating, castile, transparent, hard-water, grit, liquid, tar, and medicated. Grit soaps contain an abrasive for removing grease and stains. Hard-water soaps contain oils that lather well in hard water. Certain medicated soaps may have a slightly additional antiseptic value, but all soaps have a good antiseptic value because the lather washes away germs. In considering toilet soaps, one must bear in mind the two fundamental purposes of such soaps: (a) to cleanse and (b) to be mild or neutral. There are no other important considerations.

It is important for the housewife to become familiar with the various types of soaps that can be used for different purposes. For instance, silk, rayon, and wool require neutral soaps and careful handling. Laundry soaps, bleaches, and powders should be used with a full knowledge of their intended purposes.

Guides in Buying Soaps

1. An inferior brand of soap can easily be detected by comparison with one of the numerous good brands of soap on the market.
2. Avoid buying any soap in any class that is very much above the average price a pound.
3. A soap that is suitable for washing badly soiled garments in hard water is too strong for fine fabrics. In the laundering of a fine fabric, a relatively neutral and mild soap should be used, preferably one recommended by the manufacturer or the retailer of the fabric.
4. Use toilet soaps that are no stronger than is necessary to obtain the proper cleansing qualities. Strong soaps tend to dry out the skin and sometimes cause skin irritations.

Water picks up minerals from the earth and the atmosphere. The quantity of these dissolved minerals in the water determines its hardness. The hardness varies in different parts of the country and from one town to another.

Some soaps leave a deposit in hard water because some of the elements in the soap combine with the solids in the water. Some soaps contain elements that neutralize the solids in the water and make the soap more efficient. If the water supply is hard, a water softener plus soap will produce the best results for laundry purposes.

The Uses of Synthetic Detergents. Among the hundreds of varieties of synthetic or chemical detergents, there are those designed for toilet use, shampoos, and laundry. One of the characteristics that has made synthetic detergents popular for laundry purposes is that they can be used in hard water without water softener. Detergents are manufactured to fit varying types of water conditions. As a result of the qualities of these detergents, many people living in regions where there is hard water have found these special detergents preferable to soap; even in regions where there is soft water, these detergents are preferred by women for many uses. Therefore, one should experiment and use the detergent that produces the best results at the minimum cost.

Harold M. Lambert

Select the Right Soap or Detergent for the Intended Use and the Type of Water

Other Cleansing Agents. Other cleansing agents, such as naphtha, gasoline, and carbon tetrachloride, are used for cleansing surfaces. These are sometimes referred to as dry or waterless cleaners. Naphtha and gasoline are both explosive and extremely dangerous. Carbon tetrachloride is not explosive. Naphtha and gasoline are not only dangerous because of the possibility of being ignited by fire or electric sparks or static electricity, but they are also dangerous because of the fact that gases formed by them are explosive.

[Part 5

Buying Dentifrices and Mouthwashes. There are many good dentifrices on the market that are honestly labeled and advertised. It is true that one usually pays a pretty high price for a small tube of dentifrice. There are some people who claim that the price is exorbitant. By pointing out that certain ingredients can be obtained and mixed together to form a good dentifrice, they attempt to prove that the consumer is cheated. If one wishes to prepare his own dentifrice, he may use ordinary salt, soda, or magnesia. Any of these will make a satisfactory tooth powder. Nevertheless, if the consumer is willing to have the ingredients prepared and mixed for him, properly flavored and packaged, and finds that it is more advantageous to pay the price than to prepare his own dentifrice, no one can object to this procedure.

Authorities generally concede that almost any dentifrice will serve as a satisfactory cleansing agent and will, therefore, help to keep the teeth free from decay. However, for many years, medical and dental authorities have contended that there is no antiseptic or medicinal value in dentifrices. Some of the new dentifrices containing ammonium compounds, urea, fluoride, chlorophyll, penicillin, or other substances may tend to control tooth decay. Certain medical and dental authorities feel that still more ample evidence is needed in regard to some of these products before complete approval can be given to them.

Dental and medical authorities point out that decay of foods produces acids and these acids attack the surface of teeth. After the enamel surface has been broken, the decay spreads rapidly. It is for this reason that dental and medi-

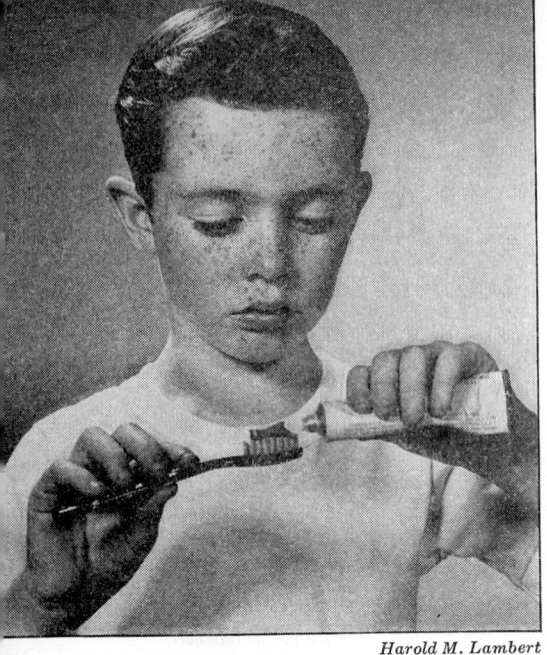

Harold M. Lambert
Children and Adults Should Scrub the Teeth Twice Daily and See a Dentist Regularly

cal authorities warn against excessive use of sugar and candy and urge the regular scrubbing of teeth to prevent the accumulation of food that will decay.

Most dental preparations are composed of common ingredients, such as chalk, soap, salt, baking soda, borax, magnesia, glycerine, alcohol, saccharin, oils, water, flavoring, and color. Claims on the labels and in the advertising of dentifrices shoud be considered in the light of the latest medical knowledge.

The Council on Dental Therapeutics of the American Dental Association does not approve so-called antiseptics that are recommended as mouthwashes. It feels that the general use of mouthwashes can be considered to serve no intrinsic purpose except to clean the mouth, largely through rinsing. Many doctors and dentists recommend a salt solution or a salt and soda solution as an effective mouthwash or gargle.

Summary of Factors in Buying Drugs and Similar Articles

1. Except for simple first aid treatment and remedies already prescribed by your doctor, you should consult your doctor and follow his advice.
2. Eyes and ears should be tested regularly and treated only by an expert.
3. There are many substances to which at least a few people are allergic.
4. Some cosmetics are useful, but many have potential danger.
5. Soaps and detergents are designed for various purposes and should be used according to their purposes.
6. A dentifrice is primarily a cleansing agent.

TEXTBOOK QUESTIONS

1. Name at least two warnings in regard to medical cures and drugs.
2. What are the differences between an oculist, optometrist and an optician?
3. What are the important conditions or elements of good lighting for reading to avoid eye strain?
4. Give as many points as you can in a good personal health program.

5. From what sources can reliable information be obtained in regard to items that will help to correct hearing defects?
6. What is an allergy?
7. Give at least three cautions that should be observed in using cosmetics.
8. What are at least three of the things that a cream or a lotion will do for the skin?
9. What will a cream or a lotion not do?
10. What is the difference between a soap and a detergent?
11. What are the desirable characteristics of a good toilet soap?
12. What are some of the advantages of synthetic detergents?
13. What basis is there for the contention that mouthwashes have an antiseptic value?
14. What is the principal cause of decay of teeth and how can this be prevented through the use of proper dentifrices?

DISCUSSION QUESTIONS

1. Discuss your opinion of the advisability of attempting to buy with the aid of a drug clerk a remedy for (a) pneumonia, (b) heart trouble, (c) burns.
2. Explain the danger of trying to treat ones self instead of going to a doctor.
3. What are the advantages of regular physical examinations when you are not ill?
4. Manufacturers of drugs and cosmetics have been blamed for diseases or ailments that resulted from the fact that certain persons were allergic to particular ingredients in the drugs or cosmetics. Discuss this situation.
5. (a) Study the lighting in your classroom and try to judge whether it is adequate. (b) Explain the kind of lighting condition that you use at home for study at night and explain whether you feel that it is good.
6. In your opinion, may an advertisement for a cosmetic legally assert that the cosmetic will eliminate wrinkles in the skin?
7. Explain why some remedies and cosmetics are safe for some people but not for others. What do you recommend as a guide?
8. Will mouthwashes tend to eliminate bad breath?
9. Give your opinion of some of the advantages of some of the newer chemicals included in modern dentifrices.

PROBLEMS

1. From among your family and acquaintances make a list of the persons whom you know to be allergic to drugs or cosmetics containing certain ingredients. Explain the results.
2. Check all of the soaps and detergents used regularly in your home. Give a list of the brand names and indicate whether each is a soap or a synthetic detergent.
3. Check your own study lamp to find whether it has adequate foot candles for study purposes and whether it is the proper kind of light. Try to borrow a light meter or take your lamp to someplace to have it checked.
4. Obtain the label from an empty medicine container that you find at home, or copy the information from such a container. Submit the label or the information with a report on the following: (a) ingredients, (b) quantity, (c) instructions, (d) warnings, and (e) any other important information. Point out any ways in which you think the label violates the Federal law.

COMMUNITY PROBLEMS AND PROJECTS

1. Investigate to see whether your own state has a law controlling the advertising, the labeling, and the selling of drugs and cosmetics. Report the significant points of the law if there is one.
2. As a class project, the girls in the class are to obtain and bring to class for comparison different brands of the same common type of facial cream. Keep a record of the brand and the price and the results, bearing in mind that a cream is primarily a moistening, massaging, and softening agent for the skin.
3. As a class project for boys, bring to class different brands of tooth paste or tooth powder. Keep a record of prices and, after trying each brand, make a report on the relative values.
4. At the time this book was published the American Dental Association had a label or seal of approval for tooth paste, but this seal had not been granted to any manufacturer of tooth paste with ingredients to prevent or retard tooth decay. Check to find out whether any seals of approval have been issued and are being carried in advertising or on the product.

Chapter 18

How Your Bank Operates

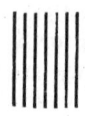

Purpose of the Chapter. Banks are very important in the business and economic development of a community. They constitute an important factor in determining our level of living. Most persons have need to use bank services in the conduct of their personal business affairs. This chapter will help you understand how banks operate.

You will find answers to these questions.
1. What are the functions of banks?
2. What is the primary function of the Federal Reserve System?
3. How are bank stockholders and customers protected?
4. What role do banks play in the economic and business development of a community?
5. How does a bank make a profit?
6. How are checks collected and cleared?

Banks and Their Functions. A *bank* is a financial institution authorized by its charter to receive deposits of money subject to withdrawal by the depositor either on demand or after notice has been given, to make loans, to pay interest, and to perform other functions as authorized by its charter. Depositors are creditors of a bank because the bank owes them money. A bank may invest or loan the money deposited in it subject to specific regulations. The income of a bank is primarily from such investments and loans.

A *commercial bank* is distinguished from other types of banks by the fact that it is authorized by its charter to receive deposits subject to withdrawal upon demand, such as checking accounts. It may within specified regulations make loans for relatively short periods of time ranging from 30 to 90 days. Commercial banks serve the day-to-day needs of both business firms and individuals. The charters of most commercial banks also permit them within certain regulations to receive time or savings deposits and to make loans for a year or longer in length.

A *savings bank* is a financial institution that may accept time deposits on which interest is paid to depositors. Savings banks may be stock companies or mutual companies. A stock savings bank is one that is owned and operated by stockholders. Profits go to the stockholders. A mutual savings bank is one that is owned by the depositors and is operated primarily for their benefit. Mutual savings banks are explained in Chapter 25. Some commercial banks operate what they call savings departments.

The savings bank or the savings department of a commercial bank ordinarily will make loans for a longer period of time than a commercial bank. Loans may extend for one year or more. The following customs are relatively uniform among savings banks and the savings departments of commercial banks:

(a) Deposits are usually accepted for amounts as small as one dollar.
(b) Checks cannot be drawn against deposits.
(c) The bank reserves the right to demand several days' notice before the withdrawal of funds.

Some banks chartered by states are authorized to serve in capacities of trust such as operating trust funds, managing real estate, or serving as administrator or executor to manage or settle an estate. A bank having this privilege is known as a *trust company*. If the bank also serves as a trust company both the words bank and trust are often included in the name of the institution.

The trend is toward banks becoming multiple-purpose or combination institutions serving commercial, savings, and trust functions.

Some other financial institutions that technically are not banks nevertheless serve some of the same functions as banks such as accepting deposits, paying interest on certain types of deposits, and making loans. Illustrative of financial institutions in this category are savings and loan associations and credit unions.

Kinds of Banks as to Organization. Banks classified according to their authorization are (1) state banks and (2) national banks. In addition to these types of banks, there are federal reserve banks or bankers' banks. These banks deal largely with individual banks that are members of the Federal Reserve System, but they also have dealings with other banks.

A *state bank* is a bank that is organized as a corporation. It obtains its authority through a charter granted by the state in which it operates. It may be a commercial bank, a savings bank, a trust company, or an investment bank. A state bank may also be a member of the Federal Reserve System.

A *national bank* obtains its charter from the Federal Government and is subject to the regulations of the Federal Reserve System and the banking laws enacted by the Federal Government. A national bank is always organized as a corporation.

There are many other financial agencies that fit into the national plan of savings, investment, and the transfer of funds. Various mutual savings societies are organized under special laws and operate under particular rules. A popular type of mutual savings association that also makes loans to its members is a credit union.

Savings and loan associations, which are discussed in Chapter 25, are of a wide variety in different states. Two other important banking institutions are the federal land bank and the home loan bank.

Organization of the Federal Reserve System. The banking system that is the outgrowth of the Federal Reserve Act passed in 1913 is called the Federal Reserve System. Under the Federal Reserve Act the country was divided into the twelve districts. In each district there is a federal reserve bank, which has a separate and distinct organization and is managed by a board of directors. Each member bank in the district in which the federal reserve bank is located must subscribe to capital stock of the federal reserve bank equal in amount to 6 per cent of its paid-up capital and surplus. In the past, however, a federal reserve bank has called for payment of only a part of the stock subscribed for by a member bank.

A federal reserve bank is operated under a board of directors of nine persons. Six of them are elected by the member banks in the district and three are appointed by the Board of Governors of the Federal Reserve System. The twelve federal reserve banks are coordinated by this Board of Governors consisting of seven members. The members of the Board of Governors are appointed by the President of the United States for a term of fourteen years. The federal reserve banks may rightfully be called bankers' banks for their stock is owned by the member banks. They do not accept deposits of individuals or businesses.

Functions of the Federal Reserve System. In many respects a federal reserve bank is similar to an ordinary state or national bank. Both are corporations operating under a charter, both issue stock, both receive deposits, both pay checks drawn on deposits, both discount (buy) ordinary promissory notes, and both make loans according to law. They do essentially the same things except that the federal reserve banks deal largely with member banks, although under certain conditions they make certain types of loans to responsible business enterprises. The theory of the Federal Reserve System is that the funds of the entire United States should be organized so as to permit the rapid shifting of money and credit from one place to another to take care of supply and demand.

The four most important functions of the federal reserve banks are as follows:

(a) Issuing notes (paper currency).
(b) Centralizing bank reserves.
(c) Making loans to member banks.
(d) Rediscounting (purchasing) notes submitted by member banks.

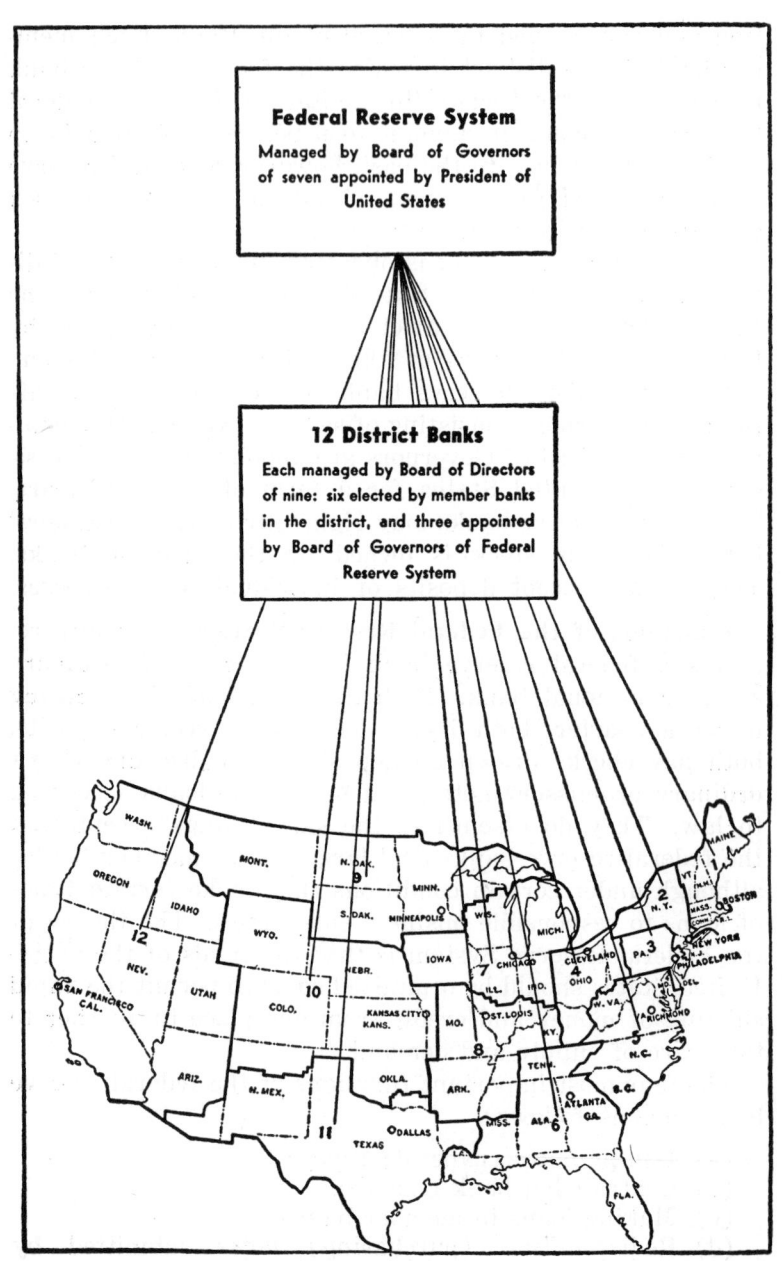

Federal Reserve System

Managed by Board of Governors of seven appointed by President of United States

12 District Banks

Each managed by Board of Directors of nine: six elected by member banks in the district, and three appointed by Board of Governors of Federal Reserve System

Federal Reserve System

The Federal Reserve System provides one type of note, the federal reserve note, that is our main source of currency. It serves as credit money and is accepted in all business channels as legal tender. The federal reserve banks act as the agent of the United States Government in issuing this type of note.

A member bank must maintain a deposit in the federal reserve bank equal to a fixed percentage of its own deposits. This percentage is governed by the Federal Reserve Board and may be changed from time to time. The deposit is known as a *reserve* or a *reserve deposit*. The deposits of all member banks combined comprise a centralized reserve in a federal reserve bank. Each bank, of course, must also keep on hand a sufficient amount of cash to take care of the demands of its customers. The deposits in the federal reserve banks make it unnecessary, however, for member banks to keep a great amount of cash on hand, for these deposits are practically the same as cash in that they are available quickly. This system causes a federal reserve bank to act more or less as a financial reservoir for its district. Each member bank can draw upon the pool or reserves. The pooling of a portion of the funds of each member bank serves to strengthen every bank in the district.

Member banks may obtain a loan from a federal reserve bank by turning over to the federal reserve bank government bonds, notes, or other bonds to guarantee the payment of the loan when it is due. Bonds, notes, or other negotiable paper when used for this purpose are known as *collateral*. The federal reserve bank either gives the local bank credit by increasing its reserve or by issuing to it federal reserve notes (paper money).

Another way a member bank may borrow from its federal reserve bank is to rediscount, or sell, the notes it holds to the federal bank. Discounting a note means exchanging it for cash or credit before its maturity (due) date. The amount received is equal to its face value less the interest from the date of discount to the date of maturity. For example, a customer may give a business firm a $1,000 note for 60 days in payment of goods. The business firm not

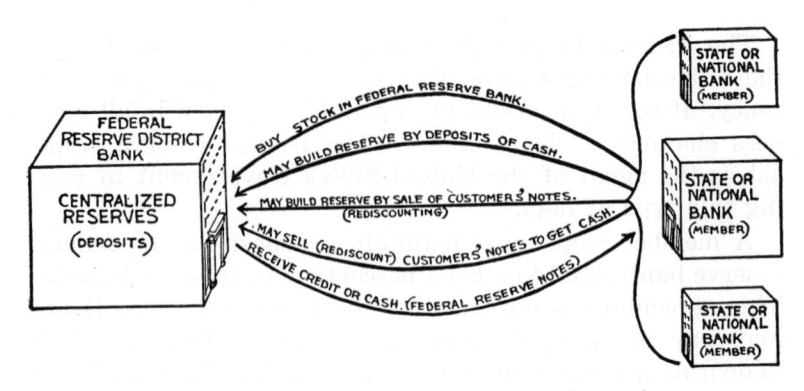

Relations of Federal Reserve Banks with Member Banks

wishing to wait 60 days for its money may take the note to a bank and discount (or sell) it. The note may be discounted anytime before maturity. If it is discounted 30 days before maturity and the rate of discount is six per cent, the business firm will receive cash or credit amounting to $995. At maturity, the original signer of the note will pay the face of the note plus interest at the agreed rate.

Rediscounting a note is a process whereby the bank now holding the discounted note in the foregoing illustration sends it to its federal reserve bank and receives credit or cash. Assuming that the member bank rediscounts the note on the day it is received from the customer and that the rediscount rate is 3 per cent, the bank would receive $997.50 which is $2.50 more than it gave the business firm that sold it originally. Not only did the bank make a profit of $2.50 but it also received $997.50 in reserve credit or in cash (federal reserve notes) which it may now loan to another customer. Inasmuch as the member bank purchased a note from the business firm for $995 and recovered the entire amount immediately from the federal reserve bank, credit actually was created. By this process business firms and individuals can expand business very rapidly as long as the local bank can provide funds to discount (buy) notes from customers.

Regulating Business Expansion. One of the most important functions of the Federal Reserve System is to prevent too rapid expansion of business which may be caused by local banks loaning money too freely to business firms. When business expands too rapidly prices and wages increase rapidly. This economic condition is known as *inflation*. Another equally important function is to stimulate the expansion of business when business activity is relatively low. This is done by making money available to local banks at a relatively low rate of discount which in turn enables the local banks to loan more money to business firms. When business activities decrease rapidly, and prices and wages also decrease, there is a condition known as *deflation*.

Adjusting the rediscount rate upward or downward is the most effective way the Federal Reserve Board has in controlling credit. Generally speaking when it is difficult to borrow money, we say money is scarce. If the Federal Reserve Board believes business should be encouraged to expand and enlarge through greater borrowing, it reduces the rediscount rate. When money is plentiful, that is relatively easy to borrow, the Federal Reserve Board may increase the rediscount rate if it feels expansion should be restricted or kept under control.

The rediscount rate of the federal reserve banks is usually lower than the discount rate of the member banks. We saw in the illustration in the preceding paragraphs how the difference between the two rates made a profit of $2.50 for the member bank on one transaction. The bank not only made a profit due to the difference between the two rates but also received either a reserve deposit in the federal reserve bank or cash (federal reserve notes). If its total cash had a safe relation to its deposits, the member bank could then lend more money to its customers. This operation would therefore be profitable to the member bank.

Suppose, however, the Federal Reserve Board in Washington issued instructions to all federal reserve banks to raise the rediscount rate to 5 or 5½ per cent. This increase in the rate would mean that member banks could not continue to make loans and to rediscount the notes profitably. Individual member banks would therefore lend only what they could on their own resources and would not rediscount the notes. As the banks would be limited in the amount of loans they could make, businesses would be limited in their expansion. This process is referred to as the *control over bank credit*.

Economists tell us that many of our depressions are caused by business firms and individuals borrowing too much in proportion to their net worth in an effort to expand and enlarge their business. This condition is sometimes referred to as overexpansion. The control over expansion is, however, not so direct and so easily exercised as is indicated in the foregoing example. Because of uncontrollable influences the action of the federal reserve banks is not always as effective as might be hoped. For instance, an individual bank might raise the interest rate on its loans and still find the rediscounting process profitable. In such a case, the raising of the interest rate would tend to discourage customers from borrowing, because it would make borrowing unprofitable. But if money is plentiful, the federal reserve banks have no means of controlling expansion through the lending of individual banks, because the individual banks do not find it necessary to rediscount their notes with the federal reserve bank. It is only when money is scarce that the federal reserve bank can restrict expansion by raising the rediscount rate.

When money is scarce, the federal reserve bank can in some cases encourage expansion by lowering the rediscount rate. Banks can lower their interest rates and rediscount their notes with the federal reserve bank and obtain more reserves and cash to use as the basis for additional lending. For instance, if the rediscount rate in the preceding example had been lowered to 1 per cent, the bank would have made a profit of $3.34 on the $1,000 loan instead of a profit of $2.50. A profit of this kind on such transactions would have encouraged the member banks to continue making loans and rediscounting the notes. Business, in turn, would have been encouraged to expand.

Economic Role of Financial Institutions. Banks promote good management of one's personal, financial affairs. They make saving easy, and they encourage wise spending. Economic and business development is stimulated by banks and other financial institutions making loans to individuals and business firms. Most people could never own a home if they had to pay cash for it. Much of the goods we buy such as automobiles and household appliances are bought on credit which ordinarily means that some financial institution such as a bank, loan company, or credit union has loaned money for the purchase.

Many business firms need loans to get started and to operate. One of the major functions of banks, savings associations, and credit unions is to encourage and stimulate business and economic development through extending credit in the form of loans. Imagine how different economic conditions in your community would be without the credit services of banks and other loan-making agencies.

Financial institutions make a contribution toward raising the level of living. Credit, whether given to individuals directly or to the business firms from which they buy, makes more goods available to more people.

Financial institutions receiving deposits from customers serve an economic function by centralizing the money not currently being used in a community thus making it available for loans to individuals and business firms.

Although financial institutions such as banks are organized to make a profit, the owners and managers are motivated by a sincere desire to encourage and stimulate business and economic development.

Customer and Stockholder Protection. The establishment of new banks is controlled by state and federal laws. These laws are designed to protect stockholders and depositors by making certain the business is financially sound and that there are adequate funds available for the operating needs of the new bank. Depositors are also protected by the laws and regulations under which new banks are formed. These laws insure ample reserves to protect deposits of customers.

Bank operations are subject to state and Federal regulations pertaining to capital stock, surplus, and reserves; policies and practices for making loans; and other regulations to safeguard both stockholders and depositors.

State and Federal laws limit banks, according to their classification, in the types of loans that they can make. State banks are governed by the laws of their respective states. Members of the Federal Reserve System are governed by strict restrictions pertaining to the types of loans they can make and the conditions under which they may make them.

Deposit Insurance. Protection of depositors against loss due to bank failure has been provided through insurance on bank deposits. This insurance is administered by the Federal Deposit Insurance Corporation, which all national banks are compelled to join and other banks may join voluntarily. Each individual account in a bank having this insurance is insured up to ten thousand dollars.

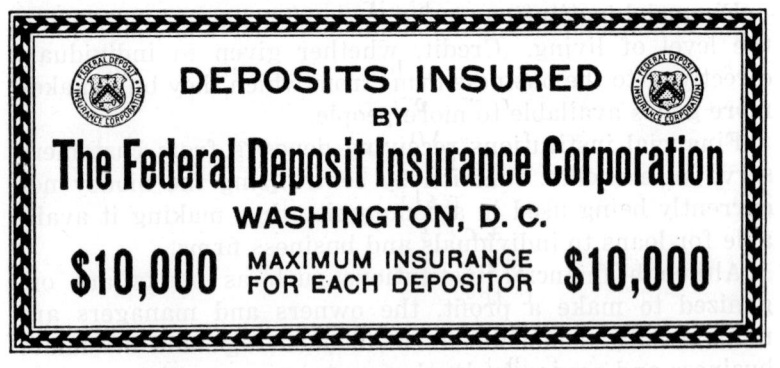

DEPOSITS INSURED BY The Federal Deposit Insurance Corporation WASHINGTON, D. C. $10,000 MAXIMUM INSURANCE FOR EACH DEPOSITOR $10,000

A Sign Announcing That a Bank's Deposits Are Insured

Bank Management. The directors and officers of a bank are charged with legal and ethical responsibility to establish policies that will insure sound operations. The formulation of policies and procedures is an important function of management particularly in regard to setting interest rates on deposits and loans, making loans, maintaining reserves, and offering services to customers.

An example of internal management is the practice now followed by many banks in having a continuous check on and examination of the records to detect mistakes and to lessen the chances of fraud.

Bank Income, Expenses, and Profits. A bank has two basic sources of income. One source is dividends or interest that may be received from bank investments. The second and primary source of income is interest received on loans made to customers. If a bank could not lend money, it could not earn a satisfactory income with which to pay interest to depositors and to cover its operating costs. A bank has practically no money to lend except what is deposited by individuals and business concerns. Thus, the bank must use customers' deposits in order to have an income.

The number and variety of costs involved in operating a bank are very great. Although many record keeping machines are used, people are required to operate them. The nature of banking operations demands complete and accurate records. High costs are incurred in maintaining such records.

Each check drawn on a bank constitutes a cost to the bank that must be borne out of income. An account with a small balance against which several checks a month are drawn may result in a loss to the bank. Some banks partially offset this loss by making service charges on checking accounts and other services.

Generally speaking, bank profits are very conservative when compared to the profits of business and industrial firms. Banks are entitled to a reasonable profit just as all other business enterprises operating under the free enterprise system.

Clearing Checks Between Banks. A problem arises when a customer of a particular bank either cashes or deposits a check that was drawn on some other bank. In order to be reimbursed for the amount of the check the customer's bank must collect from the bank on which the check was drawn. Banks located near each other can make such collections easily by messenger. In many instances, there are checks to be collected by both banks. The clearing of checks is more complicated in large cities and among banks widely separated geographically.

In order to solve the problem of clearing checks, clearinghouse associations have been established in many cities.

A *clearinghouse* is a voluntary association of banks which may have as its purpose the solving of problems common to the member banks. Among those problems are the clearing of checks and making of collections between banks, setting of banking hours, determining interest rates, considering loan policies, and many other similar problems.

The clearing of checks is illustrated in the chart below:

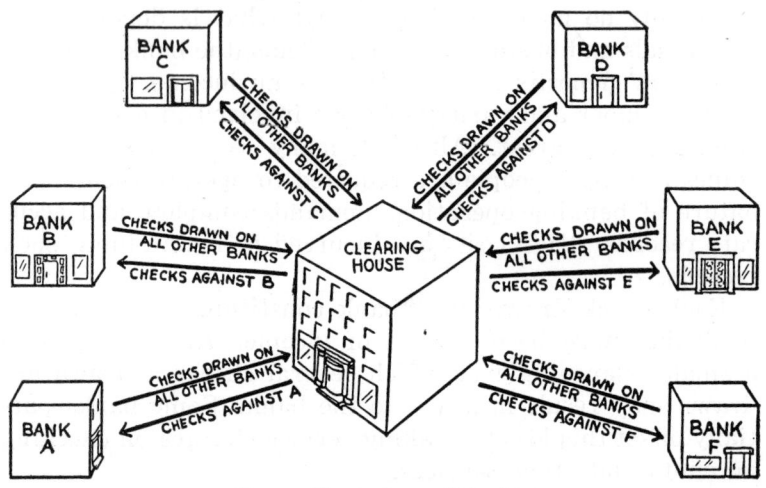

How a Clearinghouse Operates

A common practice in a clearinghouse is for representatives of the banks that are members to meet at the clearinghouse at an appointed hour each morning to exchange checks drawn on other member banks. If the total amounts of the checks exchanged by two banks are not the same, the difference is settled by check from the one bank to the other. In some instances these payments are made to the clearinghouse which, in turn, settles with each bank. Some clearinghouses also have an afternoon hour for clearing checks. At the afternoon clearing, checks having insufficient funds, fraudulent signatures, or that are otherwise unacceptable are returned to the banks that accepted them.

Federal reserve banks serve as a clearinghouse for member banks in their respective territories. Small banks often have an arrangement with a correspondent bank in another city to clear checks drawn on other banks in that area.

> ### *Summary of Banks and Bank Operations*
>
> 1. Banks serve business firms and individuals by accepting demand and time deposits, making loans, and operating trust funds.
> 2. The primary objective of the Federal Reserve System is to achieve economic stability through the control of credit.
> 3. Banks have an important role in the economic and business development of a community.
> 4. Unlike most other types of business, customers and stockholders of banks are protected by many strict regulations.
> 5. Bank policies and procedures are formulated by careful planning of directors and officers.
> 6. Bank income is practically limited to interest on loans; profits are small compared to other types of business enterprise.

TEXTBOOK QUESTIONS

1. What is a bank?
2. What is the essential difference between a commercial bank and a savings bank?
3. Do any commercial banks accept savings deposits?
4. What functions may a trust company serve that commercial and savings banks do not serve?
5. How are banks classified according to their authorization and organization?
6. What is the difference between a state bank and a national bank?
7. What is the supreme governing body of the Federal Reserve System?
8. What are the four most important functions of the federal reserve banks?
9. What notes are issued by federal reserve banks and circulated as currency?
10. How may a member bank obtain a loan from its federal reserve bank?
11. How do member banks build up reserves in the federal reserve bank?
12. Explain how the Federal Reserve System may regulate business expansion.
13. In what ways do banks and other financial institutions help people and communities?
14. What protection against loss from bank failure do customers and stockholders have?

15. What are the primary sources of income for banks?
16. Name some ways in which the Federal Reserve System regulates the loans made by member banks.
17. Why are clearinghouses necessary?

DISCUSSION QUESTIONS

1. Explain why you think it would not be possible to operate modern business under our present monetary system without the aid of banks as agents for pooling money and expanding credit.
2. Explain how loans made to business firms can serve as the basis for increasing the supply of currency.
3. Explain what you consider to be the main advantage of the centralized reserves of the federal reserve banks.
4. The raising of the rediscount rate of the Federal Reserve Board is supposed to curtail business expansion. Can you think of any cases in which this would not be very effective? Explain your answer.
5. Theoretically the Federal Reserve System is in a position to encourage business expansion when it is needed by reducing the rediscount rate. Can you explain any situation when you think this would not be effective?
6. What would happen if every depositor in a bank wanted his money immediately and, when he demanded it, the bank attempted to furnish it?
7. Discuss the various ways in which banks serve the people and business firms of the community. What would be the effect on the conduct of personal business affairs if banks discontinued their services?
8. Discuss how both customers and stockholders are protected.
9. Mr. Jayner has a checking account at the Planters Bank and Trust Company. During the past month Mr. Jayner wrote 28 checks, and he now has an account balance of $58.50. The bank notified Mr. Jayner today that his account has incurred a service charge of $1.37 for the month. Do you think the bank is justified in making the service charge?

PROBLEMS

1. Assume that money is scarce and a bank needs to rediscount some loans in order to get additional currency. It made a $1,000 loan at the rate of 3 per cent for 60 days. (a) What interest is collected by the bank in advance? (b) The bank rediscounts this note immediately with the federal reserve bank at a rediscount rate of 1 per cent. How much currency or reserve credit would the bank receive? (c) How much profit would the bank make on the transaction?

2. From newspaper reports or banks learn the present rates that are being charged on commercial loans and the present rediscount rate of the federal reserve banks. On the basis of the average existing rate on commercial loans and the present rediscount rate, compute the amount of profit that a bank can make by lending money and rediscounting the note, assuming that there are no miscellaneous service charges.
3. Banks offer many services to individuals and families. Not always do we make wise use of these services. Answers to the following questions will help you understand when and how to make use of bank services. It may be necessary to go to one of your local banks to get information to answer some of them; the answers to others may be obtained from bank employees and from people who have had experience in using bank services.
   (a) Under what conditions is it advisable to open and maintain a checking account at a bank?
   (b) Under what conditions is it advisable to open a savings account at a bank?
   (c) When would one be justified to request a bank to loan money to purchase a home?
   (d) When would one be justified in requesting a bank to loan money to pay for personal items such as expenses of going to school, clothes, etc.? Home appliances and automobiles?

COMMUNITY PROBLEMS AND PROJECTS

1. One means of determining the banking activities of any community is through bank clearances, which means the monetary volume of checks cleared through the local clearinghouse. From the financial page of your newspaper or any other source obtain information in regard to bank clearings for a recent month. Compare these with clearings for the same month in the year previous or in some other year, and give your conclusions as to the local business activity.
2. Make a list of the banks in your town, city, or county. Classify them according to the discussion in this chapter. If you find any special types of banks not discussed in this chapter, list them separately and describe them.

Chapter 19

How to Use Your Bank

> **Purpose of the Chapter.** Many banking services that are available to individuals and business firms are indispensable in modern living. An understanding of these services is necessary and essential in order to use them effectively in the conduct of business affairs. This chapter will explain how you may use the services of your bank.
>
> You will find answers to these questions:
> 1. What are the major bank services of interest to individuals?
> 2. What are the essential features of each type of service?
> 3. How are they operated? What procedures are used?
> 4. How can individuals make the most effective use of banks in the management of personal business affairs?

Using a Checking Account. The instruments ordinarily used in maintaining a checking account are deposit slips, a bankbook or deposit receipts, and a checkbook. A deposit slip should be made out by the depositor giving the bank teller a list of the items being deposited. Evidence of having made a deposit should be given to the depositor by the bank teller. The evidence may be an entry in the depositor's bankbook or a deposit receipt. Entries in the depositor's bankbook give the date of a deposit, the amount, and usually the initials of the teller who recorded the entry. Many banks are now using automatic teller's machines by which a deposit is entered by machine. A printed deposit receipt from the machine is given to the depositor.

A deposit slip should show the amount of the currency and coins separately, and a list of all checks should be

```
┌─────────────────────────────────────────────┐
│  No. 142          Cincinnati July 7    19—  │
│        Merchants National Bank  13-94       │
│                                    420      │
│  PAY TO THE                                  │
│  ORDER OF  D. M. Mason            $ 189 65  │
│  One hundred eighty-nine and 65/100 DOLLARS │
│                        L. M. Sanderson      │
└─────────────────────────────────────────────┘

A Check

given. Many banks now prefer that the checks should be listed by giving the transit number of the bank on which a check is drawn as shown in the illustration below. The numbering system was established by the American Bankers' Association. An example of a transit number is 13-94 at the right of the bank's name in the illustration of a check above. The number below the line (420) is the sorting number used by the clearinghouse or bank.

Another way of listing checks on a deposit slip is by the name of the bank, such as First National Bank, when the bank on which a check is drawn is located in the city where the deposit is being made. When depositing a check drawn on a bank in another city, the name of the city and state is given.

**Columbia Bank**

Deposited By
L. M. Sanderson
By J. Jones
July 6 19—

PLEASE LIST EACH CHECK SEPARATELY

| | Dollars | Cents |
|---|---|---|
| CURRENCY | 2 3 | |
| SILVER LESS THAN ONE DOLLAR | 2 | 42 |
| CHECKS AS FOLLOWS: 48-1 | 160 | — |
| 86-144 | 140 | — |
| | | |
| | | |
| | | |
| | | |
| TOTAL $ | 325 | 42 |

SEE THAT ALL CHECKS ARE ENDORSED

A Deposit Slip
```

Ewing Galloway

Keep Your Checkbook Balance Up to Date

The depositor should record the deposit on a stub of his checkbook. Disbursements by check should also be recorded on the checkbook stubs. The illustration on page 329 is an example of an ordinary check. A *check* is a written order in which one person directs a bank to pay to another person a certain amount of money. If a counter check is used to withdraw cash from the account, this withdrawal should likewise be recorded on a check stub. A *counter check* is a check without a stub that is available on the counter of any bank to be used at the convenience of a customer who may have forgotten his checkbook. It should be used in the same way that a person might borrow a blank check from a friend in order to write a check. He should make a note of the check and as quickly as possible record it on a stub in his checkbook. Many people simply tear out and destroy a blank check in the checkbook and use the stub for recording a counter check. Checkbook stubs should be kept up to date so that the correct balance will be shown.

Balances in customers' checking accounts provide money for banks to use in making loans to borrowers. Although a checking account does not earn interest, the facilities provided by it are valuable. The following are some of the advantages:

(a) A personal check is a convenient way to pay bills.
(b) Usually it is more economical to pay bills by check through the mails than to make a trip to the places where accounts are to be paid.
(c) The check stubs and canceled checks provide a record of expenditures, deposits, and bank balances.
(d) Money in a checking account is safe from theft or loss.
(e) A canceled check is proof of payment; therefore, it serves as a receipt.
(f) A checking account helps to enhance one's personal business standing; it also serves as a reference.

A Checkbook Stub

Reconciliation of Bank Statement. The checkbook balance and the bank balance as given on the bank's monthly statement should be reconciled monthly. The purpose of reconciliation is to see whether the checkbook balance is correct on the date on which the reconciliation is made and to detect errors, if any, in the bank statements. It is the depositor's responsibility to reconcile the bank balance monthly and to report any discrepancies to the bank immediately.

STATEMENT OF YOUR ACCOUNT WITH						
MERCHANTS NATIONAL BANK CLEVELAND, OHIO REPORT PROMPTLY ANY CHANGE IN YOUR ADDRESS			Walter A. Kline 236 Mt. Vernon Avenue Cleveland 9, Ohio			
CHECKS			DEPOSITS		THE LAST AMOUNT IN THIS COLUMN IS YOUR BALANCE	
		BALANCE FORWARD	Apr. 4	300.00		
125.00	7.16			6	167.84
21.65	3.75	14.12		9	128.32
			184.75	12	313.07
46.20	18.40			13	248.47
			100.00	19	348.47
75.00	33.65		99.95	23	339.77
66.80	5.30			27	267.67
8.85	33.19	.21		30	225.42
PLEASE EXAMINE AT ONCE AND REPORT ANY DISCREPANCIES OR ERRORS TO OUR AUDITOR WITHIN TEN DAYS.			VOUCHERS RETURNED 14 SHEET NUMBER			

A Bank Statement

Reconciliation involves checkbook balance, bank statement balance, outstanding checks, deposits made but not recorded at the time the bank statement was prepared, and charges against the checking account for such items as service charges on checking accounts and deductions for the monthly purchase of a government bond.

On the back of many bank statements a form for and the steps in reconciling a bank statement are given. Most banks also have leaflets available in which the reconciliation process is given.

Service Charges on a Checking Account. There are several different bank operations involved for every check a customer writes. These operations require not only machines and equipment but also the time of bank employees. The two primary factors that affect the bank's cost of operating a checking account are the size of the balance carried and the number of entries made each month. Banks actually suffer a loss in handling checking accounts that do not carry substantial balances.

Monthly service charges are levied by most banks because of the cost involved in the bank's handling of customers' checking accounts. Service charge rates are often set by the local clearinghouse association. There is little uniformity among the many plans for service charges.

A simple plan that has been in use for many years is making a charge of a specified amount, say $1.00, if the balance falls below $100 at any time during the month; a smaller charge if the balance is between $100 and $300; and no charge if the balance is above $300 at all times.

Another type of service charge on checking accounts takes into account the balance maintained, the number of items deposited, and the number of checks cashed. In some cases, a certain number of free checks is allowed when the minimum balance has been less than $100, the number being increased as the amount of the minimum balance increases.

For the convenience and use of persons who find it difficult to maintain a minimum balance consistently, some banks have established special checking accounts. These are known by various means such as "Check-master," "Thrifti-checks," and "Pay-as-you-go Check Way." No minimum balance is required. However, for every check written a fee is charged. In some cases, banks issue a special checkbook, containing 10 or more checks for which the depositor pays a set fee usually 10 cents a check.

Usually the service charge on one's account is a relatively small amount each month. The convenience of having a checking account far more than compensates for the cost. The service charge on checking accounts is necessary and legitimate when the average balance is small and the number of checks written is large.

> **Your Obligations as a Depositor**
>
> 1. Keep an accurate record of each check on the check stub.
> 2. Keep a sufficient balance in your account; do not overdraw. (To overdraw an account is a criminal offense in most states.)
> 3. Reconcile your checkbook and bankbook balances once a month.
> 4. Keep all canceled checks for at least a year; keep important canceled checks indefinitely.

Joint Accounts. Often two persons will want to use the same bank checking account or savings account. Such an account, which is called a *joint* or *survivorship account,* is usually opened by a man and his wife. Each must fill out a signature card, and either person has authority to withdraw funds during the life of both parties. Upon the death of either party, the survivor has full right to the funds after furnishing the bank with proof that all state tax claims have been paid. In most states when one of the parties operating a joint account dies, the bank is forbidden by law to honor any further checks until any claims by the state are settled.

A joint or survivorship checking or savings account for a man and his wife is a particular aid to good management of family finances. It gives each of them a share in and a sense of responsibility for management of the business affairs of the family.

Stopping Payment on a Check. When a check is lost or stolen, the bank should be requested to stop payment. The request may be given orally or in writing; but if it is given orally, it should also be followed by a written notice. Banks usually have a special form that may be used for this purpose. Although banks will attempt to stop the payment, they may not assume responsibility for damage or loss if inadvertently the check is paid. You may also have occasion to stop payment on a check for other reasons. For example, let us suppose that you have written a check for payment to someone and have discovered that you have been cheated, or you have issued a check for merchandise that is found to be unsatisfactory. You may stop payment on the check.

Postdating Checks. The postdating of a check is legal and sometimes convenient, but the privilege should not be abused. For instance, on February 10 you might issue a check dated February 15. The check is not payable until February 15. Banks will not cash it before that date, although some banks will accept it for deposit if the difference in dates is not more than one or two days.

Postdating of checks usually arises out of a situation in which one is paying an obligation in advance of the time it is due. Let us assume, for example, that one has a debt of $100 coming due on June 20, and he wishes to pay it on June 15 before going on his vacation. If he does not want the check cashed until June 20, he can postdate it. Bankers ordinarily discourage the practice of postdating checks.

Bank Drafts and Special Checks. Sometimes you may wish to make a payment to someone who will not accept your personal check. It could be an important payment in a distant city; it might be a deposit for the buying of a house; or it could be any one of several other situations. In such cases you may go to a bank and obtain a certified check, a bank draft, a bank money order, or a cashier's check, any one of which may serve your purpose.

A *certified check* is an ordinary check drawn by a depositor in the usual way but presented to the bank for certification by the drawer or by some holder. The bank stamps or writes a certification on the check as indicated in the illustration. The amount of the check is deducted from the depositor's balance, and the check becomes an obligation of the bank rather than of the depositor. The bank guarantees its payment. One disadvantage of a certified check to the depositor is that it will not be returned with his canceled checks; hence, he will not have available the endorsed check to serve as a receipt. If for any reason a certified check is returned to the maker, it should not be

A Certified Check

destroyed but redeposited in the maker's checking account at the bank. Otherwise, the balance of the checking account will be short for the amount of the check was deducted when it was certified. A small charge depending upon the size of the check is made by the bank.

A *bank draft* is a check of a bank upon funds deposited to its credit with some other bank. A bank draft is a convenient means of transferring money when the individual who is making payment is not known in the part of the country to which the money is to be sent. He may obtain the draft by purchasing it from a bank. People will usually accept a bank draft provided the bank that has drawn it is known. A certified check has practically the same status as a bank draft, provided the bank is known and has a good reputation. A small fee also is charged by the bank for issuing a bank draft for you.

A Bank Draft

A *cashier's check* is one a bank draws on itself. It is used to pay bills owed by the bank. Also one may buy a cashier's check to transmit money to another person in much the same way as a person buys a bank draft.

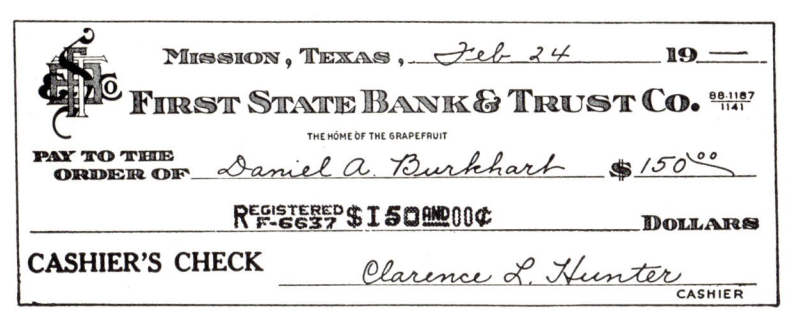

```
           MISSION, TEXAS,  Feb 24        19___
           FIRST STATE BANK & TRUST CO.  88-1187
                                          1141
                      THE HOME OF THE GRAPEFRUIT
PAY TO THE
  ORDER OF   Daniel A. Burkhart    $ 150 00
           REGISTERED $150 AND 00¢
           RF-6637                        DOLLARS
CASHIER'S CHECK    Clarence L. Hunter
                                          CASHIER
```

A Cashier's Check

The *bank money order*, in many banks, is replacing the cashier's check wholly or in part as a means of transmitting customer's money to another person. The bank money order serves essentially the same function in transmitting money for a customer as the cashier's check. However, the name of the remitter is on the bank money order, and usually it is not on a cashier's check.

The fee is usually substantially less for bank money orders, bank drafts, and cashier's checks than it is for postal money orders which also have as their function the transmission of money to another person. A typical fee for a bank money order is 10 cents for $5, 15 cents for $50, and 15 cents for each additional $50. A postal money order costs 10 cents for $5, 15 cents for $10, 25 cents for $50, and 35 cents for $100.

Savings Account. Savings accounts may be maintained in what are commonly known as savings banks or in the savings departments of other banks. The bankbook is the most important instrument in operating a savings account. In it are recorded all deposits and all withdrawals. Deposit slips are used as a record of deposits, and receipts as a record of withdrawals; but the bankbook must be presented each time money is deposited or withdrawn. Checks cannot be written on savings deposits, and many banks require advance notice of the withdrawal of savings.

```
┌─────────────────────────────────────────────────────────┐
│            MERCHANTS NATIONAL BANK                      │
│               SAVINGS DEPARTMENT                        │
│                             BOOK NO. 23056              │
│                    CINCINNATI, O. June 5     19__       │
│  Received of the SAVINGS DEPARTMENT of MERCHANTS NATIONAL BANK │
│  the sum of Two Hundred Fifty-three    00/100 DOLLARS $253.00 │
│  NON NEGOTIABLE RECEIPT       L. M. Sanderson           │
│    FOR COUNTER USE ONLY         DEPOSITORS SIGNATURE    │
└─────────────────────────────────────────────────────────┘
```

A Withdrawal Slip for a Savings Account

Savings accounts in banks usually pay interest. Saving by depositing money in a bank is a conservative means of investing, but it is usually a safe means as compared with investments in many types of securities. There is some difference in the yield of interest, depending upon the number of times a year the interest is calculated. Obviously, the income from a savings account is greater when interest is compounded semiannually than when it is computed annually at the same rate.

Trust Functions of Banks. The trust functions of banks have proved especially useful for people who wish to preserve their wealth for the benefit of dependents. Many wills include clauses that appoint certain trust companies or trust departments of banks to administer the estates left to wives and children. A more complete discussion of what one should know about wills is given in Chapter 31.

The trust officer in a bank not only serves, in a sense, as the business manager of an estate left in his care, but he also may serve as a trustee for a fund that has been created to serve some special purpose such as provide an income for a charitable organization or money for the care of a park.

Safe-Deposit Boxes. Safe-deposit boxes in the vaults of banks are provided on a rental basis. Such a box provides protection against burglary and fire, and should be used for valuables that are not safe in the home or in the business office. Each customer has a key to the box that he rents, and the bank has a control key. Both keys are necessary to unlock the box; neither one alone will unlock it. Sometimes a question is asked whether the bank has a master key that would unlock all boxes. The answer is that the bank cannot open safe-deposit boxes. In case of a lost customer's key, the bank may in the presence of witnesses and legal representatives of the renter of the box have a locksmith drill the lock to open it.

A bank cannot open a private safe-deposit box except upon the order of a court. In most states, if a safe-deposit box is registered in the names of a man and his wife, the bank is legally required to seal the box upon notice of the death of either person. The box may not then be opened except on the order of a court. When it is opened a list is made of taxable items in the box by a legal tax representative, and the contents are then turned over to the survivor. Of course, the amount of tax assessed against the contents will have to be paid.

Financial and Tax Advice. Most bankers have the problem of advising those who apply for credit. This advice must be given to individuals as well as to business owners. A wise banker will not make a loan to an individual if he believes that the loan cannot be repaid or that to repay the loan would place an undesirable hardship upon the borrower. Regardless of the character of the borrower or the security that would be pledged to the bank, the making of a loan in such a case might result in financial disaster.

Some banks maintain tax departments with a staff of lawyers and accountants who give advice on tax problems to the customers of the bank. These tax specialists, in some cases, will prepare income tax returns.

Other Bank Services. Many miscellaneous services, such as those pertaining to travel, real estate, and foreign trade are provided by banks for the convenience of customers. They also encourage business activity as well as produce additional income for themselves.

Most banks offer traveler's checks for sale to customers at a fee of about 75 cents for $100. *Traveler's checks* sold by banks usually are issued by the American Express Company or by a large well-known bank such as the National City Bank of New York or the Bank of America in California. When the checks are purchased, the buyer signs each check in the presence of a representative of the bank, and later when he cashes one of them he signs the same check again in the presence of the one cashing the check to identify himself. Traveler's checks are usually acceptable at hotels, restaurants, gasoline stations, and authorized travel ticket agents.

Certain banks operate travel departments and collect commission on travel tickets sold. They also help travelers obtain foreign exchange and credit for use in foreign countries.

Real-estate departments are sometimes operated by banks in connection with trust departments. These departments function also as service departments for depositors by maintaining or disposing of property that has been taken as security on loans.

Banks sometimes act as custodian of bonds and other securities, collecting dividends or interest for the owner. A bank also will act as an agent for a customer to take charge of his finances.

In many cities particularly in the eastern part of the United States, one or more banks in a city or town may offer a *charge account service*. A customer is given a charge account credit card which is honored in all stores in which the customer has a charge account and that cooperate with the bank. Under this plan purchases are made at stores and charged the same as on any other charge account. The price of goods bought is the same as when charged to a regular charge account. The cooperating stores send the charges they have made to customers' accounts to the bank offering the charge account service. The bank in turn sends a monthly bill to the customer accompanied by the original sales slips from each of the stores at which purchases were made. Ordinarily, the monthly bill from the bank is due in 30 days. It may be paid by check or in cash. One's bank account need not be in the bank offering the service.

Loans to Individuals by Commercial Banks. The interest banks receive on loans made to individuals and business firms is an important part of their income. Bankers, therefore, want to loan money to customers. But when a bank or other lender makes a loan there must be assurance that the borrower will pay when it becomes due. There are three ways lenders of money may be sure of a loan being repaid. First, the borrower may be a person of such character and be the owner of a sufficient amount of property that his promise is enough to guarantee payment.

Second, the borrower may give the lender a legal claim against some property which can be used to pay for the loan if the borrower fails to do so. The bonds, stocks, rights to proceeds from an insurance policy, or other personal property used to guarantee repayment of a loan are known as security or collateral. When an agreement is signed by a borrower turning certain personal property over to the lender of money to guarantee payment of the loan, the agreement is said to be a *chattel mortgage*. When land and buildings are pledged to pay a loan, if the borrower fails to pay, the agreement is known as a *real estate mortgage*. Property pledged for the payment of a loan cannot be sold by the borrower before he pays the loan for which it is pledged.

The third way a bank or other lender of money may be assured payment of a loan if the borrower does not pay when it becomes due, is to require that some other financially responsible person gives a written promise to pay the loan when it becomes due if the borrower does not pay it. Such a person is known as a *comaker* or *cosigner*, and he becomes fully responsible for the payment of the loan if the borrower does not pay when it becomes due. Thus one should never be a cosigner unless he is sure the person who is borrowing the money will pay.

Most commercial banks operate personal loan departments for the purpose of making small loans to individuals.

Loans are made for such specific purposes as buying an automobile, furniture, appliances, or financing medical and hospital bills. Ordinarily, a personal loan is limited to a relatively small amount such as 10 per cent of one's annual income. In many cases the interest is deducted in advance from the amount of the loan. Often the payment of the loan is arranged on a monthly installment plan. Commercial banks are among the most common sources for personal loans.

In Chapter 22 we shall learn more about how to obtain a small or personal loan. In Chapter 33 we shall learn the various ways of financing the purchase of a home, one of which is by borrowing money from a commercial bank on a real estate mortgage.

Negotiable Instruments. The legal relations of borrowing and lending center largely around a negotiable instrument. A *negotiable instrument* is a written evidence of some contractual obligation and is ordinarily transferable from one person to another by indorsement. It is frequently referred to as "negotiable paper" or "commercial paper."

The most common forms of negotiable instruments are (a) promissory notes and (b) checks. A *promissory note* is an unconditional written promise to pay a sum certain in money at a certain time or on demand to the bearer or the order of one who has obtained the note through legal means. The one who executes a promissory note; that is, the one who promises to pay the amount specified in the note under the terms indicated, is the *maker*. As explained in the preceding section dealing with bank loans, a person who guarantees the payment of a loan or promissory note when it becomes due if the borrower or maker does not pay is a comaker or cosigner. The person to whom the note is payable is known as the *payee*.

The person who writes a check is the *drawer*. The person to whom the check is payable is the payee. The bank on which the check is drawn is the *drawee*.

The maker of a note or the drawer of a check is unconditionally required to pay the amount specified. This obligation assumes, of course, that the transaction relating to the use of the instrument has been proper and legal. The drawer of a check is required to pay the amount of the check if the drawee (the bank) does not pay it, but there are certain limitations on this rule in many states.

The person who indorses a negotiable instrument and transfers it to someone else is known as the *indorser*. The person to whom he transfers the negotiable instrument is referred to as the *indorsee*.

Transfer of Negotiable Instruments. Much of our money consists of notes that circulate as money without indorsement. The promissory notes issued by individuals and businesses may also circulate, although they usually require an indorsement.

A person who signs a negotiable instrument as an indorser is liable under varying conditions. For instance, if he indorses a note to help a friend obtain a loan from a bank, he must pay the amount of the note to the bank or to a subsequent indorser if his friend fails to pay it when it is due. The obligation of an indorser depends upon the type of indorsement used. Four principal kinds of indorsements are used in transferring negotiable instruments. These indorsements are as follows:

(a) *Indorsement in full.* An indorsement in full is frequently referred to as a *special indorsement*. It mentions the name of the indorsee who must, in turn, indorse it in order to transfer or cash it. This type of indorsement should be used when checks are sent by mail or by messenger.

(b) *Blank indorsement.* An indorsement in blank consists in merely the name of the indorser. It makes a check or note payable to the bearer; consequently, it may be dangerous. Checks to be deposited should never be indorsed in this manner until after one is in the bank.

(c) *Qualified indorsement.* A qualified indorsement is, as its name implies, one that limits the obligation of the indorser. Assume, for instance, that a person has a check that he wishes to transfer to another. He does not wish to assume responsibility for the payment of the check if the drawer cannot or will not pay it. He may therefore use a qualified indorsement with words such as "without recourse." The qualified indorsement is infrequently used mainly because both people and banks are reluctant to accept negotiable paper for which the payee or another indorser is unwilling to assume responsibility for its payment.

Indorsement in Full

Indorsement in Blank

Qualified Indorsement

Restrictive Indorsement

Forms of Indorsement

(d) *Restrictive indorsement.* The restrictive indorsement is very common. It is one which specifies that the person to whom it is indorsed (the indorsee) may dispose of the instrument only in the manner indicated by the indorser. For instance, restrictive indorsement on checks to be deposited frequently includes the phrase "for deposit only" or "for deposit only to the account of . . ."

Ch. 19] HOW TO USE YOUR BANK 345

> *Summary of Effective Use of Banking Services*
> 1. Bank services provide an orderly and systematic way to conduct many personal business affairs.
> 2. A checking account provides a convenient and economical way to handle money transactions.
> 3. Money in a savings account is not only safe but it also earns interest.
> 4. A depositor has an obligation to follow the accepted practices and routines in using bank services.
> 5. Through banks several ways are available of transmitting money.
> 6. Bank loans are made to qualified borrowers through regular loan service and personal loan departments.
> 7. Negotiable instruments are the means by which many banking services are performed.
> 8. Customers of banks should be acquainted with the characteristic features of negotiable instruments and their uses.

TEXTBOOK QUESTIONS

1. When a bank deposit is made, what kind of receipt for the deposit is given the depositor?
2. In filling out a deposit slip, indicate the two different ways of identifying a check drawn on a local bank that is being deposited.
3. If a depositor writes a counter check what, if any, record should be made in his regular checkbook?
4. What are the advantages of a checking account?
5. Why is it that the checkbook stubs do not always show all the charges against the bank account that are shown on a bank statement?
6. Why will a monthly bank statement not always show all the money that has been deposited in the account?
7. Why is it necessary for banks to establish a charge for cashing checks?
8. Is it simply a matter of bad practice or is it illegal to write checks for more than the amount of your checking account?
9. What are the features of special checking accounts such as (a) Check-master; (b) Thrifti-checks; (c) Pay-as-you-go Check Way?
10. Ordinarily what happens to a joint checking account when one of the parties operating the account dies?

11. If you have issued a check and then decide for some good reason that you should not allow the person to whom it was issued to cash it, what can you do?
12. How can you issue a check today to somebody for payment of a transaction and still be sure that the person to whom you have issued the check cannot cash it until the desired date?
13. What is a certified check?
14. What is a bank draft?
15. What is a cashier's check?
16. What is the major difference between a cashier's check and a bank money order?
17. Which is usually the cheaper method of remitting money—the cashier's check or the postal money order?
18. Why is it not desirable for a man and his wife to have their safe-deposit box registered in both names?
19. It is often said, "Your bank is your financial advisor." Name some of the ways that a bank can help you.
20. What is the procedure for buying and cashing a traveler's check?
21. Why is a banker justified in refusing to make a loan to a person who cannot repay the loan under some definite plan?
22. (a) What is meant by security or collateral for a loan? (b) Are loans ever made without security?
23. What are some types of security for loans?
24. What is a chattel mortgage?
25. What is a comaker or cosigner?
26. In the case of a negotiable instrument, who is (a) the maker, (b) the payee, (c) the drawer, (d) the drawee, and (e) the cosigner?
27. Who is (a) the indorser; (b) the indorsee?
28. Give an example of and explain (a) an indorsement in full, (b) a blank indorsement, and (c) a restrictive indorsement.

DISCUSSION QUESTIONS

1. What would you recommend as a policy in regard to keeping the balance of your checkbook stubs up to date with the actual bank balance?
2. Some people are inclined to take the attitude, "Banks do not make mistakes; therefore why should I bother with reconciling my bank statement with my checkbook?" How do you feel about this matter?
3. Some people, because of mistakes and carelessness in keeping the records of the balances in their checking accounts, overdraw their accounts. In many states laws have been passed for the punishment of people who overdraw their accounts. Do you believe that these laws are justified?

4. Why is it a matter of good business to keep all canceled checks for at least a year?
5. What types of canceled checks would you recommend keeping indefinitely?
6. If you are interested in opening a charge account with a local business firm, how will a bank account help you?
7. Can you give some advantages and disadvantages of a joint checking account maintained by a husband and wife?
8. Some people follow a practice of postdating checks when they do not have money in the account but expect to deposit the money before the check is cashed. Give your opinion of this practice.
9. What are the essential differences between a certified check and a bank draft?
10. Why do you think a cashier's check would be more acceptable for payment to a stranger 200 miles away than your ordinary personal check?
11. If the interest rate on savings deposits in banks drops from 2 per cent to 1 per cent, what do you think such a decrease indicates as to the condition of banks?
12. Why are funds frequently left in trust with a bank instead of in the care of the widow or the children?
13. Would you recommend putting cash in a safe-deposit box? Why or why not? Discuss.
14. A man who is known to be successful and thoroughly honorable feels highly insulted when he applies for a loan at a bank and is asked for considerable information on his assets, debts, and income. He believes that the bank has no right to this confidential information. What is your opinion? Discuss the situation.
15. If you indorse a note for a friend in order to help him obtain a loan from a bank, what is your obligation?
16. What kind of indorsement would you recommend if you were away from home and were mailing a check to your bank for deposit? Why?

PROBLEMS

1. On the basis of the following information, prepare a reconciliation of the bank statement of Mr. H. L. Jones:
    (a) From checkbook stubs

    January 1—Balance on check stub, $346.53. January 2—Deposited $74.33. January 3—Paid (Check #1) $50 to L. M. James, rent for January. January 4—Paid (Check #2) $45 to Superior Cars, car payment for January. January 5—Paid (Check #3) $7.85 to Dr. Taylor, dental work. January 9—Deposited $74.33. January 14—Paid

(Check #4) $8.45 to M. L. Wheeler, life insurance for January. January 16—Deposited $74.33. January 18—Paid (Check #5) $32.24 to Figg Grocery, grocery bill to date. January 19—Paid (Check #6) $3.60 to Bell Telephone, telephone bill to date. January 23—deposited $74.33. January 24—Paid (Check #7) $48.34 to Gross Income Tax Division. January 30—Paid (Check #8) $12.50 to License Bureau, car license. January 31—Deposited $61.27. January 31—checkbook balance, $497.14.

(b) From bank statement

BANK STATEMENT for month of January, 19—

CHECKS	DEPOSITS	DATE	BALANCE
			346.53
50.00	74.33	Jan. 4	370.86
45.00		Jan. 6	325.86
7.85		Jan. 7	318.01
	74.33	Jan. 10	392.34
8.45	74.33	Jan. 17	458.22
32.24		Jan. 20	425.98
3.60		Jan. 21	422.38
	74.33	Jan. 24	496.71
.74SC *		Jan. 31	495.97

* This is a service charge deducted by the bank.

CHECKS OUTSTANDING		DEPOSITS NOT RECORDED BY BANK	
COLUMN 1	COLUMN 2	COLUMN 3	COLUMN 4
NUMBER	AMOUNT	DATE	AMOUNT
Total of checks outstanding			
Balance as on checkbook stub		Balance shown on bank statement	
Total		Total	

(c) Using the form above which is typical of those furnished by banks, prepare your reconciliation

> (1) Draw a reconciliation form like the one on the preceding page and compare check book stubs with bank statement and record in columns 1 and 2 each check written but not yet paid by bank as indicated by bank statement. Add column 2.
> (2) Compare the deposits as shown on checkbook stubs with those shown on the bank statement and record in columns 3 and 4 of the reconciliation statement the dates and amounts of any deposits not shown on the bank statement. Add column 4.
> (3) Your reconciliation is correct if the total of column 4 subtracted from column 1 is the same as the service charge. (This amount should be deducted from the balance on the check book stub.)

2. Using your own signature, write models of the four different types of indorsements that you might use on a check or a note.

COMMUNITY PROBLEMS AND PROJECTS

1. Investigate the various types of services offered by the banks in your community. Summarize these services in the form of a table, indicating what services are available in each particular institution.
2. Select a committee to go to a local bank and obtain the following: (a) All forms necessary for opening a checking account. (b) A list of the regulations governing a checking account. (c) Samples of all the forms used by depositors, such as a bank statement, a bankbook, a regular check, a counter check, and a deposit slip. Make a report on the method of opening a checking account, on the regulations governing such an account, and on the activities of depositors using such an account.
3. From your local banks obtain information in regard to personal loan privileges and regulations. Write a report of your findings, covering such important topics as interest rates, types of loans made, maximum size of loans, security required, repayment plans, and other important features.

Chapter 20

How to Obtain and Use Credit

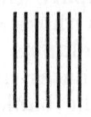

Purpose of the Chapter. Much of the business transacted in America is on the basis of trust—promises to pay later, commonly known as credit. Business as we know it could not operate without credit. Practically all persons contract debts of some kind, ranging all the way from owing for the morning newspaper for the past week to a mortgage on a home. The purpose of this chapter is to help you understand credit, its importance to you, and how to use it.

You will find answers to these questions:
1. What is credit?
2. In what ways may a consumer use credit?
3. What factors affect a person's credit standing?
4. What is one's ethical and legal responsibility for debts?
5. By what legal means may creditors force payment of debts?

The Meaning of Credit. Most transactions among business firms are conducted on a credit basis rather than on a cash basis. When a retailer buys from a wholesaler, the merchandise is charged, and a check is sent in payment at a later time. Likewise, the wholesaler purchases from the manufacturer or supplier on open account, which means that he pays later. Operating a business on strictly a cash basis would be a very difficult procedure.

Consumers also may buy on time because it is a convenient way to purchase or because they do not have cash available to pay for a purchase immediately. In either case a debt is incurred. They often borrow money with which to pay current bills for purchases of goods and services.

Credit means either an advance (or loan) of money with which to purchase goods and services or an advance of goods and services in exchange for a promise to pay at a later date. It means one is trusted to pay at a later time. In quite a different sense, credit may refer to one's potential ability to borrow money or to buy goods on time.

Consumer credit is debt incurred by a consumer for a home, goods, or services for personal and family use and consumption. However, a debt on an owner-occupied home ordinarily is financed by a long-term loan secured by a real estate mortgage and, therefore, is not commonly included in consumer credit. Debt incurred for repair or modernization of an owner-occupied home ordinarily matures within a few months and, therefore, is generally classified as consumer credit.

In the common use of the term, consumer credit is considered to be comprised of debts for goods and services for personal and family use having a maturity of less than five years. The Federal Reserve Board classifies such debts as *short-term credit* and *intermediate-term credit*.

The term consumer credit may be more easily understood if it is thought of as *consumer debt*. Practically everyone uses credit in some way every day. We incur a debt when the paperboy delivers the morning paper and when we use water and electricity for which we will be billed later. Many consumers buy on credit (go into debt temporarily) because it is more convenient to pay for several purchases at one time at a later date than it is to pay for each purchase separately.

Consumer debts may arise from purchases of goods and services for personal and family consumption or from obtaining loans for the payment of such purchases. Debts on which payments are to be made at periodic intervals are considered *installment debts* or more commonly known as *installment credit*. Debts for which the full payment is to be made in a single payment at a specified maturity date are known as *noninstallment debts* or *noninstallment credit*.

A study of consumer credit or debt outstanding on September 30, 1955, in the following table shows that approximately 78 per cent of all consumer debt is to be paid by installments and 22 per cent by single payments. It is interesting to observe that 50 per cent of all installment debts owed by consumers are for automobiles and that 40 per cent of all debts incurred by consumers are for automobiles.

Consumer Debts in the United States
September 30, 1955

NONINSTALLMENT DEBTS
(Debts to be paid in single payments)

	(MILLIONS OF DOLLARS)
Charge accounts (for goods purchased) ...	3,108
Service accounts (for such as medical or legal service)	1,829
Personal loans to customers	2,657
Total noninstallment debts	7,594

INSTALLMENT DEBTS
(Debts to be paid by periodic payments)

Debt on automobiles	13,929
Debt on other consumer goods	5,848
Loans for repair and modernization of owner-occupied homes	1,611
Personal loans to consumers	5,311
Total installment debt	26,699
Total consumer credit (consumer debt outstanding)	34,293

Source: U. S. Department of Commerce.

We shall study about credit particularly in reference to charge and service accounts in the remainder of this chapter. The problems of installment buying will be presented in Chapter 21 and personal loans as sources of credit in Chapter 22.

The Charge Account. Many stores and business firms sell merchandise on *open account* or on *charge account*. This means that at the time of the sale the title to the merchandise passes to the purchaser and that the store accepts the customer's promise to pay for it later, usually within 30 days. The customer is required to sign the sales slip as evidence that he received the merchandise.

A *service account* is similar to a charge account except that the charges made to it are for services rendered such as legal or medical service.

The first step in opening a charge account is to make application to the credit manager of the store. An illustration of an application to open an account is given on page 359. When the application is approved usually a maximum balance due on the account at any one time is established. The privilege of charging purchases to the charge account may be withdrawn by the store at any time you fail to pay the amount you owe in accordance with the terms of the account. A brief summary of the advantages of a charge account to a customer follows:

Advantages of Charge Account to Customers

1. A very convenient and simple way to buy.
2. Payment for purchases may be delayed until a future specified time.
3. A record of purchases is made automatically.
4. Money is not needed at the time of purchase; therefore the danger of loss while shopping is minimized.
5. Charge accounts make it easy to order merchandise by mail or telephone.
6. Store clerks and owners learning to know a charge customer may result in better service.
7. The privilege of charging purchases adds to one's prestige.
8. Payment for several purchases may be made at one time.

A charge account may be a disadvantage for a person who has a tendency to spend without regard to his income or ability to pay.

The usual term of payment for charge accounts is 30 days; however, it may be for a different period of time. A plan known as cycle billing that is being used by some stores makes the balance owed by a certain customer to fall due regularly on a certain day of the month regardless of the date of the last purchase. This means that a bill for a purchase made late in that customer's credit month becomes due in much less than 30 days. The reason some stores use cycle billing on charge accounts is to spread the work of sending out monthly statements over the entire month for the accounting department.

There are several types of charge accounts in use by stores. One plan permits a consumer to charge a large item like a refrigerator or a living room suite and then pay one third of the cost in each of the succeeding three months. This type is known as *divided-charge account*. Another plan is the *depositor's account*. Under this plan a customer may deposit an amount of money with the store against which purchases may be charged. A variation of the depositor's account is the *coupon* or *script account* plan in which coupons or script are issued to the customer who may pay for purchases in the store with them the same as with money.

The revolving charge account is in common use in some cities. Under this plan, the payment for purchases may be extended to four or six months. The consumer and the store representative determine at the time the account is opened the maximum amount that may be owed to the store at any one time. To illustrate the revolving charge account let us assume that the maximum amount that may be owed is set at $240 and that the store will allow the consumer a maximum of six months to pay for purchases. Equal monthly payments of $40 (240 ÷ 6 months) are to be made whenever there is an unpaid balance in the account at the end of a month. New purchases to be charged to the account may be made at any time just so the total amount owed by the consumer does not exceed the established maximum of $240. Usually a small service charge of one half to one and one half per cent is charged for this type of account.

A combination of revolving and script accounts is now used in some stores.

A *credit identification card* is issued by some business firms operating nationally such as oil companies, restaurants, hotels, airlines, and railroads. The card identifies a customer who is travelling thus enabling him to charge purchases of goods and services even though he is not known in the city where the purchase is made.

Cost of Charge Accounts to the Store. Merchants who sell on open account may be classified as follows: (a) those who have uniform prices for credit and for cash sales; (b) those who charge more for credit than for cash sales.

Selling on charge accounts adds extra costs to every sale. The principal extra costs result from (a) the clerical work necessary for recording sales and collecting accounts, (b) interest on the money that is invested in accounts receivable from customers, (c) losses due to bad debts, and (d) the greater tendency of charge customers to return goods for exchange.

In stores that do not carefully investigate a customer's ability to pay before charging sales to his account, the losses from failure to collect debts are likely to be high. One may well expect to find inflated prices in stores that recklessly advertise generous credit terms to everyone. Stores that have sound credit policies have practically no losses from bad debts. We need not assume, therefore, that a merchant who sells on credit must necessarily sell at higher prices than a merchant who sells for cash. If selling on credit increases sales, the total overhead cost of each sale may actually be decreased. The costs of selling on charge accounts, however, are reported by some stores to be as much as 6 to 8 per cent higher than costs of selling for cash. On the other hand, stores that regularly sell on charge accounts often also offer delivery services and other conveniences. These services combined with possible higher costs due to charge accounts may cause the store to sell at higher prices than a cash-and-carry store.

Cost of Charge Accounts to the Individual. The cost of selling on charge accounts is passed on either to the individual consumer on the basis of each sale, or to all buyers through generally higher prices.

Sometimes discounts are allowed to individuals in ordinary charge sales. Common terms in such a case are "2% ten days, net thirty days." These terms mean that, if the purchaser pays the amount within ten days, he may deduct a discount of 2 per cent from the amount of the bill; but if he does not desire to take advantage of the 2 per cent discount, he may pay the net amount at the end of thirty days. The person who sells on this basis is willing to forego 2 per cent of the sale value in order to obtain his money promptly. If the purchaser chooses not to take the 2 per cent discount, he is paying 2 per cent for the use of the money for twenty days. In other words, if he buys on these terms goods amounting to $100, he may take a discount of $2 at the end of ten days and therefore pay only $98. Suppose, however, that he has enough money to pay the bill but believes that he can use the money better in some other way. He therefore prefers to wait until the end of thirty days before paying the bill. By doing so, he pays $2 for using $98 for twenty days. If interest is figured on the basis of 360 days, he is paying interest at the rate of 36.72 per cent a year to use this money.

Some stores set their sales prices high enough to cover the cost of charge accounts; others use a two-price system, one for cash sales and one for sales on account. Let us assume that a television receiver is priced at $159.95 cash or $164.95 if charged payable in 30 days. The actual cost of charging the purchase to the customer's charge account is $5.00. This means that he is paying $5.00 for the use of $159.95 for 30 days. This is a rate of interest per year of 37½ per cent.

Basis for Establishing a Credit Standing. Our credit standing or credit worthiness is an indication of our ability to secure goods, services, and money in return for a promise to pay. It represents our ability to incur debts because some lender trusts us. A favorable credit standing does not come automatically. It comes as the result of slow growth. It must be nurtured, fostered, strengthened, and improved. It is an asset of tremendous value to those who develop it over a long period of years. It can be destroyed easily; it is sensitive to abuse; and it usually continues only as long as it is justified. A favorable credit standing over a period of time is enjoyed only by persons who deserve it and who have wisdom to protect it. It represents the willingness of others to accept a person's promise to pay under stipulated conditions.

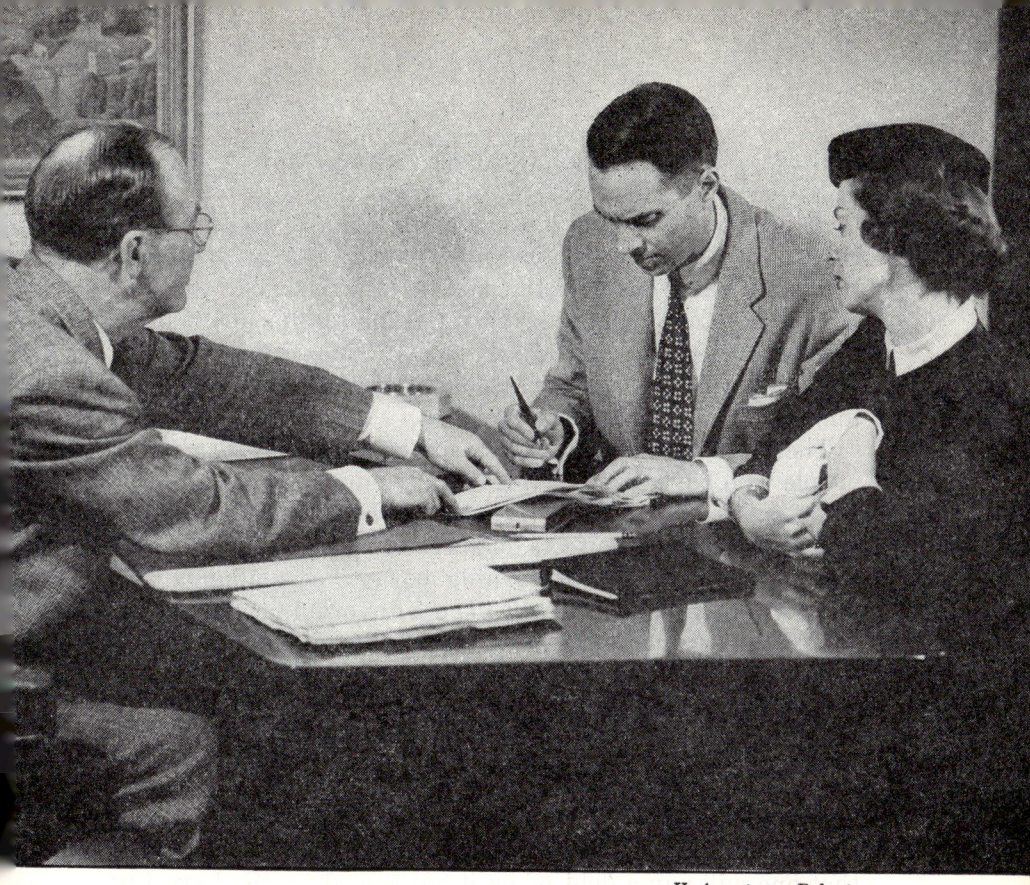

H. Armstrong Roberts

In Arranging for Credit, One Is Expected to Give Information about Himself

A commonly recognized formula for determining the credit of a person or a business consists of the "three C's"—character, capacity, and capital.

Character is the first consideration. J. P. Morgan, the famous banker, is reputed to have said that he would lend more on an individual's character than on his capital resources.

Character is revealed in one's conduct, attitudes, and achievements. It does not necessarily have any relation to one's wealth. It represents the sum total of the principles for which one stands. One's reputation is the result of how other people evaluate our character traits. We would not be able to borrow money or buy goods and services with the promise to pay later if others judge our character to be questionable.

Capacity is merely another term for earning power. It represents one's ability to earn and to pay obligations when they become due. An individual may have an honorable character and perfectly good intentions of paying an obligation; but unless he has the ability or capacity to pay, he cannot pay satisfactorily. It is often more difficult to judge character than it is to judge capacity. Capacity, or earning power, can be measured reasonably accurately, but character is an intangible quality.

The third measuring standard, *capital,* applies only to people who have property. Naturally our net worth or capital affects our ability to pay debts when they become due and, consequently, affects our credit standing. A person with temporary lack of earning power but having a substantial net worth may still have a favorable credit standing. That is others will be willing to make loans to him or to sell to him based on his promise to pay.

Capacity and capital without character will affect our credit standing adversely making it impossible to borrow money or buy goods and services on time.

How to Establish Your Line of Credit. Credit standing or credit worthiness refers to the chances or the probability that one will pay a debt when it becomes due. We have just learned that it depends upon the trust or confidence others have in our intention to pay. *Line of credit* means the maximum amount a lender or creditor will permit a customer to owe him at any one time.

Every responsible family should establish its line of credit with a good retail store or retail credit association regardless of whether it is used extensively or not. By so doing you also will take your first step in establishing your line of credit with a bank.

To establish your credit standing and your line of credit the usual procedure is to go to your favorite store and discuss the matter frankly with the credit manager or the owner, who will request information of a personal nature about your character, capacity, and capital. Such information should be provided accurately and completely. It will be kept confidential. The credit manager must have such information as a basis for determining your credit standing and your line of credit.

The illustration below shows a typical application for credit for customers of a department store. In some cases the forms are more complicated, but in general they require the same types of information.

```
LEDGER RECORD                    MEMBER OF                      DATE
                          RETAILERS CREDIT ASSOCIATION
ACCT. No.      LIMIT         Application for Account            NOTIFIED

                    SPELL CORRECTLY. SURNAME FIRST, GIVEN NAME IN FULL. STATE IF SINGLE OR WIDOW
NAME OF   Smith, Robert Allen                              NAME OF
HUSBAND                                                    WIFE     Mary Ann
RESIDENCE                                                  HOW
ADDRESS   3948 Mission Street, San Francisco, California   LONG 6 years PHONE None
FORMER
ADDRESS   237 Holliston Street, Pasadena, California
HUSBAND'S                                       WIFE'S
OCCUPATION Salesman       Fuller Brush Co.      OCCUPATION None
            POSITION          FIRM                            POSITION         FIRM
BUSINESS                                        BUSINESS
ADDRESS   1512 Van Ness Avenue                  ADDRESS
HOW LONG              HOW LONG                        ☒ OWN
PRESENT EMPLOY 5 years IN CITY 6 years    HOME  { ☐ RENT
                                  COM. ☐        BANK SIGNATURE       OTHER PROPERTY
BANK    Merchants National Bank   SAVGS. ☐      OR NAME
                     BRANCH
COMMERCIAL                                                  COMMERCIAL
REFERENCES  F. C. Nash & Co. Dept. Store, Pasadena, Calif.  REFERENCES
    "                                               "
    "                                               "
PERSONAL                                          NEAREST
REFERENCE  Mr. F. L. Roth, Manager, Fuller Brush  RELATIVE
AUTHORIZED                                        ADDRESS
BUYERS     Mary Ann Smith
SEND         TO  { ☒ RESIDENCE  TOTAL AMOUNT                      SUBSCRIBER'S
STATEMENTS       { ☐ BUSINESS   CREDIT REQUESTED $150.00  TERMS 30 days   CODE No.
       FOR THE PURPOSE OF HAVING CREDIT EXTENDED ME BY
I CERTIFY TO THE ABOVE STATEMENTS AND AGREE TO PAY MY BILLS
IN FULL IN SAN FRANCISCO DURING MONTH FOLLOWING PURCHASE.  The Emporium
APPLICATION TAKEN BY   HMK      SIGNATURE
REMARKS
```

An Application for Account

Protect Your Credit Standing. Your credit standing will soon become well known in your community; so guard it carefully. A good credit standing involves character as well as ability to pay.

Although a person may have a favorable credit standing, borrowing money and buying goods on a promise to pay should be done wisely. For example, incurring a debt for the purchase of an automobile when the payment of the obligation would mean the sacrificing of expenditures for necessary food and clothing may be unwise. On the other hand, the purchase of an automobile on an installment plan may be very wise if the family needs it for transportation to and from work.

Credit Rating Agencies. In general there are two types of credit agencies: (a) agencies that provide credit rating information on businessmen and companies, and (b) agencies that provide credit ratings of individuals.

Banks sometimes give confidential credit information on individuals and businesses. It is therefore important for a person or a business to maintain satisfactory relations with a bank if a good credit rating is desired. Information can be obtained from the local Better Business Bureau as to whether there have been any complaints on the credit of a particular person or business.

Private credit agencies collect information and issue confidential reports for the benefit of their subscribers who are retailers. Each subscriber contributes information about customers to the agency. Additional information is gathered from local newspapers, notices of change in address, death notices, and court records. Such information is valuable to the retailer in protecting himself from loss on accounts. If one of his customers moves, he will want to know of the change in address. If a customer dies, he will want to be sure that his claim is presented. If someone is taking court action against one of his customers, he will want to protect his own claim.

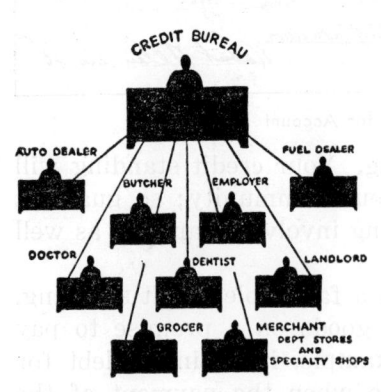

The Associated Credit Bureaus of America has 1,760 credit bureau members serving over 500,000 business firms. Any of these local credit bureaus can develop a report on any individual in North America and many foreign countries within a short period of time. Through the interchange of information the credit records of an estimated 70 million consumers are already compiled and are readily available to all members of the Associated Credit Bureaus of America. This nation-wide credit reporting system is an advantage to you if you have safeguarded your credit. You can move from one community to another, and your credit record will follow you or it can be checked upon very easily. However, a bad credit reputation also will follow you wherever you go.

Dun and Bradstreet, Incorporated, issues a book of credit ratings on commercial houses and manufacturers. The service, which is available on a subscription basis, covers the entire United States. In addition, a subscriber can obtain a special report on any businessman or professional man in any part of the country. The reliability of this agency has been established through many years of effective service to all types of businessmen.

Responsibility for Debts. Responsibility for payment of one's debts is one of the oldest moral and ethical principles recognized by man. In addition to this principle, laws have been enacted specifying man's legal responsibility for debts. Furthermore, his relationship to creditors in case he does not pay or cannot pay has been fixed by law.

A husband is responsible for debts incurred by his wife unless he gives legal written notice that from the date of the notice forward he will not be responsible for them. A merchant, therefore, may sell on account to a man's wife with confidence that the husband is responsible for payment.

Parents are not legally responsible for debts incurred by their children except when permission has been given to the children to make purchases and to charge them to the parent's account. For instance, if it has been customary for a child to use a charge account of the parents, the parents are responsible for the debts.

Minors are legally responsible for debts incurred for necessities such as medical care, clothing, and food. Such items must be suitable and appropriate. For example, even though a child of a family with a moderate income has had the privilege of using the charge account regularly, the child or the parents could not

A Minor May Legally Contract for Certain Purchases

be held responsible for an expensive mink coat sold by the store to the child. Of course, the store can insist upon having the coat returned.

Garnishment. If a debtor refuses to pay a debt, an order may be issued by a court requiring the employer of the debtor to pay the creditor a certain percentage of the debtor's wages until the full amount or an amount specified by the court has been paid. This procedure is called the *garnishment* or the *garnisheeing of wages*. Those states that permit the garnisheeing of wages have widely varying practices.

Attachment. If you owe a debt and refuse to pay or cannot pay it as agreed, you may be sued in court to force you to pay it. A common procedure in such a case is to ask the court for an attachment on some of your property until the case is settled. An *attachment* is simply a legal process whereby the property attached comes under the control of the court until the case is settled. Property upon which an attachment order has been placed may not be sold and may not be moved except by court approval.

Statute of Limitations. The *statutes of limitations* in most states set a time limit after which a creditor cannot enforce a legal claim. For instance, in one state if an account is not collected within five years, the creditor cannot sue for the amount. If the debtor, however, makes a payment or promise to pay during the five years or at any time thereafter, the account is revived or reinstated.

Bankruptcy. If a person is unable to pay his debts when they become due, he is said to be insolvent. If his debts are greater than the total fair value of his assets, a federal court may adjudge him to be *bankrupt*. Recognizing the impossibility of paying his debts, a man may petition the court to be adjudged bankrupt. This process is known as *voluntary bankruptcy*.

Any one of a person's creditors who holds a past due debt against him may also petition the court that he should be adjudged bankrupt. This process is known as *involuntary bankruptcy*.

The circumstances under which one may petition for voluntary bankruptcy are regulated by law. If the court adjudges a person to be bankrupt, a receiver is appointed, who then takes charge of the bankrupt's business, sells the property, and pays off the debts on a proportional basis among the creditors. The latest federal bankruptcy laws, under certain circumstances, provide that debtors against whom bankruptcy suits have been filed may request the court to extend the time, or to rearrange his payment plan, or to otherwise alter or modify his relation with creditors. If such request seems feasible and is granted, the debtor may be able to pay his debts in due time.

Bankruptcy discharges all of a debtor's former debts and enables him to start anew to build up property for himself again. Property acquired after bankruptcy proceedings have been completed is not subject to claims for prior debts. The great advantage of bankruptcy to creditors is that they all fare proportionately to their claims in the net proceeds resulting from the sale of the bankrupt's property.

Summary of Credit and Its Uses

1. Consumer credit is comprised of debts for goods, services and money borrowed for personal and family use.
2. Two plans of payment are commonly used for consumer debts: single payments and installment payments.
3. Approximately three fourths of consumer debts are on the installment payment plan.
4. Buying on charge accounts is primarily a convenience to consumers.
5. The cost of charging purchases should always be considered.
6. One's credit standing is an indication of the trust and confidence others have in him.
7. One's line of credit is the maximum amount of debt a particular creditor will permit.
8. A debtor has an ethical and legal responsibility for debts contracted.
9. Protections to creditors for debts not paid include the legal processes of attachment, garnishment, and bankruptcy.

TEXTBOOK QUESTIONS

1. What are two definitions of credit?
2. Why is credit so important in our business activities?
3. Is there any difference between credit and debt?
4. What is a possible disadvantage of having a charge account?
5. What is an advantage of having a credit identification card?
6. What extra costs are incurred by business in making charge sales?
7. Approximately how much more does selling on charge accounts cost than selling for cash?
8. What are the "three C's" in the formula for determining credit? Explain each.
9. List some of the information that an individual is required to give when he applies for credit.
10. What is the suggested procedure for establishing a retail credit in your community?
11. How may a merchant extend credit to you to such an extent that you may damage your credit?
12. What are some of the agencies through which credit information can be obtained?
13. In most communities how is it possible for all stores to know whether you have paid your account regularly at one store?
14. Is a wife personally responsible for the debts she incurs, or is her husband responsible? Explain your answer.
15. What is meant by garnishment?
16. What is the Statute of Limitations?
17. What relief may an individual debtor obtain under the bankruptcy laws?

DISCUSSION QUESTIONS

1. Why is character more important than capital in establishing credit?
2. Why has a creditor the right to know something about the income of a person who applies for credit?
3. From the point of view of (a) the creditor and (b) the debtor, discuss some of the evils of encouraging people to use too much credit.
4. Some merchants solicit customers to buy on account. (a) Why do you think they do so? (b) How do they plan this solicitation?
5. If you move to another city, how will a good credit rating that was established in your previous place of residence help you?
6. (a) Do you think you can open a charge account in the name of your parents and use the charge account? (b) Can you use the charge account of your parents if it has been established by them?

7. What do you think might happen to you if you owe $100 on a car and move to another city without notifying the lender?
8. If a person has become a voluntary bankrupt, why do you think it is difficult for him in the future to get credit?
9. Suppose that you owe $2,000 on a home and are six months behind in your payments. You owe a total of $200 on unsecured accounts in stores, and owe an additional $100 on household equipment on which there is a settlement mortgage. Your total assets amount to $1,200, including a $1,000 interest in the home. What relief can you obtain under the laws to straighten out your affairs and start over?

PROBLEMS

1. (a) If a department store doing a business of $500,000 a year has credit losses of $500, what is the percentage of credit losses on sales? (b) If the credit losses are $1,200, what is the percentage of loss?
2. Assume that you buy an article that is billed to you for $100 with the understanding that you may have a 1 per cent discount if you pay it within 10 days or that you have 30 days in which to pay the total net amount without the discount. (a) How much do you save by taking the discount? (b) If you consider the discount offered as interest for using the money for 20 more days, what annual rate of interest are you actually paying?

COMMUNITY PROBLEMS AND PROJECTS

1. Obtain a credit application blank used by some local store or a store in a neighboring city. (a) Fill in as much of the required information as you can, and (b) write a report explaining why each item of information is needed by the store.
2. Investigate the policies of local stores in selling for cash and on credit. Learn (a) which ones have variations in price, (b) how much the difference is, and (c) what additional carrying charges are added in the case of credit sales.
3. From local merchants, a local credit bureau, or some other local agency, obtain information with regard to (a) the percentage of merchandise sold on credit in your community, (b) the average amount of credit losses, (c) the reasons for the credit losses, and (d) the local policies with regard to uniformity in granting credit.

Chapter 21

Important Principles of Installment Buying

> **Purpose of the Chapter.** Installment payment plans enable many families and individuals to buy goods and services they need and to pay for them over a period of several months while using them. The plans for installment purchasing are numerous and vary widely in conditions and provisions. The legal relationships between buyer and seller often are complicated and frequently are not fully understood. The privilege of paying for goods and repaying loans on an installment plan has many advantages to consumers; however, the practice can be highly detrimental and harmful if basic principles are not observed. These basic principles will be discussed from the standpoint of the buyer in this chapter.
>
> You will find answers to these questions:
> 1. What is the role of installment buying in our economy?
> 2. What are the essential characteristics of installment plans?
> 3. When should one buy on the installment plan?
> 4. What are finance or carrying charges, and how are they determined?
> 5. How may one determine the actual cost of buying on the installment plan?

What Is Installment Credit? Buying on an installment plan is different from buying on charge or open account in four ways: (1) a down payment is usually required, (2) a finance or carrying charge is added to the price, (3) payments usually of equal amounts are spread over a period of time, and (4) security of the amount of the unpaid balance is taken by the seller in the form of a conditional sales contract or a chattel mortgage which will be explained later. The installment contract should always be in writing. Other characteristics of installment buying will be described in more detail as you progress through this chapter.

The Importance of Installment Buying. Estimates of the government and of various associations disclose the fact that about 60 per cent of the yearly retail sales are credit transactions. About one third of these credit sales are made on the installment plan. The percentage of consumer purchases on installment for some lines of goods is greater than for other lines. For instance, in 1954 approximately 62 per cent of all automobiles and 55 per cent of all furniture and appliances were purchased on installment plan. Of 34,293 billion dollars owed by consumers in September, 1955, approximately 77 per cent was payable on installment plans.

We learned in Chapter 2 how mass production helps us get the goods and services we want at a price we can afford to pay. But, mass production is not possible except when people buy freely. The average family has only a small reserve of money and checking account balance. Thus, purchases of major items such as automobiles, furniture, and appliances are largely dependent upon time payment plans. The ability of consumers to buy now and pay later has increased mass consumption of goods and services tremendously. If charge account privileges and other time-payment plans of purchasing such as installments were to be withdrawn making purchases wholly on a cash basis, sales would decrease rapidly, and business activity would slow down. Consumer credit, mass distribution, and mass production are closely interdependent.

Some economists believe that selling goods and services to consumers on a time payment plan is one of the major factors in making our high standard of living possible. They reason that installment selling increases the consumption of goods, which in turn increases production and thus tends to lower costs and that the greater production is, the more jobs there are at good wage rates.

Characteristics of Installment Contracts. Some agreements or credit privileges extended by merchants permit an extension of credit with regular payments, but they are not regular installment contracts. For instance, some merchants will extend credit of 60, 90, or a 120 days without requiring the signing of a time-payment contract. Regular payments are required, but this type of credit is simply an extension of the regular open-account credit. It should not be confused with an installment contract.

Every installment contract sets forth the specific terms of the purchase including the amount of the down payment, dates and amounts of future payments, finance charges, and the protections to the seller in case payments are not made as scheduled. The seller may be protected by either a chattel mortgage or a conditional sales contract, each of which provides a legal claim upon the merchandise until the obligation has been paid.

A chattel mortgage is essentially the same as any other mortgage except that it applies to goods that are ordinarily movable, such as a piano or an automobile. The laws in the states are not uniform in regard to the use of a chattel mortgage. Essentially, a seller gives title of the goods to the buyer; but the chattel mortgage permits the seller to retain a claim against the goods until the debt is paid. If the buyer fails to perform his part of the contract, the seller either automatically has a right to repossess the goods or may take legal action to repossess the goods. An example of a chattel mortgage is shown on page 369.

A *conditional sales contract* is the most common type of agreement to provide security for the seller. Under this plan the title to the goods remains with the seller until payments for the goods and interest and finance charges have been made in full. The title to the property is transferred to the buyer upon the completion of all payments. In the event that the buyer does not make his payments when due, the goods may be repossessed (taken back) by the seller.

The Uniform Conditional Sales Act, which has been enacted in ten states and one territory, provides that if the buyer has paid a substantial portion of the purchase

Ch. 21] PRINCIPLES OF INSTALLMENT BUYING 369

[Chattel Mortgage form with magnifying glass overlay]

From the pamphlet *Installment Selling—Pros and Cons*, by William Trufant Foster, the Public Affairs Committee, Inc.

Read Your Installment Contract Carefully Before Signing

An installment contract is a maze of legal technicalities, usually in fine print. If you are not sure what you are signing, take it home and study it and consult someone who knows.

price at the time the goods may be repossessed, he is entitled to get back that sum less service charges, interest, and depreciation on the goods caused by wear and tear.

In most states that do not have the Uniform Conditional Sales Act, the buyer receives no portion of his payments back in case of repossession, and if the subsequent sale price of the goods repossessed is less than the amount he still owed for them, he may be called upon to pay the difference between the two amounts.

A Conditional Sales Contract

Conditional sales contracts usually are written in triplicate. One copy is kept by the purchaser; another copy is filed in some local recording office; and the third copy is kept by the seller. The purpose of recording an installment contract is to make the record public so that anyone can determine whether a claim has been made against the property.

Installment contracts differ as to their wording and content, but a similarity is found between the conditional sales contract and the chattel mortgage contract. In each case the purchaser must agree to do certain things. For example, he must agree to make the payments as specified; he may not remove the property from the state without permission; he may not sell it to someone else without permission; and he has to keep it free from taxes and liens.

Checkpoints on Installment Contracts

The following checkpoints may serve as guides for the protection of installment buyers before signing a contract:

1. What is the cash price of the article?
2. How much money is actually advanced?
3. What are the total finance or carrying charges?
4. What are the insurance, investigation, legal, recording, and other charges in addition to the purchase price and carrying charges?
5. How does the installment rate compare with rates on other plans such as a personal loan at a bank?
6. Are all the facts about the contract known and fully understood?
7. Are all figures in the contract correct? Are all blanks spaces filled in?
8. Specifically what security has been given? Does it include merchandise previously bought or to be bought in the future?
9. May wages be assigned in case of delinquent payments?
10. Do I have the privilege of paying the total amount due and settling the contract at a reduction in cost?
11. Will a fair notice be given before repossession?
12. What equity in the property do I have in case of repossession?

Who Uses the Installment Plan? A greater percentage of consumers whose family incomes are in the range from $3,000 to $8,000 have installment debts than families with incomes lower than $3,000 or incomes greater than $8,000. From the data in the table below, it is obvious that low income families are not the greatest users of installment credit.

Installment debts are especially common among the younger families with children. Within the group of younger families with children under 18, three out of every four had installment debts in 1954. Some of these debts were for personal loans; however, the majority of them were for automobiles, furniture, household appliances, and similar items.

These facts indicate not only that buying on an installment plan is a common practice but also that it is not confined to individuals and family units of small income as is sometimes assumed.

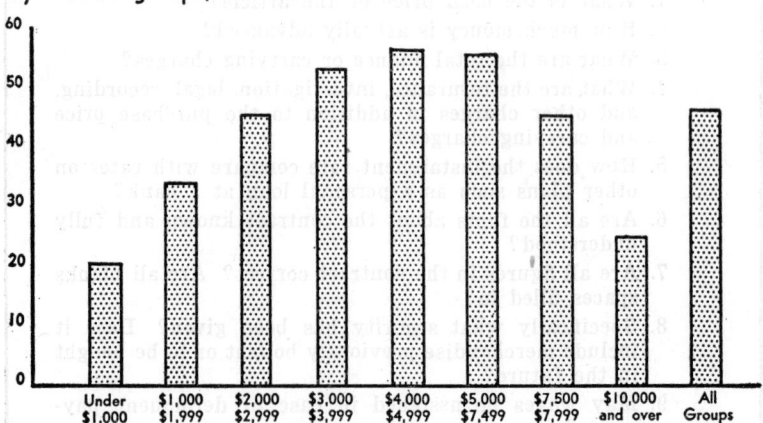

Per cent using installment credit, by income groups, in 1955

Source: Federal Reserve Board "1955 Survey of Consumer Finances"

Who Uses Installment Credit?

When to Buy on the Installment Plan. Although business activity may be stimulated by installment selling, unwise use of installment purchasing by consumers may in the long run be detrimental both to the consumer and to the business of the country as a whole.

In the 19th century and the early part of the 20th century, the philosophy of the American people was to do without the goods they wanted and probably very much needed in order to save money. When a sufficient amount of money had been saved, the purchase was made. This philosophy has changed until now the average family believes in buying goods and services when the family is young and the needs are the greatest and paying for them while they are being used and enjoyed. Installment buying is the outgrowth of this changed philosophy on the part of the American people. Like many other plans and procedures from which man benefits, installment buying must be done wisely.

Many different installment plans are in use. They differ widely in the cost of the plan to the borrower and in the terms affecting him. One should buy on installment only when he fully understands the plan offered by the seller.

Installment buying may be detrimental to the consumer if he buys luxuries or other commodities not actually needed. For example, no wise home-manager would purchase expensive clothing or elaborate jewelry on the installment plan.

On the other hand buying on an installment plan may be both economical and wise. It can be used frequently as a means of saving. It should, however, be used carefully and with common sense. For example, if one is furnishing a home, the purchase of furniture on the installment plan will be justifiable if the payments can be made without jeopardizing the budget. Using the installment plan will be better than spending all available funds to buy cheap furnishings, which would soon wear out and then have to be replaced. A railroad engineer, however, would be justified in buying a good watch on the installment plan if it were needed in his work. If a radio is needed to entertain a sick person or an automobile is required for business, installment buying is permissible and usually justified. Another example of using the installment buying privilege wisely is a young doctor starting his profession who may finance the purchase of equipment through the installment plan.

Two important personal factors to consider when entering into agreement to purchase an item on an installment plan are a person's age and his probable earning power in the years immediately ahead. As people approach retirement age their income sometimes decreases and frequently their health and strength decline making work difficult and in some cases impossible. Both health and probable earning power are affected by age.

Oftentimes the income of a family unit is committed in advance to such an extent that additional periodic payments on installment purchases are neither feasible or wise. For example, let us assume that the income of a family per month is $500, and that the family expense is $350 a month not including housing. Further, assume payments on a mortgage, taxes, and insurance on the house in which the family lives are $65 a month; on an automobile, $50 a month; and on a refrigerator, $25 a month making a total of $490 of each month's income that is committed. Under these conditions to purchase a television receiver on install-

---

Policies to Consider in Making an Installment Purchase

1. Make a substantial down payment.
2. Pay the balance as quickly as possible.
3. Buy only durable goods that will be of value long after the final payment.
4. Don't use the full extent of your installment credit.
5. Budget your income and your expenditures to be sure that you can pay all obligations.
6. Leave a safety margin for unforeseen expenses and possible reductions in income.
7. Consider before you buy whether it is more profitable and more desirable to save your money and wait until you can pay cash.
8. Check other ways to get what you want that may be cheaper.

ment with monthly payments would be very unwise. The seller and the buyer of merchandise should consider together the advisability of the buyer contracting an installment debt.

Before You Buy. Before one buys an article on the installment plan and accepts the financing plan suggested by the seller, it is well to consider the following other alternatives: (a) buying from another seller who offers better terms; (b) paying cash from accumulated savings or waiting until one has saved enough money; (c) borrowing from a bank, a credit union, or another lending agency and paying cash; (d) borrowing on a life insurance policy and paying cash.

Advantages of Installment Buying. The following are some of the recognized advantages of installment buying:
  (a) Necessities may be enjoyed before the full price is available for payment.
  (b) Better and more substantial merchandise can sometimes be obtained by utilizing the installment plan instead of paying cash for cheap merchandise.
  (c) Without the aid of installment buying, many young married people would be unable to furnish a home and start housekeeping.

Disadvantages of Installment Buying. The disadvantages of installment buying arise, not necessarily out of the faults of the system, but often out of its abuses. The following are some of the disadvantages of installment buying:
  (a) Some people buy assets because of false pride. They are encouraged to buy more expensive assets than they can afford.
  (b) When the number of dealers allowing installment purchases is limited, the person who wishes to make an installment purchase may have to accept an inferior product because the grade of goods he wants is not sold where he can make purchases on the installment plan.
  (c) The person who buys on the installment plan usually pays interest at a rate of from 6 per cent to 25 per

cent on the unpaid balance. He therefore pays more than he would have paid if he had purchased the merchandise for cash. If one uses installment buying extensively, he will cut down his total purchasing power substantially.

(d) Some people may overbuy.

(e) "Credit competition" sometimes leads businesses to put customers under pressure in the hope of selling merchandise on "easy terms."

(f) Some merchants and dealers encourage buyers to use the installment plan because the finance charge may produce additional income.

(g) Some users of the installment plan lower their standards of food, clothing, education, and environment in order to meet obligations on installment purchases.

(h) One of the greatest disadvantages is in committing oneself to future obligations. By promising to pay future income, one limits his freedom of action and cuts down his margin of safety in financial emergencies.

It is evident that installment purchases should be made only on the basis of necessity and convenience after a careful study of needs and ability to pay. In general, installment buying is recommended only for accumulating worth-while assets.

Terms of Payment. The percentage of down payment and the amount of time in which the debtor may pay vary according to the product, the amount of the down payment, and the policy of the finance company. The table on page 377 provides a summary of the usual percentages of down payment and the usual maximum periods for making payment for particular types of merchandise.

Finance Charges for Installment Service. When goods are sold on an installment plan, the seller incurs costs that would not arise with cash or charge sales. The expenses of investigation of the credit standing of the purchaser, making the loan, collecting, bookkeeping, insurance, repossessing in case of delinquent payments, reselling, bad debts, and general office expenses must be covered either by increasing

Principles of Installment Buying

PRODUCT	USUAL PERCENTAGE OF DOWN PAYMENT	USUAL TIME ALLOWED TO PAY (MONTHS)
New automobiles	25 -33⅓	18-30
Used automobiles	33⅓-40	15-21
Used automobiles (not late models)	35 -60	8-15
House trailers	25 -33⅓	24-60
Furniture	10 -25	12-24
Refrigerators	5 -10	18-36
Television receivers	25 -33⅓	12-15
Jewelry	10 -25	6-18
Men's clothing	10 -25	3- 9

Usual Down Payments and Time Allowed on Installment Sales

the sales price or by separate charges. The difference between the cash price of a commodity and the sum of the down payment on it plus all future installment payments is known as the *time balance* in which the finance charge or carrying charge is generally included. In some instances the charges are listed separately such as "charge for investigation," "insurance," and "service charge." The total *finance charge* is the cost for installment credit paid by the buyer. A finance charge is often confused with interest, but it is legally very different. Although it includes use of the money loaned to the consumer, it also includes other costs such as those already mentioned. Interest is regulated by state law; and in some states maximum finance charges are also regulated; but in many states finance or carrying charges are not regulated. The charges vary not only for different kinds of goods but also among the firms that sell on an installment plan.

Although a nominal rate of 5 to 8 per cent may be quoted for all charges on an installment plan, it must be borne in mind that this rate is not comparable to straight interest rates as we ordinarily think of them. The finance charge must include all costs. Finance charges are determined in much the same way that a merchant determines the markup on the goods he purchases for resale. He considers the money invested in the goods, the cost of advertising, and selling expenses incurred in operating his business and competition with other merchants. Then he determines his markup. The same factors plus a few additional ones are considered in determining the finance charge on installments.

In some cases the finance or carrying charges may seem to be exorbitant; and yet in most cases they are reasonable when the extra costs incident to making and collecting installment loans are considered. When dealing with a reputable business firm, finance company, or bank, it is not so much a question of whether the cost of buying on an installment plan is fair or unfair; it is a question of whether the merchandise is needed sufficiently to justify paying the amount of the finance or carrying charges.

Bad Debts and Credit Losses

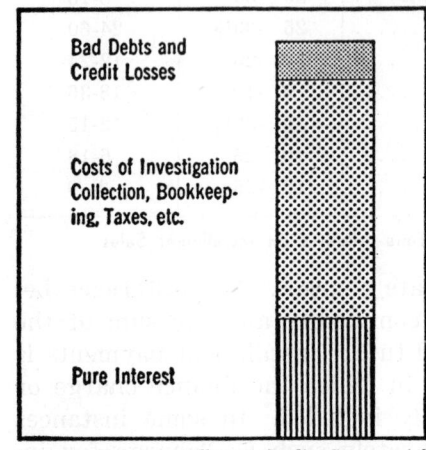

Costs of Investigation Collection, Bookkeeping, Taxes, etc.

Pure Interest

Source: *Using Installment Credit*, Commercial Credit Company.

The financing charge is not all interest; it must cover other costs which are far more important than the interest cost.

What Costs Are Included in the Financing Charge?

The following table shows typical finance charges for purchasing new automobiles on the installment plan.

AMOUNT FINANCED *	LENGTH OF CONTRACT	TOTAL FINANCE CHARGES	TOTAL AMOUNT OF LOAN	MONTHLY PAYMENT
$ 500	12 months	$33.64	$ 533.64	$ 44.47
800	12 months	53.80	853.80	71.15
1,000	12 months	67.28	1,067.28	88.94
1,200	12 months	80.64	1,280.64	106.72

* Amount the borrower gets

Computing Finance Charges. Although there are many ways to arrive at finance charges on installment transactions, they are commonly computed on either the discount basis or on the per cent-per-month basis. On the *discount basis*, a flat percentage or sometimes a flat sum is charged for making the loan. Usually the amount of the charge is proportionately higher for small than for large loans. (The percentage is not an interest rate, but a rate that includes all costs.) The discount basis is used for most installment sales and for a large share of installment loans.

The tables following show the typical finance charges on a discount basis on installment contracts for new automobiles and household appliances. In the case of automobiles the finance charge may include premiums on life insurance on the buyer of the car. Insurance on the car itself is always included in the over-all cost of a car purchased on time.

Carrying Charges on New Automobiles, Including Life Insurance on the Buyer

UNPAID BALANCE DUE	12 MONTHS	15 MONTHS	18 MONTHS	24 MONTHS
		CARRYING CHARGES		
$ 200	$13.96	$ 14.50	$ 17.26	$ 22.72
300	17.16	21.30	25.26	33.36
400	22.64	27.95	33.44	44.24
500	28.00	34.75	41.44	54.88
600	33.36	41.40	49.44	65.76
700	38.72	48.20	57.62	76.40
800	44.08	54.85	65.62	87.26
900	49.44	61.50	73.62	97.92
1000	54.80	68.30	81.80	108.80
1500	81.72	101.85	122.16	162.48

Carrying Charges on Household Appliances

100	10.76	15.05	xx	xx
150	14.52	18.15	21.72	29.04
200	17.68	24.25	28.96	36.40
250	22.76	28.55	34.22	45.68
300	29.23	32.10	38.58	51.36

NOTE: The carrying charge is added to the unpaid balance due to determine the total amount to be paid.

Carrying Charges Added to the Unpaid Balance

An example will show how the discount basis of financing is applied to an automobile installment sale transaction:

Unpaid balance on car	$300.00
Number of monthly payments	15
Finance charges, including premium for life insurance on buyer for $300 for 15 months (flat sum)	21.30
Total amount of note signed by buyer	321.30
Monthly payment (321.30 ÷ 15 months)	21.42

It will be noted that the amount of the note signed by the buyer is the sum of the amount needed to pay for the car plus finance charges.

The *per cent-per-month plan*, frequently used by small-loan companies and credit unions is illustrated by the following transaction:

Purchase price of furniture	$600.00
Down payment	200.00
Unpaid balance	$400.00
Finance charge	20.00
Amount advanced (total loan)	$420.00

Interest is to be charged at the rate of 6 per cent per year or one-half per cent per month on the unpaid balance at the beginning of the month. There are to be eight monthly payments of $52.50 plus interest. The schedule of payments on principal, charges, and interest is given below:

MONTHLY INSTALLMENT	PAYMENTS				OUTSTANDING	
	PRINCIPAL	CHARGES	INTEREST	TOTAL	ON NOTE	ON ADVANCE
1	$50.00	$2.50	$2.10	$54.60	$420.00	$400.00
2	50.00	2.50	1.84	54.34	367.50	350.00
3	50.00	2.50	1.57	54.07	315.00	300.00
4	50.00	2.50	1.31	53.81	267.50	250.00
5	50.00	2.50	1.05	53.55	210.00	200.00
6	50.00	2.50	.79	53.29	157.50	150.00
7	50.00	2.50	.53	53.03	105.00	100.00
8	50.00	2.50	.26	52.76	52.50	50.00
Total	$400.00	$20.00	$9.45	$429.45		

In the foregoing illustration, the finance charges were equally distributed among the eight months and the monthly interest charges were based upon the unpaid balance. In many instances the finance charges are also based on the unpaid balance and at the same percentage rate each month.

Figuring the Cost of an Installment Purchase. There are numerous installment plans. Some of these reveal the true cost by making a charge, in the form of interest, on the unpaid balance. In such a case the actual cost of the merchandise to the purchaser is easy to figure. On the other hand, some plans involve discounts, fees, and carrying charges which may conceal the real interest rate.

There are many ways of stating the installment costs, some of which are confusing. Therefore, in order to shop wisely for the best installment plan one must be able to compare costs. The precise calculation of installment rates involves mathematical procedures that are too complex for most people to use. However, a simple process by which a close approximation of the true interest rate will give a reliable basis for comparison of costs.

The cost of financing installment purchases may be shown in the following illustration. Let us assume an item selling for $100 is sold on the basis of 25 per cent down, the balance to be paid in eight monthly payments and that the finance charge is quoted as 6 per cent of the balance or $4.50. How much does the buyer actually borrow in this case and what interest rate on an annual basis does he pay?

Each monthly payment will reduce the principal by $9.375 ($75 ÷ 8 months). Thus, the buyer had the use of:

        $75.00 for the first month
        $65.625 for the second month
        $56.250 for the third month
        $46.875 for the fourth month
        $37.500 for the fifth month
        $28.125 for the sixth month
        $18.750 for the seventh month
        $ 9.375 for the eighth month

Or, the buyer had the use of $337.50 for one month which is the equivalent of $28.125 for a year ($337.50 ÷ 12 months).* The total finance charge was $4.50; therefore, the rate of interest actually paid by the buyer was

$$\frac{\$4.50}{\$28.125} \times 100 = 16.00 \text{ per cent per year}$$

instead of the nominal rate of 6 per cent.

The same result may also be obtained by the use of the constant-ratio formula (for the person who wishes to use an algebraic formula):

$$r = \frac{2 \times m \times i}{P(n+1)}$$

In which r equals the annual rate charged; m, the number of payments in a year, 12 if payments are made monthly and 52 if made weekly; i, the total finance charge; P, the net amount to be paid; and n, the number of installments.

---

* The average amount that the buyer had to use for one year was $28.125.

Applying the formula to the installment transaction illustrated below:

$$r = \frac{2 \times 12 \times 4.50}{75 \times (8+1)} = \frac{108}{675} = 16.00 \text{ per cent}$$

Bear in mind, however, that regardless of how the terms of an installment sale plan are stated, comparisons of the actual cost of financing can be made by calculating the interest rate. In order to make this calculation, the finance charges and the sale price of the article, not including finance charges, must be known.

In some instances, goods such as jewelry and clothing are offered for sale on monthly payments with "no charge for credit." However, a purchaser who offers cash usually will be able to buy the article for less than the stated price. The difference between the cash price he would pay and the stated price on installment with "no charge for credit" is the finance charge. Thus, the rate for financing can be calculated the same as for other installment plans.

When making comparisons of costs of financing contemplated installment purchases, it will be well for the buyer to remember that legitimate lenders of small sums find it necessary to charge from 10 to 36 per cent per year to cover their actual costs of operation and to give them a fair profit. This change is necessary because of the charges besides interest that are included in the total charge that is added to the selling price.

Warnings on Installment Buying

1. Do not allow yourself to be rushed into signing a contract until you know all the facts.
2. Refuse to sign any contract if you are not given an exact duplicate copy.
3. Do not sign any contract before all the blank spaces are filled in.
4. Do not pledge any security besides the article being purchased.

Ch. 21] Principles of Installment Buying 383

New Automobile Sales to Good Credit Risks	New Appliance Sales to Good Credit Risks	Old-model Used Car Sales to Poor Credit Risks
Low rates because: (1) amount of transaction is very large; (2) risk is very small	Higher rates because amount of transaction is small	Still higher rates because: (1) amount of transaction is small; (2) risk is high

Source: *Using Installment Credit*, Commercial Credit Company.

Interest Rates Also Depend on Risks

Finance Companies. Most stores and business firms do not have sufficient capital to finance their business if they sell on an installment plan. They need their capital to reinvest in replacement merchandise so they can have a rapid turnover. Therefore, these business firms use the services of a finance company. A finance company that deals only in installment notes arising from sales by business firms is sometimes known as a *sales finance company*. In effect, the sales finance company purchases the installment notes at a discount from the business firm at the time of the sale, thus immediately replenishing the merchant's cash. In some instances the customer's payments are made to the merchant but more often directly to the finance company.

Finance companies that make loans directly to consumers not arising from a sale of merchandise by a business firm are sometimes referred to as *consumer finance companies*. Of course, some finance companies serve customers directly and also purchase installment notes from business firms. There are approximately 8,000 finance companies in the United States who deal in installment credit. Each of the large automobile manufacturers has either an affiliated finance company or an agreement with one to handle the installment notes on cars sold by their dealers. Some finance companies confine their transactions to the purchase of one kind of installment notes such as notes arising from the sale of automobiles. Others make installment loans which may be used to purchase various kinds of durable goods, to pay existing debts, to meet emergency expenses, or for home modernization.

Well-established business firms frequently discount (or sell) installment notes arising from the sale of merchandise to their customers directly at commercial banks. In the following chapter, there will be a discussion of the roles in installment financing by banks, credit unions, finance companies, and other lending agencies.

Replevin or Repossession. When an article is sold under an installment contract and the buyer later fails to live up to his part of the contract, the seller, in order to protect himself from loss, sometimes has the right to repossess the article. The legal action necessary is usually referred to as *repossession* or *replevin*. The law of replevin differs widely in various states. In some states the law permits the seller to repossess the property, and, regardless of the amount that has been paid, he need not compensate the buyer for anything that the latter has already paid. Under the laws of many states, however, the person who repossesses an article must, according to a definite plan prescribed in the law, compensate the buyer for any interest that the latter may have had in the article.

If a Buyer on the Installment Plan Fails to Live up to the Agreement, He May Lose the Goods

Important Principles of Installment Buying

1. Installment buying stimulates mass production and thus is an important factor in our economy.
2. Installment buying really means one is borrowing money.
3. A chattel mortgage or a conditional sales contract commonly provides security for the seller.
4. Installment selling involves many extra costs that must be borne by the buyer.
5. The finance or carrying charge is the difference between the cash price and the total cost paid under installment.
6. Finance charges vary widely both in amount and in method of determining them.
7. Installment terms sometimes obscure features of great importance to the buyer.
8. The true interest rate to determine actual cost of the installment privilege can be calculated for any plan. One should shop for the most advantageous plan.
9. Buying on installment invariably costs much more than buying on charge account or for cash.
10. An installment buyer should fully understand the provisions of the contract before buying.

TEXTBOOK QUESTIONS

1. What is meant by installment credit?
2. How does installment credit affect purchasing power and buying?
3. Two general types of contracts are used in selling merchandise on the installment plan. (a) What are they? (b) When does the title pass in each case?
4. How is the seller protected under each type of installment contract?
5. What types of products are most commonly sold on the installment plan?
6. In the case of a conditional sales contract or a chattel mortgage contract, what does the purchaser usually agree to do?
7. Give at least three things you should check when entering into an installment contract.
8. Why would you not recommend buying expensive luxuries on the installment plan?
9. How could the use of the installment plan result in a saving in buying furniture?
10. Before you buy on the installment plan, what are some other alternatives to consider?

11. What are some of the advantages of installment buying?
12. What are some of the disadvantages of installment buying?
13. When a new automobile is purchased on the installment plan, what is usually (a) the down payment required? (b) the time allowed for payment?
14. What is a typical carrying charge added to the price of a household appliance for a contract covering twenty-four monthly installments when the unpaid balance due is $200?
15. What costs other than interest costs are included in finance charges?
16. What are the two commonly used methods of computing finance charges?
17. What is the major difference between a sales finance company and a consumer finance company?
18. Explain briefly the regulations in regard to replevin or repossession.
19. Mention at least two warnings in regard to installment buying.

DISCUSSION QUESTIONS

1. How should installment buying be correlated with budgeting?
2. What would happen to the sales of cars if down payments were increased to 50 per cent of the sales price of the car? What would happen if down payments were lowered to one per cent?
3. Do you see any dangers of installment buying in times of prosperity or in times of depression?
4. Does the buyer assume any obligations when he signs an installment contract?
5. What do you think might be the privilege of a seller if the buyer of an automobile under a conditional sales contract moves to another state and takes the car with him without notifying the holder of the conditional sales contract?
6. Why do you think it might be advisable for a certain family to borrow money in order to buy a washing machine instead of buying it on an installment plan?
7. What do you think of the advisability of buying jewelry on the installment plan?
8. Can you see any possibility of economic evils in installment buying?
9. Some people are induced to buy refrigerators because of the slogan "25 cents a day will buy this refrigerator." What do you think of such a plan of buying?
10. A business advertises that it sells on the installment plan at no extra charge. (a) Is this practice fair to all customers of the business? (b) What should a cash customer expect?

Ch. 21]   Principles of Installment Buying   387

11. If the law in your state or the contract that you sign requires the seller to compensate you for the financial interest that you have in an article when it is repossessed by the seller, how much would you expect to get back if you had paid $100 on a refrigerator and had used it two years?
12. Why would you not sign an installment contract if the price and the information in regard to the finance charge and monthly payments are to be filled in later with the understanding that a copy of the contract will be mailed to you?

PROBLEMS

1. From the tables on pages 377 and 379, showing the terms of payment and the carrying charges for new automobiles, compute (a) the maximum usual down payment in terms of dollars and (b) the amount added to the original unpaid balance for a carrying charge if payments are to extend over eighteen months. Assume that the delivered price of the car is $2,250.
2. On the basis of the example given on page 381, compute the annual interest rate on the purchase of a refrigerator that is sold for $165 with a down payment of $15 and installment payments of $10 a month for fifteen months, "no charge being made for the easy terms." Assume that a person paying cash could obtain the refrigerator for $150. (Remember that, regardless of the number of months involved, the average for one year is determined on the basis of twelve months.)

COMMUNITY PROBLEMS AND PROJECTS

1. Obtain the following information with regard to the purchase of an automobile: (a) the price f.o.b. the factory, (b) the delivered price, (c) the particular items and the amounts of the items that add to the cost in delivering the automobile, (d) the guarantee, (e) the service agreement, (f) the type of bill of sale used, (g) the carrying charge on the unpaid balance, and (h) the plan of paying the balance. Write a report summarizing the information that you have obtained.
2. Obtain a copy of either a chattel mortgage or a conditional sales contract (whichever is most commonly used and is legally permitted in your state) and analyze this contract by submitting your answers to the following questions: (a) When does the title pass? (b) How may the title be transferred? (c) What happens if there is a default of any payment? (d) Are there any warranties? (e) What other rights, privileges, or limitations of use are extended to the buyer?

Chapter 22

How to Obtain a Small Loan

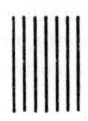

> **Purpose of the Chapter.** The consumer often finds it necessary to borrow money in small amounts. There are several sources from which such loans may be obtained. The conditions under which the loans are made and the terms of the loans vary widely. Borrowing money wisely means that one must know the advantages and disadvantages of each of the sources of loans as a basis for deciding where to borrow. Problems relative to borrowing are discussed in this chapter.
>
> You will find answers to these questions:
> 1. What principles may guide one in borrowing?
> 2. How are small loans classified?
> 3. What should a consumer know about borrowing from each of the major sources of small loans?

Need for Small Loans. Both individuals and families occasionally need to borrow money for periods of time ranging from a few days up to five years. Loans to meet personal and family needs are relatively small in amount, the average being about $200. They are known as *short-term* and *intermediate-term loans* whereas loans for the purchase of real estate are usually classified as *long-term loans*. Money may be needed for emergencies such as unexpected medical and hospital bills. In many instances, small loans enable families to buy necessary household equipment, to make permanent additions and improvements to the home, and to do other things that cannot wait until the money could be saved. Borrowing money to go to school in many instances falls in the small loan class.

Before borrowing one should always consider how great his need really is for the goods or service he intends to buy with the money. Under some circumstances one may be exercising very good judgment to borrow money, and under other conditions it may be very unwise to borrow. The advantages and disadvantages of borrowing for a specific purpose should be carefully determined and analyzed as a basis for making one's decision.

Once it has been decided that a small loan is needed, you should shop for a loan with the same care that you would use in shopping for furniture or appliances for the home. The primary factors to be considered in shopping for a loan are the reliability of the lender, the real cost of the loan to the borrower, and the special terms or conditions of the loan that affect the borrower, such as the provisions for security of the loan, payments, and claims that may arise against wages or other property in case of inability to make payments when they fall due.

In order for you to be able to borrow money, you must establish a good credit rating in ordinary buying. If you have a good credit reputation, you can borrow the money you need when you need it. Small loans may be obtained from a variety of sources such as banks, under some circumstances from savings and loan associations, insurance companies, credit unions, consumer finance companies, pawnbrokers, and others. The range of costs for a loan is exceedingly great, and the conditions or terms of loans vary widely.

Types of Loans. There are two types of loans as to the methods of repayment. One type of loan permits you to repay in a lump sum. The other type of loan permits you to repay in regular installments.

There are also two types of loans as to security. One type is an *unsecured loan*. In other words, you merely sign a contract, binding yourself to the terms of the contract. Your character and honor are sufficient to enable you to obtain the loan. If you fail to abide by the contract, you can be sued, of course, for the amount due. The other type is a secured loan. A *secured loan* means that you have to pledge or turn over to the lender some kind of property called collateral. The lender has a claim against this property until you repay the loan. If you fail to repay the loan, he can keep the property or sell it to satisfy his claim against you.

Another type of protection that a lender sometimes requires is the signature of an additional person who becomes jointly responsible with you and promises to pay if you fail to do so. As we learned in Chapter 19, this person is called a cosigner or a comaker. The illustration below shows a loan agreement signed by comakers.

Providing Security. Bonds and stocks are used frequently as collateral security for loans. The security may also consist of such items as furniture or livestock. Loans of this type can usually be obtained from banks. When security loans of this type are obtained, bonds or stocks are usually turned over to the bank or other lending agency to be kept until the loan is repaid. A bank will ordinarily lend about 50 per cent of the value of stocks or bonds that are traded on recognized exchanges.

A Personal Loan Agreement

An agreement is usually signed, giving the lender authority to keep the security (the pledged property) so that it becomes his property if the loan is not repaid. When money is borrowed from a bank or other agency for the purchase of some specific item, such as an automobile or household equipment, a chattel mortgage is usually given. This provides written evidence of the security. The lender can make you turn over to him the property if you fail to repay the loan. Chattel mortgages were discussed in Chapter 21.

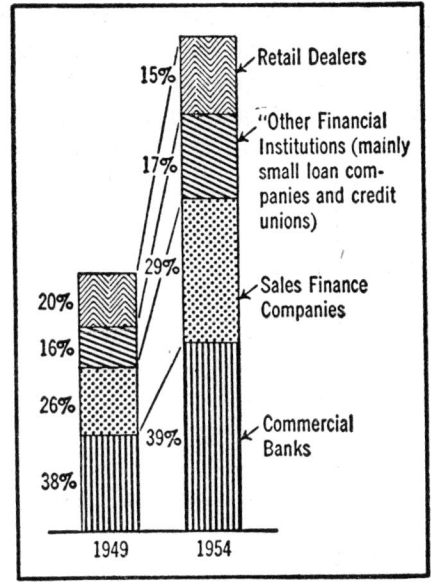

Source: *Using Installment Credit*, Commercial Credit Company.

More Than Two-Thirds of All Consumer Installment Debt Is Owed to Commercial Banks and Sales Finance Companies

A common practice of banks and loan companies is to deduct interest on a loan in advance on a discount basis as was explained in Chapter 21. Consumer finance companies and credit unions generally compute interest as a per cent-per-month on the unpaid balance.

Interest Rates. Interest rates vary according to the states and the types of lending institutions. Statutes in most states govern the interest rates of such institutions as pawnshops and loan associations. The state banking laws and the rules of the Federal Reserve System govern largely the interest rates of banks, although the demand for and the supply of money have important influences on interest rates on bank loans.

In nearly all of the states, there are two interest rates recognized by law. One is known as the *legal rate*, which is applicable if no rate is specified in a contract. For example, let us assume that a man purchased a plot of land for $1,200 on which he was to pay $200 down and $1,000 in six months with no interest. If he did not pay the $1,000 until nine months after the purchase was made, he could be charged interest for the three months the $1,000 was past due at the legal rate by law in his state.

When Borrowing Money, One Signs a Note

The other interest rate is known as the *maximum interest rate*, sometimes referred to as the *contract rate*. It is the maximum rate that it would be possible to charge by law for the use of money. For example, assume that A needs money desperately and that he would be willing to pay B $125 in 30 days if B would loan him $100 today. This would be $25 interest for one month or on an annual basis would be $300 or 300 per cent interest. In most states having a maximum or contract interest rate such an agreement would not be legal.

A typical legal rate is 6 per cent per year and a typical maximum or contract rate is 8 per cent. In some states, however, the range may be from 6 per cent to 30 per cent.

Sources of Loans. Consumers may borrow money from several sources. The distinguishing features of personal loans from each of the various sources should be known when one seeks a loan. Particularly you will want to know the practice of each of the possible sources from which you may borrow regarding the actual interest charge, the kind of security required, and the amount that may be obtained. The table on page 393 gives a brief statement of the outstanding characteristics of personal loans from various

CHARACTERISTICS OF PERSONAL LOANS COMPARED BY SOURCES

SOURCE OF LOAN	TRUE ANNUAL INTEREST RATE FOR $100 LOAN REPAYABLE IN ONE YEAR	SECURITY REQUIRED	RANGE OF AMOUNT OF LOANS
Commercial Banks, Personal Loan Departments	6-24%; 12%, common	Cosigner; chattel mortgage on acceptable property	$50-$3,500
Industrial Banks and Loan Companies, Personal Loan Departments	6-24%; 16%, common	Cosigner; chattel mortgage on acceptable property	$50-$5,000
Savings Banks and Savings and Loan Associations	5-12%; 6%, common	Usually first-mortgages only; in a few states secured by personal property (under strict regulations)	Value of shares owned or savings account balance; or limited to small secured loan
Life Insurance Companies	4-6%	Loan value of policy	95-100% of cash value of policy
Consumer Finance Companies	16-42%; usually 2½ to 3% a month on unpaid balance	Cosigner; chattel mortgage; occasionally on signature only	$25-$300; $500 in some states; higher in a few
Credit Unions	6-12%; 1% a month on unpaid balance, common	Depends upon credit committee action	$1 up, depending upon rules of credit union; $400 maximum for federally chartered unless secured
Pawnbrokers	24-120%; 36%, common	Pledged or pawned personal property at arbitrary per cent of current value	$1-$500; depends upon state laws
Unlicensed Lenders	50-1,500%; 250 to 300%, common	No pattern; varies	$5-$1,000; some higher

common sources. This table will serve as a guide to your study of the major kinds and sources of loans that are explained in the remainder of the chapter.

Borrowing from Banks. Approximately 40 per cent of the total indebtedness of consumers (not including mortgages on their homes) is owed to commercial banks and industrial banks and loan companies. Commercial banks commonly operate personal or small loan departments. They make both installment loans and single-payment loans. Borrowing on an installment loan plan from banks to purchase automobiles and appliances and to meet emergencies was explained in Chapter 21.

Industrial banks and loan companies operating in more than half the states were originally organized primarily to make loans to industrial workers. In some states, they may not use the word bank in their title and are, therefore, known as industrial loan companies. The *Morris Plan* bank or company is a typical example of an industrial bank or loan company.

The functions of industrial banks and loan companies are in many respects similar to those of commercial banks except that some cannot receive funds for deposit and do not provide checking account services. The personal or small loan departments of commercial banks and of industrial banks and loan companies serve consumers in practically the same way. Both are regulated by the laws of the states in which they operate.

Commercial and industrial banks handle personal loans on stated discount rates ranging from 3.3 to 12 per cent. Since the installment method of payment of personal loans makes the annual true rate of interest roughly double the stated discount rate, the true cost of interest on commercial and industrial bank loans is approximately 6 to 24 per cent.

There are several ways of figuring the actual yearly interest rate on loans of this type, but the simple formula explained in Chapter 21 for figuring the interest rates on installment contracts can also be used in figuring the approximate interest rates on bank loans in cases when the interest is not charged on the unpaid balance at the time of each monthly payment. The maximum amount that may be borrowed on small bank loans varies by states with the limits somewhat higher in some states for industrial banks than for commercial banks.

Commercial banks are able to make personal loans at lower costs to borrowers than are most other lenders because the funds they loan are obtained from deposits of customers on which relatively low rates of interest are paid.

Borrowing from Savings Banks and Savings and Loan Associations. In most states, savings banks and savings and loan associations make loans only on homes. Their purpose is to promote savings thus encouraging home ownership. Most of them make only first mortgage loans; however, in a few states savings banks and savings and loan associations are permitted to make personal loans under very strict regulations. The interest charges on personal loans when made ranges from 5 to 12 per cent.

Borrowing on Life Insurance Policies. Life insurance policies, except term insurance, accumulate a cash value as premiums are paid year after year. A policyholder may borrow from his insurance company up to the loan value of his policy. A table of loan values at the end of each year is shown in most policies. Most policies are so written that a loan up to the cash value of the policy must be granted if application is made for it. In some states insurance companies may require a 90-day to 180-day advance notice before making a loan on a policy.

The rate of interest you will pay on an insurance loan will be from 4 to 6 per cent. There is no credit investigation; therefore, no fee. The insurance company has no control over the use to which you put the money. The loan may be for a short or long period; and you do not need to repay it at all if you do not choose to do so. If interest is not paid, it will be added to the amount of the loan. In case of death before the loan is repaid, the amount of the loan plus accumulated interest will be deducted from the death benefits of the policy.

When one borrows on life insurance the insurance protection is reduced by the amount of the loan because the loan is deducted before the amount of the insurance is paid. Since it is relatively easy to borrow on life insurance and the insurance companies usually do not try to seek repayment of the loan, one may be slow to make repayments and, therefore, not have adequate insurance when needed.

Borrowing from Consumer Finance Companies. Small loan companies, now commonly known as consumer finance companies, have been established in many states primarily to make loans to wage earners and others of moderate means who have not established a credit rating and who may not have security to be used as collateral for bank loans. They rank next to commercial banks in the total amount of loans made to consumers annually. It is estimated that one out of every seven families borrows from consumer finance companies every year. These companies are legitimate institutions and fill an important place in our economic system. The licensed consumer finance company should not be confused with loan sharks.

Some 37 or 38 states have enacted laws governing small-loan companies that have been modeled to some extent after the Uniform Small-Loan Law. This law was an outgrowth of an investigation in 1910 by the Russell Sage Foundation, in which it was found that many people not having established credit ratings were being driven to loan sharks to borrow money at exorbitant rates of interest and under undesirable terms. In 1948 the Uniform Small-Loan Law was supplemented by the Model Consumer Finance Act. By 1955, effective versions of the Uniform Small-Loan Law and Model Consumer Finance Act had been enacted in 37 states and Hawaii; inoperative or ineffective laws had been enacted in seven states and the District of Columbia; and no law had been passed in four states. The states having ineffective and inoperative laws are Alabama, Delaware, District of Columbia, Georgia, Mississippi, North Carolina, Tennessee, and Texas. The states having no small-loan laws are Arkansas, Montana, North Dakota, and South Carolina. These laws may be changed at any time. You should inform yourself as to your local law.

In general the state laws modeled after the Uniform Small-Loan Law and the Model Consumer Finance Act provide that: (a) The lender must be licensed by the state; (b) State supervision of small-loan companies is required; (c) Maximum monthly rates of charge and maximum amount of loans are prescribed; (d) Amount of the loan, security, payment schedule, and monthly rate of charge must be disclosed in the loan agreement, a copy of which is given to the borrower; (e) Prepayment privileges on a pro rata time basis must be granted; (f) Lenders are prohibited from obtaining judgment against a borrower before notifying the borrower; and (g) Concealed and unauthorized charges, and false and misleading advertising are prohibited. Consumer finance companies now operating in states having effective regulations are licensed by the state. A prospective borrower should ascertain that the finance company with which he is dealing has and displays such a license. In most states without effective small-loan laws, state licenses to lend money are not generally required. No borrower should deal with any consumer finance company that is not licensed by the state and is not under state supervision. If there is any question about a consumer finance company, information can be obtained from such organizations as the better business bureau, the chamber of commerce, and the local welfare organization.

Consumer finance companies usually quote interest rates on a monthly basis on unpaid balances. The small-loan laws in most states require that the stated rate must be calculated on the decreasing periodic balance rather than on the entire original amount of the loan. Banks and installment sellers are not subject to this regulation. A typical rate of charge for consumer finance companies is $2\frac{1}{2}$ or 3 per cent a month on unpaid balances up to $100, and 2 or $2\frac{1}{2}$ per cent on balances from $100 to $300. This means that the true annual rates range from 16 to 42 per cent. One should consult the regulations in the small-loan law

MONTH	AMOUNT PAID ON LOAN	MONTHLY INTEREST CHARGES	TOTAL PAYMENT
1	$ 8.33	$ 3.00	$ 11.33
2	8.33	2.75	11.08
3	8.33	2.50	10.84
4	8.34	2.25	10.58
5	8.33	2.00	10.33
6	8.33	1.75	10.09
7	8.34	1.50	9.83
8	8.33	1.25	9.58
9	8.34	1.00	9.34
10	8.33	.75	9.08
11	8.33	.50	8.83
12	8.34	.25	8.59
Totals	$100.00	$19.50	$119.50

Repaying a Small Loan

in his state before borrowing to learn what the maximum rate of charge and amount of the loan may be.

The table above illustrates how a loan of $100 at the rate of 3 per cent a month is repaid in one year on the level principal payment plan. Some loan companies permit and even suggest level total payments (interest and principal combined).

Many borrowers wonder why obtaining small loans costs more than the flat 6 per cent or less that is charged on larger loans. Let us take the case of a loan of $50 to a stranger who applies to the lending agency for the first time. Let us also assume that the interest on a loan of this size, to be paid in ten monthly installments, would be $2.75. The agency lending the money has to investigate the applicant, close the loan, keep bookkeeping records, collect the money, allow for a certain percentage of loss on bad loans, and earn something on the investment. When one takes this into consideration, it can be seen why rates are higher on small loans than on large loans. With the same amount of effort, the lending agency could handle a $5,000 loan. Legitimate consumer finance companies have found it impossible to operate in states having laws that make them subject to the (maximum) contract interest rates in those states.

About 70 per cent of the loans made by consumer finance companies are secured by a chattel mortgage on household furniture or some other item of property; and the remainder are made on the borrower's signature only. The loans usually run 10 to 20 months. Consumer finance companies frequently will make a smaller loan than a bank, and they are not as selective as banks.

Borrowing from Credit Unions. A credit union is a cooperative organization of people who agree to accumulate and pool their savings and to make loans to each other at low interest from the accumulated fund. Its members are comprised of people who work for the same employer; who are members of the same church, labor union, or fraternal order; or who live in the same community. There are now more than 16,000 credit unions and 8 million members in the United States. They are chartered either under Federal or state laws. The Federal Credit Union Act of 1934 is administered by the United States Department of Health, Welfare, and Education.

Membership is required for one to become eligible to borrow money from a credit union. It is obtained by buying one or more shares which usually sell for $5 each. Savings to buy more shares are encouraged, and dividends ranging from 3 to 6 per cent a year are ordinarily paid to members. The members manage and operate the credit union, each having one vote regardless of the number of shares he owns.

Loans may be made to members out of accumulated capital. A credit committee elected by the members passes on the applications. Loans as small as $5 are sometimes made; the maximum amount for loans may be determined by the board of directors provided it does not exceed $400 for unsecured loans for credit unions organized under Federal law. Many members would find it impossible to borrow at a bank due to lack of security.

Repayments of loans ordinarily are made weekly, semimonthly, or monthly. Although more than half of the loans are not secured, comakers sometimes sign the notes with the borrower, and occasionally a chattel mortgage is made

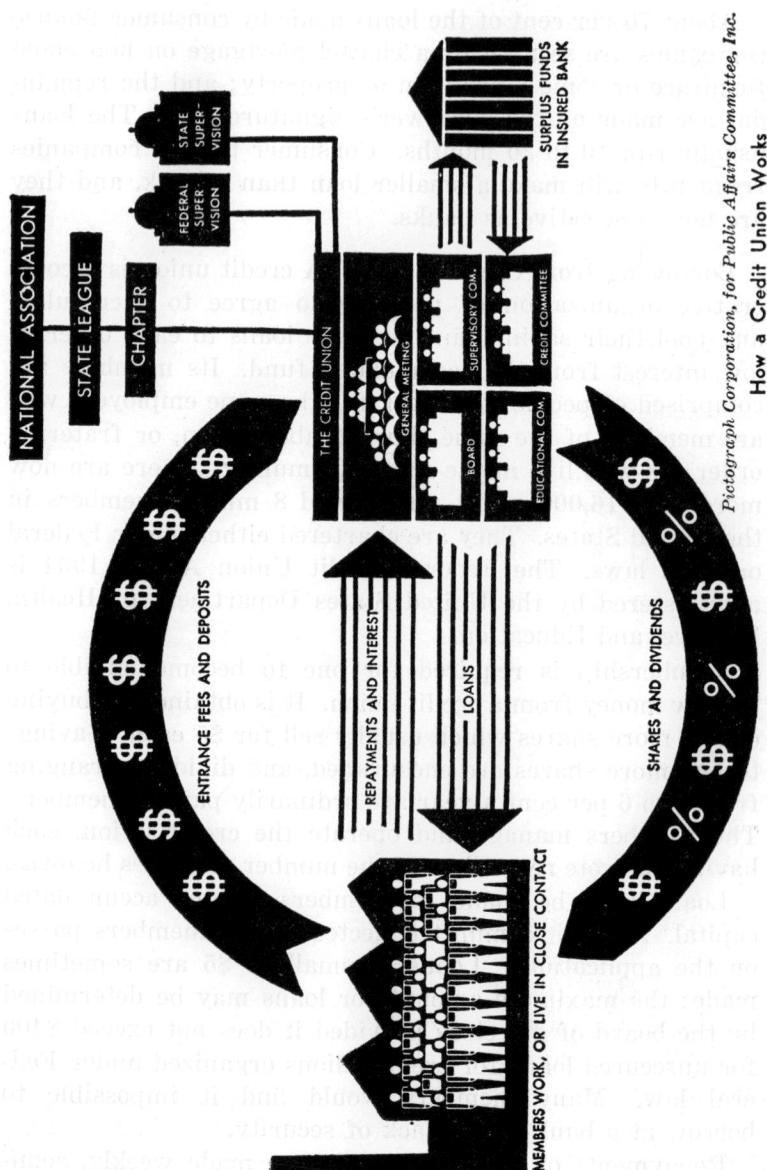

How a Credit Union Works

to secure the loan. Loans may not be made for periods of time longer than three years.

The interest rates charged by credit unions range from ½ to 1 per cent a month on unpaid monthly balances. A loan of $100 to be repaid in twelve equal monthly installments with interest at 1 per cent a month (12 per cent a year) on unpaid balance due at the end of the previous month would be $6.50. At first this appears to be at a rate of 6½ per cent per year. But the borrower did not have the entire $100 for a whole year. At the end of each month he reduced the amount he owed by $8.33. This is a savings in interest over most loan departments of commercial banks and consumer finance companies of $3 to $15. Interest rates can be low because expenses of operation are low. Most credit unions have little or no expenses for rent, salary, credit investigations, or collections. They are exempt from Federal income taxes. As long as a credit union is small, the office space for its operations usually is provided by the company for whom the members work or the group to which they belong. A credit committee makes all credit investigations. Losses from bad debts are negligible.

The primary advantages of a credit union are that savings are made easy and loans are available at relatively low interest rates. The disadvantages are that many people do not have access to membership and hence cannot borrow, and that some prefer not to reveal their personal financial affairs to fellow members.

Borrowing from Pawnbrokers. The rate of interest charged on loans obtained from pawnbrokers usually is extremely high ranging from 24 per cent to 120 per cent and higher on an annual basis.

To obtain a loan from a pawnbroker, one must turn over personal property, such as jewelry or tools, as a pledge or pawn. The maximum amount of the loan is usually extremely low in proportion to the value of the property; it is seldom more than 50 per cent of the appraised value.

If the loan is not paid by a specified time or within the length of time provided by state law, the property pawned may be sold. If there is a surplus, it is supposed to be given to the borrower. Loans from pawnbrokers must be paid in full before pledged property will be returned.

Borrowing from Unlicensed Lenders. There are still some states that do not have any small-loan laws. In these states the unlicensed lenders, commonly known as *loan sharks*, are sometimes sources of loans for many persons with low incomes who need an occasional loan. Unlicensed lenders also operate in states that do have regulatory laws. The person who patronizes an unlicensed lender is the one who needs credit the worst and who needs the most protection. Studies have shown that the lowest rate commonly charged by these illegal lenders is 120 per cent a year. It is common for the rate to be 240 per cent a year, and examples have been found of rates as high as 1,200 per cent a year.

The rates alone are not the only evils. Some of these unscrupulous lenders never allow their clients to get out of debt. The borrower is sometimes required to pay the whole loan at one time or no payment will be accepted. He is constantly in debt because he can never get enough money together to pay the whole loan.

Guides in Borrowing

1. Be sure you borrow from a company that is under state supervision.
2. Borrow no more than is necessary.
3. Borrow no more than you can repay according to your agreement.
4. Be sure that you understand your obligations and the obligations of the lender.
5. Be sure that you understand the amount of the loan, the cost of the loan, and the specific details with regard to repayment.
6. Read the contract carefully before you sign it.
7. Be sure that you get credit for every payment and receive a canceled contract when you have completed the payments.

The only sensible practice for a person who needs money is to patronize a licensed lending agency. If he is being treated unfairly, he should seek advice from such an agency as the local better business bureau or the legal aid society if he cannot afford to obtain regular legal advice from an attorney.

Summary of Principles for Borrowing

1. One's real need should be determined before borrowing money to purchase goods or services.
2. One should shop for a loan as carefully as he would for the purchase of an expensive commodity.
3. Most loans require security of some kind.
4. The range of costs for small loans is very great.
5. True interest rates on an installment payment plan are approximately double stated discount rates.
6. Each of six or seven primary sources of small loans serve some particular needs of consumers.
7. The true dollar cost of a loan should be considered before borrowing.
8. Personal loan departments of commercial banks and industrial banks rank first in the volume of loans made; consumer finance companies, second.

TEXTBOOK QUESTIONS

1. If a person needs to borrow money, what factors should he consider in selecting a lender?
2. What is the difference between a secured loan and an unsecured loan?
3. When a lender requires a borrower to have a third party sign the personal loan agreement, what is the third party's responsibility to the lender?
4. Do all lenders of money follow the same practices in collecting interest on loans? Explain.
5. A borrower agreed to repay a noninterest bearing loan in six months. He could not make payment in the specified time but paid the loan in nine months. Was the lender entitled to any interest?
6. What is a Morris Plan bank?

7. What is the economic function of a savings and loan association?
8. If an insured person borrows money on an insurance policy but dies before the loan is repaid, how do these circumstances affect the proceeds of the insurance?
9. Why is there a need for small loan agencies?
10. We sometimes speak of "uniform small-loan laws." Is there any uniformity in these laws in various states?
11. Why do many small loans cost more than the flat 6 per cent or less that is charged on large loans?
12. What is a credit union?
13. How can a credit union afford to charge lower rates of interest than can some of the other lending agencies?
14. If a person has no collateral security or insurance that could be used in obtaining a loan, and cannot find anyone to sign a note as a comaker, what are some of his other choices in obtaining a loan?
15. Why should one avoid patronizing an unlicensed lender?
16. Give at least three of the guides that have been suggested for borrowing.

DISCUSSION QUESTIONS

1. Why should one be careful in signing a note as a comaker?
2. What is one of the disadvantages of borrowing money on insurance?
3. What are some of the good features of borrowing on insurance?
4. Explain the difference between a character loan and a chattel mortgage loan.
5. If $1,000 is borrowed for a period of three years, which is the most advantageous plan of repayment (that is, the most economical): weekly installments, monthly installments, or payment in one amount at the end of the three years?
6. Why do you believe that it is necessary to have special small-loan laws?
7. Why is the interest rate on a small bank loan of $100 to an individual higher than the rate on a bank loan of $50,000 to a businessman?
8. Indicate two ways in which you could detect an unlicensed lender.
9. In what way do you think borrowing is related to budgeting?

PROBLEMS

1. Assume that you obtain a loan for $300 on your insurance policy at 6 per cent interest for one year. Compute the actual rate of interest that you pay, assuming that the interest is paid in advance and that the full amount of the loan must be repaid at the end of the year.
2. Mr. D. H. Collins borrowed from the Merchants' National Bank $500 on a 90-day note. The bank gave him cash for the face of the note less interest at 5 per cent for 90 days. (a) How much cash did he receive? (b) How much cash did he pay at maturity?
3. Assume that you obtained from a small-loan agency a loan of $100, to be paid back in ten monthly installments of $10 each. The interest of $6 and the loan service charge of $1 are deducted in advance. Figure the actual interest rate according to the formula given in Chapter 21.

COMMUNITY PROBLEMS AND PROJECTS

1. From your telephone directory or from some other source of information, make a list of all the places where small loans may be obtained in your community (not including regular banks). Classify them according to the types of lending institutions discussed in this chapter.
2. Find out whether there are small-loan laws in your state or your local community and make a study of the nominal and the actual interest rates charged by small-loan agencies. Write a report.
3. Investigate in your community to see whether the regular commercial banks have small-loan departments. Obtain information in regard to types of loans, sizes of loans, security required, terms of payment, and interest rates. Write a report setting forth this information.

Chapter 23

How to Keep Personal and Family Budgets

> **Purpose of the Chapter.** The success of most families in obtaining the things they want depends largely on how carefully they plan their expenditures. The purpose of this chapter is to show how the spending of income can be planned through a budget to help a family live within its income and still obtain the things that are needed and wanted.
>
> You will find answers to these questions:
> 1. What is a budget?
> 2. How can income be estimated?
> 3. How can expenses be estimated?
> 4. How can budgeting be simplified?
> 5. Is it necessary to account for every penny?

What Is a Budget? A *budget* is a systematic plan for using the money we earn to buy as many as possible of the things we want. It involves (a) estimating what our income will be for a certain period of time, and (b) planning our expenditures. *Income* includes not only what we receive in wages or salaries but also net profits from business, dividends on stocks owned, and interest received on investments. One must consider the total amount earned in wages and salaries and not just the take-home pay. *Expenditures* include such items as food and clothing, withholdings from wages or salary; the amounts we pay for such permanent property as a radio, television, an automobile, or a home; payments on loans; and savings. Usually a budget is an estimate of income and a plan for expenditures for a year.

For most families budgeting is necessary for saving. Budgeting can be fun, but failure to budget may result in financial tragedy for a family. A budget should be flexible and simple. Any budget plan must have reasonable goals and should be subject to change because of unforseen circumstances. It is foolish to attempt to account for every penny because that would create a hardship on every member of the family and cause the budget plan to break down.

Business firms and divisions of government prepare budgets to serve as guides for expenditures. Organizations such as churches and clubs also make budgets to govern their financial transactions. Family units and individuals whose incomes go the farthest in buying the things they want always have a financial plan for expenditures.

A budget need not be complicated. It is a device for keeping our expenditures within our income with some allowance, if possible, for savings. A budget gives one a sense of security. It makes living pleasant and successful because expenditures can be made as need for them arises. If we spend our money recklessly without consideration of income, we may deprive ourselves of the things we need

All Members of a Family Should Plan the Budget

Essential

Food (include taxes)
  Food purchased
  Meals purchased
Clothing (include taxes)
  Clothes purchased
  Material used to make
    clothes
  Shoes
  Repairs and alterations on
    clothing
  Hats

Housing
  Rent or payments on home
  Taxes
  Insurance
  Repairs
  Painting
  Payments on charge and
    installment accounts
  Interest on money borrowed

Operating

Family (include taxes)
  Fuel
  Light
  Telephone
  Water
  Gas
  Expenses on the yard
  Cleaning clothes
  Cleaning house
  Household supplies
  Life insurance protection
  Income and other taxes
  Accident insurance

Personal (include taxes)
  Carfare
  Toilet articles
  Jewelry and other personal
    items
  Personal allowances
Automobile (include taxes)
  Gasoline
  Oil
  Repairs
  Insurance
  License fees
  Tax
  Storage and parking fees

Development

Health
  Physician's and dentist's
    fees
  Nursing
  Medicine, drugs, and surgical supplies (include hospital care)
  Optical treatment
Recreation (include taxes)
  Theater tickets
  Vacations
  Hunting license
  Social club dues
  Concert tickets

Education
  Tuition
  Books
  School fees
  Traveling expenses in attending school
  Magazine subscriptions
  Lecture tickets
  Newspapers
Benevolence
  Church contributions
  Donations to charity

Savings and Other Assets

Savings funds
  Savings bank
  Building and loan association
Life insurance
  Cash value of policies

Social security
  Salary deductions
Assets (tangible)
  Furniture
  Automobile

Classification of Expenditures

and want most. Not only may we be unable to pay for our current expenses; we may also make it impossible to buy a home and to acquire major assets, such as an automobile or furniture. As a result, we find ourselves living from hand to mouth or even going into debt so deeply that it is impossible to find a way out.

Factors upon Which Income Is Estimated. Wages or salary may be estimated fairly well for a year in advance by considering the wages or salary received in the past year and by making adjustments that may be anticipated either because of wage increases or decreases or because of anticipated overtime or unemployment. Probably the best indication of the amounts that may be received from dividends, interest, and similar sources are the amounts received from these sources in past years. Except in periods of unusual economic conditions, such as inflation, war, or depression, or because of unforeseen conditions, as illness or accident, income for a family or an individual may be estimated with a fair degree of accuracy.

Classification of Expenditures. Expenditures may be classified in many ways. Most of the methods, however, are reasonably uniform in the grouping of expenses under the various headings. A classification of the various types of expenditures for the purpose of keeping a budget is shown on the next page. This classification of expenditures should serve as a guide only. You may have expenditures that must be included in your budget that are not listed here, and some that are listed you may not have.

The estimated expenditures for the budget period must include the payment of debts, such as monthly payments on a home or an automobile, interest charges on money borrowed, and payments that will fall due on charge and installment accounts.

If one is working for wages or a salary, certain deductions are usually made from his income. These deductions usually will include payments for social security and income taxes, which are required by law. In addition, the employee may voluntarily agree to deductions from his wages for insurance, union dues, savings, or other purposes. These are expenditures. One's income is considered to be the total salary or wage regardless of the number of deductions.

In the case of social security taxes (old-age benefits), the amount withheld is considered to be an asset because it accumulates to the credit of the individual. Although these deductions cannot be withdrawn as cash, they are eventually available at the time of retirement and therefore represent a specific type of saving. The deductions for hospital care represent expenses and are rightfully included as a

---

Information Needed in Making an Annual Budget

Factors for Estimating Income

(a) Wages or salary anticipated in the next year, considering the possibilities of increases or decreases, overtime, periods of unemployment, and time that may be lost through illness or accident.

(b) Net profits from business ventures.

(c) Dividends from shares of stock owned.

(d) Interest from bonds, savings accounts, and money loaned.

(e) Profit on sale of property.

Factors for Estimating Expenditures

(a) Estimated cost of food, clothing, housing, and transportation, which comprise the major expenditures for most people.

(b) Estimated cost of individual or family development, such as health, education, recreation and vacations, and personal needs.

(c) Amounts needed to make monthly payments on a home, payments on charge and installment accounts, and interest charges on money borrowed.

(d) Personal and income taxes; deductions or payments for social security.

(e) Premiums on life insurance and annuities.

(f) Contributions for religious and charitable purposes.

(g) Amounts from income placed in savings of various kinds.

part of one's health expense. Deductions for group insurance, which does not have a cash value, are expenses rightfully considered as a part of life insurance protection or family operating expenses. Deductions for union dues are also a part of the family operating expenses. Amounts withheld for savings bonds represent assets that accumulate to the credit of the individual; they should be recorded as one of the types of savings.

Any other payments for insurance, contributions for religious and charitable purposes, and any other similar expenditure must be included in a budget plan for expenditures. Furthermore, money saved is not available for other purposes and is, therefore, really an expenditure of the income that has been received. It also should be included in the budget.

Estimated Expenditures May Be Based on:

1. Expenditures in preceding years, which may be obtained from personal and family financial records.
2. Government reports of family expenditures.
3. Model budgets and reports of how other families spend their income.
4. Anticipated changes in cost of living.
5. Payments coming due on a home, an automobile, or on charge and installment accounts.
6. An anticipated irregular expenditure, such as replacement of the furnace.

Factors in Estimating Expenditures. The precise circumstances that may be encountered during the year cannot be predicted although sometimes one can predict an expenditure, such as for school tuition, a change in taxes, a surgical operation, or some other unusual item. After including expenditures for these predictable items, the person who is making the budget may consider that the other expenditures will be somewhat in proportion to those in the past. The amount of each type of expenditure in the budget is determined after a careful consideration of each of the items that are included in this classification.

AVERAGE FAMILY MONEY EXPENDITURE FOR SPECIFIED GROUPS OF GOODS AND SERVICES FOR NEW YORK AND NORTHEASTERN NEW JERSEY URBAN AREA

NUMBER OF CONSUMER UNITS, AVERAGE CONSUMER-UNIT SIZE, AND GROUPS OF GOODS AND SERVICES	UNDER $2,000	$2,000 TO $3,000	$3,000 TO $4,000	$4,000 TO $5,000	$5,000 TO $6,000	$6,000 TO $7,500	$7,500 TO $10,000	$10,000 AND OVER
Number of consumer families in sample	118	140	207	162	98	64	43	36
Average family size	1.8	2.5	3.0	3.2	3.2	3.7	3.6	3.6

Average Money Expenditures for Current Consumption

Current consumption: Total	$2,171	$3,110	$4,335	$5,337	$6,514	$7,695	$9,649	$20,934
Food	697	1,081	1,320	1,507	1,631	1,957	2,198	2,866
Housing	411	404	486	584	618	698	834	1,876
Fuel, light, refrigeration, and water	88	108	124	149	165	171	238	297
Household operation	102	135	176	198	293	339	522	1,657
Housefurnishings and equipment	77	165	226	329	433	386	605	571
Clothing	192	278	437	553	753	921	1,039	1,712
Automobile transportation	41	72	232	335	468	590	711	926
Other transportation	49	74	82	100	154	145	228	232
Personal care	43	64	87	102	113	137	149	224
Medical care	129	144	234	256	325	297	480	672
Recreation	60	124	204	236	280	380	336	671
Reading	21	28	37	43	47	67	56	107
Education	13	5	19	30	39	36	80	385
Tobacco	30	59	68	91	90	112	102	173
Beverages	20	47	73	110	120	145	161	346
Personal Taxes	54	108	198	282	470	651	930	5,195
Expenditure for gifts and contributions	81	94	135	192	223	335	452	1,648
Expenditure for insurance	38	100	157	181	220	273	452	935
Miscellaneous	25	20	40	59	72	55	76	441

U. S. Department of Labor, Bureau of Labor Statistics, Washington 25, D. C., 1950.

In making your estimates of expenditures, include the fixed or definitely known expenses first such as rent, payments on debts, taxes, and other similar items. Then classify your other needs in terms of (1) the things you need and want now, such as new clothes or a new stove; (2) things that you may wish to plan for, such as a new television set or a major expense for an operation; and (3) your wants and needs for the future, such as education, a home of your own, or a new car. Then provide savings in your budget to meet your future needs for expenditures.

According to the plan outlined in this chapter, the expenditures represent the cash outlay of funds as the result of paying expenses, buying assets, or using the income for investment or savings. If a person always conducts his transactions on a cash basis; that is, pays cash for everything and does not buy on account, he will always be able to live within his budget. If purchases are made through charge accounts, the payment of the bills should be considered as a regular expenditure of cash and should be included as such in the budget. One should therefore not buy anything on account without taking into consideration the payment for the purchase and how it will affect the budget.

Guides in Budgeting. After the financial facts upon which income and expenditures are estimated have been assembled, the next step in making a budget is to find out what others have been doing. The Bureau of Labor Statistics releases statistics on individual and family income and expenditures that may be helpful as a guide in making your own budget.

The table on page 412 shows the actual expenditures of families in one important area. Other government figures show that in some of the lower income groups families often spend more than they earn.

Family expenditures for various classes of items, such as food, shelter, and clothing, vary according to the number of persons in the family and according to the income of the family. The figures show how families spent their income—not necessarily how they should have spent it. These figures include only expenditures for consumption and do not include gifts, savings, or personal taxes, which must be considered in every budget.

In every model budget provision should be made for savings and purchase of important items. As the income grows larger, savings increase more rapidly than most other items. The expenditure for food increases more slowly; in fact, the percentage spent for food may decrease, but the amount spent may increase. As the income increases, the provision for recreation and development will increase. Expenditures for clothing, shelter, and operating should also increase although the percentage spent for those items decreases.

Example of Estimating Income. Let us assume that Mr. J. L. Murphy, who is married and has a son 12 years old and a daughter 8 years old, decides to make a budget to guide the family expenditures for the next year. One of Mr. Murphy's first problems in preparing a budget is to estimate his income for the year. His salary is $300 a month. He anticipates no changes in his salary. He receives two weeks' vacation in August with pay, but he plans to take a week of additional vacation without pay. In December last year Mr. Murphy received a bonus from the company in which he works, amounting to $37. The balance of his savings account earns interest at the rate of 2 per cent, compounded semi-annually. An average of $40 in June, $75 in July, $75 in August, and $50 in September has been received in the past five years for small fruits and vegetables that Mr. Murphy has sold from his suburban home. The prospects for a similar income next year are good. The following table shows the estimated income:

Income	Jan.	Feb.	Mar.	Apr.	May	June	July	Aug.	Sept.	Oct.	Nov.	Dec.	Total
Salary	$300	300	300	300	300	300	300	225	300	300	300	300	$3,525
Interest						24						32	56
Dividends												37	37
Sale, fruits and vegetables						40	75	75	50				240
Total	$300	300	300	300	300	364	375	300	350	300	300	369	$3,858

Estimated Income

Although Mr. Murphy estimates that his income will be $3,858 for the next year, in some months he will receive more money than in other months. This fact should be considered when he plans his expenditures.

Example of Estimating Expenditures. Mr. Murphy and his family followed the principles outlined in the earlier pages of this chapter in estimating their various expenditures. They studied their previous expenditures, consulted government figures, and then used some model budgets to guide them in setting up their estimated expenditures as shown in the table on page 416.

Their estimated income proved to be $3,858. They properly arranged their budget so that they would not spend as much as their income. Anything left over at the end of the year will be available in the form of cash or savings.

Comparison of Estimated Income and Estimated Expenditures. The estimated income and estimated expenditures should be compared for each month in the period covered by the budget to make certain that funds will be available for making expenditures as need for them arises. Most people plan to have some cash left at the end of each month. This cash balance may be added to the income of the month to determine the amount available for expenditures. An estimate of cash income and expenditures for the entire budget period should be prepared. Assuming that Mr. Murphy had $175 in cash, the illustration below is based upon his estimated income and expenditures.

	ESTIMATED BEGINNING CASH BALANCE	ESTIMATED INCOME	ESTIMATED CASH AVAILABLE	ESTIMATED EXPENDITURES	ESTIMATED ENDING CASH BALANCE
January	$175.00	$300.00	$475.00	$301.50	$173.50
February	173.50	300.00	473.50	300.00	173.50
March	173.50	300.00	473.50	297.00	176.50
April	176.50	300.00	476.50	301.50	175.00
May	175.00	300.00	475.00	291.50	183.50
June	183.50	300.00	483.50	345.50	138.00
July	138.00	364.00	502.00	366.50	135.50
August	135.50	375.00	510.50	303.00	207.50
September	207.50	300.00	507.50	351.00	156.50
October	156.50	350.00	506.50	302.00	204.50
November	204.50	300.00	504.50	300.00	204.50
December	204.50	300.00	504.50	369.00	135.50

Cash Estimate; Comparison of Estimated Income and Expenditures

Estimated Expenditures

	JAN.	FEB.	MAR.	APR.	MAY	JUNE	JULY	AUG.	SEPT.	OCT.	NOV.	DEC.	TOTAL
Essential:													
Food	$ 85.00	$ 85.00	$ 80.00	$ 80.00	$ 77.00	$ 77.00	$ 77.00	$ 77.00	$ 80.00	$ 80.00	$ 90.00	$ 91.00	$ 979.00
Clothing	38.00	38.00	39.00	30.00	30.00	30.00	30.00	30.00	60.00	37.00	35.00	35.00	432.00
Housing	45.00	45.00	45.00	45.00	45.00	45.00	45.00	45.00	45.00	45.00	45.00	45.00	540.00
Operating:													
Family (including tax)	46.00	46.00	46.00	43.00	43.00	43.00	50.00	46.00	46.00	47.00	50.00	75.00	581.00
Personal	5.00	5.00	5.00	5.00	5.00	5.00	5.00	6.00	6.00	6.00	5.00	5.00	63.00
Automobile	8.00	8.00	8.00	9.00	9.00	8.00	8.00	25.00	8.00	8.00	9.00	13.00	121.00
Development:													
Health	10.00	13.00	11.00	10.00	10.00	10.00	10.00	10.00	13.00	13.00	11.00	10.00	131.00
Education	4.00	4.00	4.00	4.00	4.00	4.00	5.00	4.00	4.00	4.00	4.00	4.00	49.00
Recreation	6.00	6.00	6.00	7.00	7.00	8.00	8.00	8.00	6.00	6.00	6.00	6.00	82.00
Benevolence	9.00	9.00	12.00	9.00	9.00	11.00	9.00	9.00	13.00	13.00	9.00	16.00	128.00
Savings and Assets:													
Savings Fund	10.00	10.00	10.00	23.00	20.00	40.00	40.00	5.00	23.00	12.00	5.00	8.00	206.00
Savings Bonds	25.00	25.00	25.00	25.00	25.00	25.00	25.00	25.00	25.00	25.00	25.00	25.00	300.00
Life Insurance (Cash Value)							30.00					30.00	60.00
Social Security	6.00	6.00	6.00	6.00	6.00	6.00	6.00	4.50	6.00	6.00	6.00	6.00	70.50
Other Assets	4.50			5.50	1.50	31.50	18.50	8.50	16.50				86.50
Total	$301.50	$300.00	$297.00	$301.50	$291.50	$345.50	$366.50	$303.00	$351.50	$302.00	$300.00	$369.00	$3,829.00

Economic Conditions Affect Budgeting. The person who plans his expenditures carefully year after year becomes aware of changes in economic conditions that affect his income and expenditures. Economic factors that especially influence personal and family budgets are price changes that affect the cost of living by either increasing or decreasing it, taxes, and deductions from income for social security. As taxes increase, smaller amounts remain from income for other expenditures and savings. An increase in income means little if there is a corresponding change in the cost of commodities and services we need and want.

Summary of Principles of Operating a Budget

1. Once the budget has been made and agreed upon, all members of the family must cooperate in keeping expenditures within the budget limits.
2. Revisions of the budget during the budget period may be necessary. These adjustments usually will reduce the expenditures for some items in order to provide more for other items. Hence, the family members should approve the revisions.
3. Accurate and complete records of all income and expenditures must be kept. Appropriate record forms should be used, and some member of the family should be responsible for making the entries.
4. When the major income for the month is received, the allocations should be made in the following sequence:
    The amount for savings should be deposited in the savings account or invested.
    Monthly payments for taxes, for purchase of the home, on charge and installment accounts, and on money borrowed should be made.
    Amounts budgeted for food and clothing should be set aside.
    Allowances for contributions, education, recreation, and personal expenses should be made.
5. Except in an emergency that could not be foreseen, no one should be allowed personal expenses or expenditures in any one of the classifications to overstep the amount budgeted for that purpose.
6. Periodically the actual expenditures should be compared with the estimated expenditures.

TEXTBOOK QUESTIONS

1. What is a budget?
2. What are some things included in income?
3. What items are included in expenditures?
4. In considering wages in the budget, how is the deduction for social security handled? Explain the reason.
5. Why is money placed in a savings account considered an expenditure since it is still available to you when you want it?
6. Under what classification in the budget would you include the cost of cleaning of clothes?
7. How would you classify magazine subscriptions in the budget?
8. In the budget of Mr. Murphy, how did he handle the expected sales of fruits and vegetables?
9. Does the budget ever provide for circumstances in which the expenditures for a particular month exceed the income for that month?
10. In the estimate of expenditures on page 416, the total of estimated expenditures is not the same as the total of estimated income. Why is this true and what happens to the difference?
11. How should buying on account or on the installment plan be correlated with budgeting?
12. In the planning of income and expenditures for budget purposes, what particular plan outlined in this chapter determines whether sufficient cash will be available for the expenditures that are planned?

DISCUSSION QUESTIONS

1. What is the fallacy of contending that for budgeting purposes one's income is only the "take-home" income after deductions have been made for social security and all other items, which might include group insurance or hospital insurance?
2. Why do you think part of the expenditure for life insurance is recorded as a family operating expense rather than a personal expense?
3. Why does information gathered from past experience help in establishing a budget?
4. Explain the advantages and disadvantages of model budgets.
5. Explain some of the advantages of the cash estimate that is illustrated in this chapter.
6. (a) If, at the beginning of the year, Mr. Murphy had planned to buy a radio for $50 in December, how would this item have been shown in his budget? (b) How would this item have affected the budget?

7. If Mr. Murphy finds that, according to his budget, he is not going to have enough cash in his checking account to take care of expenses, what can he do to avoid this situation?
8. Why is it recommended that the essential operating expenses and the savings should be taken care of first?

PROBLEMS

1. Mr. Hansen has $92.10 in cash in his checking account when he makes his budget. He estimates that his income will be $335 a month during the year. He also estimates that the following will be his total expenditures for each month:

January	$307.10	July	$315.52
February	335.15	August	307.43
March	288.25	September	305.31
April	305.23	October	306.37
May	297.42	November	295.26
June	300.36	December	327.93

Prepare a form similar to that on page 415, showing a comparison of the estimated income and expenditures.

2. Using the average family expenditure reported by the Department of Labor in the table on page 412, compute the percentage spent for each item in the $3,000 to $4,000 group based on the total consumption of $4,335. Compute a separate percentage for food, housing, etc.

3. Any model budgets or any collection of figures of expenditures for a particular area will not necessarily fit all other areas. Make a list of some of the ways in which you feel that budget figures for one area, which you will name, would not be reasonable where you live. Give your reasons.

COMMUNITY PROBLEMS AND PROJECTS

1. (a) List all your items of personal income and of personal expenditure. (b) Prepare a one-year budget of your income and your expenditures as described on pages 414 to 416. You will need this budget for your study of Chapter 24.
2. Make a study of the income and expenditures of your family. Either rule forms similar to those in this chapter for preparing a budget, or purchase a budget book in some store. On the basis of the information that you gain from your family and suggestions in this chapter, prepare a budget of the income and expenditures for twelve months.
3. Follow the instructions of your teacher and obtain samples of budget material from banks, savings and loan associations, finance companies, or any other source available to you. Pick the best and explain why you like it.

Chapter 24

How to Keep Personal and Family Records

Purpose of the Chapter. In order to operate a budget satisfactorily it is necessary to keep at least some simple financial records. They may be just as complete or just as simple as are necessary to meet the family requirements. In this chapter you will learn how to keep complete records and some ways of keeping more simple records.

You will find answers to these questions:
1. What do you include in a statement of assets and liabilities?
2. How do you determine your net worth?
3. What is a statement of income and expense?
4. How is budgeting related to record keeping?

Statement of Assets and Liabilities. The *assets* of an individual or family consist of property, such as money, savings accounts, cash value of life insurance policies, furniture, and an automobile. A *liability* is a debt that will require cash or some other asset to pay it. Examples of liabilities are amounts owed on a home or an automobile, money borrowed and the interest due on it, and amounts yet to be paid on charge and installments accounts. You will recall that payments becoming due must be considered in estimating expenditures for a budget.

The following form is recommended for use in making a statement of the assets and the debts of a family. This form is used for computing the net worth of a person or a family. *Net worth* is determined by deducting the total of all debts from the total of all assets. For instance, if a person owns assets worth $100 and owes debts amounting to $30, his net worth is $70. Notice that this summary disregards such items as clothing, which is worn out in a reasonably short time and must be replaced. Clothing, instead of being considered an asset, is charged off as an expense when it is purchased.

Statement of Assets and Liabilities

ASSETS OWNED BY THE FAMILY		DEBTS OWED BY THE FAMILY	
Cash in Checking Account ..$	xxx.xx	Mortgage ....$	xxx.xx
Cash in Savings Account ...	xxx.xx	Loans on Insurance	xxx.xx
Bonds	xxx.xx	Loans Owed to Bank	xxx.xx
Cash Value of Life Insurance.	xxx.xx	Amount Due on an Installment Purchase	xxx.xx
Stocks	xxx.xx		
Notes	xxx.xx	Amount Owed to Stores	xx.xx
Real Estate	xxx.xx	Other Debts:	
Social Security	xxx.xx	———————————	xxx.xx
Household Equipment	xxx.xx	———————————	xx.xx
Automobile	xxx.xx	———————————	xxx.xx
Other Assets:		———————————	xxx.xx
———————————	xxx.xx		
———————————	xxx.xx		
———————————	xx.xx	Total Debts ....$x.xxx.xx	
———————————	xx.xx	Net Worth (Ownership) .... x,xxx.xx	
Total Assets ....$x,xxx.xx		Total Debts and Net Worth. $x.xxx.xx	

(Total Assets, $x,xxx.xx, — Total Debts, $x,xxx.xx, = Net Worth, $x,xxx.xx.)

Let us take as a typical example the case of Mr. J. L. Murphy. Mr. Murphy decides to make a family survey of assets and debts to determine what the family is worth. He uses the model form for tabulating his assets and debts. It is easy for him to determine the amount he has in his checking account and savings account, for he can refer to his balances in these accounts. The cash value of his life insurance is determined by referring to the values indicated in his policies. He has no notes or stocks. The U. S. Bonds are listed at their present value. The amount listed for social security is the amount that has actually been deducted from his wages. His household equipment is valued by adding the cost of each of the more important items and disregarding miscellaneous items that are of little value and that will wear out in a short time. He sets the value of each article at less than the original cost because the equipment has been used several years and is partially worn out. He evaluates his automobile by obtaining an estimate of the trade-in value from an automobile dealer. He lists a vacant lot at the price it cost him.

He knows the amount of the loan that he owes on his life insurance. He determines the amount of a debt owed to a department store by referring to his monthly statement from that store. The following is his summary for January 1, based on these computations:

J. L. MURPHY
Statement of Assets and Liabilities, January 1, 195–

ASSETS OWNED BY THE FAMILY		DEBTS OWED BY THE FAMILY	
Cash in Checking Account ....$	175.00	Loan on Insurance ....$	100.00
Cash in Savings Account	200.00	Owed to Central Store	25.30
U. S. Savings Bonds	150.00	Total Debts	125.30
Life Insurance (Cash Value) ..	331.33		
Social Security	236.00		
Household Equipment	500.00		
Automobile	1,200.00		
Other Assets:			
Vacant Lot	250.00	Net Worth (Ownership)	2,917.03
Total Assets $3,042.33		Total Debts and Net Worth $3,042.33

(Total Assets, $3,042.33, − Total Debts, $125.30, = Net Worth, $2,917.03.)

A person may possess a great many assets; but if he owes debts almost equal to these assets, his net worth is relatively small. The difference between what he owns and what he owes represents what he is actually worth. This difference was referred to before as net worth. Mr. Murphy's net worth on January 1 is $2,917.03, the difference between his total assets, $3,042.33, and his total debts, $125.30.

The statement of Mr. Murphy's assets and liabilities is also known as a *balance sheet*. Everyone should prepare a record of this kind at least once a year in order to determine his financial standing. Notice that the balance sheet prepared by Mr. Murphy omits not only items of clothing but also such items as fire insurance on the household equipment. In preparing a balance sheet for the practical use of an individual or a family, it is not necessary to list these items. It is simpler to consider them as expenses at the time they are purchased and to disregard them as assets. An insurance policy may have been purchased in order to provide fire insurance protection for three years. Until the policy expires it has an asset value, but for all practical purposes it constitutes an expense at the time it is purchased.

Life insurance is treated differently. Each premium payment consists partly of payment for protection of the family and partly of savings derived from the increase in the cash value of the policy. The expense element is recorded under family expense; the savings element, under life insurance.

The foregoing balance sheet for Mr. Murphy showed his assets, liabilities, and net worth on the first day of the year. During the year the value of the assets and the amount of the liabilities will change. Therefore, Mr. Murphy should prepare a balance sheet again at the end of the year to show his financial status.

J. L. MURPHY
Statement of Assets and Liabilities, December 31, 195–

ASSETS OWNED BY THE FAMILY		DEBTS OWED BY THE FAMILY	
Cash in Checking Account ......$	232.00	City Savings Bank ....$	100.00
Cash in Savings Account	305.70	(due on refrigerator)	
U. S. Savings Bonds	250.00	Owed to Central Store	25.00
Life Insurance (Cash Value) ..	391.33	Total Debts	125.00
Social Security	306.50		
Household Equipment	550.00		
Automobile	1,000.00		
Other Assets:			
Vacant Lot	250.00	Net Worth (Ownership)	3,144.03
Total Assets $3,285.53		Total Debts and Net Worth $3,285.53	

(Total Assets, $3,285.53, — Total Debts, $125.00, = Net Worth, $3,160.53.)

By comparing this balance sheet with the one prepared at the beginning of the year (page 422), it is possible to compute the increase in net worth for the year. This computation is as follows:

Net worth at the end of the year $3,160.53
Net worth at the beginning of the year 2,917.03

Increase in Net Worth .... $ 243.50

Statement of Income and Expense. We may recall that income includes wages or salary received, interest and dividends received, bonus, net profits from business, and gifts. Expenditures include all expenses and all other ways in which cash is disposed of, such as the buying of furniture, payments on a home or on charge and installment accounts, or money placed in a savings account. It will be noted that there is a difference between expenditures and expenses. The difference between total expenses and total expenditures is the amount that has been put into furniture, bonds, savings, and similar items, or is available in some form of asset. The difference between one's income and his expenses for a given period of time is his net gain or loss. Part or all of the net gain may have been put in savings or some other asset. Actual income and expenditures for this year are good bases upon which to estimate income and expenditures when making a budget for next year.

If Mr. Murphy has kept records of the money he received and of the payments he has made during the year, he can easily determine the total for each class of income and expense. The statement of income and expense shown below was prepared by Mr. Murphy at the end of the year.

You will observe that the Murphys paid more for rent, food, and clothing than they anticipated in their budget

J. L. MURPHY
Statement of Income and Expense for the Year Ending December 31, 195–

Income:			
Salary Income		$3,525.00	
Interest Income		56.00	
Bonus		37.00	
Income from Sales		240.00	
Total Income			$3,858.00
Expenses:			
Essential:			
Food	$1,004.00		
Clothing	457.00		
Housing	740.00	2,201.00	
Operating:			
Family	581.00		
Personal	63.00		
Automobile	121.00	765.00	
Development:			
Health	181.00		
Education	57.50		
Recreation	82.00		
Benevolence	128.00	448.50	
Total Expenses			3,414.50
Net Gain			$ 443.50

in Chapter 23. The family had to move into a house where they were required to pay more rent. Their planning still permitted them to have a net gain for the year.

Mr. Murphy's net gain of $443.50 for the year, as shown by his statement of income and expense, is $200 greater than the increase in his net worth of $243.50 (see page 423). The reason for this difference is the depreciation of $200 on his automobile, which was not included in his statement of income and expense because that statement includes only cash items.

Other Financial Records. In case of loss by fire or theft, an inventory of the items having value, such as furniture, appliances, books, jewelry, and silverware, should be kept. Dates of purchase, from whom purchased, and cost should be shown on the record.

Though deeds to property, stock certificates, bonds, and insurance policies should be kept in a safe-deposit box, a record of these items should always be kept. Most persons can devise a record plan for listing the items that may be classified as miscellaneous.

You Should Check Your Budget Regularly. It is necessary for the Murphy family to keep records so that, as they go along, they can determine whether they are spending their money as they had planned. Transactions must be recorded daily, weekly, or monthly in accordance with a definite plan. There are many ways to keep a set of records, but the Murphy family chose a simple columnar cashbook with a column for each classification in the budget.

The illustration on page 426 shows a record of (a) income, (b) expenditures for expenses, and (c) expenditures for savings and assets. In other words, this record shows what the income is, its source, and how it is used. This type of business record is known as a *cashbook*. Items are recorded in this cashbook as they occur. In the part of the cashbook illustrated, the entries have been made for July. At the end of a month the various columns are totaled.

Observe that on July 15, Mr. Murphy recorded a salary income of $150. The amount of $7 recorded under family

Cashbook Record of Income and Expenditures

operating expenses is for a payroll deduction for Federal income tax. The amount of $12.50 recorded under savings funds is because of a deduction from his salary by the employer to purchase savings bonds. Likewise, the employer withheld an amount for social security old-age benefits. In other words, Mr. Murphy did not receive all his salary in cash because some of it was withheld for various purposes.

A total of $80.50 was withdrawn from the bank account during the month to pay for groceries. A check was written on July 30 to pay the rent, amounting to $65. Checks were written for clothing on July 1, 8, 23, and 26.

In recording an expenditure for life insurance, one must consider two elements: (a) the cost of the protection and (b) the accumulation of savings that results from the increase in the cash value. As will be explained in the chapter on insurance, most life insurance policies have a cash or loan value. This cash or loan value increases each time a premium is paid. The increases in the cash value are shown on the insurance policy. A definite portion of each premium payment (the increase in the cash value) should therefore be recorded as savings. The remainder should be recorded as a family operating expense (the cost of protection).

Having the proper cash balance available is important. The illustration below shows that the budget was planned so that there would be an adequate cash balance each month. It is appropriate to compare the income with the expenditures each month using a table similar to the following:

	BEGINNING CASH BALANCE	INCOME	CASH AVAILABLE	EXPENDITURES	ENDING CASH BALANCE
January	$175.00	$300.00	$475.00	$300.00	$175.00
February	175.00	300.00	475.00	298.50	176.50

Following the Budget. It will be observed that at the end of each month the columnar totals of the cashbook are added and the budget totals for the month are also inserted for comparison. This is important in order to see how the actual income and expenditures for that month for each classification compare with the estimated income and expenditures in the budget.

At the end of each month, total cumulative income and expenditures for each classification are included in the cashbook, together with the total cumulative budget figures up to date for the income and for each classification of expenditures. This arrangement makes it possible to compare the budget with the actual expenditures for the whole year ending on that particular date. If any expenditures are seriously exceeding the budget, it may be necessary to modify the budget or to change the spending habits. Sometimes it is possible to shift one type of expenditure to another in order to keep the total budget expenditures in line. For instance, let us assume that unusual medical expenses may arise far beyond the budget. Under such circumstances it may be necessary to reduce expenditures for recreation or clothing. It may be necessary to reduce savings so that the total expenditures will not exceed the total income.

Compare Your Records with Your Budget

Unless some comparisons are made monthly, the expenditures may get out of control and one may end the year by spending considerably more than was planned. Failure to follow the budget is a common cause for using up savings and going into debt.

Ch. 24]

Good Checkbook Stubs Aid in Keeping Records

Harold M. Lambert

Recording from Checkbook Stubs. Some definite system must be followed in recording income and expenditures. Unless a definite plan is followed, some items of income and expenditure may be omitted through error. If a checking account is used, the following procedure is recommended:

(a) Deposit all income in the checking account, and record all deposits on the checkbook stubs. If a person's income is subject to payroll deductions, the amounts deducted on each payday can be recorded on the checkbook stub when the deposit is made.

(b) Withdraw only enough cash to take care of such items as food, clothing, and personal and automobile expenditures.

(c) When cash is withdrawn from the bank for a particular purpose, make a record on the checkbook stub to indicate the purpose for which the amount is withdrawn.

(d) Write checks for all major expenditures, such as rent, bills, charge accounts, insurance, and savings.

(e) At the end of the month verify the bank statement and use the checkbook stubs as the source of information for recording all income and expenditures.

The method described above is based upon the assumption that the checkbook stub will provide all the information from which entries can be recorded in the cashbook. However, some persons may wish to use a variation of this plan that will enable them to avoid certain additional service charges on checks. This may be done by cashing the pay check and depositing in the checking account only part of the salary. Sufficient cash can be withheld to deposit in the savings account and to take care of small bills and personal allowances which are not to be paid by check.

Recording without a Checkbook. If a checking account is not used, the following procedure is recommended:

(a) When the salary payment is received, keep out only what is allotted for essential, operating, and development expenditures.
(b) Deposit the remainder in a savings account.
(c) If rent or any other major payments are not due at the time the regular income is received, the amount needed may be laid aside until the payment is due.
(d) Record in the cashbook (1) the salary and (2) the deductions for social security and the amounts withheld for any other purposes, such as income taxes, savings, group insurance, or union dues.
(e) Record each expenditure at the time of each purchase for cash or when each bill is paid. If more money has been kept out than is needed during any period, a lesser amount can be kept for the next period. For instance, let us assume that each payday $35 is withheld for essential operating expenditures and that $4 is left over one period. On the next payday $31 could be withheld.

Checking accounts may not be economical for every family, but it is advisable for every family to have at least a bank savings account. Some families, however, do not have even a savings account in a bank. In such cases only the amount of cash necessary to take care of all anticipated expenditures during the month should be withheld on payday; the rest should be placed in Postal Savings, deposited in a credit union, invested in United States Savings Bonds, or put in some other safe place.

Other Methods of Keeping Records. In almost any stationery store you can buy satisfactory forms for keeping records, or you can design your own forms.

In some families in which a fixed amount is allowed for each member of the family and a certain amount is allowed for the purchase of groceries and food, the main record is the checkbook, through which all other bills are paid. A supplementary record is kept of assets, and a file is kept of all bills due.

If one does not wish to use a columnar cashbook, such as is illustrated in this chapter, exactly the same plan can be followed by purchasing a notebook of an appropriate size and using it as follows:

(a) Use the first page as an index of expenditures. On this page list the classification of income and expenditures.

(b) Number the subsequent pages and place a title at the top of each page for each classification of income or expenditure. For example, page 2, Income; page 3, Food; page 4, Clothing; and so on through the entire list of expenditures.

(c) Record each transaction on the appropriate page in the same way that it was recorded in the cashbook in the illustration on page 426.

Summary of the Needs and Purposes of Family Records

1. Records of income and expenditures are important elements in planning a budget for the future.
2. A record of income and of some kinds of expense is needed for making Federal, state, and local tax reports.
3. A statement of assets and liabilities (debts) at a particular time lets a person know what he is worth at that time.
4. The income and expense statement for a particular period of time shows the net gain or net loss during that period.
5. Miscellaneous records of such things as insurance policies, deeds for real estate, and items of value owned are desirable in case of loss of property through fire or other emergency.

TEXTBOOK QUESTIONS

1. In the preparation of a statement of assets and liabilities (balance sheet), name at least two items that usually are placed in the left column.
2. From a statement of assets and liabilities, how can one determine his net worth or net ownership?
3. What are the two ways in which one can determine his net gain or increase in wealth at the end of a year?
4. In one year's time why is there a difference in the value of the automobile shown on the two statements of assets and liabilities of Mr. Murphy?
5. The statement of income and expenses on page 424 does not show all the expenditures. Why is this true?
6. What types of records should be kept in case of fire or theft?
7. What is a cashbook?
8. How did Mr. Murphy record all of the entries involving salary?
9. How should the purchase of a new suit be recorded?
10. If Mr. Murphy deposits $10 in a savings account, how will he record it in the cashbook?
11. How should Mr. Murphy record the purchase of gasoline?
12. How should Mr. Murphy record the payment of a dental bill?
13. Explain why two different amounts are recorded in two different columns for life insurance.
14. How is it possible for Mr. Murphy to make a careful comparison of his actual expenditures and his budget figures?
15. If a checking account is used, what recommendation is made in regard to depositing each salary check in the bank?
16. When a checking account is not used but a savings account is used, what policy is recommended in regard to depositing money in the savings account?
17. If a savings account in a bank is not used, what policy is recommended each payday in regard to money needed for expenditures and for the surplus fund?
18. Besides the columnar cashbook method of recording expenditures, what other method is recommended in this chapter?

DISCUSSION QUESTIONS

1. If a man's net worth at the beginning of the year was $1,900 and at the end of the year was $1,700, what was his net gain or loss?
2. Can you explain why the savings and assets are considered as part of the expenditures in the system explained in this chapter?

3. In the cashbook, the total of all expenditures equals the total of all income. Explain why the expenditures for savings and assets are not included in the statement of income and expense.
4. Suppose that sometime during the year Mr. Murphy's automobile had been stolen and he was not covered by insurance. How would you recommend showing this loss in his statements at the end of the year?
5. If Mr. Murphy gets $50 as a Christmas present from his employer, how will this amount be recorded in his cashbook?
6. In what column in the cashbook do you think Mr. Murphy would record such items as (a) a hunting license and (b) a parking fee?
7. What recommendations would you offer Mr. Murphy if he finds that his automobile expenses are running twice as much as planned in the budget?
8. If Mr. Murphy finds, by monthly comparisons, that expenditures for food are running over the budget, what would you recommend that he do?
9. If the income proves to be less than was originally expected, what must Mr. Murphy do?
10. What are some of the disadvantages of using a checking account?

PROBLEMS

1. Mr. Walsh has the following assets available: cash in a savings account, $150; U. S. Government savings bonds, $83; automobile, $350; cash value of life insurance, $460. He owes the following debts: account at grocery store, $15; account at department store, $23; due finance company for automobile, $100. Prepare a statement of assets and debts like the model in this chapter.
2. Mr. J. O. Jones has an insurance policy that has a cash value of $135.10. The annual premium is $46.20. After the premium for the current year has been paid, the cash value will amount to $161.20. How will Mr. Jones record the premium payment in his cashbook?
3. Assume that Mr. R. D. Malone's income was $1,819.47. Prepare his statement of income and expense for the year ending on December 31, 195-, using the following expenses:

Food	$382.15	Automobile	$52.20
Clothing	214.25	Health	28.00
Housing	490.00	Education	39.50
Family	96.20	Recreation	36.25
Personal	42.10	Benevolence	52.00

4. Mr. J. O. Mason found the following information on his checkbook stubs at the end of January. Rule a cashbook similar to the one shown on page 426, and record the transactions of Mr. Mason. Total and rule the columns of the cashbook after you have recorded all the transactions.

Jan.	2. Clothing	$ 10.00
	Food	36.00
	5. Personal allowance for Mr. Mason	5.00
	Personal allowance for Mrs. Mason	5.00
	Theater tickets	4.00
	10. Food	34.00
	Magazine subscription	2.50
	15. Salary (Less $2.40 for social security and $19.20 for withholding tax)	160.00
	Taxes on home	30.00
	20. Telephone	3.50
	Light and gas	4.00
	22. Gasoline	2.00
	Automobile repairs	5.00
	25. Church contributions	4.00
	Dentist bill	6.00
	31. Salary (Less $2.40 for social security and $19.20 for withholding tax)	160.00
	Savings deposit	15.00

COMMUNITY PROBLEMS AND PROJECTS

1. In Project No. 1 of the previous chapter you were required to prepare a budget for yourself. On the basis of the classifications of income and expenditures in that budget, prepare a cashbook for yourself in which you can record your income and expenditures. Keep an accurate record of your income and expenditures for at least two months, making comparisons at the end of each month with your budget, as Mr. Murphy did. At the end of two months submit this project to your teacher for checking.
2. Make a study of the income and the expenditures of your family. Rule a form for a cashbook or prepare a small notebook for keeping the records of your family. Record all the items of income and expenditure for one month.

Chapter 25

Planning Your Savings Program

> **Purpose of the Chapter.** Most people are not able to save money without a program, but most people can save at least a little money with a program. This chapter will show you how to start a program of saving which will eventually lead to the possibility of making investments and to greater security and happiness in the future.
>
> You will find answers to these questions:
> 1. What are some of the choices that must be made in saving?
> 2. What are important goals in savings?
> 3. What is a good saving program?
> 4. How do savings grow?
> 5. Where can you safely put your savings?

Saving Can Be Fun. Saving does not mean penny pinching. It can be fun if you will look forward to some greater future pleasures by giving up some of your present spending for foolish or unnecessary things. The question before you is whether you are willing to make a plan that will enable you to reach a desirable and pleasant goal.

Some of the decisions that you have to make are these: Do you want to waste small amounts daily just because you feel that what you spend today is not worth saving, or do you want to save it and build it into a larger amount that will be worthwhile later; do you need all the pleasures for which you spend small amounts now, or would you have a greater pleasure in a more substantial way if you save money for future use; can you decide between your real needs and spur-of-the-moment desires but still obtain some luxuries as you go along; do you have a careless philosophy of living to the fullest today and letting the future take care of itself; do you have the false belief that Social Security will take care of you comfortably in your old age?

Guides to Personal and Family Saving. A budget is the key to saving because it enables you to plan. Putting at least a little away for saving each week or each month should be planned in the same way that spending is planned. Then your savings will start to work for you by earning interest. Four principles of saving for individuals and families are:

Four Principles of Saving

1. Budget your income and expenditures.
2. Spend less than you earn.
3. Invest these savings wisely.
4. Reinvest the income from savings promptly.

Setting Goals for Savings. Most people have some definite goals in life, some things toward which they are striving. Some of these goals are really ideals and ambitions, and some are desires for material things that will add to the comfort and pleasantness of living. Regardless of the kind of goals we may have for ourselves, money is usually a factor in achieving them. Most of us have to set aside a little at a time from our income in order to accumulate enough to realize our goals. Setting aside a part of our income regularly is *saving*, and investing the amount we set aside so interest may be earned is evidence of good money management.

The time the money will be needed and the amount that will be needed for each of the goals we set for ourselves must be considered when we save for specific purposes.

When a savings fund has been established for some specific purpose, it should be used only for that purpose. One

Harold M. Lambert

An Education for a Chosen Occupation Is One of the Most Important Goals of a Savings Plan

of the major goals of a student should be to acquire adequate education for a trade or profession.

Retirement, a Goal for Saving. While many people receive old-age pensions and other forms of social security benefits when they no longer are able to work and earn for themselves, most people want a supplementary income of their own when they reach retirement age. They feel more independent and enjoy life more if they receive income from their own investments instead of depending entirely upon income from social security, even though they contributed to the fund from which their benefits may be paid. Therefore, during their best earning years many people set aside a certain amount of money each month that will be returned to them monthly with compound interest when they retire, usually at the age of 65 or 70 years. This amount received each month is known as *retirement income.*

Worthwhile Goals of Saving
1. Further education.
2. Marriage and furnishing a home.
3. Buying a home.
4. Starting a business.
5. Buying insurance for protection and future income.
6. Investments in securities for future income.
7. Buying major comforts and luxuries for better living.
8. Unemployment, hospital bills, and other emergencies.
9. Paying cash to save on the purchase of important items instead of buying on the installment plan.
10. Retirement.

Many people are covered by social security and some people have insurance annuities that will pay them an income on retirement. For most people however this income is not adequate to live on after retirement. Other means of savings must be started early in life in order to provide an adequate income after retirement.

In planning for retirement income, several factors should be considered:

(a) The amount of monthly income that is desired upon retirement.
(b) The amount of monthly savings invested at compound interest that will be required in order to produce that retirement income.
(c) The possible changes that may come about in a person's way of living. A modest home and ordinary comforts acceptable now may seem inadequate thirty or forty years from now. Therefore, plans for saving for retirement should be adjusted as permanent changes in standards of living become evident.

(d) The possibility of a decrease in the purchasing power of a dollar through a general increase in price levels (inflation). If when you reach retirement age, two dollars would be required to buy the same commodities or services that one dollar will buy now, you would need to save twice as much a month while you earn in order to live comfortably in retirement. As changes in economic conditions that appear to be permanent occur, you should, therefore, allow for them in your retirement saving plan.

Evaluating Expenditures. The judgment used in spending is an important factor in enabling us to save. If one's income is spent soon after each payday, the spending is probably not well planned.

The average family that spends its income as soon as it is received finds it impossible to take a vacation trip, or to purchase an automobile or any other items of comfort or luxury, without going into debt. If the same family were to forego certain trivial pleasures, however, and to establish a definite savings program, its members could enjoy more desirable comforts and luxuries, which require a reasonably large expenditure of money.

In making a decision with regard to buying a luxury, one should answer the question, "What will it cost me in terms of days of labor?" For example, if a stenographer earns $40 a week on the basis of a forty-hour week, she is earning at the rate of $1.00 an hour. Suppose she has enough to make a down payment on an automobile but finds that it will cost her $70.00 a month to pay for it, $8 a month for a garage, $4 a month for repairs, $6 a month for insurance, and $16.00 a month for gasoline and oil. The monthly cost will be $104. This calculation does not take into consideration that the tires will wear out and will have to be replaced, or that the automobile will wear out and that any accident will increase the maintenance costs. The minimum expenses therefore amount to $104 a month. As this stenographer is earning only $173.20 a month (four and one-third weeks in a month), it is obvious that the luxury of an automobile is not justified.

Paying as One Goes. One should not go into debt for things that will have been used or consumed before they are paid for. It may be necessary to borrow, however, to pay for medical or similar expenses. It is frequently desirable to go into debt for a major investment, such as a home, but the same thing is not true of going into debt for current purchases. The latter practice will soon lead to the destruction of the savings program.

Making a Plan for Saving. It is easy to spend all of our income and save none of it unless we have a goal or a reason for saving. The reason many people save is to have money at a future time to go to college, to establish or to buy a home or a business, or to invest to provide for a future income. Savings to meet these and similar goals must be planned in the budget of expenditures. Individuals and family units, like business firms, can never operate successfully financially without a plan. The plans for savings for special purposes usually involve planning for a sum of money to be available at some definite time in the future.

Anticipated needs can be calculated reasonably closely. For instance, the purchase of a home can be planned years in advance. A certain amount of money may be required as a down payment on the home. Money for this purpose can be saved under a definite plan. Money accumulates rapidly when a specific amount is deposited each month at compound interest. For example:

$5 deposited each month at 2 per cent interest grows to $665 in 10 years or at 4 per cent interest to $737.45 in 10 years.
$10 deposited each month at 2 per cent interest will be $1,330 in 10 years or at 4 per cent interest, $1,474.90.

These calculations are based on the assumption that (a) each deposit is made at the beginning of the month, (b) interest is compounded semiannually, and (c) interest is calculated according to the actual amount of time (each whole six-month period) that a deposit has been in the account.

Make Money Work for You. Very few people realize the cumulative power of compound interest. Interest is a very

Ch. 25] PLANNING YOUR SAVINGS PROGRAM

SEE HOW QUICKLY YOUR DOLLARS GROW IN A "PLAN-A-PURCHASE ACCOUNT"!

Weekly Savings	In 2 Years You Have*	In 3 Years You Have*
$5.00	$520.00	$780.00
$7.50	$780.00	$1,170.00
$10.00	$1,040.00	$1,560.00
$12.50	$1,300.00	$1,950.00
$15.00	$1,560.00	$2,340.00
$17.50	$1,820.00	$2,730.00
$20.00	$2,080.00	$3,120.00

* Plus compound interest

Watch Your Savings Grow

diligent and faithful worker, but it will work for one only if one has savings. This fact explains why many rich people have no difficulty in making a living. Although they cease to work, their money continues to work for them by earning interest.

The following table shows the rate at which money accumulates when interest is compounded semiannually. If the interest is compounded quarterly or monthly, the increase is greater.

INTEREST RATE	DOUBLED IN	QUADRUPLED IN	MULTIPLIED IN 47 YEARS (AGE 18 TO 65)
2 %	35.00 YEARS	70.00 YEARS	2 1/2 TIMES
2½%	28.00 YEARS	56.14 YEARS	3 1/5 TIMES
3 %	23.28 YEARS	46.58 YEARS	4 1/20 TIMES
3½%	19.98 YEARS	39.96 YEARS	5 1/10 TIMES
4 %	17.50 YEARS	35.00 YEARS	6 2/5 TIMES

If a person eighteen years of age invests one dollar at 4 per cent interest, compounded semiannually, the investment will be worth two dollars when he is thirty-five and a half years old, four dollars when he is fifty-three years old, and six dollars and forty cents when he is sixty-five years old.

The Cumulative Power of Compound Interest

Where to Put Savings. The average individual saves only a few dollars a month. Hence, he needs a place to put his savings month by month, until a sufficient amount accumulates to invest in bonds, stocks, real estate, or for some other form of permanent investment. In deciding upon a place to put savings where they will earn income, the following questions should be considered:

  (a) Will the account be safe?
  (b) Will it pay a reasonable rate of interest?
  (c) Will the savings be available at any time?
  (d) How often is interest compounded?

Of the many institutions where savings will earn interest as they accumulate, banks, savings and loan associations, postal savings, United States Savings Bonds, and credit unions are most commonly used.

Different kinds of savings institutions are governed by different practices in regard to withdrawals of savings. For example, a commercial bank usually pays the lowest rate of interest, but the assets of the bank are in more liquid form; that is, a higher percentage of cash is available on demand by depositors for withdrawals. Other types of savings institutions, such as savings and loan institutions, invest a higher amount in long-term loans, such as on real estate, and have a smaller percentage available in cash to take care of withdrawals. These institutions therefore pay a higher rate of interest, but they cannot quickly convert loans into cash with which to pay withdrawals. If too many people ask for their money at the same time some of these institutions might temporarily have difficulty in meeting the demand. Under state regulations these institutions have the privilege of postponing payments and making you wait for your money. The regulations are a means of protecting both the institution and you.

Saving Regularly Is What Counts
Ewing Galloway

Commercial Banks. *Commercial banks* are owned and operated by stockholders. Most commercial banks have savings departments and some commercial banks are organized as savings banks. These banks, owned and operated by stockholders, generally pay a fixed rate of interest.

Banks usually are conveniently located, making it easy to deposit savings at the time of cashing a pay check. The interest may be credited quarterly, semiannually, or annually. Some banks require thirty days' notice before withdrawing a deposit. This right is not always exercised, but it may be if necessary. Rates of interest on savings accounts are fairly uniform among banks. The rules and regulations of banks with regard to opening an account, making deposits, crediting interest, and withdrawing savings may influence the selection of a place to deposit savings. The deposits in all national and in many other banks are insured by the Federal Deposit Insurance Corporation to the extent of $10,000 for each depositor. However, some banks not having the insurance may be just as safe as those having it.

Mutual Savings Banks. A *mutual savings bank* is a slightly different type of bank because it is owned by the depositors. The depositors are not promised a fixed rate of interest. If there is a profit, each depositor is paid a dividend instead of interest. But, if there is no profit earned on the operations of the bank, the depositors do not get a dividend. In most other respects, however, a mutual savings bank is operated the same as any other bank.

Mutual savings banks permit you to withdraw your funds on demand or after giving notice. The laws of most states require notice of thirty to ninety days, but usually withdrawals may be made instantly on demand. In times of economic stress the state laws place additional restrictions on withdrawals. Mutual banks do not ordinarily accept checking accounts, but in a few states they do.

The accounts in most mutual savings banks are insured by the Federal Deposit Insurance Corporation up to the amount of $10,000 and in a few states all deposits are insured under the state banking laws.

Savings and Loan Associations. Savings and loan associations serve essentially the same purpose as savings banks, and many of them operate in much the same way. Although such associations have relatively uniform procedures, each is regulated by the laws of the state in which it is located. There is considerable difference in the laws of the various states.

The savings and loan association is organized for the purpose of lending money to people who do not have enough money to buy or build a home. The money that the association lends is accumulated from depositors. In many states, when a person makes deposits in a savings and loan association, he really buys shares and becomes theoretically a part owner. These shares usually earn a fixed rate of income, which generally is a slightly higher rate than interest on a savings account in a bank.

All federal savings and loan associations are members of the Federal Home Loan Bank and operate under regulations established by the Federal Government. The accounts of these associations are insured with the Federal Savings and Loan Insurance Corporation. All other savings and loan associations may have their accounts insured with the Federal Savings and Loan Insurance Corporation if they are members of the Federal Home Loan Bank and if they pass rigid insurability tests. The Federal Savings and Loan Insurance Corporation may also insure the accounts of homestead associations, and of cooperative banks organized and operated according to the laws of the state, district, or territory in which they were chartered or organized.

Under normal conditions withdrawals may be made from savings and loan associations on demand. However, under most state laws the institution is allowed thirty days in which to fill a request or a withdrawal. In times of economic stress state laws impose additional restrictions on withdrawals for the protection of the institution and the depositor.

Postal Savings. Many people who do not have ready access to a bank or who do not have faith in their local bank buy postal savings certificates at the local post office. The

United States Postal Savings System was established in 1910 and has served many depositors, especially those having small amounts to invest.

A person desiring to open a postal-savings account should apply at the nearest post office or station. Any person ten years of age or over is eligible under this plan. No person may have more than one account, and all accounts must be of a personal nature.

Deposits are acknowledged by postal-savings certificates in denominations of $1, $2, $5, $10, $20, $50, $100, $200, or $500, which are made out in the names of the depositors. These serve as receipts and are valid until paid. The certificates are not negotiable or transferable. If a certificate is lost, stolen, or destroyed, a new certificate will be issued. No depositor may have an account in excess of $2,500, exclusive of accumulated interest.

Interest accumulates at the rate of 2 per cent for each full year that a certificate is outstanding. It accumulates for a partial year at the rate of one-half per cent for each full quarter. Interest is not compounded, but a depositor may withdraw it and use it for making a new deposit. Therefore, it is advisable to withdraw interest when it has been earned.

A depositor at any time may withdraw all or any part of his postal savings by presenting a certificate for redemption. Withdrawals may be made in person, through a representative, or by mail.

United States Savings Bonds. United States Post Offices sell United States Savings Stamps and United States Savings Bonds. Banks and some savings and loan associations sell United States Savings Bonds without any charge or commission for this service. Several types of government bonds may be purchased by investors; however, the most popular among people who are saving small amounts regularly are the Series E Bonds. These bonds are available at the prices indicated in the following table and are payable in ten years at the prices indicated in the right-hand column.

	REDEMPTION
COST	VALUE
$ 18.75 increases in 9⅔ years to	$ 25.00
$ 37.50 increases in 9⅔ years to	$ 50.00
$ 75.00 increases in 9⅔ years to	$ 100.00
$150.00 increases in 9⅔ years to	$ 200.00
$375.00 increases in 9⅔ years to	$ 500.00
$750.00 increases in 9⅔ years to	$1,000.00

Any person may purchase up to, but not more than, $10,000 worth (maturity value) of bonds issued during any calendar year. In each subsequent year, however, additional bonds not exceeding the same maximum value may be purchased. Other series may be purchased in larger quantities.

The individual owner of bonds may name only one beneficiary, to whom payment will be made upon the death of the owner. A co-owner may also be named so that either or both may cash the bond.

If a savings bond is lost, stolen, or destroyed, a duplicate will be issued upon satisfactory proof. The Treasury

Table of Redemption Values of United States Savings Bonds, Series E

PERIOD AFTER ISSUE DATE	ISSUE PRICE			
	$18.75	$37.50	$75.00	$375.00
First ½ year	$18.75	$37.50	$ 75.00	$375.00
½ to 1 year	18.85	37.70	75.40	377.00
1 to 1½ years	19.05	38.10	76.20	381.00
1½ to 2 years	19.30	38.60	77.20	386.00
2 to 2½ years	19.55	39.10	78.20	391.00
2½ to 3 years	19.80	39.60	79.20	396.00
3 to 3½ years	20.05	40.10	80.20	401.00
3½ to 4 years	20.30	40.60	81.20	406.00
4 to 4½ years	20.55	41.10	82.20	411.00
4½ to 5 years	20.90	41.80	83.60	418.00
5 to 5½ years	21.25	42.50	85.00	425.00
5½ to 6 years	21.60	43.90	86.40	432.00
6 to 6½ years	21.95	44.60	87.80	439.00
6½ to 7 years	22.30	43.20	89.20	446.00
7 to 7½ years	22.65	45.30	90.60	453.00
7½ to 8 years	23.00	46.00	92.00	460.00
8 to 8½ years	23.40	46.80	93.60	468.00
8½ to 9 years	23.80	47.60	95.20	476.00
9 to 9½ years	24.20	48.40	96.80	484.00
9½ to 9⅔ years	24.60	49.20	98.40	492.00
Maturity value	$25.00	$50.00	$100.00	$500.00

Department, through the Federal Reserve Banks, provides means of safekeeping that are available without charge. To take advantage of this service, one should apply in person at the nearest Federal Reserve Bank or branch bank, or write and obtain an application blank. The owner of the bond must sign the application. If there is a co-owner, both of the owners must sign. The bond with the application should then be presented personally or by mail to the Federal Reserve Bank. A receipt is then issued.

While the rate of interest earned on United States savings bonds is not high, it is reasonable in comparison with the rate of earnings on some other savings. If a bond is held until maturity, it has an equivalent yield of 3 per cent interest, compounded semiannually.

Credit Unions. Credit unions are cooperative associations operating both as savings and lending institutions for the benefit of members. In most states credit unions have operated and are authorized to operate under state laws. With the passage of the Federal Credit Union Act, approved on June 26, 1934, Federal credit unions may be organized and operated under a Federal charter issued by the Farm Credit Administration.

Credit unions are usually formed by large groups of people with common interests. For instance, they may be formed by such groups as teachers in a large school system, workers in a large factory, store employees, and a church.

While the credit unions established under the laws of the various states are by no means uniform, there is uniformity in the organization of Federal credit unions. A member of a Federal credit union must agree to subscribe for at least one five-dollar share, payable in one sum of cash or in periodic installments. He may subscribe for a larger number of shares if he desires. He must also pay an entrance fee of 25 cents.

When a member has paid for one share, he is eligible to his proportionate share of the annual dividends that may be declared by the members. These dividends represent interest earned on the money deposited with the credit union and loaned to others.

> **Summary of a Savings Program**
>
> 1. Choices must be made between immediate spending or saving for later substantial spending.
> 2. A budget is desirable in any saving program.
> 3. Goals for saving should be established.
> 4. There are several safe places in which to put savings where interest will be earned.
> 5. Savings of a small amount each week are worthwhile and will grow at compound interest.

TEXTBOOK QUESTIONS

1. Name the four guides for personal and family saving.
2. Name at least three important goals of saving.
3. How does the possibility of a change in the purchasing power of the dollar affect savings plans for retirement?
4. If one is fully covered by social security, is saving for retirement necessary?
5. Give an example of how one must evaluate his expenditures in order to carry out a savings program successfully.
6. What kinds of items should be paid for in cash instead of going into debt to acquire them?
7. From the table given on page 441, find out (a) how long it takes to double your money at 2 per cent compound interest, (b) how long it takes to double your money at 3 per cent compound interest.
8. What facts should be considered in selecting a place to open a savings account?
9. What kind of savings institution often has the privilege of requiring you to wait to withdraw your money?
10. What are the two main types of banks in which savings may be placed and how do they differ?
11. Is a savings and loan association a bank?
12. What is the Federal Savings and Loan Insurance Corporation?
13. What is the interest rate on postal savings?
14. How may deposits be withdrawn from the Federal Postal Savings System?
15. What is the redemption value of a $25 (issue price $18.75) United States savings bond at the end of one and a half years? at the end of eight years?
16. Give examples of groups of persons who may organize credit unions.

DISCUSSION QUESTIONS

1. If a person has built up a reserve cash fund, what are some of the ways in which he can utilize this fund? (Do not include the ways mentioned in this chapter.)
2. Discuss this statement: "What is the use of saving? I always have to spend my savings for emergencies."
3. Why is it necessary to correlate budgeting, saving, and buying a home?
4. Suppose a young man finds that he is able to save $50.00 a month. After ten months he has accumulated $500 and decides to use this amount as a down payment on an automobile. It will cost him $50.00 a month to complete paying for the automobile. Is he justified in buying it?
5. Some people borrow money and also buy on account and on the installment plan in order to have furniture and luxuries comparable to those of people with larger incomes. What advice would you give to a person of this kind?
6. A particular loan company is liberal in lending on mortgages and offers a high rate of interest to depositors. If you were seeking a place to accumulate savings, would you select this loan company or one that is conservative in making loans and offers a rate of interest that is ½ per cent less.

PROBLEMS

Note: For Problems 1 and 2 use the following table, which shows the value of monthly deposits of one dollar at interest rates of 2, 3, and 4 per cent, compounded semiannually.

END OF YEAR	2%	3%	4%
1	$ 12.13	$ 12.20	$ 12.26
2	24.51	24.76	25.02
3	37.13	37.70	38.29
4	50.01	51.04	52.10
5	63.14	64.78	66.46
6	76.54	78.93	81.41
7	90.21	93.51	96.96
8	104.26	108.54	113.14
9	118.49	124.01	129.97
10	133.00	139.96	147.49
11	147.80	156.38	165.70
12	162.90	173.30	184.66
13	178.30	190.74	204.38
14	194.02	208.70	224.90
15	210.05	227.20	246.25

1. A person deposits $20 in a savings account at the beginning of each month. The interest rate is 3 per cent, compounded semiannually. How much will be in the savings account at the end of thirteen years?

2. If $5 a month is deposited in a savings account on which 3 per cent interest is compounded semiannually, how much will be available (a) in five years? (b) in ten years?
3. Using the table on page 441 showing the cumulative power of compound interest, assume that you have $1,000 to invest at 18 years of age at 3 per cent interest, compounded semiannually. How much will this amount to at age 65?
4. Assume that one U. S. savings bond is purchased for $18.75 at the end of each month for nine and one half years. Using the table of redemption values in this chapter, what will be the value of all the bonds at the end of ten years?
5. A man has an average balance of $400 in his checking account. The minimum amount that he may keep in the account without having to pay a service fee is $100. He draws no interest on the balance in his checking account. Assume that he places the surplus $300 in a savings account. Calculate the amount of interest that he will earn in ten years if interest is paid at the rate of 3 per cent and is compounded semiannually.

COMMUNITY PROBLEMS AND PROJECTS

1. Make a study of your local savings institutions, such as banks, saving and loan associations, United States Postal Savings, and credit unions. Make a detailed analysis of procedures for depositing and withdrawing and in such cases as the savings and loan associations, find out whether you become a purchaser of shares or whether you are a depositor as in a bank.
2. Make a study of local interest rates on savings accounts of all kinds. Write a report on your findings and indicate why you think the rates may change from time to time and why, at present, they may not be the same in all institutions.
3. Make a study of the cost of attending some particular college or several colleges. From the college or colleges obtain information with regard to tuition, laboratory fees, room rents, and cost of meals and laundry. Add to these amounts the cost of clothing, amusement, transportation, and any other items that you believe should be included in the cost of a college education. Make an estimate of the total cost for each of the four years of a college education. Prepare a report showing how you believe it will be possible to finance this education through (a) income from parents or relatives, (b) loans, (c) scholarships, (d) personal savings, (e) earnings made while you are in school.

Chapter 26

Principles of Investing Your Savings

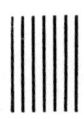

Purpose of the Chapter. A planned system of investing should follow a planned system of saving. There are many ways in which investments can be made. From the point of view of most investors the two main objectives of investing are the safety of the investment and the certainty of the income. Some of the principles of selecting investments are discussed in this chapter.

You will find answers to these questions:
1. What is the difference between investing and speculating?
2. When is a family ready to invest money?
3. What are the four important points in selecting investments?
4. What are sources of investment information?
5. What are some schemes used in selling investments?

Differences in Investing, Speculating, and Gambling. *Investing* is buying assets, such as securities, with the expectation of receiving a certain, though maybe small, income over a long period of time. *Speculating* is buying securities or other assets with the hope that the value of those securities or assets will increase in a relatively short period of time. *Gambling* is taking an unnecessary risk of losing the money paid for a lottery ticket or for a chance of extraordinary, unearned gain.

In all three cases there are risks, but the risks increase as the possibilities of large gains or losses increase. Investment and speculation both serve worthy economic functions.

451

[Part 7

For Most Families Investment Should Wait Until a Home Has Been Purchased

Harold M. Lambert

When Is a Family Ready to Invest? Ordinarily, a person or a family should not make investments in securities, such as stocks and bonds (except Government Savings Bonds), or in real estate (other than a home) until after an emergency savings fund has been established, a reasonable amount of life insurance has been planned, and a home has been secured. However, a person having a few hundred dollars to invest may be wise if he invests it in a small business that he expects to operate and manage.

Important Points in Selecting Investments. Speculations are often disguised as sound investments. Because of this fact, the prospective investor should rely on someone who is capable of giving sound advice. The banker in a small town may or may not be able to do so, although any banker is usually more capable than the average investor. Large banks have experts qualified to analyze securities and to give advice. Brokerage businesses have similar experts. The opinions of bankers and brokers are, however, sometimes biased by personal interest. Taking these facts into consideration, the prospective investor should investigate the following points with regard to a security:

(a) Suitability of the investment.
(b) Safety of the principal.
(c) Satisfactory and certain income from the investment.
(d) Marketability of the security.

Suitability of the Investment. A bond, a stock, a note, or a mortgage may prove to be safe as an investment, but it may not fit into the investment program of a particular person. The suitability of a certain investment is therefore important. The following are important considerations in determining the suitability:

(a) *Acceptable amount.* Bonds are usually available in denominations of one hundred, five hundred, or one thousand dollars, although the market value may vary. Sometimes a thousand-dollar bond can be purchased for five hundred dollars or less. When a bond sells far below its stated value, there is a cause for the loss in value that should be carefully investigated before buying.

Stocks may have stated values from one dollar to one hundred dollars, although the market value may be widely different from the stated value. Stocks with no stated value also have a wide price range.

The number of units of a bond or a stock to be purchased will be regulated by the amount that can be invested.

(b) *Variety of the investment.* There is an old saying, "Don't put all your eggs in one basket." There is, on the other hand, a contradictory saying, "Put all your eggs in one basket and watch the basket."

The first rule is probably the better one for the average investor. It means that he should distribute (by a variety of securities) his investment. By distributing his investment, he distributes his risks. If a person puts all his money into one type of security and that security decreases in value or becomes totally worthless, the loss will probably be severe. On the other hand, if a person invests his money in ten different securities and only one of them decreases in value or becomes worthless, the loss is not so severe.

Diversify Your Investments. Don't Put All Your Eggs in One Basket

Each security should be selected carefully. It is better to confine the investment to a few good securities than to purchase several questionable securities. Some brokers have a monthly purchase plan whereby a small amount may be invested monthly in selected securities.

(c) *Period of the investment.* An investment in a bond, a mortgage, or a note continues a definite period of time before the obligation matures. For instance, a bond may mature in six months or in forty to one hundred years. If a person wants to make an investment for a long period of time without the trouble of reinvesting, he should consider the date of maturity.

(d) *Value of the security as collateral.* Frequently an investor may want to use a security as collateral in obtaining a loan. If the need for obtaining a loan is a possibility, he should buy a security that will be acceptable to a bank as collateral. Securities that do not have a ready market are not desirable as collateral.

(e) *Income periods.* Bonds have definite dates on which interest is payable. The interest may be calculated quarterly, semiannually, or annually, and the specific dates of payment are set. Stocks may have quarterly, semiannual, or annual dividend dates. The person who has a diversified investment program may want to buy securities that have interest and dividend dates that fit into the complete investment program and assure a relatively steady income.

Bonds in some cases are callable before maturity. In such a case the corporation or other institution that issued the bonds may call them in and pay the owners at a specified rate. If a person wishes to invest his money in bonds for a definite length of time without the bother of reinvesting, he will want to determine whether the bonds are callable. A good income-producing bond may soon be called in unexpectedly.

Safety of the Principal. Any good investment involves the protection of the principal. If there is any question about the safety of the principal, the investment should not be made. The following are some tests of the safety of the principal of corporation securities:

Ch. 26]   PRINCIPLES OF INVESTING YOUR SAVINGS   455

(a) *Ability of the management of the corporation issuing the security.* Competent management is indispensable to the success of any business. Before purchasing a stock or a bond, the investor should make certain that those who manage the business have ability. Ability should have been demonstrated through successful previous operations, through the standing of the enterprise, and through the personal records of the managers.

(b) *Reliability of the managers of the corporation and of the investment promoters.* The integrity of the managers of the business and the promoters of the sale of the security should be investigated thoroughly. No one should buy a security issued by an unknown company. The statement of an unknown person should not be accepted without investigating through a person of known integrity and ability.

(c) *Past performance of the corporation.* The past performance of the business should be measured by the assets and the earning record. The outstanding bonds and the outstanding stock should have a very conservative relation to the assets. Any well-established company with securities listed on the open market can be investigated through the stock exchanges and banks, or through such listings of securities as those given in *Poor's Manuals* and *Moody's Manuals*. From these same sources information can be obtained with regard to the earning performance of the corporation.

(d) *The future earning position of the corporation.* Some investments in once well-established companies have been lost because of technical developments, changes in consumer buying habits, or loss of markets. Although there is no way of judging the future earnings of a given company except by the past performance of the company, consideration must be given to whatever will likely affect the future of the company.

Comparisons should be made between different companies. If a company has found it difficult to pay operating costs and interest on indebtedness and still have a comfortable margin for dividends, it is not advisable to purchase a bond or a stock of this company. At least there is no reason to believe that the investment is conservative.

As was explained in Chapter 7, the Federal Government, through the Securities and Exchange Commission, regulates the sale of securities through registered security exchanges. A good policy for any investor is to buy only a security that is registered and approved in his own state, and registered and approved by the Securities and Exchange Commission. If one is buying a security through an exchange, the safest practice is to purchase through an exchange registered by the Securities and Exchange Commission.

The safety of the principal is also involved in any other kind of investment, such as in a government bond or in real estate. Your investment in a government bond is as safe as the government itself. Cities, counties, and states have credit and financial ratings just the same as businesses.

There are three main factors to be considered as to the safety of the principal when one invests in real estate. First is the question of whether you get a good and legal title to the property, second is the question of location, and third is the question of economic conditions. Checking on the title involves legal assistance, and in checking on the location one should make sure that it is in a location that will not decrease in value. For instance, some residential neighborhoods are going down in value gradually while others are increasing in value principally because of the location. Economic conditions affect the value of real estate just as they affect the value of all other investments. These factors will be discussed in more detail in later chapters.

Satisfactory Income from the Investment. The safety of the principal is more important than a satisfactory income. If the principal is lost, there will be no income. The following are considerations with regard to the income:

(a) *Rate of return.* It should be remembered that a sound investment does not have a yield that is higher than the average rate of interest used to attract investors. A conservative rate of interest on a good bond will be determined by the conditions that exist at the time the bond is offered for sale. A high-grade bond sometimes pays no more than 2 or 3 per cent interest on the face value. If the bond sells below its face value, it may, however, pay a higher rate on the basis of its actual selling price. When the rate of return offered on a bond is $\frac{1}{2}$ per cent to 2 per cent above the rate of interest on high-grade government bonds, special care should be taken in investigating the quality of the security. If some of the tests of quality cannot be met by the bond, the reason for this failure should be determined.

(b) *Guaranteed rate of return.* A bond assures a definite rate of interest. If the company fails to pay the interest, the bondholder has a legal right of action to obtain the property (or income, in the case of debenture bonds) that has been pledged by the issuer of the bonds. Preferred stock also carries a stipulated rate of dividend and has preference in the distribution of earnings to stockholders. The earnings on common stock are regulated in many ways. A corporation is not obligated to pay any established rate of dividend on such stock. There may be two or three grades of common stock, one of which has preference with regard to sharing in the profits of the company.

(c) *Regularity of the income.* Most investors are interested in having a steady and reliable income. The continuous payment of interest or dividends is therefore one of the first considerations in evaluating a security. The prospects of future income from the security can be judged on the basis of the records of past earnings of the company. In most cases it is very simple to determine whether a company has paid its interest and dividends regularly in the past. Unless the prospects of future income can be judged, the purchase of the security on the basis of the return is largely a speculation.

(d) *Margin of safety.* A good corporation for investment purposes should earn considerably more money than is paid out as bond interest and stock dividends. Unless the corporation is regularly earning more than is needed for these purposes, there is not an adequate margin of safety. The margin of earnings regulates not only the safety of the income that is paid to the investor but also the safety of the principal. If past records show that the company has had difficulty in earning enough to pay interest and dividends, it is questionable whether it could pay interest and dividends under any unusual circumstances.

Marketability of the Security. Although an investor, in the true sense of the word, is not interested in buying a security with the thought of selling it immediately, he must give consideration to this possibility.

Guides to the Sound Investment of Savings

1. Your investment program should be built in the following sequence:
   (a) Accumulate several hundred dollars in bank savings accounts and in United States savings bonds for emergency use.
   (b) Buy life insurance for protection and for future income.
   (c) Buy a home as soon as possible.
   (d) If you wish to work for yourself, invest in a business enterprise for profit.
   (e) Buy high-grade stocks and bonds or real estate for income purposes.
2. In selecting investments consider:
   (a) The suitability of the investment as a part of your investment program.
   (b) The safety of the principal.
   (c) The certainty of income from the investment.
   (d) The marketability of the security, that is, the ease with which it can be sold if necessary.
3. Investigate every possible source of information about the security before buying. Be sure to obtain the rating of the corporation in standard manuals. Consult the Securities and Exchange Commission if in doubt.
4. Become acquainted with the protection to investors provided by state and Federal laws.
5. Select the type of investment (real estate, bonds, stocks, investment trust shares, or a business) to fit your investment program, considering the date you may need your funds and the amount of time you have available to manage your investments.

There are two main types of markets through which stocks and bonds are easily bought and sold. These are the local stock exchanges in various cities and the national exchanges located in New York City. The two national exchanges are the New York Stock Exchange and the American Stock Exchange. Local stock exchanges in the various cities have connections with the national exchanges.

Brokers deal on stock exchanges. They represent buyers and sellers of securities. Banks will also handle these transactions through a broker. A security which is said to be *listed* on a stock exchange is one on which there are regular quoted prices on either local or national exchanges. It may be listed and traded on both national and local exchanges.

The buying and selling of stocks on a security exchange is by the auction method. A stock may be offered for sale at a certain price or someone may bid for the same stock at a different price. A sale is made when someone buys it at the price offered. These offers and bids are going on regularly so that anyone owning a stock has a pretty good idea of the price at which the stock can be sold.

Some securities are *unlisted*. These are securities that are not listed on stock exchanges but may be bought and sold through individual brokers or may be bought and sold on exchanges without being listed. They are usually stocks in which there are not regular transactions. The market for these stocks is therefore not quite so dependable as it is for listed securities. An unlisted stock may be equally as good as a listed stock, but it is generally not considered so conservative an investment as a listed stock because it is not so easily sold. Unless a security can be disposed of by some satisfactory means, it may have to be sold at a sacrifice in an emergency, or perhaps it cannot be sold at any price. A security that is listed on an organized exchange is usually salable. If there are no buyers who want it, however, it may prove to be an undesirable investment for a person who wants to be able to convert his investment quickly into cash. A security that is not listed on an exchange may be handled by certain exchanges and brokers without being listed.

[Part 7

Listed Securities Are
Regularly Sold Through
Exchanges
Harold M. Lambert

Sources of Information about Investments. The main sources of information for the inexperienced investor are:

Banks
Investment brokers
Newspapers and
  financial journals
State securities com-
  missions
Investment services
Local better business bureau
Local chamber of commerce
Securities and Exchange
  Commission

If one is in doubt about any corporation in which he is considering investing money, he should write to the Federal Securities and Exchange Commission and his state securities commission. From these sources he can determine whether the corporation is properly registered, and he can obtain information in regard to the organization, the capitalization, and the indebtedness.

Bankers and long-established and reputable investment brokers are in a position to give sound advice about the desirability of securities. However, having securities for sale, they may be biased in their judgment.

Many newspapers and journals publish information regarding investments. This information should always be verified by comparing it with that available from other sources. Other investment data are available in weekly and monthly bulletins and periodicals. Some of these services are expensive; others are not.

Methods of Deception Used by Investment Promoters. In spite of the fact that most of our financial transactions are conducted in an ethical and honorable manner, everyone must recognize the fact that some people try

Ch. 26]   PRINCIPLES OF INVESTING YOUR SAVINGS   461

to make their living by defrauding others. Most of the fraudulent promoters prey upon people who desire to "get rich quick." The National Better Business Bureau has issued a bulletin entitled *What an Investor Should Know*. The following paragraphs are quoted from that bulletin:

Beware of "Get Rich Quick" Investment Schemes

"The swindler relies for success upon the universal human desire to make money—as much money as possible, as quickly as possible. The average salesman in order to make a sale has to convince his prospects of two things: first, that they want something and, second, that what he has to offer will satisfy that want. For the swindler, the task is simplified. Everyone wants to make money. The swindler needs only to convince his prospects that his particular proposition will enable them to do so. To accomplish this end, he appeals to their greed, prejudices, and self-esteem. He takes advantage of their lack of investment knowledge. Above all, he tries to prevent them from making an investigation or to discredit what he knows in advance will be the outcome of that investigation.

"Thus, if a hesitant investor suggests that he would like to consult his banker, the swindler will seek to discourage him. 'Don't ask your banker for advice,' the glib-tongued salesman will argue. 'Don't tell him why you're drawing out your money. He'll be sure to tell you not to do it. And why not? He's paying you 2 per cent on your money and investing it to bring him in five times that much. Be smart and put your money in that kind of proposition yourself—the kind I'm offering you.'

"Sometimes the argument works. And suppose the investor does consult the banker and the latter disapproves of the 'investment.' Wasn't that what the salesman predicted? And isn't the banker acting from selfish motives?

"Another favorite trick is to attempt to discredit the banker, better business bureau, or other source of disinterested information by trying to tie it up with the 'interests.' 'The Better Business Bureau is the tool of Wall Street,' the swindler rants. 'The monopolies don't want us to go into production because they know we'll cut into their profits. The big shots tried to buy us out and failed and now they're trying to throw suspicion on us. They want to keep the gravy for themselves. We believe in giving the little fellow a chance.'

"The prospect, being a little fellow himself, is likely to lend a sympathetic ear to this fantastic tale of persecution. He may not know that 'little fellows' or small stockholders own a majority of the stock of most large corporations.

"Under different circumstances, however, the dishonest promoter is far from reticent in claiming endorsement of his proposition by 'big names.' This financier owns 5,000 shares in the company, that prominent industrialist has bought 10,000, he assures his listener. (An examination of the list of corporation stockholders would tell a different story.) Or he will exhibit an imposing list of directors. Frequently such names may have been used without consent. Sometimes prominent men do lend their names thoughtlessly to promotions of dubious merit.

"Unfounded comparisons with successful companies are also part of the sharper's stock in trade. 'Look at Homestake!' he urges. 'A few hundred dollars put in that company originally would be worth millions now. Our mine has even better prospects today.' He fails to state that, for every successful mining company, there have been thousands of failures—all with marvelous 'prospects.'

"Flattery is often an effective weapon in dulling the suspicions of the investor. 'We're limiting this offer to a few important people like you.' 'You're one of the first to have a chance to take advantage of this opportunity. You're right in on the ground floor.' 'This is strictly inside information. I wouldn't take a chance of passing the tip along to everyone.' These timeworn arguments are calculated to make the investor feel important and put him in an amiable frame of mind to part with his money.

"Promises are cheap but effective—promises that a stock will be listed on a stock exchange; promises that a dividend will be declared at an early date; promises to redeem the stock whenever the investor wants to surrender it; promises that are beguiling but fail to materialize. Sometimes the promise is made in the form of a guarantee. But a guarantee is only as strong as the company behind it. Guarantees may be worthless and often are.

"Claims of Government approval are also made with marked success. 'If our offering were not strictly on the level,' the swindler argues, 'the Government would put us out of business. We couldn't use the United States mails unless we were all right.' If this argument were true, there would be no such thing as fraud.

"One point in common to all these arguments which swindlers have used so successfully is that the arguments have practically no bearing on the intrinsic value of the investment offered. The value can be determined only on a basis of facts."

A new development is the sale of uranium mining stocks. There are hundreds of these promotion schemes for the sale of cheap stocks to people who hope to make a large fortune by investing just a few dollars. Most of these are highly speculative and in many instances are a poor gamble.

Summary of Investment Principles

1. Most people should invest, but not speculate or gamble.
2. Most families should buy a home before making other investments.
3. The important choices to consider in selecting investments are:
   a. Suitability of investment
   b. Safety of the principal
   c. Satisfactory and certain income
   d. Marketability
4. Do not listen to tipsters, but consult only reliable sources of investment information.
5. Beware of the typical methods of deception practiced by unscrupulous promoters.

TEXTBOOK QUESTIONS

1. Explain the differences between investing, speculating, and gambling.
2. What elements in the financial plans of a family should come before investing?
3. What are the four points that an investor should consider in regard to any investment?
4. What are the five points that determine whether a security is suitable for a particular investment program?
5. Give the four tests of safety for a corporation security.
6. Name some factors that you should consider as to the safety of your investment in real estate.
7. What are the four factors that help to determine whether an investment will pay a satisfactory income?
8. What is meant by the marketability of a security?
9. What are some of the sources from which the inexperienced investor can obtain information on investments?
10. Give at least two questions that the better business bureau recommends should be asked of persons selling securities.
11. What devices does a swindler use to convince his victims?
12. What does the swindler often tell the victim when the latter desires to obtain advice from his banker?
13. What argument do fraudulent promoters sometimes use against the better business bureau as a source of investment information?
14. What is the fallacy of comparing a new venture with a profitable existing venture of a similar type?
15. What is meant by "being let in on the ground floor"? Why should an investor be cautious when such an assurance is made.

DISCUSSION QUESTIONS

1. If a friend of yours tells you about a stock that is not paying dividends but that he has heard will soon begin to pay dividends, would the buying of this stock be a speculation, an investment, or a gamble?
2. "A bond is an investment; a stock is a speculation." Discuss this statement. Is it true or false?
3. Would you reject a stock because it is not sold actively on a market?
4. Which do you think would pay the higher rate of interest: (a) a good bond with poor marketability, or (b) a good bond with good marketability? Why?
5. A person who is earning 3 per cent interest on a savings account considers buying bonds that pay interest at a net rate of 4 per cent. Discuss the merits and the demerits of this plan.

6. (a) What is your opinion of the securities of mining corporations? (b) Is the average person justified in buying such securities? (c) Who should buy these securities?
7. Why should an investor not consider solicitations made by telephone?
8. Why would it be absurd for you to believe a stranger who, in trying to sell you a certain stock, stated that you were one of the few invited to participate in the investment?
9. Just because stock in a seemingly legitimate oil venture is offered for sale in the producing region, is there assurance that the oil property is valuable?
10. What is your opinion of the so-called "penny" stocks being sold in uranium mining companies?

PROBLEMS

1. A man considers paying $18,000 cash for a house for investment purposes with the idea of renting it. (a) The house is now occupied by a family that is paying $120 a month rent. This amount is considered reasonable compared with the rent on other similar homes. (b) The statistics of real-estate agents show that, on the average, rented houses are vacant one month out of every year. (c) The house will require immediate repairs costing $250 and annual repairs of about $120. The taxes on the property amount to $108 a year; there are no assessments. (d) The loss from depreciation each year is estimated to be $400. (e) The commission of the real-estate agent in buying the house, and the cost of transferring and recording the title, will amount to $150. (1) Calculate the total cost of the house, including both the property and the cost of having the title transferred and recorded. (2) Calculate the total operating costs, the net income, and the percentage of net income based on the original investment. (3) Do you think the purchase of the house would be a good investment?
2. Mr. Stinson has ten shares of each of ten different preferred stocks. The total value amounts to $6,323. He also has ten different bonds valued at a total of $1,116. Ten shares of stock valued at $46 a share become worthless. Mr. Brown has fifty shares of stock in three different corporations, the total value of which is $5,200, and ten bonds, the total value of which is $1,046. Fifty shares of Mr. Brown's stock are the same kind as the ten shares of Mr. Stinson's stock that became worthless. (a) Figure Mr. Stinson's percentage of loss on his total investment. (b) Figure Mr. Brown's percentage of loss on his total investment. (c) Can you draw any conclusions?

3. A stenographer who had saved $1,000 asked her banker what investments he would recommend. He recommended a United States Government bond. She purchased it for $1,045. She obtained $30 a year as interest. (a) What was the rate of yield? (b) Was there any relation between the yield and the chance of loss?

COMMUNITY PROBLEMS AND PROJECTS

1. Investigate from all sources possible in your community the various kinds of promotion and sale of stocks in uranium and gold mines, especially stocks issued in foreign countries, but sold in the United States. What is your opinion of these?
2. Select as an investment some local piece of residential real estate that is offered for sale. (a) Make a study of the total cost of the property, including the costs of purchasing it and the expenses of upkeep and depreciation. (b) Compute the amount of income that can be expected from the property and the percentage of income based on the cost.
3. From a daily newspaper select ten stocks and ten bonds, or follow the instructions of your teacher in selecting the securities. Determine the current market prices and dividend and interest rates. (a) Record the market price quoted Monday through Friday on each stock and on each bond for a period of two months. (b) Average the prices of the stocks and those of the bonds for each day of the period. (c) Draw a graph that shows a comparison of the fluctuation in the average prices of the stocks and of that in the average prices of the bonds. (d) Draw some conclusions with regard to these price fluctuations.
4. Investigate the investment services of a local bank. Write a report describing how this bank can serve you as an investor.

Chapter 27

Information You Need About Investments

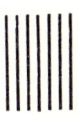

> **Purpose of the Chapter.** In the two previous chapters you have learned about plans for saving and how to determine a satisfactory investment program. This chapter will deal with a detailed description of and an analysis of the different kinds of investment opportunities.
>
> You will find answers to these questions:
> 1. What factors determine the desirability of real estate as an investment?
> 2. What different opportunities exist for investment in a business?
> 3. What are the different kinds and characteristics of securities of corporations?
> 4. What is an investment trust or mutual fund?
> 5. What are the differences between speculative and non-speculative securities?

Government Securities. Most government securities are considered safe and conservative investments whether they are federal, state, county, or local bond issues. The income from some of these is exempted from certain kinds of taxation. Because they are considered safe investments, the rate of interest income is relatively low.

Real Estate. When real estate is purchased as an investment, the following points should be considered carefully after the desirability of the location and the quality of the property have been determined:

(a) Can the property be rented?
(b) At what price can the property be rented?
(c) What will be the annual cost of repairs?
(d) What will be the taxes and assessments?
(e) What will be the yearly loss from depreciation?
(f) During what percentage of time will the property be vacant?
(g) What will be the approximate net earnings?

Real estate is subject to fluctuations in price. The current cost of a piece of property is therefore no indication of the future value. The community may change rapidly with a resulting decrease or increase in the value of the property. Because of a change in business conditions, the value of the property may be raised or lowered.

Unimproved real estate (with no buildings) is usually a speculative investment made in the hope that it can be sold at a profit. A person well acquainted with managing property may find real estate more suitable than any other type of investment; but if one is not in a position to manage real estate with buildings on it, it may not prove to be a desirable investment. Other kinds of investments may be much easier for such a person to manage.

Business Enterprise. People with money are frequently tempted to buy an interest in a partnership, or stock in a small corporation in which a friend is interested, or to lend money to a friend or a relative in business. Such investments should be made with the utmost care.

Investing in a partnership involves complicated legal responsibilities in most states. Even though one of the partners may not be actively engaged in the business, under the laws of many states he is equally responsible with the other partners. For instance, suppose that you become a part owner of a business and allow your partner to operate it. The business fails to make a profit, and the creditors demand payment. If your partner cannot pay, the creditors demand payment from you.

Many people with experience will advocate not investing in the enterprise of a friend or a relative. The friend or

Ch. 27] INFORMATION YOU NEED ABOUT INVESTMENTS 469

the relative usually feels that he has the right to operate the business as he sees fit. He may legally have the right, but sooner or later trouble may arise.

A *close corporation* is one in which the stock is owned usually by a small group of people, and sometimes by only one or two families. Those who own the greater share of the stock are generally the managers. Those who own the minority share of the stock have practically nothing to say with regard to the management, but take what dividends are allotted to them on the basis of their holdings. Those who operate the business may pay themselves large salaries and thus leave very little for distribution as dividends.

The most common type of corporation is an *open corporation*. The stock of this type of corporation is available for public sale. It will be discussed in detail in this chapter.

Mortgage Notes and Mortgage Bonds. The illustration below shows a *mortgage note,* which is a written promise to pay with interest the specified sum that is secured by the specific property described in the mortgage. A mortgage makes it impossible to sell the property on which the mortgage is given without payment of the loan that it secures. In some states mortgage bonds are used instead of mortgage notes.

```
$ 2500 00                    Youngstown, Ohio, March 15  19—
Three years ———— after date for value received, I ————
promise to pay  Jerome A. Burkhart ———————— or order,
the sum of  Twenty-five Hundred ————————— 00 DOLLARS,
                                                      100
with interest thereon at the rate of  6  per cent. per annum, payable semi annually
     This note is secured by a mortgage of even date herewith, executed and delivered by R. M. McDonough
and which is a 1st lien on land situated in  Youngstown  ,  Mahoning  County, Ohio, fully
described in said mortgage. If any installment of interest or principal be not paid when due, or within three days thereafter, or if default be
made in the performance of any of the agreements or conditions of said mortgage, the entire principal shall become immediately due and
payable at the option of the holder hereof.
     Notice of said option is hereby waived.
                                                  R. M. McDonough
Due  Mar. 15, 19 —
No.  1
```

A Mortgage Note

When a person borrows money on real estate, he usually signs (a) a mortgage and (b) a note or series of notes. He gives both the mortgage and the note or notes to the one from whom he is borrowing the money. The *mortgage* is a written contract giving the lender permission to dispose of the property to satisfy the debt in case the debt is not paid.

There are first-mortgage notes, second-mortgage notes, and third-mortgage notes. The first-mortgage note is the most common. The loan that it represents should not exceed 50 or 60 per cent of the appraised value of the property.

A first mortgage has first claim against the assets. The holder of the second mortgage cannot be paid until the claim of the first mortgage is settled. Interest rates are lower on first mortgages because these mortgages have first claim. Interest rates on second and third mortgages are higher because greater risk is involved.

A Corporation Bond Is a Loan; A Stock Represents Part Ownership

Mortgage bonds are usually issued in one of the following three ways:

(a) The mortgage company acquires the mortgage on a particular piece of property, issues a bond, and sells it to an investor.
(b) The mortgage company acquires a large mortgage; issues bonds in denominations of fifty, one hundred, or one thousand dollars; and sells these to investors.
(c) The mortgages on several pieces of property are pooled. One large bond or a number of bonds in smaller denominations are issued against these mortgages and sold to investors.

The value of mortgage bonds is measured by the value of the property behind them and the ability of this property

Ch. 27]   INFORMATION YOU NEED ABOUT INVESTMENTS   471

to provide funds for the payment of the interest and the principal on the due dates.

Stocks. A *share* of stock represents part ownership in a corporation. The two general types of stock are common stocks and preferred stocks. Ordinarily, the *common stock*

A Common-Stock Certificate

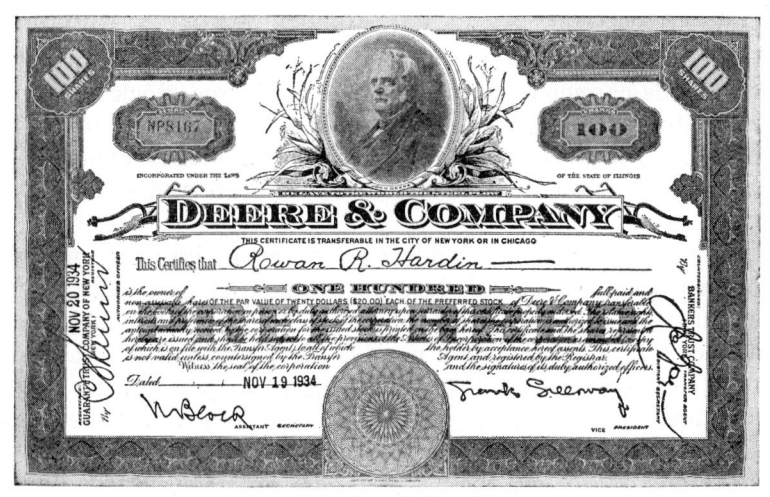

A Preferred-Stock Certificate

entitles the owners to management of the business, whereas the owners of *preferred stock* do not have management control of the business but they have certain preferred claims. The primary difference between the two kinds is that the latter usually is preferred as to dividends; that is, the owner of the preferred stock receives his stipulated share of profits before the common stockholder receives any share. Sometimes the stock is preferred as to assets in case of dissolution of the corporation. In other words, the owner of the stock preferred as to assets would receive the amount of his investment before common stockholders are paid.

There is such a great variety in each class of stock that it is difficult to distinguish between the different grades. The provisions governing a stock should be read carefully to determine one's rights and obligations. For instance, the purchase of a stock may carry with it the right to purchase at a certain price additional stock of a new issue that may be made. This right may or may not be valuable. The holders of one grade of common stock may have voting power, whereas the holders of another grade may not. When there are various grades or classes of a common stock, the public is usually urged to buy the least desirable class. The better classes are often reserved for those who are promoting the sale of the stock.

Dividends and Interest. Under the laws of most states, dividends cannot be paid on either preferred stock or common stock unless all interest has been paid on outstanding bonds. It is also a general rule that dividends cannot be paid on common stock unless those on preferred stock have been paid.

In other words, bondholders have first claim on earnings, before preferred stockholders; preferred stockholders have second claim on earnings, before common stockholders; and common stockholders receive dividends only to the extent that there are sufficient earnings to pay them. They are never promised or guaranteed. In poor years the preferred stockholders are therefore more likely than common stockholders to get their dividends; in good years, how-

Ch. 27]   INFORMATION YOU NEED ABOUT INVESTMENTS   473

ever, common stockholders have the possibility of getting much more than is paid to preferred stockholders.

Cumulative and Noncumulative Preferred Stock. The preferred stock of most companies carries with it a specified dividend rate, but the dividends may be discontinued if the corporate earnings dwindle. There is, however, one type of preferred stock that is issued under the agreement that back dividends will be paid to the holders of the stock at the regular rate if the dividends are ever discontinued temporarily. This type of preferred stock is called *cumulative*. For example, if the dividends on a preferred stock are discontinued for one year, the preferred stockholders will receive those dividends as soon as the company earns enough profits to pay them. These back dividends must be paid before any other dividends are declared.

Preferred stock may also be *noncumulative*. If the stock is noncumulative, the preferred stockholders are not guaranteed their income in case the corporation ceases temporarily to pay dividends. If the corporation does not earn a profit, dividends may not be declared. When profits are earned again, the preferred stockholders begin to receive dividends again, but they do not receive dividends for the time when no profits were earned.

Participating Preferred Stock. Some preferred stocks are classified as *participating*. In the case of such stocks, if excess earnings are still present after the regular dividend on preferred stock and a specified dividend on common stock have been distributed, the preferred stockholders will participate with the common stockholders in the surplus earnings. For example, the regular dividend rate on a preferred stock may be 6 per cent. If the earnings of the company, however, become large enough to pay a dividend at a specified rate on the common stock, in addition to the 6 per cent dividend on the preferred stock, the preferred stockholders will share with the common stockholders in the surplus earnings.

Convertible Preferred Stock. If a preferred stock is *convertible*, it may be converted into or traded for other securities of the same corporation, usually common stock, at a specified price, or one share of preferred stock is convertible into a certain specific number of shares of common stock. For example, the owner of one share of convertible preferred stock might have a stipulated privilege of trading the one share for two shares of common stock under certain conditions or at a certain time. This may have an advantage if the common stock increases in value.

Par-Value and No-Par-Value Stocks. Stocks are also designated as *par-value stocks* or *no-par-value stocks*. Par value means very little to the average investor or even to the expert, for the par value of a stock has no specific relation to the actual value. A stock may bear a par value of one hundred dollars, but may be sold for only sixty-five or seventy-five dollars. The use of a definite par value for a stock was probably intended originally to indicate the worth of the stock, but the practice of assigning par values to stocks has resulted in many abuses. For instance, there have been cases in which promoters have sold stock to unsuspecting investors on the assumption of the latter that the stock was worth approximately the par value assigned to it. Inasmuch as shares of stock represent ownership in a corporation, the stock of one person represents that part of the ownership equal to the percentage that his shares bear to the total number of shares issued. The use of no-par-value stock is intended as a means of avoiding the inference that the stock is worth a certain amount. A no-par-value stock bears no designated value. Its value, like the value of par-value stock, is regulated by what the investing public believes the stock is worth.

The stock of a corporation is either listed or unlisted on a stock market. That which is listed is more easily salable than unlisted stocks.

Bonds. *Bonds* do not represent a share in the ownership of an enterprise; they are evidence of a debt owed by the enterprise. When a business or a government issues bonds, it acknowledges that it owes the holders a certain sum of money and agrees to repay the sum on a certain date and

Ch. 27] INFORMATION YOU NEED ABOUT INVESTMENTS 475

under certain conditions. It also agrees to pay interest at a specified rate and at specified intervals.

A *short-term bond* is frequently referred to as a note and serves the same purpose as a note. A *mortgage bond* usually extends for a relatively long period of time and is essentially the same as a mortgage note. The bond shown below is a *coupon bond*. Anyone who owns a coupon bond can tear off each coupon as it becomes due and present it to his bank

A Coupon Bond

for the collection of interest. A *registered bond* is a bond that is recorded by the issuer in the name of the person to whom it has been sold. The interest on the bond will be paid only to the registered owner. From the point of view of theft, a registered bond is therefore safer than a coupon bond.

When a bond is issued, the issuing corporation usually pledges some security, such as specific property, mortgages on property, or the right to certain earnings. A railroad may pledge some of its equipment or real estate. A municipality or a county may pledge its water system or light system. A *debenture bond* is one for which no security is pledged to guarantee the safety of the principal.

Although certain property or rights are pledged to insure the safety of the principal of a mortgage investment, various difficulties are encountered if the bondholders are forced to take over the property or the rights in case the interest is not paid. It is therefore desirable to investigate bonds from the following points of view:

(a) Record of past earnings of the company and likelihood of future earnings.
(b) Record of past market prices of the bonds.
(c) Competitive and general business conditions.
(d) Marketability of the bonds.

The same general investigation should be carried on in connection with bonds of a governmental unit. The taxes of a governmental unit are comparable to the earnings of a business. The economic conditions within such a unit are comparable to the competitive conditions within an industry. Such factors have a definite effect upon the ability of the issuer of the bonds to pay interest and to repay the principal on the maturity date. State and national legislation also has a definite bearing upon the value of governmental bonds. For instance, state legislation allowing a governmental unit to postpone interest payments on bonds would have the effect of reducing the value of the bonds.

Some bonds are designated as convertible. There are so many possible stipulations in relation to convertible bonds that any particular bond should be investigated and studied carefully. A *convertible bond* is one in which there is a stipulation that permits or forces the bondholder under certain conditions to accept stock in exchange for his bond.

As a general rule, bonds are more stable than stocks because a corporation is required to pay the fixed interest on the bonds as long as it is solvent, that is, as long as it has the money with which to pay the interest.

The amount appearing on the face of a bond is called the *par value.* The interest is based on the par value. If, for various reasons, bonds cannot be sold at their par value, they are sold at less than par value; and the difference between the par value and the selling price is called *discount.* If the bonds are in demand by the investing public, they will be sold at a rate above par value; and the difference between the two values is called *premium.* The selling of bonds below par or above par is not necessarily an indication of their value. The selling of bonds below par may result from (a) unsatisfactory security that has been pledged by the issuer of the bonds, (b) an interest rate that is low in comparison with interest rates on other similar securities, or (c) unfavorable economic conditions that result in a lack of demand for bonds.

Comparisons of Bonds and Stocks. In order to illustrate different types of bonds and stocks, let us consider a corporation with $100,000 of 3 per cent first-mortgage bonds outstanding; $100,000 of 4 per cent debenture bonds; $200,000 of noncumulative 6 per cent preferred stock (2,000 shares at $100 par); and 20,000 shares of common stock. If the corporation makes a profit of $47,000 after $3,000 dollars has been paid to bondholders and after taxes have been paid, the debenture bondholders will get $4,000 in interest, and the preferred stockholders will get $12,000 in dividends, leaving a remainder of $31,000 available for the common stockholders. At the discretion of the board of directors, all or part of the amount available may be declared as a dividend to common stockholders. If a dividend of $1 a share is declared, the common stockholders will get $20,000, leaving $11,000 to be added to the surplus of the corporation.

Let us assume, however, that in another year the corporation makes only $9,000 net profit after paying taxes, but has some money in the bank. The mortgage bondholders are entitled to their interest at 3 per cent, amounting to $3,000. The debenture bondholders have a first claim on whatever earnings there are left. They are therefore paid $4,000, leaving $2,000 to be divided among the preferred stockholders. The common stockholders get nothing.

Investment Companies. There are several types of companies that are organized for the purpose of buying an extensive variety of securities. Stock in an investment company is sold to individual investors. These companies are called *investment companies, investment trusts,* or *mutual funds*. They vary widely as to their method of organization, their management, the type of securities they buy, and the methods by which ownership shares are sold. In all cases however the purpose is to obtain money from investors which is then reinvested in a variety of securities so that the investor in the investment fund owns a share in a distributed list of securities. For example: instead of investing $1,000 in one particular corporation, it is possible for an investor to buy $1,000 worth of shares in an investment company and thereby have an interest in perhaps 100 or more types of securities.

The purpose of an investment company is therefore to provide wide diversification of investment managed by experts, so that an individual who has only a small investment to make and who is not an expert, may have these advantages. However, in selecting an investment company in which to invest funds, it is desirable to study the purposes and organization by consulting a reliable broker. Each investment trust follows certain policies. For example, one may invest its funds principally in conservative securities which do not pay especially high dividends, but another may invest its funds in speculative securities which may have greater opportunity for growth in value.

Some investment companies follow a policy that requires the company to purchase back the shares of stock owned by investors if requested to do so and continue to sell new shares and invest the money. They are called *open-end companies*. Another type of company is called a *closed-end company*. This type of company does not continue to sell new shares and does not agree to buy back shares. In the case of the open-end company there is an assured market, but in the case of the closed-end company, the investor has to take his chance on selling his shares to any investor who might want them.

Installment Purchases of Investments. Many of the investment companies offer plans whereby an individual can invest a certain amount of money weekly or monthly. This is done through a broker or agent. The regular installments are invested in stock of the investment company.

Some brokerage firms also have installment plans for purchasing of securities of individual corporations which are recommended to satisfy the requirements of the individual investor.

Speculative or Nonspeculative Investments. In the previous chapter there was a discussion of the safety of principal and an assured income. These were given as two characteristics of a conservative investment. A speculative investment is one which is purchased with the hope and the assumption that there will be growth in value of the securities. For example, one might, after study, invest in a stock at a low price which has not been paying a very good dividend in the hope that the company will become successful and will begin to pay larger dividends. If this happens, the security will probably increase in price on the stock exchange.

	GROWTH	INCOME	SAFETY
Preferred Stock	steady	steady	good
Common Stock	best	variable	least
Bonds	generally none	very steady	best

Generally, government bonds of various types are considered among the most conservative investments. Therefore, let us look at corporation securities in order to determine their aspects in regard to income safety, growth, and income. Their relative merits are indicated in a general way in the following table.

There are some exceptions to the information given above. For example, convertible bonds and convertible preferred stock may produce a good steady income and are reasonably safe. The investor also has the opportunity of converting these into common stock if the company makes good profits. Some of the very high grade common stocks and convertible preferred stocks also grow in value. It can be seen from this discussion that one needs expert advice or needs to be well informed when he invests his money.

Summary of Investment Information

1. A real estate investment is not suitable for all persons.
2. Mortgage notes, bonds, and various kinds of stocks represent the various securities of a corporation available for investment purposes.
3. Government bonds are a conservative type of investment.
4. Investment companies will provide distribution of investment and expert analysis.
5. Speculative securities are primarily for the persons who can afford to take a chance on the growth in value of securities.

TEXTBOOK QUESTIONS

1. How are government securities classified as to safety and income rates?
2. When real estate is to be purchased as an investment, what are some of the factors that should be investigated in determining its desirability?
3. Why should a person not buy real estate as an investment unless he has the time and the energy to take care of it?
4. Why do some people advise against investing in an enterprise managed by a friend?
5. What is a close corporation?
6. Why is it sometimes inadvisable to buy stock in a close corporation?
7. Express briefly the difference between a mortgage note and a mortgage bond.

Ch. 27] INFORMATION YOU NEED ABOUT INVESTMENTS   481

8. In what ways are mortgage bonds usually issued?
9. What are the two general types of stocks?
10. Do all stocks have the same voting power?
11. Distinguish between cumulative stock and noncumulative stock.
12. What is meant by participating stock? To what general type of stock does the term apply?
13. What is an investment company, investment trust, or mutual fund, and how does it operate?
14. In what ways does a bond differ from a stock?
15. (a) If a $100 bond is selling for $90, is it selling at a premium or a discount? (b) What are some of the reasons why bonds sell below their par value?
16. Distinguish between an open-end investment trust and a closed-end investment trust.
17. What does one hope to gain by purchasing a speculative stock?

DISCUSSION QUESTIONS

1. Discuss the merits of real estate as an investment for an elderly woman.
2. You have an opportunity to invest some money with two other men in a partnership in a neighboring town. You expect to continue your work and to allow the other two persons to operate the business. Discuss the disadvantages of this plan.
3. In some states it has been difficult, if not impossible, during financial depressions, for mortgage holders to foreclose on the property pledged as security for the payment of the interest and of the principal due them. How do you think such a condition affects (a) the mortgage holder; (b) the future market for mortgages; and (c) the interest rates?
4. Quite often corporations split their stock. For example, each stockholder will be given two new shares for one old share. Under this plan is there any change in ownership? Why do you think prices sometimes rise after a stock split. (For example, one share may be selling for $100 and if two new shares are traded for one old share, the value would be assumed to be $50 each but the market price might quickly rise to $51 or $52 each.)
5. Some people believe that, if a person is going to buy stock, he should buy common stock instead of preferred stock. Why do you think that they are of this opinion?
6. Assume that you are contemplating buying some common stock in either of two outstanding corporations of approximately equal size. Both corporations have good reputations and good records of past earnings. They have issued approximately the same number of shares of stock. One has

cumulative preferred stock and one grade of common stock; the other has noncumulative preferred stock and one grade of common stock. From your point of view, which common stock would be more desirable? Why?
7. What kind of preferred stock combines some of the features of a preferred stock and a common stock?
8. Can you explain why shares in investment trusts are placed ahead of or given preference as an investment over mortgages, preferred stocks, common stocks, and improved real estate?

PROBLEMS

1. There is more involved in bonds and stocks as investments than it is possible to describe in this chapter. From a library or some other source, obtain a book on investments that discusses bonds and stocks. Write a report of at least 500 words in which you present additional information about stocks and bonds that is not included in this chapter.
2. Obtain from a library, or some other source, one of the important financial services that provides investment information. Write a report of at least 500 words describing the kinds of information available, and include in your report some specific information quoted from the financial service pertaining to a particular corporation.
3. From a library obtain copies of the reports from one of the investment services and write a report of at least 500 words in regard to municipal bonds, including some specific information about a particular municipal bond issue.
4. Examine a bond, a mortgage, or a stock. Read carefully all of the information and report the essentials, such as the obligations, interest rates, or dividends, etc.

COMMUNITY PROBLEMS AND PROJECTS

1. From a local newspaper, your local banker, or a financial journal, obtain the price quoted (at the close of the previous day) on some stock specified by your teacher. (a) Determine the rate of the latest dividend. (b) Calculate the cost of buying one hundred shares. (c) Using the rate of the latest dividend, compute the rate of net income on the basis of the cost.
2. Visit a stock exchange or the office of a stock broker and study the procedures of buying and selling stocks and write a report on the results of your investigation.
3. Investigate at least one investment company, investment trust, or mutual fund. Find out how it is organized, the policies of investment, and its history as to dividends.

Chapter 28

How Insurance Protects You

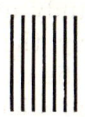

Purpose of the Chapter. There are many risks which will make family plans quite uncertain. The proper insurance will make it possible for a family to plan with certainty and without the fear of loss. The purpose of this chapter is to provide an introduction to the study of all types of insurance and to show how insurance companies operate.

You will find answers to these questions:
1. What are the underlying principles on which insurance rates are established?
2. How are insurance companies organized and operated?
3. How are insurance companies regulated?
4. What is meant by extended coverage of a fire insurance policy?
5. What are the main features of the various kinds of automobile insurance?
6. What are the features of health and accident insurance?
7. Can you insure property belonging to someone else?

The Nature of Insurance. Whenever one person transfers to another the risk of loss due to fire, theft, death, injury, or damage of any kind, he is insuring himself against loss. The major risk-bearing agency in modern society is the insurance company. An insurance company can bear the risks that individuals cannot afford to bear because it spreads the losses of a few persons over the entire group insured.

An insurance company can estimate in advance the probable losses it must bear by applying the law of averages, also called the law or theory of probability. Strange as it may seem, a large number of uncertainties may be combined to form certainties that can be predicted with reasonable accuracy. The death expectancy of individuals is a good example. For many years insurance companies have compiled statistics regarding the number of deaths of individuals. From a study of these figures it is possible to determine very nearly the exact number of people in a given group who will die each year. The insurance companies, of course, cannot predict who will die, but they can estimate with reasonable accuracy how many will die. It is on the basis of these figures that life insurance rates are calculated.

It may seem strange at first that a fire insurance company, for instance, can assume the risk of paying all losses and yet charge each policyholder only a small fee. Frequently the total yearly fee is as low as one tenth of 1 per cent of the possible loss. The reason why insurance companies can follow this practice is that they know from the theory of probability what losses can be expected. They can therefore keep in a reserve fund a sufficient amount to pay each loss as it occurs. It is true that unusual circumstances, such as an exceptionally large fire, may cause unforeseen losses; but, over a long period of time, losses are predictable. The surplus fund that an insurance company keeps is used as a protection against unusual losses.

Here is an example of how insurance companies can help individuals to protect themselves from losses that they cannot afford. Let us assume that the Midland Insurance Company carries fire insurance on 100,000 homes; each home owner pays an average of $25 a year for insurance. The company would collect $2,500,000 from the owners of the property with which to pay its operating expenses and losses due to fires. The rates charged are based on past experiences so that the insurance company should take in enough money to pay losses when they occur. The insurance company takes a calculated risk; while each property owner pays a certain amount each year so that if his home is burned, he will be paid for his loss by the insurance company. Most property owners can afford to pay $25 a year, but they cannot afford a $5,000 fire loss. In a sense, therefore, the 100,000 home owners are pooling or sharing their risks, and the insurance company is the agent that handles the financial matters.

Some Important Insurance Terms. An insurance agreement is a form of contract. An insurance contract is called a *policy*. The person who buys an insurance policy pays periodically what is called a *premium*. He is known as the *policyholder, insured,* or *assured*. The party from whom he buys the insurance and who agrees to make good the loss is called the *insurer* or *underwriter*. The possibility of a loss is called a *risk*, and the maximum amount that is to be paid in case of a loss is called the *face value*. The person to whom the proceeds of an insurance policy are payable in case of loss is called a *beneficiary*. If there is no beneficiary of a life insurance policy, the money becomes a part of a fund called an *estate* (composed of the dead person's property) which is disposed of according to law or according to the provisions of a will left by the insured.

How Insurance Companies Operate. Premiums are paid weekly, monthly, quarterly, semiannually, or yearly, the time of payment depending upon the kind of insurance, the type of policy, and the nature of the company. The funds collected from policyholders are used by the companies in somewhat the same manner as cash deposits are used by banks. In other words, insurance companies use the funds paid by policyholders in making investments that will earn an income. The insurance companies must, of course, keep a reasonable amount of cash available to pay the claims of policyholders in case of fire, accident, death, ill health, or other similar happenings.

There are two general types of insurance companies. One is known as the *stock company*; and the other, as the *mutual company*. The stock company is a corporation that is formed according to the laws of the particular state. The stockholders own the company and elect directors, who in turn hire executives to run the business. The stockholders are, however, not necessarily policyholders. An insurance company of this type obtains money from the sale of stock to stockholders, as well as from the collection of premiums from policyholders and income earned in investments. The profits of the company are paid to the stockholders, who are the owners of the business.

A mutual company must also be organized under the laws of the particular state. The policyholders in such a company are, however, the owners. Each person or business concern that is insured in a mutual company becomes a member of the company and is entitled to a share in the

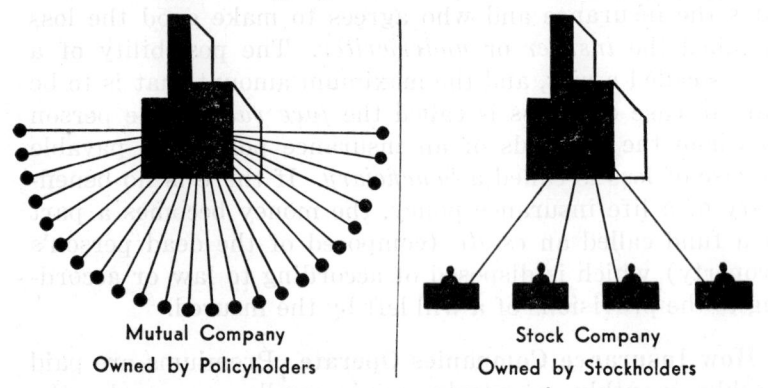

Mutual Company
Owned by Policyholders

Stock Company
Owned by Stockholders

ownership, the control, and the earnings. There are no stockholders as in a stock company.

Insurance policies are either *participating* or *nonparticipating policies*. The premium charged for a participating policy is higher than that for a nonparticipating policy. But holders of participating policies receive dividends which reduce the cost to the policyholder. Mutual companies sell only participating policies. Stock companies sell nonparticipating policies, and sometimes participating policies as well. The dividends which holders of participating policies receive are the excess of premiums paid over what proved to be needed to furnish the insurance protection.

In case a mutual company has to pay out more money than normally expected, due to epidemics or other unforseeable events, it can reduce dividends to its (participating) policyholders. In a stock company such losses (under nonparticipating policies) would be met by drawing upon stockholders' capital and surplus funds. Mutual companies do not have the right to assess policyholders to cover unexpected losses, although there are various types of assessments or benefit associations (not companies) that sometimes are permitted by charter to do so.

Regulation of Insurance. Insurance is such an important factor in the stability of modern business that all states have found it necessary to place some regulation upon insurance companies.

Each state has a special insurance law and usually designates some official whose duty it is to administer and enforce the law. The most important function of state regulation is to make sure that all insurance companies are able to pay all obligations as they become due.

State regulation also protects insurance buyers from fraud. Most states require reports from insurance companies, as well as inspection of the securities, accounting records, and business methods of the companies. In most states, insurance companies are regulated as to the ways in which they can invest the money collected from policyholders. These investments are usually confined to high-grade bonds of the Federal Government, of states, utilities, and cities, and high-grade real-estate mortgages and mortgage bonds. If an individual followed the example of a good insurance company in investing funds, he would be following an investment policy that is far above the average.

LIFE INSURANCE ASSETS

44.4% SECURITIES OF BUSINESS AND INDUSTRY
30.7% MORTGAGES
UNITED STATES GOVERNMENT SECURITIES 10.7%
2.7% REAL ESTATE
4.2% MISCELLANEOUS
3.7% POLICY LOANS
3.6% ALL OTHER GOV'T. BONDS

Institute of Life Insurance

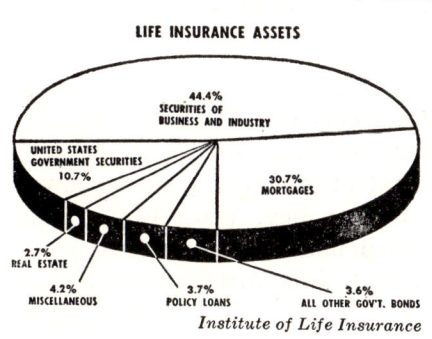

How Insurance Companies Invest Their Dollars

Although special bureaus provide information for establishing fire and casualty rates, the state governments retain the right to regulate these rates.

Life Insurance. There are various uses of life insurance. Besides using life insurance for family protection, a person may have his life insured so that when he dies his debts can be paid.

Because of the great importance of life insurance, it will be covered in detail in Chapters 30 and 31.

Fire Insurance. *Fire insurance* provides funds to replace buildings or materials destroyed by fire. Many business concerns carry fire insurance on buildings, furniture and equipment, machinery, raw materials, and finished goods. Insurance on a building usually does not cover the machinery, stock, and equipment. In buying fire insurance, one should know just what is covered by the policy.

Standard fire insurance policies formerly did not provide protection for an unoccupied or vacant house if the house was vacant for a specified length of time. However, insurance companies have changed their policies so that an insured house is still covered by insurance even though it becomes vacant. The old regulation is still in effect, however on business property. On vacant business property, special arrangements have to be made with the insurance company for fire insurance coverage if the property becomes vacant. Therefore, if one wants coverage on vacant business property, it is necessary to notify the insurance company when the property becomes vacant.

Fire Insurance, Extended Coverage. Extended coverage is also an important feature of many fire insurance contracts. For a small additional premium, a property owner may obtain, with his regular policy, protection against damage from wind storms, tornadoes, lightning, rain, water, smoke, explosion, hail, riots, falling aircraft, or damage from motor vehicles.

How Fire Insurance Operates. A person usually insures his property for a specified amount. For example, Mr. Thompson's property may be valued at five thousand dollars. If there is a garage on the property, the insurance company will require a separate valuation for the house and the garage. Suppose the lot is valued at one thousand dollars; the house, at thirty-eight hundred dollars; and the garage, at two hundred dollars. Mr. Thompson decides

Harold M. Lambert

"Extended Coverage" on Fire Insurance Provides Protection from Windstorm Damage

to insure his house for thirty-eight hundred dollars and his garage for two hundred dollars. If the house is burned completely, he can collect the maximum amount of his policy, which is thirty-eight hundred dollars, if the face of the policy is not more than the value of the house. If it is not burned completely, the insurance company has the privilege of replacing it as nearly as possible in its original condition. Suppose, however, he insures his house for only two thousand dollars. If it is completely destroyed, he can collect only two thousand dollars.

Proof of Fire Loss. A person who carries any kind of insurance should protect his policy carefully, for it is the first evidence of claim in case of loss. If possible, insurance policies should be kept in one place and a record of them in another place so they both could not be destroyed by the same fire. If they are stolen, destroyed, or lost, they can be replaced by requesting the company to furnish duplicate policies. Even if a policy cannot be presented, however, as evidence of claim in case of loss, the claim will be paid after sufficient identification has been made.

When property is insured against fire or theft, it is extremely important to keep a record of the property that is insured. In case of loss the insurance company will require some kind of evidence to serve as the basis for paying the loss. The insurance company will frequently accept a sworn statement as to the loss. The safest practice, however, is to keep some type of inventory record of the insured property.

No.	Article	Date of Purchase	Cost	Description
	Carpets,			
	Chairs,			
	Clock,			
	Couch,			
	Curtains,			
	Cushions,			
	Jardinieres,			
	Lamps,			
	Mirrors,			
	Piano,			
	Stool and Cover,			
	Rugs,			
	Shades.			
	Window Fixtures,			
	Tables,			
	Tapestry,			
	Pictures,*			
	Vases,			
	Smoking Stand,			
	Draperies,			
	Radio,			

See Special List

A Sample Record for Household Furniture That Is Insured

A record of insured property should be kept in a place where it will not be destroyed in case the property that is insured is destroyed. A policy may contain a clause that makes it mandatory for the insured person to maintain an inventory record. A safe-deposit box is a good place to keep it.

How Coinsurance Operates. *Coinsurance* is a type of insurance commonly used in business. In fire insurance policies the coinsurance clause (assuming an 80 per cent clause) limits the company's liability if the insurance is not equal to, or more than, 80 per cent of the total risk. Having met this requirement, any loss will be covered up to the total amount of the insurance. If the insurance is equal to only half the property value, then the insured is automatically a coinsurer for the other half. The insurance company will pay him only one-half of any losses, and he alone bears the rest. Some fire insurance companies are now writing policies with a coinsurance clause covering residential property. Coinsurance clauses of a similar but different nature are found in accident and health, and casualty insurance policies.

Transportation Insurance. Insurance covering goods in transportation is called *transportation insurance* (automobile insurance is a form of transportation insurance), and is often generally classified as *marine insurance* because the early transportation insurance covered merchandise shipped by boat. This type of insurance has many uses. If a shipment is sent by water, the person who owns the goods will want protection against damage, theft, and loss. The person who owns the goods may obtain this insurance, or the company that transports them may provide it as a part of the cost of transportation. The transportation company may carry its own insurance and pay its own losses, or it may insure its shipments with another company.

Shipments hauled by express companies are usually insured, and the cost of the insurance is included in the transportation charges. Railway freight shipments may be sent insured or uninsured. Parcel-post packages may also be sent in either way.

Automobile Insurance. *Automobile insurance* is one of the most common types of casualty insurance. It may cover potential loss caused by fire, theft, collision, property damage, bodily injury, a tornado, a windstorm, rain, flood, or the like involving the insured automobile.

Bodily-injury insurance provides protection against loss arising from the death or injury of any person. It is also very important insurance which is required by law in some states. Law suits for damages in case you injure another person can often run as high as $200,000.

Ordinarily bodily-injury insurance should be carried for not less than twenty-five thousand dollars in case of the injury of a single person, or not less than fifty thousand dollars in case of the injury of more than one person. Most claims can be settled within the limits of these amounts.

> ### Kinds of Automobile Insurance
> 1. Bodily-injury insurance, covering damage to other people.
> 2. Fire and theft insurance.
> 3. Property-damage insurance, covering damage done to other people's property.
> 4. Comprehensive insurance, including fire and theft coverage, and providing protection against tornadoes, hail, flood, lightning, wind storm, earthquake, riots, glass breakage, robbery, and pilferage.
> 5. Collision insurance, covering damage to one's own car.
> 6. Medical payments insurance.

If twenty-five thousand dollars' worth of bodily-injury insurance is carried as protection against loss due to a single injury, the person who is injured can collect from the insurance company an amount not exceeding twenty-five thousand dollars. In the case of injury to more than one person, the maximum protection is fifty thousand dollars. The extent of the injury must be determined by a court or established by an agreement between the injured person and the insurance company. A good insurance company will take care of all legal details. If the amount of damages exceeds the amount of insurance, the insured person will have to pay the difference.

Almost every owner of an automobile agrees that *fire and theft insurance* is desirable. There are relatively few automobile owners who do not carry this protection. The insurance rates are low because the risks are low and they are spread among a great number of automobile owners. It formerly was the custom for companies to issue policies in which they agreed to pay a fixed amount in case of the loss of the automobile by fire or theft. The most common practice now is to issue policies that state that the market value of the automobile at the time of loss will be paid. Most policies are worded in such a manner that the insurance company may replace the car with a similar one or pay the market value at the time of loss, regardless of the amount of insurance carried on the car. When there is only a partial loss, the insurance company repairs the damage or pays the amount of cash equivalent to the cost of the repairs. Most policies include protection against loss due to fire and theft while an automobile is being transported on a boat or a railroad.

Although fire and theft insurance are the most widely used forms of automobile insurance, property-damage and bodily-injury insurance are probably the most important. Some states have passed legislation that makes it necessary for automobile owners to take out these types of insurance before they can obtain licenses for their cars.

Property-damage insurance provides protection against losses resulting from damage to an automobile or some other property of another person. It is a very important type of insurance and is becoming increasingly important because of various state laws. Many state laws require that if you have an accident in which you may be at fault, you either must be covered by insurance or must post a bond immediately. If you are covered by adequate insurance with a reliable company, the insurance company will handle the claim for you.

Ordinarily it is considered wise not to carry less than five thousand dollars' worth of property-damage insurance. If an automobile driver who carries five thousand dollars' worth of property-damage insurance damages the automobile of another person or the front of a store, for instance, the person whose property has been damaged may collect damages from the insurance company to the extent of five thousand dollars.

In most automobile insurance policies it is possible to obtain for a small extra charge what is called *comprehensive insurance*. This kind of insurance provides a general coverage of many risks, such as tornado, wind storm, rain, and glass breakage covering damage to the car that is covered by the insurance.

Collision insurance is usually meant to be protection against loss arising from damage to one's own car. This type of insurance is unpopular because the cost is high. The cost is high because of the many minor damages to automobiles. Most people feel that it is less expensive to assume the risk of loss from collision than it is to carry a collision insurance policy. The rates on this type of policy are considerably less if one is willing to assume the risk on minor injuries and hold the insurance company liable only on major damages. Many people carry this type of insurance. For instance, a policy may have a deductible clause, such as a $25 or $50 deductible clause. In the case of the $25 deductible clause, the owner of the car would stand the loss from damages up to $25 on any one collision. The insurance company would pay the loss from damages above that amount.

Medical-payments insurance is really a supplement to automobile bodily-injury insurance. It provides for payments for medical, surgical, hospital, and other similar expenses caused by accidental injury to any occupant of the insured automobile, including the policyholder. The limit of the amount that will be paid is specified in the policy.

Health and Accident Insurance. One may obtain at low cost policies covering accidents and sickness. Some of these

Bodily Injury Can Result in Large Claims for Damages

Harold M. Lambert

Your Automobile Insurance May Be Void

Under certain circumstances insurance companies reserve the right, either by clauses in the insurance policy or by state law, to void a policy. In other words, the insurance company ceases to be responsible under the contract if certain things are done or if they are failed to be done by the owner or someone authorized by the owner to drive the car. (Remember, of course, that an unauthorized person driving an insured car is not covered by insurance on the car and the owner is not responsible.) The following are some cases in which your insurance policy may become void, and you will be without protection in case of an accident:

1. If the car is taken into Mexico, Alaska, or other places outside the limits of the United States.
2. If explosives are carried.
3. If the car pulls a trailer not covered by provisions of the insurance policy. (This is not always true.)
4. If you fail to report an accident promptly and honestly in writing to the company.
5. If you agree or authorize someone to agree for you to assume liability for injuries to any person or damages to other property. (The best thing to do is to tell the other person that you are covered by insurance and will report it to your insurance company.)
6. If you or an authorized user of the car does not protect the car and prevent it from further damage after an accident.
7. If you fail to assist and cooperate with the insurance company in settling any claim.
8. If you fail to turn over to your insurance company every demand notice or legal summons received in connection with any accident.

policies provide payments for lost time resulting from an accident or sickness. The policies that provide payments only in case of loss of a leg, loss of an arm, or some other specified injury are of very little practical value to most people because these types of accidents seldom occur; however, the costs are low. For persons in hazardous occupations such insurance may be desirable even though it may cost more than for persons in non-hazardous occupations.

Special clauses are sometimes included in regular insurance policies that provide some protection against accidents and sickness. For instance, there may be a waiver of the premium in case of disability, or there may be a payment of twice the face value of the policy if death results from an accident. It is possible to buy single-trip insurance, such as for a trip on an airplane or a railroad.

Features of Health and Accident Insurance

1. May provide a specified income while the insured is ill or disabled.
2. May provide a lump-sum payment for specified types of injuries or illnesses.
3. May provide money to pay medical or hospital bills or other special expenses due to accidents or illnesses.

Hospital Expense Insurance. *Hospitalization insurance* provides for payment of hospital charges for room, board, and miscellaneous services. These insurance payments are for a certain amount per day and for a stated number of days. Blue Cross plans provide similar benefits, but pay the hospital directly.

Surgical Expense Insurance. *Surgical insurance* provides for payments of surgical expenses according to a schedule of fees payable for each type of operation. Schedules paying a top fee of $200 to $300 are usual. Blue Shield plans provide similar benefits, but pay the doctor directly.

Medical Expense Insurance. Expenses for medical treatment in the home, hospital, or the doctor's office and for physical examination can be covered by *medical expense insurance.*

Major Medical Expense Insurance. *Major medical expense insurance* pays for costs that are above the hospital, surgical, and medical expense coverages, paying up to $5,000 or $7,500. The costly items of nursing care and use of special appliances are covered in these policies. Major medical coverage does not pay the first $300 or $500 of expenses since these are assumed to be covered by basic hospital and surgical policies. The insured is usually a coinsurer for the expenses above the deductible amount, which means that he pays some portion, usually 25 per cent, of these expenses.

Loss of Income Insurance. The type of insurance that replaces income lost because of inability to work, sickness, or accident is called *disability insurance*. The income payments usually continue for a specified number of weeks or months, or under some policies for life.

Personal Liability Insurance. Several companies write at a very low cost a comprehensive *personal liability insurance* policy covering claims resulting from injuries to temporary help in the home, from hitting someone with a golf ball, from damage caused by children, from injuries caused by a dog, and from numerous other types of accidents that might result in claims and law suits.

Theft Insurance. Insurance may be obtained to cover loss due to theft or embezzlement. *Theft insurance* may cover specified items such as money, or it may cover all the merchandise and equipment of a company. Insurance of this type is frequently referred to as burglary insurance, although the theft may be performed by an employee of the company. Banks and companies that handle large amounts of money carry insurance against robbery.

Many businesses carry insurance that protects them from loss in case of theft or embezzlement by dishonest employees. Some employees who handle large sums of money are covered by *fidelity bonds*. If such an employee proves dishonest, the company can recover from the insurance company the loss to the extent of the bond. A fidelity bond is one form of insurance.

Many people carry theft insurance on property in the home. Some of these policies cover theft either inside or outside the home. One special policy that is called *personal floater* covers the theft of personal items such as a watch regardless of where it is stolen.

Consumer-Credit Insurance. Several types of insurance have been discussed up to this point. There are hundreds of other types of insurance protection that can be purchased. However, these cannot all be discussed in detail. There is one more type of insurance that is of interest to many consumers. It is called *consumer-credit insurance*. It follows essentially the same principle as buying a life insurance policy when you go in debt to purchase a home. If you die, the life insurance policy will pay the remaining debt on the home.

Many sellers of automobiles and household equipment provide the same kind of insurance when selling on the installment plan. The cost of the insurance is included in the financial charges so that if the purchaser becomes ill or dies, the payments are made from the insurance.

Can You Carry Multiple Insurance? Insurance covering the same property may be carried in more than one company. Multiple insurance has no advantage if you carry full protection in more than one company, however, because one can collect only the amount of his loss. If the policies of two or more companies cover part or all of the value of the property, both insurance companies will share in the loss. For example, if you carry $4,000 worth of fire insurance in one company and $2,000 in another and if the loss amounts to $3,000, the first company will pay $2,000 and the second company will pay $1,000 of the loss.

Insurable Interest. Insurance may be secured only by persons having what is known as an *insurable interest*. Everyone has an insurable interest in his own life. Whether a person has an insurable interest in the life of another depends upon whether he will be deprived of some benefit by the death of the other. One need not be a relative of a person in order to insure that person's life. A creditor, under some circumstances, may insure the life of a debtor. Close kinship is often, but not necessarily, sufficient to constitute an insurable interest.

When property is insured against loss due to fire or other causes, the purpose of the insurance is considered to be the protection of the interest of the person who buys the insurance. The policyholder must have an insurable interest in the property. A person is considered to have an insurable interest in property if there is a reasonable expectation that he will derive a financial benefit from the existence of the property or will suffer a loss from the damage or the destruction of the property. For instance, both the owner of a home and the person who holds a mortgage on the home have an insurable interest. If the property is not insured and is later destroyed, the owner will lose the money he has invested in it, and the person who owns the mortgage may lose the money that is due him on the mortgage.

In the case of property the insurable interest ordinarily must exist at the time of the loss; otherwise, the contract is not enforceable. For example, a person might carry some insurance on property that he rents and occupies. If he moves out of the property without canceling the insurance, he could not collect for a fire loss in case the building burns after he moves.

Most mortgages contain a clause that requires the owner of the property to carry enough insurance to protect the mortgagee, the person lending the money.

Assignment of Insurance. If you carry an insurance policy on property that you sell, you cannot transfer the insurance policy to the new owner without the approval of the insurance company. The insurance company need not contract with the new owner, but with the approval of the insurance company the policy can be assigned or transferred to the new owner or to the mortgage holder. The transfer is called an *assignment*.

If there is any change in the title to insured property, the protection under the policy usually becomes void. For instance, if a house is insured by Mr. Smith and is sold to Mr. Howard, the insurance policy taken out by Mr. Smith becomes void, for it was written to protect the latter's interest and cannot be transferred without the consent of the insurance company. An exception to this rule arises in case of the death of the person who has purchased the insurance.

If such person dies, his heirs are protected under the insurance.

Life insurance does not become void if there is a change in the insurable interest. For example, a policy taken out by a corporation on the life of its president is still valid even though he retires or is discharged.

Analysis of Insurance Needs. Nearly everyone is interested in some kind of insurance. He is therefore confronted with the problem of choosing what insurance to buy, how much to buy, and from whom to buy. In some cases the person does not have any choice as to whether he will carry insurance or not. If he has purchased a home, and a bank or a loan association holds a mortgage on the home, he will be required to insure the home. In an increasingly large number of states, a person cannot obtain an automobile license without buying bodily-injury and property-damage insurance.

The mere fact that a person has never suffered a loss is no reason to believe that he will continue to be so fortunate. One cannot assume the attitude, "It has not happened to me thus far. What reason is there to expect it to happen?" One must look upon the buying of insurance from the point of view of (a) the cost of carrying insurance, (b) the results of not carrying insurance, and (c) the benefits of carrying insurance. It is just as foolish to carry too much insurance as it is not to carry any. A person would be foolish to use all his surplus income for buying life insurance.

A person who has a million dollars and who owns a large estate might not find it desirable to insure a small building on that estate or a motor boat that he owns, for the loss of either of these would not cause him any special handicap. On the other hand, a person who owns his own home and has only a small amount of additional savings should, by all means, insure the home. If he did not carry insurance and the home were destroyed, he would have difficulty in replacing it.

If a person owns a small cottage that he uses during his summer vacation, he may debate whether to insure it. The loss of the cottage would be inconvenient, but it would not impose upon him a great financial loss. If the insurance rate on a cottage of this type is high, the insurance will not be justified. On the other hand, if the same man owns a small building that he uses for a workshop in making a living, he will want to insure it even though its value may not be equal to that of the summer cottage. The destruction of the workshop would result in a severe handicap.

The use of insurance should be looked upon as a means of enabling one to carry out fixed plans through life without the hazards of uncertainty. Insurance makes plans certain, whereas the lack of it makes plans uncertain. A sudden large loss might disrupt an otherwise good plan.

Summary of Insurance Protection

1. Insurance is possible through certain small payments collected from many people to pay a large loss that may occur to any person.
2. Insurance rates are determined by past experience and are based upon the law of averages.
3. Insurance companies are generally stock companies or mutual companies and are either participating or nonparticipating.
4. There are several forms of automobile insurance and it is important to carry the principle forms of insurance.
5. Health, accident, hospital, medical, and surgical are types of insurance important to family protection.
6. Some people can assume their own risks without worry.
7. Anyone can insure property if he has a real interest in it.

TEXTBOOK QUESTIONS

1. Explain briefly how losses, such as those due to fires, deaths, accidents, or the like, are predictable.
2. Give an example of how an insurance company collects money from individuals in small amounts to protect each individual from a major loss.
3. What is an insurance contract called?

4. Who is the insured or the assured?
5. Who is the beneficiary?
6. Explain the fundamental difference between a stock company and a mutual company in the insurance business.
7. What is the difference between a participating policy and a nonparticipating policy?
8. How are insurance companies regulated?
9. What is extended coverage on fire insurance policies?
10. Explain briefly how regular fire insurance operates on a residence as to the amount carried and the payment of claims.
11. What precaution should be used in order that proof of loss can be provided in case of loss of insured property?
12. State briefly how coinsurance operates.
13. Under the agreements in most automobile insurance policies, what options does the insurance company have if the automobile is destroyed by fire?
14. If a person has a collision insurance policy on an automobile with a $25 deductible clause, how much will the insurance company pay if the car is damaged in an accident to the extent of $35?
15. (a) What is bodily-injury insurance on an automobile? (b) What is property-damage insurance?
16. What is medical-payment insurance in connection with automobile insurance?
17. Indicate the three principle features that may be found in health and accident policies.
18. Name some of the kinds of insurance that will provide protection for sickness, accidents, and loss of income.
19. What is the nature of a personal floater theft policy?
20. What is consumer-credit insurance?
21. If you carry full fire insurance protection on your house in each of two different companies, can you collect the full amount of fire loss from each of these companies?
22. What is meant by an insurable interest?
23. On what basis is a person considered to have an insurable interest in the life or the property that is insured?
24. Explain how one may have an insurable interest in property at the time the property is insured but may not have an insurable interest at the time the property is destroyed.

25. Explain the difference between the insurance needs of the wealthy person on a small cottage that he uses for his vacations and the insurance needs on a small workshop used by another man in making a living.

DISCUSSION QUESTIONS

1. (a) How could an insurance company determine rates for insurance against loss due to rain? (b) Do you think such rates would be high or low as compared with the rates for automobile insurance? Why?
2. If a city has strict building ordinances and strict inspection of buildings, how would fire insurance rates be affected?
3. If you were buying automobile insurance, what consideration would you give to the type of policy and the general attitude of the company in paying claims?
4. What, in your opinion, represents the more serious risk of an automobile owner: (a) the risk of property damage or (b) the risk of injury to a person? Why?
5. If your automobile insurance policy provides $10,000 protection against injury to a person and the court awards damages of $12,000 to the injured person, how is the claim settled?
6. What do you think of an accident policy that provides protection against such risks as loss of one leg, loss of both arms, loss of one eye, and other similar hazards?
7. Explain why you do or do not have an insurable interest in (a) the life of your brother, (b) your neighbor's house, and (c) a house on which you are holding a mortgage.

PROBLEMS

1. Assume that the straight fire insurance rates on a home are $5 a thousand and that a new fire alarm system and fire department in a city will reduce this rate to $3.50 a thousand. (a) What will be the savings in insurance on a house valued at $12,000, assuming that the entire value of the house is covered? (b) If these improvements will increase the tax rates $1 a thousand on all real estate, what savings will there be to the same owner, assuming that the house and lot combined are valued at $14,000?

2. In a certain city the hospital care plan costs a family with two children $12.75 quarterly for the semiprivate plan. During the past three years the hospital bills of the Harrison family have amounted to $70, $65, and $120. Assume that under the hospital care plan all these bills would have been reimbursable. Figure to what extent the hospital care plan would have saved the family money annually. Use the average amount of the hospital bills per year in making the comparison.

3. Obtain a policy for fire insurance on a home. Study its clauses and regulations. Write a report on it.

4. Obtain an automobile insurance policy of some kind. Study its clauses and make a report on its features. Point out some of the ways in which the automobile owner may not be protected adequately by the policy.

COMMUNITY PROBLEMS AND PROJECTS

1. A fifty-dollar deductible collision insurance policy on an automobile has cost Mr. Fall an average of $42 a year for ten years. At the end of the tenth year he had a wreck costing $650 to repair his car. How much has he saved or lost by carrying the insurance as compared with assuming his own risk and paying all of his own damages?

2. Consult an automobile insurance agent about special rates that are either higher or lower than regular rates for children, persons with a bad accident record, boys as compared with girls, persons who have had driver education as compared with those who have not, or any other classes of people.

3. Investigate the hospital care insurance available in your community. Report on the rates and the features of the contract both for individuals and families.

4. Investigate the fire insurance rates in your community by talking to an insurance agent or some other qualified person. Find out the conditions for the cheapest rates on a house and the factors that cause higher rates.

Chapter 29

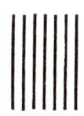

Social Security

> **Purpose of the Chapter.** Social legislation is that which deals with social or economic welfare of all citizens. In this particular chapter social security refers to the various state and federal laws that provide insurance protection against such risks and hazards as unemployment, old-age, disability, and accidents.
>
> You will find answers to these questions:
> 1. Is private life insurance necessary?
> 2. Why do we need social security legislation?
> 3. What are the two main phases of the Federal Social Security Act?
> 4. Who are covered by unemployment insurance?
> 5. Who are covered by old-age insurance?
> 6. What are the benefits received from old-age insurance?

Does Social Security Replace Life Insurance? Some persons have gained the impression that the Social Security Act makes it unnecessary for a person to carry other insurance. If a person wants to have more income when he retires, he must provide that income through other insurance, an investment, or savings. Furthermore, he may want insurance to provide a certain fixed sum for his dependents upon his death. He will have to use regular insurance to provide for this type of protection.

A relatively new development in recent years has been in the field of special retirement plans sponsored by employers and unions, sometimes separately and sometimes jointly. In planning for one's total program of savings, insurance, and retirement plans, all of these factors must be taken into consideration. Social security old-age pensions are only a supplement to other forms of saving and insurance.

Reasons for Social Security Laws. Economic insecurity has always been one of the basic problems of life, but in an industrialized, money-dependent society there are certain new factors that increase this insecurity. In the early history of our country, as explained in the beginning chapters of this book, the home was an independent unit taking care of old people and young people alike through good times and bad times. But our society has become more complicated. Old age is a more critical problem in an industrialized society. Money savings would take care of old age if they were large enough and if they were safely invested, but many among our population are not able to save enough for old age. Unemployment, depressions, accidents, and sickness cause other economic risks.

Our society, in total, is wealthy enough and productive enough to be able to take care of all individuals. Legislation, therefore, has been enacted to protect and aid those who cannot help themselves. Some of the first social legislation involved workmen's compensation for accidents and illness. One of the first states to enact old-age pension laws was the state of Arizona. We now have social security legislation on a much more comprehensive basis. The comprehensive Federal plan is the one that will be discussed in detail in this chapter.

The Federal Social Security Act. The Federal Social Security Act involves two phases, (a) benefits for unemployment, and (b) benefits for old age, death, the needy aged, dependent children, and the blind. The first phase of this program is handled primarily through state agencies with Federal assistance. The second phase of this program is administered directly by the Federal Government, and the taxes for it are collected by the Federal Government.

Wages and Taxes. Under the current social security laws, a worker's wages are taxable for old-age benefits to the extent of the first $4,200 earned each year at the rate of

2¼ per cent (2¾ per cent starting 1960). For purposes of unemployment insurance the first $3,000 earned in a year is taxable, but in most states the employee is not taxed.

Who Are Covered by Old-Age Insurance? Generally speaking, old-age benefits have applied to workers in factories, offices, stores, mines, shops, mills, farm workers, some state employees, household workers, members of the clergy on a voluntary basis, certain Federal workers, fishermen, members of the armed services, and people who take work home.

Self-employed workers are also covered. Self-employed workers include independent contractors; independent businessmen; partners in business; independent commission salesmen and agents, life insurance agents, commission truck drivers; newspaper and magazine distributors over 18 years of age; architects; professional engineers; accountants; funeral directors; farmers; lawyers; dentists; osteopaths; chiropractors; veterinarians; naturopaths; optometrists; and other similar workers.

Who Are Not Covered by Federal Old-Age Insurance? Some workers still are not covered by Federal laws that apply to old-age benefits and unemployment benefits. Obviously, these classifications may be changed from time to time by changes in the federal law.

Some types of workers specifically excluded are employees of foreign governments or international organizations, newspaper workers under eighteen; members of the clergy, except on a voluntary basis; student workers employed by schools, student nurses; interns; doctors; a child under 21 working for a parent; a parent working for a child; a wife working for a husband; or a husband working for a wife.

How to Apply for Social Security Coverage. When one accepts his first job in an occupation covered by the Social Security Act, he should fill out an "Application for Social Security Number." This can be obtained from the employer or the nearest social security office. He will then be issued a social security card with a number on it. The Federal

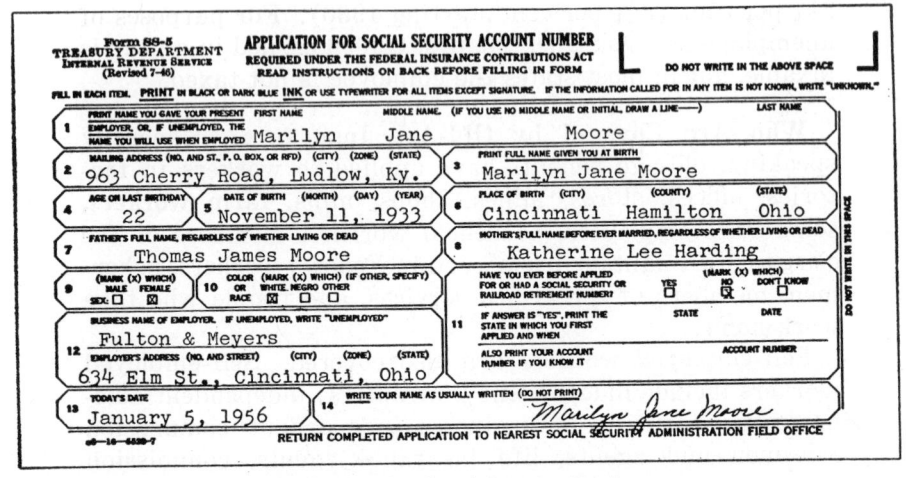

Application for Social Security Number

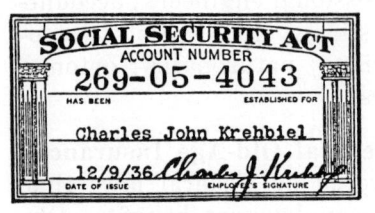

A Social Security Card

Government keeps a separate account for each individual listed under the account number shown on the card. This account is credited for all payments made by the employer into the fund and for all deductions that the employer makes for this purpose from the employee's wages.

Record of Deductions. Every individual who is subject to social security taxes should keep a record of his wages and the amount of taxes paid. The employer is required by law to furnish regularly to each employee a written statement or statements showing the wages paid to the employee during the year. Each statement must be suitable for permanent retention. It may cover one, two, three, or four quarters of the year.

Whenever an employee changes employment, he should see that his new employer has his correct social security number so that he will receive credit for any wages that are earned. That is the responsibility of the employee to be sure he uses the right number.

Check Your Social Security Account. Mistakes may be made in one's social security account. The regulations provide that any insured person may check his account for accuracy, but any mistake more than five years old will not be corrected. Therefore, any person with a social security account should check it for accuracy and compare it with his own records at least once every five years. A convenient card usually obtainable at the post office is provided for this purpose. A sample of this card is shown below.

Unemployment Insurance. Under the Social Security Act each state has set up its own law providing for an unemployment insurance system. This plan is operated in cooperation with the Federal Government. In most cases the tax is levied directly against the employer, but in some cases

A Card for Checking the Accuracy of Social Security Entries

the employee also shares in the tax. In only five states the employee is required to pay a tax for disability or unemployment contributions.

Who Are Covered by Unemployment Insurance? The Federal and state unemployment insurance that is operated under the social security laws applies to workers in factories, offices, stores, mines, shops, mills, and other places of business and industry. However, these laws do not cover farmers, domestic help, Federal employees, teachers and other professional workers, and several other groups.

Unemployment Compensation. An unemployed person is entitled to compensation if he has been engaged in a specified occupation for a specified length of time prior to his unemployment.

In order to obtain unemployment insurance benefits, the worker must meet the following qualifications, besides those previously specified:

- (a) He must be unemployed through no fault of his own.
- (b) He must register at a public employment office for a job.
- (c) He must make a claim for benefits.
- (d) He must be able and available for work.
- (e) He must be totally unemployed for the amount of time specified in his state.

Causes for Denying or Forfeiting Unemployment Benefits

1. Participating in a strike. (Some states have exceptions to this rule.)
2. Voluntarily quitting work without a good cause. (The waiting period is usually longer, and the number of weeks of benefits is usually less.)
3. Being discharged for misconduct. (The waiting period is usually longer, and the number of weeks of benefits is usually less.)
4. Refusing to apply for or to accept suitable work. (Usually the waiting period is longer, and the benefits may be cut off entirely.)
5. Intentionally misrepresenting facts. (Payments are usually forfeited for the remainder of the current year.)
6. Being discharged for theft and found guilty.

Old-Age Insurance. Under the Social Security Act a reserve fund is accumulated as in the case of life insurance. The employer and the employee must contribute regularly to the Federal Government a certain percentage of the employee's wages. This contribution is computed on the first $4,200 of income paid to the employee during any calendar year. The part contributed by the employee is deducted by the employer from the employee's wages. The percentage is subject to change by law; but, regardless of the rate in effect in any particular year, the employer pays a certain percentage as a payroll tax and the employee pays the same percentage as a portion of his wages that is laid aside for old-age benefits.

Old-Age Benefits. Because the Social Security Act is subject to change by new legislation, it is impossible to predict exactly what benefits a person may expect when he attains retirement age. Nevertheless, the following illustration shows old-age benefits that have been computed on the basis of existing rates and the present plan of figuring such benefits.

Old-Age and Survivors' Benefits for a Fully Covered Worker
Starting after January 1, 1955
(Based on the assumption that no low years are dropped out)

STATUS OF RETIRED OR DECEASED WORKER OR OF FAMILY	AVERAGE MONTHLY WAGE $150	AVERAGE MONTHLY WAGE $200	AVERAGE MONTHLY WAGE $250	AVERAGE MONTHLY WAGE $300	AVERAGE MONTHLY WAGE $350
	MONTHLY BENEFITS	MONTHLY BENEFITS	MONTHLY BENEFITS	MONTHLY BENEFITS	MONTHLY BENEFITS
Worker—no dependents	$ 68.50	$ 78.50	$ 88.50	$ 98.50	$108.50
Worker and wife, 50 years old	68.50	78.50	88.50	98.50	108.50
Worker and wife, 65 years old	102.80	107.80	132.80	147.80	162.80
Worker, wife 50, one child	102.80	107.80	132.80	147.80	162.80
Worker, wife 65, one child	*120.00	157.00	177.10	197.10	*200.00
Widow, one child	102.80	117.80	132.80	147.80	162.80
Widow, two children	*120.00	157.10	177.20	197.10	*200.00
Widow, 50	00.00	00.00	00.00	00.00	00.00
Widow, 65	51.40	58.90	66.40	73.90	81.40
Parent	51.40	58.90	66.40	73.90	81.40

* Maximum of $200 or 80 per cent of average wage, whichever is less.

Fully Insured. After being employed in a covered occupation for ten years or forty quarters, a worker becomes fully insured for life for the purposes of old-age insurance. It is not necessary that the worker be employed full time in any quarter for it to count. A quarter is, for instance, January to March inclusive. Under certain other conditions one may become fully insured in a shorter length of time.

Primary Benefit. The primary old-age benefit that will be paid on retirement of the worker is figured on the basis of 55 per cent of the first $110 plus 20 per cent of the next $240 of the average monthly income of a fully covered person. A person who is only partially covered receives less. Under certain conditions a worker may drop out certain low income months in figuring his average monthly income. This privilege will raise the average monthly income.

Maximum and Minimum Family Benefits. The maximum benefit that a family (two or more persons) may receive for old-age insurance is $200 a month or 80 per cent of the average monthly income, whichever is lower. In no case will the monthly family benefit be less than $50 or one and one half times the primary benefit, whichever is larger.

Example of Primary Benefits. The example on page 513 shows a formula for computing the primary benefit of a young person starting to work after the new law of 1955 went into effect.

Upon reaching sixty-five years of age, Mr. Newton will receive this benefit for the rest of his life, provided he is not working and earning more than is permitted.

Besides the primary benefit, Mr. Newton may be entitled to certain supplementary benefits for dependents. Supplementary benefits are based upon primary benefits under the following conditions:

1. One half the primary benefit is allowed for wife * sixty-five years of age or older or if there is a dependent child.
2. If the wife * is entitled to a primary benefit of her own because of previous employment, she may use her own primary benefit or the benefit allowed as the wife of a defendent, whichever of the two is larger.
3. One half the primary benefit plus one fourth the primary benefit divided by the number of children is allowed for each child under eighteen and not married.
4. The total allowed for any family may not be more than 80 per cent of the worker's average monthly wage or $200, whichever is less, but in no case less than $50.

---

* Under the 1956 amendment, women workers or widows may begin receiving benefits at age 62 but at a reduced amount.

Example

Frank H. Newton became twenty-two years of age on January 15, 1955. He will be eligible for retirement benefits at age 65. Let us assume that he will have forty-three years of service consisting of ten years at $2,400 a year, ten years at $2,800 a year, ten years at $3,000 a year, and thirteen years at $4,000 a year. Frank is employed in a covered occupation. How can we figure his primary benefit?

FORMULA FOR FIGURING PRIMARY BENEFIT FOR PERSON FULLY INSURED AFTER JANUARY 1, 1955

Computation of Average Wage

(1) Add all wages earned in a covered occupation, not exceeding $4,200 a year (omit 5 years of lowest income) $122,000.00

(2) Divide this sum by the number of months in which the income was earned (516 — 60 = 456 after dropping out 5 lowest years) to get the average monthly income ..... $ 267.00 *

* When the average wage does not work out to an even multiple of $1, it is reduced to the next lower multiple of $1 (cents are dropped).

Computation of Primary Benefit

(1) Take 55 per cent of the first $110 of his average monthly income .... $ 60.50

(2) Add 20 per cent of the balance of the next $240 ($157 × .20) .... $ 31.40

(3) Primary benefit .... $ 91.90 *

* If the benefit is not a multiple of 10 cents regulations require that it be raised to next higher multiple of 10 cents.

Benefits for Survivors. Under the Federal Social Security Act, if an employee dies before reaching the age of sixty-five, his widow will be provided for. A widow * sixty-five years of age or more, whose husband was insured, is entitled to three fourths the benefits that her husband would have received if he had lived.

A widow, regardless of her age, who has one or more children under eighteen years of age will receive three fourths the monthly benefits to which her husband would

---

* Under the 1956 amendment, women workers or widows may begin receiving benefits at age 62 but at a reduced amount.

have been entitled. If only one child is left, the monthly benefit for that child is three fourths of the worker's primary benefit. However, if there are two or more children, the benefit is figured differently. In such cases, each of the children is entitled to benefits equal to one half of the primary benefit, plus one fourth of the primary benefit divided by the number of children. (For example, in the case of a father of four whose primary benefit was $94.50: ½ of $94.50 equals $47.25; ¼ of $94.50 divided by 4 equals $5.90; $47.25 plus $5.90 equals $53.15 which is raised to $53.20 or the benefit for each of the four children; but in no case is the total family benefit more than $200.)

As each child reaches eighteen years of age or becomes married, the benefit for the child will cease.

Example

Let us assume that Frank Newton, on whom previous examples are based, dies after reaching the age of 65. Since his primary benefit was $91.90, the following is the way the benefit will be computed for the widow and two children:

FORMULA—SURVIVORS' BENEFITS FULLY COVERED AFTER JANUARY 1, 1955

Survivors' Benefits

(1) Widow's benefit, three fourths of primary benefit .... $ 69.00 *
(2) Benefits for two children (each child gets one half of $91.90; plus one fourth of $91.90 divided by 2) .... $114.90 *
(3) Total benefits to family $183.90

* Raise to nearest 10 cents higher.

If the wage earner leaves no widow or unmarried children under eighteen years of age, but does leave parents who are wholly dependent upon him, each of the parents will receive a monthly payment equal to three fourths of the payment to which the wage earner was entitled at the time of his death. To receive these benefits, the parents must be sixty-five years of age or older.

Any widow will lose part of her benefits if she remarries or works in a covered occupation for more than $100 a month.

Lump-Sum Survivor Benefit. Under the 1954 amendments to the social security laws, the survivor of a fully covered or of a currently covered worker or the person paying the funeral expenses is entitled to a lump-sum death benefit. This benefit will be paid regardless of other benefits that may go to survivors. It amounts to three times the deceased worker's primary benefit but not more than $255. For example, if Mr. Newton were to die at age 65 with a primary benefit of $91.90, his widow, children, or other heirs would receive a lump-sum payment of $255. Application for this payment must be filed within two years after the death of the insured individual.

Summary of Benefits to Survivors

After the death of a worker at any age, if he has the necessary "quarters of coverage," benefits go to:

—his widow, if she is sixty-five or over, or when she reaches sixty-five;

—his children until they are eighteen;

—his widow of any age if she has such children in her care;

—his dependent parents if they are sixty-five or when they reach sixty-five, provided he leaves no widow or child under eighteen;

—lump-sum benefit to anyone who pays funeral expenses.

Special Provision for Disabled Workers.* Since the average monthly income is used to determine monthly benefits on retirement, a person who loses his income because of disability or is placed on reduced pay because of disability would have a reduction in his old-age benefits unless there were some special provision. The 1954 amendment to the law makes a special provision for such persons. After a person has been disabled for six months and it appears that it may extend for an indefinite period, he may apply to have

---

* Under the 1956 amendment, a totally and permanently disabled worker (starting July 1, 1957) may receive at age 50 a regular benefit equal to his normal primary benefit.

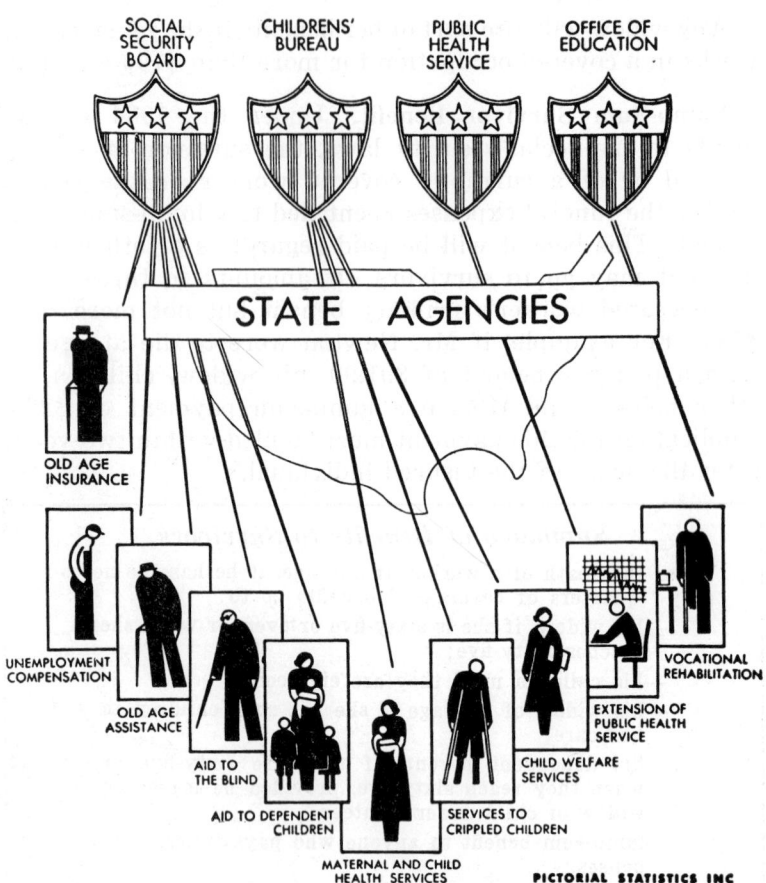

How the Social Security Program Is Administered

his earnings record "frozen." This period will then not be counted in figuring the average income for social security benefits.

Work after Age 65. Under the 1954 amendment to the Social Security Law, a retired worker can continue to receive the regular benefits and the family will receive the usual benefits if the worker is not employed and earning $1,200 a year up to age 72. If he earns more than $1,200 a year, his benefits and the benefits of the family will be reduced according to a scale established by law. After age 72 the retired worker may earn any amount without reducing his old-age benefits or the benefits of his family.

Other Social Security Assistance. The preceding discussion on social security has dealt with the benefits that are paid as a result of deductions from wages and on the basis of previous earnings. Under the Social Security Act, however, the Federal Government has made provisions for assistance to other needy groups. In general, the plan provides for funds to be furnished for (a) needy aged, (b) needy dependent children, (c) needy blind, (d) maternal welfare of infants and mothers, (e) crippled children, (f) child welfare, (g) vocational rehabilitation, and (h) public health. If a state has a plan satisfactory to the Federal Government, that state may obtain from the Federal Government a contribution up to 50 per cent of the state expenditures.

Workmen's Compensation. As was mentioned in the first part of this chapter, workmen's compensation sponsored by various states is another form of social security. The laws providing protection against accidents and sickness are quite variable. For an interpretation of these laws one should become familiar with the plan in operation in his particular state. These laws have no connection with the Federal Social Security Act.

Summary of Social Security Provisions

1. Most workers are covered by old-age and unemployment insurance benefits.
2. Old-age benefits are generally determined by the average monthly income during the time of employment.
3. Wives, widows, children, parents, and survivors of an insured worker are entitled to certain benefits under old-age insurance provisions.
4. The amount of income earned by a retired worker may affect the amount of old-age insurance he can collect.
5. Social security does not replace the need for life insurance and other retirement income.

TEXTBOOK QUESTIONS

1. Does social security replace life insurance?
2. Explain briefly the reason for social security legislation.
3. What types of insurance and benefits are provided under the Federal Social Security Act?
4. Give some examples of self-employed workers who are covered by federal old-age insurance.
5. Give some examples of workers not covered by federal old-age insurance.
6. How does one apply for a social security number?
7. How many years do you have to make a correction if you find a mistake in your social security account?
8. Who are covered by the social security unemployment benefits?
9. What are the qualifications for a person to receive unemployment compensation?
10. Give at least two causes for denying unemployment benefits to a worker or causes for forfeiting these benefits.
11. What is the age of retirement under the Federal Social Security Act?
12. What is a primary benefit under the old-age social security laws and how is it computed under the present law?
13. What is the maximum old-age or survivors benefit that would be paid to any family; what is the minimum benefit?
14. On what basis is the benefit of a widow, 65 years of age, of a retired fully covered worker computed?
15. What benefits are allowed for children under 18 who are not married?
16. (a) If a fully insured worker is dead, what benefits go to his widow if she is 65 years of age? (b) What benefits go to the widow if she is 55 years of age?
17. Some aged and dependent persons are not covered by the Social Security Act. How may these persons receive some assistance?

DISCUSSION QUESTIONS

1. Can you point out any reasons why the changes in economic conditions make social security benefits more necessary today than they were in 1700?
2. Explain how the provisions for old-age benefits under the Federal Social Security Act are a device to eliminate economic risks.

3. Employees of railroads are not included under the Social Security Act. Can you think of any reasons why?
4. Why does unemployment insurance differ in the various states although it is a part of the Federal social security program?
5. Does the Federal Social Security Act make it unnecessary to buy various forms of life insurance?
6. If a worker is fully covered when he dies, can anyone collect any benefits for funeral expenses?
7. What is the purpose of so-called "Workmen's Compensation Laws"?

PROBLEMS

1. On the basis of a 2 per cent deduction from wages for old-age benefits and the rate of 1 per cent for unemployment and sickness deductions: (a) How much will be withheld from the payroll each year for a man earning $300 a month if the withholdings for unemployment and sickness benefits are based upon the first $3,000 a year earned? (b) How much for a man earning $400 a month?
2. From the example on page 513 for the computation of primary benefits, prepare a similar table from the following figures: wages earned, not exceeding $3,600 in any year, $90,000; number of months in which income was earned, 450.
3. From the example in this chapter on page 514 showing the survivors' benefits, compute the benefits for a widow with two children under eighteen if the primary benefit is $60.

COMMUNITY PROBLEMS AND PROJECTS

1. Obtain a copy of your state law pertaining to unemployment insurance. Make a report on it, and figure out specifically how an unemployed person is compensated.
2. Make an investigation of the laws in your state affecting workmen's compensation. These laws usually cover industrial accidents and sometimes sick and death benefits. Make a written report of the important features of this law and list the occupations covered.
3. Investigate the laws in your state pertaining to assistance for the blind, and write a report explaining the aid that is available to the blind.

Chapter 30

Features of Life Insurance Contracts

> **Purpose of the Chapter.** Many people look upon life insurance as being essentially the same rate regardless of the type of policy or contract that one buys. There are many different kinds of contracts designed to serve various needs of individuals. The features of these different kinds of contracts will be explained in this chapter.
>
> You will find answers to these questions:
> 1. What is meant by legal-reserve insurance?
> 2. What is the difference between term insurance and endowment insurance?
> 3. What is the difference between ordinary life insurance and limited payment life insurance?
> 4. What is an annuity?
> 5. What are the characteristics of industrial insurance?
> 6. What is meant by nonforfeiture values?

What Is Life Insurance? *Life insurance* is a voluntary plan through which people set aside portions of their income during their earning years to make provision for the time when their income will cease by death, declining health, or retirement. It is a risk-sharing plan that provides for each member of a group protection that would be impossible for each individual to provide for himself.

Life insurance involves a specific plan or contract (the *policy*) between the insured and an insurance company in which the company promises to pay a sum of money to the person (the *beneficiary*) named in the policy at the time of the insured's death. If the insured is alive at a future date specified in the policy, a certain sum or periodic sums of money are usually paid to him, except in the case of term insurance. The promise on the part of the insurance company is given in return for the payment of a sum of money (the *premium*) to the insurance company.

Since insurance is a sort of cooperative plan through which individuals pay the same rates under similar conditions, most general forms of insurance require a physical examination and the meeting of other requirements. This is done so that the cost of the insurance and the protection of all members of the insured group will be fair. For instance, if there were no physical examinations required, a person in poor health and likely to die soon would not pay any higher rate than one in good health; or a person 25 years of age would have to pay as high a rate as one 50 years of age. A physical examination determines eligibility, therefore; and the age, and other conditions determine the rate. Sometimes persons with poor health or in extra dangerous occupations can obtain insurance but at higher rates than normal.

Legal-Reserve Insurance. *Legal-reserve*, or *level-premium*, life insurance constitutes the chief type in force today. Nearly all life insurance is of this kind.

The probability of death increases at a rapid rate as the age of the individual increases. If this increased risk were directly reflected in each year's premium, the cost would increase steadily, becoming more and more burdensome and finally impossible to pay. The practice in legal-reserve insurance is to determine a level premium that, because it is more than enough in the early years, will provide additional funds to meet the cost of protection in later years when the actual cost exceeds the level premiums. The reserves built by these additional funds are invested to earn interest until needed for policyholders as a group. These interest earnings help to pay for the cost of the protection. If an individual wants to discontinue his insurance, his share of these reserve funds is called the cash value. The cash value of a policy increases until the policy matures either as an endowment or at the end of the span of life on which the rates were calculated. The cash value is also the basis for a policy loan that will enable the policyholder to meet an emergency, to pay a future premium that is due, or to take advantage of an opportunity.

Insurance Contracts. There are many types of life insurance contracts, usually referred to as policies. Some of them are simple; others involve a combination of elements that cannot be explained without considerable detail. The following are basic types of policies: term, ordinary life, limited-payment life, single-premium life, endowment, combination, and annuity. These types of policies are explained in the following pages.

Term Insurance. *Term insurance,* as the name implies, is insurance that covers a specified period of time and is usually obtained to cover a specific need. For example, if a man has a debt that he expects to pay off in ten years, provided he lives, he can buy a ten-year term policy for the amount of the indebtedness. This insurance will pay the debt in case he dies.

Term insurance is often referred to as "pure insurance" because it provides protection only. It does not have a cash-surrender value or a loan value. One of the major advantages of term insurance is its initial low cost compared with that of other types. Term insurance makes it possible for a person to acquire more life insurance coverage at the time it is needed but when income is too low to buy permanent protection.

Although this type of insurance is considered primarily as temporary insurance, some individuals prefer to obtain insurance protection entirely through it and to establish a savings plan independently of the insurance program. Term insurance therefore has some advantage for those who can successfully save and invest.

The most common periods covered by term insurance are five years and ten years, but it may cover any period of years. Such policies are convertible into other types of contracts that provide protection over longer periods of

KINDS OF LIFE INSURANCE

	AMOUNT	PAYMENTS	TYPE OF PAYMENTS	PHYSICAL EXAM	COST
ORDINARY	$500–UP	MONTHLY QUARTERLY SEMI-YEARLY YEARLY	MAIL	YES	MEDIUM
INDUSTRIAL	$100–UP	WEEKLY	COLLECTED BY AGENT	NO	HIGH
GROUP	SMALL	DEDUCTION FROM WAGE	COLLECTED BY EMPLOYER	NO	LOW
SAVINGS BANK	$250–UP	MONTHLY QUARTERLY YEARLY	MAIL OR AT BANK	YES	LOW

PICTOGRAPH CORPORATION

years and involve the accumulation of reserves. For instance, a man may wish a large amount of protection at a low cost while he is educating his children. After they have been educated, he may convert the term insurance into some other type of insurance at a higher cost.

Ordinary Life Insurance. The *ordinary life insurance* plan may be called the basic life insurance policy for protection over a long period of years. This type of insurance is sometimes called *whole life* or *straight life insurance*. If one has dependents and is anxious to provide primarily for their protection in the event of death, the ordinary life plan is ideal. The premium rate is lower than that for any other type of permanent insurance. The policyholder has a loan or a cash-surrender value in the policy. The insured person may continue paying premiums for the entire length of his life or to age 96, at which time he is paid the face value of the insurance policy.

Most policyholders of straight life contracts actually do not pay premiums until the end of the mortality table (which may be 96, 100, or 104). A very few do. Most such people stop paying premiums and take a reduced paid-up policy, which at age 65 amounts to from 60 per cent to 70 per cent of the face value.

Limited-Payment Life Insurance. A *limited-payment life insurance* contract is the same as an ordinary life contract except that premiums are paid for a limited time, such as ten, twenty, or thirty years, instead of for life. Because premiums are paid only for a limited time, the rates are somewhat higher than for ordinary life insurance. When these premiums have been paid, the insurance policy is said to be fully paid. If the face value of the policy is, for example, ten thousand dollars, the insurance company will pay this amount whenever death occurs.

Such a contract is desirable when the earning years are limited. If a person is reasonably sure that his earning days will cease when he is fifty-five years of age, he certainly will not want to continue to pay premiums after that age. This type of policy is therefore based on the idea that the payment of premiums should cease when the person's earnings dwindle. As it is assumed, in calculating the premium rate for a limited-payment policy, that there will be fewer annual payments than in the case of the ordinary life policy, each annual payment must be larger than it would be for the ordinary life policy.

Endowment Insurance. The company that issues an *endowment policy* agrees to pay a definite sum of money at a specified time to the insured person or, in the event of death, to the beneficiaries of this person. An endowment policy costs more than a limited-payment policy for an equivalent number of years. The face amount is available, however, as cash at death or at the end of the period; whereas, in the case of the limited-payment policy, it is available only in the event of death or at age 96 or a later specified age.

An endowment policy is an excellent means of accumulating a definite amount for a future need. Short-term endowments for periods of from five to twenty years are ideal to create sums of money that will be needed to educate children, to start a child in some particular profession or business, to purchase a home, or to pay off a debt.

Frequently, and particularly in the case of young people, the short-term endowment policy should not be used. In such a case the amount of insurance that can be purchased may be limited by the comparatively high premium rates. For example, with one particular insurance company, a young man at age 20 could purchase ordinary life insurance at an annual rate of $18.22 a thousand, twenty-payment life insurance for $30.01 a thousand, twenty-year endowment insurance for $49.42 a thousand, or endowment at age 65 for $21.58 a thousand. If one is seeking maximum permanent protection at the lowest price, the ordinary life policy is the cheapest. Often in the case of young people who purchase ten- or twenty-year endowment policies, the money becomes available too early in life and the protection against death ceases, although the insured person will have a great need for the protection in later life. When the policy matures, he may even find himself physically impaired and thus uninsurable.

It is usually most desirable to obtain a long-term endowment policy so that the money will become available at about the age of sixty or later. At this stage in life the insured person may have little or no earning power. If the policy matures at that time, its face value will be available to provide comfort during the later years of life. A similar type of policy which for the same amount of annual premium places more emphasis on retirement needs and less on protection needs than does the endowment policy is the *retirement income policy*. Both the endowment and retirement income policies can be purchased to provide a specified monthly amount beginning at age 55, 60, or 65. Many estimates and surveys that have been made indicate the need for old-age income.

Other Types of Policies. Many contracts in force today involve combinations of various types of life insurance. For example, one particular type of combination policy provides a low rate for the first four or five years and a higher rate in later years. The same insurance plan would be carried out if an individual purchased a term insurance policy and then, at the end of four or five years, converted it into an ordinary life, a limited-payment life, or an endowment policy.

Another type of policy, the family income policy, provides a monthly income during the dependency years of children, then pays the face amount. This policy combines the features of term insurance with an ordinary life or limited-payment life policy. It becomes a regular policy after the term period runs out.

Annuity Contracts. Many people purchase an *annuity* by turning over to an insurance company a specified sum of money as a single premium or in regular payments. In return for this sum of money the insurance company agrees to pay a specified monthly or yearly income over a definite period of years or until the death of the insured. Some insurance contracts that are paid up can be converted into annuity contracts. In this way a specified income is assured to the person who is insured or to his beneficiaries after his death.

Annuities are not limited to wealthy people. They can be purchased for as low as one thousand dollars. An annuity contract can be purchased over a period of years by annual payments of as little as twenty-five dollars. Under the terms of the contract the insurance company will start annuity payments at the age selected by the purchaser and continue them as long as he lives. Some annuity contracts also guarantee a minimum number of payments. Any guaranteed payments not made before death will be continued to the beneficiary.

There are numerous types of annuity contracts. However, the principal feature of an annuity is guaranteed income starting at a certain age. Therefore, through an annuity one may, during his earning years, provide for an income after his retirement.

Industrial Insurance. *Industrial insurance* is the type that requires small weekly, or sometimes monthly, payments. It is commonly sold to the industrial or wage-earning group. The payment required each week is usually five cents or some multiple of five cents. This type of insurance furnishes varying amounts of protection, according to the age of the insured person and the plan selected. A fairly large proportion of industrial insurance is on the lives of children and women. Medical examinations are seldom required.

The rates reflect the cost of collecting the small premiums and the higher rates of mortality resulting from the less rigid standards of selection. Since its cost is higher in proportion to the protection provided, no one who can obtain other types of insurance should consider industrial insurance.

This type of insurance serves essentially the following useful purposes: it reaches many people who would other-

WHAT HAPPENED TO THE INDUSTRIAL POLICIES
OF 222 INSURANCE COMPANIES IN 1954?

How Terminated:

By death	Number	1,268,063
	Amount	$ 350,112,994
By maturity	Number	545,917
	Amount	$ 118,504,432
By disability	Number	743
	Amount	$ 196,893
By expiration	Number	1,289,408
	Amount	$ 543,063,706
By surrender	Number	2,624,209
	Amount	$ 909,016,851
By lapse	Number	9,561,021
	Amount	$3,871,637,475
By change	Number	374,648
	Amount	$ 106,249,743
TOTAL TERMINATIONS	Number	15,664,009
	Amount	$5,898,782,094

Source: SPECTATOR COMPENDIUM of Official Life Insurance Reports, 1954

wise not buy any insurance; it teaches these people to save and to guard against unfavorable possibilities; it enables many people who are not insurable under most of the other plans to obtain insurance.

Group Insurance. Group insurance is best used to protect the workers of a common employer. Under this plan many employees can be insured through one policy and without medical examination. The cost is determined by an analysis of the group and is based on the losses indicated by the ages, environment, occupation, and general health of the members. The rates may be increased or decreased, but they are usually low. Employers pay part or all of the premiums.

There are two types of group insurance: one is *group term insurance* that does not build up any cash value; the other is *group permanent life insurance* that does build a cash value.

When an employee covered under a group policy leaves the employment through which he has been insured, his protection stops. He may convert this protection to a regular policy (within thirty days) and will then pay annual premiums determined by his age at that time. If the employee was covered under a group permanent policy, he is usually entitled to the fully paid-up protection which has been purchased to date. Sometimes under group permanent, individual certificates are issued which resemble individual life policies. In such cases, these may be converted to regular individual policies and continued by the former employee.

Savings-Bank Insurance. For many years the state of Massachusetts has had in operation a plan of selling savings-bank insurance. Under that plan savings banks accept payments for insurance policies in the same way as they accept deposits in savings accounts. Premiums are not collected by solicitors. Savings-bank insurance was intended to supplant industrial insurance sold largely to wage-earners. It is contended that the savings-bank insurance plan is cheaper because commissions, as well as some other overhead, are eliminated.

New York and Connecticut also permit the sale of savings-bank insurance. In all cases there are certain restrictions on the amount that a person can buy. For instance, in the state of New York no person can buy more than $1,000 from a single bank or more than a total of $3,000; in Massachusetts the limit is $25,000.

Endowment Feature of All Legal-Reserve Contracts. Every straight life policy is based on a mortality table which assumes that at some high age (96, 100, or 104) all people are dead. The last age is therefore considered as the extreme of life. If, for instance, any person who has an ordinary life policy reaches that age, he will be paid the proceeds of his policy just as if he had originally purchased an endowment policy to mature at the age of ninety-six. Basically, therefore, any life insurance policy in legal-reserve companies, except a term contract, is an endowment contract that will pay to the insured person the previously determined amount if he lives to reach a designated age. If he dies before that time, the company will pay the amount to his beneficiary.

Insurance as a Form of Saving. In considering insurance as a form of saving, one must compare it with at least two other forms of saving utilized by individuals: (a) the deposit of savings in a bank and (b) the purchase of government bonds. There are advantages to each of the three forms. Certain types of insurance policies, such as the endowment policy, are in reality insurance plus the savings element. Of course, insurance savings may not accumulate so rapidly as bank savings because, in the case of insurance, payment must be made for the protection involved.

Bank savings offer no financial protection beyond the amount of the deposits and the accumulated interest. These savings can, however, be readily withdrawn. The cash value of an insurance policy can also be withdrawn. If funds are borrowed on an insurance policy, interest must be paid. Government bonds offer an excellent medium of savings because they can be bought in small denominations and pay a fair rate of interest.

Incontestable Clause. The purchaser of life insurance should understand the meaning of the *incontestable clause* in his policy. The essence of such a clause is that, if the insurance company and its agents have not discovered within a specified time (usually one or two years) that the insured person intentionally or unintentionally made misstatements of fact with regard to diseases or other information required in the application, the insurance company cannot contest the validity of the policy. In other words, if any error has been made, it is the responsibility of the insurance company to discover such a fact within the time limit specified in the incontestable clause.

When a misstatement is made in the age of the insured, the policy is not canceled, but the amount payable under the contract will be the amount that could have been obtained at his true age by the actual premiums paid. For instance, if the insured has understated his age by five years, each premium payment is less than the premium for his true age. He is entitled to protection equal only to the amount that his premium payments based on his true age would have purchased.

Some contracts have specific war clauses limiting the liability of the insurance company, but most contracts do not have these clauses. War restrictions may apply to death, disability, and accident benefits.

All standard policies permit the insured person to ride in a licensed airplane on an established route; but if one has ridden in an airplane or expects to ride in an airplane, he should give these facts in his insurance application. Some of the policies written during the early days of the airplane forbid the policyholder to ride in an airplane under any circumstances. Insurance companies will, however, without charge, grant such policyholders, upon application, a supplementary clause that can be attached to their insurance policies. This clause permits those policyholders to ride in airplanes without jeopardizing the validity of their policies.

The Use of Dividends. Dividends paid participating policyholders can be used in the following ways:

(a) They may be obtained in cash.
(b) They may be used to reduce the amount of the next premium payment.
(c) They may be used to purchase additional insurance.
(d) They may be left with the company to accumulate at an interest rate prescribed by the company. This accumulated amount may be used later for any purpose, or it may be withdrawn in cash. If the insured dies before using the accumulated dividends, the beneficiary will be paid the face amount of the policy, plus the amount of the accumulated dividends and interest. When dividends accumulate, ordinary life policies may be paid up eventually, and other policies may be paid up faster than normal.

Nonforfeiture Values. All legal-reserve life insurance companies provide a choice of nonforfeiture values to a policyholder who stops paying premiums on any policy except term insurance. These are cash value, extended term insurance, paid-up insurance, and automatic premium loans. The following is an explanation of these nonforfeiture values:

(a) Each policy states the *cash value*, which is the amount of money that will be paid to the insured if the policy is canceled. It is stated in his contract as required by law.
(b) If one wishes to continue the maximum amount of insurance protection without paying premiums, he may accept *extended term insurance*. This continues the face value of the policy for as long as the accumulated cash value will pay the premium.
(c) Under the *paid-up insurance* plan, the cash value is used to buy a reduced amount of fully paid insurance.
(d) If one elects the *automatic premium loan* plan, the company will automatically pay any overdue premiums by means of a policy loan. If you make no further choice and do not pay any further premiums, the policy will be continued in force until such time as the total indebtedness equals the cash surrender value. At that time the policy is terminated without further value.

If one is not able to keep up the payments on his life insurance policy, he may exchange it for an identical policy of smaller amount. If a different type of policy, such as an ordinary life instead of an endowment policy, is desired, it may be necessary to meet again the requirements for insurability.

Time of Premium Payments. Read your insurance policy carefully concerning your obligations in regard to premiums. Premiums are due on the date mentioned in your policy. They must be paid to the home office or to an authorized representative. Most companies do not give a receipt unless requested. A canceled check serves as a receipt. You may change the frequency of your premium payments upon written request to the insurance company. For example, you may have been paying premiums quarterly, but upon written request you can arrange to pay premiums annually, thereby saving a little money.

Life insurance policies generally allow what is called a *grace period*. This is a period ranging from twenty-eight to thirty-one days after the date the premium is due. If the premium is paid during this grace period, there is no penalty to the policyholder. However, if you die within this period, the unpaid premium will be collected from the amount paid to the beneficiary.

If the premium is not paid during the grace period, the policy lapses. This means the termination of the contract and the loss of protection unless the policy has a value that will automatically continue part or all of the insurance for a time. However, if you stop payments of premiums, you may reinstate your insurance policy provided you have not surrendered your policy for a cash settlement. In order to reinstate it, you must meet all requirements of any person buying a new policy. You will be required to take a new physical examination and pay all the overdue premiums with interest or the increase in cash value. Some policies also have other requirements for reinstatement.

Change of Beneficiary. When anyone buys a life insurance policy, he names a beneficiary or his policy becomes payable to the estate upon his death. If you decide to change your beneficiary, you may do so at any time by filling out forms furnished by the insurance company. This may be done provided you have reserved this right in your policy. If you have not reserved the right to change your beneficiary, you must get the written consent of the original beneficiary before naming a new one.

If the beneficiary you have named should die before you do, your insurance will be paid to your estate. Because of this possibility, you may name second and third beneficiaries so that if the first one dies, the estate will be paid to the next in order.

Assignment of Your Policy. If you have reserved the right to change the beneficiary of your life insurance policy, it can be assigned as security for a loan. Banks will lend money on some life insurance policies provided the policy is assigned to the bank as security for the loan.

Some Limitations in Insurance Policies. Some life insurance contracts contain limitations on travel in foreign countries, travel by air, and war risks. If you have an insurance policy, it is well to study the special clauses providing limitations. Some policies do not provide protection in case of death due to a war. Most policies now provide protection for travel on a scheduled commercial air line or on a nonscheduled private plane with a licensed commercial pilot. These are usually inserted in the back of your policy as riders. Many of the clauses are no longer in effect.

Some special travel insurance policies provide protection only on scheduled air lines and other scheduled public transportation, such as busses and railroads, but do not provide protection when traveling on nonscheduled or private airplanes or vehicles.

The risk of suicide is usually not covered by an insurance policy if it occurs during the first year or two of the contract. If suicide occurs during that time, however, the insurance company will return the premiums.

Extra Benefits. Some insurance policies have provisions whereby it is not necessary to pay the premiums if the insured is permanently disabled. Still others have extra benefits that provide twice the amount of death benefit if the insured dies as a result of an accident instead of from natural causes.

Each company sets its own standard practices. However, the clauses in policies of the same type issued by one company in different states may not always be alike, for the various clauses must conform to the laws of the states in which the company operates and the policies are issued.

Summary of Life Insurance Features

1. A life insurance policy is a contract.
2. Nearly all life insurance premiums are paid at a constant rate.
3. Term insurance is the cheapest, but does not accumulate a cash value.
4. Straight life insurance is the cheapest permanent insurance.
5. Endowment or variations of endowment insurance build the greatest cash values.
6. Several features may be combined in one policy.
7. Group insurance and industrial insurance generally do not require a physical examination.

TEXTBOOK QUESTIONS

1. What is life insurance?
2. In life insurance, who is the beneficiary?
3. What is meant by the premium on a life insurance policy?
4. How can a company selling participating policies reduce its net costs to policyholders by selecting carefully the best risks?
5. Why is legal-reserve insurance sometimes referred to as "level-premium insurance"?
6. Why does not the premium on a legal-reserve insurance policy increase as one grows older and the risk of death becomes greater?
7. What are the recognized basic types of life insurance policies?
8. What is the most important merit of term insurance?

Ch. 30]   FEATURES OF LIFE INSURANCE CONTRACTS   535

9. Is ordinary life insurance recommended for permanent or temporary insurance?
10. In what ways does a limited-payment life policy differ from an ordinary life policy?
11. What is the difference between endowment insurance and limited-payment life insurance?
12. What is one good use of an endowment policy?
13. Why is a short-term endowment policy sometimes not desirable for a young person?
14. As compared with a limited-payment life or an endowment policy, does an ordinary life policy have a lower or a higher premium rate for protection?
15. Describe an annuity in a few words.
16. Why are the rates on industrial insurance high?
17. Do group insurance policies require a medical examination?
18. What is the asserted advantage of savings-bank insurance?
19. If a person has dependents and wants to buy permanent insurance that will provide the maximum amount of protection for the minimum amount of money, what type of policy is recommended?
20. What is the incontestable clause in a life insurance policy?
21. In what way may a policyholder use dividends?
22. What are the four common nonforfeiture values of legal-reserve life insurance?
23. Explain what is meant by the grace period and tell what happens if the premium on a life insurance policy is not paid during that period.
24. If you have not reserved the right to change your beneficiary in your life insurance policy, what must you do in order to change the beneficiary?
25. How can an insurance policy sometimes be used to obtain a mortgage from a bank?

DISCUSSION QUESTIONS

1. "Insurance is the opposite of gambling." Explain this statement.
2. If you borrow some money to buy a home and want to obtain a life insurance policy at the lowest possible cost as a protection until the loan is paid, what kind of insurance will you buy?

3. While he is in school, a student obtains some assistance from his widowed mother. Most of her savings are needed for financing his education, but he earns some of his own money. He hopes to finish school and then to support his mother. He believes that he should carry some insurance to protect his mother. What kind of insurance do you recommend? Why?
4. Under certain circumstances is a limited-payment policy similar to an ordinary life policy?
5. What is the advantage of a limited-payment life policy to a person whose earnings can reasonably be expected to cease at some definite time?
6. Mr. Brown has no dependents, but he wants to buy some insurance so that he can accumulate the maximum amount of savings with reasonable protection and at the same time save some money that can be used to buy a home in ten years. What kind of policy will best suit his needs?
7. Explain why it is necessary to pass a physical examination to qualify for most regular insurance policies. Is there any difference in the case of group insurance?
8. If you want to obtain an insurance policy that will provide permanent protection, become paid up eventually, and have a cash-surrender or a loan value, what kind of policy will you obtain?
9. Which type of policy provides the greatest element of saving but the least element of protection in proportion to the premiums?
10. If one has purchased a twenty-payment life insurance policy of a participating type, what practice would you recommend if it is desired to pay the policy up before the end of twenty years?
11. Explain how the automatic premium loan plan works with legal-reserve life insurance.
12. Assume that you have been sixty days delinquent on paying a premium on a life insurance policy. Is there anything you can do to reinstate it?
13. Describe a circumstance in which the beneficiary of a life insurance policy would have a right to object to changing the beneficiary.
14. (a) Will riding on a regular commercial airline jeopardize insurance policies? (b) In what way will riding in a private plane or operating a private plane jeopardize an insurance policy?

PROBLEMS

1. According to the life insurance contract of one company, it will pay to the widow of the insured for each $1,000 of insurance, a monthly income of the following amounts for at least ten, or at least twenty years, and for as long thereafter as she lives:

AGE OF WIDOW	10 YEARS CERTAIN AND FOR LIFE	20 YEARS CERTAIN AND FOR LIFE
35	$3.22	$3.18
40	3.43	3.37
45	3.70	3.59
50	4.02	3.84
55	4.42	4.12
60	4.90	4.41

On a $10,000 policy (a) how much will the widow at the age of 40 receive each month on a ten year certain basis? (b) a widow at age 55 on a twenty year certain basis?

2. A certain insurance company sells a twenty-year endowment policy at age 25 at the premium rate of $49.27 per year per thousand dollars. The average dividends on policies of this company in recent years have been $6.72 per thousand dollars. Assuming that the dividend rate will continue and that the dividends will be used to reduce the premium, how much will be paid into the insurance company on a $1,000 policy in twenty years?

COMMUNITY PROBLEMS AND PROJECTS

1. Obtain a copy of a form used in applying for an insurance policy and fill out the form for yourself.
2. Obtain an insurance policy at home or from some insurance agent. Examine it carefully in regard to rates, dividends, and special clauses. Make a list of the facts that you learned from an examination of this policy.
3. Examine and study carefully some of the special low priced health and accident insurance policies sometimes sold by mail. Determine exactly what is covered by the insurance and what the exclusions are (not covered by insurance).

Chapter 31

How to Buy Life Insurance

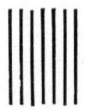

> **Purpose of the Chapter.** In buying life insurance it is important to select the right company, the right insurance agent, and the right policy or contract. The right agent will be able to give you correct professional advice in buying the proper contracts and in buying insurance in the proper amount to satisfy your budget. These problems will be discussed in this chapter.
>
> You will find answers to these questions:
> 1. How can you select an insurance company?
> 2. How can you compare rates on participating and nonparticipating policies?
> 3. How can you select an insurance agent?
> 4. What are the objectives of a good insurance program?
> 5. Why is it important to write a will?

Selecting a Company. To sell life insurance, a company must be licensed in each state in which it operates. From the point of view of the buyer it is desirable to inquire about the standing and reputation of an insurance company from which you plan to purchase a policy. You can get a copy of the company's latest annual report from the agent or by writing to the home office. You can check on a company's standing and reputation with local people—your banker, your lawyer, and local businessmen. You can write to the state insurance commissioner. You should also be sure that the company is licensed in your state.

In comparing the cost of a policy of one company with another, only equivalent contracts should be considered.

538

Caution is necessary since policies which may appear to be identical often differ significantly in nonforfeiture benefits, in settlement values, or in other policy provisions. Under a nonparticipating policy the premium is the final cost to the policyholder. Under a participating policy future dividends must be deducted from premiums to arrive at the final cost. The two tables appearing below show the rates on various policies of two typical companies. After deducting the average dividends of Company B, the rates of that company may or may not be lower than those of Company A.

Annual Premium Rates

AGE OF INSURED AT ISSUANCE OF POLICY	ORDINARY LIFE ($1,000)	20-PAYMENT LIFE ($1,000)	20-YEAR ENDOWMENT ($1,000)	5-YEAR TERM CONVERTIBLE ($1,000)
Company A, nonparticipating				
20	$13.80	$24.90	$46.04	$ 6.13
25	15.75	27.18	46.16	6.31
30	18.16	29.84	46.38	6.59
35	21.42	33.08	46.96	7.34
40	25.57	36.87	48.08	8.91
45	31.01	41.55	49.66	11.78
50	37.96	47.08	52.62	16.61
55	47.11	53.61	56.90	24.00
Company B, participating				
20	$18.21	$29.99	$49.41	$ 7.14
25	20.72	32.82	50.00	7.83
30	23.83	36.05	50.85	8.86
35	27.72	39.81	52.14	10.41
40	32.68	44.25	54.10	12.73
45	39.07	49.65	57.06	16.30
50	47.39	56.43	61.65	21.79
55	58.40	65.33	68.59	30.24

Some participating companies set their original rates higher than do other participating companies. Higher dividends should be expected from the former than from the latter companies. Tables are published which show the dividends which are being paid by each company under its participating policies. Insurance salesmen can furnish this information.

Let us assume, for example that the average annual dividend over the first ten years in Company B is $3.41 for each $1,000 of ordinary life insurance issued at age 20. For the first ten years, the net cost per year is $14.80 after deducting the average dividend. Over the first twenty years, the average annual dividend might be $4.57 and then the average annual cost would be $13.64. (These dividends correspond to the rates given in the tables.)

The cost of an insurance policy differs between companies, but competition tends to restrict these differences. The difference in cost between insurance bought on the participating, as compared with nonparticipating basis, can be measured accurately only over a long period of time.

Guides in Selecting an Insurance Company

1. Compare rates between companies, including dividends.
2. Select only a company that has a good reputation.
3. Deal only with a reputable agent.
4. In comparing the same or similar policies of different companies, do not compare cost alone, but be sure that they are identical in every respect. For example, some policies have a disability clause which relieves you from the responsibility of paying premiums in case of illness or other disability.
5. The dividend rate or other factors will not necessarily remain the same in the future for any company.

Selecting an Insurance Agent. As a general rule, insurance salesmen are honorable and consider seriously the needs of clients. The buyer of insurance should bear in mind that even an honorable insurance salesman may be so eager to sell that he may make a recommendation sometimes just to please the person who is buying the insurance, even though it may not be the best possible recommendation. The buyer of insurance must therefore learn the first principles of insurance so that he may judge the merits of an insurance salesman's recommendations.

A reliable agent who is working for a reliable company will give good advice to prospective purchasers of insurance. In making application for an insurance policy, the individual is usually required to indicate the amount of

Compare Agents, Companies, and Policies Before Buying

Ewing Galloway

insurance he already owns. This information gives the insurance company an opportunity to determine whether the applicant is justified in purchasing additional insurance.

A good life insurance agent is one who not only has an adequate knowledge of life insurance but who also has learned how to help people determine their insurance needs and fit insurance policies to those needs. If a person wants to obtain the best use of his insurance dollars, he must find such an agent and put his trust in him as he would in his doctor or lawyer. Only then can the agent help him:

1. Plan insurance protection to fit his needs and those of his dependents.
2. Build an insurance program that will include the savings he wants for his retirement and for specific purposes such as college education of his children.
3. Fit the purchasing of policies to his present and probable future income.
4. Revise his program periodically and help the insured build onto it, as the first three factors change.

Selecting a Policy. In buying insurance and in comparing one policy with another, one must consider: (a) the uses for which the insurance is intended, (b) his present and expected income, (c) the cost of the insurance, and (d) his willingness and capacity to save.

In examining any policy, one should compare the cash-surrender value, the paid-up insurance, and the extended insurance with those of other policies. The next problem is to choose the best policy for one's individual needs.

Planning Your Program. No one can decide how much insurance to carry on a particular life without knowing all the circumstances surrounding the person and his family. The amount of an expenditure for insurance should be governed by the budget.

Three Key Objectives

1. Adequate protection for specific needs.
2. Adequate savings through insurance.
3. Fitting the premium payments to the income available in your budget.

In the case of most insurance policies a part of the expenditure constitutes a saving, while the remaining part of it constitutes an expense for the protection obtained. The saving is a result of the gradual increase in the cash value or the loan value of the policy. Expenditures for insurance should therefore be considered from the point of view of savings and expenses.

Life insurance should be designed primarily to replace income lost to a family when the husband and father dies. Except for certain sums that may be needed at the time of death, the proceeds of the insurance should be looked upon as an income that will be paid regularly under some prescribed plan to the family of the deceased husband and father. A total of $10,000 may sound like a large sum of money, and it really is, as you will find when you try to save that sum. But at 2 or 3 per cent interest, $10,000 will only provide $200 or $300 a year of income from interest. Life insurance policies can be arranged to provide monthly checks consisting of both principal and interest instead of a lump-sum payment or instead of just interest.

For example, the proceeds of a $10,000 insurance policy will pay $100 a month for nine years and six months. The proceeds of a $20,000 policy will pay $100 a month for twenty-two years and ten months. Other methods of payment may enable a person to work out almost any desired program of income for his family after his death. His life

Ewing Galloway
Insurance Is Mainly for the Protection and Support of Dependents

insurance agent should be quite helpful in arranging the details of adequate protection and proper payments.

When the head of a family dies, the scale of living must be lowered in most cases. Many families are entitled to social security benefits, but these are seldom sufficient to take care of all the needs; however, they do supplement the insurance program and should be taken into consideration. Unless an insurance program is planned, the family will have to depend upon its own earning power or upon the income from other property already accumulated. Most families are not qualified to manage investments.

The following chart illustrates the readjustments that are necessary upon the death of the father and husband. At the time of death there are certain unusual expenses involved. Then comes the readjustment period when the family may have to move into a smaller house and prepare for living on a smaller income. In many families there is a problem of educating the children until they are self-supporting, and then providing an income for the widow.

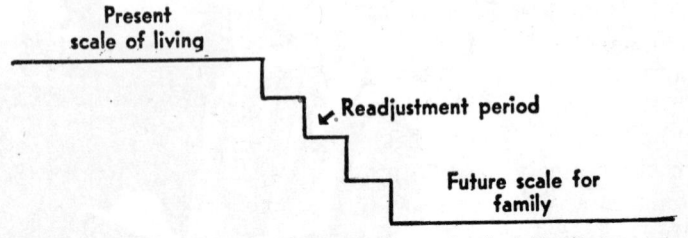

```
Present
scale of living
    └─────┐
          │  ↙ Readjustment period
          └─────┐
                │  Future scale for
                │     family
                └─────────────────
```

The Insurance Program Should Provide for a Gradual Readjustment in the Scale of Living

An Example of a Planned Insurance Program. Let us take for an example the Nelson family. Assume that Mr. and Mrs. Nelson are both forty years of age, and that they have two children, thirteen and fifteen years of age. Mr. Nelson wants to plan his insurance program so that, if he should die, his family will have a reasonable income based upon his maximum ability to provide this income through insurance. He feels that he can afford to spend about $50 a month for insurance premiums and then proceeds to build his program based upon this expenditure.

Mr. and Mrs. Nelson feel that at least $1,000 will be necessary to take care of funeral and other expenses. They do not have any mortgage or other substantial debts that will have to be paid.

Under the present social security laws, if Mr. Nelson died during the current year, Mrs. Nelson would receive, unless she remarries or dies, a monthly income for five years, or until the youngest child reaches age eighteen. She will receive for each child a monthly income until that child reaches eighteen, unless the child marries, quits school, or dies before reaching eighteen. Assuming that Mr. Nelson has paid social security taxes on the maximum income for social security purposes and is fully covered under the new law, the benefit payments will be $200 a month for three years (until the first child reaches eighteen), and then $162.80 a month for two more years (until the other child reaches eighteen). Mrs. Nelson will not receive any further social security benefits until age sixty-five, at which time she will receive $81.40 a month for life. If she remarries, those benefits will cease.

Obviously the Nelsons must supplement these probable benefits, for they will not be sufficient for the needs of the family; and, if Mrs. Nelson or the children are forced to go to work, they will lose all or part of the benefits. Income will be badly needed while the children are in school. After both the children reach eighteen, Mrs. Nelson will need an income to replace the social security benefits.

Mr. Nelson owns a $10,000 straight life insurance policy bought at age twenty-five. He and Mrs. Nelson decide that a $1,000 straight life policy, payable in a lump sum, would be desirable for a cleanup fund at the time of death. They also feel that for approximately a year following his death she will need extra income to carry her through the readjustment period. They find that a policy with a face value of approximately $1,189 will provide an income of $100 a month for twelve months following his death.

The big problem is to provide a satisfactory monthly income after the first year and through the years when Mrs. Nelson will not have any social security benefits. The $10,000 policy already owned will pay $100 a month to Mrs. Nelson for nine years and six months after his death. After consulting an insurance agent, it was decided to purchase another $10,000 straight life policy with certain unusual features about it. Under the provisions of this policy Mrs. Nelson will be paid $100 a month to age sixty-five and thereafter will be paid $56.10 a month. The premium payments on this policy for the first twenty-five years are $401.80 a year and thereafter are $255.60.

The following table shows the amount, the purposes, and the annual cost of this program:

AMOUNT OF INSURANCE	PURPOSE AND AMOUNT OF PROTECTION	ANNUAL PREMIUM*
$ 1,000	$1,000 cash for cleanup fund	$ 32.18
1,189	$100 a month for readjustment period of 12 months	41.25
10,000	$100 a month for 9 years and 6 months for education of children	210.20
10,000	$100 a month until age 65, then $56.10 until death	401.80
$22,189	Total Insurance Required	$685.43

* The dividends will reduce the total annual premium.

A Sample Insurance Plan

Now let us see how this program works out from the point of view of monthly income for Mrs. Nelson's family until the death of Mrs. Nelson. The following table shows the monthly income from insurance and social security benefits, with the total monthly income given in the last column.

YEAR	MONTHLY PROCEEDS FROM INSURANCE	MONTHLY PROCEEDS FROM SOCIAL SECURITY	MONTHLY TOTAL
1 *	$300.00 *	$200.00	$500.00
2	200.00	200.00	400.00
3	200.00	200.00	400.00
4	200.00	162.80	320.00
5	200.00	162.80	320.00
6	200.00	none	200.00
7	200.00	none	200.00
8	200.00	none	200.00
9 (and six months)	200.00	none	200.00
10–25	100.00	none	100.00
26 to end of life	56.10	81.40	137.50

* And a lump-sum payment of $1,000.

Proceeds from Mr. Nelson's Insurance and Social Security Benefits

Amount of Insurance Based on Income. When a married person's income is small, he needs insurance because he must have some protection for his dependents. The amount that is set aside for insurance should be budgeted in the same manner as his other expenditures. As a person's salary increases, the amount spent for insurance should also increase. The only people who do not need life insurance are those who have investments which provide a certain income sufficient to support the dependents.

The amount of insurance that should be bought is a special problem in the case of each individual. It must be determined by considering the income, the necessary expenditures, the accumulation of a cash savings fund, and the care of dependents. There are, however, reasonable percentages that have proved to be satisfactory. The table at the top of the next page shows the percentages of insurance expenditures recommended for individuals.

An analysis of this table discloses that a person earning three thousand dollars a year should expect to spend from 5½ to 7 per cent of his income for insurance. Obviously, the percentage expended in any particular case will depend

ANNUAL INCOME	PERCENTAGE	ANNUAL OUTLAY
$2,500	5–6½	$125 to $162.50
3,000	5½–7	165 to 210
3,500	6–8½	210 to 297.50
4,000	6½–9	260 to 360
4,500	7–9½	315 to 427.50
5,000	7½–10	375 to 500

The Amount of Income to Spend for Life Insurance

upon (a) one's standard of living, (b) one's sense of responsibility, (c) the cost of living, (d) the number of dependents, and (e) the type of insurance that is bought.

The amount and the type of insurance that is purchased should be based upon a carefully thought-out insurance plan and should be taken into consideration in the family budget.

Amount of Insurance Required for a Future Income. Another way to determine the amount of insurance that should be purchased is to determine the amount that one needs to provide a future income in any one of three ways:

(a) By creating a cash estate, which will be invested to provide an income.
(b) By buying sufficient insurance to yield a fixed amount of income for life after a certain age.
(c) By arranging with the insurance company to use the proceeds of the insurance policy for paying a fixed income to dependents after the death of the insured.

Under the first plan the person can consider his insurance and his other savings in computing the amount of income that will be available. Suppose, for example, that a person has planned his insurance program so that the cash proceeds available at his contemplated retirement age of sixty will amount to $25,000. If this amount is invested at 3½ per cent, it will pay an annual income of $875. This income, plus the income from other savings and investments, will represent the sum that the person may expect for use after he retires, provided he does spend part of the principal.

Under the second plan it is possible for a person to make a contract with an insurance company whereby the proceeds of insurance are to provide (a) a guaranteed income for life or (b) a guaranteed income for life with a cash settlement if death occurs within a certain period. The following table shows the monthly income guaranteed by one insurance company for each $1,000 of the proceeds from insurance. The payments given in this table are guaranteed for life. Tables such as this vary, of course, according to the companies with which the contracts of life insurance have been made.

BEGINNING AT AGE	GUARANTEED MONTHLY INCOME FOR LIFE FOR EACH $1,000 IN INSURANCE FUND
50	$4.51
55	5.07
60	5.80
65	6.75
70	8.02

Monthly Income for Life (No Refund)

For example, if a person has, under this plan, a $10,000 matured endowment policy at the age of fifty, he will receive from the insurance company $45.10 a month for the rest of his life. Some settlement options guarantee such payments for a certain number of years, such as fifteen or twenty years, and for life thereafter if the person lives longer. If he does not live beyond the fixed number of years, his beneficiary will get a specified cash settlement.

Under the third plan the person who is insured can provide for the proceeds of his insurance to be left with the insurance company after his death so that his dependents can be paid a fixed income for a specified number of years. The following table shows the proceeds that must be left with the company to provide fixed monthly payments of $50 to $150 for a period of five to fifteen years:

NUMBER OF MONTHLY PAYMENTS	$50	$70	$75	$90	$100	$125	$150	NUMBER OF YEARS PAYABLE
60	$2,792	$ 3,909	$ 4,188	$ 5,026	$ 5,585	$ 6,981	$ 8,377	5
72	3,303	4,624	4,954	5,945	6,606	8,277	9,909	6
84	3,799	5,318	5,698	6,838	7,598	9,497	11,396	7
96	4,280	5,992	6,420	7,704	8,560	10,700	12,840	8
108	4,748	6,646	7,121	8,546	9,495	11,869	14,242	9
120	5,201	7,281	7,801	9,362	10,402	13,002	15,603	10
132	5,642	7,898	8,462	10,155	11,283	14,104	16,924	11
144	6,069	8,497	9,104	10,924	12,138	15,173	18,207	12
156	6,484	9,078	9,727	11,672	12,969	16,211	19,454	13
168	6,888	9,642	10,331	12,398	13,775	17,219	20,662	14
180	7,279	10,190	10,918	13,102	14,557	18,197	21,836	15

The Cash Value Needed to Provide a Fixed Monthly Income for Dependents for a Certain Number of Years if 3 Per Cent Interest Is Paid (The Interest Rate May Be Lower Than 3 Per Cent)

From this table it is apparent that, when a person dies, the proceeds from his insurance policy must amount to $5,201 to guarantee a payment of $50 a month to his dependents for a period of ten years. The values vary, of course, according to the companies.

The buying of insurance should be just one part of the plan of building up savings and providing for the protection of dependents. In deciding how much insurance to buy, a person should consider his entire financial program.

Insurance, Estates, Wills. As you have learned through your study of life insurance, a beneficiary may be named to collect the proceeds of a life insurance policy. If no beneficiary is named, the proceeds go into what is called an *estate*, which includes money and other property of the deceased. An estate must be administered according to the laws of the state. The distribution of money or other property can therefore be regulated, to a certain extent, before one's death by designating beneficiaries of life insurance policies and by making a will.

A *will* consists simply of instructions that a person gives before his death as to the distribution of his property after his death. It may be changed or revoked at any time during the maker's life. Even though there is a will, creditors must be paid; and a will may not deprive the wife or husband from his rightful share in property according to the laws of the state.

If you make a will, you should select and name in the will an *executor* who may be a member of the family, a friend, or a lawyer. A lawyer is entitled to a fee for his services. The function of the executor is to prepare tax returns, pay the taxes, investigate claims against the estate, pay the debts that are due, determine the value of the property, distribute the property as instructed in the will, and make a report to the Probate Court.

If a valid will is not left by the deceased person or if an executor has not been named, the court will appoint an *administrator* to settle the estate and distribute the property according to the laws of the state. The duties of the administrator are the same as those of the executor.

If it is possible to designate two persons to serve as executors, these are called *coexecutors*. Sometimes under a will, the property, or part of the property, is left in trust to be managed by a trust company, the trust department of a bank, or an individual called a *trustee*. Sometimes an individual is named as a trustee along with a trust company or the trust department of a bank in which case this person is called a *cotrustee*. Trustees are required to carry out the instructions which may be limited and specific or may be very broad and general. In most states the trustees must obtain the approval of the Probate Court before taking any important action.

Should You Make a Will? Many people in moderate circumstances do not feel that it is desirable to make a will. They feel that wills are only for rich people. However, if you own only a moderate amount of property, your heirs will have less trouble and less expense if you make a will; and you are more likely to have your wishes carried out with a will than you are without it.

Even when a small amount of money or property is involved there are dangers in assuming that it is not necessary to make a will. The situation is different in every state, but many things can happen which may not be according to the plans or wishes of the person who died. For example, a husband may assume that all of his property will automatically go to his wife, but in the absence of a will in some states where there is a wife and one child, the wife would get one third and the child would get two thirds of the estate. In some states if there are no children, the wife would get part of the property and the rest would go to the mother, brother, sister, or other relatives. There are many other things that can happen.

There are mistaken ideas of many people that any kind of written instructions will serve as a valid will. That belief is not correct. Because of the fact that there are different laws in various states, the making of a home-made will is sometimes risky. A lawyer should therefore be consulted. Usually a lawyer will draw up a simple will at very low cost.

Summary of Life Insurance and Wills

1. Select a good agent of a good company.
2. Buy the proper contract for protection or savings or both.
3. Buy the right amount of insurance.
4. The distribution of property is less expensive with a will than without it.
5. Provided the will does not conflict with the laws of the state, the property may be distributed according to the wishes of the maker of the will.
6. If a husband dies, leaving a wife and children, without a will, someone must administer the estate. Even though the wife administers the estate, she usually will have to provide a bond and make regular reports as to the handling of the estate for the children.

TEXTBOOK QUESTIONS

1. How can you judge the standing or reputation of a life insurance company?
2. When the listed premium rates of companies are compared, what should be considered in computing the net rates?
3. What are some guides or factors in selecting an insurance company?
4. What kind of insurance agent should one select?
5. What are the three key objectives of a life insurance program?
6. What types of policies would you use for the following purposes: (a) when a special need must be covered for a short period; (b) when future obligations will be more important than present obligations; (c) when it is more important to get protection for a large amount than to avoid the payment of premiums in old age; (d) when the accumulation of a savings fund is the main objective?
7. In the case of a family, who is the main person whose life is insured and why?
8. Why is it considered desirable to have a set amount of life insurance paid in cash immediately on the death of the insured?
9. From the table at the top of page 548 determine the guaranteed monthly income of a person who retires at the age of sixty if he has $12,000 in an insurance fund.

10. From the table on page 548 determine how much the cash value of insurance must be to pay the dependents of the insured a monthly income of $90 a month for 108 months.
11. What are some of the disadvantages if a young man buys all the endowment insurance that his income will permit?
12. If your employer offers you protection under a group insurance policy, is it desirable for you to participate in this kind of insurance?
13. What is a will?
14. What is the difference between an executor and an administrator?
15. Why should one make a will?

DISCUSSION QUESTIONS

1. If you start buying life insurance at age thirty and there is inflation (a general increase in prices and the cost of living), what happens to the value of the money that is paid to you in your old age or to a beneficiary on your death? In other words, explain the effect of inflation on insurance.
2. If the situation in the previous question is reversed and there is deflation, what is the effect on insurance?
3. Why do insurance companies spend considerable money each year in publishing health advertisements and in conducting health campaigns?
4. Give some reasons why it is so important to buy insurance from a good agent representing a good company and how you can determine whether you will be saving properly.
5. (a) When a person applies for an insurance policy, why does the insurance agent ask how much insurance the person already owns? (b) Why is it desirable for the person to tell how much he owns?
6. A man forty years of age knows that in the position in which he works he must retire at the age of sixty. He would like to buy an ordinary life policy, but he wants all premium payments to cease by the time he retires. What options are open to him?
7. A man plans to go into business. He knows that he needs insurance protection, but he wants to buy insurance that will provide the maximum loan value. What kind of insurance would you recommend?
8. What kind of insurance program would you recommend for a young unmarried man of seventeen years of age who expects to finish a college education and go into business for himself?
9. In the case of Mr. and Mrs. Nelson discussed in this chapter, what would you recommend as an improvement in the program provided additional insurance could be afforded?

10. (a) Why is it undesirable for a person to carry too much insurance? (b) What is too much insurance?
11. Explain why one should avoid borrowing money to pay the first premium on a life insurance policy.

PROBLEMS

1. Suppose Company B, the rates of which are listed on page 539, has been paying an average dividend of $6.42 a thousand on an ordinary life policy. Is the net rate lower or higher than the rate on the equivalent policy of Company A? (Base your figures on the rates for a person who is thirty years of age.)
2. A man thirty-five years of age has two children, aged four and eight. He has a good position and has almost paid for his home. He has $500 in a savings account, an endowment policy of $2,000, and an ordinary life policy of $5,000. His budget provides for a yearly saving of approximately $200. He decides that he wants to spend approximately $100 of this amount for insurance that will provide the maximum amount of protection, but will become paid up before he is sixty years of age. What kind of policy and how much insurance can he buy from Company A, the rates of which are listed in the table on page 539.
3. A man, age twenty, who is planning to marry, has $200 a year available for insurance. He wants to be assured of having $2,000 to use as a payment on a home by the time he is forty years of age. He also wants the maximum amount of protection from his insurance. Outline a plan of insurance for him based on the rates of Company A (page 539).

COMMUNITY PROBLEMS AND PROJECTS

1. If your parents are paying insurance premiums monthly, quarterly, or semiannually, calculate the amount of savings that would be accumulated if the money were deposited in a savings account and used to pay the premiums annually.
2. If your family will permit you to do so, analyze their present insurance program and then give your recommendations as to changes or improvements in the program, including the use of dividends, the authorized beneficiary, and the settlement provisions.
3. Consult an insurance agent and ask him to give you the figures in regard to the types of policies, amounts, first-year premiums, and recommended use of the proceeds for a program for your family. The program should be based upon a stipulated yearly premium that can be afforded in the family budget.

Chapter 32

Renting or Buying a Home

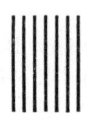

Purpose of the Chapter. Everyone must have a home, but the problem of the family is to decide whether to rent or lease a home or apartment, or whether to buy or build a home. The purpose of this chapter is to show the advantages and disadvantages of renting, buying, and building.

You will find answers to these questions:
1. When is it best to rent instead of to own a home?
2. When is it best to own instead of to rent a home?
3. What is the difference between renting from month to month or signing a written lease?
4. What are the advantages and disadvantages of owning a home?
5. How can you determine whether you can afford to own a home and how much you can pay?
6. What is the minimum down payment required?
7. What are the monthly and yearly costs of buying a home as compared with renting?

Who Should Own a Home? Regardless of the advantages that are claimed for owning a home, one should consider the problem carefully. Even though owning a home may appear desirable, it may be economically unwise to buy or to build a house. For instance, if one expects to move soon to another town, if property values are declining, if insufficient capital is available to make the down payment, or if there is any likelihood that payments on the home cannot be made, buying a home would be unwise. All the costs of owning a home should be carefully computed and these should then be considered in the family budget.

When You Should Rent, Not Buy

1. When you expect to move soon to another town.
2. When prices are declining.
3. When you do not have enough money for a substantial down payment.
4. When your budget will not allow for the payments and other expenses involved.

When You Should Own, Not Rent

1. When you expect to stay in the community.
2. When prices of real estate are stable or increasing.
3. When you have enough money to make a substantial down payment.
4. When your budget will allow for necessary payments and other expenses involved.

Renting with or without a Written Lease. The first consideration in renting a home, whether a house or an apartment, is to determine the advisability of renting for a shorter, indefinite period or for a longer, definite period. Renting a home from month to month gives a person greater freedom to move and to take advantage of decreases in rentals as conditions change. A person who may find it necessary to move at an uncertain future date because of a change in his work should try to avoid signing a lease, particularly one covering a long period.

In some communities it is very difficult under normal circumstances to obtain a home without a written lease. Property owners naturally do not want to run the risk of the property being vacant frequently. They therefore prefer the protection of a written lease for a specified length of time.

A person who rents for an indefinite period is subject to the necessity of moving if the owner wants the property for some other purpose. In most states, however, the custom or law requires the property owner to give at least thirty days' notice. If legal action is necessary to force the renter to move, still more time will be required before the property must be vacated.

Points to Investigate in Renting

1. Is the location desirable?
2. Is the external appearance good?
3. Is the internal appearance good?
4. Are the number of rooms and their size and arrangement satisfactory?
5. Are the lighting and heating adequate?
6. Are the laundry, plumbing, and sanitary facilities satisfactory?
7. Does the building have shades, awnings, or other similar equipment?
8. Will the landlord paint and redecorate where necessary?
9. Will the landlord take care of the necessary repairs?
10. Is the character of the neighborhood satisfactory?
11. In the case of an apartment, are yard privileges granted?
12. If you are renting an apartment, who pays for the heat, water, electricity, and other services?

Length and Expiration of the Lease. A period when rentals are going down is a bad time to obtain a long lease. A period when rentals have reached a low level or have started to rise is a good time to obtain a long lease.

In some communities most leases expire at the same time, usually at the end of April or May. If your lease expires when other leases are expiring, you will have a better opportunity to obtain another home.

Many families find that it pays them to select a home carefully with the intention of occupying it for several years. By leasing for a long period, they can reduce moving costs and become better established in the community. By staying in one place a long time, a family has an opportunity to develop a garden and to improve the property. Landlords are usually willing to keep property in good repair if the tenants indicate a desire to stay a reasonable length of time. People who lease property will therefore usually find it advantageous to obtain a lease for one year with the privilege of extending the lease one or more years.

Advantages of Owning a Home. There is little doubt that any family who can own a home should own a home if they meet the requirements that have already been discussed. Owning a home places certain responsibilities upon the home owner, but these responsibilities help to make the family feel secure and a more permanent part of the community. When the home is finally paid for, the family will be more secure in case the earnings of the family decrease. The family at least will have a place to live.

Ordinarily, the best time to buy a home is not when prices of real estate are high, but, on the other hand, this is usually the time when the family has its greatest income and is able to save enough money to make a substantial down payment. Therefore, the answer to when a family should buy is determined largely by the following factors:

1. Does the family have enough money saved to make a substantial down payment?
2. Is the future income reasonably assured so that the monthly payments on the home can be continued with a margin of safety?
3. Can an adequate home in a satisfactory location be purchased or built with the down payment that can be made, and the monthly payments that will fit the budget?

Advantages of Owning a Home

1. It will give you a sense of security and a home in your old age.
2. It will force you to establish a purpose and a plan of saving.
3. It will add prestige, improve your credit rating, and add stability to the family.
4. It will give you enjoyment and pride.

Can You Pay for It? All authorities in home management, financing, and home building insist that no family should buy a home until a very careful budget plan has been worked out. After shopping for a satisfactory home in a desirable location that will take care of the family for a reasonable time in the future, a budget should then be prepared that will take into consideration the down payment and all of the carrying and operating charges, including the payment on principal. Ways of figuring these estimates will be discussed later in this chapter.

If a person buys a house for cash, he should not invest so much that he must use all the funds that he has laid aside for use in an emergency. For instance, if he uses all his cash to purchase a house, he may not have any reserve to use in case of a serious illness or some other emergency. A person who acquires a house by means of borrowed money makes a serious mistake if he buys beyond his capacity to pay the interest charge and to repay the loan. When one borrows money to buy a home, the loan must be repaid in installments. These include payments on the principal and interest on the unpaid balance.

If the loan is too great, he may become discouraged because of the necessity of cutting down the level of living and thus depriving his family of necessities that are required to maintain health. He may even lose the house through foreclosure proceedings (see Chapter 34).

In buying a house or renting, many young people gamble to the extent of assuming that their earnings will increase. They therefore undertake a greater obligation than they should. If future earnings do not become greater, or if they become less, discouragement inevitably results. One of the first questions that should arise in the mind of a prospective renter or purchaser is the percentage of earnings to be expended in providing the home.

The amount that a person may spend as the interest and the principal on a loan on a home is always a question. Studies have been made to determine reasonable amounts that should be spent in acquiring a home. Builders, realtors, and lenders of money estimate that about 23 per cent of the assured income of a family may safely be spent in buying a home. This total should include both interest and principal.

If a person who has been renting a house decides to buy it, he will be required to make greater expenditures than those required formerly in renting. If it has not been possible for him to save money regularly in the past, it will probably not be possible to finance the purchase of the home. Some people do, however, undertake such a purchase because they are then forced to follow some definite plan of saving. The purchase of a home may result in systematic saving in order to pay for the investment.

Minimum Down Payment. As will be explained in Chapter 33, there are many ways of financing the purchase of a home, but usually a person must pay part of the original price in cash.

Conservative financial advisors recommend that a person who buys a home should pay 20 to 25 per cent of the purchase price in cash. It is frequently impossible to obtain a first-mortgage loan of more than 50 or 60 per cent of the value of a house. The plans developed under the Federal Housing Administration permit a minimum cash investment of from 10 to 20 per cent. The difference must be paid in cash, or an additional loan must be obtained from another source.

Veterans are entitled to obtain loans under favorable conditions which involve very small down payments and low interest rates. However, they must qualify for these loans under special regulations and there must be adequate evidence provided that the veteran will have enough income to make the regular payments on the loan. These loans are discussed in Chapter 33.

Analysis of Financing Costs. The table on the next page shows the first-year cost of financing a home. This information was collected for prospective home owners by the Bureau of Standards of the United States Department of Commerce. The various income groups are listed according to the approximate cost of the home that a person in each income group can afford. This table assumes that an initial cash payment of 20 per cent of the total value will be made when the home is purchased.

The fact is recognized that families having the same annual income may not be able to devote the same amount toward purchasing a home. For example, a family having four or five children and living in a city may not be able

	$7,000	$8,000	$9,000	$10,000	$14,000
1. Value of house and lot	$7,000	$8,000	$9,000	$10,000	$14,000
2. Annual income	2,800 to 4,200	3,200 to 4,800	3,600 to 5,400	4,000 to 6,000	5,600 to 8,400
3. Cash down payment (20% of value)	1,400	1,600	1,800	2,000	2,800
4. Amount of loan (80% of value)	5,600	6,400	7,200	8,000	11,200
5. Amounts of yearly payments (10% of total value)	700	800	900	1,000	1,400
5-A. Interest (5%)	280	320	360	400	560
5-B. Payment of principal	420	480	540	600	840
6. Taxes and assessments (2%)	140	160	180	200	280
7. Insurance (.5%)	35	40	45	50	70
8. Upkeep (1.5%)	105	120	135	150	210
9. Total first-year cost (5 plus 6, 7, 8)	980	1,120	1,260	1,400	1,960
9-A. Expense (5-A plus 6, 7, 8)	560	640	720	800	1,020
*9-B. Saving (9 minus 9-A)	420	480	540	600	940

* Although this amount represents the apparent monetary saving, there is a hidden expense called depreciation because of the wearing out due to the increase in age of the house. A 2 per cent allowance for depreciation on the value of the house itself would be a fair estimate of the loss from this cause.

The First-Year Cost of Financing a Home

to put much aside for buying a home; but another family with only one or two children and located possibly in a small village can afford to apply a larger proportion of its income for the same purpose.

The following is an explanation of the items in the table:

Item 1. Value of house and lot. The value of the house and the lot is the basis upon which the expenses in this table have been computed. The value of the lot will usually be from 8 to 20 per cent of the total amount.

Item 2. Annual income. Because of the wide variation the incomes have been grouped. No rule can be set that will apply to all classes. It is assumed in this table, however, that the value of the house and the lot will be between $1\frac{2}{3}$ and $2\frac{1}{2}$ times the annual income. For example, a family with an income of $3,000 could expect to pay from $5,000 to $7,500 for a home. The average amount to pay for a home will be about double the annual income, but usually not more than $2\frac{1}{2}$ times the annual income. As the income of the family becomes larger, a higher percentage of the income can be spent for a home.

Item 3. First cash payment. The cash payment should not be below 20 per cent of the value of the house and the lot. It should be much higher if possible. The greater the down payment, the better, for the financing is then simpler and the cost is less. Occasionally a home can be purchased with a down payment of less than 20 per cent, but even under normal conditions a down payment of 20 per cent is dangerously low for many people. It is unwise to make so small an initial payment unless there is a good margin for saving. When there is a shortage of money for lending purposes, the loan is difficult to obtain if only a small down payment can be made. Furthermore, the interest charge at such a time is high.

Item 4. Amount of loan. After the amount of the initial cash payment has been deducted from the value of the house and the lot, the difference represents the amount of the loan.

Item 5. Amount of yearly payments. In this table the yearly payments are the same in amount. Under some plans of financing, however, the payment is reduced as the loan is paid off. Item 5A represents the amount of each payment that is applicable as interest; and item 5B, the amount that is applicable as amortization of the principal. With a small down payment the interest rate is usually higher than with a large down payment. If it is necessary to obtain a second mortgage, the interest rate is less favorable.

The interest rate will depend upon local conditions at the time the loan is made. It is generally considered best to pay off a loan on a home within fifteen years or less. If interest rates are unfavorable at the time the loan is to be made, the loan can be obtained for a short time in the hope that it can be renewed later at a lower rate.

Various plans of financing require weekly payments, semimonthly payments, monthly payments, semiannual payments, or annual payments. The plan of payment should be fully understood before any contract is signed.

Item 6. Taxes and assessments. Local taxes on real estate usually range from $1\frac{1}{2}$ to $2\frac{1}{2}$ per cent of the market value of the property. Occasionally there are assessments against the property for a sidewalk, a street, lights, or other facilities; but ordinarily the assessments on residential property are not high. In this table 2 per cent has been allowed for taxes and assessments.

Item 7. Insurance. Fire insurance rates rarely amount to more than $\frac{1}{2}$ per cent of the value of the house. The allowance made in this table is liberal because it has been figured on the basis of the value of the house and the lot.

Item 8. Upkeep. The cost of maintaining a home will vary considerably, depending upon the condition of the property, the age of the house, and the type of construction. The yearly cost of maintenance may, however, be estimated reasonably at $1\frac{1}{2}$ per cent of the total value.

Item 9. Total first-year cost. The total first-year cost of the home includes the total annual payment plus taxes, assessments, insurance, and upkeep. Item 9A represents the yearly expense. The difference between the total cost for the year and the total expense is the saving (item 9B). In other words, this is the amount of investment that the buyer has accumulated during the first year. The rest of his money has been used for interest and expenses of maintaining the house. Item 9A is equivalent to the rent.

Buying Compared with Renting. Whether to buy or to rent a home is the problem of each individual. A person frequently rents because (a) he desires freedom of movement, (b) he is unable to arrange a plan of financing a home, (c) he believes that it is cheaper to rent, (d) he doubts the investment value of owning a home, or (e) he does not care to assume the obligation of paying for a home. If a person needs a permanent home and can buy it, the following table will serve as a guide in comparing the cost of buying a home with the cost of renting one:

1. Value of house and lot	$7,000	$8,000	$9,000	$10,000	$14,000
2. Annual income	2,800 to 4,200	3,200 to 4,800	3,600 to 5,400	4,000 to 6,000	5,600 to 8,400
3. First-year cost of buying a house Expense Saving	980 560 420	1,120 640 480	1,260 720 540	1,400 800 600	1,960 1,020 940
4. Annual cost of renting a house A Example B Example C Example D Example	480 530 660 720	540 720 750 810	600 810 840 900	660 900 930 990	840 960 1,080 1,200

For instance, if one is considering an $8,000 house and is paying $750 a year rent (Example C), there would be a cash expense saving of $110 a year by owning a house ($750 − $640 = $110).

Comparison of Cost of Buying with Cost of Renting

This table does not tell the whole story because it does not take into consideration the matter of depreciation. The tables on the next page show how one may compare renting with owning a home. Let us assume that the family is paying a rent of $70 a month and that it would cost $8,000 to buy a home of equal quality. Basing the first-year cost of owning a home on the table on page 560, it will be observed that in this particular case it costs $24 a year less to own a home than to rent. In this example it is assumed that there is a down payment of $1,600 and that

COST OF RENTING	COST OF OWNING
Rent $840	Interest $320
	Taxes 150
	Assessments 10
	Repairs and Upkeep 120
	Depreciation 144
	Insurance 40
	Interest Loss on Investment 32
Total $840	Total $816

Cost of Renting Compared with the First-Year Cost of Owning a Home

interest is paid at the rate of 5 per cent on the unpaid balance. Since the family has an investment of $1,600 in the home, it is assumed that they are losing interest at the rate of 2 per cent, which they could be earning on this money if it were in a savings account. It is also assumed that the house is worth $7,200 and the lot is worth $800 and that the depreciation rate on the house is 2 per cent a year.

Not all of the costs of owning a home are cash expenditures. The depreciation represents a loss in value of the home each year based upon 2 per cent of the value of the house itself. Of the total cost, $32 represents the loss of interest that could have been earned if the down payment were in a savings account earning 2 per cent interest; in a sense this is equivalent to a cash outlay of $32. The family pays an additional amount of $480 a year to apply on the principal. For budgeting purposes the family therefore needs to compare the total cash outlay with the cost of renting to determine whether or not the family can afford to buy. This will be figured as follows:

RENTING	OWNING
Rent $840	Interest .... $ 320
	Taxes 150
	Assessments 10
	Repairs and Upkeep ... 120
	Insurance 40
	Interest Loss on Investment 32
	Payment on Principal .. 480
Total Cash Outlay $840	Total Cash Outlay $1,152

Cash Outlay for Renting Compared with the First-Year Outlay for Owning a Home

Ewing Galloway

There Are Many Things to Consider When You Build

The first-year cash outlay for owning a home is $312 greater than the outlay for renting. This illustrates the fact that even though a person is able to pay rent, an additional sum may be needed each year to buy.

In buying an old home there is another factor that is important. Very often it is necessary to repair or remodel the house before moving in. It may need a new roof, a new furnace, or other types of repairs. Sometimes a new room must be added. These costs must all be taken into consideration in the budget.

Five Ways to Build

1. Engage the complete services of an architect.
2. Engage the limited services of an architect with stock plans.
3. Engage a contractor or builder, using stock plans.
4. Buy stock plans and arrange with several contractors for different parts of construction.
5. Buy a pre-fabricated house and engage a builder to erect it.

As a family grows in size and moves from an apartment into a house or from a smaller house into a larger house, there usually are additional costs involved because of the necessity of buying new rugs or furniture for the larger home. These costs must be included in the budget.

New House, Old House, or Build Your Own Home? Most families do not have unlimited money with which to purchase the ideal home that they would like to buy. It is necessary therefore to make certain choices to get the most satisfactory home for the money that is available. Very often an entirely new home will cost more than an old home for the same housing facilities. However, a new home that is built probably will cost less for repairs for many years. On the other hand, some old homes that are in excellent condition may be better buys than new homes. A new home may hold its value better than an old home, but in either case, it is well to consult a reliable friend who can help you judge the value. Appraisals that are

---

Cautions in Building

1. The plans should be well designed, and the finished house will be satisfactory to the entire family.
2. The plans should meet the requirements of building codes and local restrictions.
3. The specifications should be complete, and there should be no extra charge for additional work.
4. The contractor should have a reputation for good work, financial responsibility, and fair dealing.
5. The contract should specify clearly the amount of the payments and the conditions under which the payments are to be made.
6. The contractor should be responsible for loss due to fire or to personal injury during the construction period.
7. The property should be subject to final inspection before acceptance and final payment.
8. All agreements should be in writing and have been approved by a lawyer.
9. You should have worked out a plan of financing a home that you can afford.
10. It should be a good time to build.

made in attempting to obtain a loan will usually help to determine values. The appraisal will be discussed in the next chapter.

If you intend to build a home, there are five choices recommended by the National Better Business Bureau.

In some cases it is possible to engage the limited services of an architect by submitting to him ready-made plans and asking him to make certain alterations, having him arrange for the proper placement of the house on the lot, and arranging for the awarding of contracts and supervision of the building.

Pre-fabricated homes sometimes save some of the cost of building. If you have the ability, you can do some of the construction yourself, but generally it is desirable to engage a competent builder to do at least the main part of the work.

Selecting a Home Site. There are many factors that help to determine choices of a place to live. Some of these are listed in the table below.

Factors in Selecting a Home Site

1. Accessibility, transportation, and cost of transportation.
2. Improvements, including water, sewer, gas, electricity, pavements, and street lights.
3. Assessments against the property that must be paid by the owner or future assessments that will be made for improvements.
4. The insurance rates, which are largely determined by fire and police protection.
5. Rates for taxes, water, electricity, and other services.
6. Building and zoning restrictions which will protect and preserve the characteristics of the community.
7. General land values and characteristics of the land, including drainage of the lot and type of soil. (Filled land is undesirable.)
8. Characteristics of the neighborhood which include schools, churches, hospitals, parks, general cleanliness, neatness of surrounding property, shopping district, social life, kind of neighbors, and nearness to factories, railroads, main highways, dumps, etc.

Some communities are improving; some are well established and their nature is evident; some communities that are new are hard to judge as to their future development; some are going down hill because property is deteriorating, factories are moving in, and people are moving out into better areas. These factors should be studied carefully if you want to protect your investment and live in a good community.

Summary of Renting or Buying

1. Some people should rent, but others should own a home.
2. There are important factors to check in renting a home.
3. A budget will determine whether you can afford to buy a home.
4. Financial advisors recommend a down payment of 20 to 25 per cent on the purchase of a home.
5. A new home is not always the best buy.
6. Investigate carefully the location of the new home.

TEXTBOOK QUESTIONS

1. (a) Indicate some circumstances under which it is better to rent than to own a home. (b) When is it better to own instead of renting?
2. When is it desirable to make (a) a short-term lease? (b) a long-term lease?
3. What are some of the advantages of a long lease?
4. What are some of the advantages of owning a home?
5. What factors help to determine when a family should buy a home?
6. What percentage of income is considered the maximum amount that one may safely spend a year in buying a home?
7. What is the minimum down payment that conservative financial advisors recommend for a person who buys his home?
8. What is a reasonable estimate of the cost of fire insurance based on the cost of a house?
9. What is a safe estimate of the cost of upkeep based on the total value of a home?
10. Explain why depreciation needs to be taken into consideration in figuring the cost of owning a home.

11. If one invests $1,000 in the purchase of a home, explain why the loss of interest on this investment is part of the cost of owning the home.
12. From the point of a cash outlay, why does owning a home and making regular monthly payments require more expenditure than renting?
13. Indicate at least three of the most important cautions in building a home.
14. When one buys an old home as compared with a newer home, what are some of the additional costs that may have to be taken into consideration besides the purchase price of the home?
15. What are the five different ways that one can go about building a home?
16. Name at least three cautions in building.
17. Name at least three factors that are important in selecting a home site.

DISCUSSION QUESTIONS

1. Give your opinion as to whether each of the following individuals should own or rent a home, provided each can afford to buy: (a) a traveling salesman, (b) the owner of a retail store, (c) the sales manager of a district office, (d) the office manager in a local manufacturing plant. Give reasons for your answers.
2. (a) Why is location an important factor in selecting a house to rent or to buy? (b) Are the considerations the same in both cases?
3. Mr. Moore, who is considering the purchase of a house, finds in an old community a house that is better constructed and otherwise more desirable than a newer one in a recently developed community. The two houses are offered at the same price. What do you think are some of the factors that he should consider in determining which house to select?
4. Discuss what you consider to be the merits of buying a home on the assumption that one's income will increase to such an extent that the debt can be paid off.
5. Explain how one's budget should be the controlling guide in buying a home.
6. A young couple finds that it is possible to make a down payment on a home and to pay the principal, the interest, and the taxes with the money that is ordinarily spent for rent and the additional amount that is placed in a savings account each month. They consider that they can save more by investing in a home than they can by paying rent and accumulating a savings fund. Do you agree with them? Give your reasons.

7. Under what circumstances do you think a person would be justified in making a down payment of only 5 or 10 per cent of the purchase price of a home?
8. If one has been renting a home and has been taking care of the repairs, painting, and papering of the house under the rental agreement, how should these figures be taken into consideration in making a comparison of the cost of renting and the cost of owning a home?
9. Explain some of the advantages and disadvantages of buying either an old house or a new house.
10. Can you think of any difficulties that may be involved if a person tries to handle all the details of building his own home by arranging contracts with individual workers and contractors on various parts of the work?
11. Name some of the kinds of changes in neighborhoods that cause property to go down in value and become less desirable for residential purposes.

PROBLEMS

1. Using the table on page 560 as a guide, compute the first-year cost of financing a home under the following conditions: (a) the value of the house and the lot is $12,500; (b) the first cash payment is $1,900; (c) a first mortgage is obtained on the balance of the indebtedness at 5 per cent interest, to be charged annually in advance; (d) the yearly payments of the principal and the interest are $1,250; (e) the taxes are 1.8 per cent of the value of the house and lot; (f) the insurand is .4 per cent of the value of the house ($10,000); (g) the upkeep is 1.5 per cent of the value of the house. Indicate the first-year expense and first-year savings. Note that the principal is adjusted at the end of the year.
2. Mr. Herbert French owns a house and a lot that cost $15,000. The lot is valued at $2,400. Assume that, over a period of twenty years, the valuation of the property for assessing taxes will remain at $15,000; the tax rate will stay at 2.1 per cent; the yearly cost of insurance on the house will be .35 per cent of the cost of the house; the annual cost of upkeep will be 1.5 per cent of the cost of the house; the house and the lot will be worth $12,000 at the end of the twenty years (the loss in value to be distributed equally over the twenty years); the money invested in the home would have earned a yearly income of 3.5 per cent if it had been invested in good bonds. Determine whether it is more economical for Mr. French to own his home than it would have been for him to pay a monthly rental of $120. Assume that all other costs of owning the home or of renting are negligible and that the rental rate would have remained the same.

3. Mr. Boland is paying $120 a month for rent for a house valued at $15,000. He has $3,750 that he can use for a down payment on a house valued at $15,000 and he can borrow the balance of $11,250 at 4½ per cent interest, computed semi-annually on the unpaid balance. His monthly payments on this new house would be $97.50, including principal and interest. Taxes would amount to $247.50 a year. There are no assessments; repairs and upkeep are estimated at $195 a year; depreciation is estimated at 2 per cent of the value of the house after deducting the value of the lot, which is figured at $1,500. Insurance would cost $63 a year. He would lose the interest on the $3,750 down payment because this amount is now in a savings account earning 2 per cent, compounded annually. (a) Construct a table like the one shown in this chapter, showing the cost of renting compared with the first-year cost of owning a home. (b) Construct a table similar to the one in this chapter showing the cash outlay for renting compared with the first-year outlay for owning a home.

COMMUNITY PROBLEMS AND PROJECTS

1. Pick a location in your community for a location for the building of a home. On the basis of the information in this chapter, make an evaluation of this home building site from the point of view of transportation, water, school, taxes, and all of the other factors and give your conclusions as to the desirability of the site, including the costs.
2. If you are renting your home, prepare a table similar to the one on page 560 showing the first-year cost of buying it. You can make a down payment of $2,000. Obtain the latest and most accurate information that you can in regard to interest rates, taxes, insurance, and estimated repair costs, and figure depreciation on the value of the building at 2 per cent a year. Set a reasonable value on the house according to prevailing real-estate values. If your family is the owner of the house, construct the same table and estimate the amount of rental that could be obtained from it in order to make the same comparison.
3. Analyze the total cost of rent that your family or another is paying. Compare this with the monthly cost of acquiring a home that would fit the requirements of the family. Use an actual piece of property as the basis of your study, and consider the income of the family in making the computations. Use the actual tax rate and the prevailing interest and insurance rates. Make your other computations on the basis of the tables shown on pages 560 and 564.

Chapter 33

Financing the Purchase of a Home

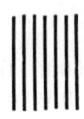

> **Purpose of the Chapter.** Nearly every person who buys or builds a home has to borrow money. There are several sources from which it can be borrowed, and there are different interest rates and arrangements for repaying the loan. The various methods of financing the purchase of a home are presented in this chapter.
>
> You will find answers to these questions:
> 1. What are the sources from which money can be borrowed?
> 2. How much will a loan cost?
> 3. How fast must a loan be paid off?
> 4. What are the obligations under a mortgage?
> 5. What special charges are there likely to be in connection with a loan?
> 6. What are meant by F.H.A. and G.I. loans?

Sources of Loans. There are several different sources from which money can be borrowed to finance the purchase of a home. Generally, these include savings and loan associations, life insurance companies, banks, trust companies, mortgage companies, and private investors. There are other special types of lenders in some cities. Certain types of institutions, such as savings and loan associations, make a specialty of lending money for the purchase of homes. The illustration on page 573 shows the proportion of total debts on homes financed by the more important types of lenders.

Appraisals. When one applies for a loan from any lending agency, it is necessary to fill out an application. The lender will then insist upon having experts make an *appraisal*, which is an examination of the property and the setting of its value. This is done to determine its value and condition. The appraisal is important to the lender and to the borrower because it should help to disclose any defects and should help to determine a fair value of the property. There is usually a special fee charged with the application for the appraisal.

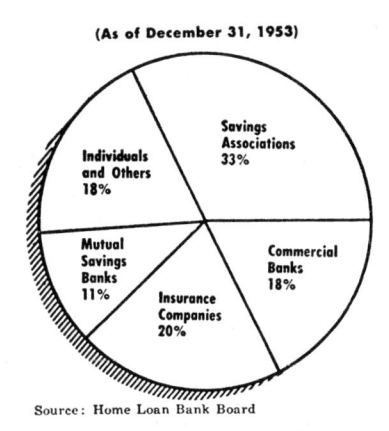

(As of December 31, 1953)

Savings Associations 33%
Individuals and Others 18%
Mutual Savings Banks 11%
Insurance Companies 20%
Commercial Banks 18%

Source: Home Loan Bank Board

Proportion of Total Home Mortgage Loans by Type of Lender

Mortgage. A *real estate mortgage* is a contract between the borrower and the lender for purposes of buying property. It stipulates the conditions under which the money is lent and must be repaid. It serves as security for the loan and grants certain privileges to the lender if the loan is not repaid according to agreement. The features of a mortgage are discussed in the next chapter. In addition, the borrower may also be required to sign a series of notes coming due periodically.

An old type of mortgage (but seldom used now) is one which runs for a period of time such as five to ten years. In the meantime the borrower is required to pay interest on the debt at specified intervals. At the end of the term of the mortgage the entire amount must be repaid or a new mortgage must be obtained to take its place.

Most mortgages on homes provide for periodic payments of a part of the principal and the accumulated interest. This is sometimes called a *partial-payment mortgage*. Payments are arranged so that at the end of the term specified in the mortgage the entire loan will be paid off. There are several different types of this mortgage.

Some mortgage contracts are called *package deals*. The payments not only include interest and principal, but also include insurance on the building, taxes, and sometimes even life insurance on the borrower.

There is also a type of mortgage that is sometimes called an *open-end mortgage* which permits a borrower, after having made substantial repayments on the loan, to borrow additional sums under the same mortgage contract without arranging for an additional loan. This extra money may be needed from time to time for making repairs.

Savings and Loan Associations. A savings and loan association is an organization created for the promotion of thrift and home ownership. Associations of this type use various plans for accumulating funds to be used in lending. The members of an association usually subscribe for shares and make regular payments on their subscriptions until the sum of these installment payments, added to the dividends obtained through the lending operations, equals the matured, or face, value of the shares. Some associations require no subscription but accept deposits of any amount. The money obtained by savings and loan associations from its subscribers and depositors is used for the purpose of making loans to persons buying or building homes.

Savings and loan associations are relatively liberal in their lending. They extend loans for reasonably long periods, usually ten to twenty years. They frequently appraise property at a value equal to the full market price. First-mortgage loans are sometimes made on property to the extent of from 60 to 80 per cent of the valuation. The liberality in lending depends largely on local and general business conditions and on the availability of funds.

As a guide to families interested in borrowing money, the following table was prepared by the United States Savings and Loan League, which is an organization of savings and loan associations. The first two columns show the income available by families for housing purposes, and the remaining columns show the usual amount that can be borrowed and paid off under different plans at different rates through a savings and loan association.

Income Available for Housing		Amount of Loan Which Income for Housing Will Finance							
		At 5 Per Cent			At 5½ Per Cent			At 6 Per Cent		
Monthly	Annual	10 Yrs.	15 Yrs.	20 Yrs.	10 Yrs.	15 Yrs.	20 Yrs.	10 Yrs.	15 Yrs.	20 Yrs.
$ 15	$ 180	$ 1,070	$ 1,320	$ 1,500	$ 1,050	$ 1,280	$ 1,440	$ 1,030	$ 1,240	$ 1,395
20	240	1,430	1,760	2,000	1,400	1,700	1,920	1,635	1,645	1,845
25	300	1,790	2,210	2,500	1,750	2,140	2,400	1,720	2,110	2,360
30	360	2,140	2,650	3,000	2,090	2,570	2,880	2,070	2,540	2,830
35	420	2,500	3,090	3,500	2,440	2,990	3,360	2,410	2,960	3,310
40	480	2,860	3,530	4,000	2,800	3,420	3,840	2,760	3,380	3,780
50	600	3,570	4,410	5,000	3,490	4,270	4,800	3,450	4,230	4,720
60	720	4,290	5,290	6,000	4,200	5,120	5,760	4,140	5,070	5,670
80	960	5,710	7,060	8,000	5,580	6,840	7,670	5,520	6,760	7,560
100	1,200	7,140	8,820	10,000	6,980	8,540	9,590	6,700	8,450	9,450
125	1,500	8,930	11,030	12,500	8,730	10,680	11,990	8,620	10,560	11,810
150	1,800	10,620	13,200	14,970	10,380	12,780	14,360	10,230	12,590	14,150
175	2,100	12,390	15,400	17,460	12,110	14,910	16,760	11,940	14,690	16,510
200	2,400	14,160	17,600	19,960	13,850	17,050	19,150	13,650	16,790	18,870
225	2,700	15,930	19,800	22,450	15,580	19,180	21,540	15,350	18,890	21,230
250	3,000	17,700	22,000	24,950	17,310	21,300	23,940	17,060	20,980	23,590

Life Insurance Companies. In recent years life insurance companies have invested considerable money in loans on real estate. The loans of such a company are commonly placed through local agents, such as banks, trust companies, mortgage companies, and individuals. The applicant for a loan is required to supply the agent with information as to the risk. Special forms are usually filled out for this purpose.

The appraiser for an insurance company will usually be very conservative in setting a value as the basis of the loan. The loan usually will not be granted for more than 50 per cent of the appraised value of the property. The loans of insurance companies run for periods as long as fifteen years. Interest is charged at the rate prevailing in the locality in which the loan is made, and is usually payable semiannually. In some cases payments on the principal can be made semiannually; in others they can be made monthly. Provision in many cases is made for allowing the borrower to pay off the loan after the third year.

Banks. An important source of borrowing on homes is a bank, especially a savings bank. When application is made for a loan, an officer of the bank or a committee usually visits the property and makes an appraisal. The size of the loan that such a bank can make is generally restricted by state law (or Federal regulations in the case of national banks) to a certain percentage of the value of the property. In some states this is 50 per cent, but in others it is as high as 60 per cent. State laws do not, however, restrict the banks with respect to making liberal or conservative appraisals. A liberal bank in a state that limits loans to 50 per cent of the property value might lend more than a conservative bank in a state that limits loans to 60 per cent of the property value.

Some banks extend loans for only short periods, such as three, five, or ten years. Short-term loans can usually be renewed, but a charge may be made for the privilege of extension. Unless the property has been taken care of satisfactorily, it is difficult to renew the loan.

Trust Companies. Trust companies and the trust departments of banks usually have funds available for real-estate loans. The lending policies and methods of trust companies are similar to those of savings banks.

Mortgage Companies. In many large communities mortgage companies are an important factor in home financing. There are two classes of these companies. One class lends on first, or senior, mortgages; and the other lends on second, or junior, mortgages. There is a great lack of uniformity in the policies and the methods of these companies. They are usually not placed under such legal restrictions as are savings and loan associations, banks, trust companies, and insurance companies. They ordinarily do not lend in excess of 50 per cent of the valuation of the property. When a higher amount is lent, a commission may be charged.

Private Investors. Private investors, who are unorganized, are free to operate as they please so long as they keep within the bounds of state laws on lending. They usually follow the methods of the lending institutions in their communities. They are frequently willing to lend a higher percentage of the property value than are savings and loan associations, banks, trust companies, or insurance companies. They do so especially when it is possible for them to get a slightly higher rate of interest.

The person who borrows from a lending institution can usually depend on being able to renew his mortgage if he has been prompt with his payments. When he borrows from an individual, however, there is nothing but personal assurance that the loan can be renewed. Such unforeseen circumstances as the death of the lender may cause an embarrassing situation for the borrower.

Second-Mortgage Borrowing. In communities where lending agencies are unwilling to make loans equal to from 60 to 75 per cent of the value of the home, some borrowers find it necessary to use two loans, a first mortgage and a second mortgage.

The following example shows the relationship between a first and a second mortgage: A person purchases a house valued at $12,000. He pays $3,000 in cash and is successful in obtaining a first-mortgage loan of $6,000. He obtains the loan by signing a series of notes that will become due at specified intervals. The interest on the notes is 5 per cent. To protect the lender, he gives a real-estate mortgage.

A second-mortgage loan is negotiated for the remainder of the purchase price, $3,000. The borrower signs a series of notes and a second-mortgage contract. The interest on the second mortgage is at a higher rate (6 per cent) than the interest on the first mortgage because the holder of the second mortgage has a greater risk of loss. The lender holds the second-mortgage contract. If the payments are not made when they become due, the first-mortgage holder or the second-mortgage holder, or both, depending upon the laws of the particular state, have the option of suing for the disposal of the property to satisfy the claims against it. The first-mortgage holder has first claim on the proceeds from the sale; the second-mortgage holder has second claim.

Land Contracts. A common form of financing used by home buyers who can make a down payment of only 10 to 15 per cent involves a *land contract*. This plan is popular in the central part of the United States. It is an agreement between the buyer and the seller of the property, under the terms of which the buyer usually makes a small down payment and agrees to pay the full purchase price in installments. The seller does not give the buyer legal ownership of the property, but agrees to convey the title to him when a certain percentage of the purchase price (usually approximately 50 per cent) has been paid. When the title is transferred, the seller usually accepts a first-mortgage note or the buyer either takes care of the unpaid balance or obtains a loan from someone else to pay the balance due the original seller.

This type of borrowing makes the purchase of a home possible for a large number of people who might be unable to buy in any other way. It is advantageous to real-estate operators because it enables the seller to hold the title of the property until the buyer has invested a sufficient amount in the home to indicate that he can satisfactorily complete payment and assume the obligation of ownership. In case the buyer fails to live up to his agreement, the seller has a better opportunity to take possession of the property than if the title had been transferred.

Renewing a Mortgage. In obtaining a loan on a home, the borrower should take into consideration what will happen to the mortgage obligation at the time it matures. Sometimes difficulty arises because the loan cannot be paid at maturity. Some mortgages require regular payments of the principal and interest, whereas others require payment of the interest regularly and payment of the entire principal at a specified date.

A mortgage that extends for a long period is safest. If a mortgage extends for only three, four, or five years, the person who borrows the money should obtain some assurance that the mortgage can be renewed or that a new loan can be obtained from some source. Suppose, for example, that a person will require ten years to pay for a home, but that he obtains a loan that will be due in three years. During the three years he will not be able to repay much of the principal. At the end of that period he must either have the loan renewed or obtain a new loan. He otherwise will run the risk of foreclosure on his property. The cost of the renewal of the loan should be predetermined, for this expense must be considered as part of the total cost of financing the home. If there is a charge, it should not be much.

Figuring Rates. The final decision in choosing an agency to finance the purchase or the building of a home should be based upon the reputation of the agency and the economy with which the home can be financed. The method of calculating the interest charges and the expenses involved in obtaining the loan should be investigated.

Different types of financial institutions have considerable variation in their plans of charging interest. For instance, some loan companies calculate interest annually; others calculate it semiannually or quarterly. Occasionally the interest is figured on the basis of the original amount of the loan, extended over the entire time during which the loan is being paid off. This method results in the borrower's paying an unusually high rate of interest on the outstanding amount of the loan, provided periodic payments are made on the principal. The table below shows how a $1,000 loan at 5 per cent interest is partially retired during the first year by monthly payments of $10 each, the interest being calculated monthly on the unpaid balance.

MONTH	MONTHLY PAYMENT	PART OF PAYMENT APPLIED TO INTEREST	PART OF PAYMENT APPLIED TO PRINCIPAL	PRINCIPAL DUE AFTER INSTALLMENT PAYMENT
1	$ 10.00	$ 4.17	$ 5.83	$994.17
2	10.00	4.14	5.86	988.31
3	10.00	4.12	5.88	982.43
4	10.00	4.09	5.91	976.52
5	10.00	4.07	5.93	970.59
6	10.00	4.04	5.96	964.63
7	10.00	4.02	5.98	958.65
8	10.00	3.99	6.01	952.64
9	10.00	3.97	6.03	946.61
10	10.00	3.94	6.06	940.55
11	10.00	3.92	6.08	934.47
12	10.00	3.89	6.11	928.36
	$120.00	$48.36	$71.64	$928.36

How a $1,000 Loan Is Reduced During the First Year, with Interest at 5 Per Cent, When the Interest Is Computed Monthly on the Unpaid Balance

Extra Charges. When loans are obtained, special care should be used to detect any extra charges. Premiums, commissions, and bonuses on loans result in higher interest rates for the borrowers. When a loan is obtained from some sources, the lender charges a commission for granting it. If, for example, a $40 commission is charged on a $1,000 loan that will extend for ten years, the actual amount of cash available from the loan is $960. The interest, however, must be paid on the $1,000. The actual rate of interest is therefore greater than the nominal rate.

There are other additional charges that must be considered in obtaining a loan. In some states a tax is levied. In practically every state there is a fee for having the deed recorded. The cost of having the title examined is usually from $25 to $80. The cost of an appraisal should not exceed $10 to $25. Some lenders require title insurance, which is also charged to the borrower. Ordinarily these costs are borne by the person who obtains the loan, but occasionally they are paid by the company granting the loan.

Federal Housing Administration. The Federal Housing Administration is commonly known as the FHA. The FHA provides Federal insurance on loans that are obtained through an approved lending agency, such as a bank. If the FHA approves the loan, the money can be borrowed from the regular lending agency. The lending agency is protected because the FHA insures the loan, guaranteeing its payment. Money may be borrowed for repairing or improving a home, buying or building a new home, buying an existing home, or buying a multiple-family dwelling, such as an apartment building.

From the point of view of an individual seeking a loan, an FHA loan is usually no better than many other types of loans, except that a qualified person who can make only a small down payment can sometimes obtain an FHA loan, when he might not be able to make a sufficient down payment to obtain any other kind of loan.

Where and How to Apply for FHA Loans. Any regular lending agency, such as a building and loan association, life insurance company, bank, trust company, mortgage company, or private investor, can help an individual apply for an FHA loan. A contractor, an architect, or a real-estate agent can also help a buyer of a home to apply for an FHA loan. If a loan is desired for repairing or improving a home, assistance can be obtained through a contractor or a dealer in building supplies.

Ewing Galloway
These Homes Were Financed by Means of FHA Loans

Charges and Payment Plans of the FHA. A loan obtained under the FHA may be repaid over periods of fifteen, twenty, or twenty-five years, or in a lump sum at any time. If a new home is being purchased, the minimum down payment is 10 per cent, and the mortgage insurance is one half of 1 per cent on the decreasing annual balance of the loan. If an existing home is being purchased or refinanced, the minimum cash down payment is 20 per cent, and the mortgage insurance charge is one half of 1 per cent on the decreasing annual balance. The maximum interest rate in each case is 5 per cent a year on the decreasing monthly balance. In other words, the monthly payments remain the same, but in each successive month more is applied to the principal and less to interest and mortgage insurance.

TYPICAL MONTHLY CHARGES	ON A $5,000 LOAN		
	15 YEARS	20 YEARS	25 YEARS
Principal and Interest	$38.25	$31.65	$27.80
Mortgage Insurance Premium	.97	1.00	1.01
Subtotal	39.22	32.65	28.81
Taxes (Estimated)	7.00	7.00	7.00
Fire Insurance (Estimated)	1.88	1.88	1.88
Total	$48.10	$41.53	$37.69

Typical Monthly Charges on Insured FHA Loans

G. I. Loans. For persons who performed service in the Armed Forces during World War II, special privileges are granted under the Servicemen's Readjustment Act. These privileges are similar to those obtainable under FHA loans. The loan must be obtained through a regular lending agency. It is then guaranteed by the Federal Government. This privilege enables veterans to obtain real estate and borrow money for business or agricultural purposes on very favorable terms. G. I. loans are insured by the Veterans Administration in essentially the same way that FHA loans are insured. If a veteran fails to repay his loan, the Veterans Administration has a claim against the borrower and has the privilege of deducting this amount from any pension, insurance dividend, or any other compensation due the veteran.

The maximum interest rate that a lender may charge on a G. I. loan is 4½ per cent, and the Veterans Administration adds its charge for insurance. A down payment is urged and recommended, but the G. I. loan law permits the Veterans Administration to guarantee loans with no down payment if the lender is willing to make the loan for the full amount of the purchase price.

Life Insurance and Real Estate. When one borrows money to buy a home for his family, he likes to feel sure that the loan will be repaid and that his family will have a home even though he dies. A buyer of real estate may purchase term life insurance sufficient to repay the amount of the loan on the real estate if he should die. Then if the buyer dies, proceeds from his life insurance will repay the loan.

The lender also likes to have some assurance that the loan will be repaid even though the buyer dies. Although the lender will have a mortgage claim against the property, he probably will not like to take the property away from a family if the head of the family dies. Some lenders require the buyers to obtain life insurance for this purpose. The lender is happy, and the family has a home without any debt on it. Therefore, life insurance serves an important function in the field of real estate.

Ch. 33]   FINANCING THE PURCHASE OF A HOME   583

Summary of Financing Plans

1. A mortgage is a contract between the borrower and the lender.
2. An appraisal is necessary and desirable.
3. There are several sources of loans with different rates and arrangements for repayments.
4. A land contract helps a buyer to purchase a home without a down payment.
5. The extra charges should be studied in obtaining any loan.
6. The F.H.A. and V.A. insure certain types of loans obtained through regular lenders.

TEXTBOOK QUESTIONS

1. Name the most common sources of loans on real estate.
2. What is meant by appraisal?
3. What is a real estate mortgage?
4. What is an open-end mortgage?
5. (a) What is the purpose of a savings and loan association? (b) How much will such an organization usually lend on property?
6. When borrowing from a life insurance company, what is the maximum percentage of the appraised value that an insurance company will usually lend?
7. Explain the typical policies of mortgage companies in lending on real estate.
8. Explain how money can be borrowed on more than one mortgage on the same piece of property.
9. Which is the safer type of mortgage from the point of view of the borrower: (a) a mortgage that extends for a short term of three or four years or (b) one that extends for a long term of from ten to fifteen years? Why?
10. What are the principal features of a land contract?
11. What happens when a mortgage matures or expires?
12. What are some of the extra charges that must be paid by the borrower of money?
13. For what purposes may FHA loans be obtained?
14. Who can assist a person in obtaining an FHA loan?
15. Over what period of payment may an FHA loan be extended?
16. What are the minimum down payments under FHA loans?
17. What are the principal advantages of a G. I. loan?
18. How is life insurance sometimes used in connection with borrowing to buy a home so that the family will be protected if the husband and father dies?

DISCUSSION QUESTIONS

1. If you want to borrow the greatest possible amount of money on a particular piece of real estate, from what source would you most likely obtain that amount, assuming that all sources of loans are available to you? Give your reasons.
2. For many borrowers on real estate what is the objection to a loan that is obtained for a period of years, such as five, at which time the entire amount is due but there are no payments except interest requested during the five years?
3. What do you think of the so-called package deals whereby the repayment of a loan on real estate includes interest, principal, taxes, and insurance?
4. Give the advantages and disadvantages of second mortgages from the point of view of (a) the borrower and (b) the lender.
5. If a person has bought a home and has agreed to pay off the mortgage at the rate of $50 a month, (a) can you see any advantage in his paying $60 or $70 a month if this amount is available? (b) Under what circumstances might there be such an advantage?
6. If a person is considering an FHA loan as compared with an ordinary loan from a saving and loan association or a bank, what factors in relation to the monthly payments must be taken into consideration to determine which is the more economical method of purchase and which is the more desirable?
7. Some insurance companies that make loans on real estate include as part of the interest or the service charge an amount that is sufficient to pay for insurance on the life of the borrower during the period in which the loan will be repaid. Can you see any advantages or disadvantages in this plan? Discuss them.

PROBLEMS

1. Mr. and Mrs. Osborne have $3,000 in a savings account which has been earning 3 per cent interest, calculated annually. They buy an $18,000 home, using the $3,000 as a down payment. They succeed in obtaining a first mortgage for $10,000 at 5 per cent interest and a second-mortgage loan for the remainder of the purchase price at 6 per cent interest. Considering the loss of the interest on their savings as a part of the cost, figure the total interest cost during the first year if the interest on the loans is computed annually.
2. (a) In this chapter is a table on page 579 showing how a $1,000 loan is reduced during the first year with interest at 5 per cent when the interest is computed monthly on the

unpaid balance. Prepare a similar table for a $1,000 loan at the same rate of interest computed quarterly on the unpaid balance. (b) What is the difference in the interest charged between this method and the one shown in the chapter?
3. (a) On the basis of the table on page 581, compute the total amount (principal payments, interest, mortgage insurance, taxes, and fire insurance) paid on a $5,000 loan covering fifteen years. (b) Subtract from the total amount paid (the answer to the preceding part) the amount of the loan in order to determine the total expense. (c) Divide the total expense by the number of months in the loan period to determine the average monthly expense. (Your answer to this part is not the total monthly expense, because it does not include such items as depreciation and repairs.)

COMMUNITY PROBLEMS AND PROJECTS

1. From your nearest Veterans Administration office or from the Veterans Administration in Washington, obtain the latest regulations and procedures for a war veteran to obtain a real estate loan. Make a report of information that you have obtained.
2. From your nearest FHA office or the FHA in Washington obtain information as to the procedures necessary for obtaining an FHA loan. Write a report on your findings.
3. Investigate the various local sources of loans on real estate. For each type of source find out (a) the percentage of the appraised value of property that will be lent, (b) the rate of interest, (c) the length of time during which a loan may extend, (d) the method of payment, (e) the dates on which interest is computed, and (f) any additional charges in obtaining a loan.
4. Obtain a sample form required by a bank, a building and loan association, or an insurance company for making an application for a loan. Fill out the blank, basing your figures on some particular piece of property, preferably your own home.

Chapter 34

Legal Problems of Obtaining A Home

Purpose of the Chapter. You do not need to be a lawyer to understand some of the legal problems of renting or buying real estate. However, a study of many of these legal problems will easily prove that you do need a lawyer in handling real estate transactions. The purpose of the chapter is to point out the legal rights and responsibilities of the landlord, the tenant, the seller, and the purchaser.

You will find answers to these questions:

1. What are the important points that should be included in a lease?
2. What are the rights and duties of both the landlord and the tenant?
3. In what ways can you be sure of obtaining a clear title to real estate?
4. What are the characteristics of different kinds of deeds?
5. What is meant by escrow?
6. What is a mortgage and how is a mortgage foreclosed?

Renting or Leasing

Relations of Landlord and Tenant. If you are the owner of a house and, by agreement, allow this property to be occupied and controlled by another, you are a *landlord*. The one who occupies the property is the *tenant*. The tenant has the right of possession and use of the property although he must respect the rights of the landlord. After the expiration of the agreement, the landlord has the right to regain possession of the property.

Leasing. The agreement between the landlord and the tenant is known as a *lease*. The landlord is the *lessor*, and the tenant is the *lessee*. The lease may be oral or written, the form depending upon the laws of the state governing the form. A written lease is desirable in many cases because it clearly defines the rights of the landlord and the tenant. In some states the lessor and the lessee must sign their names before a witness, such as a notary public.

Usual Content of a Lease

1. The date.
2. The names of the landlord and the tenant.
3. A description and an identification of the property.
4. The length of the tenancy period.
5. The amount of the payment.
6. The manner of payment.
7. A statement of the conditions and the agreements.
8. The signatures of the tenant and the landlord.

The lessor grants the lessee the privilege of using the property without interference, provided the terms of the contract are carried out. The lease may state specifically the rights of each party, but some other legal rights of the lessee and the lessor may not be mentioned in the lease.

Is Leasing the Same as Renting? Generally speaking, leasing and renting mean the same thing, but some people think of renting as meaning occupying property without a written agreement and of leasing as meaning occupying property with a written agreement. The term renting, however, is properly applied to the occupation of property both with and without a written agreement.

A person may occupy property under an agreement covering an indefinite period; he may occupy property for an indefinite period, the agreement being terminable at the will of either party; or he may occupy property under an

This Lease Witnesseth:

THAT John G. Turner does
HEREBY LEASE TO William F. Goodall
the premises situate in the   City   of Portland in the County of
Multnomah   and State of   Oregon   described as follows:
Dwelling House, No. 1229 Melbourne Road, Portland, Oregon

with the appurtenances thereto, for the term of two years   commencing
April 2,   19 , at a rental of eighty-five
dollars per month , payable monthly.

SAID LESSEE AGREES to pay said rent, unless said premises shall be destroyed or rendered untenantable by fire or other unavoidable accident; to not commit or suffer waste; to not use said premises for any unlawful purpose; to not assign this lease, or under-let said premises, or any part thereof, or permit the sale of. his interest herein by legal process, without the written consent of said lessor ; to not use said premises or any part thereof in violation of any law relating to intoxicating liquors; and at the expiration of this lease, to surrender said premises in as good condition as they now are, or may be put by said lessor reasonable wear and unavoidable casualties, condemnation or appropriation excepted. Upon non-payment of any of said rent for ten days, after it shall become due, and without demand made therefore; or the bankruptcy or insolvency of lessee or assigns, or the appointment of a receiver or trustee of the property of lessee or assigns or if this lease pass to any person or persons by operation of law; or the breach of any of the other agreements herein contained, the lessor may terminate this lease and re-enter and re-possess said premises.

SAID LESSOR AGREES (said lessee having performed his obligations under this lease) that said lessee shall quietly hold and occupy said premises during said term without any hindrance or molestation by said lessor , his heir or any person lawfully claiming under them.

Signed this second   day of April   A. D. 19
IN PRESENCE OF:

Gene Rainier   *John G. Turner*

Carl Noble   *William F. Goodall*

A Lease

agreement covering a definite period. Any of these agreements may be written or oral, but the first two are more likely to be oral agreements.

Rights and Duties of the Tenant. The tenant of a piece of property is entitled to peaceful possession of it. If he is deprived of that, he may sue for damages. The tenant is also entitled to use the property for any purpose for which it is adapted, unless he is forbidden certain uses by the agreement. The property may not be used for unlawful purposes.

The tenant is under obligation to make repairs, but not improvements. For example, if the child of a tenant breaks a window, it ordinarily is the responsibility of the tenant to replace the window. He must pay his rent when it is due. Unless the lease states otherwise, the rent is not due until the end of each month.

If the lease is for a definite period of time, the tenant is not obligated to give notice when he vacates the property. The lease may be terminated, however, before the expiration of the period if an agreement is reached with the landlord. If the lease is for an indefinite period of time, the tenant must notify the landlord of his intention to give up the lease. The form and the time of notice are regulated by the customs or the laws of the community.

Auburn, Maine, June 1, 195–

Mr. Harry Becker:

I hereby give you notice that I will quit and deliver possession, July 1, 195–, of the premises at No. 417 Reading Road, in the city of Auburn, Maine, which I now hold as tenant under you.

Robert Mason

A Tenant's Notice of Intention to Terminate a Lease

The tenant should inspect carefully the property that he rents or leases. In the absence of any agreement with the landlord, he accepts the property with the risk of defects, except those hidden, being present. For example, if a tenant accepts a house with an obviously defective screen door, the landlord may not be responsible for fixing it except by agreement. However, if the tenant accepts the property in the summer and finds that the furnace will not function in the fall, the landlord is probably responsible because this is a hidden defect that could not easily be determined in the summer. In most states the tenant is liable for injuries to guests resulting from defects that he should have known and remedied.

Rights and Duties of the Landlord. A landlord does not have the right to enter the premises of a tenant except to do what is necessary to protect the property. He must not interfere with the tenant's right of possession. If the tenant abandons the property, however, the landlord may take possession. At the expiration of the lease the landlord is entitled to take possession of the property. If the tenant refuses possession, the landlord may force him to give possession through legal proceedings.

The Tenant Has the Right to the Undisturbed Use of the Property. The Landlord Has No Right to Enter the Property to Show It to a Prospective Buyer

The landlord is entitled to receive the rent as specified in the lease. In some states, through legal proceedings, he may seize personal property of the tenant and have it sold to pay the rent that is in arrears.

In some states the landlord is under no obligation to make repairs or to pay for improvements on the property unless such an agreement has been made with the tenant. In most states, however, he is obligated to keep the house in habitable condition. Unless the lease specifies otherwise, taxes and assessments must be paid by the landlord.

When a tenant occupies property for an indefinite period of time, the landlord may obtain possession of it by giving notice. The form and the time of the notice are regulated by local customs or laws.

> Cleveland, Ohio, April 30, 195–
>
> Mr. Ronald Cramer:
>
> I hereby notify you to surrender possession of the premises at 5942 Ridge Avenue, Cleveland, Ohio, on or before June 1, 195–. Your lease of the said premises expires on June 1, and I shall take possession of the property on that date.
>
> James Royalson

A Landlord's Notice Requesting a Tenant to Vacate Property

When the landlord retains control over a part of the property—as in the case of a landlord who leases part of a building to a tenant—he is liable for certain injuries caused by the defective condition of the part of the property over which he has control. For instance, Mr. Adams owns a two-story building. He lives on the first floor and retains control over the porch and the yard, but he rents the second floor to Mr. Brown. If Mr. Brown or a member of his family is injured as a result of the defective condition of the porch or the sidewalk, Mr. Adams is liable for the injuries. The landlord is also liable, in most cases, for injuries to any friend or guest of the tenant who may have been injured because of defects in the property which the landlord controls and therefore is obligated to maintain.

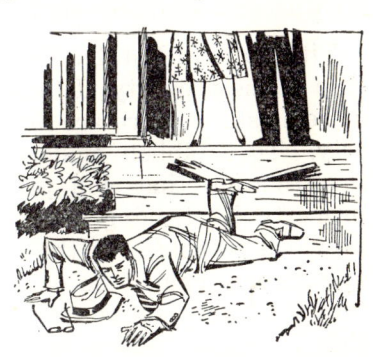

Unless There Are Specific Laws to the Contrary, the Tenant Is Responsible for Injuries Arising from Defective Conditions of the Property

Improvements and Fixtures. In the absence of an agreement to the contrary, the improvements that are attached to the property become a part of the property and therefore belong to the owner. For instance, if a tenant builds a shed or a garage upon the lot belonging to his landlord, he cannot tear it down or take it away without permission.

If a tenant constructs shelves or cupboards in the house that he has rented or leased, he ordinarily cannot take them away when he leaves. In some cases, however, courts have held that such fixtures attached with nails become a part of the property, whereas fixtures attached with screws may be removed.

Buying Real Estate

Agreements Must Be in Writing. State laws require that most agreements relating to the purchase and sale of real estate be in writing in order to be effective or legally binding on the parties involved. Therefore, in buying or selling real estate the safest practice is to have all agreements in writing and properly signed.

Title to Real Estate. The *title* to real estate is the ownership of the property. If a person has a clear title to a piece of real estate, there are no other claims against that property. To establish evidence of a clear title involves an investigation that will prove the true ownership of the property by tracing the history and the legality of the previous transfers of the title. Usually a loan on a piece of property cannot be obtained until the lender is certain that the title is satisfactory. The charge for examining the title is usually added to the loan or is paid as a special charge.

Each legal transfer of the title to a piece of property is recorded in a register of deeds, usually kept in the courthouse. It is therefore advisable to have a competent lawyer examine the records and determine whether there is a clear title to the property.

In some states, individuals and companies specialize in the practice of making examinations of the titles to property. A condensation of the information taken from the recorded history of the property is referred to as an *abstract of title*. The report of the individual or the company making the abstract is called an *opinion of the title*. It is also possible to obtain a *title-guarantee policy* from such a company. This policy guarantees that the title is clear and no claims are against it.

In order to eliminate uncertainties and to reduce the expense of transferring the titles to property, some states have established a special system of registering titles. This is known as the *Torrens System*. For instance, the owner of land applies for a registration of the title to his land. An officer then examines the records, and, if the title is good, he issues a *certificate of title*. Each time the title is transferred thereafter, a new certificate is issued. Under this system an abstract is usually not necessary.

Deeds, the Written Evidence of Title. There are two general types of deeds: (a) the warranty deed and (b) the quitclaim deed. The *warranty deed* * is the more common. It is written evidence of the ownership of a piece of real property and serves as a means of conveying the title from one person to another. The one who transfers the title to the property is called the *grantor* of the deed, and the one to whom the title is transferred is called the *grantee* of the deed. Such a deed not only purports to convey the interest of the grantor to the grantee, but also involves stipulations that certain facts relating to the title are true. A warranty deed is illustrated on page 594.

A *quitclaim deed* merely relinquishes the interest that the grantor may have in the property. The grantee assumes the risk that the title may not be good. In some communities a quitclaim deed is used instead of a warranty deed.

Consider this example: Mr. Allis desires to transfer real estate to Mr. Bush. He grants a warranty deed as evidence of the transfer of the title. In investigating the title, Mr. Bush discovers that a former owner, Mr. Carter, at one time had a claim against the property. Mr. Bush is therefore not quite sure that the claim has been settled fully. To protect his rights that are granted in the warranty deed, Mr. Bush gets Mr. Carter to grant a quitclaim deed relinquishing any rights that the latter may have had in the property.

The important elements in a deed are the description of the property, signature, seal, witnesses, acknowledgment, delivery, and acceptance. The laws in different states vary in some respects. To assure a clear title, the person execut-

---

* In a few states there is also a grant deed that is a limited warranty deed.

Know all men by these presents:

That Joseph Bentley and Marie Bentley, his wife **in consideration of** One thousand dollars ($1,000) **to** them **paid by** Walter Rathburn the receipt whereof is hereby acknowledged, do hereby **Grant, Bargain, Sell and Convey** to the said Walter Rathburn, his heirs and assigns forever: Lot sixteen (16) block three (3) in the Avonlea subdivision and all the **Estate, Title and Interest** of the said Grantors either in Law or Equity, of, in and to the said premises; **Together** with all the privileges and appurtenances to the same belonging, and all the rents, issues and profits thereof; **To have and to hold** the same to the only proper use of the said Grantee his heirs and assigns forever. And the said Joseph Bentley and Marie Bentley for themselves and their heirs, executors and administrators, do hereby Covenant with the said Walter Rathburn, his heirs and assigns, that they are the true and lawful owner s of the said premises, and have full power to convey the same; and that the title so conveyed is **Clear, Free and Unincumbered**; And further, That they do **Warrant and Will Defend** the same against all claim or claims, of all persons whomsoever;

In Witness Whereof, The said Joseph Bentley and Marie Bentley who hereby release all their right and expectancy of **Dower** in the said premises, have hereunto set their hands this fourteenth day of October in the year of our Lord one thousand nine hundred _____.

Signed and acknowledged in presence of—

P. M. Davis
E. R. Hall

Joseph Bentley
Marie Bentley

State of Virginia, **County of** Norfolk, ss.

Be it Remembered, That on this fourteenth day of October in the year of our Lord one thousand nine hundred and _____ before me, the subscriber, a Notary Public in and for said county, personally came Joseph Bentley and Marie Bentley the grantors in the foregoing Deed, and acknowledged the signing thereof to be their voluntary act and deed.

In Testimony Whereof, I have hereunto subscribed my name and affixed my official seal on the day and year last aforesaid.

E. R. Stern
Notary Public.

A Warranty Deed

ing the deed should become familiar with local laws. For instance, the laws in various states differ with regard to the ownership of property by man and wife. Some states require the signatures of both, whereas others require only one signature. In some states the witnesses must sign in the presence of one another, whereas in others they may sign only in the presence of an authorized public officer. Because of the many technicalities, the average person should obtain legal advice in granting a deed or taking the title to real estate. It is best to let a lawyer write all the legal papers.

Sales Contract. Often before the actual transfer of the title of real estate, an agreement is reached between the buyer and the seller. This agreement, which should not be confused with a deed, is referred to as a *contract of sale,* a *contract to convey,* or a *land contract.* It is a contract in which the seller agrees to sell under certain conditions and the buyer agrees to buy under certain conditions.

What Is Meant by Escrow? In bringing the sale of real estate to a conclusion, the seller sometimes will prepare a deed transferring ownership of the property to the buyer. He will then place this deed in the hands of a third party who is authorized to deliver the deed to the new owner when certain conditions have been fulfilled. This process is called placing the deed in *escrow.* For example, a deed may be placed in escrow until the buyer submits a certified check or bank draft in complete payment. Then the deed is turned over to the buyer. Money may also be placed in escrow to pay for work when it is completed.

Joint Ownership. In most states a husband and a wife may own real estate together. When property is owned under such a condition, the husband and the wife are considered to own it jointly, neither being the owner of any particular part. Our law in this respect is fashioned after the English law.

Under the laws of *joint ownership,* when either dies, the survivor becomes sole owner of the property. In such a case the survivor is said to become a *tenant by entirety.*

> **Legal Steps in Buying Real Property**
>
> 1. Writing and signing a contract of sale.
> 2. Making a survey of the property to determine its exact size, location, and shape to be sure that the property is exactly as described.
> 3. Making a title search to determine whether the seller has a clear title to the property.
> 4. Signing a mortgage if money is borrowed.
> 5. Obtaining a clearly drawn and legally accurate deed from the seller.
> 6. Recording the deed in the proper place of registration in the county in which the land is located.

In some states, however, the manner in which the title will pass to the survivor must be indicated in the deed.

There are laws in most states that grant what is called a *dower right* or *dower interest*. This right is conferred upon the wife, who has a legal right to share in the property of her husband. A similar right is granted to the husband, who shares in the property of his wife. This right is known as *curtesy*. Some of these rights have been abolished in certain states, and the laws are not uniform. The laws of many states, however, prohibit either the husband or the wife from selling property unless the signatures of both appear on the deed. This rule holds good even though the property may be recorded in the name of only one.

In many states when property that has been owned jointly by a husband and a wife becomes the sole property of the survivor, it is not subject to an inheritance tax or a state tax, for the survivor is not considered to inherit the property.

Mortgage, A Contract Between Lender and Borrower. If you borrow money to buy or build a home, you will be required to sign a mortgage, which is given to the person from whom you borrow the money. A mortgage is a contract between the lender and the borrower which states the rights and the obligations of each person. The mortgage states, among other things, how the interest and the principal must be paid and the rights of the lender in case the payments are not made as agreed.

Mortgages are not the same in all states, although they have similar characteristics. Every mortgage should be in writing, and usually the signature should be witnessed. The correct wording can be found in statute books, and a special legal form on which to draw up the mortgage can be obtained.

In some states a *mortgage bond* is commonly used instead of a mortgage. In other states the instrument is referred to as a *mortgage contract*. Regardless of its title the legal instrument that is used specifies the amount of the indebtedness and the method of payment. The mortgage is given as security for the payment of the debt. In some transactions in which a mortgage is issued, the borrower must also sign a note or series of notes that will become due on certain dates.

In most states the laws require that a mortgage, in order to be effective protection against subsequent buyers or mortgagees, must be recorded in the county in which the property is located. This procedure enables other interested people to discover any claims against the property.

Rights and Duties of the Mortgagor and the Mortgagee. Any person who owns an interest in land, buildings, or even crops raised on land, may mortgage that interest. The person who owns the land and borrows the money through a mortgage is called the *mortgagor*. The person who lends the money and holds the mortgage as evidence of his claim is called the *mortgagee*. In the eyes of the law the mortgagor is the legal owner of the property. The property is merely pledged as security for the payment of a debt, and the mortgage is the written contract acknowledging the debt. A mortgage on real estate includes equipment that has become so permanently attached to the real estate that it is considered a part of it. If a piece of land is mortgaged, and a house is later built on the land, the house will be included in the mortgage, for it has become a part of the land.

The mortgagor is under duty to refrain from destroying or damaging the property. The mortgagee must not interfere with the occupancy of the property except through agreement with the mortgagor or through legal procedure. If a mortgagee sells a mortgage to a third person, he should give the mortgagor a notice of transfer.

When the indebtedness is paid, the mortgage is automatically canceled. It is wise, however, for the mortgagor to obtain the mortgage, the mortgage note, and a statement acknowledging the discharge of the obligation. The notice acknowledging the discharge of the obligation should be recorded in the proper place of registration, usually the county courthouse.

Mortgage Foreclosure. If the mortgagor fails to fulfill his obligation, the mortgagee has the right of *foreclosure*, that is, of bringing a law suit to obtain possession of the property and title to it. Foreclosure may consist of (a) a court order that transfers the title to the property from the mortgagor to the mortgagee, or (b) a court order that requires the property to be sold to pay the mortgagee.

Although a mortgage contract usually specifies that the mortgagor loses all rights to the mortgaged property if the obligation is not performed at a specified time, the laws in most states permit the mortgagor to regain his interest in the property by fulfilling his contract at any time before the foreclosure of the mortgage.

If the proceeds from the sale of the property exceed the total of the indebtedness and the expenses incident to the sale, the mortgagor gets the difference. If the proceeds are less than the amount of the indebtedness, the mortgagee has a right, in most states, to obtain a judgment against the mortgagor for the difference. This judgment is referred to as a *deficiency judgment*. Because of the possibilities of a deficiency judgment, the mortgagor does not release himself, under the laws of some states, from his obligation merely by giving up his property. For example, Mr. and Mrs. Charles purchased a home. They paid $2,000 in cash and borrowed $8,000 on a mortgage to pay for the home. They failed to repay the money as agreed. The person

> **Things to Investigate in Buying Real Estate**
>
> 1. What unsettled claims are there against the property?
> 2. Are any assessments or taxes due?
> 3. Are any street, sidewalk, or sewer improvements likely for which there will be future additional assessments?
> 4. Do any unfavorable zoning laws affect the property?
> 5. Is the property mortgaged? If so, can the mortgage be transferred to the new owner?
> 6. Have arrangements been made for the proper insurance on the property at the time of purchase?
> 7. Have you checked the fees to be charged by the lawyer?
> 8. Are all agreements in writing, including the settlement of old claims against the property?

who loaned the money and held the mortgage foreclosed through the proper legal proceedings. The property was sold to settle the claim, which at the time of the foreclosure amounted to $7,500. The property was sold for $7,000, which was paid to the holder of the mortgage (mortgagee), leaving a deficiency of $500. The court granted a deficiency judgment of $500 against Mr. and Mrs. Charles, which they are required to pay to the mortgagee.

One piece of property may have as many as three mortgages. If it is sold through foreclosure proceedings, the mortgagees must be protected according to the preference given to their respective mortgages.

In many states a mortgagor who has lost his property through foreclosure is given a certain time (usually one year) in which he may redeem or recover his property after the foreclosure. The property may be redeemed by paying the amount due plus interest at a stipulated rate.

Claims Against Real Estate. Any claim on real estate that arises from a debt is referred to as a lien. A mortgage is one type of lien. A *mechanic's lien* is another. For instance, a contractor who has constructed a building may hold a lien against the property for the payment of the amount due him. A *judgment* rendered by a court as the result of a lawsuit is still another kind of lien.

Summary of Legal Problems

1. Renting and leasing are legally the same and agreements may be written or oral.
2. A tenant has a right to peaceful and uninterrupted possession of the property.
3. A tenant is generally obligated to make normal repairs, but not improvements.
4. Agreements in regard to purchasing or selling real estate must be in writing.
5. A deed is a written evidence of title or ownership of real estate.
6. A man and a wife may jointly own property but the laws of joint ownership are not the same in different states.
7. A mortgage is a contract between lender and borrower and involves many different rights and obligations.

TEXTBOOK QUESTIONS

1. (a) Who is a landlord? (b) Who is a tenant?
2. (a) Who is a lessor? (b) Who is a lessee?
3. Why is a written lease desirable?
4. What information is usually embodied in a formal lease?
5. What is the distinction between renting and leasing?
6. May a tenant use the property for any purposes that he wishes?
7. In the absence of any agreement, when is rent usually due?
8. Under what circumstances must a tenant notify the landlord of his intention to give up the use of the property?
9. Is the landlord or the tenant liable for damages if an invited guest of the tenant is injured on the property?
10. May the landlord enter the premises of a tenant any time he wishes?
11. If the tenant fails to pay his rent, what may the landlord do in order to ensure payment of the amount that is due as rent?
12. Must the landlord make repairs and improvements that are demanded by the tenant?
13. A tenant who intends to move wishes to tear down and take with him any improvements he has made. May he do so?
14. Are oral agreements in regard to purchasing or selling real estate enforceable?

15. Through what process is it possible to determine who is the legal owner of a piece of real estate and what claims, such as a mortgage, are held against the property?
16. What protection can one obtain against the possibility that the title to a piece of property may not be good?
17. What is the advantage of the Torrens System of registering land?
18. (a) What are the two general types of deeds? (b) In what ways do they differ?
19. What is the difference between a contract of sale and a deed?
20. What is meant by escrow?
21. Is it always true that, if property is recorded only in the name of the husband, he alone has the right to sell it?
22. Name the legal steps in buying real property.
23. What is meant by joint ownership of real property?
24. If the mortgagor fails to pay the claim against the mortgaged property, what right has the mortgagee?
25. After the mortgage on real estate has been foreclosed, is there any means by which the mortgagor may recover the property?
26. What is a mechanic's lien?

DISCUSSION QUESTIONS

1. (a) Name some of the advantages of a written lease to a lessee. (b) Name some of the disadvantages.
2. (a) Name some of the advantages of a written lease to a lessor. (b) Name some of the disadvantages.
3. (a) May a tenant change the property that he has leased by making physical alterations? (b) May he repair it without the consent of the owner?
4. When Mr. Brown visited Mr. Cooper, he injured himself on a broken step. Mr. Cooper has rented the house from Mr. Thompson. Who is responsible for the injury?
5. Is a refrigerator or a stove considered part of a house or an apartment that is mortgaged? Explain your answer in detail.
6. If a mortgage on a home is foreclosed: (a) Who gets the extra money if the property is sold for more than the mortgage claim? (b) What may happen if the amount obtained from the sale is not sufficient to pay the mortgage? (c) What, if anything, can be done by the mortgagor to get his property back again?
7. When banks or other lending agencies lend money on a new home that has just been completed, why does the lender often require the builder to give proof that the plumber, the carpenter, and other types of workers and suppliers have been paid or that arrangements have been made to pay them?

PROBLEMS

1. Mr. Osborn, who had rented a house to Mr. Chace, wanted to sell the house. In the absence of the Chace family he unlocked the door and showed the house to a prospective buyer. When Mr. Chace learned what Mr. Osborn had done, he objected and insisted that Mr. Osborn had no right to enter the house. Mr. Osborn insisted that he did have the right to enter his own house. What is your opinion? Why?
2. Mr. Kelley rented a house to Mr. Packer and later sold the property to Mr. Sims. Mr. Sims wanted immediate possession of the property. Mr. Packer insisted that he had an agreement with Mr. Kelley to the effect that he might stay on the property as long as he wished. This agreement was, however, not written. (a) Do you think Mr. Sims can obtain possession of the property? (b) In what way do you think he can obtain possession?
3. Mr. Duval granted a mortgage on his house and lot in favor of the Central Savings and Loan Association, to which he owed some money. The mortgage was not recorded. Mr. True accepted a deed from Mr. Duval in good faith and without knowing that a mortgage had been granted to the Central Savings and Loan Association. The Central Savings and Loan Association insisted that it still had a legal claim against the property. Mr. True insisted that the property was free from a mortgage. Who was right? Why?

COMMUNITY PROBLEMS AND PROJECTS

1. Obtain copies of your state laws pertaining to the foreclosure of mortgages. Write a report on the legal rights of the mortgagor and the mortgagee. Point out whether there is any possibility of repossessing property after the mortgage has been foreclosed.
2. Investigate the procedure in your community for recording a deed, a mortgage, or a lease. Find out the place of recording, the details of procedure, and the fee.
3. Learn what is the common procedure in your community for leasing and renting. Find out whether it is a custom to have leases begin and end in some particular month of the year. Also investigate the customary procedure in giving notices, the forms of leases, and the obligations of tenant and landlord. Try to obtain a sample of a lease form or a complete lease.
4. Obtain copies of the legal forms required in granting a mortgage. Fill out the necessary forms, using an imaginary piece of property, and write an explanation of the procedure and the use of the forms.

Chapter 35

Wealth, Production, and Income

Purpose of the Chapter. Every individual has need for understanding the relationship of the business and economic system to his personal economic affairs. This relationship involves problems pertaining to money, wealth, income, production, and wages. The purpose of this chapter is to provide a background of knowledge for understanding the relationship of these problems to consumers.

You will find answers to these questions:

1. What are money, wealth, production, and income?
2. How does production affect consumers?
3. What is the relationship of machines to national prosperity?
4. How does the introduction of new machinery affect our income and our standard of living?
5. What is the difference between money wages and real wages?

Meaning of Money, Wealth, and Income. Usually we speak of a person with considerable money as being wealthy. Actually *money* is a convenient means of measuring wealth and is a medium of exchange; but money in itself is not wealth, except the metal in metallic money or the small amount of paper in paper money. In the economic sense, one is wealthy, not because he has money, but only because his money enables him to buy the goods and services. The goods that he owns are wealth. A nation is not wealthy in terms of its money, but in terms of its resources.

Wealth consists of useful, tangible goods. This book is wealth. The factory in which the book was printed is wealth. Wealth consists of goods that satisfy human wants directly or indirectly.

Wealth has other characteristics; the goods comprising wealth must be scarce enough to be wanted by people; they must have usefulness or serve some purpose; and they must have value. Air is so free that it is not economic wealth, but oxygen taken from the air and placed in tanks to be sold is wealth.

Income is the product of wealth; it results from the wise use of goods and services to satisfy the desires of people. Therefore, *income* is one's share of new wealth that he has helped to create by using his labor or his stored-up wealth. One might think of income as the amount of wealth he has created during a week or a month. The baker through his labor and by the use of his equipment converts flour and other ingredients into bread. People want bread; therefore the baker, by satisfying the desire of people for bread, earns income. Income, whether of individuals or nations, results from combining wealth (material goods having value), and the physical or mental work of people.

Ordinarily, income is measured in terms of money, but it may be in the form of goods and services. A farmer on a completely self-sufficient farm would have an income because he would produce certain goods that he would consume and some that he might save; however, he might not have any money income.

Wealth and Money. The concepts of wealth and income given here are basic to an understanding of many other phases of business and economic life.

One might be on a barren island with millions of dollars in money, but without any tangible goods. The money would be useless, for it could not be used to procure food or clothing, or to satisfy other needs. If this same person had jewels or several automobiles, or a hundred new suits of clothes in addition to the money, these goods would be of little value to him, for he could not use them. They would not be wealth so far as he is concerned, for they would not be useful. If his money could be used, however, to obtain goods to satisfy his needs, it could be exchanged for wealth. The jewels would represent wealth if they satisfied a need. The automobiles would also be wealth only if they satisfied a need. From this explanation we can see that wealth is comprised of usable goods and that money is of no value unless it can be used to buy the goods and services we want.

Some of the soldiers on the islands in the Pacific in World War II learned some lessons in regard to money and wealth. When they first arrived, they were anxious to send grass skirts home to their friends. In a few minutes a native could make a grass skirt that he could sell for two dollars; but when the natives accumulated handfuls of paper money and found that there was nothing to buy with the money, they discovered that their labors were useless. Barter then became the basis of exchange for the grass skirts. Any soldier who had a knife, cigarettes, food, or a trinket was able to barter it for a grass skirt, but the natives did not want paper currency. Thus money decreased in value because it would not buy the goods the natives wanted; it was plentiful. The other goods used in exchange, such as the knives and cigarettes, had value because they were relatively scarce and people wanted them.

Money in itself is of no value unless it can be used. It is possible to imagine a condition of barter, such as existed in earlier periods of time, in which various products and services were exchanged between individuals. A person's wealth and relative prosperity depended upon what products or services he could exchange for other things. Under such conditions one's wealth directly depended upon what he could produce so long as people wanted the goods or services produced. This condition is equally applicable today. The more one produces of goods and services wanted by others, the greater his income is and hence the greater his wealth becomes. In other words, the more one produces, the higher his standard or level of living may be.

Producing Economic Goods. Producing goods consists in part of changing their form or location to make them more

[Part 10

The Welder Creates Form Utility

Ewing Galloway

useful in satisfying the desires and wants of people. To make goods more useful usually requires a combination of labor, the use of equipment, and the knowledge and skill of management. A person who makes goods more useful is a producer of wealth.

Anyone who makes goods more useful in satisfying wants is said to create *utility*. In order that a commodity may have the power to satisfy a desire or a want, it must be in the proper physical form; it must be at the place where it is needed; it must be available when needed; and usually it must be owned or capable of being owned by the person who wants it. As explained in Chapter 2 the most common types of utilities, therefore, are (a) *form utility*, (b) *time utility*, and (c) *place utility*. Production is the creation of utility. Anyone who helps create goods in the proper form, at the proper time, and in the proper place so that they can be used is a producer of goods.

From this description of the production of goods, it is evident that the man who works with his hands, the man who operates a machine, the bank which finances business activity, the railroad which transports the goods, the telegraph company which facilitates business transactions, the wholesaler and the retailer which handle the goods, the salesman who sells the goods, and many others contribute to the production of goods.

Performing Economic Services. Another type of producer is one who performs services that satisfy human wants directly. These people are producing economic services, but these services do not relate to any economic activity dealing directly with the production of wealth.

An opera singer is a producer, not because he creates any utility in wealth, but because he satisfies a human want directly. Teachers, lawyers, physicians, and actors are also producers because they satisfy human wants directly. A stenographer who works for a doctor is performing an economic service that directly satisfies a human want. This stenographer is not a producer of goods or wealth, but there is no doubt that her services are useful. Another type of stenographer may be indirectly a producer of wealth, as, for example, a stenographer in a wholesale grocery firm. She is performing a service that is one step in creating place utility in goods. Without her help, the distributor would be unable to create place utility.

It should be observed that one may produce a desirable economic service that satisfies directly a human want; but in doing so, that person is not producing wealth because this type of service is not tangible goods.

Factors of Production. The five elements of production are considered to be: (a) *natural resources,* or land; (b) *labor;* (c) *capital,* or tools and machinery; (d) *management;* and (e) *government.* Some refer to these elements as nature; labor, including both physical and mental; capital; management; and government.

Clearly, men cannot produce anything without the aid of nature, for nature furnishes all raw materials with which we work, such as mineral and vegetable resources. Very little wealth is produced except through the application of physical and mental labor to natural resources. The term capital is applied to tools and machinery because the economist uses it to designate any kind of goods used for producing wealth. Government is considered a factor in production because it provides such services as protection, regulation, and information. The function of management in production is to integrate the other four factors, natural resources, labor, capital, and government services in such a manner as to produce usable goods desired by people.

In our present industrial society, man cannot produce efficiently without the aid of technical equipment, such as tools and special knowledge. As the wealth of a nation is measured by its ability to produce goods, the more goods the individual can produce, the greater the wealth of the country and the individuals in it. In the United States the use of tools and machinery has reached a relatively high stage of development. It has been estimated that the average amount of capital equipment used in United States factories is almost fourteen thousand dollars' worth for every worker. In some countries, industrial development has been retarded, and national and individual wealth and income are low.

Machine production doubtless increases individual income. It must be remembered, however, that machines are necessary to make machines. A vacuum cleaner makes the housewife's work easier and more efficient, but a factory and the labor of many people are required to produce the vacuum cleaner.

The problem of the business manager is to develop an effective combination of the right proportions of natural resources, labor, capital, management, and government. This combination will, of course, vary from one industry to another; but the problem of the proper adjustment of these five factors is a basic one by which the efficiency of the business manager is determined.

Specialization and Production. Specialization, sometimes referred to as *division of labor,* is one of the outstanding characteristics of large-scale production. The trades, crafts, all phases of skilled labor, and the professions have been developed by dividing large tasks among several special occupational workers in order that each one might do only the small part in which he is a specialist.

Under a plan of specialization of labor no one attempts to produce everything that he needs to satisfy his wants. Consequently, there are now hundreds of different kinds of occupations, and most workers specialize in some particular type of work. There was a time when one person with one or more helpers could do all the work in constructing a house. Now a house is constructed by specialized carpenters, bricklayers, plumbers, painters, and plasterers. Even the lathing, the laying of the floor, the roofing, and the concrete work are done by specialized workmen. Although the total task of constructing a house is broken down into several special jobs, the work of the various specialists must be coordinated. Specialization, then consists not only of dividing a given piece of work among specialists, but also of coordinating their work. Planning and coordinating is the work of management.

Advantages of Specialization. Some of the advantages of specialization are: (a) it increases production, hence the amount of wealth and income; (b) it encourages the development of greater skill; (c) it saves time; (d) it lowers production costs; (e) it makes possible the employment of persons who may otherwise be unemployable; (f) it permits the continuous and economical use of tools and equipment; and (g) it develops a spirit of interdependence.

Disadvantages of Specialization. Some of the disadvantages of specialization are serious, but they do not necessarily affect the production of wealth. Among the disadvantages are: (a) workers become greatly dependent upon one another; (b) work may become monotonous and deadening to the worker; (c) a worker finds it difficult to change from one occupation to another; (d) a worker may not have as much pride in his workmanship; (e) the efficient worker does not have an opportunity to learn how to perform other tasks; and (f) a worker who loses his position may have difficulty finding another or adjusting to another because it may require other skills and knowledges.

Limiting Production. Periodically in our economic history various groups—including government, labor, farmers, manufacturers, and others—have attempted to restrict production in order to maintain prices and personal profits. Certain individuals have been afraid that machines would take the place of men. Some labor leaders feel that by reducing the length of the working day or the working week, income can be spread among more workers.

A common practice for some producers of food crops has been to destroy part of the crops rather than to market them because the marketing of large surpluses would depress the prices. For them, the marketing of a small quantity at a good price is profitable, whereas the marketing of a large quantity at a low price might be unprofitable.

Any restriction on production by any particular group may be of temporary advantage to that group. Temporary restriction and control of production may be necessary and helpful to our whole society in order to correct maladjustments in our economic system. However, if several groups or all groups restrict production in the same manner, we all suffer because we have less goods to consume. Maximum prosperity will come about by maximum production by every individual so that his goods are available at a low price to everyone else and so that, in turn, the goods that other people produce are available to him at low prices. Permanent advantage cannot be realized by a group, whether it be a producer of agricultural products, machines, or clothing, by restricting production to make prices high. Not only will such a course of action contribute to forcing prices of all commodities and services higher, a policy from which no one benefits, but it also will encourage the development of substitutes for the product which is being controlled. In other words, maximum prosperity depends upon maximum production rather than on restriction of production. Some economists believe the greater the percentage of our people who are employed, the greater will be their buying power, and their demand for goods and services will make maximum production necessary.

The principle that maximum prosperity depends upon maximum production rather than upon restricted production is applicable to the individual worker as well as to an industry or a business enterprise. The employee who produces as much as he can each day and week consistent with his physical strength and health helps to raise the level of living for all people—for the nation as a whole. The worker who produces less than he is capable of producing, yet draws compensation for a full day's work, automatically contributes to higher price levels, which means that wages received will buy less. As a result, the level of living falls.

Men, Machines, and Productivity. Men using machines have greater productive capacity than men working without machines. Productivity is the key to prosperity. A nation improves its standard of living through increases in productivity. Future progress depends upon raising the output of each man. Greater production for each man-hour is possible through the increasing use of machine power. Machines are now the helping hand of men in modern industry. A man with his hands alone can make a very limited quantity of any product. With the aid of a few tools he can increase his production. With the aid of machinery he is often able to multiply his production ten or twenty times or more.

Machines Increase Man's Productivity Many Times

Increased output or production per man per day by using machines has two distinctly favorable results:
- (a) *Workers have more leisure time.* They can produce more per hour, hence the number of hours of work per week can be reduced without curtailing production.
- (b) *Increased output per man per day tends to increase the worker's daily wage.* The increased output makes goods available to more people at lower costs, hence the standard of living is improved.

Most of us fail to realize the advantages that we have gained from the use of machines. It is estimated, for instance, that thirty years ago it required approximately 9 hours of a factory worker's wages to buy a pair of shoes. Today it requires approximately 3½ hours. Thirty years ago if a factory worker wanted to buy an electric light bulb, he would have had to spend the wages that he would have earned in about 105 minutes. Today he can buy an electric light bulb with the wages he has earned in 10 to 12 minutes.

Effects of New Machinery. New machines and new processes invented and discovered, especially during the past thirty years, are great aids to workers, enabling them to produce more per day and often with less effort. This development in industry is referred to as *technology*. With the introduction of automatic machines and processes to factory and office operations, especially since World War II, technology has progressed to a new stage known as automation. *Automation* generally is accepted to mean a continuous operation in production such as the assembly line through the use of automatic equipment. This equipment automatically performs routine operations, regulates the flow of materials being processed, and controls the quality of production.

As the effects of technology resulted in many changes in routine operations in factories, some workers were fearful of technological unemployment feeling that machines would be substituted for men or that machines aiding workers would increase the output per man to the extent that the number of workers would be reduced. These fears have been proved largely ungrounded. It is true that when major inventions are introduced, there is usually a certain amount of unemployment as a direct result of the introduction of the new machinery. In the long run, however, most new inventions not only provide more goods for all of us to use, but also create new types of jobs and thus eventually take care of persons displaced from previous jobs. For instance, the invention of the automobile displaced many employees who had manufactured wagons and other horse-drawn vehicles; but the automobile has created new jobs in automobile factories and filling stations, in the oil industry, in the steel industry, and in the rubber industry.

Many workers now look upon automation in the factory as a competitor to labor. Again there is fear of technological unemployment. Undoubtedly there will be temporary dislocation of labor, and readjustment of workers to new jobs will be necessary. In taking a larger view of industry, however, we find machines are not competitors of man, and automation is not a threat to the security of labor. Rather machines are man's helpers. They enable him to produce more in a shorter period of time with less physical discomfort and strain. In individual cases a machine may be a competitor of man for a particular job. Automation may affect a particular worker adversely by eliminating his job entirely. But, in the long run technology and automation will reduce the number of hours a week a man will need to work to earn the same amount he earned before the changes took place. There is a strong possibility that not only will he work fewer hours for his weekly wage but also that he will receive more in terms of purchasing power for his week's work. That is the way we have made progress in the past.

The economic soundness of using machines, either man-controlled or automatically controlled, in producing goods is unquestioned. However, the problem created by temporary unemployment caused by new inventions is one that must be met through the cooperative efforts of industry and labor.

Electrical Appliances in United States Homes

APPLIANCE	PER CENT OF HOMES
Mechanical refrigeration	89
Washing machines	76
Vacuum cleaners	59
Electric ranges	24

Source: *Electrical Manufacturing*, January, 1955.

These Machines Make Housework Easier

One would not think of going back to the hoe and spade instead of the tractor plow, the hand-drawn cart instead of the truck, the broom instead of the vacuum sweeper, or the wood fireplace instead of the modern kitchen range. Yet, probably these new inventions when introduced caused temporary dislocations of workers and made adjustments to new jobs necessary.

Wealth and Purchasing Power. The *private wealth* of a nation is comprised of all things that have a value in terms of money owned by individuals. *National wealth* is comprised of all of the material things having value in terms of money that are owned by either individuals or government. Thus, automobiles, household appliances, furniture, farms, houses, factories, and all buildings both publicly and privately owned are among the things included in national wealth.

Earlier in this chapter, it was said that income is the product of wealth. The prosperity of people depends largely upon their income. However, the per capita wealth of the nation means very little in determining the prosperity of the nation. Even the average income of the citizens does not determine the prosperity of the whole country. A nation may be very wealthy and, in total, may have a large income; but unless this income is divided reasonably over the entire population, there will be a lack of purchasing power.

According to available information the per capita national wealth of the United States exceeds that of every other nation in the world. When our per capita national wealth is compared with that of countries, such as Brazil, we find that ours is as much as four times as great. One reason is that much of our production is performed by high-speed machinery, whereas production in countries such as Brazil is performed largely by hand.

Although we state our income in terms of dollars, the real test of its value is what it will buy or its purchasing power. Another measure of income is the time one must work to buy a certain article. For example, if you must work five hours to buy a pair of shoes and someone else earns a pair of the same price in three hours, you know

Time Required for Average Worker to Earn One Unit Each of Eight Staple Foods in the United States and 19 Other Countries
(Minutes to earn one unit)

COUNTRY	TOTAL MINUTES	WHEAT FLOUR (LB.)	BREAD (LB.)	BUTTER (LB.)	CHEESE (LB.)	EGGS (DOZ.)	POTATOES (LB.)	LARD (LB.)	SUGAR (LB.)
United States	98	4	6	31	22	22	2	7	4
Average for 19 foreign countries	356	12	10	116	56	94	5	42	22
Australia	123	4	5	30	23	52	3	—	6
Austria	561	12	13	148	136	124	6	94	28
Canada	133	4	6	39	35	39	2	12	6
Chili	522	13	14	167	96	105	6	108	13
Czechoslovakia	346	8	6	93	58	92	2	70	17
Denmark	219	7	10	57	43	61	2	35	4
Finland	349	12	14	106	74	74	3	49	17
France	560	17	9	169	164	96	9	71	25
Germany	285	11	10	129	—	105	4	—	26
Great Britain	168	7	6	37	18	66	3	22	9
Hungary	471	17	11	160	—	106	4	133	40
Ireland	291	6	7	76	61	94	4	33	10
Israel	147	8	4	40	20	64	3	—	8
Italy	567	17	15	183	133	102	8	66	43
Netherlands	515	14	12	163	105	128	4	66	23
Norway	180	6	5	58	25	75	3	—	8
Sweden	171	7	10	60	28	54	3	—	9
Switzerland	310	19	17	117	35	76	5	39	12
USSR	852	36	19	373	—	291	11	—	122

Source: *Monthly Labor Review*, February, 1951.

your income per hour is much less than his. Likewise, the relative prosperity of the people of various countries may be measured by comparing the minutes of times people in those countries must work to earn certain staple commodities.

The amounts of time required to earn a given quantity of eight staple foods in the United States and 19 foreign countries are compared in the table on page 615. The figures are based upon current wage rates and current retail prices in these countries in 1951, the latest date for which figures from all of the countries are available. It is commonly said that prices of food in the United States are high. The average worker must work much longer periods of time, however, to earn the same food in many other countries. For example, from the table it may be seen that the average worker in the United States must work one hour and 38 minutes to earn enough to buy one unit of the eight foods listed in the table, where as the average worker in the 19 other countries combined would work an average of five hours and 56 minutes to earn the same amount of food in those countries. Relatively speaking, the purchasing power of wages for an hour of labor in the United States is almost four times greater than the average purchasing power of an hour of labor in those 19 countries.

Real Wages. It is impossible to determine whether a person is earning a high or a low wage without a knowledge of the prices that he has to pay for the goods and services that he uses. One's *wages* is the amount earned before deductions for taxes, insurance, and other items. One's *real wages* is the amount of goods and services that may be purchased with the money earned. In other words, the measure of real wages is the purchasing power of one's earnings.

For instance, assume that a man is earning forty dollars a week and paying certain prices for food, clothing, and rent. Suppose the prices of necessities increase 50 per cent, and his wages increase 25 per cent. He has had a substantial increase in wages, but he still is not earning real wages that are equal to his former wages of forty dollars.

His increased wages of fifty dollars will not buy so much as his former wages of forty dollars did.

Let us take another example. Let us assume that one's wages are increased from $60 a week to $66 a week. Let us also assume that the cost of living increases from $40 a week to $44 a week. Is the wage earner any better off financially? No. His real wages have not increased, although his monetary wages have increased. Of course, it is easier to pay off any debts that he has incurred because he is paying off the debts with dollars that are worth less than they were when he incurred the debts. However, if he has saved money in the bank, this money is worth less than when he saved it because the dollars will buy less now than when he saved the money.

Real Wages Are Not Money; They Are What Money Will Buy

Summary of What Money, Wealth, Production, and Income Mean to Consumers

1. Wealth consists of useful, tangible goods wanted by man.
2. Money has value only in acquiring the goods we want.
3. Income results from the production and use of goods to satisfy human wants.
4. Production consists primarily of making goods useful to man.
5. Maximum, not limited, production by every person is the key to maximum prosperity.
6. The use of machines in production reduces the unit cost of goods for consumers; more goods are sold, thereby making more jobs for more people.
7. Machines increase a worker's productive capacity resulting in less hours of work a week for the same wage.
8. Using semiautomatic and automatic machines in production in the long run is sound economically and for the good of all people.
9. The measure of the prosperity of a nation is how adequately the income of people supplies their economic wants and needs.

TEXTBOOK QUESTIONS

1. What is money?
2. What is wealth?
3. Is money wealth? Explain.
4. What is income?
5. Why may a native on an isolated island in the Pacific prefer to accept some kind of goods instead of money?
6. Explain what makes money valuable.
7. Name and explain the three most important types of utilities created by a producer.
8. Give an example of a strictly nonproductive activity.
9. Explain the two types or classes of producers.
10. What are the five elements of production?
11. What is capital?
12. What are the advantages of specialization?
13. What are the disadvantages of specialization?
14. Why do some producers of food crops destroy part of them?
15. Upon what does maximum prosperity depend?
16. What have been the two general good effects of the use of machines in production?
17. Give an example of how the productiveness of machinery helps us to buy more with each hour of labor.
18. What is meant by automation?
19. What is meant by technological unemployment?
20. How does the United States rank with other nations in respect to the buying power of one hour's wages?
21. What is meant by real wages?

DISCUSSION QUESTIONS

1. A man is said to be worth a million dollars. Does this statement mean that he has a million dollars in cash?
2. Can new wealth be produced by labor or by wealth alone, or must the two always join forces?
3. Of what value is ten thousand dollars in cash to an individual alone on an island?
4. Does the production of harmful narcotics represent the production of wealth?
5. Some people criticize the use of the term *nonproductive activities* to designate the activities of organizations such as banks, stock exchanges, and wholesalers. Are the activities of such organizations nonproductive?
6. Why are the services of some people more valuable than the services of others?
7. If a large machine is installed in a factory to do the work of ten men, what will be the result from the point of view of the total production of wealth?

Ch. 35] WEALTH, PRODUCTION, AND INCOME

8. What are some of the advantages that nature provides for production?
9. Has specialization in production increased the average standard of living?
10. Some producers have been known to destroy part of their products in order to raise prices. They have obtained more for the small supply that they sold than they would have received for the entire quantity. What is the result of such a practice?
11. In what way has the automobile increased both employment and the production of wealth?
12. In times of war people are usually very busy. Does this fact mean that the production of wealth is increasing rapidly?
13. If the machine has made a forty-hour week possible, do you think it would be advisable to continue to decrease the working week to as low as ten or twenty hours a week?
14. Is technological unemployment a permanent type of unemployment?

PROBLEMS

1. (a) If production by everyone was increased 20 per cent, what do you think would be the general result from the point of view of individual and national welfare?
   (b) What would be the result if there were a 20 per cent decrease in the efficiency of production?
2. Point out the functions that each of the following three factors performs in the production of an automobile: (a) nature, (b) man, and (c) machinery.
3. The amount of money of all kinds in circulation in 1955 totaled about $29 billion while the national income for that year totaled about $300 billion. Explain how it is possible for everyone to earn a cash income when there is less than a month's supply of cash in circulation.

COMMUNITY PROBLEMS AND PROJECTS

1. Compare the income of your community with that of your state. Your local chamber of commerce may be able to supply you with the figures.
2. From your personal observation and investigation, make a list of ten examples of producers of each of the following types of utilities: (a) form utility, (b) time utility, and (c) place utility.
3. Make a study of the natural resources available in your state. Give as much information in regard to each resource as possible. If you can get the figures, compare the resources of your state with those of others.

Chapter 36

How We Share in the National Income

Purpose of the Chapter. As a group, we continuously produce a gigantic stream of wealth in the form of goods and services. Each of us shares to a small extent in this great wealth through the income we receive. The income we receive may be in various forms. Not all of us, of course, receive equal amounts. The purpose of this chapter is to show how we divide our national wealth and income.

You will find answers to these questions:
1. What entitles a person to a share in national income?
2. What affects the share of total income received by each of the following: (a) Labor and managers, (b) Lenders of money, (c) Land owners, (d) Owners of business, and (e) Government?
3. What entitles owners of business to receive a share in income?
4. Why do some persons receive more income than others?

Who Shares in Income? The national income for a given period of time consists of the net total of goods and services produced by all of the people. The value of these goods and services is measured in terms of money.

In industry the results of production are divided among those who represent the factors involved in the production of goods and services. These factors, usually classified as natural resources, labor, capital, management, and government were discussed in Chapter 35. The results of productive effort are divided in the form of wages, interest, rents,

620

profits, and taxes. These are various forms of income. Wages go to the workers; interest goes to those from whom funds have been borrowed; rents go to the owners of land or other resources; profits go to the owners of business or industrial enterprises; and taxes go to government for the services it performs.

The owner of a business may own the land on which his business is located. He therefore may pay no rent. If he owes no money, he does not pay any interest. The only two elements involved in such a case are wages and profits. Society as a whole, however, shares in the income of the business through the taxes that are paid. It may be said, therefore, that the results of productive effort are divided into wages, interest, rents, profits, and taxes.

Sharing in Several Forms of Income. One may share in several of the forms of income from production. For instance, Mr. Jones, the owner of a garage, has a house that he rents. In this way he shares in rent. He has some money in a savings bank and gets interest on it. In this way he shares in interest. From the business that he operates, he probably draws a weekly or monthly salary. In this way he shares in wages. Since he owns the business, he earns

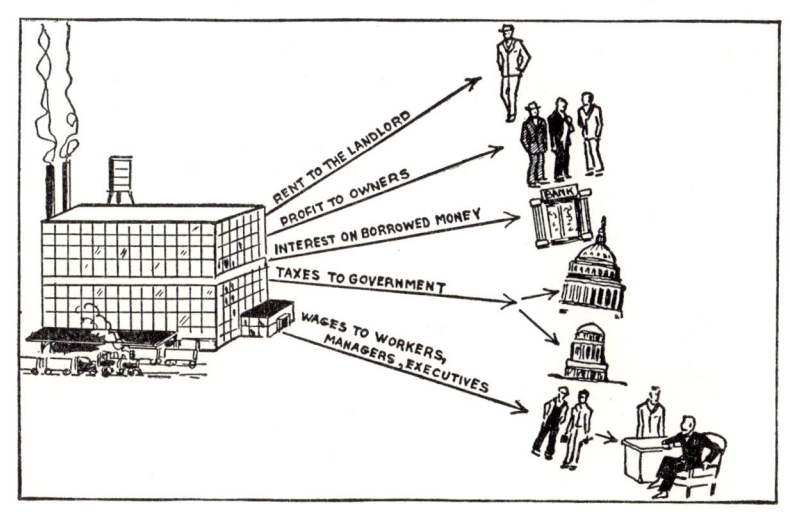

The Results of Production Are Divided Through Wages, Interest, Rents, Profits, and Taxes

profits, if there are any after all the expenses of operating the business have been paid. If he owns some stock in a corporation, he shares also in the profits of that business.

Illustration of Sharing in Income. Studying the income and the expenses of a business provides a concrete picture of the ways in which those who represent the various factors of production share in the income from production. The Eureka Manufacturing Company, a corporation, is organized to produce electric fans. The corporation is owned by the stockholders. The stockholders, through their board of directors, hire a manager to operate the business. The manager rents a building and land. He borrows money from a bank in order to buy equipment and to help pay the expenses that will be incurred in making sales. He also hires people to do the work in the factory and in the office, and to sell the goods.

At the end of the first year the manager prepares for the stockholders a statement to show how those who represent the various factors of production will share in the income. The income and expense statement of the Eureka Manufacturing Company is shown below.

This statement briefly illustrates how rent, wages, interest, profits, and taxes represent the distribution of the income of the Eureka Manufacturing Company. After all other deductions have been made, the balance of the income,

EUREKA MANUFACTURING COMPANY
Income and Expense Statement for the Year 195–

Income from Sales	135,000 00	
Cost of Merchandise Sold	97,000 00	
Gross Profit		38,000 00
Rent of Land and Building	2,800 00	
Wages of Clerks and Factory Workers	11,800 00	
Salary of Manager	4,200 00	
Interest on Borrowed Money	3,900 00	
Taxes	2,500 00	
Other Expenses (Supplies, Insurance, etc.)	9,300 00	
Total Expenses		34,500 00
Net Profit (to Owners)		3,500 00

Statement Showing the Sharing in the Fruits of Production

or net profit, goes to the stockholders, who own the business. If there is nothing left after the other items have been deducted, the owners do not get any share of the income. If there is a loss, the owners are the ones who lose.

Wages, Labor's Share of Income. Wages constitute that part of the national income which belongs to those who perform either mental or physical labor. Wages are the prices paid for the services of labor and management. The price of labor in terms of money places a value on labor.

The price of labor is determined in the same manner as the price of any product. In the absence of any control, the price is determined by the supply and the demand. The supply consists of the workers who are offering their services for sale. The demand consists of the needs of employers for workers. The principle of supply and demand of labor is as effective for an occupation as for all labor taken collectively. For example, except when there are wage controls, the ratio of the available supply of stenographers seeking employment to the demand affects the wages stenographers may receive.

An employer in determining the wage he can pay his workers must take into consideration the price that he can obtain for his goods and how much the worker can produce. The price for which a product will sell can be determined reasonably well from the prices at which other similar products are selling. In order to produce goods that can be sold in competition with others, the employer must estimate accurately the cost of rent, the cost of wages, and amounts of other expenses. The cost of materials can be computed with reasonable accuracy. The financial statement on page 622 is an example of the kind of analysis that an employer must make. He will have to pay the prevailing rates of wages, just as he will have to pay the prevailing prices for materials. He may not always be able to make a profit.

If the manager of a factory contemplates hiring more employees at the existing price that is being paid for labor, his problem is to decide whether the additional goods that will be produced by the new employees will earn additional profit. If more goods are needed for sale, and if the labor can be hired at a wage that will allow a profit on the additional production, new workers will be employed.

The Supply of Labor. As there are thousands of occupations, various classifications may be made of them. A common classification is that based on the kinds of labor required by the occupations: (a) unskilled, (b) semiskilled, (c) skilled, (d) clerical and semiprofessional, and (e) professional. The first three groups represent manual labor; the last two, work of a service type. The occupations in the last two groups are sometimes referred to as "white-collar" occupations. The requirements of the various occupations differ greatly. Consequently, a worker may not be able to transfer from one type of occupation to another. An unskilled day laborer could scarcely become an engineer; but many engineers could serve, if need be, as day laborers.

The supply of labor is indicated by the number of workers who are seeking employment in each kind of work at each of the wage rates offered in the occupation. If the wage rate for an occupation is low, a relatively small number of workers will be available; but as the wage rate increases, the larger will be the number of workers who will seek employment in that occupation.

The fact that there are many occupations for which a large number of persons can qualify affects the supply of labor. The attractiveness and the working conditions of certain occupations also affect the supply. Many persons prefer clerical occupations, even at low wages, because they believe the working conditions in such occupations are more desirable than those in occupations requiring manual labor. The desire to live in certain sections of the country or in a city affects the supply of labor. Many other factors influence the supply of labor, such as minimum age at which employment may begin, economic condition of older workers who may wish to retire, amount and cost of training, and the policies of organized labor.

The Demand for Labor. The demand for labor is the result of the demand for the products of labor. If, for any reason, the demand for a product or a service declines or disappears, the demand for the labor that produces it will likewise decline or disappear. The worker will therefore become unemployed unless he is able to shift to a new type of work. The development of a demand for a new product or service may result in abnormally high wages for the comparatively few workers able to produce the product or provide the service.

Wage rates, above the minimum required by law, are determined by demand and supply; but many conditions may affect either factor. Demand may fall off because of the lack of purchasing power on the part of consumers. Supply, too, may be affected in many ways. One common method of regulating supply is through the unionization of workers. Other factors that may affect demand and supply are the substitution of other types of labor and an increase in the use of machines.

Wage Inequalities. How is it possible to explain why one worker gets six dollars a day and another gets fifteen dollars a day? Why are those who do some of the more disagreeable work of the world rather poorly paid? Without having evaluated the reasons for this condition, one might assume that every person who is earning only six dollars a day would try to get a job in which he could earn more. There are reasons for these wage inequalities.

Education and training are two of the most important factors causing wage inequalities. Natural ability is another. The supply of people who can handle the low-paying positions is greater than the supply of those who can handle the better positions. If a certain kind of work demands more training and knowledge than another, an employer is willing to pay more for someone to do this work. Essentially, however, the wages in each group are determined according to the supply of labor in that group. The supply of labor becomes smaller as we progress from the lowest group to the highest. The supply in the highest group is often very limited. Why does a baseball star or a radio performer get fifty thousand dollars or more a year, even though either occupation may be rather pleasant? Clearly, the answer rests in the matter of supply and demand. If the public refused to pay for (or did not demand) such services, or if the persons who render those services could be found with ease, the salaries in that group would, of course, decline.

Legislation Affecting the Wages of Labor. After considering the regulation of wages and hours of labor for many years, Congress in 1938 passed the Fair Labor Standards Act, commonly known as the Wage-Hour Law. The law directly regulates the extent to which children may be employed in industry, fixed the minimum rates of pay for labor, and limited the standard work periods a week. The Wage-Hour Law defines as "oppressive child labor" the employment of children under 16 years of age subject to certain conditions and under 18 years in hazardous occupations.

The minimum wage rate per hour was to change gradually from 25 cents in 1938 to 40 cents by October, 1945, and the maximum standard work week was to change gradually from 44 hours in 1938 to 40 hours by June, 1940. As a result of amendments effective in 1950 and 1956, the minimum wage rate is $1.00 an hour, with an overtime rate of 150 per cent of the basic hourly rate for the number of hours worked over 40 hours per week.

The Wage-Hour Law applies only to interstate industries; however, it tends to influence minimum wages and maximum hours in all industries. Furthermore, the law encourages state labor legislation; many states have now enacted labor laws patterned generally after the Federal law.

The Walsh-Healy Act and the Bacon-Davis Act supplement the Wage-Hour Law by regulating the minimum wages that may be paid by a contractor who is producing under contract for the Federal Government.

Minimum wage rates and maximum work periods a week are protections to employees, especially when wages are dropping. The effect is to force industry to operate efficiently enough to meet the wage-hour standards or to discontinue business.

In addition to the wages and hours legislation for the protection of labor, several other kinds of laws enacted by states and the Federal Government regulate collective bargaining in labor-management negotiations, child labor, employment of women, and employers' liability and workmen's compensation in the event of accidents.

Interest, Capital's Share of Income. Funds are borrowed to serve three purposes: (a) to enable individuals to buy goods and services before having accumulated sufficient savings to pay for them, (b) to enable individuals and business firms to increase their productive capacity, and (c) to provide governments with funds to be used in both production and consumption. The amount paid for the use of borrowed funds is *interest*. Another concept of interest is that it is that portion of national income attributable to the use of capital, not including land. Usually, however, interest is considered the payment for the use of money borrowed.

The interest that one must pay to obtain the use of money is the price at which the services of the money can be obtained. The rate of interest is established by supply and demand in the same way that wages are determined by supply and demand. However, government agencies, such as the Federal Reserve Board and the United States Treasury, also influence interest rates as described in Chapter 18.

Suppose, for example, that Mr. Jacobs, the owner of a department store, needs to borrow five thousand dollars to buy a stock of goods for his fall season. He goes to an individual or a bank and inquires about the rate that is being charged on loans made at that time. If the rate quoted him is too high, he may go to another individual or bank. Frequently the rate of interest asked by one bank may be the same as that asked by another in the same community. In some cases, however, one bank may have more money on hand to lend than another, and may therefore be willing to take a lower rate of interest in order to make the loan. When large loans are being negotiated, the bargaining for rates of interest is frequently prolonged and carefully considered on a competitive basis.

When banks have available plenty of money for which there is no immediate need, they are usually anxious to lend it. If there are very few business firms that wish to borrow money, there is a lack of demand. As a result the rates on loans are low. When, on the other hand, banks have already lent most of their funds and there is an active demand for loans, the rates are high.

These simple laws of supply and demand, however, do not work exactly as described because of governmental controls and psychological factors. When profits and the prospects of profits are good, borrowers are willing to pay higher rates of interest if necessary, and banks are willing to lend money because they can charge good rates and because they are reasonably sure that the loans will be repaid. The government, through its monetary controls and lending activities, may cause low interest rates and a plentiful supply of money when prospects of business are good.

In times of depression, there is usually plenty of money lying idle in banks; rates are low; but loans are hard to get because banks and others are afraid to lend money in view of the risk involved. The interest rate is important because it determines the amount of national income that is distributed to those who supply capital.

Why Is Interest Paid? If money is to be borrowed for business purposes, the amount that can be paid for its use is determined by the amount of profit that can be made from business operations. If interest rates are high, businessmen are less likely to borrow, but they will borrow if there is a sufficient chance for a profit. The borrower's willingness is dependent upon the intensity of his needs and what other alternatives he has. For example, if one had to pay 20 per cent interest on a loan to finance the purchase of a home, the borrower would probably find it far less expensive to rent a home.

Risk in Lending Money. The person who lends money takes a risk just as does the person who rents an automobile to another. If the automobile is damaged and there is no means of collecting money to pay for the damages, the owner will suffer a loss. The person who owns the automobile has a right, therefore, to charge for its use and for the risk that he takes in renting it. Likewise, if a person lends money and it is not repaid, he suffers a loss. A person who lends money is entitled to a reasonable rate for the services performed by his money and also as compensation for the risk that he is taking. If the risk is great, the rate should be high; if the risk is negligible, the rate should be low.

Rent, Landowner's Share in Income. In an economic sense, land includes all natural resources. Thus it includes farms, urban building sites, minerals, forests, water, and even air, because all are natural resources. In many instances, land has man-made improvements, such as buildings, permanent equipment, or dams. These and similar improvements increase the usefulness of the land and hence its value.

In the ordinary use of the term, rent is the contract price received from a tenant for the temporary use of land including buildings and other improvements. In a more restricted sense, *economic rent* is that portion of income that is due solely to the land without buildings and other improvements. The more productive the land is, the greater the economic rent. When we speak of rent as a source of income, we refer to the contract price paid for the use of land and its improvements.

What Regulates the Cost of Rent of Land? Why should some farm land rent for one dollar a year an acre while other farm land rents for ten dollars an acre? Why should a building on one street in a city rent for twenty-five cents a square foot while a building on another street rents for one dollar a square foot?

Rent in such cases depends upon the usefulness, the productivity, and the desirability of the property. For example, a piece of land that will produce fifty bushels of wheat to an acre is theoretically worth at least twice as much as land that will produce only twenty-five bushels to an acre. Richness of the soil, mineral deposits, and location with regard to water or transportation facilities are a few of the many factors that have their bearing on the value of land. If an individual has land available for rent, he can obtain a rent only in proportion to the productivity of the land measured in comparison with that of competing land. The law of supply and demand applies to land just as it does to wages and interest.

Rent and Prices. Only a slight relationship exists between the rent that a producer pays for the use of the land in production and the price that he charges for his product. If the rent on any particular piece of land becomes so high that a reasonable profit cannot be made by the renter, this land will go out of use unless the rent is lowered, or it will have to be used for another purpose for which it is better suited.

Merchants sometimes advertise that, because their rent is lower, they can sell merchandise at a lower price than other merchants. Their statements are sometimes, but not always, true. Other factors, such as the quantity that can be sold, affect the price at which merchandise can be sold. The fallacy of the argument that low rents make it possible to sell at low prices lies in the fact that the rent of land is determined by supply and demand.

The merchant in the center of a large city pays a high rent, but he has many times as many customers as the merchant in an outlying district. He probably sells his goods faster and therefore needs less borrowed capital to finance his purchases. The person in an outlying community or a small town has fewer customers and sells his goods more slowly. His rate of profit is not any higher, and frequently is lower, than that of the city merchant.

Profit, The Owner's Share of Income. *Profit* is the share of income from an enterprise remaining for the owner after distributing the shares to which all others have claim. The rent share is paid to the owner of the land and permanent equipment leased; the interest share, to the one from whom funds have been borrowed; the wages, to laborers and employed management; and taxes, to local and Federal governments. Anything left over out of income after these claims have been paid is the property of the owner. It is his profit. If the income in a given period is not large enough to pay the claims of rent, interest, wages, and taxes, the loss must come out of previously accumulated surplus or must be paid by the owners.

The economist and the accountant do not compute profit the same way. *Pure profit* as computed by the economist is the amount of income remaining after all expenses have been deducted in which he includes economic rent for the use of land owned by the business firm and an amount which he refers to as interest for the use of equipment and buildings also owned by the business. *Net profit* as computed by the accountant is the amount of income remaining after paying all expenses that require money to satisfy. These expenses do not include economic rent for land and interest on capital investment owned by the business, as no money was required to satisfy them. It is easily seen that the pure profit from a month's operations would be less than the net profit for the same period.

In order to induce men to invest in a business enterprise and to devote their time and energy to its management and operation, the business must hold the possibility of profit after allowances are made for normal return on investment and for the wages of management.

Competition and Profits. On the average, the profits of a business are limited to a fair return on the investment and a reasonable compensation for risk. Sooner or later competition retards the increase in profits. New competition always tends to develop when someone makes a success of a business.

If one businessman has a secret that will enable him to operate at a profit that is greater than the profits of competitors, he has an important advantage. If his competitors learn the secret and become as skillful as he, the latter will lose his advantage.

As a result of the risks that a businessman takes, he sometimes receives an additional earning; but the risks, on the other hand, cause many businessmen to become bankrupt. As a business manager, the man of much ability and wide training receives a higher rate of income than a man of lesser competence. Likewise, an employee who is well trained and has much ability receives a higher rate of income than a less capable employee.

Risks and Profits. A business must build up a surplus to take care of times when there will be no profits. In order to build a surplus, a reasonably high rate of profit must be earned when business is good. If there is no surplus, adverse times may cause a business to fail. Building a surplus out of profits from income enables businessmen to take the risks involved in ownership and management.

Many people who work for wages or a salary think that the man who owns or manages a business has an easy life and that his profits are far greater than they rightfully should be. They overlook the fact that he often works long hours in his place of business and at home. He risks not only his money but also his health. He must plan ahead when the employed person is resting or is enjoying recreation. He must often meet acute competition. These are some of the reasons why many men are willing to take positions and to let their employers do the worrying and planning.

Businessmen are entitled to a profit for the risk of losing on their investment and for performing the arduous tasks of ownership and management. Estimates indicate that 60 per cent of those who enter business fail or quit.

Actual Distribution of National Income. The national income varies from year to year according to the productivity of the nation; it is influenced by business conditions in general. Since 1929, the national income has ranged from a low of 40 billion dollars in 1933 to a high of more than 305 billion dollars in 1953.

In 1954, the national income was 299.8 billion dollars. If equally divided among all men, women, and children in the United States, this would have given each an income of approximately $1,770 for the year or about $34 a week ($1,770 ÷ 52 weeks).

Of course, many people received more than the average share of income and many received less. In some sections

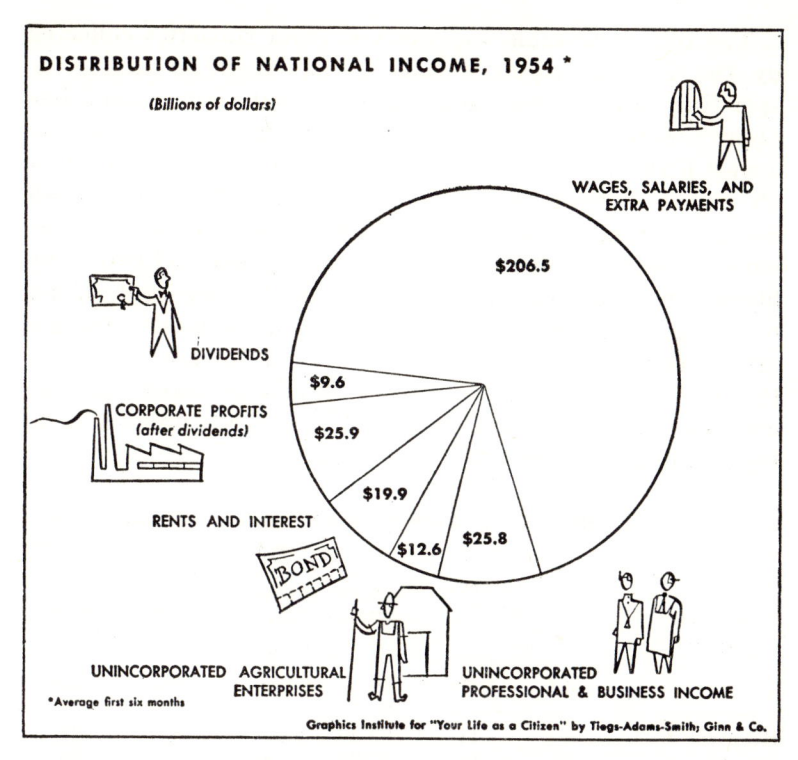

DISTRIBUTION OF NATIONAL INCOME, 1954 *
(Billions of dollars)

- WAGES, SALARIES, AND EXTRA PAYMENTS — $206.5
- DIVIDENDS — $9.6
- CORPORATE PROFITS (after dividends) — $25.9
- RENTS AND INTEREST — $19.9
- $12.6
- $25.8
- UNINCORPORATED AGRICULTURAL ENTERPRISES
- UNINCORPORATED PROFESSIONAL & BUSINESS INCOME

*Average first six months

Graphics Institute for "Your Life as a Citizen" by Tiegs-Adams-Smith; Ginn & Co.

of the country average per capita income is higher than in other sections. Although the average total income received per person in the United States in 1954 was $1,770, in the State of Delaware it was $2,361 and in Mississippi, $873.

How the National Income Was Shared in 1954
(Billions of Dollars)

DIVISION OF INCOME	INCOME	PER CENT
Wages and salaries of employees	207.9	69.3
Owner's income		
From farms	12.0	4.0
From business and professions	25.9	8.6
Rental income of persons	10.5	3.5
Net interest	9.5	3.2
Corporation profits before paying taxes	34.0	11.4
Total national income	299.8	100.0

Source: U. S. Department of Commerce.

The following table was derived from statistics collected by the Federal Reserve Board. The average family or spending unit as defined by the Federal Government has approximately three persons. During the year 1954, the lowest fifth (income) of our families received 4 per cent of all money income; however, they had 5 per cent of all money income after Federal taxes were deducted. The lowest family income in this group was below $1,000. The highest fifth of our families received 44 per cent of all money income; they had 42 per cent of all money income after Federal taxes were deducted. The lowest income in this family group was $6,000. It should be noted that the average income in each group was probably quite a little higher than the lowest income in the group.

Money Income Received by Each Fifth of Families, 1950 and 1954

INCOME FIFTH	PERCENTAGE OF TOTAL MONEY INCOME		LOWEST INCOME WITHIN FIFTH		PERCENTAGE OF DISPOSABLE MONEY INCOME (AFTER TAXES)	
	1954	1950	1954	1950	1954	1950
Hightest fifth	44	44	$6,000	$4,950	42	42
Second fifth .	24	24	4,350	3,550	23	24
Third fifth ..	17	17	3,120	2,510	18	18
Fourth fifth .	11	11	1,760	1,430	12	12
Lowest fifth .	4	4	(a)	(a)	5	4

(a) Data not available.
Source: *1955 Survey of Consumer Finances.*
 Federal Reserve Bulletin, June, 1955, pp. 616-17.

Numerous factors account for the inequality of income distribution among people. Among these factors, personal traits, habits, and abilities are among the most important. We are just not alike in our earning ability. Other factors, such as general economic conditions in the geographical area in which one lives and works, education, accumulated savings, and employment opportunities also affect the amount any one person may earn.

It must be remembered also that money income is not the real answer; what the money will buy is important.

> *Summary of How We Share Our Income*
>
> 1. Annual national income consists of the total goods and services produced by all of the people.
> 2. The total annual national income is received in money during the year by:
>   a. Labor and management in the form of wages
>   b. Lenders of money, in interest
>   c. Land owners, in rent
>   d. Owners of business, in profits, and
>   e. Government, in taxes
> 3. The primary factors affecting the share of income owners get from profits are competition and managerial ability.
> 4. Managers and owners are entitled to a just share in income for the risk they assume.
> 5. The primary causes of inequality in receiving shares in national income are differences among people in education, training, ability, and drive.

TEXTBOOK QUESTIONS

1. In what sense do all share in the national wealth?
2. Of what does the national income consist?
3. In what five forms are the results of productive effort of industry distributed?
4. How may a person share in more than one form of income?
5. According to the statement of the Eureka Manufacturing Company on page 622, how much profit is available for the owners?
6. Upon what does individual income depend?
7. What determines whether an employer will hire additional workers?
8. The price of labor is said to be determined to some extent by the supply of and the demand for labor. What is meant by (a) the supply? (b) the demand?
9. What effect does a shortage of workers tend to have on wages?
10. What factors tend to cause wage inequalities?
11. As amended, the Wage-Hour Law now provides for what minimum hourly rate?
12. What is the justification for paying interest?
13. What factors besides the law of supply and demand affect interest rates?
14. What determines the value of land?

15. Why is the rental rate on a piece of business property in the center of a city higher than in an outlying district?
16. What is profit?
17. Explain how competition tends to control profits and prices.
18. What was the average income per person in the United States in 1954?

DISCUSSION QUESTIONS

1. In how many forms of income may a farmer who owns and works his own farm share?
2. Explain how a manager of a small business shares in different kinds of income, although his total income is the profit from his business.
3. Why do wages depend not only on the skill of an individual but also on his ability to market his skill?
4. Why are there differences in the amount of wealth individuals have and in the amount of income they receive?
5. What is a fair wage for a man? Upon what does it depend?
6. Why will the wages of unskilled workers always be low in comparison with those of other workers?
7. Does higher education result in higher wages always? usually?
8. Trace the Wage-Hour Law from 1938 to 1956.
9. Why do reduced interest rates on loans encourage borrowing?
10. Sometimes when there is plenty of business activity and good profits can be made, how are interest rates affected by a program of the Federal Government of lending large sums of money to corporations at low interest rates?
11. A merchant in the downtown section of a city advertises that he sells a large volume of goods and that he therefore can sell at lower prices than competitors. Discuss this statement.
12. Assume that there is only one hardware store in a city of 10,000 population. Since there is only one store, the owner charges very high prices and makes an exceptionally large profit. What natural economic controls are likely to remedy this situation? Explain.
13. Does a dividend paid to a stockholder represent a share of income in the form of wages, rent, interest, or profits? Explain your answer.

PROBLEMS

1. In one particular state a proposed new law would increase a tax $20 on each $1,000 of valuation of city real estate. If a piece of property were worth $7,000 and were being rented, how much would the landlord have to increase the monthly rent in order to pay the additional tax?

2. A person has $300,000 invested in the Eureka Manufacturing Company. This amount represents all the stock of the company. On the basis of the financial statement shown on page 622, compute the percentage of income earned on the investment.
3. A businessman finds that he can borrow $5,000 for three months at 4 per cent and make a gross profit of $100 on the transaction in which the $5,000 will be used. After deducting the $50 interest charge, he will make a net profit of $50. If the interest rate were 6 per cent, what would be the profitableness of the transaction?
4. From Department of Commerce figures, determine what per cent of national income went to wages and salaries in 1954 and later years.
5. In 1954 what per cent of families earned $6,000 or more? What per cent of the national income did they receive? What per cent of the families earned less than $1,760? What per cent of the national income did they receive? These figures may be obtained from the table in this chapter referring to money income received by families.

COMMUNITY PROBLEMS AND PROJECTS

1. Wages vary according to occupations and localities. For your own community investigate (a) the wage rates for various classifications of local workers and (b) the minimum wage rates that have been established for various classes of workers. Compare the wage rates in your community with those in other communities. Compare the wage rates with the costs of living in order to determine the real wages.
2. Investigate the prevailing interest rates in your community for (a) loans on real estate, (b) loans on securities, (c) commercial loans, and (d) other types of loans. Find out how they compare with the rates of the year before, of five years ago, and of ten years ago. Give a report to indicate the reasons for the variations.
3. Compare rental rates on two similar pieces of property, either residential or business, each in a different section of your community. Explain these differences in rates.
4. List as many as possible of the risks involved in operating a business for profit.

Chapter 37

The Functions of Money and Credit

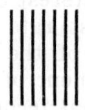

Purpose of the Chapter. Modern business would be impossible without money and credit. Practices in production, exchange, distribution, and consumption are all based upon money and credit. As individuals we use money and credit constantly in obtaining the economic goods and services we want and need. It is very important to us that we should understand what money and credit are and how they serve us. The purpose of this chapter is to provide an understanding of them.

You will find answers to these questions:
1. What are the functions of money?
2. What is the relation between the value of money and prices?
3. What is credit?
4. How are credit instruments used in business transactions?
5. How may banks expand the use of money through credit?

Functions of Money. Anyone is willing to take money in payment for goods or services. A person may accept goods as payment, but not so willingly as money. If you have canned vegetables and want to trade them for clothing, you may have some difficulty in finding a person who will be willing to make the exchange of goods. Nevertheless, you probably can find someone eventually. Today, in many rural communities, eggs are brought in by farmers and traded for clothing, food, or other products. For most of us, trading is not satisfactory or convenient.

638

Ch. 37]   THE FUNCTIONS OF MONEY AND CREDIT   639

The use of money has arisen because of the need for some medium that will be accepted in exchange for any product or service. Money is therefore defined as a *medium of exchange.* Money serves as a medium of exchange, for the person who has one type of goods can sell the goods for money and can use that money for buying what he wants. In this way money simplifies the process of exchange. In the selling of goods for money and the buying of other goods for money, the value of each type of goods is established in terms of money. Money is therefore also a *measure* or *standard of value.*

A person may receive his wage or salary for a month but prefer not to spend it until some future time. In this instance, money becomes a *store of value.* It represents accumulated purchasing power; it is value earned, but not yet spent. In another sense, money is a *standard of deferred payment.* For instance, a person may contract a debt today which is to run five years before coming due. Both prices and the demand for the goods may change materially in five years. Instead of saying that one owes

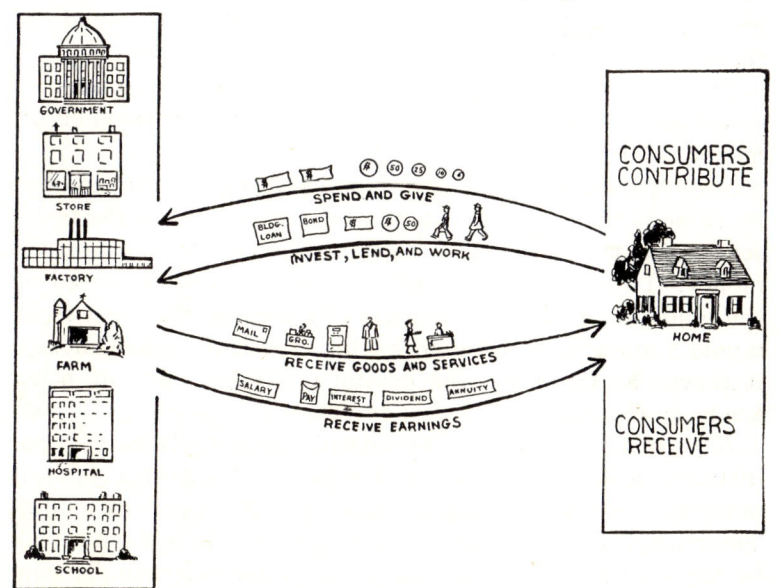

How Money Serves All Members of Society

a creditor five years from now three weeks' wages or 90 bushels of corn or one half of a television receiver, we state the amount of the debt in terms of dollars.

True wealth consists of goods. Through the use of money it is possible to accumulate wealth (or the means of obtaining wealth; that is, purchasing power) without having to amass and store actual goods. Money, except metallic money, is therefore only a right or claim to wealth. All the money in the world would not be of any value to a person if he could not use it in exchange for goods and services. To have value, money must therefore be readily exchangeable for goods and services. Whenever anyone has accumulated money, he is wealthy as long as money is exchangeable for goods and services. If money ceases to be of value, he is no longer wealthy. In such a case only those who have in their possession actual goods are wealthy.

Kinds of Money. If one were to trace the matter back through history, he would find many varieties of money. Gold and silver have been used frequently for making money, largely because of the fact that the coins made of these metals have a value in themselves.

The money of most civilized countries can be classified essentially as standard money, representative money, credit money, and token money.

Standard money is the term applied to money that obtains its value from the standard metal contained in it—the metal selected as the measure of value in the country issuing the money. The value of a gold coin, for example, is based on the gold that is in it if the country issuing the coin is on a gold standard. Since gold in this case is standard money, it serves as the basis for establishing the value of other kinds of money.

Representative money consists of paper certificates. For instance, a silver certificate is representative money; it is not standard money, but merely a claim to standard money. The reason for using representative money is to keep metallic money out of circulation. Paper money is usually considered more satisfactory for circulation and less costly to

Ch. 37] THE FUNCTIONS OF MONEY AND CREDIT 641

use. These paper certificates serve the same purposes as coins. Each piece of representative money certifies that the government is holding in its treasury enough actual metallic money to pay every holder of a certificate if that holder wishes metallic money instead of the certificate. Under the plan of issuing representative money, the government must keep in its vaults exactly the same amount of metallic money as the total value of the certificates it issues.

Theoretically, under this system of issuing money, the holder of a certificate can obtain standard money on demand. A government may, however, under special laws nationalize the metallic or standard money, such as gold or silver. In the United States gold has been nationalized, which means that it is not legal for any individual to possess gold coins, gold bullion, or gold certificates. These gold items are held by the Federal Government. By nationalizing this money, the Government prevents the hoarding of it and gains certain controls.

While the holder of a certificate may be assured that the issuing government has in its vaults metal equal in value to

United States Money in Circulation by Denomination
(Outside Treasury and Federal Reserve Banks)
September 30, 1955

COIN AND DENOMINA- TION CURRENCY	AMOUNT (IN MILLIONS)
Coin	1,887
$1 bills	1,252
$2 bills	72
$5 bills	2,072
$10 bills	6,495
$20 bills	9,711
$50 bills	2,653
$100 bills	5,518
$500 bills	308
$1,000 bills	442
$5,000 bills	4
$10,000 bills	9
Unassorted	1
Total	30,422

Source: *Federal Reserve Bulletin,* November, 1955, p. 1235.

the amount of the certificates issued, he cannot always obtain the actual metallic money. The security behind the certificate is, however, just as good as ever. All people who hold the certificates within their own countries are in the same relative position. Actual metallic money is therefore used largely only for exchange between nations.

Credit money is actually not money in the sense of standard money or representative money. It represents the promise of a government or of a bank to pay money on demand. Neither the government nor the bank that issues the credit money is required to keep on hand an amount of standard money equal to the total value of the notes in circulation. Examples of this kind of money are the Federal Reserve Notes which are secured partially by gold certificates and partially by rediscounted commercial paper. (See Chapter 18.) This is by far the most common type of currency now in use.

Token money consists of coins that contain metal of less value than that indicated by them. These coins are usually made of silver, nickel, or copper. Token money is used largely for making change and is not available in large denominations. Inasmuch as gold coins are no longer in circulation, all coins that are now in circulation are token money.

The theory of issuing token money is that it may be exchanged on demand for standard money. When monetary metals are nationalized, however, token money cannot be exchanged for standard money by people within the country.

Money in the United States
(In millions of dollars)

YEAR	MONEY IN CIRCULATION (PAPER AND METALLIC)	DEMAND DEPOSITS IN BANKS (CHECKBOOK MONEY)
1939	7,598	29,793
1945	28,515	75,851
1950	27,741	92,272
1954	30,509	106,550
1955 *	30,422	104,900

* September 30.
Source: *Federal Reserve Bulletin.*

Ch. 37]   THE FUNCTIONS OF MONEY AND CREDIT   643

The actual value of the metal in token money must always be less than the value indicated by the coin. If, for instance, the actual silver in a twenty-five cent piece were worth fifty cents, silver coins would go out of circulation and would be hoarded because of their silver content, or would be melted and sold as uncoined silver. Laws prohibiting the use of coins as a source of silver could scarcely prevent such action.

In a sense balances in checking accounts are the same as money, for they can be used to pay bills and to buy goods. Therefore, the total amount of money actually available for financial transactions of business firms and individuals is the sum of the paper money and coins in circulation plus the total of the balances in checking accounts.

Paper Currency Now Being Issued. In the United States the following types of notes, or paper money, are being issued currently: (a) United States notes, (b) silver certificates, and (c) Federal reserve notes. The United States notes are commonly referred to as "greenbacks." Upon them will be found an inscription similar to the following: "The United States of America will pay to the bearer one dollar." Silver certificates in denominations of $1, $5, and

United States Money in Circulation
(Includes paper currency held outside the continental limits of the United States)

	AMOUNT (IN MILLIONS)
Gold Certificates *	34
Federal Reserve Notes	25,806
Standard Silver Dollars	227
Silver Certificates and Treasury Notes of 1890 ...	2,155
United States Notes	316
Federal Reserve Bank Notes	158
National Bank Notes	66
Subsidiary Silver Coin	1,219
Minor Coin	441
Total	30,422

* Gold Certificates are not in circulation within the United States; in addition to the amount held outside continental United States, Federal Reserve Banks hold 21,020 millions of dollars in these certificates.
Source: Circulation Statement of U. S. Money, September 30, 1955.

$10 are issued by the United States Treasury against standard silver dollars held in the Treasury. Federal reserve notes are issued by federal reserve banks in denominations of $5, $10, $20, $50, $100, $500, $1,000, $5,000, and $10,000. These are secured by deposits of gold certificates and other securities held by the federal reserve banks.

Standards of Money. The money values of the civilized world are based upon either gold or silver. Most countries are on either the gold standard or the silver standard. A few countries follow a *bimetal policy*; that is, both gold and silver are used in one country as the standard, or measure of value, of money.

U. S. Treasury Department
United States Bullion Depository, Fort Knox, Kentucky

Prior to 1873 United States currency could be converted either directly or indirectly by the bearer upon request to the United States Treasury to either gold dollars or silver dollars. In the period from 1873 to 1933, we had a gold standard instead of the bimetallic standard of the earlier period, and currency could be converted into gold. Thus, we were said to have a *monometallic standard*, meaning that the value of our currency was based upon one metal, gold. The gold dollar coin contained 23.22 grains of fine gold.

Under an act of Congress in May, 1933, amended in January, 1934, the right of a bearer of United States currency to convert the currency to gold was rescinded, and the President was given authority to reduce by 50 per cent the standard upon which the value of the dollar was based if economic conditions warranted. Accordingly, the amount of gold upon which the value of the dollar is based was reduced from 23.22 grains to 13.71 grains of fine gold. The standard has not been changed since 1934. It may be said that our currency is based upon gold bullion, the value of which is determined by the government. Since gold does not circulate, all money in the United States may be classified as *fiduciary*; that is, it is accepted on faith in the United States Government rather than on the promise of the government to redeem in metal the face value of the currency. The government does have gold and silver bullion as security for paper money; however, the paper money is not redeemable in gold or silver bullion.

Reducing the amount of gold upon which the value of a dollar is based means that more dollars ordinarily will be required to buy goods that are offered for sale than before the standard is reduced. This condition is referred to as inflation; that is, the value of money is reduced.

The primary effect on the consumer of devaluing of the dollar and the consequent inflating of prices is that the purchasing power of his dollars of income and savings decreases. The effect on foreign trade is that it is more difficult to import goods but easier to export them. When the dollar of the United States becomes worth less in terms of foreign money, foreign money will buy more after inflation than it did before inflation.

Purchasing Power of Money. Prices of commodities and services vary inversely with the purchasing power or value of money. In other words, when general price levels are high, we say that the value of money is low. When prices are high, it takes more money to buy the same amount of goods than it did when prices were low. If prices begin to fall, we say that the purchasing power of money increases, for the dollar will buy more than it would formerly buy at the higher prices. The purchasing power or value of money is measured by the quantity of goods that a given amount of money will buy. Of course, the quantity of goods a dollar will buy depends upon the price of the goods.

The purchasing power of the dollar at one time is frequently compared with the purchasing power of a dollar at another time by a device known as a *price index number*. The United States Department of Commerce and the Bureau of Labor Statistics prepare price index numbers on many groups of commodities.

Purchasing Power of the Dollar
September 30, 1955

PRICES	PRICE INDEX BASE 1935–1939 = 100	PRICE INDEX BASE 1947–1949 = 100
All wholesale prices	46.8	89.5
All consumer prices	46.9	87.0
Retail food prices	52.1	89.6

Source: Department of Commerce.

The figures above mean that on September 30, 1955, a dollar would buy on an average 46.8 per cent as much goods at wholesale prices as it did in the 1935-1939 period and 89.5 per cent as much as in the 1947-1949 period. Similar comparisons can be made of consumer prices and retail food prices. Roughly, a dollar would buy approximately one half as much in 1955 as in 1939 and nine-tenths as much as in 1949.

Your prosperity is determined not by the number of dollars you earn but by the amount of goods and services they will buy. In other words, the purchasing power of money is of great importance to you.

Economists are not in complete agreement as to the forces that control the value of money. However, supply and demand affect both commodity prices and the value of money.

What Is Credit? In Chapter 20 we learned that a credit transaction is one in which one party to a business transaction receives either a loan of money or an advance of goods on the promise to repay the other party to the transaction at a specified later time. The person who makes a loan or advances goods to another on a promise to pay later must trust that person. Trust is based primarily on one's character, his earning power, and the amount of property he owns. Promises to pay are stated in terms of money.

Credit may be divided into two major classes: (1) business and agricultural credit and (2) consumer credit. *Business and agricultural credit* is used to finance the transactions of business and farming. *Consumer credit* is a means of financing the transactions of individuals for personal and family needs. Through the use of credit, business firms and farmers may increase their productivity by buying more machinery and more goods to sell or more cattle to feed. Wise use of credit by consumers may increase their productivity and earning power.

Business and Consumer Short-term and
Intermediate-term Debts
(In billions of dollars)

YEAR	BUSINESS AND AGRICULTURAL CREDIT	CONSUMER CREDIT	TOTAL
1949	$13.9	$17.1	$31.0
1953	23.4	29.5	52.9
1954	22.4	30.1	52.1
1955 *	24.7	34.3	58.0

* September 30.
Source: *Economic Indicators*, November, 1955.

The table above shows the amount of current debts not including mortgage debt. This means that both business firms and consumers are paying for many commodities while they use them. One may observe that the amount of debt was almost twice as much in 1955 as in 1949.

Credit Instruments. Any instrument that is used instead of metallic or paper money is a *credit instrument*. The most common type of credit instrument is the *bank check*. A person accepts a check with the confidence that it will be honored by the bank when it is presented for payment.

Checks are also used in transactions between banks. These are called *bank drafts*. The illustration on page 336 is a bank draft. Checks of this type are also sold to individuals who might have difficulty in transferring money by their personal checks. A bank draft is an order in which one bank directs another bank to pay a certain sum of the money it has on deposit in the latter. Suppose, for example, a person in St. Louis wishes to pay one thousand dollars to someone in San Francisco. He can go to a bank in St. Louis and buy a draft drawn on a San Francisco bank and made payable to his creditor. When the person in San Francisco receives the draft, he can collect the amount from any bank in San Francisco. If the man in St. Louis sent his personal check, it might not be honored because he is not known there. The bank draft will be honored, however, because the bank is known.

Bill of exchange is a general term that includes commercial *time drafts* or *sight drafts, trade acceptances,* and

A Commercial Time Draft

checks. Three original parties are involved in a bill of exchange: (a) the party who gives or issues the bill of exchange is called the *drawer*; (b) the party who is ordered to pay is called the *drawee*; (c) the party to whom payment is to be made is called the *payee.*

A Commercial Sight Draft

A *note* is a promise to pay to another a certain sum of money for value received. The time and the method of payment are indicated in the note. Interest may or may not be involved. Promissory notes are issued by individuals and businesses. Credit money (Federal Reserve notes) issued by the Government is a type of promissory note.

How Credit Expands the Use of Money. The expansion of credit through banking is presented here in order to give a complete picture of the functions of credit.

The process of expanding credit by a member bank discounting customers' notes at the Federal Reserve Bank in its district was explained in Chapter 18. An illustration here will further explain the effect of rediscounting customers' notes on increasing a bank's ability to loan more money to customers, therefore, creating more credit.

The following simple bank statement shows the status of the Central National Bank at a specific time:

Balance Sheet of Central National Bank

Assets:		Liabilities and Ownership:	
Cash	$ 80,000	Amount Due Depositors	$100,000
Bonds	120,000	Capital Stock	150,000
Deposits in Federal Reserve Bank	20,000	Surplus	50,000
Equipment	20,000		
Building	60,000	Total Liabilities and Ownership	$300,000
Total Assets	$300,000		

The American Manufacturing Company, a customer of this bank, obtains a loan of $10,000 for three months at 6 per cent and gives as security its promissory note. The bank deducts (discounts) its interest in advance and gives the customer credit for $9,850 in its account. The latter may use this credit by writing checks to the extent of $9,850. The note, which is a credit instrument, has become an asset of the bank, for it represents a promise of the American Manufacturing Company to pay $10,000 at the end of three months. After the loan has been made, the statement of the bank appears as shown on page 650.

It is evident that there has been no increase in the amount of money, but there has been an increase in the use of money. The deposits are almost 10 per cent larger than they were previously.

Balance Sheet of Central National Bank

ASSETS:		LIABILITIES AND OWNERSHIP:	
Cash	$ 80,000	Amount Due Depositors	$109,850
Bonds	120,000	Capital Stock	150,000
Deposits in Federal Reserve Bank	20,000	Surplus	50,000
Loans to Customers	**10,000**	Undivided Profits (Interest)	150
Equipment	20,000		
Building	60,000		
Total Assets	$310,000	Total Liabilities and Ownership	$310,000

Since this bank is a member of the Federal Reserve System, it can sell the note of the American Manufacturing Company at a federal reserve bank. When the note is sold to the federal reserve bank, it is rediscounted. The Federal Reserve Bank Board regulates the rediscount rate. Suppose, for example, the note is rediscounted in this case at 3 per cent. The bank accepts federal reserve notes (lawful money) for $5,000 and leaves the remainder on deposit in the federal reserve bank. The statement of the Central National Bank then is as follows:

Balance Sheet of Central National Bank

ASSETS:		LIABILITIES AND OWNERSHIP:	
Cash	$ **85,000**	Amount Due Depositors	$109,850
Bonds	120,000	Capital Stock	150,000
Deposits in Federal Reserve Bank	**24,925**	Surplus	50,000
Equipment	20,000	Undivided Profits	75
Building	60,000		
Total Assets	$309,925	Total Liabilities and Ownership	$309,925

The Central National Bank now has $5,000 more cash that can be loaned to customers and it has $4,925 more on deposit in the federal reserve bank which also increases its capacity to make loans to customers. This process of expanding the use of money by means of credit could continue indefinitely. Under present laws the expansion of credit can continue until the reserve in the federal reserve bank drops to a specified percentage of the bank's deposits.

Credit is also expanded in other ways. Let us assume that individuals go to a store and buy on account. The merchant obtains credit from the wholesaler to buy new merchandise; the wholesaler obtains credit from the manufacturer to buy merchandise; the manufacturer borrows money from the bank. He does not receive actual cash, but receives credit to his account on which he can write checks.

Ch. 37]   THE FUNCTIONS OF MONEY AND CREDIT   651

Most of these transactions, from the individual consumer's credit through to the manufacturer, are handled by the use of checks, making it necessary to use little currency in the transactions.

Checks may be drawn against most demand deposits in banks. Debts may be paid and goods purchased with checks just as with money. Some economists, therefore, believe that demand deposits should be considered along with currency and coins in determining the amount of money in circulation. From the foregoing points it is evident that banks perform an important function in expanding the use of money.

The illustration below shows how people place their money in various institutions and how this money is loaned out again. For example, when one buys life insurance he actually becomes a creditor of the life insurance company. The life insurance company lends the money to others.

Idle money does not stimulate business; but if money is used to buy goods or is lent for productive purposes, production is increased, more workers are needed, and business

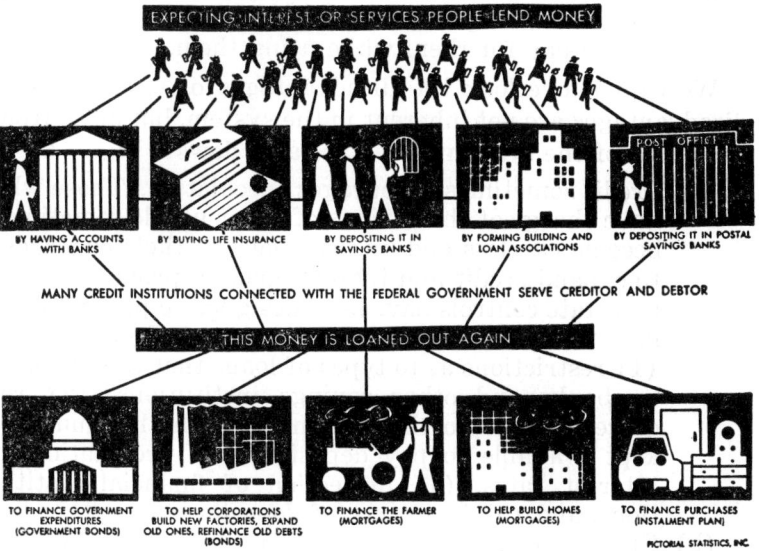

From Maxwell S. Stewart, *Debts—Good or Bad?*
The Public Affairs Committee, Inc., New York City

Creditor and Debtor Relationships in Expanding the Use of Money

is improved. The illustration on page 651 also shows how the money of individuals is lent to various institutions and is then used for various productive purposes.

Advantages and Disadvantages of Credit. After a system of credit is established, it is impossible for an economic system to operate on its existing scale without the use of continued credit. The following are some of the advantages of credit:

(a) Credit reduces the use of precious metals in coins.
(b) Credit saves time and expense by providing a safer and more convenient means of doing business.
(c) Credit helps production by making funds available for productive enterprises. For instance, a person without funds, but with ability and character, can obtain credit to use in producing new wealth.
(d) Credit helps the accumulation and the use of money for productive processes. An individual may not be able to use his savings funds for productive purposes, but he can safely put them to use by lending them to some productive enterprise.
(e) Credit enables consumers to buy houses, appliances, and other things needed for personal and family use and to pay for them while using them.

We cannot overlook the disadvantages of credit. These disadvantages are not inherent in the system, but arise from the abuse of the system. They are as follows:

(a) Credit sometimes encourages speculation. Those who have charge of the savings of other people sometimes become careless and unscrupulous in their eagerness to expand credit and thereby make a profit. Federal and state controls have been designed to prevent such bad practices. The most common safeguards are (1) restrictions as to types of loans that can be made by banks and other savings institutions, (2) requirements as to the amount of cash that must be kept available to pay depositors, (3) regulation of interest rates, (4) inspection of financial institutions, and (5) insurance of deposits.
(b) Credit sometimes causes extravagance and carelessness in the people who obtain it. Since the person who obtains credit is not using his own money but is

using the money of other people, he should not fail to appreciate the trust of credit.

(c) Credit may expand certain industries so much that they become relatively too large or experience "mushroom" growth. Certain industries may grow too rapidly on the basis of installment or other types of credit. Industrial expansion that takes place largely on the basis of consumer credit depends upon the consumer's future earning power. Should this future earning power fail to materialize, these industries are likely to experience a severe contraction of their business. If an industry bases its expansion on a large proportion of cash business, it is not likely to grow so rapidly, but is also not likely to experience a serious contraction of its business because of the curtailment of consumer purchasing.

(d) Because business can be expanded rapidly or contracted rapidly through the use of credit, businessmen are quite susceptible to confidence or pessimism. Credit causes one businessman to be dependent upon others. In order to extend credit, he must have faith in other businessmen and faith in the future. If credit relations become strained, many businesses may fail and a business recession may set in.

Summary of What Consumers Need to Know about Money and Credit

1. Modern business could not be carried on without money and credit.
2. The Federal Government controls the standard by which the value of a dollar is determined.
3. The real value of money to a consumer is measured by the amount of goods it will buy.
4. Credit is involved in a business transaction in which money is loaned or goods are advanced upon a promise to pay later.
5. Through the use of credit instruments banks and business firms expand the use of money.
6. Our business and economic system is dependent upon the use of credit.
7. Abuse and misuse of credit privileges should be avoided.

TEXTBOOK QUESTIONS

1. Why has the need for money arisen?
2. If money ceases to be of value, who are the only persons to possess wealth?
3. What is standard money?
4. What is representative money?
5. Under what circumstances can a person who possesses representative money obtain silver coins for it?
6. What is credit money?
7. What is token money?
8. What are the two most common standards of money?
9. How does a change in the gold content of a dollar affect prices?
10. What is the relation between value of money and prices?
11. What is meant by a dollar that is worth only 46.8 cents in purchasing power?
12. What use is made of business and agricultural credit?
13. What use is made of consumers' credit?
14. Explain what is meant by a credit instrument.
15. What is the most common type of credit instrument?
16. When a business borrows from a bank, how does the transaction affect the financial statement of the bank?
17. What can a bank which is a member of the Federal Reserve System do with notes that it obtains from businesses and individuals?
18. What are some of the advantages of credit?
19. What are some of the disadvantages of credit?

DISCUSSION QUESTIONS

1. "Money is a standard of value." Explain this statement.
2. (a) Is a bond wealth? (b) Is a silver certificate wealth?
3. Why do you think it would not be desirable to use iron as a standard of money?
4. What is the difference between standard and representative money?
5. Why are postage stamps sometimes accepted as money?
6. What are the types of paper money currently issued in the United States?
7. From the point of view of foreign trade, what, in your opinion, would be the effect of a sudden decrease in the value of the United States dollar?
8. Why did the purchasing power of a dollar fall from 1939 to 1955?
9. In what way does the use of credit act just as an increase in the amount of money?
10. What is the difference between a bank check and a bank draft?

Ch. 37]   THE FUNCTIONS OF MONEY AND CREDIT

11. Study the balance sheet of the Central National Bank that is shown on page 649. Explain what would be the effect on the depositors (a) if $10,000 worth of additional stock were sold, and (b) if the bank used $50,000 of its cash to buy an equal amount of its own stock from its stockholders.
12. Why do you think some bankers need to keep more cash than others in order to be sure that they have enough to pay depositors on demand?
13. Explain the function of banks in expanding credit.

PROBLEMS

1. Make a chart of the purchasing power of a dollar from 1941 to 1955. Figures may be obtained from the *World Almanac* or government publications.
2. List and define as many credit instruments as you can find.
3. There is about 30 billion dollars worth of money now printed and coined. Bank deposits total 105 billion dollars. How can there be on deposit more than five times as much money as there is in existence?
4. Refer to the first balance sheet of the Central National Bank on page 649. Make a new statement, assuming that depositors have withdrawn $70,000 in cash.
5. Refer to the first balance sheet of the Central National Bank on page 649. This bank lends $100,000 to customers at 6 per cent for thirty days and deducts the interest in advance. How much actual cash does the bank lend (if it deducts interest in advance)? Since the balance sheet shows only $80,000 cash on hand, where would the bank get the money to loan? Do you think it wise for the bank to loan this amount? Why? Prepare a new balance sheet showing the conditions of the bank at this particular time. Assume that the customers receive the loans in the form of credits to their accounts.

COMMUNITY PROBLEMS AND PROJECTS

1. From a bank, a federal reserve bank, your local chamber of commerce, the United States Treasury, or from any other source, obtain the latest information in regard to foreign exchange rates. If it is possible, make a comparison with the rates ten years ago. Report your conclusions.
2. Take some local example, such as a retail store, and trace the flow of credit back through to the source of raw materials. Illustrate your report with a sketch showing the various hands through which the product has traveled and the various persons and institutions that have probably provided credit.

Chapter 38

How Values and Prices Are Established

Purpose of the Chapter. Every person is affected by prices. Prices affect wages, interest rates, savings, the buying of commodities, the making of investments, and many other activities. The purpose of this chapter is to help you understand the significance of prices for consumers, why they change, and some of the factors that affect them.

You will find answers to these questions:
1. What is meant by the price system?
2. What is the relation of production and consumption to prices?
3. How does the law of supply and demand affect prices?
4. How do competition and monopoly affect prices?
5. What is the relationship of money and credit to prices?
6. By what means do state and Federal Governments control prices?

Barter System Versus Price System. In the days of barter, the person who produced wheat traded his wheat to the person who made saddles. The person who raised cows traded his cows to the person who raised flax. The person who made shoes traded his shoes to the farmer who produced potatoes. There was no single medium of exchange. A person enjoyed a variety of the necessities of life in proportion to his ability to produce and to exchange what he had produced for other things that he needed and wanted.

In the days of barter the value of wheat as compared to that of shoes depended largely upon the supply and the degree of usefulness of each product. When wheat was plentiful and shoes were scarce and difficult to produce, a considerable amount of wheat was required in return for shoes. When people found that a great many others had wheat to trade, but very few people had shoes to trade, more people began to produce shoes. As the supply of shoes increased, more shoes were required in return for wheat. Under the barter system, therefore, the supply of products regulated to a large extent the relative values of products. When the demand for a product was great, the product could be traded easily for other products. As the demand decreased, trading became more difficult.

Under the price system, the product one makes or one's labor is exchanged for money, and the money is used to buy goods and services. *Price* is the exchange value of goods or services stated in terms of money. For example, the price of wheat is the amount of money that is required to buy a bushel of wheat. All prices are stated in terms of money. Thus money serves not only as the medium for exchanging one kind of goods or services for another, but it is a measure or standard of value by which prices are determined. Under the price system, a general rise in all prices or a general fall in all prices may occur. A general rise or fall in prices means that the purchasing power or value of money has changed. Inflation results in higher prices in general, which means that the value or purchasing power of money has decreased.

Price is a powerful influence in our lives. In periods of rising prices, the man who has plenty of money can pay the prices of goods and services. A man whose expenses are almost as great as his income, however, will find that he must choose the goods and services he wants and needs most. He probably will continue to produce as much goods as he did before the increase in prices; but until his money income is increased, he will be unable to buy as many goods and services as he did before the general price rise.

Relation Between Production and Price. No businessman wishes to produce unless he receives enough money to pay all his costs. Costs include wages, raw materials, insurance, rent, interest, transportation, and many other items. Some businessmen will continue temporarily to produce goods without profit in the hope that they will eventually make enough profit to repay them for their previous losses.

Price tends to govern production. For instance, if the price of wheat goes up while the price of corn and hogs remains the same, as many farmers as possible will shift to the production of wheat. Then the production of wheat will rise, while the production of corn and hogs will decrease.

Production, in turn, tends to govern price. If too many farmers have shifted to the production of wheat, as indicated above, the supply of wheat will increase and the price will go down. Because of the decrease in the supply of corn and hogs, the price of corn and hogs will rise. Then there is likely to be a new shift in production. These examples serve to illustrate the fact that there is a constant interplay of price and supply, each influencing the other.

The fluctuation in price and supply, however, will generally be steadied by a basic factor: the cost of production. If price long remains much above the cost of production, new competitors will usually enter the field; supply will increase; and the price will be driven down. On the other hand, if the price falls below the cost of production and remains there long, some producers will drop out or will decrease production; supply will be curtailed; and the price will rise.

Ordinarily the businessman computes the cost of manufacturing, adds a reasonable profit, and announces the total as the price of his goods. If the price is based upon efficient manufacture and if conditions are normal, the manufacturer will be able to sell the goods at that price. There are always competitors who will sell at cut prices; but under normal conditions efficient manufacturers can go ahead and produce without lowering prices because the person who cuts prices and thus eliminates profit for a temporary advantage cannot long endure such a situation.

Production cannot be continued indefinitely unless the selling price is greater than the costs of production. More efficient methods of production permit the lowering of the selling price. It is for this reason that the first producers

Courtesy of the Los Angeles Chamber of Commerce

Production of Fruit Is Often Much Greater than the Quantity Offered by Sale Through the Grower's Cooperative. The Quantity Offered for Sale Tends to Control Price; and Price Tends to Control the Amount Offered for Sale

driven out of a field are those who are the least efficient. Their departure may cut the supply enough to steady prices above the production costs of the more efficient.

As a summary: high prices stimulate production, low prices discourage it; high production tends to depress prices, low production tends to raise prices.

Our Federal Government has influenced both the price and the quantity of production of agricultural products through subsidy and guaranteed prices. A *subsidy* is a direct payment to the producer. There is a further discussion of government controls later in this chapter.

Relation Between Price and Goods Offered for Sale. The amount of goods and services offered for sale is governed considerably by the price. If the price is favorable to the producer, he will offer large quantities of his product for sale. If the price is not favorable, he will not produce. Similarly, a farmer may have harvested 10,000 bushels of wheat. If the price of wheat is $2.30 a bushel, he may sell all of his wheat; but if it is only $1.50 a bushel, he may sell only enough to supply him with sufficient cash until he can dispose of the rest at a better price. A southern cotton-grower may have harvested 1,000 bales of cotton. If he can get 30 cents a pound for his cotton, he may sell all the bales; but if he can get only 12 cents a pound, he may be willing to sell only 500 bales. Price therefore tends to regulate supply.

Theoretically, *supply* represents the quantity of goods offered for sale. If the supply increases—in other words, if more goods are offered for sale—the price tends to be lowered. If the supply continues to increase, the price will eventually reach a level that closely approximates the cost of production. When the price goes below this point, producers frequently fail and go into bankruptcy, for they cannot continue to produce without profit. The supply then tends to decrease, and the price becomes more stable. As the supply decreases, the price rises.

An opportune time to buy is when the supply is great and the demand is low. This condition is called a *buyer's market*. When the demand is high and the supply is low, the condition is referred to as a *seller's market*. In the first case the buyer has the bargaining advantage; in the second the seller has this advantage.

How Consumption Is Influenced by Prices. The person who buys goods wants to pay the lowest price possible. This is because he is selfishly interested in getting all he can for his money. The business man usually has to buy this way to make a profit.

As the price of a commodity increases, the number of people who buy that commodity at the price asked decreases. Take the example of clothing. Normally an increase in the price of clothing will reduce the amount of clothing bought unless the incomes of people are increased. As a general rule, the quantity of the article that is sold will decrease as the price rises, and will increase as the price drops. This general principle is, however, subject to modifications because of the influence of demand, supply, competition, monopoly, money, credit, and various other factors.

Relation Between Demand and Price. *Demand* is a schedule of amounts of a commodity that would be purchased at various prices. A commodity is said to have an *elastic demand* when a change in price will bring about considerable change in the amount of that commodity that will be purchased. The demand for a commodity is *inelastic* when a change in prices will bring about little or no change in the quantity of the commodity purchased.

As an example, elastic demand is the type in which the amount of goods and services bought increases readily as the price decreases, as in the case of automobiles. Many of the motor-car manufacturers have discovered the fact that, by reducing the price of their cars, they can sell a much larger number. The sale of a larger number will enable them to produce cars at lower per unit cost. Their reduction in price in many instances has resulted in their making more profit than they made at the previous higher price.

A hypothetical example of the elastic demand for automobiles will serve to illustrate the general principle of elastic demand. The following table shows (a) the decreasing prices of a car, (b) the number of cars that can be sold, (c) the total receipts from sales, and (d) the profits from sales:

PRICE PER CAR	NUMBER THAT CAN BE SOLD	TOTAL RECEIPTS FROM SALES	PROFITS FROM SALES
$3,600	75,000	$270,000,000	$16,200,000
3,200	125,000	490,000,000	28,000,000
2,800	175,000	490,000,000	38,400,000
2,400	250,000	600,000,000	30,000,000

The Principle of Elastic Demand

It is evident from this analysis that the reduction in price proves profitable up to the point where the price is approximately $2,800 a car. Any further reduction in the selling price of the car results in a decrease in the total profit.

An inelastic demand is the type of demand in which the amount of goods and services bought does not change, or shows relatively little change, when the price changes. For instance, a decrease in the price of bread may cause only a slight increase in the demand. The profit becomes less at the reduced price if the cost of production remains about the same. A hypothetical example will serve best to illustrate the principle of an inelastic demand. The following table shows an example of the relation between (a) the price, (b) the quantity that can be sold, (c) the total receipts from sales, and (d) the profits from sales:

PRICE PER LOAF OF BREAD	NUMBER OF LOAVES THAT CAN BE SOLD	TOTAL RECEIPTS FROM SALES	PROFITS FROM SALES
20¢	6,000,000	$1,200,000	$120,000
18¢	6,250,000	1,125,000	90,000
16¢	6,500,000	1,040,000	12,000
14¢	6,750,000	945,000	Loss, $30,000

The Principle of Inelastic Demand

From these analyses we see that demand and price are interrelated and that demand has an important effect on price. Demand for a commodity tends to make the price increase when the supply is limited. This tendency prevails not only for commodities having a so-called inelastic demand but in a modified degree for those having an elastic demand. If, for example, there is a scarcity of wheat as well as of bread, the price of bread rises, for the producers know that they can expect a relatively constant demand. In the case of elastic demand, however, the producers try to keep prices reasonable, for they know that when prices are raised the demand decreases.

Even in the case of an inelastic demand these rules do not hold strictly true when prices get too high. Although the demand for bread is relatively inelastic, regardless of price, yet if the price were to go high enough in proportion to the price of potatoes, people with limited income would shift to the buying of potatoes as a substitute. This represents *substitution* as a principle of economics.

How Competition Affects Prices. Competition is one means of protection for the consumer, for it helps to minimize prices, to promote efficiency, and to assure buyers that they can obtain what they want at the time they want it. Fundamentally we operate on the basis of a competitive system; but as will be discussed later, we also have some regulated monopolies and occasionally price controls, which set the maximum prices allowed on various goods.

Under free competition the cost of production is an important regulatory factor in determining prices. The price of goods usually fluctuates above and below the cost of production. No producer can persistently sell goods at prices that are much higher than those of his competitors. If producers make too much profit—in other words, if they charge high prices—their customers will buy from competitors that sell at lower prices. New competitors may also enter the field. As a result of this competition, the high prices that were formerly charged will be reduced.

The efficient businessman makes more profit than the inefficient. The inefficient producer who cannot succeed in keeping his costs low finds that he cannot compete with the efficient producer. When he tries to lower his prices to compete with the efficient producer, he fails to make a profit and has to quit business.

Through competition, buyers tend to get goods at the lowest prices at which the goods can be produced. Of course, there are exceptions. Some people prefer to pay more than others. Wealthy persons frequently patronize stores where prices are higher than in ordinary stores. As a general rule, however, people will buy products at the lowest prices at which the products can be obtained.

The economic principle of substitution is also an important factor in the competitive system. If prices of cotton go to a high level, there is likely to be a shift to substitutes such as rayon. In a similar manner airlines may take passengers away from the railroads.

How Monopoly Affects Prices. In a few instances, a producer free from competition may have absolute power to determine the selling price by releasing for sale a supply of his goods or services that is less than the amount that would be purchased, thus keeping prices high. This is a situation known as *monopoly*. As there is no competition, the person who has the monopoly may try to charge what he pleases. He usually will limit production to keep prices artificially high. He undoubtedly will attempt to create demand and maintain demand so that he can get the prices he asks. Prices do not necessarily have any relation to the cost of production; rather, as has been explained, they are determined by supply and demand. Generally speaking, the price and the supply are regulated in relation to demand so that the person controlling the monopoly will obtain the greatest aggregate profit.

The telegraph and the telephone companies provide interesting examples of monopolies, or at least partial monopolies. If one telephone company has a monopoly on the telephone service in a particular city, it has control over the supply of that service. In the absence of any legal control, the telephone company could set its own rates. A rise in the rates would cause some people to quit using the telephone. If the rates were to continue to rise, the telephone company might lose so many customers that it would not be able to make a profit. State governments, however, reserve the right to regulate the rates, or prices, charged by such companies.

The production of diamonds is controlled largely by monopoly. The monopoly governs the price and keeps it high. As a result of a restriction in the supply, diamonds are in constant demand. The volume of sales is limited, however, by the high price. At the high price at which diamonds are sold, a large profit is made. If the price were lowered, the rate of profit would decrease, although the demand would increase. If the price were lowered still more, it would eventually reach a point at which the total sales would not pay the producers as much profit as that which resulted from the total sales at the former high price.

How Money Affects Prices. Money is our medium of exchange. It also serves as the basis for establishing the relative values of goods. The value of money is determined by the amount of goods that a dollar will purchase. When the value of a dollar is low, the dollar will not buy so much

Ch. 38]

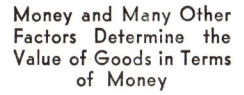

Money and Many Other Factors Determine the Value of Goods in Terms of Money

Harold M. Lambert

as when its value is high. In other words, money is cheap if it buys little, and dear if it buys much. When money changes in value, prices in general change.

On the other hand, a change in the price of a particular product does not necessarily influence the prices of other products. For example, the price of shoes may rise, but the prices of other commodities may stay at the same level. In other words, a rise in the price of shoes does not affect the prices of clothing, bread, and other commodities, since each product is evaluated individually in terms of money.

Two factors that affect the price level are (a) the quantity of money and (b) the rapidity with which money is used. The amount of money in the United States is less than the total value of goods that are being exchanged at a particular time. It is estimated that the total quantity of money in the United States changes hands from twenty to forty times a year. Ordinarily the quantity of money does not increase. The quantity has, however, been increased several times during the history of the United States by the issue of new paper money in the form of representative money or credit money. When there is an increase in the money available to buy goods and this money is used rapidly, prices tend to rise (a) because the supply of dollars is greater and (b) because the increase in rapidity with which money is used has the same effect as an increase in the amount. The general rise in prices is not always in proportion, however, to the increase in the supply of money or to the increase in turnover.

As a simple example let us consider an island on which there is a certain amount of money and a relatively inelastic supply of goods. The people who have money will soon establish the values of goods. If the total supply of money is suddenly doubled, however, everyone is in the same relative position. Each person has twice as much money as he formerly had, but he cannot buy twice as much goods because all the people want the goods in the same proportion as they formerly wanted them. If he attempts to buy goods with the same amount of money that he formerly used, he will find that other people are willing to pay more because they have more money. He will therefore have to pay just as much as anyone else. Prices in terms of money will rise because of the increase in the supply of money. In other words, increasing the supply of money has caused inflation of commodity prices.

How Credit Affects Prices. Increases and decreases in credit affect prices in very much the same way as increases and decreases in the supply of money. Since credit expands the use of money, it serves to increase the rapidity with which money is used. If a person has one hundred dollars to spend and borrows one hundred dollars, he has a total purchasing power of two hundred dollars. If, at the same time, the supply of products and services remains unchanged, prices will increase because there is an increased amount of money and credit with which to buy products and services. When money and credit are increased, however, the supply of products and services may also increase.

If the purchasing power continues to increase faster than the supply of goods and services, prices will continue to rise. When credit decreases, prices tend to decrease.

The prices of goods and their relation to the amount of money, the rapidity of use of money, and the amount of credit may be likened to weights on the ends of a pair of scales. Suppose that the scales are in balance, with the goods on one end and money and credit on the other end. If the amount of money decreases, the goods will drop in price. If the amount of money increases, the goods will rise in price. The same reactions will result from a decrease or an increase in the rapidity of use of money, or from a decrease or an increase in credit. Suppose, however, that as the prices of goods rise, the supply begins to increase. This increase in supply will tend to keep the prices down. If there is, however, a sufficiently large expansion of (a) the amount of money, (b) the rapidity of use of money, or (c) the use of credit, the prices will continue to rise. These three factors usually go hand in hand.

How Taxes Affect Prices. In general, high taxes on producers and distributors tend to increase prices, for taxes constitute part of the cost of producing any article or rendering any service. If a high tax is levied on a building, it must be included in computing the rent of the building. If a sales tax is levied on any item, such as gasoline, clothing, or drugs, regardless of the person against whom it has been assessed, it constitutes part of the cost of the product. Part or all of the taxes are usually passed on eventually to the consumer, either directly or indirectly, so that the levying of a tax against a particular product will eventually cause a rise in the price of that product. Sometimes all the tax or part of it is absorbed by the producer, resulting in a decrease in his profits. In the case of a tax on real estate, the result will be a decreased net profit from rentals if the owner does not pass the tax on to the tenant.

Such taxes as state and Federal income taxes levied on the incomes of individuals reduce the purchasing power of consumers and tend to decrease the demand for goods and services; therefore tend to lower prices.

Control of Prices. The preceding discussion of prices has assumed that there would be no control of prices. Nevertheless, prices are controlled to a certain extent by government, by businessmen, by farmers, and by workers.

The Federal Government owns and operates some industries and sometimes sets the prices of its commodities or services at less than cost and sometimes at more than cost. Among these industries owned by the Federal Government in which prices are controlled are the postal system, the Panama Canal, and the Tennessee Valley Authority. Some states also engage in production and distribution. States and municipalities own and operate many industrial and commercial enterprises, most of which are natural monopolies because they have the characteristics of a public utility. In many government-owned enterprises, prices are arbitrarily set almost without reference to costs. Deficits are paid from funds derived from taxation.

The rates for services given by public utilities, not government owned, are usually regulated or controlled by the state or Federal Government. For example, the rates for telephone service are under the control of the government. Likewise, railroad passenger rates and freight rates are controlled.

For many years, the various states have had regulations as to the maximum interest rates that may be charged for borrowed money. In more recent years the Board of Governors of the Federal Reserve System has exercised the power of control of discount or interest rates that federal reserve banks may charge member banks. This control influences the rates of interest that banks charge.

With the enactment of laws regulating the minimum wages per hour and the maximum hours per week for labor, a control of the price of labor has been in effect. Not all workers are covered by the laws, but the wages of all are influenced.

At various times, primarily since 1930, the Federal Government has extended its powers to control prices because of either a real or purported economic emergency. During the depression years of 1933 to 1936, the National

Recovery Administration, which was created by Congress, regulated minimum prices of certain specified commodities and the volume of production of some industries. The purpose was to aid in recovering from the economic depression. About the same time, the Secretary of Agriculture was empowered to set up a quantity restriction on the production of certain farm crops. If this quantity restriction on production was agreed upon by the growers of the crop, then the Government would make subsidy payments to the farmers if the market price of the crop fell below the established figure, called *parity*. This agreement to limit production and this guarantee of a specified minimum price constitute, of course, control through price supports.

Another phase of price supports for farmers is crop insurance. If market prices are lower than parity (government guaranteed price), the farmer may store his crop in a government-controlled warehouse and borrow from the Government a certain per cent of the parity value of the crop. If the price rises above the parity price guaranteed by the Government, the farmer may sell his crop, pay off his loan, and keep the difference. If the price does not rise above parity, he may sell at market price and the Government will pay him the difference between the price he obtained and parity price.

During World War II the Emergency Price Control Act regulated maximum prices for most goods. The maximum prices allowed were called *price ceilings*. The regulations affected the producers of raw materials, manufacturers, wholesalers, and retailers but did not include farm commodities, wages of labor, or the compensation of professional workers (wages were restricted through the War Labor Board). The regulations were administered by the Office of Price Administration, commonly known as OPA.

Price control, subsidies, grants of funds to certain types of industry, and government ownership of industry are economic problems that we must face.

Organized groups representing various aspects of production, distribution, and consumption attempt to obtain governmental protection or regulation on their behalf. Labor, professional, business, and farm groups practically all seek some kind of Federal legislation primarily to give them an economic advantage. Some of the legislation is undoubtedly desirable, and some is necessary. However, from the early days of the Roman Empire to the present, attempts to control price and to regulate income have created many other problems.

As citizens, we vote in state and national elections on economic issues. It is highly important that we understand clearly the issues having to do with prices, subsidies, and ownership so that we may have a basis for intelligent voting.

Summary of Principles Involving Values and Prices

1. The process by which one exchanges his labor or his products for the goods and services he needs through the medium of money is known as the price system.
2. High prices tend to increase production; whereas high production tends to depress prices.
3. As the supply of goods (quantity offered for sale) increases, the price tends to be lowered.
4. The price of a commodity influences consumption.
5. Competition tends to force a reasonable relationship between the price asked and the cost to produce.
6. When money is plentiful and credit relatively easy to obtain, prices tend to be high.
7. Taxes on producers tend to increase cost of goods, hence to increase prices.
8. Many prices are partially or completely controlled by state and Federal Governments.

TEXTBOOK QUESTIONS

1. Under the barter system what was the medium of exchange?
2. Under a barter system could there be any general rise in prices?
3. What effect does price have on production?
4. What effect does production have on price?
5. Explain how the cost of production tends to govern price.
6. How does supply affect prices?

7. What constitutes the supply of any product?
8. What is a buyer's market?
9. What is a seller's market?
10. In general, how does price affect consumption?
11. Explain in a general way what we mean by *demand*.
12. (a) What are the two types of demand? (b) Explain each.
13. Explain the economic principle of substitution.
14. In what ways does competition protect and aid the consumer?
15. In what way does competition regulate prices?
16. What effect does monopoly have on prices?
17. If you had a monopoly, in what manner would you adjust your prices?
18. In what way is the value of money determined?
19. If money changes in value, what happens to prices?
20. In what way does the use of credit affect prices?
21. How do taxes affect prices?
22. Explain two different kinds of price control.

DISCUSSION QUESTIONS

1. If we are to have an ideal economic society, why is it absolutely necessary for the prices of goods and the prices of wages to remain relatively stationary or to fluctuate up and down together?
2. How do you think a general reduction in the price of coal would affect the consumption of coal?
3. The consumption of lettuce in the United States has increased rather rapidly within the last twenty years. Why do you think this increase has taken place?
4. One store in a shopping section indicates the prices on all articles displayed in its windows. Another store does not indicate any prices. How do you account for the difference in practice?
5. The history of most new products, such as the automobile, the radio, and air-conditioning equipment, shows that the products at first sold at high prices, although they were not nearly so good as they were later. How do you account for the reduction in price?
6. Some people believe that quantity production at a low price is the solution to the problem of competition. In other words, producers can master competition by increasing their production and thus cutting down their costs. Is there any limit to the practicability of meeting competition in this way?
7. What effect does a drought in a particular section of the United States have (a) on the individual farmer in that section? (b) on farmers as a group? (c) on everyone?
8. Why are the farmers in many states encouraged to diversify their production by raising a variety of crops?

9. Assume that foreign-grown cotton can be imported at the same or lower prices than ours and that rayon and nylon are also competitors of cotton. Can you recommend any remedies?
10. (a) Give some examples of elastic demand. (b) Give some examples of inelastic demand.
11. (a) How may competition cause prices to rise? (b) How may it cause prices to decrease?
12. How do you think a sales tax affects prices?
13. What would you expect to happen if all apple growers were able to control the supply and maintain prices at a very high level?

PROBLEMS

1. From current publications and library files obtain prices quoted on some commodities today as compared with ten years ago or five years ago. Select one or more items, such as wheat, cotton, wool, eggs, cattle, or poultry. Submit a report explaining the differences that you find. Try to explain some of the reasons for these differences.
2. From your library or any other source obtain books pertaining to the agricultural problem in the United States. Study the supply and the price problems, as well as governmental controls, and write a report based on the various principles that you have learned in this chapter.

COMMUNITY PROBLEMS AND PROJECTS

1. Make a study of local price trends by keeping a record of the prices of several commodities over a period of at least two months.
2. Investigate the national production figures for a period of five years for at least two products, such as cotton goods, shoes, iron, or any other similar commodities. Draw your conclusions as to the relative adequacy of supply, and, if you can also obtain figures in regard to prices, explain the differences in prices based upon supply and demand.
3. Telephone companies, public power companies, and railroads are examples of controlled monopolies. Investigate the Federal and state laws affecting one of these types of companies and find out how prices and rates are regulated. Write a report.
4. Visit the office of the local county agricultural agent. Discuss with him the kinds of price control (or price support) now being used to protect farmers in your county. Write a report.

Chapter 39

How Business Conditions and Prices Affect Us

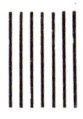

Purpose of the Chapter. Business conditions are almost always changing. We have periods of great activity and other periods of less activity. Both our income and the prices we pay for goods and services tend to fluctuate with business or economic conditions. As prices fluctuate, the purchasing power of our money changes. When the value of money changes, we are affected in various ways. The purpose of this chapter is to help you understand the business cycle and how changes in general price level affect you.

You will find answers to these questions:

1. What are indicators of trends in business conditions?
2. What do we know about the causes of the business cycle?
3. How do marked changes in prices affect business operators, people on salaries and fixed incomes, wage earners, creditors and investors, and debtors?
4. What devices are used to control inflation and deflation?
5. By what means does the Federal Government attempt to regulate business activity?

How to Determine Business Conditions. A businessman knows that his own business is bad when his sales and his profits are low. He knows that it is good when his sales and his profits are high. The condition of one business does not, however, determine general business conditions. In order to determine the general condition of business, it is necessary to know (a) the conditions in many businesses of a similar nature and (b) the conditions in a wide variety of businesses, such as the steel, lumber, and coal industries.

673

Many explanations have been given by businessmen and economists for changes in business conditions. These explanations vary widely. Some explanations credit or blame the current state of business activity on the political party in power, on labor troubles, on communism, or on conditions brought about by the weather. No one wholly satisfactory or reliable explanation has ever been given for the cyclical changes that occur in business activity.

In recent years several agencies of the Federal Government have compiled monthly and in some instances weekly statistics that are indicators of general business conditions currently. By comparison of current statistics with those of last month and previous years, the trend of general business conditions may be discernible. Among the most commonly used indicators to determine business conditions are:

1. *Gross national product,* which is the value of all goods and services produced in a period of time in the United States.
2. *National income,* which is the total income earned by those who contribute to current production. It represents the gross national product remaining after deductions are made for indirect taxes, depreciation, and the use of capital.
3. *Consumer prices,* which is the cost in dollars of nondurable goods used by consumers such as food, clothing, rent, and transportation.
4. *Industrial production,* which roughly is the quantity of durable and nondurable products manufactured and of minerals mined.
5. *Employment status and wages,* which indicate the number of persons employed and unemployed and the average hourly, weekly, and monthly wages of employees.
6. *Sales and inventories figures,* which show the dollar value of goods sold to consumers and of inventories of merchandise on hand by business.

Other figures that may indicate general business conditions are statistics dealing with such items as prices of stocks, amount of bank loans, consumer indebtedness, new construction, farm income, and imports and exports.

Ch. 39] BUSINESS CONDITIONS AND PRICES 675

The foregoing statistical items along with many others are prepared and made available by the Department of Commerce, Council of Economic Advisors, Department of Labor, Department of Agriculture, Security and Exchange Commission, Federal Reserve Board, and other Federal agencies. Anyone interested in statistics for determining business conditions may subscribe to government periodicals containing such figures for a small fee.

Examples of Commonly Used Indicators of Business Conditions

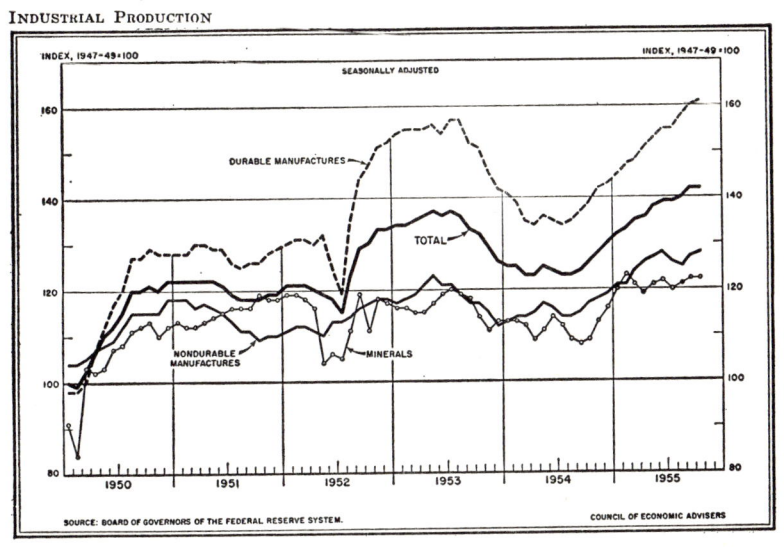

INDUSTRIAL PRODUCTION

SALES AND INVENTORIES

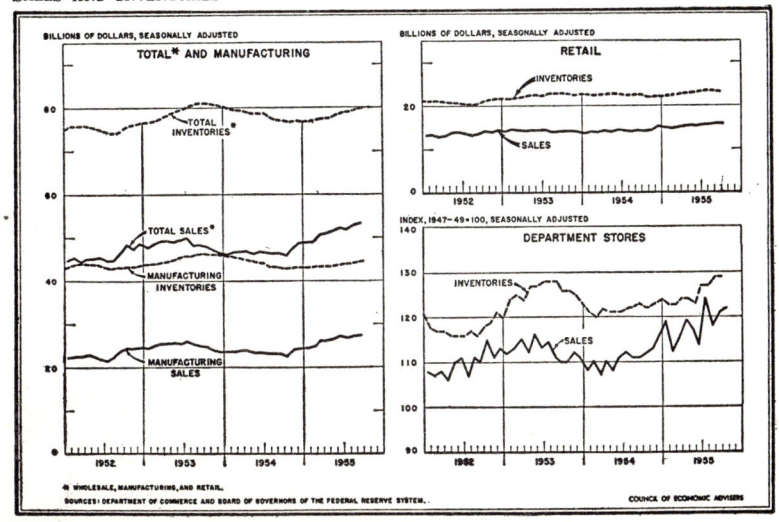

Source: *Economic Indicators*, November, 1955

Two charts are given on page 675 showing typical examples of the indicators of business conditions. The changes in the figures on these and many other charts from month to month may serve as indicators of the trends in business conditions in general.

Business Cycle. By the time the average person reaches the age of maturity, he reads and hears the term business cycle. Just what is a business cycle? The *business cycle* is computed from the various business indicators that show the "ups and downs" of business. It usually extends over a period of from three to nine years and includes alternating periods of prosperity and depression. The average person is aware that business conditions change, but he is not always aware of the causes or of the significance of the changes. Even experts disagree on the analysis of the business cycle, but the following discussion will give an elementary understanding of the problem.

The Federal Government and business interests are trying to find ways of eliminating the "downs" or at least reducing their severity.

Analysis of the Business Cycle. A business cycle may be measured from the low point of one depression to the low point of the next depression, or from the high point of one period of prosperity to the high point of the next period of prosperity. The illustration at the left shows the four phases of a business cycle. The four phases are referred to as (a) prosperity, (b) decline, (c) depression, and (d) recovery.

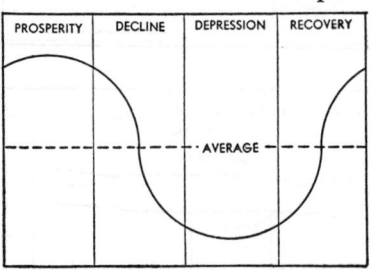

The Business Cycle Extends from One High Point to the Next High Point, or from One Low Point to Another, and Includes Periods of Prosperity, Decline, Depression and Recovery

Prosperity. Starting with a period of prosperity, let us analyze the characteristics of the various phases of the business cycle. In periods of *prosperity* most people have work. Wages and prices are relatively high as compared with those in other periods of the cycle. Most businessmen are able to make profits. Businesses and consumers buy goods generously. Eventually prices begin to rise; wages begin to increase; the prices of securities rise in anticipation of increased profits from business; many people are tempted to speculate in securities, commodities, or real estate; businesses continue to expand; money is borrowed on a large scale; interest rates are reasonably low so long as money is plentiful because the lenders see an opportunity to make profits with a very little risk.

Decline. In past periods of prosperity eventually we reached a stage when there was overproduction; the selling of the merchandise became a critical problem in business; competition became keen; profits were reduced; production began to lag; gradually employers started to reduce wages and to lay off workers; lenders became fearful and quit lending money; consumers reduced their purchases; the psychological factor of fear set in; and with these characteristics the period of *decline* had started.

The decrease in production, the curtailment of expansion of business, the curtailment of loans, the demand for payment of loans, the lowering of wages, and the laying off of workers, as well as many other factors, gradually accelerate the speed of decline and cause a decrease in the demand for manufactured products and therefore a decrease in the demand for raw materials.

We cannot overlook the human element in the business cycle. Many people watch for indications of a decline in business. They then begin to cut prices, to discharge employees, to pay off their loans as rapidly as they can, and to cease borrowing. Many of these actions cannot be helped. Merchants conduct special sales and cut prices in order to pay bank loans. As soon as production in factories is curtailed, men are thrown out of work and the purchasing power of the people is therefore decreased. Wages decrease because of the drop in prices and in the demand for workers. Many businessmen fail because they cannot make profits. The pessimism of producers sometimes prevents them from continuing to produce.

Depression. Just when the process turns into depression is difficult to determine. When business in general is bad, the period is referred to as a *depression.* In other words, business activities are depressed. In general, depression is considered to be the low point in the cycle. Prices are greatly reduced; many people are unemployed; businesses fail and sometimes banks fail. Some banks fail because they have been unable to collect loans and to keep themselves in a position to pay depositors. Others fail because people become panic-stricken and all demand their money at once.

During the time of depression very few people start in business because there is a lack of prospect for profit. People do not buy because they want to save their money in anticipation of worse conditions. Businessmen do not buy goods in large lots because they do not want to run the risk of lower prices.

PROSPERITY	DECLINE	DEPRESSION	RECOVERY
1. Labor is fully employed.	1. Profits decline.	1. Volume of business is low.	1. There is an accumulated shortage of goods.
2. Wages are high.	2. Goods are forced on to the market.	2. Buying is only for immediate requirements.	2. Most debts are paid.
3. Costs of operation increase.	3. Prices are reduced.	3. Wages are low.	3. Outlook is favorable.
4. Selling prices increase.	4. Buying is reduced.	4. Production is efficient.	4. Sales increase.
5. Stocks of goods are large.	5. Volume of business decreases.	5. Prices are low.	5. Construction increases.
6. There is new construction and expansion of business.	6. Unemployment results.	6. Costs of operation are low.	6. Borrowing begins.
7. Banks are willing to lend money.	7. Businesses cease to expand.	7. Costs of construction are low.	7. Prices begin to rise.
8. Demand for consumers' goods increases.	8. Businesses quit borrowing.	8. Stocks of goods are small.	8. Buying begins in anticipation of rising prices.
9. Profits are high.	9. Prices decline.	9. Shortage of goods develops.	9. People go back to work.
10. Interest rates tend to increase.	10. Creditors press for payment.	10. Interest rates are low.	10. Businesses begin to operate at a profit.
11. Dividends are high.	11. Failures increase.	11. Demand for loans is low.	11. Production increases.
12. Production is high.	12. Mortgages are foreclosed.	12. Unemployment is high.	

Characteristics of the Business Cycle

Recovery. Eventually *recovery* begins. Prices and costs readjust themselves. Producers find that they can sell goods at a profit because the goods are produced cheaply. The production of cheap goods begins to stimulate buying. Banks offer low rates of interest to encourage businessmen to borrow. Wage rates slowly begin to rise as prices of commodities, prices of securities, and dividends begin to increase.

Causes of the Business Cycle. There will always be a certain amount of fluctuation in profits, in the total amount of business that is done, and in the incomes of individuals. If we could prevent the extreme fluctuations, we would have the cure for declines and depressions.

There are certain rather basic reasons on which most economists and financial experts agree as causes that lead to a depression. Some of these were mentioned in the description of the business cycle. The following factors are considered very fundamental in understanding the causes of a depression and the development of cures:

(a) Purchasing power usually lags behind production power. Not enough of the income received from production is put back into purchasing power, and the income from production is not sufficiently widely distributed among all the population to create widespread purchasing power.

(b) At the same time that buying power has lagged behind production, surpluses are built up on the shelves of merchants, in warehouses, and at the mines. Lenders begin to get nervous. They ask for the repayment of their loans. Those who borrowed the money have to pay off the loans and curtail their businesses. They begin dumping goods on to the market and discharging their employees in an attempt to keep going.

(c) In all of this process there is usually an attempt to stabilize prices and to keep them at a high level, and also to stabilize wages; but prices usually do not come down fast enough to keep in balance with the purchasing power, particularly when large numbers of individuals are thrown out of employment. Probably the greatest problem is keeping purchasing power in balance with production and prices.

(d) Tied up with the factors mentioned above is the fact that many consumers have bought more than they can pay for quickly; therefore they stop buying until they can pay their debts. Many others stop buying because of the fear of an inevitable slump.

(e) The psychological factor of fear cannot be overestimated in this whole problem, for when a decline gets started, fear accelerates it and often causes a slump that otherwise might never have happened. Fear causes scarce money and high money rates, decreased buying, discharge of employees, the calling of loans, and many other problems that push us downward.

Effects of Prices on Business Operators. For purposes of discussion business operators may be considered to be owners of individual businesses, farmers, and managers of large corporations. Their problems are largely the same in relation to price changes. In periods of rising prices business operators face increasing costs of production, such as the costs represented by labor, materials, rent, and interest. Business operators must then raise their own prices and receive more for their products; otherwise their profits will decrease.

Sometimes individual owners of various businesses find that they are gradually paying more for the products and the services that they use, but are unable to raise their own prices. This fact applies especially to farmers. There have been times when farmers have had to pay high prices for equipment, clothing, and labor, and high rates of interest and taxes; but, because of the low prices of farm products, they were unable to earn profits from their farms.

When prices drop, producers usually find themselves with a supply of goods on hand. These goods were produced at higher cost; and now, because prices have dropped, they cannot be sold at a price that will provide a profit based on the cost of production. The producer must suffer a loss.

Effects of Prices on People with Fixed Incomes. In times of falling prices the person with a fixed income is fortunate. A fixed income is one that does not vary in times of rising or falling prices. The income from some good investment, such as high-grade bonds, is an example. Those who were fortunate enough to have their investments in United States Government bonds during the last depression were assured a fixed income. Their real income increased, for their dollars bought more products than when prices were higher.

When prices rise, the person with a fixed income is in an unfavorable position. The income in terms of dollars remains the same, but these dollars will buy less in terms of commodities and services. Therefore, people who live on a pension or a fixed investment income suffer when prices rise.

Effects of Prices on Salaried Workers. In times of falling prices salaried workers are in essentially the same position as people with fixed incomes. Salaries ordinarily do not change so quickly as prices. In other words, salary changes lag behind price changes. For a while during a period of decreased prices, salaries will remain the same, but eventually they will change. As long as the salaries remain the same, the persons who receive them are in a favorable position, for their dollars will buy more than they did during periods of high prices.

When prices rise, salaried people are in a disadvantageous position. The rise in their salaries lags behind the increase in prices. Consequently, their dollars will not buy so much as they did when prices were lower.

Teachers, governmental workers, and junior executives are in the group of salaried workers.

Effects of Prices on Wage Earners. Wage earners are considered to be those who work for hourly, daily, or weekly wages. In the absence of control through government or labor contracts, wages can usually be changed easily, often on merely a moment's notice. In the absence of such control, wage earners are therefore in an unfavorable position.

When prices begin to drop, wages also soon start to decrease. Sometimes they lag slightly behind decreases in prices, but occasionally they precede such decreases. In periods of increasing prices the income of wage earners lags behind the increase in prices. Wages usually increase, however, before salaries.

Ordinarily wage agreements function advantageously for workers during periods of decreasing prices, but disadvantageously during periods of increasing prices. If a wage agreement has been made prior to a general price level

CONSUMER PRICE INDEX (1953 = 100)

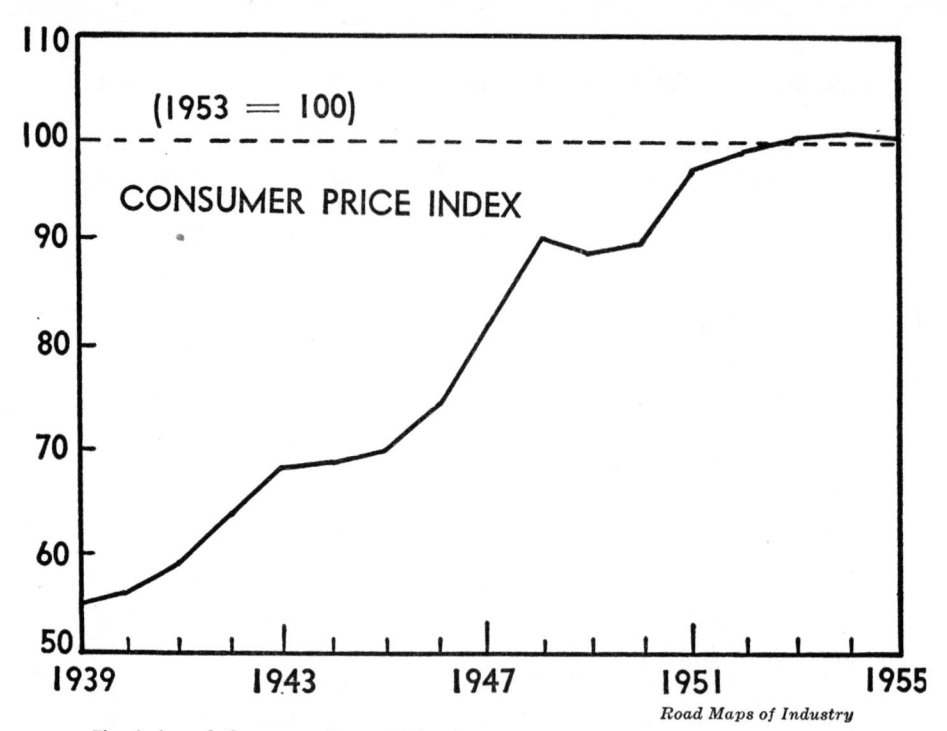

Road Maps of Industry

The Index of Consumer Prices Helps Determine Real Wages or the Purchasing Power of the Dollar

decline, the wage earner is protected from lower wages. However, if the general price level rises, the purchasing power of the worker's wages decreases accordingly, and an increase in wages while the agreement is still effective may be difficult to obtain. In a few cases, wage agreements have been made for relatively long periods of time, that is, three to five years but with stipulations that adjustments be made with the rise and fall of the cost of living index. Such labor contracts are said to contain *escalator clause agreements*.

Prices, Cost of Living, and Real Wages. The cost of living as compared with our monetary wages will determine **real wages**. The Federal Government and other agencies collect figures to establish an index of the cost of living. These indexes usually compare the cost of living of a family at one particular time with that of a previous base period to determine whether prices have increased or decreased. The table on page 683 shows the index of cost of living in selected large cities. The base period used for comparison is

CONSUMER PRICE INDEX BY SELECTED LARGE CITIES
1954
Index: 1947–49 = 100

CITY	ALL ITEMS	FOOD	CLOTHING	GAS AND ELECTRICITY	HOUSE FURNISHINGS	HOUSEHOLD OPERATION	MEDICAL CARE
Average: 46 large cities	119.7	110.4	104.3	109.1	105.4	117.7	126.3
Baltimore	115.1	111.4	102.5	100.0	99.1	112.6	133.4
Chicago	128.5	108.2	106.2	106.2	108.4	121.1	126.1
Cleveland	120.3	109.7	104.1	106.8	103.0	110.9	130.8
Detroit	122.4	113.0	102.4	109.0	109.0	110.3	127.6
Kansas City, Mo.	120.6	108.5	104.6	118.0	104.5	122.5	136.0
Los Angeles	125.1	110.7	104.7	113.6	106.7	108.1	122.9
New York	116.1	110.1	103.7	108.2	105.0	119.1	124.6
Philadelphia	114.5	112.6	105.8	102.3	109.3	114.7	133.7
San Francisco	117.8	111.8	101.9	130.1	105.2	108.9	123.7
Washington, D. C.	117.2	110.1	102.3	114.3	106.9	117.0	118.6

Source: *Statistical Abstract of the United States*, 1955.

1947–49. For instance, for all items in 46 large cities in 1954, it would cost $1.20 to buy the same items that could have been purchased for $1 during the period of 1947–49.

We can use this table to determine real wages. For example, if the income of a family in Baltimore during the period of 1947–49 averaged $5,000 a year, it would have had to earn $5,755 in 1954 to maintain the same real wage; 115.1 per cent of $5,000 = $5,755. Stating it another way, the $5,755 in 1954 would not have purchased any more than the $5,000 income would have purchased during the base period; $5,755 ÷ 115.1 per cent = $5,000.

Effects of Prices on Creditors and Investors. A fall in prices benefits the creditor and the investor. After prices fall, the person who has borrowed money must pay interest in dollars that will buy more than they would have at the time he obtained the loan, for dollars are now more difficult to obtain. If the loan is repaid while prices are low, the dollars are more valuable than those that were borrowed. The creditor or the investor is therefore in an advantageous position. In periods of rising prices just the reverse is true; creditors and investors are in a disadvantageous position.

Effects of Prices on Debtors. In periods of decreasing prices the debtor is in a disadvantageous position; but in periods of increasing prices he is in an advantageous position. The farmer presents a good example of the position of debtors. For instance, during World War I many farmers bought farms at high prices. They contracted debts to pay for these farms and expected to pay off the debts from their earnings. When they contracted their debts, farm products were selling at high prices. As prices fell, their earnings decreased. In other words, dollars became scarce. They still had to pay the same amount on their debts, but more bushels of wheat or more hours of work were required to get the money to pay the debt. As a result many farmers lost their farms through the foreclosure of mortgages. Many other people lost their homes in this way.

Obviously, it is wise to make an investment during periods of low prices and to sell during periods of high prices.

Price Lag. From the foregoing discussion it is evident that interest rates and certain types of salaries and wages lag behind when prices rise or fall. There is also a lag between wholesale prices and retail prices. Wholesale prices usually change first. If all prices, interest rates, wages, rents, and taxes would rise and fall simultaneously, neither consumers nor businessmen would be adversely affected by changes in the business cycle.

Inflation. In several of the previous discussions in this and earlier chapters examples are given of what happens when we have so-called inflation. When prices are inflated or forced up beyond their normal level, the value of money decreases. The previous discussion shows what happens to all types of individuals when this continues to occur. New price levels are established and, until the earning power of individuals catches up with the cost of living, all suffer because the money that they earn will buy less than previously. When inflation continues over a long period of time, it tends to decrease the purchasing power of all kinds of savings that have been put into banks, insurance companies, and other investments, because when those savings are needed for future use, each dollar will buy less than it would have bought at the time the money was saved.

The only way to prevent inflation is to hold both prices and incomes down. This is a well-recognized principle, but it is seldom put into practice. It was established by our Federal Government as a definite practice in World War II after the disastrous experiences in World War I. It was only partially

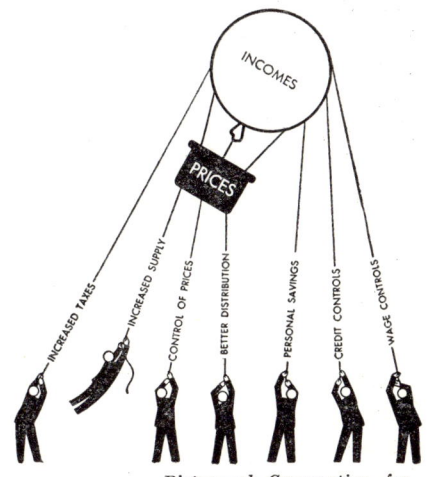

Pictograph Corporation, for Public Affairs Committee, Inc.

Devices Which Are Used or Can Be Used to Prevent Inflation

successful, however, because various individuals and groups of individuals gradually succeeded in attempts to increase their incomes. During World War II, prices did not rise as rapidly as during World War I; however, when the controls on prices were lifted in 1947, the general price level of commodities and services rose very rapidly.

The illustration on page 685 shows the common devices that may be used for controlling inflation—increased taxes, increased supplies, better distribution, personal savings, and control of prices, credit, and wages. Very few of these were used during the First World War, but most of them were used during the Second World War. Thus, we know it is possible to control inflation and to help preserve a better real wage.

Deflation. A rapid fall in general prices and income extending over a period of a few months results in *deflation*. The value of money increases; however, it is scarce, and most people have little of it. Falling prices and curtailed incomes can be highly disadvantageous to people in certain situations. For example, merchants who have a large inventory of goods bought at high prices will find it necessary to sell it at a loss. Money that one has saved and income from investments will buy more in periods of deflation than in normal times or in periods of inflation.

For the protection of business firms and individuals, the Federal Government has tried to stimulate business activity and thus control deflation through various means. Some of the devices used by government to control deflation are as follows: stimulate production; subsidize certain kinds of business; encourage people to spend savings; improve service; extend credit; make borrowing easier; increase public works.

Government Control of Business Activity. Ideally, business activity should be at a level that employment would be available to all who want it at a fair rate of wages, business firms could make a reasonable profit, income would be high enough to maintain a high standard of living for all the people, and at the same time prices would not be unreasonably high. Of course, general business conditions can never be wholly pleasing to all people, for some would always want certain things advantageous to them even though they would be disadvantageous to others. The Federal Government has attempted to control over-all business activity to avoid extreme rises in prices during periods of emergency such as in World War II and to stimulate business activity in depression periods such as in 1930–37. In other words, there is an attempt to control extreme fluctuations in business activity that would result in marked inflation or deflation.

One of the early attempts of the Federal Government to influence directly business conditions was the development of the Federal Reserve System following a period of economic distress in 1907. While the primary purpose of the Federal Reserve System was to regulate the supply of money and credit and to adjust interest rates, it in effect stimulates business activity or slows it down, either of which influences the business cycle.

In the Employment Act of 1946, provision was made for a Council of Economic Advisers, the primary purpose of

---

Summary of What We Should Know about Business Conditions and Prices

1. Trends in business activity are indicated in changes in reliable figures pertaining to income, production, prices, employment, and other factors.
2. The various phases of the business cycle have distinctly different effects on business firms, people on salaries and with fixed incomes, wage earners, creditors and investors, and debtors.
3. Ordinarily extreme fluctuations in general business activity are not caused by one but rather by a combination of several factors.
4. Sharply rising prices result in lowering the purchasing power of wages and income, an economic condition known as inflation.
5. In periods of decreasing prices, the purchasing power of savings and wages increase, but chances to earn wages or an income diminish. This economic condition is known as deflation.

which is to recommend to the President economic policies for the maintenance of employment, production, and purchasing power and to avoid the extreme fluctuations in business activity that lead to periods of inflation and depression. The Council is required to make a report to the President on the economic conditions of the nation in December each year. The recommendations of the President in his Economic Report to Congress are ordinarily based upon or at least substantially influenced by the report made to him by the Council of Economic Advisers. The Council thus becomes the central governmental agency for analyzing and interpreting business conditions for the guidance of Congress.

TEXTBOOK QUESTIONS

1. In order to judge the general conditions of business, what is it necessary to know?
2. What is meant by gross national product?
3. What Federal agencies provide information about prices, wages, and production?
4. How many years are usually covered by a business cycle?
5. What are some of the characteristic indications of prosperity?
6. What are some of the characteristic indications of a decline in the business cycle?
7. What are some of the characteristic indications of a depression?
8. What are some of the indications that are characteristic of a period of recovery?
9. Give possible causes of changes in the business cycle, particularly causes of a decline.
10. What effect on business operators has a fall in prices? a rise in prices?
11. If a person has a fixed income, how is he affected (a) when prices rise? (b) when prices drop?
12. How are salaried workers affected (a) by rising prices? (b) by falling prices?
13. In the absence of wage-control agreements, how are wage earners affected (a) when prices rise? (b) when prices drop?
14. What attempt has been made to tie wages and cost of living together?

15. Explain the meaning of the index of cost of living.
16. (a) How is a creditor affected as prices rise? (b) How is he affected as prices fall?
17. How are debtors affected by price changes?
18. What is meant by price lag?
19. Explain why the value of money is decreased when there is inflation.
20. How may inflation be prevented?
21. What devices may the Federal Government use to control deflation?

DISCUSSION QUESTIONS

1. How is it possible to determine if business conditions are prosperous or not?
2. How is the amount of payments made by checks drawn on bank accounts an indicator of business conditions?
3. Do you think that there is a sharp dividing point when business activity makes the change from one phase to another in the business cycle?
4. Why does the overexpansion of business lead to a decline in the business cycle?
5. Name some factors in a period of decline that you believe contribute to the speed of the decline.
6. (a) How is recovery aided by the elimination of inefficient producers? (b) How are wage earners benefited by the elimination of inefficient producers?
7. How do you think the element of fear affects decline and recovery?
8. How does credit affect a decline in business?
9. Excessive installment selling is sometimes given as one of the main reasons for the beginning of a business depression. Why?
10. Why does production become efficient during a depression?
11. (a) When prices and profits increase, who has the greater advantage: the owner of bonds or the owner of stocks? (b) Who has the greater advantage during periods of decreasing prices and profits?
12. Some people yearn for the return of the days when two dollars would buy plenty of food for the average family for one week. Did people live any better in those times than they do during periods of high prices?
13. If a person buys a house during a period of depression and gives a mortgage, how is he affected when conditions improve?
14. Why should persons who own insurance fear inflation?

PROBLEMS

1. Assume that the cost of living index in your city today is 150 and that Mrs. James A. Barclay, a widow, has $50,000 in bonds from which she gets interest at 3 per cent. If the cost of living index is 200 per cent five years later, how is Mrs. Barclay affected?
2. Two years ago Mr. Nelson earned $70 a week. Although his wages have remained the same, the figures of the United States Department of Labor disclose that the general price level has increased 20 per cent. (a) What are his real wages now as compared with his real wages of two years ago? (b) How much would he have to earn now to buy what his wages bought two years ago? (c) How much would he have had to earn two years ago to buy what his present wages buy?
3. A person who earns $4,000 a year owes a $2,000 debt and sets aside 10 per cent of his salary each month to pay on the interest and the principal of the debt. How much should he be able to set aside each month to pay on the debt if the general price level rises 20 per cent and his salary increases accordingly?

COMMUNITY PROBLEMS AND PROJECTS

1. On the basis of the principles discussed in this chapter, make a report showing whether the present is the time to buy real estate or whether it is the time to save money in anticipation of buying later.
2. Using two or more sources of information, prepare a report on the outlook of business conditions. If you find any differences of opinion, explain these and point out why current observers of business conditions feel that such conditions are improving or are becoming worse.
3. (a) Obtain the latest figures on the cost of living in various cities of the United States. On the basis of the cost of living designated for your city or the city nearest your home, prepare a report in which you compare the present price level with the former price level and present wages with former wages. (b) From local people find out what wages are earned now in comparison with those that were earned formerly. Draw some conclusions with regard to real wages.

Chapter 40

How the Consumer Buys Services with Taxes

Purpose of the Chapter. Consumers receive the benefits of many services and protections that governments—local, state, and national—provide. We have to pay for these services just as though they were purchased from private organizations. It is presumed that these services can be provided more efficiently and more economically by government agencies than by private organizations. As consumers of governmental services, we are, therefore, very much interested in getting maximum benefits from the taxes we pay. The consumer is also interested in tariffs (a form of tax) because they, too, affect him both directly and indirectly. The purpose of this chapter is to help you understand how taxes and tariffs affect you.

You will find answers to these questions:

1. What are the meaning and the purposes of taxes?
2. What are the essential characteristics of each of the principal kinds of taxes?
3. What proportion of the income of the average person is spent in buying government services through taxes?
4. What effect do tariffs have on marketing, prices, labor, agriculture, manufacturing, and consumers?

Taxes

What Are Taxes? The average citizen looks upon taxes as a burden and as something to be avoided if possible. If there were a better understanding of the purposes and the uses of taxation, citizens would have a more kindly attitude toward being taxed.

691

692   Economic Problems of the Consumer   [Part 10

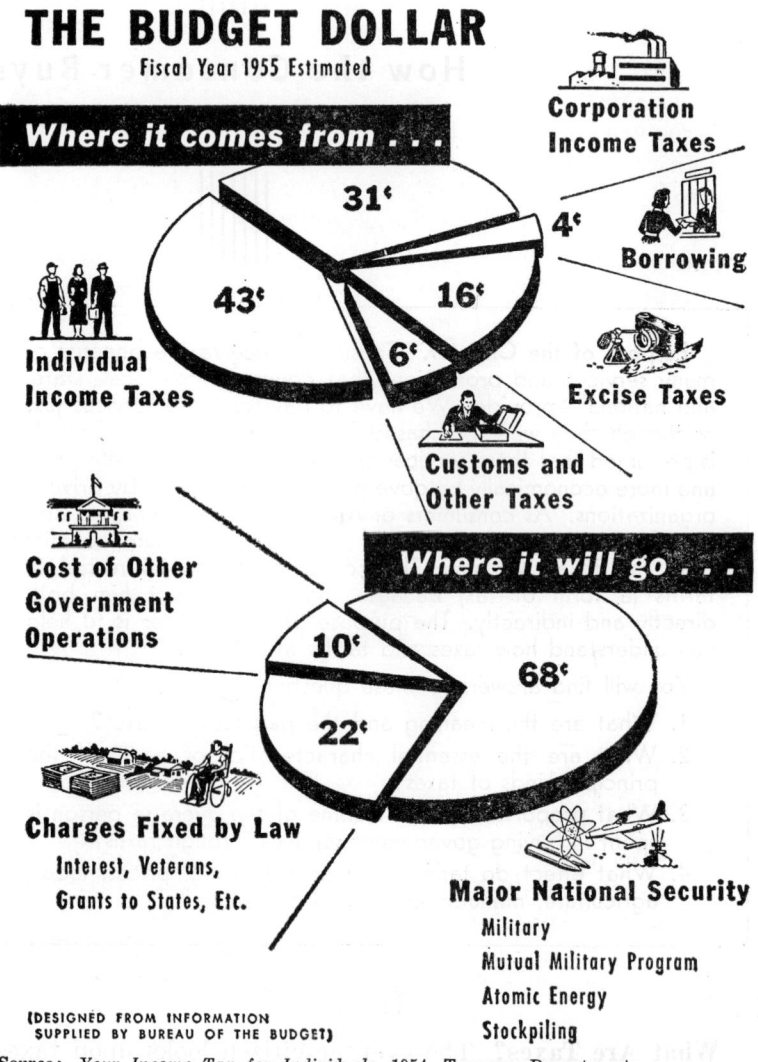

THE BUDGET DOLLAR
Fiscal Year 1955 Estimated

Where it comes from . . .

- 31¢
- 43¢ — Individual Income Taxes
- 16¢ — Corporation Income Taxes
- 4¢ — Borrowing
- 6¢ — Excise Taxes
- Customs and Other Taxes

Where it will go . . .

- 10¢ — Cost of Other Government Operations
- 68¢ — Major National Security
  Military
  Mutual Military Program
  Atomic Energy
  Stockpiling
- 22¢ — Charges Fixed by Law
  Interest, Veterans, Grants to States, Etc.

(DESIGNED FROM INFORMATION SUPPLIED BY BUREAU OF THE BUDGET)

Source: *Your Income Tax for Individuals*, 1954, Treasury Department.

Sources of Federal Taxes and How Money Is Spent

Without government our present economic system could not operate. Inasmuch as government helps our economic society to operate, it must share in the fruits of production. Obviously, those who benefit from the use of governmental agencies must pay for these services.

Taxes are imposed, directly or indirectly, by the citizens of a city, a county, a state, or a country. A tax, after it is imposed, requires a compulsory contribution of money to be made to the government in payment for services for the common good. Taxes therefore have no specific application to special benefits conferred on individuals. They are for the common good, and they are compulsory.

This definition distinguishes taxation from other payments to governmental agencies. For instance, a postage stamp pays for a service, but its use is not compulsory unless the service is desired. Citizens who violate laws have to pay fines as penalties. The fines are compulsory, but they are not taxes; they are penalties. Every person in a state may pay a tax for some general improvement in the state, but an assessment on certain property for the construction of a street or a sewer does not constitute a tax. It is a payment for the improvement of the property. In most cases assessments are voluntary. The majority of property owners who are to benefit from the improvement agree to the assessment.

Purposes of Taxes. Taxes levied to provide revenue come under the taxing power of the government. In the past, most taxes have been for the purpose of raising revenue to pay for the costs of government. Taxes levied for regulatory purposes come under the government's right of police power. As a rule, our government has not used taxation as a means of removing inequalities in wealth among people, but some taxes tend to do this.

Our governmental bodies must first determine what services should be provided at public cost. They must then decide the problem of assessing each citizen to pay for these services. In the levying of taxes, exact justice can never be attained. Even the simplest tax is frequently purely arbitrary. In general, there have been attempts to levy taxes so that each citizen would contribute in proportion to his ability and to the benefits that he derived. No tax can be levied, however, without affecting some particular interest of citizens and without falling more heavily on one group than on another.

When governmental agencies need new sources of revenue, they must devise new taxes or raise the rates of the existing taxes. Because of a general feeling among taxpayers that all taxes are bad, there is a constant effort to shift the burden of taxes from one class of taxpayers to another. In the early history of the United States, the Federal Government was supported largely by import duties. It is reported that at one time Congress considered distributing a surplus of money that had been collected from these taxes. As our country has developed, the multiplicity of governmental units and services has caused a need for increased revenues. New forms of taxation have consequently been created.

Government Finances and Taxes. The financial operations of local, state, and Federal governments are affected by income and expenditures much the same as individuals. Income or revenue of governments is thought of primarily as coming from taxes of some kind. However, some revenue may be received from such sources as tariffs and government-owned utilities.

When expenditures exceed income, governments must borrow. Hence, we may have local, state, and Federal debts. As consumers we are interested in three phases of government financial operations. First, we want to know how much government services and protections cost per person; second, how much the average person must pay in taxes to support government; and finally, the amount of government indebtedness per person.

The per capita expenditures for Federal, state, and local governments for four selected years are shown in the following table. The effect of war on government expenditures is reflected in the figures for 1944. In 1954, the total expenditures of Federal, state, and local governments was 103 billions of dollars; for Federal Government, $72 billions;

Per Capita Expenditures of Federal, State and Local Governments for Selected Years from 1940 to 1954
(Expenditures do not include debt retirement)

	1940	1944 *	1950	1954
Federal	$ 70.33	$710.48	$274.60	$451.95
State	27.38	31.35	85.62	93.35
Local	37.47	34.91	95.48	107.39
Total	135.04	776.48	455.23	652.20

* Includes expenditures for war year.
Sources: Treasury Department and Department of Commerce.

state, $14.7 billions; and local, $17 billions. Since 1952, state and local expenditures amount to about one fourth and Federal expenditures about three fourths of the total spent for government services.

The average total amount of taxes paid by each person in the United States is shown in the table below. By reference to the table it may be noted that the average amount of total taxes paid per capita in 1954 is approximately $80 less than the per capita government expenditures for that year. This difference, of course, must be paid out of accumulated surplus or from money borrowed.

Tax Receipts of Federal, State, and Local Governments, Per Capita, for Selected Years 1940-1954

	1940	1944	1950	1954
Federal	$ 42.96	$312.71	$253.80	$426.65
State	31.92	40.72	60.59	78.17
Local	34.38	35.17	53.73	67.59
Total	109.96	388.04	367.79	572.00

Sources: Treasury Department and Department of Commerce.

The per capita Federal, state, and local debt represents an accumulated excess of expenditures over revenue received by governmental units. The table on page 696 shows the public debts per capita.

The per capita income in 1954 was $1,770. The total per capita taxes paid in the same year was $572. Thus, after paying Federal, state, and local taxes each person had remaining on an average $1,198 of income to spend as he wished. This is called *disposable personal income.*

Per Capita Federal, State, and Local Debt
at End of Selected Years 1942-1953

	1942	1948	1953
Federal	$541	$1,727	$1,681
State	24	26	50
Local	123	103	163
Total	688	1,855	1,893

Source: Department of Commerce.

Benefits of Taxes. In a primitive civilization there is little need for taxes because few services are expected. As civilization develops, greater demands are made for public services. Citizens rarely realize, however, what additional tax burdens these demands cause. Services, whether produced by governments or private enterprises, cost money. Any additional service rendered by a government must be paid for by some group of citizens. The real question to the consumer is, How can I get the service most economically and effectively? Does my tax money produce more service in the hands of government than it would in the hands of private enterprise? The question is not answered easily. Most taxpayers consider only how much they pay in taxes. An important consideration is how tax money is spent.

When new services are added, new sources of income must be discovered by governmental agencies. If one type of tax will not provide the income, another type must be tried.

People who vote for taxes should first weigh the advantages of the services that will be provided by the taxes. The advantages should be evaluated in the light of the benefit to the entire community. It should be remembered that no public service is free; someone has to pay. The person who ultimately bears the burden is the taxpayer.

Direct and Indirect Taxes. Taxes are frequently classified as direct and indirect. This distinction is not entirely accurate. A *direct tax* is one that is levied upon a particular group of persons or organizations without the possibility of the cost of the tax being passed on to others. An *indirect tax* is one that is levied upon a group of individuals or organizations but that can be passed on indirectly to others.

A tax on real estate is usually considered to be a direct tax because it must be paid by the owner of the real estate. Nevertheless, the tax on real estate can be passed on to the renter by charging higher rent. From this point of view it may be considered as an indirect tax.

Some sales taxes are direct, and others are indirect. If a sales tax is charged on the total sales of a merchant, it will probably be passed on indirectly to the individual customers through increased prices; whereas if the tax is added to each sale, it is direct because it is paid by the consumer.

A number of states have a *poll tax*. In some cases it is imposed on every voter; in others, it is imposed on every male person who is of voting age. A poll tax is one tax that cannot be escaped and cannot be passed on to anyone else.

There are many excise taxes, some of which are direct and others, indirect. An *excise tax* is one that is levied upon the commodities, facilities, privileges, or occupations within a country. It should be distinguished from an import tax. Some excise taxes are supposed to be direct, but many of them become indirect. For example, a Federal excise tax on cigarettes is imposed as a direct tax upon the merchant, but he includes it in his selling price. The consumer therefore pays the tax. This process is referred to as "shifting the tax burden." Whenever the cost of a product is increased to include a tax, the tax is being passed on to the buyers.

Many of the taxes on gasoline were supposed to be direct taxes on the producers or the distributors, but they have become indirect taxes by being passed on to the consumers through an increase in the retail price. They thus resemble many other taxes that are supposed to be direct but that result in being indirect. Legislators have discovered that the least "painful" taxes are the ones that arouse least opposition. Indirect taxes are considered in this class.

Hidden Taxes. Many of the so-called indirect taxes are referred to as *hidden taxes* because most people are not aware of the fact that they are paying those taxes. For instance, one may pay a sales tax when he purchases a new radio. The purchaser is aware of paying that tax, but he is not aware of paying many others that are included in the selling price. For instance, taxes have been paid on the labor that was required to produce the radio or on raw materials that were needed in manufacturing the radio. Taxes have been paid on the factory in which the radio was manufactured. Transportation costs have been included in the selling price. The transportation companies that handled the radio have included a certain amount of taxes in their charges. Most of these taxes cannot be traced definitely to their original sources, but it has been estimated that hidden taxes represent almost 20 per cent of every dollar of retail sales.

Property Taxes. A *property tax* is one levied upon real estate or any personal property that has value and that may be bought or sold. The property tax is one of the oldest forms of tax. Until recent years it provided the greatest source of revenue; and, although it does not represent an ideal form of taxation, it is still one of the main sources of revenue in most taxing districts. The illustration below shows a typical form of tax bill for real estate.

It is difficult to bring about changes in methods of property taxation because rents have been adjusted to the property

A Real-Estate Tax Bill

taxes. In some states different types of property are taxed at different rates. Some forms of personal property are exempt entirely. A new form of property tax is the tax on intangible property, such as money, deposits, and securities.

One of the most important arguments for a property tax is that, since property receives protection from the government, the owners should be required to pay for the protection. In the early days when our tax system was established, the ownership of real estate was a reasonably good index of the ability to pay taxes. Now, however, there are many persons who do not own real property but who have much greater incomes than some other people who own real estate. The ownership of real estate, therefore, should not be the only means of determining one's ability to pay taxes.

Property tax rates may be stated in terms of mills, dollars per thousand, percentages, or other units. The total tax rate on property is the sum of the separate rates on property imposed by the various units of government that are empowered to levy a tax. The following is an example of how the total tax rate on property is comprised of the sum of the separate rates, levied by different units:

State unit	.015
City unit	.017
County unit	.009
School district	.028
Total tax rate	.059

This tax rate means that the taxpayer will be assessed property taxes at the rate of 5.9 per cent of the assessed value of his property. Property valuations or assessments are not always computed fairly, for they are based on judgment. Judgment is sure to vary. If one person's piece of property is valued low and another person's property is valued high, the latter person pays a greater tax in proportion to the actual value of his property.

Who Pays Property Taxes? A property tax is supposed to be a direct tax. If a person lives on the real estate on which he is paying taxes, the tax is reasonably direct. If the property is rented, however, and the tax is figured in the cost of maintaining the property, the renter actually pays the tax. In some cases it may be shared by the owner and the renter.

Sales or Consumption Taxes. There are two principal forms of the sales tax (sometimes called excise tax): (a) general and (b) selective.

General sales taxes are of several different kinds, among the most common of which are: the retail sales tax, levied on retailers; the wholesale tax; the gross income tax, usually levied on all income from sales both of commodities and of services; the gross sales tax, which is applicable to all sales including manufacturers'; and the gross profit tax, levied on gross profit. Taxes on luxuries, amusements, and gasoline are good examples of selective or commodity taxes.

An argument in favor of the sales tax is that many who do not pay other taxes are thus required to contribute to the support of government. Many people argue also that this tax meets one of the basic requirements of taxation not only by charging those who have the ability to pay, but also by charging them in proportion to the ability to pay. The general sales tax is obviously open to many criticisms. For instance, it places a heavy burden especially upon those who scarcely can earn a living. Some of these objections are overcome, however, by the selective sales tax.

Some sales taxes are supposed to be levied on producers and wholesalers and not to be passed on to consumers. The consumer, however, usually pays the tax because it is passed on to him indirectly through a rise in prices. In many cases a sales tax is without question a direct tax on the consumer. The retail price is quoted, and the tax is added to it. For instance: retail price, 25 cents; sales tax, 1 cent.

Business or Service Taxes. Business or service taxes can rightfully be called privilege taxes. They are sometimes also referred to as benefit taxes. Those who pay them derive a privilege from Federal, state, or local governments. Franchise taxes, occupational taxes, and severance taxes come within this classification. The tax on gasoline is sometimes classed as a benefit tax, for it is usually levied to pay for the construction and maintenance of roads.

Franchise taxes are those charged to public utilities and certain other companies that are granted concessions or privileges. In most states all corporations must pay a franchise tax for the privilege of doing business within the state.

The occupational tax has been the subject of controversy and legal action in many communities. In some states and in some cities, it has been ruled illegal. An *occupational tax* is that levied on businesses for the privilege of "occupying" a location within the city for the purpose of doing business. In some respects it serves as a license tax.

A *severance tax* is levied by a state as a charge against the consumption of natural resources. For instance, certain states charge a percentage on the oil that is pumped, the ore that is mined, and the timber that is cut. These taxes are levied on the assumption that the state is granting the privilege of a profit to be derived from the consumption of natural resources.

Other good examples of service taxes are those imposed on corporations, particularly on life insurance companies. Since a corporation is an artificial being created by the state, it is subject to the regulations of the state and must pay for the privilege of its existence. Life insurance companies usually pay on the basis of their gross or net income.

Business or service taxes are direct taxes for those on whom they are imposed, although they frequently result in indirect taxes on the consumers. In some states certain taxes have been imposed on public utilities without the possibility of the taxes being passed on to the consumers. For instance, a state may impose a 2 per cent tax on the sale of electricity and gas. The public utility may be restrained from passing this charge on to the consumer since the rates have already been established and cannot be raised. The corporation must therefore pay the tax without passing it on to the consumers.

Inheritance and Gift Taxes. During the twentieth century the growth of inheritance, estate, legacy, or succession taxes has been very rapid. Such taxes, commonly referred to as death taxes, are now levied under Federal and state laws. The theory behind the legislation is that wealth should not be allowed to accumulate, through successive generations, in the hands of a few people, and that large estates should be broken up. Those who argue for inheritance taxes assert that there is no natural right of descendants, that property rights cease with death, and that the state merely confers a favor upon descendants by permitting a person before his death to make a plan disposing of his property in their favor. The administration of inheritance taxes is therefore a social and an economic problem.

Two general types of inheritance taxes are: (a) the estate tax and (b) the share, or inheritance, tax. The Federal Government largely employs the estate tax, whereas most states employ the share tax.

The *estate tax* is calculated on the entire amount of the net estate, regardless of the interests of the beneficiaries.

The *inheritance tax* or *share tax* may be taken out of each share of the will, provided the will so specifies. In the absence of a specification in the will, the tax is taken out of the part of the estate remaining after specific bequests have been distributed. The rate of this tax may vary according to the individuals who share in the estate. Under most state laws the portions of an estate that go to distant relatives are subjected to higher taxes than the portions going to close relatives.

A *gift tax* is levied upon a gift from one person to another. Ordinarily, gift taxes are levied to prevent avoidance of estate and inheritance taxes.

Under this type of taxation the beneficiaries of an estate are the ones who bear the tax burden. In other words, the state deprives them of part of the estate. This tax is a good example of a tax that cannot be shifted to others.

Those who argue against inheritance and gift taxes assert that an estate is built as the result of one's business skill, foresight, and labor; descendants therefore have a natural right to the proceeds of the estate. It is also contended that such taxes tend to discourage initiative and thrift.

Income Taxes. The principal source of revenue of the United States Government is the income tax. In 1954, approximately 45 per cent of its revenue came from individual income tax, approximately 30 per cent from corporate income and excess profits tax, and the remainder from miscellaneous sources.

In theory the income tax is sound and just. It is one of the fairest direct taxes because it is levied in reasonable proportion to one's ability to pay. While property is considered as evidence of ability to pay, it may not be good evidence. An actual income is, however, good evidence of the ability to pay. Although the theory may be correct, the particular rates charged on various incomes are nevertheless subject to debate. Most authoritative economists approve of the income tax, although they do not agree as to the method of its application. One of the weaknesses of the income tax is that, in times of reduced earnings, the revenue from it shrinks rapidly. Property taxes are not subject to such violent fluctuations.

The income tax is also imposed in many states. The state income-tax laws are patterned largely after the Federal law, although they are usually not so complicated and the rates vary. The legal accounting procedure governing the operation of the Federal income-tax law has become quite complicated. The interpretation of many of the stipulations of the law has been clarified through court decisions. The law may be changed by Congress, but the principles remain the same.

Who Pays Income Tax? The Federal income tax applies to both business firms and individuals. The rates of tax and the regulations relative to exemptions, methods of payment, and the items constituting deductible expenses are different for business firms than for individuals. All business and professional firms must file income tax returns, either as individuals or as corporations. Usually business firms have tax accountants compute their taxes for them.

Every individual who has a gross income of $600 or more for the taxable year must file a return. Age is no factor, and it makes no difference whether the individual is single or married. The amount of the net income is immaterial. Even if the deductions and the credits are such that no tax is payable, a return still must be filed. Failure to file a return when required to do so may result in certain penalties being imposed. The United States Treasury Department furnishes complete instructions as a guide yearly to taxpayers.

Tax Payments Withheld from Wages. Since January 1, 1943, employers have been required to withhold a percentage of the wages paid to their employees for Federal income tax purposes.

Each employee is required to furnish his employer with a signed withholding exemption certificate setting forth the number of income tax exemptions that he claims. The employer may use either a percentage method or a wage bracket (table) method in determining the amounts to be withheld each payday. The amounts withheld by the employer must be paid to the collector of internal revenue or a bank designated as a United States depositary. At the end of each year the employer must furnish each employee with a written statement showing the amount withheld from his wages during the year. If the amount withheld is more than the actual amount of the tax, the excess will be refunded; if it is less, the employee will be required to pay the difference to the collector of internal revenue.

Having the Federal taxes withheld and paid by one's employer does not relieve a person from filing an income tax return. Persons whose income is primarily from wages and not over $5,000 a year may file Form 1040A, which virtually means that the collector of internal revenue computes the tax for you. Of the approximately 56 million individuals who file Federal income tax returns annually, it is estimated that about 40 million may use the short form of return. Persons who have an income in excess of $5,000 or whose income is from other than wages are required to file a more detailed statement (Form 1040) of their income and deductible expenses.

A declaration of estimated income tax for the year must be filed by April 15 by persons who expect to receive more

Ch. 40] THE CONSUMER BUYS SERVICES WITH TAXES   705

Form W-2 (Goes with tax return)

31-0560780
Jone's Grocery Store
5101 Park Lane
Madison 5, Wisconsin

WITHHOLDING TAX STATEMENT
1955 Federal Taxes Withheld From Wages
Copy B—For Employee's Tax Return

Type or print EMPLOYER'S identification number, name, and address above.

SOCIAL SECURITY INFORMATION		INCOME TAX INFORMATION	
$652.65 Total F.I.C.A. Wages* paid in 1955	$13.05 F.I.C.A. employee tax withheld, if any	$625.65 Total Wages* paid in 1955	$65.20 Federal Income Tax withheld, if any

269-09-9087
Robert E. Clark
1624 Beacon Street
Madison 5, Wisconsin

EMPLOYEE: See instructions on other side.

Type or print EMPLOYEE'S social security account no., name, and address above.   *Before payroll deductions.
FORM W-2—U. S. Treasury Department, Internal Revenue Service

Form W-2 (Kept by employee)

31-0560780
Jone's Grocery Store
5101 Park Lane
Madison 5, Wisconsin

WITHHOLDING TAX STATEMENT
1955 Federal Taxes Withheld From Wages
Copy C—For Employee's Records

Type or print EMPLOYER'S identification number, name, and address above.

SOCIAL SECURITY INFORMATION		INCOME TAX INFORMATION	
$652.65 Total F.I.C.A. Wages* paid in 1955	$13.05 F.I.C.A. employee tax withheld, if any	$625.65 Total Wages* paid in 1955	$65.20 Federal Income Tax withheld, if any

269-09-9087
Robert E. Clark
1624 Beacon Street
Madison 5, Wisconsin

NOTICE: If your wages were subject to Social Security taxes, but are not shown, your Social Security wages are the same as wages shown under "INCOME TAX INFORMATION," but not more than $4,200.
Keep this copy as part of your tax records.

Type or print EMPLOYEE'S social security account no., name, and address above.   *Before payroll deductions.
FORM W-2—U. S. Treasury Department, Internal Revenue Service

Form 1040A (Back)

11. EXEMPTIONS FOR YOURSELF AND WIFE

Check blocks which apply.
Check for wife if she had no income OR if her income is included in this return.

(a) Regular $600 exemption............ [X] Yourself [ ] Wife
(b) 65 or over at end of 1955......... [ ] Yourself [ ] Wife
(c) Blind at end of 1955.............. [ ] Yourself [ ] Wife

Enter number of blocks checked →

12. EXEMPTIONS FOR YOUR CHILDREN AND OTHER DEPENDENTS (List below)

NAME ▶Enter figure 1 in the last column to right for each name listed	Relationship	Did dependent live in your home?	Answer ONLY for dependents other than your children		
			Did dependent have gross income of $600 or more?	Amount YOU spent for dependent's support. If 100% write "ALL"	Amount spent by OTHERS including dependent from own funds

13. Enter total number of exemptions listed in items 11 and 12 above ▶

SIGN HERE
I declare under the penalties of perjury that this is a true, correct, and complete return to the best of my knowledge and belief.
Robert E. Clark   1/15/56
(Your signature)   (Date)   (If this is a joint return, wife's signature)   (Date)

873298-0 ● To assure split-income benefits, husband and wife must include all their income and, even though only one has income, BOTH MUST SIGN.

Form 1040A (Front)

Read instructions carefully.
List your exemptions and sign on other side.

U. S. INDIVIDUAL INCOME TAX RETURN—1955
If you use this form, the Internal Revenue Service will figure your tax.

Enclose Forms W-2, Copy B.
PLEASE DO NOT BEND, PIN, OR TEAR THIS CARD.

Please print.

1. Name (If this is a joint return of husband and wife, use first names of both)
   Robert E. Clark
   Home address (Number and street or rural route)
   1624 Beacon Street
   City, town, or post office   Zone   State
   Madison   5   Wisconsin

2. Your Social Security No.   296 09 9087
3. Wife's Social Security No.
4. Do you owe any Federal tax for prior years? [ ] Yes [X] No
5. Is your wife (husband) making a separate return? [ ] Yes [ ] No
   If "Yes," write her (his) name

6. EMPLOYER'S NAME—Write (W) before name of each of wife's employers. Where employed
   Jone's Grocery Store, Madison 5, Wis.
7. WAGES, ETC. $ 652 65
8. INCOME TAX WITHHELD $ 65 20

9. Other income (if over $100, use Form 1040)
   a. Yours   4 15   xxxxxxxxxx xxx
   b. Wife's   xxxxxxxxxx xxx

10. Totals (if income is $5,000 or more, use Form 1040) $ 656 80 $ 65 20

U. S. TREASURY DEPARTMENT
INTERNAL REVENUE SERVICE
FORM **1040A**

Please do not write in these spaces
873297-0

than $100 of income from sources other than wages subject to withholding.

Social Security Taxes. Under the Social Security Act the Federal Government collects Federal payroll taxes for (a) old-age benefits and (b) unemployment insurance. These are often called social security taxes. Employers and employees make payments to the Federal Government for old-age benefits. The Federal unemployment insurance tax does not provide for the payment of unemployment insurance benefits, but imposes on employers a tax against which credit is allowed for payments that the employers make to state unemployment compensation funds. Every state has an unemployment compensation act. In some cases the employers pay all the tax, but in others the employees as well as the employers contribute to the tax.

The Federal payroll taxes do not cover all forms of employment. There are various exemptions, and these may be changed from time to time by amendments to the law.

Special Taxes. Various special taxes are levied by the Federal Government, state governments, and local governments. Many of these, such as the tax on legal papers (deeds, notes, and mortgages), are *stamp taxes;* that is, they are collected through the use of revenue stamps. Some are customs taxes on imports; others, excise taxes in the form of automobile, dog, and hunting and fishing licenses; and still others, special licenses for conducting certain types of businesses.

State Trade Barriers. The Federal Constitution theoretically regulates the commerce among the states. State taxing systems and the so-called port-of-entry systems of taxing goods as they enter states have, however, resulted in tariffs on imports of goods into the various states.

These various state trade barriers tend to nullify the provisions of the Federal Constitution that provide for free trade among states. Any increased tendency in this respect will serve to work to the serious disadvantage of consumers and businesses.

Tariffs

Purposes of Tariffs. *Tariffs*, sometimes known as *customs duties*, are taxes levied on exports or imports, usually the latter. Tariffs are levied on two bases, *ad valorem* and *specific*. The former is a percentage of the value of a commodity; the latter is a given payment on a unit of the commodity, as per bushel or per ton. Tariffs may be levied for purposes of (a) revenue, (b) protection of an industry or of labor, or (c) both. While tariffs produce a revenue, the amount of revenue from tariffs is relatively insignificant in relation to the total amount of income that is necessary to run the government. Most of our tariffs are intended to protects business interests and labor. They are sometimes used to protect industries that are vital in our national defense. Tariffs are also used to protect infant industries and certain other industries that might be destroyed by competition of foreign goods.

How Tariffs Affect Production. The common practice of placing tariffs on foreign products is the result of the desire of domestic producers to have the national market to themselves. While a tariff on an import gives the domestic producers some control over the market, it also tends to limit their foreign markets because foreign countries tend to retaliate and place tariffs on products produced in a country with high tariffs like the United States. Of course,

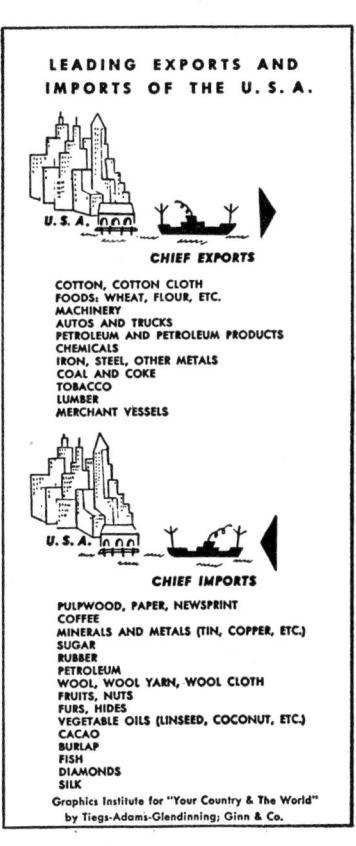

LEADING EXPORTS AND IMPORTS OF THE U. S. A.

CHIEF EXPORTS

COTTON, COTTON CLOTH
FOODS: WHEAT, FLOUR, ETC.
MACHINERY
AUTOS AND TRUCKS
PETROLEUM AND PETROLEUM PRODUCTS
CHEMICALS
IRON, STEEL, OTHER METALS
COAL AND COKE
TOBACCO
LUMBER
MERCHANT VESSELS

CHIEF IMPORTS

PULPWOOD, PAPER, NEWSPRINT
COFFEE
MINERALS AND METALS (TIN, COPPER, ETC.)
SUGAR
RUBBER
PETROLEUM
WOOL, WOOL YARN, WOOL CLOTH
FRUITS, NUTS
FURS, HIDES
VEGETABLE OILS (LINSEED, COCONUT, ETC.)
CACAO
BURLAP
FISH
DIAMONDS
SILK

Graphics Institute for "Your Country & The World" by Tiegs-Adams-Glendinning; Ginn & Co.

Principal Imports and Exports

our high tariff policy affects various producers differently. From the point of view of a manufacturer whose entire market is in this country, a high tariff is desirable; from that of a manufacturer whose main business is abroad, a high tariff may be unfortunate.

Most students of tariff problems agree that a sudden reduction in tariffs would not be desirable, although they believe that tariffs should be reduced over a long period of time. A sudden reduction in tariffs would result in unemployment and the decay of certain industries that have been artificially built up by a high tariff policy. These results would have a serious effect on our economy.

How Tariffs Affect Prices. From the consumer's point of view a tariff on a foreign product is simply a tax. Tariffs, although they protect certain manufacturers or other producers, necessarily result in higher price levels. Most consumers are quite unaware of the fact that they daily have to pay high prices for certain commodities or have to accept similar inferior products at lower prices simply because of the existence of tariffs. A tariff is a hidden tax. For example, woolen blankets are manufactured in certain foreign countries and sold at prices much lower than the prices prevailing in the United States. If a person in this country wishes to purchase a woolen blanket that was produced abroad, he must pay the foreign price of the blanket plus the tariff. He may, however, purchase a similar blanket produced in this country, but he will have to pay a price that is approximately the cost of the foreign-produced blanket plus the tariff. Or the consumer has the alternative of purchasing a lower-grade blanket at a price approximately the same as the price of the foreign blanket without the tariff.

How Tariffs Affect Labor. One of the most frequent statements favoring a high tariff is that such tariffs protect workers from the competition of foreign countries where labor is cheap and standards of living are low. Whether or not this argument has a basis of fact depends upon (a) the purchasing power of the worker's dollar and

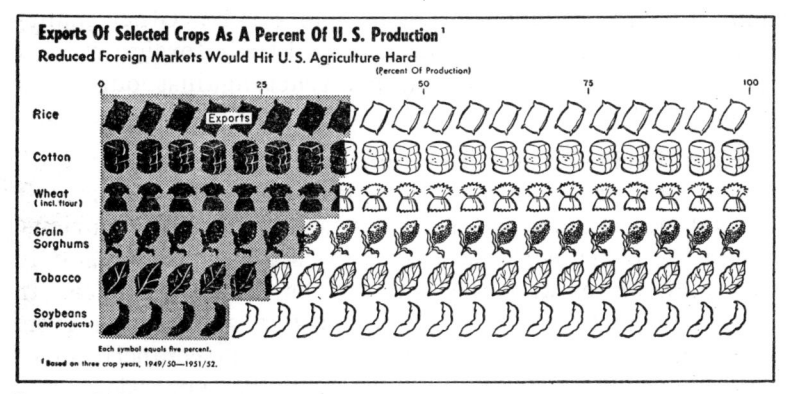

Exports Of Selected Crops As A Percent Of U. S. Production [1]
Reduced Foreign Markets Would Hit U. S. Agriculture Hard

Source: Public Advisory Board for Mutual Security

Agricultural Exports

(b) whether or not the benefits of the tariff accrue to the manufacturer or the worker. If a general high tariff results in a high price level, obviously the worker's wages will not purchase so much as they would if the price level were lower.

How Tariffs Affect Agriculture. Tariffs affect farmers in two ways. They affect the things the farmers must buy that are manufactured products; and they affect, in some cases, the products the farmers sell. In the United States the major farm crops have been protected by high tariffs, although the tariffs on some agricultural products have been reduced. There have also been tariffs on clothing, machinery, and other products that a farmer must have. Thus the advantages that a farmer might gain from higher prices on his crops are offset by higher prices he must pay for the products he buys.

How Tariffs Affect Manufacturing. Very early in the history of the United States, certain manufacturers, notably in the textile field, sought governmental protection by the encouragement of high tariffs. They argued that infant industries would be protected and encouraged and that in case of war certain industries were necessary; they also defended the idea that high tariffs brought about high standards of living. Manufacturers whose market is largely domestic are the chief gainers from tariffs. Other manufacturers may actually be injured and their foreign market destroyed when foreign nations react against our tariff policies.

How Tariffs Affect the Consumer. Although an individual as a producer may gain from tariffs, as a consumer he suffers because high tariffs are generally injurious. From the consumer's point of view solely, tariffs result in (a) high prices and (b) a narrower range of choice. In some few instances tariffs may protect a consumer from cheap and shoddy goods. In general, the competition of foreign products would necessarily make domestic manufacturers more efficient so that they could compete with foreigners and not have to withdraw from the market. As productive efficiency is always to the consumer's advantage, tariffs indirectly serve to discourage efficiency and therefore penalize the consumer. In general, it may be said that high tariffs decrease the consumer's purchasing power.

Conflicting Theories. The tariff problem has long been a source of political and economic debate. Economists have generally agreed that low tariffs or no tariffs are desirable from a national and a consumer point of view, but political representatives have usually been powerful enough to overcome the opposition to tariffs. There are many pros and cons with respect to tariffs. The tariff advocates point out that tariffs keep out cheap foreign products made by low-paid labor; that they maintain industries necessary in case of war; that they promote young and weak industries; and that they help to make the nation self-sufficient. Economists and others point out that tariffs reduce productivity by limiting specialization and markets; that they penalize the consumer; that they help, not labor, but only particular groups; that they create international animosities and ill will.

The dominant point of view seems to be that tariffs are undesirable; but in a world in which national rivalries are increasing, it is difficult to reduce them. Then, too, if tariffs are reduced, certain industries, especially those in which foreign competition is strong, will be affected adversely.

> ### Summary of Consumers' Interests in Taxes and Tariffs
>
> 1. A tax is a compulsory payment for governmental services.
> 2. Most taxes are to pay costs of government; some to regulate certain aspects of business.
> 3. Governmental expenditures, income, and indebtedness are of particular interest to consumers.
> 4. Many common services are provided by local, state, and Federal Governments.
> 5. The principal kinds of tax for revenue purposes are income, property, sales, service, death, and gift taxes.
> 6. Tariffs produce a negligible portion of Federal income; they are levied primarily to protect the interests of certain groups.

TEXTBOOK QUESTIONS

1. Why should consumers be concerned with taxes?
2. It is easy to demand new public services, but is is not always easy to pay for them. What should be considered before establishing a new public service?
3. What do we mean by "shifting the tax burden"?
4. What is meant by disposable personal income?
5. What is (a) a direct tax? (b) an indirect tax?
6. What is meant by the term hidden taxes?
7. Give an example of (a) a tax on tangible property; (b) a tax on intangible property.
8. (a) Who pays the property tax on real estate that is rented? (b) Is such a tax direct or indirect?
9. What are the most common kinds of general sales taxes?
10. Why is the franchise tax of a corporation sometimes called a privilege tax?
11. What is a severance tax?
12. What are the two types of inheritance taxes? Explain each.
13. (a) Is the income tax a direct tax or an indirect tax? (b) What is its principal weakness from the point of view of government?
14. Who must file Federal income tax returns?
15. Explain how a worker pays his income tax as he earns his wage.
16. For what two purposes are taxes collected under the Federal Social Security Act and the various state acts relating to it?

17. How do the state trade barriers, such as taxes on goods made outside the state, affect the consumer?
18. What are the main purposes of levying tariffs on imports?
19. From the consumer's point of view what is a tariff on a foreign product that is imported?
20. From the point of view of labor what is the advantage of a tariff?

DISCUSSION QUESTIONS

1. (a) Distinguish between a tax on gasoline to pay for roads in all parts of a state, and an assessment on adjoining property to pay for the paving of a new street. (b) What are the benefits derived in each case? (c) Why is one a tax and the other not a tax?
2. A new viaduct and an arterial boulevard are constructed from the center of a city into an outlying district. Part of the cost is paid from a general tax fund, and part is obtained through the assessment of adjoining property owners. Some taxpayers believe that the entire cost should be paid by the adjoining property owners. Would this plan be fair or unfair?
3. Give your arguments against a policy of continued governmental borrowing to take care of deficits.
4. If a government spends more than it receives, where does it secure money?
5. (a) What do you think would be one of the most "painful" taxes to a man who owns considerable real estate? (b) What would probably be one of the least "painful"?
6. The statement is frequently made that rents adjust themselves to taxation. What do you think is meant by this statement?
7. Suppose a sales tax of 2 per cent were levied by a state on all commodities and services. If this tax were the only state tax, why would it be fair or unfair?
8. What is the theory or purpose of inheritance taxes?
9. From the point of view of the ability to pay, which type of tax do you think is most fair—a sales tax, an income tax, or a property tax? Why?
10. (a) In terms of the ability to pay, who bears the greatest percentage of a sales tax in proportion to his earnings? (b) Who bears the least?
11. Why are there many conflicting opinions on the subject of tariffs?
12. The statement is often made that high tariffs mean high prices. Why is this statement true?

PROBLEMS

1. If a real-estate tax rate is listed as .0224, what is the total tax for a half year on real estate with an assessed valuation of $6,430?
2. The tax valuation of the real estate in a certain city is approximately 80 per cent of the actual value, and the tax rate is .0189. Mr. Allison builds a new house that costs $8,000. What is a reasonable estimate of the taxes on this property that he will have to pay each year?
3. The real property in City X is listed at a tax valuation of $812,446. The rates for the various taxing bodies that share in the income from the tax are as follows: state unit, .002; county unit, .003; city unit, .018; school unit, .013. (a) What is the total tax rate on the real property in the city? (b) What is the estimated yearly income from the tax for each of the taxing bodies?
4. Assume that 2 per cent of a worker's yearly wage of $3,500 is deducted for social security taxes. (a) How much is withheld for social security taxes? (b) If the employer must match a worker's social security contribution and contribute an additional 3 per cent of wages paid for unemployment insurance, how much do wage taxes cost the employer?

COMMUNITY PROBLEMS AND PROJECTS

1. Make a list of the specific types of taxes in your community.
2. Make a study of some particular tax in your community and find out (a) the rates of taxation, (b) the basis on which the taxes are levied, (c) how taxes are collected, and (d) for what purposes the tax money is used.
3. Determine how much it costs your community to provide education for each high school pupil a year.
4. From local sources determine the amount of taxes that a person pays during one year in connection with the operation of an automobile.

INDEX

A

Abstract of title, 592
Acceptance, 129
Acceptances, trade, 648
Accident insurance, health and, 494
Accounts, advantages of charge, 353; charge, 352; checking, 328; joint or survivorship, 334; savings, 337
Administrator, 549
Ad valorem, 707
Advertisements, how to read, 181
Advertising, 53, 169; absurdities of, 179; aid to buyer, 171; cost of, 176; Federal control of, 116; guides in analyzing, 182; honest and dishonest, 178; how to interpret, 169; informative, 181; legal implications of, 183; meaningless statements in, 180; misleading, 179; state control of, 117
Agencies, public, 119
Agent, selecting insurance, 540
Agreements, defective, 139
Agricultural Marketing Service, 106
Agriculture, tariffs affect, 709; U. S. Department of, 105
Allergy, 300
American Bankers' Association, transit number, 329
American Dental Association, 89
American economic system, 15
American Gas Association, 90
American Home Economics Association, 97
American Institute of Homeopathy, standards of, 193
American Institute of Laundering, 193
American Medical Association, 87
American Pharmaceutical Association, standards of, 193
American Society for Testing Materials, 91
American Standards Association, 90
Annuity insurance, 526
Appeal, sales, types of, 173
Appeals, illustrated, 175
Appraisals, 573
Assembling, 49
Assets, 420
Assets and liabilities, statement of, 421
Assignment of insurance, 499
Assignment of life insurance policy, 533
Assured, 485
Attachment, 362
Auction market, 58
Automatic premium loan plan, 531
Automation, 612
Automobile, depreciation, 269; supplies and accessories, 272
Automobile insurance, 491
Automobiles, buying, 266; delivery cost of, 267; used, buying, 270
Averages, law of, 483
Axminster rugs, 291

B

Balance sheet, 422
Balanced diet, examples of, 215
Bank check, 647
Bank credit, control over, 320
Bank drafts, 336, 647
Bank income, 323
Bank money order, 337
Bank services, 339
Bank statement, 331; reconciliation of, 331
Bankrupt, involuntary, 362; voluntary, 362
Bankruptcy, 362
Banks, 312; commercial, 443; kinds of, as to organization, 314; Morris Plan, 395; mutual savings, 443; savings, 313; source of borrowing on homes, 575; trust functions of, 338
Bargain, legal, 134; legitimate, 153
Bargain sales, examples of, 154
Barter, 605
Barter system versus price system, 656
Basic seven food groups, 209
Beef chart, 228
Beneficiary, 485, 520; change of, 532
Benefits, old-age, 511; primary, 512
Benefits to survivors, 513; summary of, 515
Better business bureaus, 85
Bill of exchange, 648
Bill of sale, 139
Bimetal policy, 644
Blank indorsement, 343
Blue sky laws, 121
Board of directors, 37
Bodily-injury insurance, 491
Bond, convertible, 477; coupon, 475; coupon, illustrated, 475; debenture, 476; discount on, 477; mortgage, 469, 475, 597; par-value of, 477; premium of, 477; registered, 476; short-term, 475
Bonds, 474; fidelity, 497; United States savings, redemption values of, 446
Bonds and stocks, comparisons of, 477
Borrowing, guides in, 402; second mortgage, 577

715

716 INDEX

Borrowing from banks, 394
Borrowing from consumer finance companies, 396
Borrowing from credit unions, 399
Borrowing on life insurance policies, 395
Breach of warranty, 142
Broker, 57
Brussels carpets and rugs, 291
Budget, checking regularly, 425; defined, 406; following the, 427; information needed in making annual, 410; principles of operating, 417
Budget spending plan, advantages of, 151
Budgeting, economic conditions affect, 417; guides in, 413
Building a house, 565; cautions in, 566
Bureau of Labor Statistics, 119
Bureau of Standards, National, 102
Business, 13; development to meet needs, 14; elements of, 29; function of, 15; government operation of, 70; government regulation of, 75; government regulation of, reasons for, 74
Business activity, government control of, 686
Business conditions, how to determine, 673
Business cycle, 676; causes of, 679
Business enterprise, 468
Business operators, effects of prices on, 680
Business organization, forms of, 35
Business services, people who render, 16
Business taxes, 700
Butter, grading of, 231
Buyer, remedies of, 143
Buyer's market, 660
Buying, best time for, 154; guides in, 156; installment, importance of, 367; methods of, 151; mistakes in, 164; policies in, 155
Buying a home, 554
Buying compared with renting, 563
Buying foods, summary, 237
Buying real property, legal steps in, 596
Buy-points for fresh fruits, 234
Buy-points for fresh vegetables, 236
Buying practices, money-saving, in fresh fruits and vegetables, 234
Bylaws of corporation, 37

C

Calcium, 210
Calorie, 210
Canned foods, determining quality of, 220; labeling of, 218
Canned fruits and vegetables, grades for, 196; quality characteristics of, 221
Canned goods, guides in buying, 223
Canners Association, National, 98
Cans, sizes of, 222
Capacity, 357
Capital, 358, 607
Capital's share of income, 627
Carbohydrates, 208
Carpets, types of, 288
Cashbook, 425; illustrated, 426
Cashier's check, 337
Cash value, 531
Ceilings, price, 669
Certificate, stock, 471
Certificate of title, 593
Certified check, 335
Chair joint, illustrated, 283
Change of beneficiary, 532
Character, 357
Charge accounts, 352; advantages of, 353
Charter of corporation, 37
Chattel mortgage, 341

Check, bank, 647; cashier's, 337; certified, 335; counter, 330; defined, 330; illustrated, 329; stopping payment on, 334
Checkbook, recording without, 430
Checkbook stub, recording from, 429
Checking account, 328, 332; service charges on, 332; using, 328
Checks, clearing between banks, 323; postdating, 335; special, 335; traveler's, 340
Cheese, grading of, 231
Choice, problems of, 23
City inspector's seal, 121
City protection, 121
Clause, incontestable, 530
Cleansing agents, 307
Clearinghouse, 324
Close corporation, 38, 469
Cloth, kinds of, 240
Clothing, judging quality of, 249; planning and selecting, 248
Coexecutors, 550
Coinsurance, 490
Collateral, 317
Collision insurance, 493
Color tested, 193
Comaker, 341
Combination policy, 525
Commerce, United States Department of, 101
Commercial banks, 312, 443
Commercial paper, 342
Commercial sight draft, 648
Commercial standards, 103
Commercial time draft, illustrated, 648
Commission markets, 57
Commission merchant, 57
Common stock, 471
Communicating, 55
Compensation, unemployment, 510
Competent parties in contracts, 131
Competition, 33; effect on prices, 662
Competition and profits, 631
Competitive system, 34

INDEX

Compound interest, cumulative power of, 441
Comprehensive insurance, 493
Conditional sales contract, 368; illustrated, 370
Consideration in contracts, 135
Consumer, 2; benefits to, from Department of Commerce, 101; how government affects, 66; tariffs affect, 710
Consumer co-operative, 41
Consumer credit, 351
Consumer-credit insurance, 498
Consumer economics, 2
Consumer finance companies, borrowing from, 396
Consumer Price Index, 120, 682
Consumers' research organizations, 94
Consumers, foreign policy may affect, 79
Consumers Union of U. S., Inc., 96
Consumption taxes, 700
Contract, conditional sales, 368; conditional sales, illustrated, 368; defined, 127
Contract of sale, 595
Contract rate, 392
Contracts, competent parties in, 131; consideration in, 135; express, 137; implied, 137; installment, characteristics of, 368; installment, points to check in, 371; insurance, 522; land, 577; oral, 136; proper form of, 136; void, 139; voidable, 132, 139; written, 136; written, primary essentials of, 139
Contract to convey, 595
Control of prices, 668
Control over bank credit, 320
Convertible bond, 477
Convertible preferred stock, 473

Convey, contract to, 595
Co-operatives, 40; consumer, 41; retail, 41
Copper, 210
Corporation, 37; close, 38, 469; open, 39, 469; organization of, 38
Cosigner, 341
Cosmetic, defined, 110
Cosmetics, 301; cautions about, 303
Counter check, 330
Coupon bond, 475; illustrated, 475
Cream, 230
Creams and lotions, function of, 302
Credit, advantages and disadvantages of, 652; application for, 359; basis for establishing, 356; business and agricultural, 647; consumer, 351, 647; defined, 351; effect on prices, 666; expands use of money, 649; how to establish, 358; installment, 351, 366; protecting, 359
Credit instrument, 647
Credit money, 642
Credit rating agencies, 359
Credit unions, 400, 447
Creditors and investors, effects of prices on, 684
Cumulative power of compound interest, 441
Cumulative preferred stock, 473
Currency, paper, 643
Curtesy, 596
Customs duties, 707
Cut-pile carpets, 288
Cycle, business, 670; business, causes of, 679

D

Dairy products, grades for, 199
Dealer, 57
Debenture bond, 476
Debtors, effects of prices on, 684
Deception, methods of, used by investment promoters, 460

Decline, 677
Deed, placing in escrow, 595; quitclaim, 593; warranty, 593
Deeds, 593
Defective agreements, 139
Deficiency judgment, 598
Deflation, 686
Delivery cost of automobiles, 267
Demand, 661; elastic, 661; inelastic, 661
Demand and price, relation between, 661
Demand for labor, 624
Demonstrations, 162
Dental Association, American, 89
Dentifrices, 309
Department of Agriculture, 105
Department of Commerce, 101
Department of Health, Education, and Welfare, standards of, 190
Department of Labor, 119
Deposit insurance, 322
Deposit slip, 329
Depositor, obligations of, 334
Depreciation, automobile, 269
Depression, 678
Detergent, defined, 305
Detergents, synthetic, uses of, 307
Diet, examples of balanced, 215
Direct marketing, 61
Direct taxes, 696
Directors, board of, 37
Disability insurance, 497
Discount, 477
Dishonest advertising, 178
Distribution, cost of, 63; defined, 15
Distributive system, 48
Dividends, 530; on stock, 472
Division of labor, 18, 608
Dollar, purchasing power of, 8
Dower interest, 596
Dower right, 596
Down payment, minimum, 559

718 INDEX

Drafts, bank, 336, 647; commercial sight, 648; commercial time, 648
Drawee, 342
Drawer, 342
Drawers, construction of, 283
Drug, defined, 110
Drugs, guides in buying, 298; how to buy, 295
Duties, customs, 707
Dyers and Cleaners, National Association of, 92

E

Economic problems, 9
Economic rent, 629
Economic services, performing, 606
Economic voting, 8
Economic wants, satisfaction of, 2
Economics, 2
Eggs, grades for, 198
Eggs, U. S. graded, 232
Elastic demand, 661
Electrical Testing Laboratories, Inc., 94
Elementary utility, 16
Emotional appeal, 173; illustrated, 175
Endowment feature of legal-reserve contracts, 529
Endowment insurance, 524
Enterprise, business, 468
Entirety, tenant by, 595
Escrow, 595
Estate, 485
Estate tax, 702
Estates, 549
Exchange, 58; bill of, 648; medium of, 639
Exchange Commission, Securities and, 120
Excise tax, 197
Executor, 549
Expenditures, 406; classification of, 408; evaluating, 439; example of estimating, 415; factors to be considered in estimating, 411; family, 412
Expenditures and income, comparison of estimated, 415

Expenditures of Federal, state, and local governments, 80
Expense, statement of income and, 423
Express contracts, 137
Express warranties, 141
Extended coverage, 488
Extended term insurance, 531
Eyes, care of, 297

F

Fabric, defined, 240
Fabrics, guides for selection of, 246; how to buy, 240
Fabrics, labels, information to look for, 247
Fabrics, selection of, 243; wool, 241
Face value, 485
Fair Labor Standards Act, 626
Fair trade laws, 113
Family expenditures, 412
Family income policy, 526
Family saving, guides to, 436
Fats, 208
Federal Food, Drug, and Cosmetic Act, 108
Federal Food and Drug Administration, 107
Federal Housing Administration, 580; loans, 580
Federal Old-Age Insurance, 507
Federal reserve banks, relations of, with member banks, 318
Federal Reserve System, 314; functions of, 315
Federal Social Security Act, 506
Federal specifications, 103
Federal Trade Commission, 111; functions of, 112; standards of, 191
Federal Trade Commission Act, 113
FHA loans, 580
Fidelity bonds, 497
Fiduciary, 645
Fill, standard, 190
Filled Milk Act, 111
Finance, public, 79

Finance companies, 383
Financial advice, 339
Financial records, 425
Financing, 56
Financing a home, first-year cost of, 560
Financing charges, computing, 378, 579
Financing costs, analysis of, 559
Finish of furniture, 298
Fire and theft insurance, 492
Fire insurance, 488
Fire Underwriters, National Board of, 89
Fixed incomes, effects of prices on people with, 680
Flammable Fabrics Act, 119
Flat-weave rugs, 288
Floor coverings, smooth surfaced, 290
Food, Drug, and Cosmetic Act, Federal, 108
Food and Drug Administration, Federal, 107
Food dollar, guides for obtaining most for, 208
Food groups, basic seven, 209
Food management, 206
Food nutrients, functions and sources, 212
Food requirements, 213
Foods, canned, labeling of, 218; determining quality of canned, 220; frozen, 226; functions of, 210; how to buy, 217; packaged, 225; types of, 208; U. S. grades for, 217
Foreclosure, mortgage, 598
Foreign policy, consumers affected by, 79
Form utility, 16
Fort Knox depository, 644
Frames of upholstered furniture, 285
Franchise, 42
Franchise taxes, 701
Fraud, preventing, 140
Free enterprise system, 32
Freezers, home, buying, 262

INDEX

719

Fresh fruits, buying points, 234
Fresh fruits and vegetables, grades for, 195, 237; judging quality of, 233
Fresh vegetables, buying points, 236
Frozen foods, 226
Fruits, fresh, buying points, 234
Fruits and vegetables, grades for canned, 196; grades for fresh, 195, 237; judging the quality of fresh, 233; quality characteristics of canned, 221
Furniture, coverings of upholstered, 286; finish of, 298; frames of upholstered, 285; joints in, 282; selecting, 277; stuffing in upholstered, 285; upholstered, guides in selection of, 288; veneer in, 281
Furniture wood, 279
Furs, durability and cost of, 252; how to buy, 251
Fur Products Labeling Act, 118
Fur Products Name Guide, 119

G

Gambling, 451
Garnisheeing, 362
Garnishment, 362
Gas Association, American, 90
Gasoline consumption, 270
Gift taxes, 702
Gold supply, 644
G. I. loans, 582
Goods offered for sale and price, relation between, 659
Government, 607; protection of citizens by, 76; services performed by, 68
Governmental agencies, 78; consumers affected by, 79
Governmental operations, 77

Governmental services, 66
Government inspection of food, 200
Government, operation of business, 70; regulation of business, 75; regulation of business, reasons for, 74
Governments, expenditures of Federal, state, and local, 80
Grace period, 532
Grade, defined, 188
Grading, 51, 106; of butter, 231; of cheese, 231
Grades for canned fruits and vegetables, 196; for dairy products, 199; for eggs, 198; for fresh fruits and vegetables, 195; for meat, 199, 226; for poultry, eggs, and dairy products, 197
Grantee, 593
Grantor, 593
Greenbacks, 643
Group insurance, 528
Group permanent life insurance, 528
Group term insurance, 528

H

Health and accident insurance, 494
Health program, 299
Health Service, Public, 107
Hearing aids, 300
Hedging, 59
Hidden taxes, 697
Home, advantages of owning, 556; analysis of financing costs, 559; financing purchase of, 572; first-year cost of financing, 752; when to buy, 555; when to rent, 555
Home appliances and equipment, guides in buying, 259
Home Economics Association, American, 97
Home freezers and refrigerators, guides in buying, 262
Homeopathic Pharmacopoeia, 193

Homeopathy, American Institute of, standards of, 193
Home site, factors in selecting, 567
Honest advertising, 178
Hospitalization insurance, 496
House, building, 565; cautions in building, 566
Housing Administration, Federal, 580
Human-interest appeal, 752

I

Implied contracts, 137
Implied warranties, 141
Import Milk Act, 111
Improvements in property, 591
Income, 406, 604; bank, 323; capital's share of, 627; distribution of national, 632; example of estimating, 414; national, 620; sharing in, 621; sharing in, illustration of, 622
Income and expenditures, comparison of estimated, 415
Income and expense, statement of, 423
Income taxes, 703
Incomes, effects of prices on people with fixed, 680
Income taxes, who pays, 703
Incontestable clause, 530
Index, consumers' price, 682
Indirect marketing, 61
Indirect taxes, 696
Indorsee, 343
Indorsement, blank, 343; forms of, illustrated, 344; qualified, 343; restrictive, 344; special, 343
Indorsement in full, 343
Indorser, 343
Industrial banks, 394
Industrial insurance, 526
Inelastic demand, 661
Inflation, 319, 685
Informative advertising, 181

Informative label, model outline for, 202
Informative labeling, 200
Inheritance taxes, 702
Inspection, government, of food, 200
Installment buying, advantages of, 375; disadvantages of, 375; importance of, 367; warnings on, 382
Installment contracts, characteristics of, 368; points to check in, 371
Installment credit, 351, 366
Installment plan, when to use, 372
Installment purchase, figuring cost of, 380; policies to consider in making, 374
Installment service, charges for, 376
Institute of Homeopathy, American, standards of, 193
Instrument, credit, 647
Insurable interest, 498
Insurance, amount based on income, 546; amount required for future income, 547; annuity, 526; assignment of, 499; automobile, 491; bodily-injury, 491; collision, 493; consumer-credit, 498; comprehensive, 493; deposit, 322; disability, 497; endowment, 524; extended term, 531; fire, 488; fire and theft, 492; form of saving, 529; group, 528; group permanent life, 528; group term, 528; health and accident, 494; hospitalization, 496; industrial, 526; kinds of, 523; legal reserve, 521; level premium, 521; life, 487, 520; limited payment life, 524; major medical expense, 496; marine, 491; medical expense, 496; medical payments, 494; multiple, 498; nature of, 483; old age, 507, 510; ordinary life, 523; paid-up, 531; personal liability, 497; property-damage, 493; regulation of, 487; retirement income, 525; savings bank, 528; straight life, 523; surgical, 496; term, 522; theft, 497; transportation, 491; unemployment, 509; whole life, 523
Insurance companies, operation of, 485
Insurance company, guides in selecting, 540
Insurance contracts, 522
Insurance needs, analysis of, 500
Insurance policies, extra benefits of, 533; limitations in, 533
Insurance program, example of planned, 544; planning, 542
Insurance terms, 485
Insured, 485
Insurer, 485
Intangible wants, 1
Interdependence, development of, 24
Interest, cumulative power of compound, 441; defined, 627; insurable, 498; why is it paid, 628
Interest on stock, 472
Interest rates, 391
International market, 59
Investment companies, 478
Investment promoters, methods of deception used by, 460
Investment of savings, guide to, 458
Investments, important points in selecting, 452; satisfactory income from, 456; sources of information about, 460; suitability of, 453
Investors, private, 576
Iodine, 210
Iron, 210

J

Job lots, 60
Jobber, 60
Joint accounts, 334
Joint of chair, illustrated, 299
Joints in furniture, 282
Joint ownership, 595
Judgment, 599
Judgment, deficiency, 598

L

Label, defined, 190; how to read, 157; informative, model outline for, 202; self-certifying, 105
Labeling, informative, 200; of canned foods, 218; of fur products, 118; of wool products, 118
Labeling information, voluntary, 219
Labor, 607; demand for, 624; Department of, 119; division of, 18, 608; legislation affecting wages of, 626; supply of, 624; tariffs affect, 708
Labor's share of income, 623
Labor Statistics, Bureau of, 119
Lag, price, 685
Land contract, 577
Landlord, 586; rights and duties of, 590
Laundering, American Institute of, 193
Law of averages, 483
Lease, 587; illustrated, 588; length and expiration of, 556; renting with or without written, 555
Legal advice, when to use, 125
Legal aid societies, 87
Legal bargain, 134
Legal rate, 391
Legal-reserve contracts, endowment feature of, 529
Legal reserve insurance, 521
Legislation affecting wages of labor, 626
Lenders, unlicensed, 402
Lessee, 587
Lessor, 587

Index

Level of living, 3; raising of, 4
Level-premium insurance, 521
Liability, 420
Liability insurance, personal, 497
Lien, mechanic's, 599
Life insurance, 487, 520; group permanent, 528; kinds of, 520; limited payment, 524; ordinary, 523; straight, 523; whole, 523
Life insurance and real estate, 582
Life insurance company, selecting, 538
Life insurance companies, as source for loans on real estate, 575
Life insurance policy, assignment of, 533; borrowing on, 395; limitations in, 533
Limitations, statute of, 362
Limitations in insurance policies, 533
Limited-payment life insurance, 524
Listed stock, 459
Living, cost of, 682; level of, 3; raising, 4; standard of, 3
Loan, assignment of life insurance policy as security for, 533; repaying small, 398
Loan associations, savings and, 574
Loan plan, automatic premium, 531
Loans, G. I., 582; need for small, 388; personal, 390; sources of, 392; types of, 389
Loans from banks, personal, 390
Loans to individuals, made by banks, 341
Local market, 59
Loop-pile carpets, 288
Lotions and creams, function of, 302
Lump-sum survivor benefit from social security, 515

M

Machines in production, advantages of, 611
Magazines, aid in consumer protection, 97
Mail, buying by, 151
Major medical expense insurance, 496
Maker of a note, 342
Management, 607
Management, food, 206
Mandatory labeling information, 194
Man-made fibers, 242; characteristics of, 244
Manufacturing, tariffs affect, 709
Marbling, 227
Margarine, 232
Marine insurance, 491
Market, buyer's, 660; seller's, 660
Marketability of security, 458
Marketing, direct, 61; functions of, 48; indirect, 61
Marketing system, 15
Markets, 56; auction, 58; commission, 57; international, 59; local, 59; national, 59; organized, 58; regional, 59; retail, 58; wholesale, 57; world, 59
Mass production, 15; benefits of, 20
Meaningless statements in advertising, 180
Meat, grades for, 199, 226, 227; judging quality of, 226
Mechanic's lien, 599
Medical Association, American, 87
Medical expense insurance, 496
Medical-payments insurance, 494
Medium of exchange, 639
Men, 611
Menus for different types of people, 214
Merchandising, 55
Merchant, commission, 57
Middleman, 60
Milk, 230
Milk grading, 230
Miller-Tydings Act, 113

Minerals, 210
Money, 603; credit, 642; credit expands use of, 649; functions of, 638; kinds of, 640; prices affected by, 664; purchasing power of, 645; representative, 640; risk in lending, 628; standard, 640; standards of, 644; token, 642
Money and credit, functions of, 638
Monometallic standard, 644
Monopoly, 43, 664; effect on prices, 664
Morris Plan banks, 394
Mortgage, 470; chattel, 341; open-end, 574; partial-payment, 573; real estate, 573; renewing, 578
Mortgage bond, 469, 475, 597
Mortgage companies, 576
Mortgage contract, 597
Mortgagee, 597; rights and duties of, 597
Mortgage foreclosure, 598
Mortgage note, 469
Mortgagor, 597; rights and duties of, 597
Mouthwashes, 308
Multiple insurance, 498
Mutual assent, 128
Mutual company, 485
Mutual savings bank, 443

N

National Association of Dyers and Cleaners, 92
National bank, 314
National Board of Fire Underwriters, 89
National Bureau of Standards, 102
National Canners Association, 98
National Formulary, 193
National income, 620; distribution of, 632
National market, 59
National wealth, 614
Natural resources, 607
Negotiable instruments, 342; transfer of, 342
Negotiable paper, 342
Net profit, 631
Net worth, 420

722 INDEX

New and Nonofficial Remedies, 88
Newspapers, aid in consumer protection, 97
Noncumulative preferred stock, 473
Nonforfeiture values, 531
Nonparticipating insurance policies, 486
No-par-value stock, 474
Note, illustrated, 392; mortgage, 469; promissory, 342; rediscounting, 318

O

Occupational tax, 701
Oculist, 297
Offer, essential characteristics of, 129; termination of, 130
Offeror, 129
Officers of corporation, 37
Oil consumption, 270
Old-age benefits, 511
Old-age insurance, 507, 510
Open corporation, 39, 469
Open-end mortgage, 574
Opinion of the title, 592
Optician, 297
Option, 131
Optometrist, 297
Oral contracts, 136
Ordinary life insurance, 523
Organized market, 58
Organized marketing, 23
Owner's share of income, 630
Ownership, joint, 595

P

Packing, vacuum packing, 225
Paid-up insurance, 531
Paper currency, 643
Partial-payment mortgage, 573
Parity, 669
Participating insurance policies, 486
Participating preferred stock, 473
Partnership, 36
Par value, 477
Par value stock, 474

Passing of title, 142
Pawnbrokers, 401
Payee, 342
Payment, terms of, 376
Personal liability insurance, 497
Personal loan agreement, 390
Personal saving, guides to, 436
Personal selling, 52
Pharmaceutical Association, American, standards of, 193
Phosphorus, 210
Place utility, 16
Policy, 485, 520
Policy, selecting, 541
Poll tax, 697
Possession utility, 16
Postal savings, 444
Postdating checks, 335
Post Office Department, 120
Poultry, eggs, and dairy products, grades for, 197
Poultry, grades for, 197; grades for, dressed, 229; judging quality of, 229
Preferred stock, 472; convertible, 473; cumulative, 473; noncumulative, 473; participating, 473
Premium, 477, 521
Premium loan plan, automatic, 531
Premium payments, time of, 532
Price, defined, 657
Price and demand, relation between, 661
Price and goods offered for sale, relation between, 659
Price and production, relation between, 657
Price ceilings, 669
Price index, consumer, 120, 682
Price lag, 685
Prices, affected by competition, 662; affected by monopoly, 663; control of, 668; credit affects, 666; effects on business operators by, 680; effects on credi-

tors and investors, 684; effects on debtors by, 684; effects on people with fixed incomes, 680; effects on salaried workers by, 681; effects on wage earners by, 681; how affect real income, 7; money affects, 664; rent and, 630; taxes affect, 667; tariffs affect, 708
Price system versus barter system, 656
Primary benefits, 512
Principal, safety of, 454
Printers' Ink Model Statute, 117
Private enterprise, 32
Private investors, 576
Private testing laboratories, 92
Private wealth, 614
Problems, economic, 9
Production, affected by tariffs, 707; factors of, 607; limiting, 610; mass, 15
Production and price, relation between, 657
Profit, defined, 630; net, 631; pure, 631
Profits, competition and, 631; risks and, 632
Profit system, 34
Promissory note, 342
Property-damage insurance, 493
Property, improvements in, 591; legal steps in buying real, 596
Property taxes, 698; who pays, 699
Proprietorship, 35
Prosperity, 676
Protection, city, 121
Proteins, 208
Proxy, 38
Public Health Service, 107
Public agencies, 119
Public finance, 79
Public utilities, 42
Puffs, trade, 141
Purchasing power of dollar, changes in, 8; effect of, 6
Purchasing power of money, 645

Purchasing power, wealth and, 614
Pure profit, 631

Q

Qualified indorsement, 343
Quality characteristics of canned fruits and vegetables, 221
Quality of canned foods, determining, 220
Quitclaim deed, 593

R

Ranges, guides in buying, 262
Rates of interest, 391; figuring, 579
Rational appeal, 173
Real estate, 467; buying, 592; life insurance and, 582; things to investigate in buying, 599; title to, 592
Real estate mortgage, 573
Real property, legal steps in buying, 596
Real wages, 616
Reason-why appeal, 173
Reconciliation of bank statement, 331
Records, methods of keeping, 430
Recovery, 678
Rediscounting, 318
Refrigerators and home freezers, guides in buying, 262
Regional market, 59
Registered bond, 476
Renewing a mortgage, 578
Rent, economic, 629
Rent and prices, 630
Rent of land, what regulates cost of, 629
Renting, buying compared with, 564; points to investigate in, 556
Repaying small loan, 398
Replevin, 384
Repossession, 384
Representative money, 640
Reprocessed wool, 241
Resources, natural, 607

Restrictive indorsement, 344
Retail co-operative, 41
Retailers Credit Association, 359
Retail market, 58
Retirement, 437
Retirement income insurance, 525
Risk bearing, 56
Risk in lending money, 628
Risks and profits, 632
Rug cushions, 290
Rugs, basic types, features and quality of, 291; guides in buying, 290; types of, 288

S

Safe-deposit boxes, 338
Salaried workers, effects of prices on, 681
Sale, bill of, 139; contract of, 595
Sales appeal, types of, 173
Sales contract, 595; conditional, 368
Sales taxes, 700
Saving, defined, 436; goals for, 438; guides to personal and family, 436; insurance as form of, 529; making plan for, 440
Savings account, 337
Savings and loan associations, 444, 574; borrowing from, 395
Savings bank insurance, 528
Savings banks, 313; borrowing from, 395
Savings bonds, United States, 445; United States, redemption values of, 446
Savings, postal, 444
Second-mortgage borrowing, 577
Secured loan, 389
Securities, Federal and state regulation of, 120
Securities and Exchange Commission, 120
Security, social, 505
Self-certifying label, 105
Seller's market, 660
Seller, remedies of, 143

Selling, personal, 52
Service account, 353
Service taxes, 700
Services, business, people who render, 16; provided through taxes, 69
Severance tax, 701
Share of stock, 471
Shoes, how to buy, 251
Shopping procedures, 152
Short-term bond, 475
Short-term consumer credit, 351
Sight drafts, commercial, 648
Simplified practice, 104
Sizes of cans, 222
Small loan, repaying, 398
Small loans, need for, 388
Smooth-surfaced floor coverings, 290
Soap, defined, 305
Soaps, guides in buying, 306; uses of, 305
Social security, 505
Social security assistance, 517
Social security benefits to survivors, 513
Social security coverage, how to apply for, 507
Social security laws, reasons for, 506
Social security taxes, 706
Society for Testing Materials, American, 91
Specialization, 18, 608; advantages of, 609; disadvantages of, 609
Special indorsement, 343
Specific, 707
Specifications, Federal, 103
Speculating, 451
Spread, 63
Stamp taxes, 706
Standard, defined, 187
Standardizing, 51
Standard money, 640
Standard of living, 3
Standard of value, 639
Standards, commercial, 103
Standards Association, American, 90
Standards of Federal Trade Commission, 191
Standards of U. S. Department of Commerce, 191

724 INDEX

Standards of U. S. Department of Health, Education, and Welfare, 190
State bank, 314
State control of advertising, 117
State trade barriers, 706
Statement, bank, 332; reconciliation of, 331
Statement of income and expense, 423
Statute of limitations, 362
Stimulating demand, 51
Stock, 37; common, 471; convertible preferred, 473; cumulative preferred, 473; listed, 459; noncumulative preferred, 473; no-par-value, 474; participating preferred, 473; par-value, 474; preferred, 472; shares of, 471; unlisted, 459
Stock certificate, 471
Stock company, 485
Stocks and bonds, comparisons of, 477
Stopping payment on check, 334
Stores, buying in, 152
Storing, 50
Straight life insurance, 523
Stubs, recording from checkbook, 429
Stuffing in upholstered furniture, 285
Substitution, 662
Supply, 660; of labor, 624
Surgical insurance, 496
Survivors, social security, benefits to, 513
Survivorship account, 334

T

Tangible wants, 1
Tariffs, 707; agriculture affected by, 709; consumer affected by, 710; labor affected by, 708; manufacturing affected by, 709; prices affected by, 708; production affected by, 707; purposes of, 707

Tax, estate, 702; excise, 697; occupational, 701; poll, 697; severance, 701
Tax advice, 339
Tax bill, real estate, 698
Tax payments withheld from wages, 704
Taxes, 691
Taxes, benefits of, 696; business, 700; consumption, 700; direct, 696; franchise, 701; gift, 702; hidden, 697; income, 703; indirect, 696; inheritance, 702; prices affected by, 667; property, 698; purposes of, 693; sales, 700; service, 700; services provided through, 69; social security, 706; special, 706; stamp, 706
Tea Act, 111
Technology, 612
Telephone buying, 151
Tenant, 586; rights and duties of, 589
Tenant by entirety, 595
Term insurance, 522
Terms of payment, 376
Testimonials, 180
Testing, 161
Testing laboratories, private, 92
Testing services, 163
Theft insurance, 497
Time drafts, commercial, 648
Time utility, 16
Title, certificate of, 593; opinion of, 592; passing of, 142
Title-guarantee policy, 592
Title to real estate, 592
Today's Health, 89
Token money, 642
Torrens System, 593
Trade acceptances, 648
Trade barriers, state, 706
Trade-mark Act, 119
Trade names and terms, 157
Trade puff, 141
Transit number, ABA, 329
Transportation insurance, 491
Transporting, 55

Traveler's checks, 340
Trust companies, 313, 576
Trust functions of banks, 338
Trusts, investment, 478

U

Underwriter, 485
Underwriters' Laboratories, Inc., 89; standards of, 192
Underwriters, National Board of Fire, 89
Unemployment benefits, causes for denying or forfeiting, 510
Unemployment compensation, 510
Unemployment insurance, 509
Uniform Conditional Sales Act, 368
Uniform Small-Loan Law, 396
Unions, credit, 400, 447
United States bullion depository, 644
United States Department of Agriculture, 105
United States Department of Commerce, 101; standards of, 191
United States Department of Health, Education, and Welfare, standards of, 190
United States Department of Labor, 119
U. S. Pharmacopoeia, 193; standards of, 193
United States Post Office Department, 120
United States saving bonds, 445; redemption values of, 446
Unlicensed lenders, 402
Unlisted stock, 459
Unsecured loan, 389
Upholstered furniture, coverings of, 286; frames of, 285; guides in selecton of, 288; stuffing in, 285
Unlisted stock, 459
Used automobiles, buying, 270
Used fur, 118
Utilities, public, 42

Utility, 606; elementary, 16; form, 16; place, 16; possession, 16; time, 16

V

Vacuum packing, 225
Value, cash, 531; standard of, 639
Vegetables, fresh, buying points, 236; grades for canned fruits and, 196; grades for fresh fruits and, 195; quality characteristics of canned fruits and, 221
Velvet rugs, 291
Veneer, in furniture, 281
Virgin wool, 241
Vitamins, 210
Void, 139
Voidable contracts, 139
Voluntary bankrupt, 362
Voluntary labeling information, 194, 219
Voting, economic, 8
Voting system, 34

W

Wage earners, effects of prices on, 681
Wage-Hour Law, 626
Wage inequalities, 625
Wages, defined, 616; real, 616; taxes and, 506
Wages of labor, legislation affecting, 626
Walsh-Healy Act, 626
Wants, intangible, 1; tangible, 1
Warranties, 141; express, 141; implied, 141
Warranty, breach of, 142
Warranty deed, 593; illustrated, 594
Warp, 245
Waste fur, 119
Wealth, 604; national, 614; private, 614
Wealth and purchasing power, 614
Weave, 241
Weighted fabric, 245
Wheeler-Lea Act, 116
Whole life insurance, 523
Wholesale markets, 57
Wills, 549; reasons for making, 550
Wilton rugs, 291
Wood for furniture, 279
Wool product, defined, 118
Wool, reprocessed, 241; re-used, 241; virgin, 241
Wool Products Labeling Act, 118
Woolen yarn, 241
Workers, effects of prices on salaried, 681
Workmen's Compensation, 517
World market, 59
Worsted yarn, 242
Written contract, 136
Written contract, primary essentials of, 139

Y

Yarn, woolen, 241; worsted, 242